News Reporting and Writing

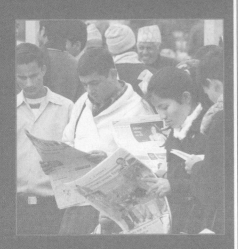

News Reporting and Writing

Ninth Edition

The Missouri Group

Brian S. Brooks
George Kennedy
Daryl R. Moen
Don Ranly
School of Journalism
University of Missouri

Bedford/St. Martin's
Boston ▪ New York

For Bedford/St. Martin's

Executive Editor for Communication: Erika Gutierrez
Editor: Lai Moy
Developmental Editor: Linda Stern
Editorial Assistant: Ada Fung
Production Supervisor: Jennifer Peterson
Marketing Manager: Casey Carroll
Marketing Assistant: Zoe Kazmierski
Project Management: Books By Design, Inc.
Text Design: Books By Design, Inc.
Photo Researcher: Emily Teresa
Cover Design: Billy Boardman
Cover Photo: *U.S. Troops and Iraqi Police Fight Gun Battle in Tal Afar.* Charles Crain (L), a reporter working for *Time* magazine, takes notes during a gun battle between insurgents and the 1st Battalion, 5th Infantry Stryker Brigade Combat Team of the 25th Infantry Division, January 16, 2005, in Tal Afar, Iraq. A routine patrol in the insurgent stronghold turned into an hour-long running gun battle, with a combined U.S. and Iraqi police force battling insurgents across alleys and down boulevards. © Chris Hondros/Getty Images.
Composition: Books By Design, Inc.
Printing and Binding: RR Donnelley & Sons Company

President: Joan E. Feinberg
Editorial Director: Denise B. Wydra
Director of Development: Erica T. Appel
Director of Marketing: Karen Melton Soeltz
Director of Editing, Design, and Production: Marcia Cohen
Manager, Publisher Services: Emily Berleth

Library of Congress Control Number: 2007925327

Manufactured in the United States of America.

2   1   0   9   8   7
f   e   d   c   b   a

For information, write: Bedford/St. Martin's, 75 Arlington Street, Boston, MA 02116 (617-399-4000)

ISBN-10: 0-312-46419-3
ISBN-13: 978-0-312-46419-6

Acknowledgments

Acknowledgments and copyrights appear at the back of the book on pages 555–58, which constitute an extension of the copyright page.

Preface

How many of your students get and read a newspaper daily? Good question, especially in this age of multiple media outlets where traditional newspapers and television stations are being overshadowed by online papers, blogs, webcasts, text messages and podcasts. Motivated by the rapid growth of information pipelines, we went out to visit convergent news rooms in Tampa and Sarasota, we talked with dozens of journalists around the country and we read scores of articles in every medium to pose an even more important question: "What new skills do new journalists require?" Despite innovative technologies, one theme emerged: Editors want journalists who can report fully and write clearly. We were pleased to see that even in this crazy, convergent world, the keys to being a good journalist are still as fundamental as that. As teachers ourselves, we recognize your need to keep up with the revolutionary changes occurring in news rooms without losing sight of the unchanging foundations of our profession. We also recognize the need to practice what we preach. So, as we've done in all previous editions of this book, we use current examples and issues. We write as you want your students to write — clearly and descriptively.

To see what's new in this ninth edition of *News Reporting and Writing*, you need look no further than the first page of Chapter 1. There you'll meet three students whose internships introduce them — and your students — to the new journalistic world of gathering information and telling stories in multiple media. Yet you'll quickly see that the essentials haven't changed: the bedrock importance of accuracy and fairness, the central role of journalism in a free society, and the requirement that journalists tell stories that are relevant, useful and interesting.

Focusing on Fundamentals in a New Journalistic World

In this new edition, we acknowledge the changing face of journalism. We explore the possibilities of convergence, examine the emerging phenomenon of citizen journalism and explain the opportunities for reporting and storytelling offered by Web 2.0, the more powerful Internet. However, the heart of the book is still the emphasis on the basic skills of interviewing, reporting and writing. We also remain committed to teaching the fundamentals that make good journalists good: accurate research, effective reporting, solid writing and engaging storytelling.

That said, we continue to emphasize the importance of fair and accurate research, especially when conducted online. A rewritten Chapter 5 guides students through the wilderness of online information sources and shows them how to ensure credibility in the Internet age. Recognizing the need to address the emergence of diverse media outlets, we have extensively revised Chapter 8 to demonstrate writing techniques that students can use for effective storytelling in print or on the Web. Whether students write for a blog, an online news source or a traditional newspaper, good writing skills are an absolute must, as is understanding how to apply those skills within a news-telling structure. Thus Chapter 9 now explains the most important story structures and how to use them. Chapter 20 offers the latest examples of online storytelling.

Addressing Student Challenges

Again and again, instructors across the country lament that their students either lack basic writing skills or come into the classroom unable to make the distinction between journalistic writing and essay writing. The ninth edition of *News Reporting and Writing* addresses these challenges by providing more writing help than ever before.

- **New annotated model stories.** Seven annotated news stories help students apply basic writing skills and identify the difference between the news article and the essay; the annotations walk them through well-structured articles from the classic inverted pyramid structure—the core of all journalistic writing—to the news narrative.
- **The inverted pyramid and beyond.** Chapters 7 to 9, which we've revised heavily, now clarify the role of the inverted pyramid in journalistic writing and explain the alternative structures to the inverted pyramid. Students will find more advice for when and why to use these structures and concrete guidance for putting them into action.
- **Even more writing help online.** The Exercise Central for AP Style Web site offers thousands of questions that help students improve grammar and punctuation skills. New exercises help students learn to write in the Associated Press style.

Keeping Students Critically Aware

The revisions in this new edition of *News Reporting and Writing* emphasize critical awareness; while we stress that students must continually hone their basic skills, we also insist that students remain aware of everything affecting the face of journalism today, including current trends, the ever-expanding audience of news consumers, and breaking stories concerning local, national and world events. The ninth edition offers

- **Updated preparation for today's news rooms.** A completely rewritten Chapter 2 clearly explains the impact of convergence, citizen journalism and reader participation on how news is reported today.
- **Improved emphasis on globalism and multicultural issues.** Throughout the book, we stress the importance of being sensitive to and writing well for a broad range of audiences.
- **New up-to-the-moment RSS feeds on the book's Companion Web site.** RSS feeds have been added to the book's Companion Web site (bedfordstmartins .com/newsreporting) in order to bring students breaking news all the time, making it easier than ever for them to stay on top of the issues of the day.

Resources for Students and Instructors

The following ancillaries are available with this edition:

Workbook for NEWS REPORTING AND WRITING, Ninth Edition. Supplementing the activities at the end of each chapter in the text, the workbook provides students with the extra practice they need to develop and master the principles of journalism.

Instructor's Manual to Accompany NEWS REPORTING AND WRITING, Ninth Edition. This manual contains sample syllabuses and chapter overviews as well as answers to the end-of-chapter questions from the main text and answers to all the questions in the workbook.

Companion Web site (bedfordstmartins.com/newsreporting). Here students can find links to research tools and online exercises, as well as up-to-the-moment RSS feeds providing students with breaking news all the time.

Exercise Central for AP Style (bedfordstmartins.com/apexercises). Revised for this new edition, this free database offers more than 2,500 questions targeting the 20 common grammar and usage errors most commonly made by journalism students. In addition, it provides a new set of exercises that focus on mastering the Associated Press style of writing.

Crisis Coverage CD-ROM. Created by Robert Bergland, Jeanette Browning and Professor Bergland's students at Missouri Western State College, this multimedia CD-ROM provides unique simulation exercises that allow students to practice journalism in real time using text, audio and video clips. *Crisis Coverage* is free when packaged with the text.

ACKNOWLEDGMENTS

Our colleagues and students at the University of Missouri have given us invaluable feedback on the book, for which we are grateful.

We especially appreciate the contributions of Dr. Sandra Davidson, an attorney and journalism faculty colleague, who revised the law chapter; Marty Steffens, who holds the Society of American Business Editors and Writers Chair in Business and Financial Journalism, for revising our business chapter, and our colleagues in our broadcast department for reviewing the chapter on writing for radio and television.

In addition, we would like to thank all of the instructors who thoughtfully reviewed the text: Chet Benson, Clark College; Gregory A. Borchard, Hank Greenspun School of Journalism and Media Studies, University of Nevada; Bonnie Newman Davis, Virginia Commonwealth University; Russell E. Eshleman Jr., Pennsylvania State University; Michael Robert Evans, Indiana University; Deidra Jackson, University of Mississippi; Barbara Kelley, Santa Clara University; Suzanne McBride, Columbia College; Dennis J. McCarthy, St. Louis University; James E.

Mueller, University of North Texas; Jane Gibson Natt, Purdue University; Bruce L. Plopper, University of Arkansas at Little Rock; William Rainbolt, University at Albany; Karen Rathe, University of Washington; Jennifer Shapiro, Broward Community College; Michael Skube, Elon University; and Lisa C. Watson, California State University Monterey Bay.

We have worked with editors at Bedford/St. Martin's for 28 years now. With each edition, they have challenged us to improve, and we appreciate their work. We would like to acknowledge the expert work of our development editor, Linda Stern, who kept us in line and on time. Thanks are also due to Erika Gutierrez, Lai Moy, Erica Appel and Ada Fung. We are equally grateful to the production team, which includes Emily Berleth and Nancy Benjamin of Books By Design, as well as our photo researcher, Emily Teresa. We'd like to extend further thanks to our marketing team, Casey Carroll and Zoe Kazmierski. Last, but most certainly not least, we want to express our appreciation to our wives—Anne, Robin, Nancy and Eva Joan—who have been wonderful partners in this undertaking.

As always, we value your comments.

You can reach us via e-mail at Brooksbs@missouri.edu; Kennedyg@missouri.edu; Moend@missouri.edu; or Ranlyd@missouri.edu.

Brian S. Brooks
George Kennedy
Daryl R. Moen
Don Ranly

Contents

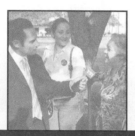

PART TWO   REPORTING TOOLS

3   Interviewing   42

6   Reporting with Numbers   112

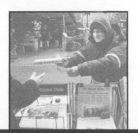

PART THREE **STORYTELLING**

8   Writing to Be Read   160

9 Alternatives to the Inverted Pyramid 186

PART FOUR   BASIC STORIES

PART FIVE   BEAT REPORTING

14 Covering a Beat   298

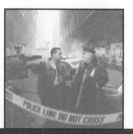

PART SIX   SPECIALIZED TECHNIQUES

18   Investigative Reporting   380

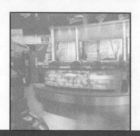

PART SEVEN   **WRITING FOR SPECIFIC MEDIA**

PART EIGHT   RIGHTS AND RESPONSIBILITIES

22 Media Law   464

News Reporting and Writing

The Nature of News

1

IN THIS CHAPTER
YOU WILL LEARN:

1. What news is.

2. How journalism and audiences are changing.

3. How the unchanging principles of accuracy and fairness will help you meet the challenges of permanent change.

Like many journalism students, Amanda Hicks, Emily Goldstein and Matt Sokoloff landed summer internships. Amanda worked at *The Roanoke (Va.) Times*, Emily at *The Dallas Morning News* and Matt at *ABC World News* in New York. But none of Amanda's or Emily's work appeared on paper, and Matt didn't get on the air. Instead, Amanda created slide shows and audio commentaries, among other things. Emily's assignments included putting together an interactive survey. Matt worked on podcasts (downloadable programs designed to be played on iPods or personal computers) and on a show designed for iTunes.

Their experiences in the new world of journalism suggested what their professional futures can be. Amanda concluded, "I hope to someday advance to a level where I can shape a truly converged newsroom. That may sound ambitious, but from what I've seen in the short time I've worked in media, audiences and journalists are ready for a change."

To assess the impact of that change, the Project for Excellence in Journalism set out to capture a day in the life of the media. Researchers studied the news as it was reported over 24 hours by three national newspapers, the three main cable news networks, the three major broadcast networks, PBS, seven news Web sites, seven popular blogs and the local media in three cities. That added up to 2,125 stories available through 57 outlets, plus 112 blog postings. They even looked at *The Daily Show*, a mock TV news show hosted by the comedian Jon Stewart.

Here's what that study showed: "What people learn depends heavily on where they go for news. The medium may not be the message, but it no doubt influences it. In print, online and on the network evening newscasts this day, violence in Iraq, a false alarm in Washington and protests in Afghanistan were the top stories. . . . On local TV and radio, weather, traffic and local crime dominated. . . . As the media fragment nowadays, consumers must choose strategically to get a complete diet. The notion of relying on a single or primary source for news—one-stop shopping—may no longer make sense."

Still, journalists in the 21st century are doing what journalists have always done. They are telling the world its stories. As Amanda, Emily and Matt learned, how they tell those stories, however, has changed. Communication from the most remote locations is instant. The Internet gives news consumers the ability to read, watch or listen whenever they wish—and to respond. Traditional print and broadcast media are joining forces and sharing resources in the latest trend, something called convergence.

CONVERGENCE IN JOURNALISM

Convergence is the term that describes efforts to use the different strengths of different media to reach broader audiences and tell the world's stories in new ways. Still in its early days, convergence already demands of journalists new skills and new flexibility. Print reporters find themselves summarizing their stories into a television camera. Videographers find themselves selecting images to be published in the partner newspaper. Both print and broadcast journalists look for Web links to connect their stories to the worldwide audience and nearly infinite capacity of the Internet. Cell phones and iPods provide new outlets and require new storytelling techniques.

The technological revolution also has exploded traditional definitions of just who is a journalist. Millions of people across the world have launched **blogs**. Although one estimate is that only 5 percent of those sites include original reporting, and although most have tiny audiences, many have become influential voices in the public conversation. In an effort to add personality and encourage interactivity with audience members, traditional news organizations are encouraging staff members to write blogs.

Increasingly, members of the public are being invited to respond to stories that are published or broadcast. Citizens are even being enlisted as amateur reporters. To take one example, *The (Fort Myers, Fla.) News-Press* asked its readers for help in an investigation of whether a local sewer district was overcharging customers. Not only did readers provide their own examples, but some who were professional engineers volunteered to study documents and share their expertise with the newspaper and the entire community. The result: a communitywide conversation that led to reductions in sewer rates. The Gannett Co., owner of *The News-Press*, calls this "crowdsourcing." A better label might be "citizen sourcing."

Some fundamentals haven't changed. One constant is journalists' definition of news itself. Another is the importance of accuracy and fairness. The core is still the essential role of journalism in a democratic society.

The basic skills required of every journalist haven't changed either, despite the revolution in technology. Whatever the medium, the skills of news-gathering and storytelling are essential to good journalism.

WHAT NEWS IS

The criteria that professional reporters and editors use to decide what news is can be summarized in three words:

Relevance

Usefulness

Interest

These criteria apply generally, but each journalist and each news organization uses them in a specific context that gives them particular meaning. That context is supplied by the audience.

Let's look at an example:

By Amos Bridges
news@ColumbiaMissourian.com

As if high school freshmen didn't have it hard enough, a recent study says only about one in three will graduate with the courses needed to get into even the nation's least selective four-year colleges.

Nationwide, only 70 percent of all students entering high school will graduate, says a study from the Manhattan Institute, a New York think tank that advocates vouchers and school choice. Fewer than half of those—32 percent of all students—have transcripts that will get them into four-year programs with what the study defines as the least demanding course requirements.

The study, "Public High School Graduation and College Readiness Rates in the United States," says that to have "any reasonable hope of attending" a four-year college, students need to have taken four years of English, three years of math and two years each of natural science, social science and foreign language. These requirements were developed by looking at four-year institutions researchers deemed "representative of the lowest level of prestige and selectivity."

The high school graduation rate in Columbia is about 79 percent, just short of the state average of 82.5 percent, according to data from the Missouri Department of Elementary and Secondary Education, or DESE. But more Columbia students enter four-year schools the year after they graduate—65 percent, compared to 40 percent statewide. . . .

This is the top of a story that appeared in a morning newspaper. The full story goes on to explain how local and state graduation requirements compare with the national standards and what the hometown university requires for admission. Along with it ran a box labeled "More online." That contained the Web site addresses for the national report and the state department of education. Readers could then go online and see for themselves much of the raw material on which the story was based.

Now consider this story's value to its audience. The story is relevant. Education touches the core of any community, especially a college town such as Columbia. Every parent, every student, every teacher has a direct stake in this subject. The story and the accompanying Web sites are useful because they allow readers to assess just where they, and those they care about, stand in relation to peers and competitors across the country. Relevance and usefulness add up to a high level of interest.

This story would have been a challenge for television journalists. Statistics and comparisons don't lend themselves to compelling pictures, which television demands. So the TV version would probably rely on video of students studying, on-camera interviews with experts and charts conveying essential numbers. The presentation would be different in each medium, but the news values that make the story important and the reporting skills required to tell it would be the same. Later chapters will help you learn those skills. For now, let's look a little more closely at news values, the criteria journalists use to decide which stories are worth telling.

Relevance, usefulness and interest are the broad guidelines for judging the news value of any event, issue or personality. Within those broad standards, journalists look for more specific elements in each potential story. The most important are the following.

- **Impact.** The potential impact of a story is another way of measuring its relevance and usefulness. How many people are affected by an event or idea? How seriously does it affect them? The wider and heavier the impact, the better the story. Sometimes, of course, impact isn't immediately obvious. Sometimes it isn't very exciting. The challenge for good journalism is making such dull but important stories lively and interesting. That may require relying on the next three elements.

- **Conflict.** A recurring theme in all storytelling—whether the stories told are journalism, literature or drama—is conflict. Struggles between people, among nations or with natural forces make fascinating reading. Conflict is such a basic element of life that journalists must resist the temptation to overdramatize or oversimplify it.

- **Novelty.** Novelty is another element common to journalism and other kinds of stories. People or events may be interesting and therefore newsworthy just because they are unusual or bizarre.

- **Prominence.** Names make news. The bigger the name, the bigger the news. Ordinary people have always been intrigued by the doings of the rich and famous. Both prominence and novelty also can be, and often are, exaggerated to produce "news" that lacks real relevance and usefulness.

- **Proximity.** Generally, people are more interested in and concerned about what happens close to home. When they read or listen to national or international news, they often want to know how it relates to their own community. Some newspapers are experimenting with "hyperlocal" coverage, as they seek to reconnect with readers by reporting at the neighborhood level, sometimes by soliciting contributions from residents, or citizen journalists. Independent Web sites devoted to this kind of extremely local coverage are springing up across the country.

- **Timeliness.** News is supposed to be new. If news is to be relevant and useful, it must be timely. For example, it is more useful to write about an issue facing the city council before it is decided than afterward. Timely reporting gives people a chance to be participants in public affairs rather than mere spectators.

Notice that this list suggests two important things about news. First, not all news is serious, life-and-death stuff. Journalism has been described as "a culture's conversation with itself." The conversation that holds a culture together includes talk of crime, politics and world affairs, of course, but it also includes talk of everyday life. It includes humor and gossip. All of that can be news. Second, news is more than collections of facts. Telling the news usually means telling stories. The narrative, the humanity, the drama of storytelling is the art of journalism. To gather the facts for their stories, journalists use many of the same techniques used by sociologists, political scientists and historians. But to tell their stories so that those facts can be understood, journalists often use the techniques of other storytellers, such as novelists and screenwriters.

Differences among the news media give different weights to those criteria and require different approaches to telling stories. For example, newspapers and magazines are better than television or radio for explaining the impact of an issue or the causes of a conflict. Scholars have learned that, although most people say they get most of their news from television, few can remember very much of what they've seen or heard on a newscast. But print can't compete with television in speed or emotional power. The differing strengths and limitations of each medium make it more likely that you'll find a lengthy explanatory story in a newspaper or magazine, while you're more likely to learn of an event from television, radio or the Internet. The newspaper lets you read the details of a budget or a box score, but television shows you the worker whose job was cut or the player scoring the winning basket. The unique power of online journalism is that it brings together the immediacy of television and the comprehensive authority of print, with endless opportunities to pursue your interests through the Web. And you can join the public conversation by posting comments to an existing blog or launching your own.

> **❙❙**(On television) superficiality is not just built into the lack of time. It's that we spend a lot of time not on the phone, not in the library, but trying to show visually what we're talking about.**❙❙**
>
> — Sam Donaldson, ABC News correspondent

The most exciting — and, to some traditional journalists, most worrisome — development is **citizen journalism**. This is news coverage, usually online, by people who don't work for commercial companies. Some citizen journalists are producing regular reporting for growing audiences. Their focus may be on local communities, as is the case with www.backfence.com and www.yourhub.com. Or it may be broader, as with the activist www.indymedia.org, an international collective that publishes online editions in a number of major cities, with a strongly anti-establishment slant.

Few of these citizen journalism outlets are profitable, and many are deliberately nonprofit. Their goal, whether local or international, is to cover communities and issues that even local newspapers and broadcast stations don't reach. Their staffs are a mix of trained journalists and interested amateurs. Their audiences are people who don't feel adequately served by the traditional media. Some observers have likened them to the pamphleteers who were the pioneers of American journalism two centuries ago.

THE ROLE OF JOURNALISM AND THE CHALLENGES IT FACES

The First Amendment to the U.S. Constitution protects the five freedoms that the nation's founders considered essential to a democracy: the freedom of speech, religion, the press, petition and assembly. In the 1830s, the French aristocrat Alexis de Tocqueville came to study the United States and wrote his classic *Democracy in America*. He was struck by the central role played by the only journalism available then, the newspapers. "We should underrate their importance if we thought they just guaranteed liberty; they maintain civilization," he wrote.

More than 200 years after they were guaranteed, the First Amendment freedoms are still essential and still under threat. After September 11, 2001, a new emphasis on national and personal security tempted government officials and citizens alike to question just how much freedom is compatible with safety. The role of journalism in guaranteeing liberty and maintaining civilization is challenged by those who make news and those who need it.

American journalism is also under threat from growing public skepticism about how well today's journalists are fulfilling their historic roles. In a national survey conducted in 2005 by researchers at the Missouri School of Journalism, 85 percent of those responding said they see bias in news coverage. Half said journalism is too sensational. Seventy percent said the news media are often influenced by powerful people and organizations. Nearly two-thirds said journalists often invade people's privacy. (Still, 56 percent said they trust the information provided by their local newspaper, and 58 percent said the same for local television and radio.)

In that same survey, however, 93 percent said freedom of the press is important to our system of government, 75 percent said journalism helps them understand what is going on in America, and 75 percent said journalism helps them be more thoughtful about public issues. More than 80 percent said investigative reporting is important, and two-thirds said journalists are good watchdogs over public officials. Even though both daily newspaper circulation and television news viewing have declined in recent years, 76 percent in the survey said they watch local TV news at least three days a week, and 66 percent said they read a local newspaper at least three days a week.

What these citizens seem to be saying is that the work journalists do is important, but journalists aren't doing it well enough. The past decade has seen the emergence of several major efforts to improve the performance of American journalism.

One of those efforts has been driven by an informal association called the Committee of Concerned Journalists and the related Project for Excellence in Journalism. The project conducts regular research on journalism and issues reports, which can be accessed on its Web site, www.journalism.org. Among the reports are annual "State of the News Media" assessments of the quality of local television news. Another product of these reformers is a book that every student and practitioner of journalism should read. Written by two leaders of the committee and the project, Bill Kovach and Tom Rosenstiel, the book is *The Elements of Journalism.*

The book argues that "the purpose of journalism is to provide people with the information they need to be free and self-governing." It proposes nine principles to achieve this purpose:

1. Journalism's first obligation is to the truth.
2. Its first loyalty is to citizens.
3. Its essence is a discipline of verification.
4. Its practitioners must maintain an independence from those they cover.
5. It must serve as an independent monitor of power.

TIPS

Audiences of the 21st Century

● By 2010, married couples will no longer make up a majority of households.

● By 2025, Americans over 64 will outnumber teenagers 2-1.

● By 2050, one-fifth of the U.S. population will be Hispanic.

— All from *Undercovered: The New USA*, published by New Directions for News

6. It must provide a forum for public criticism and compromise.
7. It must strive to make the significant interesting and relevant.
8. It must keep the news comprehensive and proportional.
9. Its practitioners must be allowed to exercise their personal conscience.

In these principles, you can hear echoes of the Journalist's Creed, written nearly a century before by Walter Williams, founding dean of the world's first journalism school, at the University of Missouri. Williams wrote that "the public journal is a public trust . . . (and) acceptance of a lesser interest than the public interest is a violation of that trust."

These efforts to reform, or restore, journalism recognize these vital functions of journalists in a free society:

- **Journalists report the news.** The first and most obvious function, it is the foundation of the rest. Reporters cover Congress and council meetings, describe accidents and disasters, show the horrors of war and the highlights of football games. This reporting takes many forms—live television, online bulletins, next-day newspaper analyses, long-form magazine narratives. No wonder journalism has been called the first rough draft of history.

- **Journalists monitor power.** Most often, Americans are concerned about the power of government. Lately, private power has become more of a worry and more a source of news. Monitoring is required even if power is used legitimately—when governments raise taxes or take us to war, for example, or businesses close plants or cut healthcare benefits for employees. When the power is used illegally or immorally, another important function comes into play.

- **Journalists uncover injustice.** A television reporter learns that one brand of tires and one model of car are involved in a disproportionate number of fatal accidents. A newspaper discovers that prisoners on death row were convicted unfairly. In those cases and thousands more, journalists bring to light dangerous or illegal abuses that might otherwise go unchecked.

- **Journalists tell compelling stories that delight us and some that dismay us.** *The (New Orleans) Times-Picayune*'s coverage of Hurricane Katrina and its aftermath, in print and online, did both. George Packer wrote gripping accounts of the Iraq war for *The New Yorker* and then turned them into a book, *The Assassin's Gate*. Television's *60 Minutes* and *Frontline* tell the stories of true-life dramas. Bloggers bring firsthand experiences and, often, great passion to their posts.

- **Journalists sustain communities.** These may be small towns, cities or even virtual communities of people connected only by the Internet. By their reporting, monitoring, revealing and storytelling, journalists serve as the nervous system of the community. They convey information and argument. Their work is, in the words of the late journalism scholar James Carey, the community's "conversation with itself."

Other scholars use other terms for this combination of vital functions. One is "agenda-setting," the placing of issues on the public agenda for discussion and decision. Another is "gate-keeping," the process by which some events and ideas become news and others do not. Now that the Internet has flooded the world with information, another role is emerging—that of "navigation," guiding readers and viewers through oceans of fact, rumor and fantasy in search of solid meaning.

Richard Saul Wurman has examined this new need in his book *Information Anxiety*, another work every journalist should read. In it, Wurman says that most news could be divided into three categories: hope, absurdity and catastrophe. Journalists typically focus on absurdity and catastrophe. Readers and viewers hunger for hope. Instead of merely pointing out problems, a journalism of hope would identify possible solutions, provide examples and tell people where to go for information or to get involved. (You'll notice a resemblance to civic journalism in Wurman's prescriptions.)

Wurman's other point relates directly to navigation. Mere information is not the most important product of journalism, he points out. Understanding is what's essential to effective communication. As journalists improve their ability to tell stories that are relevant and useful, they are more likely to convey understanding. Lacking that, citizens drift, and sometimes drown, in the ever-deepening sea of information.

> **❚❚**The computer is an icon for our age, but reason and imagination, which yield understanding, are yet to be programmable.**❚❚**
>
> — Richard Saul Wurman

ACCURACY, FAIRNESS AND THE PROBLEM OF OBJECTIVITY

The goal toward which most journalists strive has seldom been expressed any better than in a phrase used by Bob Woodward, a reporter, author and editor at *The Washington Post.* Woodward was defending in court an investigative story published by the *Post.* The story, he said, was "the best obtainable version of the truth."

A grander-sounding goal would be "the truth," unmodified. But Woodward's phrase, while paying homage to the ideal, recognizes the realities of life and the limitations of journalism. Despite centuries of argument, philosophers and theologians are still unable to agree on what truth is. Even if there were agreement on that basic question, how likely is it that the Roman Catholic Church and the Planned Parenthood organization would agree on the "truth" about abortion, or that a president and an opposition presidential candidate would agree on the "truth" about the state of the American economy?

In American daily journalism, that kind of dispute is left to be argued among the partisans on all sides, on the editorial pages and in commentaries. The reporter's usual role is simply to find and write the facts. The trouble is, that task rarely turns out often to be simple.

Sometimes it's hard to get the facts. The committee searching for a new university president announces that the field of candidates has been narrowed to five, but the names of the five are not released. Committee members are sworn to secrecy. What can you do to get the names? Should you try?

Sometimes it's hard to tell what the facts mean. The state Supreme Court refuses to hear a case in which legislators are questioning the constitutionality of a state spending limit. The court says only that there is no "justiciable controversy." What does that mean? Who won? Is the ruling good news or bad news, and for whom?

Sometimes it's even hard to tell what is fact. A presidential commission, after a yearlong study, says there is no widespread hunger in America. Is the conclusion a fact? Or is the fact only what the commission said? And how can you determine whether the commission is correct?

Daily journalism presents still more complications. As a reporter, you usually have only a few hours—or at most a few days—to try to learn as many facts as possible. Then, even in such a limited time, you may accumulate information enough for a story of 2,000 words, only to be told that there is space or time enough for only 1,000 or fewer. The new media offer more space but no more time for reporting. When you take into account all these realities and limitations, you can see that reaching the best obtainable version of the truth is challenge enough for any journalist.

How can you tell when the goal has been reached? Seldom, if ever, is there a definitive answer. But there are two questions every responsible journalist should ask about every story before being satisfied: Is it accurate? Is it fair?

Accuracy and Fairness

Accuracy is the most important characteristic of any story, great or small, long or short. Accuracy is essential in every detail. Every name must be spelled correctly; every quote must be just what was said; every set of numbers must add up. And that still isn't good enough. You can get the details right and still mislead unless you are accurate with context, too. The same statement may have widely different meanings depending on the circumstances in which it was uttered and the tone in which it was spoken. Circumstances and intent affect the meaning of actions as well. You will never have the best obtainable version of the truth unless your version is built on accurate reporting of detail and context.

Nor can you approach the truth without being fair. Accuracy and fairness are related, but they are not the same. The relationship and the difference show clearly in this analogy from the world of sports:

The referee in a basketball game is similar, in some ways, to a reporter. Each is supposed to be an impartial observer, calling developments as he or she sees them. (Of course, the referee's job is to make judgments on those developments, while the reporter's is just to describe them. Rendering judgment is the role of columnists, bloggers and other opinion writers.) Television has brought to sports

ON THE JOB

Road to a Dream Job

As politics analyst for www.washingtonpost.com, Terry Neal had a dream job. He described it as "a bit of a strange hybrid between news and opinion." He loved it. "It allows me to bring my perspective to the political news of the day in a way that is entertaining and accessible to the masses of people who find politics interesting and important, but who don't make their living at it." Still, he gave it up to become an editor helping to direct the *Post*'s local coverage. It was another move in a career full of movement.

He didn't follow a straightforward route to the top. When he was in journalism school, and even after he graduated, he wasn't sure journalism was what he wanted for a career. Like many other journalism majors, he felt the lure of law school. Ultimately, he was hooked on journalism by an internship at the Fort Lauderdale, Fla., *Sun-Sentinel*. "I really fell in love with journalism," he recalls.

After he graduated, a reporting job at the *Sun-Sentinel* led to an offer from *The Miami Herald*. There he began by covering local government and won a "plum assignment" to the state capital bureau in Tallahassee. "It had never been my plan in college to pursue a career as a political reporter, but I seemed to fall naturally into that niche. By this time, law school was a long-faded aspiration. I had found my calling."

After he covered Jeb Bush's first run for governor of Florida, *The Washington Post* found Terry. Three years on the metro desk, reporting on local and state politics, earned him a promotion to the national desk. At the age of 30, he was the *Post*'s youngest national politics reporter.

"I traveled around the country writing about congressional and gubernatorial races. I spent a lot of time on the Hill, particularly in 1998, during the whole Monica Lewinsky mess. And I got to know the White House, traveling occasionally with both President Clinton and Vice President Gore on *Air Force One* and *Air Force Two*."

It got even better. He was assigned to cover the presidential campaign and spent a year and a half "following George W. Bush around the country, flying on his campaign plane, hanging out in Austin and filing dispatches."

But the best journalists are often restless. In Terry Neal's case, his hunger for something new led him into public relations at Burson-Marsteller, "advising major corporate clients on media strategy and that sort of thing."

He made money and spent more nights at home, "but I always felt somewhat out of place," he realized. "I never could really wrap my mind around being an advocate. I missed journalism." So when the columnist position came open at the *Post*'s Web site, he applied.

Now, he says, "I feel like I'm back home. Sometimes you have to leave something to remind you that you miss it. . . . Sometimes you just become what you do."

the instant replay, in which a key play—for example, whether a player was fouled while taking a shot—can be examined again and again, often from an angle different from the referee's view. Sometimes the replay shows an apparent outcome different from the one the official called. Perhaps the players actually didn't make contact. Perhaps what looked like an attempted shot was really a pass. The difference may be due to human error on the official's part, or it may be due to the differences in angle and in viewpoint. Referees recognize this problem. They try to deal with it by obtaining the best possible view of every play and by conferring with their colleagues on some close calls. Still, every official knows that an occasional mistake will be made. That is unavoidable. What can, and must, be avoided is unfairness. Referees must be fair, and both players and fans must believe they are fair. Otherwise, their judgments will not be accepted; they will not be trusted.

With news, too, there are different viewpoints from which every event or issue can be observed. Each viewpoint may yield a different interpretation of what is occurring and of what it means. There is also, in journalism as in sports, the possibility of human error, even by the most careful reporters.

Fairness requires that you as a reporter try to find every viewpoint on a story. Rarely will there be only one; often there are more than two. Fairness requires that you allow ample opportunity for response to anyone who is being attacked or whose integrity is being questioned in a story. Fairness requires, above all, that you make every effort to avoid following your own biases in your reporting and your writing.

Bias

The research summarized earlier suggests that citizens don't think journalists do enough to keep bias out of the news. More than eight out of 10 in a national survey said they see bias at least sometimes. Of those, about twice as many said the bias seemed to be liberal as thought it conservative. A chorus of critics claims that journalists lean to the left. A smaller chorus complains of a rightward tilt. Books and cable television talk shows add heat, if not light, to the criticism. How valid is it?

One answer is that American journalism has many biases built into it. For example, journalists are biased toward conflict. War is a better story than peace. Journalists are biased toward novelty. Airplanes that don't crash are seldom reported. Journalists are biased toward celebrity. Thousands of babies are adopted every year, but Madonna's adoption makes news.

There's a less obvious but even more important bias, too. This one probably accounts for much of the criticism. It is hidden in the job description of journalism. What do journalists say they do? What are they proudest of? What do they honor?

Journalists describe themselves as the outside agitator, the afflicter of the comfortable and the comforter of the afflicted. They see their job as being the watchdog of the powerful, the voice of the voiceless, the surrogate for the ordinary citizen, the protector of the abused and downtrodden. Journalists expect themselves to be forever skeptical, consistently open-minded, respectful of differences, sensitive to what sociologists call "the other." Neither patriotism nor religion is exempt from their critical examination.

Does that job description seem more "liberal" or more "conservative"? Conservatives generally are respectful of authority and supportive of the status quo. Is it any surprise, then, that the overwhelming majority of conservatives and many liberals see a liberal bias in journalism? Notice that this bias has little or nothing to do with partisan politics.

Now suppose we had a journalism that wasn't questioning, disrespectful of authority, open to new ideas, dogging the powerful and speaking for the weak. Who would benefit, and who would suffer? Would society and democracy be better or worse off?

While American journalism may seem superficially to be liberal, at a deeper level it is profoundly conservative. Think of the foundation stones on which the American way of life is based. Among them are capitalism, the two-party system, the myths of the ethnic melting pot and of social mobility. When was the last time you saw any of those questioned seriously in the mainstream press? And do you remember Hurricane Katrina and its aftermath? Issues of race and class were thrust into the news. Journalists don't often talk about those, either.

One conclusion suggested by this analysis is that in societies that aren't free—such as 18th-century America—a free press is a revolutionary instrument. In a society such as 21st-century America that considers itself free and is, overall, self-satisfied, the free press becomes, at a fundamental level, conservative.

Objectivity

The rules that mainstream journalists follow in attempting to arrive at the best obtainable version of the truth are commonly summarized as objectivity. Objectivity has been and still is accepted as a working credo by most American journalists, students and teachers of journalism. It has been exalted by leaders of the profession as an essential, if unattainable, ideal. Its critics, by contrast, have attacked objectivity as, in the phrase of sociologist Gaye Tuchman, a "strategic ritual" that conceals a multitude of professional sins while producing superficial and often misleading coverage.

In his classic *Discovering the News*, Michael Schudson traces the rise of objectivity to the post-World War I period, when scholars and journalists alike turned to the methods and the language of science in an attempt to make sense of a world that was being turned upside down by the influence of Freud and Marx, the emergence of new economic forces and the erosion of traditional values. Objectivity was a reliance on observable facts, but it was also a methodology for freeing factual reporting from the biases and values of source, writer or reader. It was itself a value, an ideal.

Schudson wrote, "Journalists came to believe in objectivity, to the extent that they did, because they wanted to, needed to, were forced by ordinary human aspiration to seek escape from their own deep convictions of doubt and drift."

Objectivity, then, was a way of applying to the art of journalism the methods of science. Those methods emphasized reliance on observable fact. They also included the use of a variety of transparent techniques for pursuing truth and verifying facts. In science, transparency means that the researchers explain their objectives, their methods, their findings and their limitations. In journalism, only part of that methodology is usually followed.

In *The Elements of Journalism*, Kovach and Rosenstiel worry that a kind of phony objectivity has replaced the original concept. The objectivity of science does not require neutrality or the artificial balance of two sides in a dispute. Scientists are free, and expected, to state their conclusions, as long as they report how they reached those conclusions. However, as usually practiced today, journalistic objectivity employs both neutrality and balance, sometimes instead of the kind of openness that is essential in science. This misunderstanding, or misapplication, of the real principles of objectivity has opened the way for critics to call for its abandonment. Journalists would be more honest, these critics argue, if they were open about their biases. In much of Europe, for example, journalists practice, and audiences expect, openly biased reporting.

> **"**You go into journalism because you can do good, have fun and learn.**"**
>
> — The late Molly Ivins, reporter and columnist

The problem with that approach is easy to see in European journalism or, closer to home, in the opinionated journalism of partisan publications, cable television or many blogs. One-sided reports appeal to audiences that share the reporter's bias, but they repel those who don't. Fairness and accuracy too often are casualties in this journalism of assertion rather than of verification.

Properly understood, objectivity provides the journalistic method most likely to yield the best obtainable version of the truth. True objectivity, Kovach and Rosenstiel argue, would add scientific rigor to journalistic art. Without that, journalists and audiences alike can be misled.

In 1947 the Hutchins Commission on freedom of the press concluded that what a free society needs from journalists is "a truthful, comprehensive and intelligent account of the day's events in a context which gives them meaning." The goal of this chapter is to show you how the journalists of today and tomorrow understand that need, how they are trying to meet it, and the complexity of the task. The rest of the book will help you develop the skills you'll need to take up the challenge. There are few challenges so important or so rewarding.

Suggested Readings

Journalism reviews: Any issue of the *Columbia Journalism Review*, the *American Journalism Review*, *Quill* or *The American Editor*, the bulletin of the American Society of Newspaper Editors, offers reports and analyses of the most important issues of contemporary journalism.

Kovach, Bill and Rosenstiel, Tom. *The Elements of Journalism*. New York: Crown Publishers, 2001. This little book is packed with practical advice and inspiration, a kind of applied ethics for journalists in any medium.

Schudson, Michael. *Discovering the News: A Social History of American Newspapers*. New York: Basic Books, 1978. This well-written study traces the development of objectivity in American journalism.

Wurman, Richard Saul. *Information Anxiety*. New York: Doubleday, 1990. This guide for consumers of information can also serve as a guide for journalists as they seek to provide understanding.

Suggested Web Sites

www.asne.org
The American Society of Newspaper Editors is the most important of the industry's professional organizations. This Web site will give you access to the society's landmark credibility project, including the results of a major study of Americans' attitudes toward, and uses of, journalism.

www.cjr.org
The *Columbia Journalism Review* is the oldest of the magazines devoted to critical analysis of journalists' performance. You'll find critiques of major stories and essays on ethics, along with book reviews and trade news. *American Journalism Review* (**www.ajr.org**) offers similar content.

www. journalism.org
This site of the Project for Excellence in Journalism contains relevant research and articles on the current state of journalism. See especially "State of the News Media" reports for the most comprehensive look at the current performance of all the major news media.

www.poynter.org
This site is an excellent starting point. The Poynter Institute is the leading center of continuing professional education for journalists. On this site you'll find not only a guide to the services and resources of the institute itself but links to the sites of every major professional organization and a variety of other useful resources.

Exercises

1. The Project for Excellence in Journalism is monitoring the news flow through dozens of different channels. Visit **www.journalism.org** and examine that flow. Which reports seem most thorough? Which reveal their biases? Which are you most inclined to believe?

2. Spend some time with the citizen journalists at **www.Villagesoup.com** and **www.indymedia.org**. Compare what you find with the stories in the mainstream media from those areas. Where do you see overlapping coverage, and what stories are different in each medium? Which sources seem to serve the citizens best?

3. Most Americans say they get most of their news from television. Watch an evening newscast on one of the major networks. Read *The New York Times* or *USA Today* for the same day. Compare the number of stories, the topics and the depth of coverage. How well informed are those television-dependent Americans?

4. Get copies of today's issue of your local newspaper, a paper from a city at least 50 miles away and a paper of national circulation, such as *USA Today* or *The Wall Street Journal*. Analyze the front page according to the criteria discussed in this chapter.

    What can you tell about the editors' understanding of each paper's audience by looking at the selection of stories?

    If you find stories on the same topic on two or more front pages, determine if they are written differently for different audiences. Are there any attempts to localize national stories? Suggest any possibilities you can think of.

On the basis of what you've learned in this chapter, do you agree or disagree with the editors' news judgments? Why?

5. As a class project, visit or invite to your class the editor of your local paper and the news director of a local television station. Study their products ahead of time, and then interview them about how they decide the value of news stories, how they assess the reliability of sources and how they try to ensure accuracy.

6. Take a drive on the information superhighway. Sample some of the sources you find. Describe briefly at least five sources of information you can use as a journalist and at least five sources of news you can use as a consumer.

Redefining News:
Citizen Journalism
and Convergence

2

When terrorists planted bombs in the London subway in the summer of 2005, the first images of the disaster came from survivors who used their mobile phones to take photos and transmit them to the outside world from below ground. When a tsunami hammered Indonesia months earlier and Hurricane Katrina ravaged the U.S. Gulf Coast in 2005, some of the first photos came from such phones.

That phenomenon—**citizen journalism**—isn't restricted to still photographs. Citizen-generated articles, audio files and video are cropping up on Web sites around the world, much of it on established sites of the mainstream media.

Those media sites are produced in news rooms that have begun to look different from those of the past. Even in newspaper news rooms, reporters and editors now prepare audio and video for the paper's Web site or for allied radio and television stations. They also write blogs and engage readers in online dialogues in ways that just a few years ago would have been unthinkable. Those in the radio and television business now write articles for the station's Web site that more closely resemble newspaper or magazine stories than copy to be broadcast. All are gearing up to provide news bulletins (and soon video clips) to mobile telephones. And they are focusing on the Web, which many see as the most important news platform of the future.

Journalists call this **convergence**. It's the melding of traditional media into something entirely new—the concept that consumers should be able to get news on their own terms, however and whenever they want it.

These two trends—citizen journalism and convergence—are driving fundamental changes in the media industry. In this chapter, we look at how they are altering the face of the industry and perhaps even changing the very definition of "news."

CITIZEN JOURNALISM

The Public Drives Change

Many journalists would define "news" as information that comes from trained professionals. The public, on the other hand, couldn't care less about the source; if it's interesting or informative, it's news. And regardless of whether the information comes from a neighbor or from a blogger in California or China or Chile, it can have importance and credibility in the mind of the consumer.

One of the first to understand the significance of this change was Dan Gillmor, a veteran newspaperman and former columnist for the *San Jose Mercury News* who has become a leading advocate for citizen journalism. In *We the Media: Grassroots Journalism by the People, for the People*, Gillmor writes of Sept. 11, 2001:

We watched—again and again—the awful events. Consumers of news learned the *what* about the attacks, thanks to the television networks that showed the horror so graphically. Then we learned some of the *how* and *why* as print publications and thoughtful broadcasters worked to bring depth to events that defied mere words. Journalists did some of their finest work and made me proud to be one of them.

But something else, something profound, was happening this time around: News was being produced by regular people who had something to say and show, and not solely by the "official" news organizations that had traditionally decided how the first draft of history would look. This time, the first draft of history was being written, in part, by the former audience. It was possible—it was inevitable—because of new publishing tools available on the Internet.

Another kind of reporting emerged during those appalling hours and days. Via emails, mailing lists, chat groups, personal Web journals—all nonstandard news sources—we received valuable context that the major American media couldn't, or wouldn't, provide. We were witnessing—and in many cases were part of—the future of news.

Make no mistake about it: Technology has brought us to this point. Today, anyone can be a publisher thanks to technological improvements that permit inexpensive printing, the ability to create digital audio and video with ease, and the simplicity of distributing text, photos, audio and video over the Internet. In South Korea, a citizen journalism Web site called OhmyNews adopted the slogan, "Every citizen is a reporter." At the OhmyNews site, that's true, and the model is rapidly spreading worldwide.

So what does all this mean for those who would become professional journalists? It means you won't have a one-way channel of communication through which to talk to your audience. The audience will want to talk back and participate in the process of gathering and distributing news. It also means you're likely to be working with citizens who aren't trained journalists and therefore may have little sense of the concept of verification—checking information that goes into the news report to make sure it is as correct as humanly possible. Already, mainstream news organizations are starting to feel the change.

MSNBC.msn.com, a joint venture of Microsoft and NBC News and the companion site of the MSNBC cable news channel, is a mainstream media outlet that has embraced the concept of citizen journalism (see Figure 2.1). On the front page of the MSNBC site, readers are advised, "MSNBC is looking for your help. If you are a witness to a big news event, send us your video and photos at CJ@MSNBC.com." Readers are even given assignments:

- **Assignment 1: Rebuilding homes and lives.** Was your home severely damaged or destroyed after Hurricane Katrina or Hurricane Rita? If you are rebuilding, tell us your story. You may also send text, pictures and video to CJ@MSNBC.com.
- **Assignment 2: Returning home.** Did you evacuate because of Hurricane Katrina and/or Hurricane Rita and return home? If you would like to share your stories and/or images, please click the link above or email CJ@MSNBC.com.

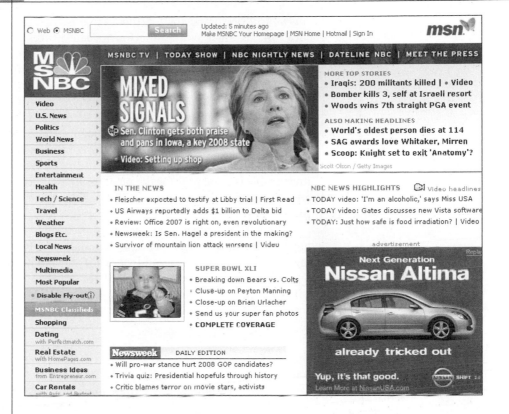

Figure 2.1
Budding journalists can participate in the news dialogue at MSNBC.com, where they are asked to submit photos, videos and stories of events they witness.

- **Assignment 3: Pinched at the pump.** How have high gas prices impacted your life? Send us your stories.

That's quite a departure from the norm. Historically, journalism in the United States and around the world has been a form of one-way communication. In its infancy, early journalists like Thomas Paine used it as a soapbox through which to influence public opinion. Later, as the craft was professionalized, the partisan press of early America yielded, in large part, to a more balanced approach founded on the elusive concept of objectivity. But journalism remained a one-way channel: reporters writing about or broadcasting information to the masses.

In that environment, the concept of journalist as **gatekeeper** prevailed. Editors decided what stories would go in the paper or the newscast. They were the powerful gatekeepers who decided what the public got to read and see.

Today, it's clear that the concept of editor as gatekeeper has largely evaporated. In a world in which anyone can be a reporter or a publisher, the media have been democratized. For those who truly believe that multiple voices give rise to a better-educated electorate, on its face that's a good thing.

But what of the quality of information produced by untrained journalists? As noted by Bill Kovach and Tom Rosenstiel in their seminal work, *The Elements of*

Journalism, one of the great virtues of mainstream journalism is the process of verification. In other words, the journalistic process of checking and rechecking information and using multiple sources provides some assurance that a report is reasonably accurate. Such rigor is often missing in citizen journalism reports, which sometimes are little more than opinion pieces.

That doesn't diminish the fact that in the eyes of the public, citizen-generated content has great value. Indeed, some of it is good, and some of it is excellent. Many mainstream journalists now recognize the value of citizen-produced content, and more and more are embracing citizens as partners in the news-gathering process. After all, a citizen-provided exclusive photograph that otherwise would be unavailable is a real plus for the medium that publishes it. And a citizen expert can add depth and explanation to a story that a nonexpert reporter would be hard-pressed to produce.

Even if journalists don't accept the change—and some are resistant—it's happening. The public, you see, is demanding it. Readers and viewers seek a dialogue with those who run and work for their newspapers, magazines, radio and television stations, and Web sites. They want to be part of the discussion. So whether imperfect or not, citizen journalism is here to stay.

Reject It or Embrace It?

When citizen journalism first appeared, most mainstream media rejected it as unprofessional. Many journalists felt threatened by it. But many in the public found it liberating and saw citizen journalism as a way of striking back at the established media, which they distrusted or viewed as biased. A rather nasty dialogue resulted on several blogs as journalists reacted.

Today, however, many media companies have taken Gillmor's advice to embrace citizen journalism as a complement to the traditional news report and as a way to reconnect with readers and viewers. There's no doubt that those who are allowed to contribute to the news feel a sense of satisfaction with the fruit of their labors and a real connection to the media outlets that publish their work. And, of course, there's the reality that citizen journalism brings a fresh perspective to the news.

As a result, the mainstream media are not only allowing but also encouraging increased dialogue with the audience—in effect, giving readers and viewers the chance to talk back, air their opinions and contribute new information. The growth of such media is phenomenal:

- Across the country, newspaper and television station Web sites contain blogs by reporters and editors that attempt to make the news-gathering process more transparent and that provide a chance for the audience to react.

- In some communities, newspapers have popped up that are written and photographed entirely by readers with the help of professional editors. Two examples are *The Northwest Voice* in Bakersfield, Calif., and *My Missourian* in Columbia, Mo. Both are published by their sponsoring mainstream newspapers and both have companion Web sites full of citizen-generated content.

Figure 2.2
On Bluffton Today, regular citizens are able to post their own blogs, upload pictures or even send in a news tip, which makes the site an interactive forum for information exchange.

- Community Web sites packed with citizen-generated blogs abound. A notable example is BlufftonToday.com, an effort of the *Bluffton Today* newspaper in Bluffton, S.C. (see Figure 2.2). It's a dramatic departure from the usual newspaper Web site, which is often little more than a regurgitation of the contents of that day's newspaper. BlufftonToday.com contains community blogs, expert blogs and staff blogs. As a result, everyone is part of the dialogue.

Many editors and publishers now realize that readers and viewers want to talk back, and they are allowing that to happen. In the process, they are connecting with the audience in ways that were never before possible. As they do so, the media are creating positive discussions with audiences that quite recently felt talked to and alienated.

The trend, then, is toward Big Media's using the phenomenon of citizen journalism to its advantage. Citizen journalism isn't going away, so it's time for the news media to embrace it. Citizen journalism is not, as some feared, a significant threat to mainstream journalism. It does, however, require journalists to welcome the public to the discussion.

The Coming of Web 2.0

In its initial forms, the Web was merely a replica of traditional media forms: Publishers published, and consumers consumed. Call it Web 1.0. Although that's certainly

ON THE JOB

Journalism for a New Century

Less than five years after he graduated, Adrian Holovaty was invited back to his alma mater to be the graduation speaker. His rapid ascent to the top tier of journalism is directly attributable to these undeniable facts: He's intelligent, and he understands where the media need to go.

After graduation, Holovaty went to the *Lawrence (Kan.) Journal-World*, a recognized leader among newspaper companies trying to figure out how to manage the inevitable transition from print to the Web. He then designed www.chicago crime.org, an innovative Web site that helped the people of Greater Chicago better understand crime in their community. The site won a Batten Award for Innovation in Journalism and captured the attention of the media industry. *The Washington Post* came calling and named Holovaty editor of editorial innovations, a new position.

In his speech, Holovaty urged graduates of his alma mater to follow him:

The fire should be burning under each and every one of you. You should be yearning — aching — to bring this industry into a new age. Your generation — our generation — is going to be the one to do it.

You're going to be the people breaking the rules. You're going to be the people inventing new ones. You'll be the person who says, "Hey, let's try this new way of getting our journalism out to the public." . . .

You'll be the person who asks, "Why are we doing things the way we are?" and when the top editor says, "Because that's the way they've always been done," you'll openly question that. "Because we've always done it that way" doesn't cut it. "Because we've always done it that way" is blatantly unacceptable, blatantly lazy, and you need to call that out.

In his brief time in the industry, Holovaty has done just that. He's helping to reinvent journalism for a new century.

the way most of the Web still works, Web 2.0 is arriving, and it differs from Web 1.0 in three fundamental ways:

- Members of the public become publishers.
- Members of the public help to decide what's news and how it's presented.
- Members of the public build communities to help process information.

Blogs have become a major means of receiving information and reacting to it. Podcasts and the ability to deliver them over the Internet have made it inexpensive for citizens to become broadcasters. **Wikis** (for example, Wikipedia) allow people to share information and edit that information as they see fit (see Figure 2.3). People who were once only news consumers are now news editors and publishers.

They also are their own news aggregators. Serious news consumers can use **RSS feeds** to automate the collection of news from various sites on the Internet. Combined with video-capture devices like TiVo, such software allows consumers to read, listen to or watch the news on their own terms—when, where and how they want it. In addition, news from mainstream Web sites like that of *The New York Times* (nytimes.com) is easily combined with news from nontraditional sites like the Drudge Report or RocWiki.org, a newspaper edited entirely by readers in Rochester, N.Y.

The world's largest newspaper-industry trade association, ifra, compiled this list of exemplary Web 2.0 sites to demonstrate how the Web is evolving:

- **Rollyo.com**, a search engine that searches only the sites you're interested in.
- **Flock.com**, a Mozilla-based browser incorporating an RSS aggregator and blogging.
- **Del.icio.us**, a site that enables consumers to bookmark and tag content that interests them and get insight into the tagging of others.
- **Basecamphq.com**, group collaboration software.
- **Zimbra.com**, a Web 2.0 rival to Microsoft Outlook.
- **Flickr.com**, a site (now owned by Yahoo!) that enables users to publish, share and collaborate on picture albums.
- **Dropcash.com**, fund-raising software.

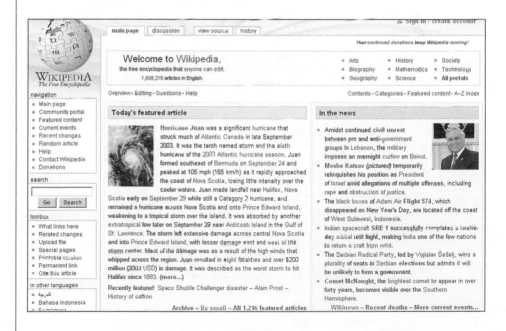

Figure 2.3

Wikipedia, one of the best-known wiki Web sites, employs a technology that allows anyone to add, edit or remove content from their online encyclopedia.

Web 2.0 is all about collaboration and sharing, the very forces that are driving citizen journalism.

Forms of Citizen Journalism

In an article in Online Journalism Review, J.D. Lasica sorted the media forms used in citizen journalism into six types:

- **Audience participation** (user comments attached to news stories, personal blogs, photos or video footage captured from mobile phone cameras, local news written by members of the community). Mainstream media outlets like MSNBC.com give readers the chance to post comments and other items on their sites.
- **Independent news or information Web sites** (ConsumerReports.org, the Drudge Report). These sites are published by groups that are not associated with traditional media.
- **Participatory news sites** (*My Missourian*, *The Northwest Voice*). On participatory news sites, readers get to write, take photos and publish their work, perhaps even in newspaper format, with the assistance of professional editors. Most have companion Web sites.
- **Collaborative and contributory news sites** (Slashdot, Kuro5hin). These sites, often featuring a specific subject-matter area, are based on reader comments and contribution.
- **Thin media** (mailing lists, e-mail newsletters). The targeted news content of mailing lists and e-mail newsletters is directed to those with narrowly defined interests.
- **Personal broadcasting sites** (KenRadio). On these sites, the operators provide news-based subject matter in a specific area of interest, such as technology. The result is downloadable audio or video in various formats, including Windows Media, QuickTime, podcasts and vodcasts (video podcasts) (see Figure 2.4).

Many consumers wouldn't stop there. Is *The Daily Show* a news program? It is to many young adults and others, even though the show is clearly intended to be entertainment, not a serious news report. Is the information found on social-networking sites like Facebook and MySpace news? It is for many. The public, then, is using its newfound power in the news marketplace to shake the very definition of traditional news. If it's something someone wants or needs to know, no matter the source, it's news.

Managing the Change

If citizen journalism and its enabler, Web 2.0, are changing the way news is consumed, the question becomes, How should journalists adapt to that change? Robert Cauthorn, chief executive officer of CityTools, urges journalists to forget news and concentrate on storytelling.

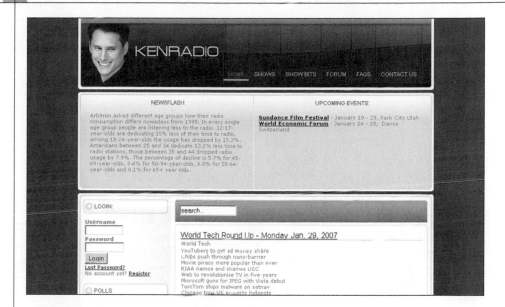

Figure 2.4
Listeners can tune into KenRadio to hear a daily live talk-radio show on technology and media news from around the world.

And that storytelling, Cauthorn believes, should be collaborative in nature. "If you let people write on your Web sites," he told a group of worldwide publishers, "they are on your side. Let people comment on your stories. Don't seek to dominate the discussion, which is the usual media role. You cannot stop the trend toward distributed discussion."

To illustrate his point, Cauthorn points out that Digg, a Web site devoted to covering technology, now has more daily traffic than the Web site of *The New York Times*, despite the *Times'* valuable brand. Digg got to that point by sharing the authority to cover technology news with its readers. Readers can write for the site, and all members then rate the articles. The rating system provides some assurance that the highest-ranked articles are authoritative.

"Allow your readers to become stars," Cauthorn says. "That builds loyalty." Some understand Cauthorn's message. Bakersfield.com, for example, is a community Web site published by the *Bakersfield Californian* and its Web site. The site allows citizens to set up their own blogs, right on the newspaper's Web site (see Figure 2.5).

YourHub.com attempts to connect readers right down to the neighborhood level. The concept is to create discussion about things of great concern in tiny portions of a community. For many publishers, this hyperlocal approach bears watching. People are passionate about their schools and neighborhoods, and engaging them in a discussion about those things has value.

That's exactly what Cauthorn is trying to do with his new venture, CityTools. The idea is to connect people and categorize information at the neighborhood

> **"**We're in the very early days of citizen journalism (or grassroots media, or we media or whatever you choose to call it). Every day, people are taking photos of and writing about their experiences in natural disasters and other news events, then submitting them to news organizations, Web sites and blogs. And most often, they're not getting paid for it.**"**
>
> — Steve Outing, Enthusiast Group founder

Figure 2.5

Although affiliated with *The Bakersfield Californian*, Bakotopia is entirely community-run. Users can create a profile, share videos and photos, post events and connect with other users.

level. Readers are able to rate all content, creating an online community valuable to everyone in the area.

Well-tailored content, whether geographic in nature or designed to appeal to users with common interests, offers great commercial opportunities for publishers. Such online communities make it possible to offer **contextual advertising**, advertising related to the content, which is exactly the kind of targeted advertising for which agencies are willing to pay a premium. It's also the kind of local advertising that newspapers and television stations have been unable to offer. The potential result is a new stream of revenue.

The concept of building online communities to which information and advertising can be marketed is merely an extension of an old staple, the intensely local news carried by weekly newspapers. In this case, however, the readers get to talk back.

But is this content news? Well, that depends on your definition. More important, it depends on the definition of your audience. If people crave the information, it probably qualifies as news.

Rob Curley, vice president for new product development at Washingtonpost .Newsweek Interactive, understands the value and appeal of hyperlocal content. Prior to joining WPNI, Curley worked at newspapers in Kansas and Florida to build Web sites with database-driven coverage. Curley's formula includes restaurant guides, guides of things to do today and guides tailored to the uniqueness of communities. In Lawrence, Kan., for example, he created the definitive Web site on all things related to the University of Kansas Jayhawks teams.

While working for the *Naples Daily News* in Florida, Curley designed a database that provided copious detail about the community's annual charity wine dinners. Lavish dinners catered by some of the world's leading chefs were the province of Naples' high society, but everyone in the city—or around the world—could share in the experience by going to the Naples Web site. There you could find the menus for the dinners, held at the homes of Naples' wealthiest citizens, and photos of the event. You also could find details of the wines offered at the related wine auction and the prices they brought.

Another of Curley's axioms is that content should be platform-independent. If the customer wants it in the newspaper, on television or on the Web site, fine. But if the reader would prefer an instant message or an e-mail reminder, that should be available, too. He's now gearing up to provide content on third-generation mobile phones: **3G technology** will allow delivery of video over telephones, an innovation that's already commonplace in Japan, Korea and parts of Europe. When the network infrastructure is in place, it is expected to take the United States by storm. Publishers must be ready.

CONVERGENCE

Different News Rooms, Different Skills

It's clear that if mainstream journalists are to become players in the new media marketplace, they have to become multimedia journalists. They must understand not only the basics of writing and editing but also the fundamentals of audio and video production, blogging, mobile phone technology and more.

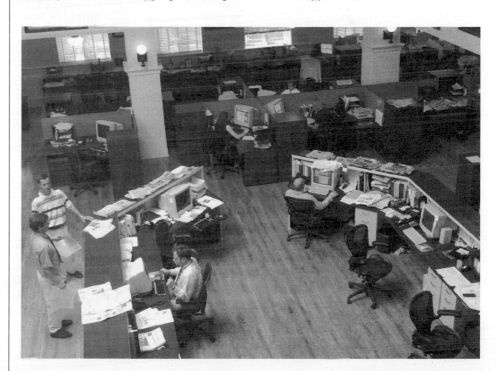

The convergent news room of the *Lawrence (Kan.) Journal-World*.

"What I'm looking for," a Florida newspaper editor said, "is someone who can cover the Super Bowl for my newspaper, then do a completely different story for our Web site that takes advantage of the strengths of that medium. Then I want that same person to be able to do a standup for the television station."

That quotation speaks volumes about the changing face of the media industry. Historically, journalists were trained for jobs as newspaper reporters or magazine designers, television reporters or producers, photojournalists, or a host of other roles. But rarely was one reporter expected to be able to function across media boundaries — in print, in broadcast and in online media. Today, that's changing.

Increasingly, editors like the one in Florida are looking for journalists who can function in the world of convergence, that is, cross-media collaboration. From coast to coast, newspapers are striking alliances with television stations, sometimes owned by the same company and sometimes not. Other newspapers are collaborating with radio stations and expect their reporters to produce not only written reports of a meeting but also audio reports. Almost all of them must produce for the Web.

> **"**Paper won't disappear (in the future), but paperless media will soak up more of our time. We will eventually become paperless the way we once became horseless. Horses are still around, but they are ridden by hobbyists, not consumers.**"**
>
> — Paul Saffo, Institute for the Future

If citizen journalism is challenging the norms of traditional journalism, and perhaps even redefining news, convergence is changing the industry itself. "Convergence" is the hottest buzzword in the media industry these days, but defining it isn't easy.

In the definition of some, convergence occurs when a newspaper or television station starts publishing material on the Internet. According to others, convergence occurs when print reporters start carrying tape recorders and produce material for radio as well as print, or when advertising salespeople start selling ads for radio as well as newspapers.

While those may indeed be forms of convergence, in its most complete sense convergence involves alliances of four communication forms:

- Print (usually a newspaper or magazine).
- Broadcast or cable television, and perhaps radio.
- The Internet.
- Mobile phones and other wireless devices.

Without question, those last two are essential to any serious definition of convergence. Why? Because the Internet and wireless devices such as mobile telephones and **personal digital assistants** allow consumers to search for and find information they want and need whenever and wherever they like, a possibility generally absent in traditional media. With the newspaper you can search through the stock listings for the closing share price of Merck, the pharmaceutical giant. But you cannot read about Merck's chances of winning federal approval for its latest drug unless the newspaper's editors happen to provide that story for you. On the Internet, a simple search produces the story.

Perhaps the best definition of "convergence" is this: Convergence is the practice of sharing and cross-promoting content from a variety of media, some interactive, through news-room collaborations and partnerships. However one defines it, one thing is certain: Convergence is changing the face of the media landscape.

Enlightened editors and publishers of this new era—people like Curley—believe the key to success is giving readers what they want when they want it. That's precisely the attitude of those driving the most successful convergence experiments in the United States. *The Tampa Tribune*-WFLA-Tampa Bay Online convergence effort of Media General in Tampa is the most celebrated of those experiments. It also is one of the oldest, having started in 2000 (see Figure 2.6).

Several years after the convergence craze occurred, the converged news room in Tampa has little trouble getting either breaking or routine news onto all three platforms, says Gil Thelen, former publisher of *The Tampa Tribune* and the original leader of the effort. But it wasn't easy to get to that point. Some employees quit rather than learn new ways of doing things. Others stayed and complained but ultimately adjusted.

"Right now we're all trying to think multimedia," Kate MacCormack, team leader for pop culture at the *Tribune*, told Online Journalism Review. "But I can say (that for someone trained in newspaper journalism) it's just really, really hard. . . . Every moment, every day you need to think outside the box on what could be done, but you want to take care of your world first. We're still struggling with that." Still, crossover reporting in Tampa has become increasingly common:

- A *Tribune* story about a passenger who landed a plane after the pilot became ill carried the bylines of both a *Tribune* reporter and the WFLA anchor.

- A report on dog bites ran as a two-part WFLA series, a front-page *Tribune* story and a TBO.com package.

- A *Tribune* story on the removal of a statue from a shopping center included a picture by the photo editor, who also shot video for WFLA.

Figure 2.6
The *Tampa Tribune*-WFLA-Tampa Bay Online collaboration was one of the earliest and most successful media convergences. Readers are able to find video footage of breaking news provided by News Channel 8 alongside the *Tribune*'s print story in one place on the Tampa Bay Online Web site.

But differences in the way television and newspaper reporters have traditionally operated can cause trouble for converged operations. That became evident in Dallas when *The Dallas Morning News* and WFAA, both owned by the Belo Corp., started cooperating. How was the *Morning News'* television critic supposed to critique a show on the television station with which the newspaper partnered? Would anything he wrote be seen as biased? Not sure, the newspaper decided that, for the time being, it would not do any television criticism at all.

On other fronts, things were easier. When the television station and the newspaper decided to have their movie critics collaborate, both agreed that the *Morning News'* more stringent ethical standards, which called for refusing freebies from any source, would prevail (see Chapter 15). That agreement signaled a cultural shift for the television station — but arguably a positive one.

Without a doubt, more and more media companies are headed in this direction. Gannett, the nation's largest newspaper company, announced in late 2006 the creation of what it calls Gannett Information Centers. The concept, piloted at several Gannett newspapers, is simple, as described by Gannett CEO Craig Dubow in a letter to Gannett employees:

> The Information Center is a way to gather and disseminate news and information across all platforms, 24/7. The Information Center will let us gather the very local news and information that customers want, then distribute it when, where and how our customers seek it.

In Dubow's words, the result of the pilot projects was remarkable:

> Breaking news on the Web and updating for the newspaper draws more people to both those media. Asking the community for help gets it — and delivers the newspaper into the heart of community conversations once again. Rich and deep databases with local, local information gathered efficiently are central to the whole process. The changes impact all media, and the public has approved. Results include stronger newspapers, more popular Web sites and more opportunities to attract the customers advertisers want.

With testimonials like that, it's certain that the rest of the industry will follow.

Why Convergence?

Although converged news rooms may be the wave of the future, most news rooms today are decidedly traditional. For every Tampa-like convergence operation, there are hundreds of traditional newspaper or television news rooms. Those news rooms typically look much as they did 25 years ago except for their embedded online operations. Today, almost every television station or newspaper has a Web site.

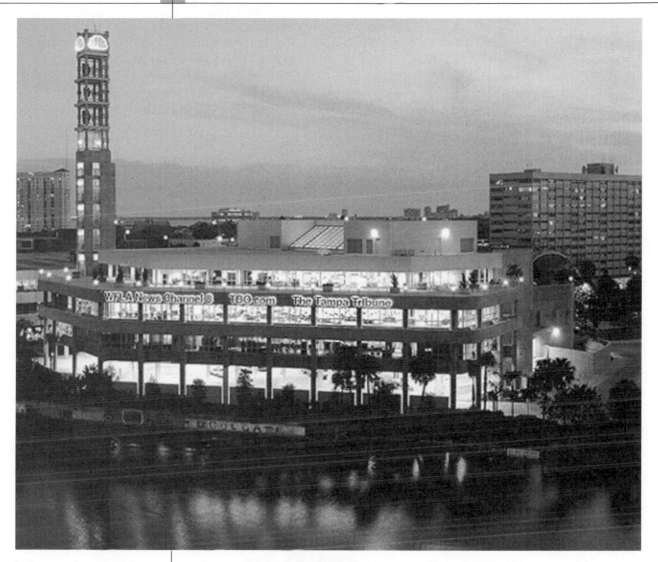

In Tampa, where one company owns the newspaper, a TV station and Web sites, a new building offers a workplace design to encourage convergence.

It's also true that most traditional news operations are still profitable. It's not at all unusual for a daily newspaper to earn a profit of 20 cents or more on every dollar it brings through the door—less than 20 years ago but still significant. Many television stations earn even more. What, then, explains the interest in convergence? It's quite simple, really. Most media-industry financial trends are headed in the wrong direction. Audiences, and therefore profits, are shrinking, and media-industry managers are worried. Many see convergence as the long-term answer to their problems.

To understand today's media-industry climate, consider these facts about newspapers, published by the Newspaper Association of America, the industry's leading U.S. trade organization:

- The daily newspaper industry is in decline. There were 1,452 daily newspapers in the United States at the end of 2005, compared with 1,745 as recently as 1980.

- In 1970, 78 percent of the nation's adults read a newspaper daily, but by 2005 that percentage had declined to 51. Worse, survey after survey has revealed that the biggest decline is among readers 34 and younger. That statistic sounds an ominous note for the future: As older readers die, there is no one to replace them. Research suggests that those who fail to develop the newspaper reading habit early will not acquire it later in life.

- Newspaper circulation is plummeting. According to the Audit Bureau of Circulation, newspaper readership is declining precipitously in major markets, and the trend is accelerating.

But if the newspaper industry is dying, as some argue, it is far from dead. Consider this:

- Newspapers remain one of the most profitable industries around, helped in large part by their near-monopoly situation in most cities.

- The number of weekly newspapers has increased slightly—from 6,580 in 1996 to 6,659 in 2005. And weekly circulation grew by almost 4 million copies during that time.

- Newspapers now trail both television and direct mail in the amount of advertising they attract, but they still capture a large share of the U.S. advertising dollar (see Figure 2.7).

Newspapers' competitors have their own problems. Network and local television both have experienced audience declines and the resulting pressure on advertising revenue. The creation of new U.S. broadcast networks like FOX and CW has fragmented television audiences, and the proliferation of cable channels has divided those audiences into even smaller segments.

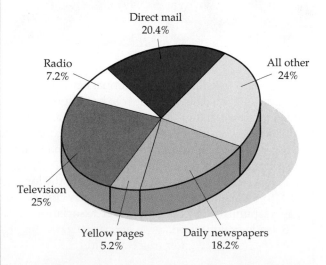

Figure 2.7
Newspapers once led in the percentage of advertising revenue, but in recent years both television and direct mail have surpassed them. *(Source: Newspaper Association of America.)*

Direct mail
20.4%

All other
24%

Radio
7.2%

Television
25%

Yellow pages
5.2%

Daily newspapers
18.2%

Cable channels are worrisome indeed for network television; unlike the networks, they are ideally positioned to deliver targeted audiences to advertisers because of their focus on specific areas of information (sports, health and fitness, children, and so on). Like newspapers, network television is best able to deliver mass audiences, not the cohesive audiences that many advertisers covet. Radio does a better job of targeting specific audiences, but its impact on the media industry, as measured by its share of advertising dollars, is relatively small, and most stations don't even cover news these days.

Magazines, like radio and cable television, deliver targeted audiences to advertisers, but they do so at a rapidly increasing cost, and together they account for only about 5 percent of U.S. advertising dollars. In the long term, magazines, like newspapers, are threatened by rising production costs, and their distribution relies heavily on ever-escalating postal rates.

The only reasonable conclusion is that the future lies with Internet-based media, perhaps in combination with the existing media. Users are able to interact with online material in ways that are not possible in traditional media, and any type of media—text, video, audio, still photographs and graphics—can be delivered online. Citizen journalists can and will play a role in the production of that content, which is a feat more difficult to accomplish with traditional media.

All of this explains why convergence is so appealing to media managers, even if convergence is shaking the very norms of traditional journalism.

Traditional Media: Where Are They Headed?

If the Internet is the news medium of the future, as many believe, where does that leave the existing media? It leaves them in a position of change, to be sure, but most are jockeying for a good seat in the new arena.

Newspapers hold the franchise for local news coverage, and they are unlikely to let that slip away without a fight. No startup site like CityTools can hope to duplicate the news-gathering apparatus already in place at the local paper (see Figure 2.8). Even with the much-publicized cuts in newspaper staffing that have occurred nationwide in recent years, most newspapers employ many more journalists than all the television stations in their markets combined. But they also are reorganizing news rooms to tackle the new realities (see Figure 2.9), which means there are increased opportunities for tech-savvy graduates of journalism programs.

Although there may be fewer newspapers in the future, the medium won't go away any time soon. The reality is that newspapers are embracing the Web. Almost all have Web sites, and a few have even begun to figure out how to make the medium complement, rather than duplicate, their existing products.

Similarly, the Internet will not usurp television in the near future. The Internet is not yet where it needs to be to challenge television, but its real potential in the video realm is its ability to deliver news and entertainment programming on demand. Station and network executives are scrambling to figure out how to do this too; high-speed, fiber-optic Internet connections into the home might be the answer. Television stations are following newspapers' lead and trying to determine how the Internet figures into their future.

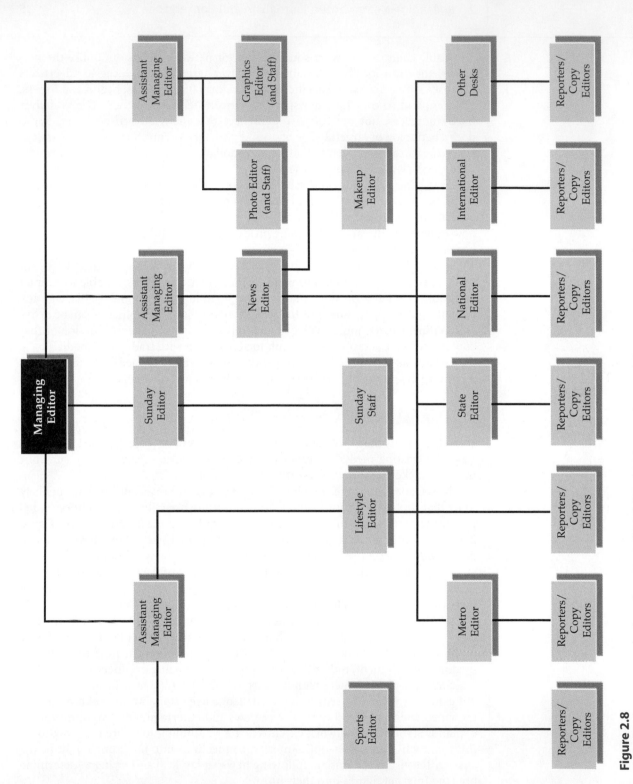

Figure 2.8
Typical news room organization of a metropolitan daily newspaper.

How decisions are made using the team concept

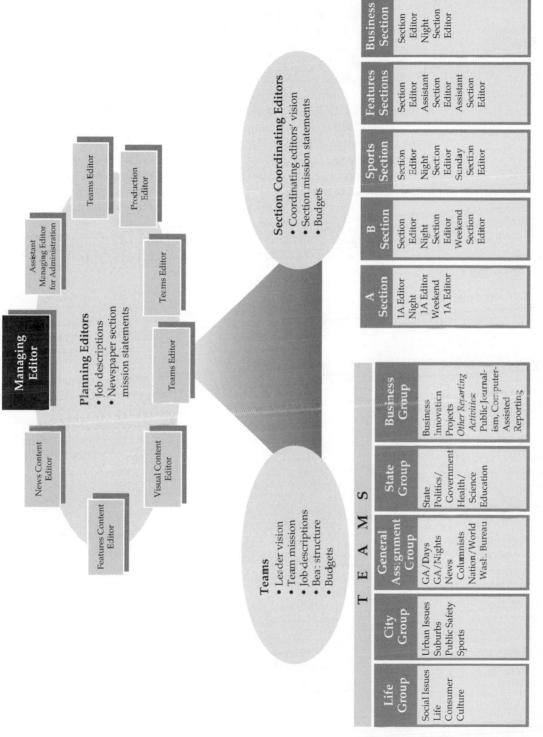

Managing Editor

Assistant Managing Editor for Administration

Teams Editor

Production Editor

News Content Editor

Features Content Editor

Visual Content Editor

Teams Editor

Teams Editor

Planning Editors
• Job descriptions
• Newspaper section mission statements

Section Coordinating Editors
• Coordinating editors' vision
• Section mission statements
• Budgets

A Section	B Section	Sports Section	Features Sections	Business Section
1A Editor Night 1A Editor Weekend 1A Editor	Section Editor Night Section Editor Weekend Section Editor	Section Editor Night Section Editor Sunday Section Editor	Section Editor Assistant Section Editor Assistant Section Editor	Section Editor Night Section Editor

Teams
• Leader vision
• Team mission
• Job descriptions
• Beat structure
• Budgets

T E A M S

Life Group	City Group	General Assignment Group	State Group	Business Group
Social Issues Life Consumer Culture	Urban Issues Suburbs Public Safety Sports	GA/Days GA/Nights News Columnists Nation/World Wash. Bureau	State Politics/ Government Health/ Science Education	Business Innovation Projects *Other Reporting Activities* Public Journalism, Computer-Assisted Reporting

Figure 2.9

Some newspapers are now organizing into teams rather than using traditional beat systems, and teams may be responsible for content in both the print and online editions. This organizational chart is based on a model provided by the Minneapolis *Star Tribune.*

Magazines, too, are embracing the Internet. There are even a few Internet-only magazines, like Slate. Newsletters, many of which have small circulations, are finding the Internet a more suitable, cost-efficient place for their content than the printed page.

Clearly, we're in a period of evolution. As more and more content moves to the Internet, traditional media outlets will begin to decline. Online distribution just makes sense. It's less expensive than carrier or mail delivery for newspapers and magazines, and it doesn't require a huge investment in printing presses or involve the environmentally unfriendly production of paper in massive quantities. Online delivery gives the media industry a means of providing audio and video on demand in place of traditional television, most of which the viewer must watch when the station chooses to transmit it, not necessarily when the viewer wants to consume it.

Still, it's important to remember that this is an evolutionary process. For the lifetimes of those entering the field of journalism today, there will still be newspapers, magazines and television stations. That means there will be jobs in those media—good jobs (see the box "Jobs in Journalism" and Figure 2.10). But those

Jobs in Journalism

Jobs abound for those who seek to enter the media industry. Here are a few of the possibilities for each medium. Entry-level jobs that beginners are likely to land are marked with asterisks.

Newspapers (Daily and Weekly)
Reporter*
Copy editor*
Page designer*
Information graphics specialist*
Photographer*
Assignment editor
News editor
Managing editor
Executive editor
Columnist

Magazines
Writer*
Fact checker*
Copy editor*
Page designer*
Senior writer

Senior editor
Contributing writer
Managing editor
Editor
Columnist

Television
Reporter*
Producer*
Desk assistant*
Videographer*
Anchor
News director
Executive producer

Radio
Reporter*
Producer*

Anchor
News director

Online Media
Producer*
Graphics specialist*
Executive producer (titles vary)

Other Jobs
Advertising sales*
Advertising copywriter*
Advertising account manager*
Public relations practitioner*
Account executive
Art director
Media critic
Foreign correspondent

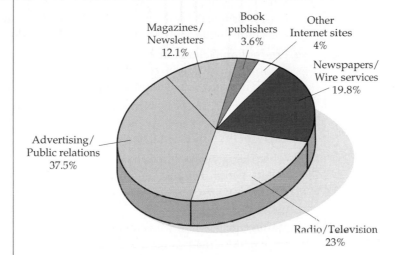

Figure 2.10
Where journalism students seek work. *(Source: Annual Survey of Journalism and Mass Communication Students, 2005, University of Georgia Grady School of Journalism.)*

entering the field also should prepare for a multimedia world. A newspaper designer might also be asked to design the newspaper's Web site. Similarly, a television reporter might be asked to write a story for the Internet or for a collaborating newspaper. It's a multimedia world in which convergence will increasingly reign.

JOURNALISM JOBS

Training to become a journalist prepares you for many jobs. Some are obvious, some not. Most jobs, regardless of the medium, fall into one of these categories.

- **Writing and reporting.** At newspapers, most writing jobs are full-time staff positions, but many magazines rely much more heavily on freelance writers who are paid by the story. The skills of reporting and writing go together. No one in journalism can be a good writer without first being a good reporter.

- **Editing.** Great jobs abound for those who can edit well. Newspapers, magazines, radio and television stations, and some Web sites have copy editors, assignment editors and editorial assistants. At newspapers, the entry-level position of copy editor often pays more than the entry-level position of reporter because copy editors are in greater demand.

- **Photography and video.** Printed publications and Web sites use lots of photographs and therefore need photographers. At newspapers, most are staff photographers, but at many magazines freelance photography is more common. Video is becoming important for all media operations that run Web sites. No longer is video merely the province of television.

- **Art and design.** Designers are needed in all media. There are jobs for newspaper and magazine designers and Web designers. Even television stations employ designers for their Web sites. There also is an increasing demand for information graphics specialists—people who produce maps, charts and graphs.

- **Production.** Television producers are in high demand. It's quite possible to become a news producer right out of journalism school. Web producers are also in demand, and additional production jobs exist in the print media.

- **Tech support.** Those who combine a knowledge of journalism with computer literacy can find jobs anywhere. Media outlets around the world have a strong interest in computer-literate journalists.

- **Advertising and public relations.** Advertising and public relations often are taught within schools and departments of journalism. Jobs in this field abound, and they range from advertising sales to creative design to account management.

- **Management.** Many who enter the journalism field eventually become assignment editors, managing editors or executive editors. These jobs pay more than reporting and editing positions and are a natural progression for reporters and copy editors.

Suggested Readings

De Wolk, Roland. *Introduction to Online Journalism: Publishing News and Information.* Boston: Allyn & Bacon, 2001. An overview of online journalism.

Gillmor, Dan. *We the Media: Grassroots Journalism By the People, For the People.* Sebastopol, Calif.: O'Reilly Media, 2006. This vital treatise on the importance of citizen journalism was written by a longtime newspaper reporter and editor.

Hewitt, Hugh. *Blog: Understanding the Information Reformation That's Changing Your World.* Nashville, Tenn.: Thomas Nelson, 2005. Hewitt, a conservative attorney and commentator, provides his view of the importance of blogs.

Suggested Web Sites

www.cbsnews.com/sections/publiceye/main500486.shtml
Public Eye lets viewers have an inside look at decision making at CBS News.

www.magazine.org
The professional organization for magazine journalists is the Magazine Publishers of America.

www.naa.org
The Newspaper Association of America, based in Reston, Va., is the newspaper industry's leading trade association.

www.nab.org
The National Association of Broadcasters is the primary trade organization of the broadcast industry.

www.onlinenewsassociation.org
The Online News Association was organized in 1999.

Exercises

1. Find two newspaper Web sites that carry staff-generated blogs. Compare and contrast them.

2. Analyze a citizen journalism site in your community or in your area. How does the information found there compare with the news on your local newspaper's Web site?

3. Provide a definition of "news" that incorporates the new realities of citizen journalism.

4. The Internet is a useful source of information for journalists. Using the Internet, locate information on the most recent U.S. census and report the following:

a. The population of your state.
b. The population of your city.
c. The range of income levels in your city and the percentages of the population that fall within those income levels.
d. The demographic breakdown of your city by race.

5. Make a list of at least 10 sources of information available on the Internet that would be good resources for journalists. Explain why and describe how you would assess the reliability of the information from each source.

Interviewing

3

Bill Reiter knew he was onto a great story. The problem was how to *get* it. Reiter was only about a year into his first job out of journalism school. He was 22. He was from Iowa. He was white. The story was the life of Edith McClinton. Mrs. McClinton had lived through the turbulent birth of the civil rights era in Little Rock, Ark. She had overcome poverty, racism and blindness to achieve professional success and personal dignity. She was 89 years old and African-American.

Reiter discovered immediately that telling Mrs. McClinton's story would require all the skills he had learned in school and some he would have to develop on the spot. Here's his recollection:

> Interviewing Mrs. McClinton was difficult for a number of reasons. Her age alone presented a pretty daunting challenge. Some days, she was in fine spirits and her memory was sharp as anyone's. But some days we'd be talking for five or 10 minutes and then I'd lose her. . . .
>
> Another problem was my paper. The *Arkansas Democrat Gazette* does not have an excellent reputation with the black community. Early on, Mrs. McClinton and her daughter Joyce (who lives with her and takes care of her) made it clear that they didn't trust my paper and that they didn't trust me. So that's where it started.

By the time it ended eight months later, Reiter had earned the family's trust and written a seven-part, front-page narrative telling the story of race in Arkansas through the experiences of one courageous woman. The series ended with this quote from Mrs. McClinton:

> "Great things can come from freedom," she says. "I take my freedom and pass it on to my children and my grandchildren."

Not every interview is that difficult, time-consuming or important. But every successful interview begins with establishing trust and ends with telling a story.

Interviewing—having conversations with sources—is the key to most stories you will write. Your ability to make people comfortable being with you is often the difference between mediocre reporting and good reporting.

Information is the raw material of a journalist. While some of it is gathered from records and some from observation, most of it is gathered in person-to-person conversations. The skills that go into those conversations are the most basic reporting tools of any reporter for any medium. You try first to talk to *primary sources*, those who witnessed the event or have authority over documents. If you can't get to the primary source, you may be forced to go to a *secondary source*, one who talked to witnesses, such as public safety officials or lawyers or the next-door neighbor.

Even when you are doing a profile, determine how your source knows your profile subject. Does your source work with the subject? Then he or she is probably not much of an authority on the subject's after-hours activities. Does the source play poker with the person? Then he or she probably doesn't know the subject in the workplace. Once you know how your source knows what he or she knows, then you can start the conversation.

If you're interviewing for television, broadcast or webcast (an audio and/or video report sent over the Internet), your goals and techniques may be different from those of a print reporter, but the basics are the same.

PREPARING FOR THE INTERVIEW

How you prepare for the interview depends in part on what kind of a story you intend to write. You may be doing a news story, a personality profile or an investigative piece. In each case, you check the newspaper library and search online databases, talk to other reporters and, if there's enough time, read magazine articles and books.

To prepare for a news story, you pay more attention to clips about the subject matter of the story than to those about the personality of the individual to be interviewed. To prepare for a profile, you look for personality quirks and the subject's interests, family, friends, travels and habits. To prepare for an investigative piece, you want to know both your subject matter and the person you are interviewing. In all these stories, do not overlook other reporters and editors who know something about the person or subject. Let's look at each of these three types of stories more closely.

> Interviews are best used to solicit reactions and interpretations, not to gather facts. Good reporters do their fact-gathering before their interviews.

The News Story

One day Paul Leavitt made a routine telephone call to a law-enforcement source. Leavitt, then assistant city editor for *The Des Moines (Iowa) Register*, was working on a story. He knew the source from his days as a county government and courts reporter for the *Register*.

He expected the story, and the interview, to be routine. Polk County was building a new jail. Leavitt wanted to find out about progress on the new building. The source pleaded ignorance. He said, "Oh, Leavitt, I don't know. I haven't had time to keep up on that, what with all these meetings on the pope's visit."

Leavitt didn't say anything right away. A less astute reporter might have let the source know he was surprised. The pope in Des Moines? Are you kidding? Instead, Leavitt remembered a story he had read about an Iowan who had extended an invitation for the pope to stop in Iowa during his American visit. At the time, Leavitt had thought the Iowan didn't have much of a chance. When the Vatican had announced the pope's visit to the United States, people from every state were bartering for a chance to bask in the worldwide limelight.

Still, the source's slip of the tongue seemed genuine. Leavitt finally replied, "Oh, yeah, that's right. When's he coming, anyway?"

"October 4," the source said.

Before the conversation ended, Leavitt had learned of a meeting among the Secret Service, the Vatican, the U.S. State Department and Iowa law-enforcement

ON THE JOB

Telling Compelling Stories

Bill Reiter, now with *The Kansas City Star*, formerly worked as a reporter for *The Des Moines (Iowa) Register*. His experience at his first job after college, in Little Rock, Ark., introduces this chapter. Here he talks about interviewing, about building trust, about getting the material to tell compelling stories:

"My goal was to write a series that would take our readers inside the lives of homeless teenagers. The task seemed daunting. I had to find these young people, build enough trust to enter their world and somehow show the complex problems and dilemmas that kept them on the street.

"So, knowing they were out there but not sure where to go, I followed the first rule of reporting, the one my college professors drilled into me. . . . I left the office. I stopped folks who looked like they might be homeless. I went by a shelter. I talked to a police officer whose beat takes him to poor parts of town. It didn't take long to hear that the man to see about life on the street was a homeless-youth outreach worker named Howard Matalba."

Matalba introduced Bill to his world and to Gabrielle, a pregnant teenager. Bill explains:

"I spent the next three months with Gabrielle. I wandered town with her, listened for hours to her complaining, filled notebook after notebook with quotes that never made the newspaper. I ate with her at the soup kitchen, followed her when she applied for food stamps and stuck around when she and her boyfriend snuggled up together on a bench or against a building. . . . I was there when Gabrielle applied for an apartment, when she ran out of money and food, and when she took back her boyfriend despite his abusive tendencies. I was there when she gave birth to her daughter. . . .

"My reporting came with costs. I was knocked down by a homeless man, I was punched and scratched by a homeless 19-year-old girl. I conquered my fear of heights because one of my sources, with me right behind him, scuttled over a rickety train bridge on his way to town. I worked nights and weekends, wandered for miles in the cold, and was told in no uncertain terms by a group of homeless men that they'd kill me if I came back. I went back anyway, again and again. . . .

"I looked for moments, dialogue and action that gave life to the issue I was writing about. I didn't rely on quotes that reconstructed something I wanted to write about. Instead, I wrote down what my sources actually said to each other, not what they said to me. I relaxed, acted like myself and remembered the people I was writing about had been through a lot."

His series ran on Page One of the *Register* and set Des Moines talking. For Bill Reiter, that's what counts.

officials to discuss the trip. He also had learned when the pope would arrive, where he would arrive, where he would celebrate Mass and when he would leave.

As a result, the *Register* stunned its readers the next morning with a copyrighted story saying the pope would speak in Des Moines. The story was printed three weeks before the Vatican released its official itinerary of the visit. Other area reporters scoffed at the story. One newspaper even printed a story poking fun at the thought of a pope hobnobbing in an Iowa cornfield.

Leavitt and the *Register* were vindicated. As scheduled, the pope arrived Oct. 4—and celebrated Mass in an Iowa cornfield.

Remembering his conversation with the source, and how a routine question had turned into a bona fide scoop, Leavitt said, "I don't even remember what the original question was."

Leavitt probably would not have gotten the story had he not remembered the earlier story about the invitation and known something else about interviewing: When a source unwittingly gives you a scoop, sometimes it is best to act as if you already know it. That may encourage the source to give you more information.

The Profile

A reporter who decided to write a profile of a local freelance writer prepared differently. Because the reporter had used the writer as a source in an earlier story, she knew something about her. She needed to know more, so she looked in *Contemporary Authors* and found biographical information. She also asked the writer to send her copies of some of the articles she had written. Before the reporter went to see the freelancer, she read several of the articles. She also interviewed the editor at one of the magazines that bought the writer's material.

The reporter was prepared. Or so she thought. She had to pass one more test. The writer was an animal lover, and when the reporter arrived, she first had to make friends with a handful of dogs. Fortunately, she loved dogs. That immediately established rapport with the freelancer. The resulting story was full of lively detail:

> Joan Gilbert stretches lazily to soft sunbeams and chirping birds. She dresses casually in blue denim shorts and a plaid, short-sleeved blouse. She and her favorite work companions, five playful dogs, file out the door of her little white house to begin their day with a lazy walk in the surrounding woods. When she returns, she'll contentedly sit down at her typewriter. Such is work.
>
> Joan Gilbert is a freelance writer.

Walt Harrington, author of *American Profiles*, specialized in writing in-depth personality profiles when he worked for *The Washington Post Magazine*. In his book, he says he spent one to three months on each profile. For profiles on former President George H.W. Bush and journalist Carl Bernstein, he conducted about 80 interviews each. He also accompanied his subjects. Few journalists are afforded the luxury of three months to work on a profile, but whether you do eight or 80 interviews, the lessons are still the same: Be prepared. Be there.

The Investigative Piece

The casual atmosphere of the Joan Gilbert interview is not always possible for the investigative reporter. An adversarial relationship determines both the preparation required for an investigative piece and the atmosphere of the interview itself. An investigative reporter is like an attorney in a courtroom. Wise attorneys know in advance what the answers to their questions will be. So do investigative reporters. Preparation is essential.

In the early stages of the investigation, you conduct some fishing-expedition interviews: Because you don't know how much the source knows, you cast around. Start with people on the fringes. Gather as much as you can from them. Study the records. Only after you have most of the evidence do you confront your central character. You start with a large circle and gradually draw it smaller.

Getting the interview is sometimes as big a challenge as the interview itself. Sources who believe you are working on a story that will be critical of them or their friends often try to avoid you. Steve Weinberg, author of an unauthorized biography of industrialist Armand Hammer, had to overcome the suspicion of many former Hammer associates. Their former boss had told all of them not to talk to Weinberg. Instead of calling, Weinberg approached them by mail. "I sent letters, examples of my previous work, explained what I wanted to cover and why I was doing it without Hammer's blessing," Weinberg says.

He recommends that you use a letter or an e-mail to share some of what you know about the story that might surprise or impress the source. For instance, a reference such as "And last week, when I was checking all the land records . . ." would indicate the depth of your research.

In his letter to former Hammer assistants, Weinberg talked about how Hammer was one of the most important people in the history of business. The letters opened doors to all seven of Hammer's former executive assistants whom Weinberg contacted.

Weinberg, former director of Investigative Reporters and Editors, an international organization of journalists involved in investigative reporting, also offers to show the sources relevant portions of his manuscript as an accuracy check. (An *accuracy check* just verifies the facts. It does not give the source the option of choosing what goes in and what stays out of a story.) He makes it clear in writing that he maintains control of the content.

Requesting an interview in writing can allow you to make your best case for getting it. And an offer to allow your sources to review the story assures them that you are serious about accuracy. E-mail makes both the request and the offer simpler and faster.

Ed Bradley, whose successful interviews were shown for years on the CBS show *60 Minutes*, died in 2006. In an obituary, Patricia Sullivan of *The Washington Post* wrote that Bradley always looked interested and listened closely.

"Although colleagues such as Mike Wallace and Dan Rather would pounce on a subject, Bradley would wait, letting his patience and silence draw out both nervous and experienced subjects. His questions were rarely accusatory but always pointed," she wrote. As an example, she showed how he phrased a tough question

TIPS

Before the Interview

● Know the subject.
  · Seek specific information.
  · Research the subject.
  · List the questions.

● Know the person.
  · Know salient biographical information.
  · Know the person's expertise regarding the subject matter.

TIPS

Set Up the Interview

● Set the time.
  · At interviewee's convenience — but suggest a time.
  · Length of time needed.
  · Possible return visits.

● Set the place.
  · Interviewee's turf.
  · Neutral turf.

without sounding as if he were making an accusation when he interviewed Secretary of State Condoleezza Rice: "(Richard) Clarke has alleged that the Bush administration underestimated the threat from al Qaeda, didn't act as if terrorism was an imminent and urgent problem. Was it?"

BROADCAST INTERVIEWS

When you're interviewing someone in front of a camera, the basic rules of interviewing don't change. Some of your objectives and techniques, however, do.

The first thing to remember is that broadcast journalism is a performance. Television journalists, at least those who appear on camera, are also performers. Sure, they have to report and write, but they also have to be able to tell their stories with both words and body language to people who are watching and listening — not reading. An important part of the television reporter's performance is the interview.

Both print and broadcast reporters often interview to develop information that can be used in further reporting. Interviews on camera usually have a different goal. That goal is the *soundbite*, the few seconds of words with accompanying video that convey not only information but emotion. Print is a medium that mainly provides information. Television is a medium of emotion. The best interviews for television are those that reveal how a situation feels to the participants or witnesses.

Al Tompkins, the Poynter Institute's group leader for broadcast and online journalism, offers what he calls "a new set of interviewing tools" intended to produce better storytelling for television. You can find these and other tools at www.poynter.org. Here are some that show both differences and similarities in print and television interviewing:

- **Ask both objective and subjective questions.** To gather facts, ask objective questions: "When?" "Where?" "How much?" But subjective questions usually produce the best soundbites. "Why?" "Tell me more. . . ." "Can you explain . . . ?"

- **Focus on one issue at a time.** Vague, complicated questions produce vague, complicated, hard-to-follow answers. Remember that readers can review until they understand, but viewers can't rewind an interview. Help them follow the story by taking your interviewee through it one step at a time.

- **Ask open-ended questions.** For print, you often want a simple yes or no. That kind of answer stops a television interview. Open-ended questions encourage conversation, and conversation makes a good interview. (For more on this, see "Open-Ended Questions" later in this chapter.)

- **Keep questions short.** Make the interviewee do the talking. Tompkins points out that short questions are more likely to produce focused responses. They also keep the viewer's attention on the person being interviewed and what she or he has to say.

- **Build to the point.** The best interviews are like the best stories. They don't give away the punch line in the first few words. Ask soft, easy questions to encourage relaxation and trust. Then move to the heart of the issue.

TIPS

Discuss Arrangements

- Will you bring a recording device?

- Will you bring a photographer?

- Will you let the interviewee check the accuracy of quotes?

- **Be honest.** As true for television as for print and online, the importance of honesty is too often overlooked by rookie reporters. You do neither your source nor yourself a favor if you lead the source to expect an interview about softball when you have an indictment in mind. Tell the source ahead of time that you'll want to ask some tough questions. Say—and mean it—that you want to get the whole story, to be fair. Then politely but firmly dig in. As Tompkins notes, honesty has the added benefit of helping you defend yourself against any later accusations of malice.

SETTING UP THE INTERVIEW

Most interviews are conducted in the source's office. However, especially if the story is a profile or a feature, it usually is better to get the source away from his or her work. If you are doing a story about a rabbi's hobby of collecting butterflies, seek a setting appropriate to the topic. Suggest meeting where the rabbi keeps the collection.

For some interviews, it is to your advantage to get the source on neutral territory. If you have some questions for the provost or a public official, suggest meeting in a coffee shop at a quiet time. A person has more power in his or her official surroundings.

It is important, too, to let the source know how much time you need and whether you expect to return for further information. And if you don't already know how the source might react to a recording device, ask when you are making the appointment.

Be sure to dress appropriately for the interview. Something as trifling as your appearance may determine whether you will have a successful interview. You would

This reporter dresses to fit in with the marchers he is interviewing. He gains their confidence by being friendly and attentive.

hardly wear cutoff shorts into a university president's suite, and you wouldn't wear a three-piece suit to talk to underground revolutionaries. It is your right to wear your hair however you wish, pierce your body and wear whatever clothes you want, but it is the source's prerogative to refuse to talk to you.

PREPARING QUESTIONS

You have now done the appropriate homework. You have made an appointment and told the source how much time you will need. You are properly attired. Before you leave, you may want to write down a list of questions to ask. They will guide you through the interview and prevent you from missing important topics altogether. The best way to encourage a spontaneous conversation is to have your questions prepared. You'll be more relaxed. The thinking you must do to write the questions will help prepare you for the interview. Having questions prepared relieves you of the need to be mentally searching for the next question as the source is answering the last one. If you are trying to think of the next question, you will not be paying close attention to what is being said, and you might miss the most important part of the interview.

Researching Questions

Preparing the questions for an interview is hard work, even for veterans. If you are writing for your campus newspaper, seek suggestions from other staff members. You will find ideas in the newspaper's electronic database. If you anticipate a troublesome interview with the chancellor, you might want to seek advice from faculty members, too. What questions would they ask if they were you? Often, they have more background knowledge, or they might have heard some of the faculty talk around campus. Staff members are also valuable sources of information.

Although you may ask all of your prepared questions in some interviews, in most you probably will use only some of them. Still, you will have benefited from preparing the questions in two important ways. First, even when you don't use many questions, the work you did thinking of them helped prepare you for the interview. Second, sources who see that you have a prepared list often are impressed with your seriousness.

On the basis of the information you have gathered already, you know what you want to ask. Now you must be careful about how you ask the questions.

Phrasing Questions

A young monk asked his superior if he could smoke while he prayed, and he was rebuked sharply. A friend advised him to rephrase the question. "Ask him if you can pray while you smoke," he said. The young monk was discovering that how questions are structured often determines the answer. Journalists face the same challenge. Reporters have missed many stories because they didn't know how to ask questions.

Quantitative researchers have shown how only a slight wording change affects the results of a survey. If you want to know whether citizens favor a city plan to beautify the downtown area, you can ask the question in several ways:

- Do you favor the city council's plan to beautify the downtown area?
- The city council plans to spend $3 million beautifying the downtown area. Are you in favor of this?
- Do you think the downtown area needs physical changes?
- Which of the following actions do you favor?
  - Prohibiting all automobile traffic in an area bounded by Providence Road, Ash Street, College Avenue and Elm Street.
  - Having all the downtown storefronts remodeled to carry out a single theme and putting in brick streets, shrubbery and benches.
  - None of the above.

How you structure that question may affect the survey results by several percentage points. Similarly, how you ask questions in an interview may affect the response.

By the phrasing of the question, many reporters signal the response they expect or the prejudices they have. For instance, a reporter who says, "Don't you think that the city council should allocate more money to the parks and recreation department?" is not only asking a question but also influencing the source or betraying a bias. A neutral phrasing would be "Do you think the city council should allocate more money to the parks and recreation department?" Another common way of asking a leading question is this: "Are you going to vote against this amendment like the other legislators I've talked to?" A neutral phrasing would be "How are you planning to vote on this amendment?" To avoid leading or even irritating your source, ask neutral questions.

Also ask one question at a time. Journalists at press conferences sometimes jump up and ask two or three questions at a time. The source then chooses the one he or she wishes to answer and ignores the rest. That will often happen in one-on-one interviews, too.

In situations where you have to ask embarrassing or awkward questions, Jeff Truesdell of *People* magazine suggests demonstrating empathy. "Say, 'I'm sorry I have to ask this,' or 'I can't believe I'm asking this but here goes,' or 'My editors will want to know'—editors in absentia make for great fall guys—or 'Let me play devil's advocate here,'" Truesdell suggests. "Acknowledge that there are unpleasant questions, apologize for asking, and then ask."

Sometimes a reporter unwittingly blocks a response by the phrasing of the question. A reporter who was investigating possible job discrimination against women conducted several interviews before she told her city editor she didn't think the women with whom she talked were being frank with her. "When I ask them if they have ever been discriminated against, they always tell me no. But three times now during the course of the interviews, they have said things that indicate they have been. How do I get them to tell me about it?" she asked.

TIPS

When You Arrive at the Interview

- Control the seating arrangement.
- Place the recording device at the optimum spot.
- Warm up the person briefly with small talk.
- Set the ground rules.
- Put everything on the record.

"Perhaps it's the way you are asking the question," the city editor replied. "When you ask the women whether they have ever been discriminated against, you are forcing them to answer yes or no. Don't be so blunt. Ask them if others with the same qualifications at work have advanced faster than they have. Ask if they are paid the same amount as men for the same work. Ask them what they think they would be doing today if they were male. Ask them if they know of any qualified women who were denied jobs."

The city editor was giving the reporter examples of both open- and closed-ended questions. Each has its specific strengths.

Open-Ended Questions

Open-ended questions allow the respondent some flexibility. Women may not respond frankly when asked whether they have ever been discriminated against. The question calls for a yes-no response. But an open-ended question such as "What would you be doing today if you were a man?" is not so personal. It does not sound as threatening to the respondent. In response to an open-ended question, the source often reveals more than he or she realizes or intends to.

A sportswriter who was interviewing a pro scout at a college football game wanted to know whom the scout was there to see. When the scout diplomatically declined to be specific, the reporter tried another approach. He asked a series of questions:

- "What kinds of qualities does a pro scout look for in an athlete?"
- "Do you think any of the players here today have those talents?"
- "Whom would you put into that category?"

The reporter worked from the general to the specific until he had the information he wanted. Open-ended questions are less direct and less threatening. They are more exploratory and more flexible. However, if you want to know a person's biographical data, don't ask, "Can you tell me about yourself?"

Closed-Ended Questions

Eventually, the reporter needs to close in on a subject, to pin down details, to get the respondent to be specific. **Closed-ended questions** are designed to elicit specific responses.

Instead of asking the mayor, "What did you think of the conference in Washington, D.C.?" you ask, "What did you learn in the session 'Funds You May Not Know Are Available'?" Instead of asking a previous employee to appraise the chancellor-designate's managerial abilities, you ask, "How well does she listen to the people who work for her?" "Do the people who work for her have specific job duties?" "Does she explain her decisions?"

A vague question invites a vague answer. By asking a specific question, you are more likely to get a specific answer. You are also communicating to your source that you have done your homework and that you are looking for precise details.

Knowing exactly when to ask a closed-ended question or when to be less specific is not something you can plan ahead of time. The type of information you are seeking and the chemistry between the interviewer and the source are the determining factors. You must make on-the-spot decisions. The important thing is to keep rephrasing the question until the source answers it adequately. Gary Smith wrote in *Intimate Journalism*, "A lot of my reporting comes from asking a question three different ways. Sometimes the third go at it is what produces the nugget, but even if the answers aren't wonderful or the quotes usable, they can still confirm or correct my impressions."

Every reporter seeks anecdotes, and closed-ended questions help elicit them. "What is the funniest thing you've ever done?" "The weirdest?" "What's the saddest thing that ever happened to you?" When the source talks in generalities, ask a close-ended question to get to specifics. "You say Mary is a practical joker. Can you think of an example of a practical joke she played on someone?" The answers to these types of questions yield the anecdotal nuggets that make your story readable.

Closed-Ended Questions	**Open-Ended Questions**
Do you like the proposal?	What are the strengths of the proposal? What are the weaknesses?
Did you have trouble coping when your child was in the car accident?	How did you cope after your child was in the car accident? Why did you attend counseling sessions?
Did you keep your promise to diet today?	What did you eat today?
Did you give the theater teacher permission to stage the play?	What did you tell the theater teacher when she asked if they could perform the play?
Do you use iChat in your work?	How do you use iChat in your work?

ESTABLISHING RAPPORT

The most basic requirement of any successful interview is a reasonable degree of trust between reporter and source. Usually, as a reporter you have to earn that trust. Wright Thompson, who now works for ESPN, tells about the time he wanted to do a story for *The Kansas City Star* about a former college football player named Ernest Blackwell, who had gone on a rampage in his neighborhood, shot a child and almost kicked another to death. He collapsed on a police gurney afterward and died en route to the hospital. No one could figure out what happened. Media outlet after media outlet approached the family. All were turned down.

"When I called, I had a line. I told them I was going to talk to the cops and was going to do a story about Ernest. The police, I told them, would give me more than enough detail about the last five minutes of Ernest's life. Then I said, 'I think there's a lot more to his life than the last five minutes. I think he deserves to be remembered for how he lived and not just how he died.'" Thompson's reasoning won him the interview. His conclusion: "Have a plan. You must give someone a reason why it's better if they talk to you than if they don't."

Because he earned the trust of the Blackwell family, he was able to develop the insights that allowed him to write this:

Those who knew him wonder how Blackwell arrived on that day with so much rage in his heart, so much bad intent. Truth is, none of them could peer into the man's soul and see the hate that grew until it reached the breaking point.

On Aug. 11, 2004, Blackwell could take no more.

"Lord, why didn't I see the signs?" says his aunt Joyce Strong, who mostly raised Blackwell. "Why didn't I see he was reaching out for help? He must have been a ticking time bomb waiting to go off."

That's the payoff on the investment in building trust.

You probably won't have many assignments that are this difficult. It always helps, though, to have a plan. It also helps to have the honesty and empathy that lead strangers to be honest with you. Act like a human being.

Rapport—the relationship between the reporter and the source—is crucial to the success of the interview. The relationship is sometimes relaxed, sometimes strained. Often it is somewhere in between. The type of relationship you try to establish with your source is determined by the kind of story you are doing. Several approaches are possible.

Interview Approaches

For most news stories and personality profiles, the reporter gains a great deal if the subject is at ease. Often that can be accomplished by starting with small talk. Ask about a trophy, the plants or an engraved pen. Bring up something humorous you have found during your research. Ask about something you know the source will want to talk about. In other interviews, if you think the subject might be skeptical about your knowledge of the field, open with a question that demonstrates your knowledge.

Rapport also depends on where you conduct the interview. Many people, especially those unaccustomed to being interviewed, feel more comfortable in their workplace. Go to them. Talk to the businessperson in the office, to the athlete in the locker room, to the conductor in the concert hall. In some cases, though, you may get a better interview elsewhere if the source cannot relax at the workplace or is frequently interrupted. Reporters have talked to politicians during car rides between campaign appearances. They've gone sailing with businesspeople and hunting with athletes. One student reporter doing a feature on a police chief spent a weekend with the chief, who was painting his home. To do a profile, which requires more than one interview, vary the location. New surroundings can make a difference.

Lisa Kremer, reporting the story of a mountain avalanche for *The (Tacoma, Wash.) News Tribune*, recognized that where she interviewed the rescuers was important. She approached the climbers at a restaurant and said she wanted to talk to them. They weren't sure they wanted to talk to her. "I said, 'Would you be more comfortable here at the restaurant? I could sit down right now. Or would you rather go back to the hotel?'"

Establishing rapport with interview subjects helps a reporter get better story information.

They said they would meet her at the hotel. They did, and she got the interviews.

There are times when the reporter would rather have the source edgy, nervous or even scared. When you are doing an investigation, you may want the key characters to feel uneasy. You may pretend you know more than you actually do. You want them to know that the material you have is substantive and serious. Seymour Hersh, a Pulitzer Prize-winning investigative reporter, uses this tactic. *Time* magazine once quoted a government official commenting on Hersh: "He wheedles, cajoles, pleads, threatens, asks a leading question, uses little tidbits as if he knew the whole story. When he finishes you feel like a wet rag."

In some cases, however, it is better even in an investigation to take a low-key approach. Let the source relax. Talk around the subject but gradually bring the discussion to the key issues. The surprise element may work in your favor.

So may the sympathetic approach. When the source is speaking, you may nod or punctuate the source's responses with comments such as "That's interesting." Sources who think you are sympathetic are more likely to volunteer information. Researchers have found, for instance, that a simple "mm-hmmm" affects the length of the answer interviewers get.

Other Practical Considerations

Where you sit in relation to the person you are interviewing can be important. Unless you deliberately are trying to make those interviewed feel uncomfortable, do not sit directly in front of them. Permit your sources to establish eye contact if and when they wish.

Some people are even more disturbed by the way a reporter takes notes. A tape recorder ensures accuracy of quotes, but it makes many speakers self-conscious or

Masson v. Malcolm: A Cautionary Tale

The "fabricated quotes" case of Masson v. Malcolm is a bad soap opera. The lead characters are writer Janet Malcolm, the defendant, and psychoanalyst Jeffrey Masson, the plaintiff.

Here is the main scenario:

Masson became disillusioned with Freudian psychology when he was serving as projects director of the Sigmund Freud Archives in London. He was fired for advancing his controversial theories about Freud in 1981. Malcolm wanted to write about the situation. She established a rapport with Masson and taped more than 40 hours' worth of interviews. But she said she did not tape-record all of their conversations, especially those that occurred when they were walking or traveling in her car.

Malcolm wrote about Masson for *The New Yorker* in 1983. Book publisher Alfred A. Knopf later published a book from that material. The placement of quota-tion marks around certain statements in these works provoked a dispute between subject and author. Malcolm wrote that Masson said his superiors at the Sigmund Freud Archives considered him "an intellectual gigolo — you get your pleasure from him, but you don't take him out in public." Masson said he never said that. A tape recording shows that he said, "I was, in a sense, much too junior within the hierarchy of analysis for these important training analysts to be caught dead with me."

Did he call himself an "intellectual gigolo" or not? It is a catchy phrase. Masson claimed that quote and others were fabricated. He sued *The New Yorker*, Knopf and Malcolm for libel.

In 1989, the 9th U.S. Circuit Court of Appeals ruled in favor of the defendants. The court said that an author may "under certain circumstances, fictionalize quotations to some extent." Because Masson had conceded that he was a public figure, he had to prove "actual malice" — knowledge of falsity or reckless regard (see Chapter 22).

The court said:

Malice will not be inferred from evidence showing that the quoted language does not contain the exact words used by the plaintiff provided that the fabricated quotations are either *"rational interpretations of ambiguous" remarks made by the public figure … or do not "alter the substantive content" of unambiguous remarks actually made by the public figure.* (Italics added.)

In 1991 the Supreme Court overturned the 9th Circuit's decision, rejecting the lower court's "rational interpretation" standard. The Court said that "quotation marks indicate that the author is not interpreting the speaker's ambiguous statement, but is attempting to convey what the speaker said."

The Court said:

Were we to assess quotations under a rational interpretation standard, we would give journalists the freedom to place statements in their subjects' mouths without fear of liability. By eliminating any method of distinguishing between the statements of the subject and the interpretation of the author, we would diminish to a great degree the trustworthiness of the printed word and eliminate the real meaning of quotations. Not only public figures but the press doubtless would suffer under such a rule.

The Court clearly was trying to protect the sanctity of quotation marks, but the Court also made it clear that not every change in a quotation is going to lead

nervous. If you have permission to use a tape recorder, place it in an inconspicuous spot and ignore it except to make sure it is working properly. Writing notes longhand may interfere with your ability to digest what is being said. But not taking any notes at all is risky. Only a few reporters can leave an interview and accurately write down what was said. Certainly no one can do it and reproduce direct quotes verbatim. You should learn shorthand or develop a note-taking system of your own.

to a lawsuit. To some extent, some reporters do clean up quotes. Some reporters correct errors in grammar. Some delete "uh" or "um" without using ellipsis points. Those changes will not get a reporter into trouble. The change in words has to result in a material change in the meaning of a statement for actual malice to be present. But courts are going to look hard at cases where a writer has put words in a speaker's mouth.

The Supreme Court remanded the case. In 1992, the 9th Circuit let Knopf off the hook, saying, in effect, that Knopf relied on *The New Yorker* in concluding that Malcolm's manuscript was accurate.

In June 1993, a jury heard the case. It found two fabricated quotes libelous — the "intellectual gigolo" quote was not one of them. Here are the two quotes:

Malcolm quoted Masson as describing his plans for Maresfield Gardens, the home of the Freud Archives, which he hoped to occupy after the death of Anna Freud, Sigmund's child: "I would have renovated it, opened it up, brought it to life. Maresfield Gardens would have been a center of scholarship, but it would also have been a place of *sex, women, fun.* (Italics added.) It would have been like the change in *The Wizard of Oz,* from black-and-white into color." He said on tape of his meeting with a London analyst: ". . . we were going to pass women on to each other, and we were going to have a great time together when I lived in the Freud house. We'd have great parties and . . . we were going to live it up."

The second quotation involved the placement of the sentence "Well, he had the wrong man." Masson is recounting being fired by the director of the archives. The director says Masson is upsetting Anna Freud and that might kill her. Malcolm quotes Masson talking to the director:

"What have I done? You're doing it. You're firing me. What am I supposed to do — be grateful to you?" "You could be silent about it. . . ." "Why should I do that?" "Because it is the honorable thing to do." "Well, he had the wrong man."

Masson seems to be calling himself dishonorable. On the tape, the conversation, starting with the director, says:

"You could be silent about it." . . . "Why?" . . . "Because it's the honorable thing to do and you will save face. And who knows? If you never speak about it and you quietly and humbly accept our judgment, who knows that in a few years if we don't bring you back?" Well, he had the wrong man.

While agreeing the two quotes were libelous, the jury deadlocked on damages. The judge ordered a retrial on all issues — liability as well as damages. But another defendant dropped by the wayside. The jurors did not think *The New Yorker* deliberately published false quotes, so the judge dismissed the case against the magazine.

In November 1994, a jury decided in favor of defendant Malcolm.

Then, belatedly, in August 1995, Malcolm recovered a lost notebook containing her notes on some of the contested conversations.

The moral is clear. Material changes in quotations are perilous. They can lead to long court cases and expensive attorney's fees even if ultimately there is no liability for damages.

— Sandra Davidson

Be sure that you address the people you are interviewing correctly. If you are unsure how they should be addressed — Mrs., Miss, Dr., Professor — ask them.

If you are interviewing someone from a culture or race different from your own, recognize and avoid your own stereotypes. Perhaps you feel that an Islamic woman should not wear a veil when she attends school in the United States. Instead of letting your feelings influence your actions, respect her beliefs. As a reporter, take pride in the ability to move among all cultures. This requires that you read about cultural differences. It might help you to know that Chinese people are generally uncomfortable with too much eye contact. Many Arabs consider it improper for a man to look into a woman's eyes. No one knows everything about every culture, but you can prepare for some situations, and you can also recognize what you don't know.

ENSURING ACCURACY AND FAIRNESS

Accuracy is a major problem in all interviews. Both the question and the answer may be ambiguous. You may not understand what is said. You may record it incorrectly. You may not know the context of the remarks. Your biases may interfere with the message.

Knowing the background of your sources, having a comfortable relationship with them and keeping good notes are important elements of accuracy. All those were missing when a journalism student, two weeks into an internship at a major daily, interviewed the public information officer for a sheriff's department about criminal activity in and around a shelter for battered women. The reporter had never met the source. She took notes on her phone interview with the deputy and others in whatever notebook happened to be nearby. She didn't record the time, date or even the source's name. There were no notes showing context, just fragments of quotes, scrawled in nearly illegible handwriting.

After the story was published, the developer of the shelter sued. Questioned by attorneys, the deputy swore that the reporter misunderstood him and used some of his comments out of context. In several cases, he contended, she completed her fragmentary notes by putting her own words in his mouth. He testified that most reporters come to see him to get acquainted. Many call back to check his quotes on sensitive or complex stories. She did neither.

When the court ordered the reporter to produce and explain her notes, she had trouble reconstructing them. She had to admit on several occasions that she wasn't sure what the fragments meant.

The accuracy of your story is only as good as your notes. David Finkel, whose story on a family's TV-watching habits became a Pulitzer Prize finalist, took extra steps to be certain his material was accurate. Observing what his subject was watching, he obtained transcripts of the shows so he could quote accurately from them. If he knew transcripts would not be available, he set his tape recorder near the TV to record the program.

When you finish your interview, go back over the key points in your notes to confirm them. Read back quotes to be sure that you have them right. Realize, too, that you will need to confirm some of the information you get from other, perhaps more authoritative, sources. And if your interview produces allegations against other people or organizations, you will need to talk to those named.

Figures stated during an interview must be double-checked. The mere statement of a statistic, even by a reliable source, does not ensure accuracy.

"Today one has the impression that the interviewer is not listening to what you say, nor does he think it important, because he believes that the tape recorder hears everything. But he's wrong, it doesn't hear the beating of the heart, which is the most important part of the interview.**"**

— Gabriel García Márquez, Colombian writer and Nobel laureate

Some possibilities for making errors or introducing bias are unavoidable, but others are not. To ensure the most accurate and complete reporting possible, you should use all the techniques available to obtain a good interview, including observing, understanding what you hear and asking follow-up questions. Let's examine these and other techniques.

Observing

TIPS

Before You Leave the Interview

● Ask if there's anything else the interviewee wants to say.

● Check facts — spellings, dates, statistics, quotes.

● Set a time for rechecking facts, quotes.

● Discuss when and where the interview might appear.

● Ask the interviewee if he or she wants extra copies.

Some reporters look but do not see. The detail they miss may be the difference between a routine story and one that is a delight to read. Your powers of observation may enable you to discover a story beyond your source's words. Is the subject nervous? What kinds of questions are striking home? The mayor may deny that he is going to fire the police chief, but if you notice the chief's personnel file sitting on an adjacent worktable, you may have reason to continue the investigation.

Wright Thompson says, "It's all about the scenes. Don't just ask questions. Be an observer." Like any good writer, he offers an example to show what he means:

> I was doing a story about former Heisman Trophy winner Eric Crouch. It was almost exactly one year since he'd won the trophy, and that year had been tough for him. He'd quit pro football and had been forced to ask some hard questions about his life. As we sat in an Omaha bar, a clip of him running the football came on the television. One of the women at the table said, "You're on TV, Eric." I remember he looked up at the screen and spat, "That's not me, man." Then he took a shot of liquor. No amount of interviewing could breathe life into the idea that he had changed like that scene.

Understanding

Understanding what you see is crucial to the news-gathering process. So is understanding what you hear. It is not enough merely to record what is being said; you must also digest it.

Sometimes what you don't hear may be the message. The reporter who was trying to find out if the mayor was going to fire the police chief asked several questions about the chief's performance. What struck the reporter during the interview was the mayor's lack of enthusiasm for the chief. That unintentional tip kept the reporter working on the story until he confirmed it.

Asking Follow-Up Questions

If you understand what the source is saying, you can ask meaningful follow-up questions. There is nothing worse than briefing your city editor on the interview and having the editor ask you, "Well, did you ask . . . ?" Having to say no is embarrassing.

Even if you go into an interview armed with a list of questions, the most important questions will probably be the ones you ask in response to an answer. A reporter who was doing a story on bidding procedures was interviewing the mayor. The reporter asked how bid specifications were written. In the course of his reply, the mayor mentioned that the president of a construction firm had assured him the last bid specifications were adequate. The alert reporter picked up on the statement:

TIPS

After the Interview

- Organize your notes — immediately.

- Craft a proper lead.

- Write a coherent story.

- Check accuracy with the interviewee.

"When did you talk to him?"

"About three weeks ago," the mayor said.

"That's before the specifications were published, wasn't it?"

"Yes, we asked him to look them over for us."

"Did he find anything wrong with the way they were written?"

"Oh, he changed a few minor things. Nothing important."

"Did officials of any other construction firms see the bid specifications before they were advertised?"

"No, he was the only one."

Gradually, on the basis of one offhand comment by the mayor, the reporter was able to piece together a solid story on the questionable relationship between the city and the construction firm. You should end nearly every interview with the same question: "Is there anything I haven't asked that I should?"

Other Techniques

Although most questions are designed to get information, some are asked as a delaying tactic. A reporter who is taking notes may fall behind. One good trick for catching up is just to say, "Hold on a second—let me get that" or "Say that again, please." Other questions are intended to encourage a longer response. "Tell me more about that" encourages the speaker to add more detail.

You don't have to be stalling for time to say you don't understand. Don't be embarrassed to admit you haven't grasped something. It is better to admit to one person you don't understand something than to advertise your ignorance in newsprint or on the airwaves in front of thousands.

Another device for making the source talk on is not a question at all; it is a pause. You are signaling the source that you expect more. But the lack of a response from you is much more ambiguous than "Tell me more about that." It may indicate that you were skeptical of what was just said, that you didn't understand, that the answer was inadequate or several other possibilities. The source will be forced to react.

Many dull interviews become interesting after they end. There are two things you should always do when you finish your questions: Check key facts, figures and quotes and then put away your pen but keep your ears open. You are not breaching any ethical rule if you continue to ask questions after you have put away your pen or turned off the tape recorder. That's when some sources loosen up.

Quickly review your notes and check facts, especially dates, numbers, quotes, spellings and titles. Besides helping you get it right, this shows the source you are careful. If necessary, arrange a time when you can call to check other parts of the story or clear up questions you may have as you are writing. Researchers have found that more than half of direct quotations are inaccurate, even when the interview is tape-recorded. That reflects a sloppiness that is unacceptable. Make sure you are the exception.

As a matter of courtesy, tell the source when the story might appear. You may even offer to send along an extra copy of the article when it's completed.

Reporters should do research after an interview to ascertain specific figures when a source provides an estimate. For example, if a shop owner says he runs one of 20 pizza parlors in town, check with the city business-license office to get the exact number.

Suggested Readings

Biagi, Shirley. *Interviews That Work*. Belmont, Calif.: Wadsworth Publishing Co., 1992. A complete guide to interviewing techniques. The instruction is interspersed with interviews of journalists describing their techniques.

Harrington, Walt. *American Profiles*. Columbia: University of Missouri Press, 1992. Fifteen excellent profiles and the author's explanation of how and why he does what he does.

Malcolm, Janet. *The Journalist and the Murderer*. New York: Knopf, 1990. Using the Joe McGinnis–Jeffrey MacDonald case, the author accuses all journalists of being "confidence men" who betray their sources.

Metzler, Ken. *The Writer's Guide to Gathering Information by Asking Questions*, Third Edition. Needham Heights, Mass.: Allyn & Bacon, 1997. An invaluable, in-depth look at problems of interviewing.

Paterno, Susan. "The Question Man." *American Journalism Review*, October 2000. http://ajr.org/Article.asp?id=676. An interview with John Sawatsky, who has specialized in interviewing techniques, particularly in how to phrase questions.

Scanlon, Christopher, ed. *Best Newspaper Writing*. St. Petersburg, Fla.: Poynter Institute for Media Studies. Reprints of winners of American Society of Newspaper Editors Distinguished Writing Awards and interviews with the authors make this an invaluable resource. It is published annually.

Suggested Web Sites

www.poewar.com
The Writer's Resource Center offers advice on a variety of writers' concerns, including interviewing.

www.poynter.org
The Poynter Institute site offers an array of help for journalists. Among the lists are bibliographies on interviewing and a regular column on reporting and writing techniques by Chip Scanlan.

www.wwcd.org/action/ampu/crosscult.html#WORKING
"Working on Common Cross-cultural Communication Challenges," a good, short overview of problems of communicating across cultures, is written by Marcelle E. DuPraw, National Institute for Dispute Resolution, and Marya Axner, consultant in leadership development and diversity awareness.

Exercises

1. Learn to gather background on your sources. Write a memo of up to two pages about your state's senior U.S. senator. Concentrate on those details that will allow you to focus on how the senator views the issue of illegal immigration. Indicate the sources of your information. Do an Internet search on the senator.

2. List five open-ended questions you would ask the senator.

3. List five closed-ended questions you would ask.

4. Interview a student also enrolled in your reporting class. Write a two- or three-page story. Be sure to focus on one aspect of the student's life. Ask your classmate to read the story and to mark errors of fact and perception. The instructor will read your story and the critique.

5. Your instructor will give you a news item. Prepare a list of questions you would ask to do a follow-up interview. As each question is read aloud in class, cross it off your list. See if you can come up with the most original and appropriate questions.

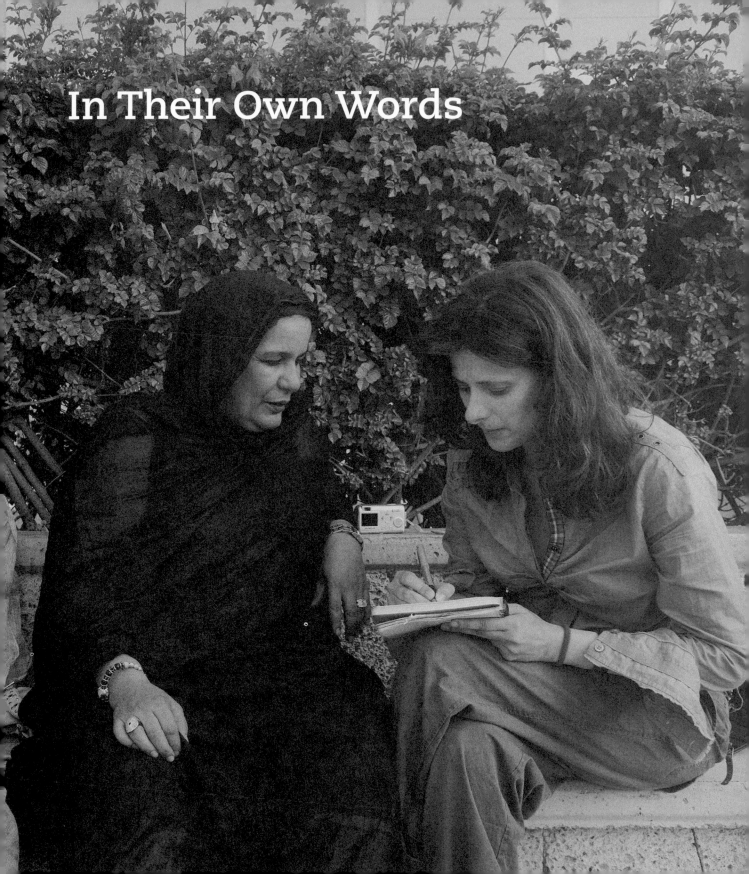

In Their Own Words

4

"Bureaucracy has murdered people in the greater New Orleans area, and bureaucracy needs to stand trial before Congress today," he said. "Take whatever idiot they have at the top, give me a better idiot. Give me a caring idiot. Give me a sensitive idiot. Just don't give me the same idiot."

These words of Jefferson Parish president Aaron Broussard, reported on CBS New, are a reporter's dream come true.

Direct quotes add color and credibility to your story. By using direct quotes, you are telling readers that you are putting them directly in touch with the speaker. Like a letter, direct quotes are personal. Quotation marks signal the reader that something special is coming. Direct quotes provide a story with a change of pace, a breath of air. They also loosen up a clump of dense type.

As Paula LaRoque, former writing coach and assistant managing editor of *The Dallas Morning News*, said, "The right quotes, carefully selected and presented, enliven and humanize a story and help make it clear, credible, immediate and dramatic. Yet many quotations in journalism are dull, repetitive, ill-phrased, ungrammatical, nonsensical, self-serving or just plain dumb."

Now that's a quotation worth quoting!

But not everything people say is worth quoting. You need to learn what to quote directly, when to use partial quotes and when to paraphrase. You also must learn how and how often to attribute quotations and other information. Like a researcher, you must know when information must be tied to a source. However, attributing a remark or some information does not excuse you from a possible libel suit. And, of course, you want to be fair.

Being fair sometimes is difficult when sources do not want to be quoted. For that reason you also must learn how to deal with off-the-record quotes and background information.

WHAT TO QUOTE DIRECTLY

Crisp, succinct, meaningful quotes spice up any story. But you can overdo a good thing. You need direct **quotes**—the exact words that a source says or writes—in your stories, but you also need to develop your skill in recognizing what is worth quoting. Let's look at the basic guidelines.

Unique Material

When you can say, "Ah, I never heard that before," you can be quite sure your readers would like to know exactly what the speaker said. Instead of quoting someone at length, look for the kernel. Sometimes it is something surprising, something neither you nor your readers would expect that person to say. For example, on *Good Morning America*, Barbara Bush, the president's mother, told interviewer Diane Sawyer she would watch none of TV's coverage of the war on Iraq. Then she said, "Why should we hear about body bags and deaths and how many, what day it's going to happen? It's not relevant. So why should I waste my beautiful mind on something like that?"

When singer Dolly Parton was asked how she felt about dumb-blonde jokes, she replied: "I'm not offended at all because I know I'm not a dumb blonde. I also know I'm not a blonde."

Striking statements like these should be quoted, but not always. The *Arizona Daily Star* did a profile of a chef who writes a weekly column. Describing his food philosophy, the chef said, "I have a food philosophy, but it's a kind of an angry one. I'd eat a baby if you cooked it right. Yeah, that's pretty much it."

The *Star*'s reader advocate wrote that at least a half dozen readers objected. Said one, "Shame on the chef for saying it, and shame on the *Star* for printing it."

There is no reason to place simple, factual material inside quotation marks. Here is a segment of copy from a story about similarities in the careers of a father and son that needed no quotes at all:

> "My son was born on campus," says the elder Denney, 208 Westridge Drive, a professor in regional and community affairs.
>
> "In fact, he was born in the same hospital that I met my wife," he says, explaining he was in Noyes Hospital with a fractured spine when she was a student nurse.
>
> Since that time, he has earned his bachelor's degree "technically in agriculture with a major in biological science and conservation."

Although the quoted material is informative, it contains nothing particularly interesting, surprising, disturbing, new or even different. It should be written:

> Denney, of 208 Westridge Drive, is a professor in regional and community affairs. While hospitalized in Noyes Hospital with a fractured spine, he met a student nurse who became his wife. Eight years later, his son was born at the same hospital.
>
> The son has since earned a bachelor's degree in agriculture with a major in biological science and conservation.

The first version has 72 words; the second, with 60 words, is tighter and better because it eliminates the wordy, uninteresting quotes.

A direct quotation should say something significant. Also, a direct quotation should not simply repeat what has been said indirectly. It should move the story forward. Here's a passage from a *USA Today* story about a proposed law that would bar health-insurance companies, employers and managed-care plans from discriminating against people because of their genetic makeup:

> Fear of insurance discrimination based on the results of genetic tests has been on the rise for years. "It stops

" I often quote myself. It adds spice to my conversation. **"**

— George Bernard Shaw, playwright

TIPS

Use direct quotes when

- Someone says something unique.
- Someone says something uniquely.
- Someone important says something important.

many people cold from getting tested," says Karen Clarke, a genetics counselor at Johns Hopkins University in Baltimore.

The quotation is useful, it is informative, and it moves the story forward.

Sometimes spoken material is unique not because of individual remarks that are surprising or new but because of extended dialogue that can tell the story more effectively than writers can in their own words. A quotation comes from a source speaking to the reporter. **Dialogue** occurs when two or more sources or characters are speaking to each other. The writer of the following story made excellent use of dialogue:

Lou Provancha pushed his wire-rimmed glasses up on his nose and leaned toward the man in the wheelchair.

"What is today, Jake?" he asked.

Jake twisted slightly and stared at the floor.

"Jake," Provancha said. "Jake, look up here."

A long silence filled the tiny, cluttered room on the sixth floor of the University Medical Center.

Provancha, a licensed practical nurse at the hospital, glanced at the reporter. "Jake was in a coma a week ago," he explained. "He couldn't talk."

Provancha pointed to a wooden board propped up on the table beside him.

"Jake, what is today? What does it say here? What is this word? I've got my finger pointed right at it."

Jake squinted at the word. With a sudden effort, like a man heaving a bag of cement mix onto a truck bed, he said: "Tuesday."

Provancha grinned. It was a small victory for both of them.

The shaggy-haired nurse was coaxing his patient step-by-step back into the world he had known before a car accident pitched him into a two-month-long coma, with its resulting disorientation and memory loss.

Here's another example of how dialogue can move the story along and "show" rather than "tell." The story is about the restoration of old cars. A father is passing on a rare technique to his son:

When the lead is smooth and the irregularities filled to his satisfaction, he reaches for his file.

"How long has it been since you've done this?" his son asks.

"It's been at least 20 years."

"How do you tin it so it won't melt and all run off on the floor?"

"Very carefully."

Before the lesson is finished, a customer and two other shop workers have joined the group watching Larry at work. This is a skill few people know.

"I don't like the way this lead melts," he says.

"That's what it does when there's not enough tin?" his son asks.

"Tin helps it stick."

"Why do you pull the file instead of pushing it?"

"So I can see better."

"I would already have the fiberglass on and be done by now."

"I know, but anything worthwhile you have to work for."

Notice the careful instruction and concerned advice from a teacher-father. His last sentence contains one of life's lessons: "I know, but anything worthwhile you have to work for."

The Unique Expression

When you can say, "Ah, I've never heard it said that way before," you know you have something quotable. Be on the lookout for the clever, the colorful, the colloquial. For example, an elderly man talking about his organic garden said, "It's hard to tell people to watch what they eat. You eat health, you know."

A professor lecturing on graphic design said, "When you think it looks like a mistake, it is." The same professor once explained that elements in a design should not call attention to themselves: "You don't walk up to a beautiful painting in someone's home and say, 'That's a beautiful frame!'"

A computer trainer said to a reporter: "Teaching kids computers is like leading ducks to water. But teaching adults computers is like trying to teach chickens to swim."

Sometimes something said uniquely is a colloquialism. Colloquialisms can add color and life to your copy. A person from Louisiana may say, "I was just fixing to leave when the phone rang." In parts of the South you're apt to hear, "I might could do that." A person from around Lancaster, Pa., might "make the light out" when turning off the lights. And people in and around Fort Wayne, Ind., "redd up" the dishes after a meal, meaning that they wash them and put them where they belong.

Important Quotes by Important People

If citizen Joe Smith says, "Something must be done about this teachers' strike," you may or may not consider it worth quoting. But if the mayor says, "Something must be done about this teachers' strike," many papers would print the quote. Generally, reporters quote public officials or known personalities in their news stories (although not everything the famous say is worth quoting). Remember, prominence is an important property of news.

Quoting sources that readers are likely to know lends authority, credibility and interest to your story. Presumably, a meteorologist knows something about the weather, a doctor about health, a chemistry professor about chemicals. However, it is unlikely that a television star knows a great deal about cameras, even if he or she makes commercials about cameras.

Important, knowledgeable people are good sources for quotes even if what they say is not unique or said uniquely. A story with no quotes often lacks life and substance though there is no set number you should strive to include.

Accuracy

The first obligation of any reporter is to be accurate. Before there can be any discussion of whether or how to use direct quotations, you must learn to get the exact words of the source.

Although quotes from experts and public figures are generally used to strengthen a story's authority, quotes from ordinary citizens with unique experience in a newsworthy event may also add credibility.

It's not easy.

Scribbled notes from interviews, press conferences and meetings are often difficult to decipher and interpret. A study by Adrienne Leher, a professor of linguistics at the University of Arizona, shows only 13 of 98 quotations taken from Arizona newspapers proved to be verbatim when compared to recordings. Only twice, however, were the nonverbatim quotes considered "incompatible with what was intended."

During his first presidential campaign on Sept. 4, 2000, at a rally in Naperville, Ill., George W. Bush made a derogatory remark about a journalist while on stage. The remark, meant to be heard only by running mate Dick Cheney, was picked up by the microphone and several reporters' tape recorders.

The (Baltimore) Sun related the incident this way:

> As the two candidates stood onstage, gazing out over the crowd and waving, Bush remarked, "There's Adam Clymer, major-league asshole from *The New York Times*."
>
> "Oh, yeah, he is, big-time," Cheney agreed.

We know those quotations are accurate because Web sites like *USA Today*'s provided an actual audio recording. Convergence brings a whole new demand to quoting people exactly. How strange that *USA Today*'s Web site had a recording of the actual words, and yet the newspaper quoted the candidates differently:

> Standing on a stage at the start of a rally in Naperville,
> Ill., Bush was heard saying to Cheney, "There's Adam
> Clymer of *The New York Times*, a major-league asshole."
> To which Cheney replied, "Yeah, big time."

Other newspapers reported censored variations of the quotes. The *St. Petersburg Times* wrote:

> "There's Adam Clymer, major league a___h___," Bush
> told Cheney.
> > "Oh yeah, yeah. Big time," Cheney agreed.

The New York *Daily News* censored the quote this way:

> "There's Adam Clymer—major league a___hole from
> *The New York Times*," Bush noted while waving to the
> crowd.
> > "Oh, yeah, he is. Big time," Cheney said, as the
> > smiles on the two men broadened and Bush nodded
> > while continuing to wave with both arms.

One thing's for sure. Bush and Cheney said what they said. Editors might want to censor the vulgarity, but they should not change the words. Your passion for accuracy should compel you to get and record the exact words. Only then can you decide which words to put between quotation marks.

Those who edit for radio and television news can also cut in and out of quotes, and they can certainly insert them out of context. Doing so is not just inaccurate because it distorts the meaning of what people are saying; it is also unethical.

Verification

When someone important says something important but perhaps false, putting the material in quotes does not relieve you of the responsibility for the inaccuracies. Citizens, officials and candidates for office often say things that may be partially true or altogether untrue and perhaps even libelous. (See Chapter 22 for more on libel.) Quotations need verification, like any other information you gather.

In the 1950s, during the time of Sen. Joseph McCarthy's anticommunism investigations, many newspapers, in the interest of strict objectivity, day after day quoted the Wisconsin senator's charges and countercharges. (It should be pointed out that some publishers did this because they agreed with his stance and because his remarks sold newspapers.) Few papers thought it was their responsibility to quote others who were pointing out the obvious errors and inconsistencies in the demagogue's remarks. Today, however, in the interest of balance, fairness and objectivity, many papers leave out, correct or point out the errors in some quotations. This may be done in the article itself or in an accompanying story.

If candidate Joe Harkness says that his opponent Jim McGown is a member of the Ku Klux Klan, you should check before you print the charge. Good reporters don't stop looking and checking just because someone gives them some information. Look for yourself. Prisoners may have an altogether different account of a riot from the one the prison officials give you. Your story will not be complete unless you talk to all sides.

Quoting from E-mail, the Internet and Chat Rooms

When you quote from e-mail that you have received personally, you can usually be sure that the sender has written the intended words. If you have doubts, be sure to check with the writer. It's also a good idea to let the readers know that you obtained the quote through e-mail and had no personal contact with the source.

> *"When you see yourself quoted in print and you're sorry you said it, it suddenly becomes a misquotation."*
>
> —Dr. Laurence J. Peter, author of *Peter's Quotations* and *The Peter Principle*

If you quote someone from the Internet, you need to be much more careful. Be sure to verify the quote from the source, but if you can't do that, at least be sure to tell readers that the quote comes from the Internet, and then cite the URL (Internet address).

Reading what people are saying in chat rooms can be a useful thing for a reporter to do. However, quoting what people say in these chat rooms is unwise because some statements might be unverified and even libelous. Nevertheless, if you have verified the information—and identified the person who is saying it—and if you specifically state the source is a chat room, you might on occasion use such a quote. Identifying the person might well be impossible because people use screen names, aliases and pseudonyms.

PROBLEMS IN DIRECT QUOTATION

By now you realize that although you should use direct quotations, they present many challenges and problems. Let's look at some of them.

Paraphrasing Quotes

While some quotations need verification, others need clarification. Do not quote someone unless you are sure of what that person means. The reason (or excuse) "But that's what the man said" is not sufficient to use the quote. It is much better to skip a quotation altogether than to confuse the reader.

The best way to avoid confusing and unclear quotes or needlessly long and wordy quotes is to paraphrase. You must convey to the reader the meaning of the speaker. As a reporter you must have confidence that sometimes you are able to convey that meaning in fewer words and in better language than the speaker did.

You can save your editors a lot of work if you shorten quotes. Digesting, condensing and clarifying quotes take more effort than simply recording them word for word. You will not impress anyone with long quotations. On the contrary, you may be guilty of lazy writing. Here is a quote that could be cut drastically:

> "When I first started singing lessons I assumed I would be a public school teacher and maybe, if I was good enough, a voice teacher," he said. "When I graduated from the university, I still thought I would be a teacher, and I wanted to teach."

A rewrite conveys the meaning more succinctly:

> When he first started singing lessons, and even after he graduated from the university, he wanted to be a public school voice teacher.

Using Partial Quotes

It is much better to paraphrase or to use full quotes than to use fragmentary or partial quotes. Partial quotes often make for choppy, interrupted sentences. Some editors would have you avoid "orphan quotes" almost altogether. Here is an example of the overuse of partial quotes:

> The mayor said citizens should "turn off" unnecessary lights and "turn down" thermostats "to 65 degrees."

The sentence would be better with no quotation marks at all.

If a particular phrase has special significance or meaning, a partial quote may be justifiable. Sometimes you may want to put a word or phrase in quotation marks to indicate that this was precisely what the speaker said. Look at this use of a one-word quote in a story about genetic engineering in *The Atlantic Monthly*:

> By all but eliminating agricultural erosion and run-off—so Brian Noyes, the local conservation-district manager, told me—continuous no-till could "revolutionize" the area's water quality.

The writer thought it important that readers should know that "revolutionize" was not his word but the word of Brian Noyes. And he was right. "Revolutionize" is a strong word.

When you do use partial quotes, do not put quotation marks around something the speaker could not have said. Suppose a speaker told a student audience at a university, "I am pleased and thrilled with your attendance here tonight." It would be incorrect to write:

> The speaker said she was "pleased and thrilled with the students' attendance."

Partial quotes often contain an ellipsis (three spaced periods) to tell the reader that some of the words of the quote are missing. For example:

> "I have come here tonight . . . and I have crossed state lines . . . to conspire against the government."

This practice at times may be justifiable, but you should not keep the reader guessing about what is missing. Sometimes the speaker's actual meaning can be distorted by dropping certain words. If a critic writes about a three-act play, "A great hit—except for the first three acts," an ad that picks up only the first part of that quote is guilty of misrepresentation. A journalist using the technique to distort the message is no less guilty.

Capturing Dialect or Accent

Using colorful or colloquial expressions helps the writer capture a person in a particular environment. The same is true when you write the way people talk:

> "Are you gonna go?" he asked.
> "No, I'm not goin'," she replied.

In everyday speech hardly anyone enunciates perfectly. To do so would sound affected. In fiction, therefore, it is common to use spellings that match speech. But when conversation is written down in newspaper reporting, readers expect correct, full spellings. Not only is correct spelling easier to read, it is also less difficult to write. Capturing dialect consistently is difficult, as these passages from a story about a Hollywood actress illustrate:

> "Boy, it's hot out theah," she started. "I could sure use a
> nice cold beer. How about it, uh? Wanta go get a couple
> beers?"

If she said "theah," wouldn't she also say "beeah"? Perhaps she said, "How 'bout it, uh?" And if she said "wanta," maybe she also said "geta."

In another passage, the writer has the actress speaking "straight" English:

> "Would you believe I used to dress like that all the time?
> Dates didn't want to be seen with me. I was always being
> asked to change clothes before going out."

Then, later in the story, the writer has her revert to less formal speech:

> "I'm tired of pickin' up checks. I've never been ta col-
> lege, so I'd like to take a coupla classes. I wanta take
> law so I can find out who's stealing the country. And I
> wanta take geology. The San Andreas Fault is my hobby,
> y'know? I think man can beat out nature."

First the actress wanted "a couple beers." Then she wanted to take "a coupla classes." In the same passage she is tired of "pickin'" up checks, but she wants to find out who's "stealing" the country. It is unlikely she is that inconsistent in her speech.

The writer of this story tried to show us something of the character of the actress. If he wanted to convey her speech patterns, he should either have been consistent or simply reported that she talked the same off the set as on it.

Sometimes when a newspaper attempts to quote someone saying something uniquely, it betrays a bias. During the 1960 presidential election campaign, some Northern newspapers delighted in quoting Alabama Gov. George Wallace exactly, even trying to reproduce his Southern drawl. But some of these same newspapers did not try to reproduce the Boston accent of John F. Kennedy or of his brothers.

> **"The surest way to make a monkey of a man is to quote him."**
>
> — Robert Benchley, humorist

However, you should not make everyone's speech the same. Barbara King Lord, former director of editorial training for the Associated Press, laments "our frequent inability to write other than insipid speech" and "our tendency to homogenize the day-to-day speech patterns of the heterogeneous people we write about." She acknowledges that writers worry about exposing to ridicule the immigrant's halting or perhaps unconventional speech while the stockbroker's speech appears flawless.

Lord calls the argument specious. Of course, people should not be exposed to ridicule through their speech. "The point here," she says, "is simply that when the writer's intention in writing dialects, quaint expressions, nonconventional grammar, flowery or showy speech, or the Queen's English is to make a person human, that intention is not only acceptable, it's desirable."

J.R. Moehringer of the *Los Angeles Times* did this in his Pulitzer Prize-winning article for feature writing:

> "No white man gonna tell me not to march," Lucy says, jutting her chin. "Only make me march harder."

The only way you can make people human is to listen to them. Lord says reporters and writers usually hear but rarely listen. She advises reporters to "listen for expressions, turns of phrase, idiosyncratic talk," and to work that into their stories.

Nevertheless, you must be careful when quoting people for whom English is a second language. Nearly any attempt to quote them exactly will be looked upon as making fun of their English. Better that you paraphrase their comments, or as some would advise, make them speak good English. Once again, however, if you have audio from baseball star Albert Pujols on your Web site and have the same quotes in perfect, fluent English in the written text, many would see that as a serious problem. Others would say that you are hurting the uniqueness and character of the great slugger born in the Dominican Republic. These problems are as old as radio and television, but convergence of the media has increased their frequency.

Mix-Matching Questions and Answers

Writers have other problems with quotes. They often agonize over whether they may use responses to one question to answer another question. Later on in an interview or in a trial, a person may say something that answers better or more fully a question posed earlier.

The primary questions you must ask yourself are: Am I being fair? Am I distorting the meaning? Am I putting quotes together that change what the speaker intended to say? Sentences that logically go together, that logically enhance one another and that are clearly sequential can and often should be placed together.

Correcting Quotes

Perhaps the most perplexing problem tied to the proper handling of direct quotations is this: When do you, or should you, correct grammatical errors in a direct quotation? Should you expect people in news conferences or during informal interviews to speak perfect English?

Although quotation marks mean you are capturing the exact language of a speaker, it is accepted practice at many newspapers to correct mistakes in grammar and to convey a person's remarks in complete sentences. None of us regularly speaks in perfect, grammatical sentences. But if we were writing down our remarks, presumably we would write in grammatically correct English.

Reporters and editors differ widely on when or even whether to correct quotes. A reporter for the *Rocky Mountain News* quoted an attorney as saying, "Her and John gave each other things they needed and couldn't get anyplace else." The reporter said the quote was accurate but, on second thought, said it might have been better to correct the grammar to "She and John" in the written account.

You are most likely to find grammatical errors in direct quotations in the sports pages of daily newspapers. For example, "'We don't have no centers on this team,' Grimes said." Nevertheless, often you can read an entire newspaper and not find a single grammatical error in a direct quote.

Most papers have no written policy on correcting grammatical errors in direct quotations. Because so many variables are involved, these matters are handled on a case-by-case basis. Some argue you should sacrifice a bit of accuracy in the interest of promoting proper English.

However, some would let public figures be embarrassed by quoting them using incorrect grammar. Columnist James Kilpatrick asks, "When we put a statement (of a public figure) in direct quotation marks, must it be exactly what was said? My own answer is yes. On any issue of critical substance, we ought not to alter a single word."

Yet in another matter in a different column, Kilpatrick writes, "It is all very well to *tidy up a subject's syntax* (italics added) and to eliminate the ahs, ers and you-knows, but direct quotation marks are a reporter's iron-clad, honor-bound guarantee that something was actually said."

ON THE JOB

In Their Own Words

Jo Ellen Krumm was a reporter for *The North Platte (Neb.) Telegraph* and a correspondent for *The Denver Post* zone sections before returning to school for a master's degree in health/medical writing and magazine journalism.

"I never thought I'd end up being an editor," she says. But after completing her degree in 1980, she was hired as associate editor of *Muscle & Fitness* magazine. Then she became research editor, articles editor, managing editor, and finally, senior editor. After 24 years at *Muscle & Fitness*, Jo Ellen became feature editor at Cherbo Publishing Group, Inc., in Encino, Calif., where she currently works.

Both as a reporter and as an editor, Jo Ellen has had long experience with direct quotations and attribution. She offers these tips:

- Get it straight from the horse's mouth. Don't trust secondhand and thirdhand sources.
- Listen. Don't be so wrapped up in your preselected questions that you don't let your subject expound on his or her favorite theme or pet peeve. When your subject's on a roll, listen.
- Cultivate many sources. The more varied sources you have, the more information and points of view you'll obtain. If you rely on the same people all the time, you'll get similar quotes.
- Be nice. Remember that people don't have to talk to you. Usually they're doing you a favor. Even when you write something the source would prefer not be printed or broadcast, be professional and fair in your dealings with the unhappy subject.
- Think ahead. Remember, you may need your sources again.

At times it may be necessary to illustrate a person's flawed use of language. In some cases, you may wish to use "sic" in brackets to note the error, misuse or peculiarity of the quotation. "Sic," Latin for "thus," indicates that a statement was originally spoken or written exactly as quoted. It is particularly important to use "sic" for improper or unusual use of language when you are quoting a written source. However, *The Associated Press Stylebook* says not to use "sic" unless "it is in the matter being quoted." Most book editors avoid it also; some find it appropriate only when confusion may result.

And if you think there is some agreement on the subject of correcting grammar in direct quotations, read what AP says under "Quotations in the News":

Never alter quotations even to correct minor grammatical errors or word usage. Casual minor tongue slips may be removed by using ellipses but even that should be done with extreme caution. If there is a question about a quote, either don't use it or ask the speaker to clarify.

When a reporter asked Kelly McBride of the Poynter Institute about using a quote of a child who said, "Everybody be up here," McBride answered, "Fix it."
The reporter asked, "Really? I can do that?"
McBride goes on to say this in her column on Poynter Online:

> We fix grammar all the time, I explained. Often, we do it as we write the quotes down in our notebook. A week later, one of my colleagues told her (the reporter) the exact opposite. Never change anything inside the quotations marks, he said.
>   If a quote contains poor grammar, the bar for using it is surpassed when the substance of the statement contains an important fact, reveals something about the character, and is relevant to the story, he said.

Correcting quotations is even more difficult for radio and television reporters. That's why they don't worry about it as much. Writers and editors for print might remember that the quotation they use may have been heard by millions of people on radio or television. Changing the quote even slightly might make viewers and listeners question the credibility of print reports. Readers might also ask why print writers feel the need to act as press agents who wish to make their subjects look good.

That applies to celebrities of all kinds (actors, sports figures), but it might also apply to registered political candidates and elected officials. At least, some argue, news agencies should have some consistency. If a reporter quotes a farmer using incorrect grammar, then should the same be done for the mayor or for a college professor?

A letter in *The Washington Post* criticized the newspaper for quoting exactly a mother of 14 children who was annoyed at then Mayor Marion Barry's advice to stop having babies. The quote read: "And your job is to open up all those houses that's boarded up." The writer then accused the *Post* of regularly stringing together quotes of the president to make him appear articulate. The writer concluded: "I don't care whether the *Post* polishes quotes or not. I simply think that everyone—black or white, rich or poor, president or welfare mother—deserves equal treatment."

That's good advice.

Removing Redundancies

Another question you must deal with as a reporter is whether to remove redundancies and other irrelevant material by using ellipses. Again, there is no agreement in the industry. Even though some consider it wrong to clean up quotes, they do not mind omitting words and even sentences from quotes without indicating the omission by an ellipsis. Some newspapers choose not to use ellipses because they make readers wonder what was left out or, as one editor said, "because typographically they make the paper look like chicken pox."

For most reporters and editors, the answer to the problem of correcting quotes is to take out the quotation marks and to paraphrase. However, when you paraphrase, you sometimes lose a lot. The value of quotes often lies in their richness and uniqueness.

Without question, you should know the policy of your news organization regarding the use of direct quotations. But equally without question, that policy should be that you place inside quotation marks only the exact words of the speaker. Make that your personal policy, and you can't go wrong.

Deleting Obscenity, Profanity and Vulgarity

Many news organizations never allow some things people say to be printed or broadcast—even if they are said uniquely. Obscenities (words usually referring to sexual parts or functions), profanities (words used irreverently to refer to a deity or to beings people regard as divine) and vulgarities (words referring to excretory matters) are usually deleted or bleeped unless they are essential to the story. Even at major newspapers, policy often demands that an obscenity, for example, be used only with the approval of a top editor.

> **"**We, as journalists, know far more about the effect of the printed word than any citizen off the street who talks to us for a story, and that knowledge carries a responsibility with it. If someone is likely to get his head blown off because we run his name, we shouldn't run it without good reason.**"**
>
> —Bob Reuteman, city editor, *Rocky Mountain News*, quoted by Bill Hosokawa

Of course, there are legitimate reasons to use proper sex-related terms in health stories and in some crime stories, including child molestation stories. Unlike in the past, newspapers now routinely use words such as "intercourse," "oral sex," "orgasm" and "penis."

The Washington Post used such words in a 1998 article about Kenneth Starr's impeachment report of President Bill Clinton. The article details the controversy about explicit sexual description used in the report, which prompted wire service stories to run a warning that its contents "may be OFFENSIVE to some readers." The *Post* itself used terms in its article such as "oral sex," "sexual favors" and "phone sex."

Obviously, words such as "God" and "Jesus Christ" used in discussions of religion have always been acceptable to most people.

Nevertheless, the rules are different for words when used as what some call "swear" words in direct quotation. Some papers follow the *AP Stylebook* rule: "If a full quote that contains profanity, obscenity or vulgarity cannot be dropped but there is no compelling reason for the offensive language, replace letters of an offensive word with a hyphen."

The *AP Stylebook* also says not to use obscenities, profanities and vulgarities, "unless they are part of direct quotations and there is a compelling reason for them." AP style recommends flagging the story on top with a warning that the story contains language that is offensive to some.

Nevertheless, in recent years the news business has become "racier and more streetwise," writes Rita Ciolli of *Newsday*. She quotes Don Fry, of the Poynter Institute in St. Petersburg, Fla.: "There is a lot less priggishness." Fry attributes this change to entertainment programming, especially that of cable TV.

News is more likely to reflect the sensibilities of its audience. Like it or not, language that was once considered vulgar in polite society is now tolerated more widely.

In broadcasting, of course, the Federal Communications Commission, which regulates the broadcast industry, can still fine a broadcaster or suspend a license for indecency. Though that's unlikely, audiences are quick to let a station know that it has gone too far.

At times you may wish to use vulgarities to show the intensity of someone's anger, terror, frustration or bitterness. Few inside the news media condone the casual, gratuitous use of vulgarities, however.

Readers and listeners don't condone it either.

Avoiding Made-Up Quotes

Fabricating a direct quote, even from general things that a source has said or from what the source might say if given the chance, is never a good idea. Even seasoned reporters are sometimes tempted to put quotation marks around words that their sources "meant to say," or to clarify or simplify a quote. The journalist reasons that it's more important to have a clear and concise quote for the reader than to be a slave to the verbose and unclear words of the source. Bad reasoning. It's better to paraphrase.

An even worse idea is fabricating a quote that makes a source look bad or that is defamatory or perhaps even libelous. Doing so can result in a lawsuit.

In 1991, in Masson v. Malcolm, the Supreme Court ruled that suits regarding quotations can proceed to trial if the altered quote "results in a material change in the meaning conveyed by the statement."

Libel or no libel, your credibility as a reporter demands that you be scrupulously exact when you place people's words inside quotation marks. Again, when in doubt, paraphrase.

Practicing Prepublication Review

A decade ago, you would not have had a city editor tell you to check the accuracy of your direct quotations with your source. Today, it is standard practice on many newspapers. Steve Weinberg, a Missouri School of Journalism professor and former head of the Investigative Reporters and Editors, calls it PPR—prepublication review. He says, "I have practiced PPR as a newspaper staff writer, a magazine freelancer and a book author. Never have I regretted my practice. What I do regret is failing to do it during the first decade of my career because of mindless adherence to tradition."

Weinberg states candidly that it is not sensitivity to the feelings of his sources that is his primary motivator. Rather, he insists that prepublication review loosens the tongues of tight-lipped sources and gets them on the record for making their statements. Prepublication review extends also to checking the facts. Professionals insist it does not compromise their stand or make them surrender control over their stories.

Journalist Philip Weiss offers another reason why more journalists are practicing prepublication review. "The press's quiet acceptance of quote approval surely owes something to the fact that reporters are an influential elite and are themselves often the subjects of interviews," he writes. "They have had a taste of their own medicine and they don't like it."

Another reason for prepublication review is that it serves as a defense against libel. Jurors are less likely to find "reckless disregard for the truth" in an article that the source reviewed.

But what happens when sources want to change a quote? Weinberg says he makes it clear that the source is checking only for accuracy. He will consider com-

Getting good quotes in a television interview takes skill and practice.

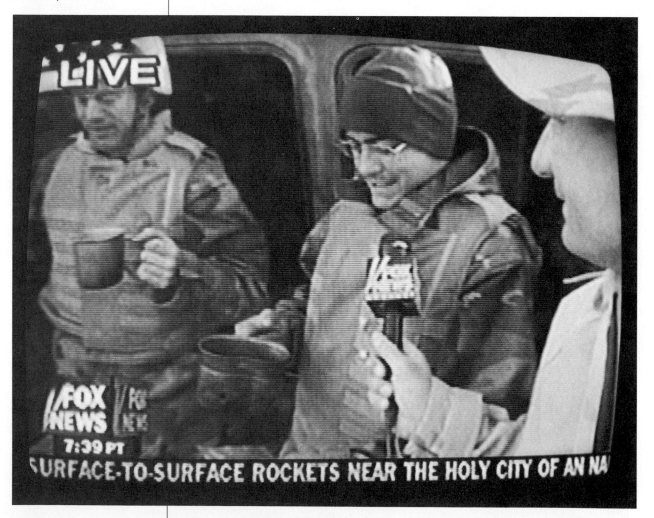

ments about interpretation, phrasing or tone, but he retains the right to change or not to change the quotes.

And what happens if someone denies saying something that is in a direct quote? That possibility is why, Weinberg says, you need to have good notes, even if they are in shorthand. Having the interview on tape is even better.

In an article in Poynter Online about reporter Judith Miller's front-page story in *The New York Times* in which she agreed to have her story reviewed by military officials prior to publication, Kelly McBride writes: "Although the conditions for Miller's access to MET Alpha unit were unusual, they are hardly unprecedented in the world of journalism. Every day, beat reporters make deals—explicit and implicit—with their sources about what to print, when to print it, and what to leave out. Rarely do they tell their readers about these deals. Sometimes they don't even tell their editors."

Nevertheless, McBride lists some conditions for when it is appropriate "to even consider letting an outsider read a story before press time":

- Is it even possible? Does your newspaper ever allow it?
- If it's possible, circumstances should be extremely limited. It must be a last resort to getting the story.
- Is this story worth it? Exploiting PPR compromises credibility and public trust.

You need to know the policy of your news organization, and someday you may want to help develop a policy that not only allows but also demands prepublication review of the facts and quotations in a story.

ATTRIBUTING DIRECT AND INDIRECT QUOTES

Now that you've learned some of the complexities of using direct quotations, let's take a look at when and how to attribute them to a source.

When to Attribute

Attribution involves giving the name, and sometimes other identifying information, about the source of a quotation or paraphrase. You should almost always attribute direct quotes—with some exceptions. You would not, for example, attribute a quotation to a 7-year-old who witnessed a gang shooting. You may not wish to attribute a quote to someone who saw a homicide suspect with the victim. To do so in either case could put the source in danger.

You should also have a good reason to allow a paragraph of direct quotations to stand without an attribution. Nevertheless, if you are quoting from a speech, an interview or a press conference and no one else is mentioned in the story, it may be excessive to put an attribution in every paragraph.

Ordinarily you should attribute indirect quotes. You should usually have a source for the information you write, and when you do, attribute the information to that source. The source can be a person or a written document. However, there are exceptions.

If you are a witness to damages or injuries, do not name yourself as a source in the story. Attribute this information to the police or to other authorities. But if you are on the scene of an accident and can see that three people were involved, you do not have to write "'Three people were involved in the accident,' Officer Osbord said." If you are unsure of the information or if there are conclusions or generalities involved, your editor probably will want you to attribute the information to an official or a witness. Avoid, however, attributing factual statements to "officials" or "authorities" or "sources." "Such constructions," writes journalist Jack Hart, "suggest that we are controlled by form and that we have forgotten about function."

Hart makes a plea for common sense regarding attributions. "Let's save them for direct quotations or paraphrased quotes laced with opinion," he writes. "Or for assertions likely to be especially sensitive. Or controversial." He says we should attribute only "if it matters."

This is good advice for the veteran. Nevertheless, although it is possible to attribute too often and although you do not always need to attribute, when you have doubts, go with the attribution.

That goes for attributing anonymous sources, too. Even though you should seldom use them, you must attribute them. Try to preserve your credibility by giving as much information as you can about the sources without revealing their names. For example, you may report "a source close to the chancellor said." For the second reference to the same source, use "the anonymous source said."

When Republican Rep. Mark Foley from Florida resigned abruptly in Sept. 2006 because of inappropriate e-mails he sent to teenage congressional pages, newspaper stories contained a flurry of anonymous sources. In this AP story, the writer gave information about the source without giving the name and noted the reason for the anonymity:

> FBI cyber sleuths are looking into the text of some of the Foley messages, checking to see how many e-mails and instant electronic messages were sent and how many computers were used, according to a law enforcement official, who spoke under condition of anonymity because of the ongoing investigation.

Notice the even more vague sourcing ("government officials") in this story from *The New York Times*:

> Federal agents on Monday began contacting men who were in the Congressional page program in recent years, said government officials briefed on the matter, who asked not to be named because they were not authorized to discuss the inquiry. The officials said the agents

TIPS

You need not attribute information to a source if you are a witness or if the information:

- Is a matter of public record.
- Is generally known.
- Is available from several sources.
- Is easily verifiable.
- Makes no assumptions.
- Contains no opinions.
- Is noncontroversial.

> were trying to find any former or current pages who had had contact with Mr. Foley and to authenticate e-mail and instant messages attributed to the former lawmaker that had circulated on the Internet in recent days.

Once again, the writer gives the reason for the anonymous source: "because they were not authorized to discuss the inquiry."

Sometimes, as in stories about crime victims, you may have to change someone's name and follow it with "not her real name" in parentheses.

How to Attribute

In composition and creative writing classes, you may have been told to avoid repeating the same word. You probably picked up your thesaurus to look for a synonym for "to say," a colorless verb. Without much research you may have found 100 or more substitutes. None of them is wrong. Indeed, writers may search long for the exact word they need to convey a particular nuance of meaning. For example:

> A presidential candidate announces the choice of a running mate.
>
> An arrested man divulges the names of his accomplices.
>
> A judge pronounces sentence.

At other times, in the interest of precise and lively writing, you may write:

> "I'll get you for that," she whispered.
>
> "I object!" he shouted.

Nevertheless, reporters and editors prefer forms of "to say" in most instances, even if they are repeated throughout a story. And there are good reasons for this word choice. "Said" is unobtrusive. Rather than appearing tiresome and repetitious, it hides in the news columns and calls no attention to itself. "Said" is also neutral. It has no connotations. To use the word "said" is to be objective.

Some of the synonyms for "said" sound innocent enough— but be careful. If you report that a city official "claimed" or "maintained" or "contended," you are implying that you do not quite believe what the official said. The word "said" is the solution to your problem. If you have evidence that what the official is saying is incorrect, you should include the correct information or evidence in your story.

In some newspaper accounts of labor negotiations, company officials always "ask" and labor leaders always "demand." "Demanding" sounds harsh and unreasonable, but "asking" sounds calm and reasonable. A reporter who uses these words in this context is taking an editorial stand—consciously or unconsciously.

Other words you may be tempted to use as a substitute for "say" are simply unacceptable because they represent improper usage. For example:

"You don't really mean that," he winked.
"Of course I do," she grinned.
"But what if someone heard you say that?" he frowned.
"Oh, you are a fool," she laughed.

You cannot "wink" a word. It is difficult, if not impossible, to "grin," "frown" or "laugh" words. But you may want to say this:

"Not again," he said, moaning.
"I'm afraid so," she said with a grin.

This usage is correct, but often it is not necessary or even helpful to add words like "moaning" or phrases like "with a grin." Sometimes, though, such words and phrases are needed to convey the meaning of the speaker.

Learning the correct words for attribution is the first step. Here are some other guidelines to follow when attributing information:

- **If a direct quote is more than one sentence long, place the attribution at the end of the first sentence.** For example:

"The car overturned at least three times," the police officer said. "None of the four passengers was hurt. Luckily, the car did not explode into flames."

That one attribution is adequate. It would be redundant to write:

"The car overturned at least three times," the police officer said. "None of the four passengers was hurt," he added. "Luckily, the car did not explode into flames," he continued.

Nor should you write:

"The car overturned at least three times. None of the four passengers was hurt. Luckily, the car did not explode into flames," the police officer said.

Although you should not keep the reader wondering who is being quoted, in most cases you should avoid placing the attribution at the beginning of a quote. Do not write:

The police officer said: "The car overturned at least three times. None of the four passengers was hurt. Luckily, the car did not explode into flames."

However, if direct quotes from two different speakers follow one another, you should start the second with the attribution to avoid confusion:

"The driver must not have seen the curve," an eyewitness said. "Once the car left the road, all I saw was a cloud of dust."

> The police officer said: "The car overturned at least three times. None of the four passengers was hurt. Luckily, the car did not explode into flames."

Notice that when an attribution precedes a direct quotation that is more than one sentence long, wire service style requires that a colon follow the attribution.

- **Do not follow a fragment of a quote with a continuing complete sentence of quotation.** Avoid constructions like this one:

> The mayor said the time had come "to turn off some lights. We all must do something to conserve electricity."

The correct form is to separate partial quotes and complete quotes:

> The time has come "to turn off some lights," the mayor said. "We all must do something to conserve electricity."

- **The first time you attribute a direct or an indirect quote, identify the speaker fully.** How fully depends on how well the speaker is known to the readers. In Springfield, Ill., it is sufficient to identify the mayor simply as Mayor Tim Davlin. But if a story in the *Chicago Tribune* referred to the mayor of Springfield, the first reference would have to be "Tim Davlin, mayor of Springfield" — unless, of course, the dateline for the story was Springfield.
- **Do not attribute direct quotes to more than one person.** For example, don't do the following:

> "Flames were shooting out everywhere," witnesses said. "Then electrical wires began falling, and voices were heard screaming."

All you have to do is eliminate the quotation marks, if indeed any witness made the statements.

- **Do not make up a source. Never attribute a statement to "a witness" unless your source is indeed that witness.** At times you may ask a witness to confirm what you have seen, but never invent quotes for anonymous witnesses. Inventing witnesses and making up quotes is dishonest, inaccurate and inexcusable. One of the many transgressions of former *New York Times* reporter Jayson Blair was that he quoted people who never existed.
- **In stories covering past news events, use the past tense in attributions, and use it throughout the story.** However, features and other stories that do not report on news events may be more effective if the attributions are consistently given in the present tense. In a feature story like a personality profile, when it is safe to assume that what the person once said, he or she would still say, you may use the present tense. For example, when you write, "'I like being mayor,' she says," you are indicating that she still enjoys the job.

- **Ordinarily, place the noun or pronoun before the verb in attributions:**

"Everything is under control," the sheriff said.

However, if you must identify a person by including a long title, it is better to begin the attribution with the verb:

"I enjoy the challenge," says Janet Berry, associate dean for graduate studies and research.

Attributing Written Sources

Do not use the word "says" when quoting from written sources. You may be general at times and say, "As *Time* magazine reported last week . . ." or "According to *Time* magazine. . . ." When you know the author of the piece, you may wish to include it: As Malcolm Gladwell wrote in the Oct. 16, 2006, issue of *The New Yorker*. . . ."

HANDLING ON- AND OFF-THE-RECORD INFORMATION

TIPS

Three Reasons for Avoiding Anonymous Sources

- You damage your credibility.
- Your source may be lying or floating a trial balloon.
- You may be sued if you later reveal your source.

Until you are a source in a story involving controversy, you may not understand why people sometimes don't want to talk to reporters or why they don't want their names in the paper. Your job would be easy if all of your sources wished to be "on the record."

Some sources for sound reasons do not want to be named. You must learn to use professional judgment in handling the material they give you. If you agree to accept their information, you must honor their requests to remain off the record. Breaching that confidence destroys trust and credibility and may get you in trouble with the law. But it is your obligation to take the information elsewhere to confirm it and get it on the record.

Perhaps no author or reporter is better known for using anonymous sources than Bob Woodward of *The Washington Post*. His 2006 book, *State of Denial*, once again upset many readers, especially those whom Woodward treated unkindly, trying to identify his many anonymous sources. Most newspapers and Web sites would not permit this use of anonymous sources, but Woodward takes more latitude in his books because he makes the decision, not an editor or news director.

Not naming sources is dangerous for three important reasons. First, such information lacks credibility and makes the reporter and the newspaper suspect.

Second, the source may be lying. He or she may be out to discredit someone or may be floating a trial balloon to test public reaction on some issue or event. Skilled diplomats and politicians know how to use reporters to take the temperature of public opinion. If the public reacts negatively, the sources will not proceed with whatever plans they leaked to the press. In such cases the press has been used—and it has become less credible.

The third reason that not naming sources is dangerous is that once you have promised anonymity to a source, you may not change your mind without risking a breach-of-contract suit. In 1991, the Supreme Court ruled 5-4 in Cohen v. Cowles Media Co. that the First Amendment does not prevent news sources from suing the press for breach of contract when the press makes confidential sources public. That's why papers such as *The Miami Herald* have a policy that only a senior editor has authority to commit the paper to a pledge of confidentiality.

Some reporters make these distinctions regarding sources and attribution:

- **Off the record.** You may not use the information.
- **Not for attribution.** You may use the information but may not attribute it.
- **Background.** You may use it with a general title for a source (for example, "a White House aide said").
- **Deep background.** You may use the information, but you may not indicate any source.

By no means is there agreement on these terms. For most people "off the record" means not for attribution. For some it means that you cannot use the information in any way. Some find no difference between "background" and "deep background."

Because there is little agreement among journalists, sources may be equally vague about the terms. Your obligation is to make sure you and your sources understand each other. Set the ground rules ahead of time. Clarify your terms.

Also be sure you know the policy of your paper in these matters. For example, many newspapers do not allow reporters to use unidentified sources unless an editor knows the source and approves the usage. Other news organizations such as the Associated Press will not carry opinions, whether positive or negative, that are expressed by an unidentified source. The news agency will cite statements of fact without attribution, but only if the story makes it clear that the person providing this material would do so only on the condition of anonymity. *The New York Times* has a policy of not allowing direct quotations of pejorative remarks by an unidentified source.

> **"**On one of Kissinger's (then Secretary of State Henry Kissinger) sojourns, humorist Art Buchwald attributed information to a 'high U.S. official with wavy hair, horn-rimmed glasses and a German accent.' **"**
>
> —Alicia C. Shepard, *American Journalism Review*

Be careful not to allow a speaker to suddenly claim something is off the record. Sometimes in the middle of an interview a source will see you taking notes and suddenly try to change the rules. "Oh, I meant to tell you, that last example was off the record." With all the tact you can muster, try, without losing the source altogether, to change the person's mind. At least, tell the person to try to avoid doing that for the rest of the interview.

Nevertheless, if a city manager or police chief wishes to have a background session with you, unless it is against newspaper policy, you should not refuse. Often these officials are trying to be as open as they can under certain circumstances. Without such background sessions the task of reporting complex issues intelligently is nearly impossible. But you must be aware that you are hearing only one point of view and that the information may be self-serving.

Miles Beller, at the time a reporter for the *Los Angeles Herald Examiner*, gave this example in *Editor & Publisher*:

> Several years ago a woman phoned this reporter and "wanted to go off the record" in regard to a Los Angeles official's "secret ownership of a Las Vegas radio station" and other questionable holdings tied to this public servant. Funny thing though, the caller plumb forgot to mention that she was working for another candidate. This bit of minutia probably just slipped her mind, what with her man trailing so badly and the election a few weeks away.

Some sources make a habit of saying everything is off the record and of giving commonplace information in background sessions. Although you should not quote a source who asks to remain off the record, you may use information if one or more of the following is true:

- The information is a matter of public record.
- It is generally known.
- It is available from several sources.
- You are a witness.

So as not to lose credibility with your source, it's a good idea to make it clear that you plan to use the information because of one or more of the preceding reasons.

Knowing when and how to attribute background information is an art you will have to give continuing special care and attention to as a reporter. Remember these two important points:

- When possible, set the ground rules with your sources ahead of time.
- Know your newspaper's policy in these matters.

Using Someone Else's Direct Quotations

If you use a direct quotation that you personally did not get from a source, always indicate the source of the quote. The Colorado Rockies' manager Clint Hurdle would not participate in a news conference attended by any reporter from *The Denver Post* because its columnist Mark Kiszla quoted right fielder Larry Walker from an interview by reporter Troy Renck. Jay Alves, the Rockies' media-relations director, said, "There were quotes taken out of context from a player that the columnist never talked to directly."

Denver Post managing editor Gary Clark stood by his reporter. "He did nothing wrong," he said in a *Post* story. "He (Troy Renck) did nothing wrong. He gave a quote to a colleague. The quote is accurate, and the Rockies do not dispute that."

Then the *Post* filed a formal complaint with Major League Baseball and the Baseball Writers Association of America.

Don't be tempted to use direct quotes you find in news releases. Don't be lazy; get your own quotes. Sources are much less likely to say things that are self-serving if they are talking to a journalist rather than a public-relations person.

Suggested Readings

Brooks, Brian S., Pinson, James L. and Wilson, Jean Gaddy. *Working With Words*, Sixth Edition. New York: Bedford/St. Martin's, 2005. The section on quotations is excellent and follows Associated Press style.

Callihan, E. L. *Grammar for Journalists*, Revised Edition. Radnor, Pa.: Chilton Book Co., 1979. This classic text contains a good section on how to punctuate, attribute and handle quotations.

Germer, Fawn. "Are Quotes Sacred?" *American Journalism Review*, Sept. 1995, pp. 34–37. Presents many views of all sides of whether and when to change quotes.

Hart, Jack. "Giving Credit When Credit Isn't Due." *Editor & Publisher*, Sept. 11, 1993, p. 2. Warns against useless attribution.

King, Barbara. "There's Real Power in Common Speech." *Ottaway News Extra*, no. 137, Winter 1989, pp. 8, 16. An excellent discussion of using real quotes from real people.

LaRoque, Paula. "People Are Using Quotes More Often—But in Many Cases They Shouldn't Be." *Quill*, March 1, 2004, p. 32. Good advice from an excellent writer, writing coach and teacher.

Stein, M. L. "9th Circuit: It's OK to Make Up Quotes." *Editor & Publisher*, Aug. 12, 1989, pp. 16, 30. Reactions from the press and lawyers to the court decision allowing quotes that are not verbatim.

Stimson, William. "Two Schools on Quoting Confuse the Reader." *Journalism Educator*, vol. 49, no. 4, Winter 1995, pp. 69–73. Strong arguments against cleaning up quotes.

Stolzfus, Duane. "Partial Pre-Publication Review Gaining Favor at Newspapers." *Newspaper Research Journal*, vol. 27, no. 4, Fall 2006, pp. 23–37. A practice long thought unconscionable among journalists gains acceptance.

Weinberg, Steve. "So What's Wrong with Pre-Publication Review?" *Quill*, May 1990, pp. 26–28. Answers objections to prepublication review.

Weinberg, Steve. "Thou Shalt Not Concoct Thy Quote." *Fineline*, July/Aug. 1991, pp. 3–4. Presents reasons for allowing sources to review quotations before publication.

Weiss, Philip. "Who Gets Quote Approval?" *Columbia Journalism Review*, May/June 1991, pp. 52–54. Discusses the growing practice of allowing sources to check quotations before publication.

Suggested Web Sites

www.instruct1.cit.cornell.edu/courses/comm352-fall2000/ quotes.html
A thorough discussion of quotes and attribution that applies to newspapers, magazines, television, radio and online journalism.

www.jerz.setonhill.edu/writing/journalism/ quotations.htm
A clear explanation of using quotes effectively. Excellent use of examples.

www.owl.english.purdue.edu/handouts/grammar/ g_quote.html
A broad discussion of how to handle quotes of all kinds.

Exercises

1. Rewrite the following story, paying special attention to the use of quotations and attribution. Note the sensitive nature of some of the quotations. Paraphrase when necessary.

Christopher O'Reilly is a remarkably happy young man, despite a bout with meningitis eight years ago that has left him paralyzed and brain-damaged.

"I am happy," O'Reilly commented, as he puffed a cigarette.

He has much to be happy about. Physical therapy has hastened his recovery since the day he awoke from a 10-week-long coma. He has lived to celebrate his 26th birthday.

"I had a helluva birthday," he said. "I seen several friends. I had big cake," he added slowly.

He lives in a house with his mother and stepfather in the rolling, green countryside near Springfield.

O'Reilly's withered legs are curled beneath him now, and his right arm is mostly paralyzed, but he can do pull-ups with his left arm. He can see and hear.

"When he came back, he wasn't worth a damn," his mother said. "The hack doctors told me he would be a vegetable all his life," she claimed.

"He couldn't talk; he could only blink. And he drooled a lot," she smiled.

Now, Chris is able to respond in incomplete sentences to questions and can carry on slow communication. "He don't talk good, but he talks," his mother commented.

It all began when he stole a neighbor's Rototiller. His probation was revoked, and he found himself in the medium-security prison in Springfield. Then came "inadequate medical treatment" in the prison system. O'Reilly's family argued that he received punishment beyond what the Eighth Amendment of the U.S. Constitution calls "cruel and unusual."

"Those prison officials were vicious," they said.

As a result, he was awarded $250,000 from the state, the largest legal settlement in federal court in 10 years. "That sounds like a lot of money. But it really isn't, you know, when you consider what happened and when you consider the worth of a human life, and the way they treated him and all, we thought we should get at least a million," his mother remarked.

O'Reilly contracted the infection of the brain after sleeping "on the concrete floor" of a confinement cell, his mother maintained. He had been placed in solitary confinement because he would not clean his cell. The disease went undiagnosed for eight days, leaving him paralyzed and brain-damaged, she said.

Now O'Reilly likes watching television. "I like TV," he grinned. "And smoking."

His mother said she "never gives up hope" that "one day" her son will "come out of it."

2. Here are some words of writer and artist John Gerstner. Write a brief story covering what Gerstner said, and use three—and only three—direct quotes.

I believe a magazine should be everything you would like your mate to be: intelligent, adventurous, stimulating, candid, helpful, spirited, nice to look at and full of surprises. I believe a magazine should feast the eye as well as feed the mind. Leafing through a magazine should be an aesthetic as well as an intellectual experience. Each page should be a synthesis of idea, concepts, words, photographs, illustrations and graphic design that arrests, intrigues and instantly communicates . . . not only the subject of the article but also some of its nuances as well—no small trick.

I believe a magazine should continually evolve and take risks. About the time a winning formula is found is about the time a new one needs formulating. The best magazines stretch themselves in every issue and surprise both readers and staff.

I believe a magazine should be a team project. No editor is an island, nor should want to be. The editor's job is to set the course and the standard. After that it's a matter of squeezing every ounce of creativity out of himself or herself and others and "arguing, procuring, tinkering and sending things back," as one magazine editor put it. And no editor or publisher should ever underestimate the role human chemistry and magic play in putting out a successful magazine.

Finally, I believe the magazine is one of journalism's highest and noblest forms. The magazine format demands not just good reporting and writing but good communicating, which entails visual as well as verbal sophistication. The best magazines move minds, raise sights and spirits, and make waves to break on distant shores. They aspire to—and sometimes achieve—the level of art.

3. Attend a meeting, a press conference or a speech and tape-record it. While there, write down the quotes you would use if you were writing the story for your local newspaper. Then listen to the tape, and check the accuracy of the quotations.

4. Interview at least two reporters, and ask them about their policies on handling sources regarding the following:

   a. Off the record
   b. Not for attribution
   c. Background
   d. Deep background

   Write an essay of at least 200 words on the subject.

5. Read the front-page section of your local daily newspaper. Note every anonymous source that you find used, and decide whether the use of the anonymous source was justified.

6. Engage a classmate in a half-hour interview about his or her life. In your story, use as many direct quotes as you think are fitting. Then check the accuracy of your quotations with your classmate.

Gathering and Verifying Information

5

IN THIS CHAPTER
YOU WILL LEARN:

1. How to use computerized sources of information to check facts.

2. How to use traditional sources of information to check facts.

3. Where to find information on the Web.

4. How the media use computers in investigative reporting.

I talian astronomer Galileo Galilei wrote in the 17th century, "All truths are easy to understand once they are discovered; the point is to discover them." Discovering the truth also is the point of journalistic reporting.

Truth is the primary defense against libel, as we shall learn in Chapter 22. But it's also at the heart of credibility, a quality that readers feel is too often lacking in today's journalism. Survey after survey shows that the public views the news media as biased and inaccurate. Reporters rank alongside used-car salespeople in prestige and trustworthiness.

That's an appalling state of affairs for a craft about which Bill Kovach and Tom Rosenstiel, authors of *The Elements of Journalism*, assert, "The essence of journalism is a discipline of verification."

The problem, as Kovach and Rosenstiel note, is that getting it right isn't easy, and it's been that way at least since the fifth century B.C., when Thucydides wrote in his account of the introduction of the Peloponnesian War:

> With regard to my factual reporting of events . . . I have made it a principle not to write down the first story that came my way, and not even to be guided by my own general impressions; either I was present myself at the events which I have described or else heard of them from eye witnesses whose reports I have checked with as much thoroughness as possible. Not that even so the truth was easy to discover: different eye witnesses gave different accounts of the same events, speaking out of partiality for one side or the other, or else from imperfect memories.

Any reporter who has ever covered a breaking news event, such as a war, a fire, an accident or a disaster, has encountered the same situation—conflicting accounts of what happened and a near inability to sort it all out. But sort it out we must. That's the job of journalists, and gathering facts is at the heart of what journalists do.

In this chapter, we'll explore the discipline of getting information—and getting it right.

ACCURATE INFORMATION: THE BASIS OF A GOOD STORY

Ask any editor whether a reporter can be a good writer without being good at information gathering, and you're likely to hear a resounding, "No!" That's because good writing depends on good reporting.

The Discipline of Multiple Sources

Good writing is of course important, as we'll explore in later chapters, but the quality of writing depends in large part on good fact-gathering, which we call good reporting. It's almost impossible to write a great story without first doing a great job of reporting. Gathering that information requires skilled interviewing, as we discussed in Chapter 3. It also requires knowing how to use the many sources of information readily available. Make no mistake about it: There are hundreds of places to find information.

Good reporters know that the worst kind of news story is one with a single source. Rarely is such a story worth publishing. Even a personality profile should be based on more than just an interview with the source. To get a fuller perspective, it's important to talk with individuals who know the subject. Gathering information from multiple sources is one of the keys to good writing and good communication. It's also the best way to ensure accuracy by verifying information. When additional sources are checked and cross-checked, the chances of a story being accurate greatly improve.

Imagine how many sources George Dohrman of the *St. Paul Pioneer Press* checked in his Pulitzer Prize-winning story about academic fraud in the University of Minnesota basketball program:

At least 20 men's basketball players at the University of Minnesota had research papers, take-home exams or other course work done for them during a five-year period, according to a former office manager in the academic counseling unit who said she did the work.

Four former players, Courtney James, Russ Archambault, Kevin Loge and Darrell Whaley, confirmed that work was prepared for them in possible violation of the student code of conduct and NCAA regulations. Another former player, Trevor Winter, said he was aware of the practice.

James, Archambault and the office manager, Jan Gangelhoff, said knowledge of the academic fraud was widespread.

"These are serious allegations," University of Minnesota President Mark Yudof said Tuesday. "We've called in legal counsel. I want to look into this promptly. But they are just allegations at this point."

Gangelhoff, 50, said that from 1993 to 1998 she estimates she did more than 400 pieces of course work for players, including some starters on the 1996-97 Final Four team.

"They bring in these high-risk kids, and they know that everything they did in high school was done for them," Gangelhoff said. "It's got to stop somewhere."

Gangelhoff said she "struggled for a long time" whether to disclose the allegations. When asked to prove them, Gangelhoff provided the *Pioneer Press* with computer files containing more than 225 examples of course work for 19 players, dating to 1994, that she says she wrote and players turned in. Gangelhoff said she kept only about half her files.

Gangelhoff also provided printed copies of five pieces of course work that she said had been turned in by students. Some of the papers had grades and instructor's comments written on them. All five pieces also appeared in Gangelhoff's computer files.

Elayne Donahue, the retired head of the academic counseling unit, said she was unaware of the fraud but warned athletic department administrators that the office manager was tutoring players in violation of department policy and was ignored. . . .

Although Gangelhoff was Dohrman's primary source, there is evidence of many other sources in just the first few paragraphs of the first story in the series.

Four former players confirmed the practice. A fifth said he was aware of it. The University of Minnesota president was asked to comment. Gangelhoff provided the newspaper with files of course work she said she produced for players. She also produced corrected copies from instructors for five of those files. Yet another source reported being aware of tutoring practices that violated athletic department policy.

As the story played out, Dohrman provided evidence of dozens of other sources that he used to get the story. In investigations, of course, dozens of sources may be necessary. But good reporters know that in any story, no matter how short, multiple sources are essential. If nothing else, multiple sources help build credibility with readers and viewers. Journalism is predicated on credibility. Without it, newspapers, magazines, radio and television stations, online sites and the rest have little to offer.

The Discipline of Verification

Journalists, when operating as they should, follow much the same investigative system used by scientists. They develop a hypothesis and then seek facts to support or reject it. In the 20th century, journalists developed the concept of objectivity—an elusive idea that was often interpreted the wrong way.

As Philip Meyer of the University of North Carolina suggests to Kovach and Rosenstiel in *The Elements of Journalism*: "I think [the] connection between journalism and science ought to emphasize objectivity of method. That's what scientific method is—our humanity, our subjective impulses ... directed toward deciding what to investigate by objective means."

What objectivity isn't, Kovach and Rosenstiel argue, is blind loyalty to the concepts of fairness and balance. Fairness, they argue, can be misunderstood if it is seen as a goal unto itself. Fairness should mean that a journalist is fair to the facts and to the public's understanding of them. It should not mean, "Am I being fair to my sources, so that none of them will be unhappy?" or "Does my story seem fair?" Those are subjective judgments that lead the journalist away from the task of independent verification.

Similarly, balance should not mean that it's necessary to get an equal number of scientists speaking on each side of the global-warming debate if an overwhelming number of scientists in fact believe that global warming is a reality.

Kovach and Rosenstiel argue that sharpening the meaning of verification and resisting the temptation to simplify it are essential to improving the credibility of what journalists write.

So, too, is the journalistic process of layered editing. At a good newspaper or magazine, once the reporter writes a story, it is subject to extensive review by several editors. Each may find facts to correct or language to clarify in the quest for a story that is as compelling—and accurate—as possible. Thus, as a story flows through the editorial process (see Figure 5.1), the goal is to make it as nearly perfect as possible.

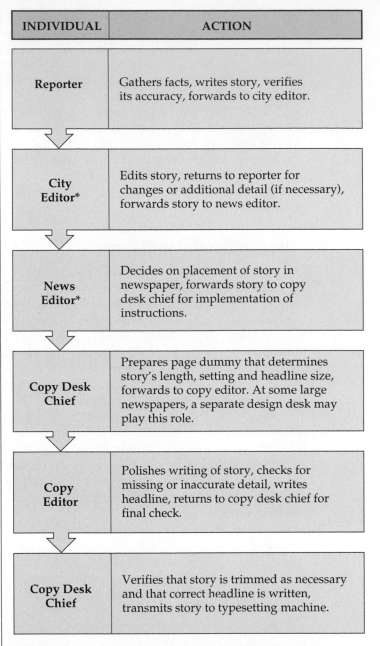

INDIVIDUAL	ACTION
Reporter	Gathers facts, writes story, verifies its accuracy, forwards to city editor.
City Editor*	Edits story, returns to reporter for changes or additional detail (if necessary), forwards story to news editor.
News Editor*	Decides on placement of story in newspaper, forwards story to copy desk chief for implementation of instructions.
Copy Desk Chief	Prepares page dummy that determines story's length, setting and headline size, forwards to copy editor. At some large newspapers, a separate design desk may play this role.
Copy Editor	Polishes writing of story, checks for missing or inaccurate detail, writes headline, returns to copy desk chief for final check.
Copy Desk Chief	Verifies that story is trimmed as necessary and that correct headline is written, transmits story to typesetting machine.

* Or assistant

Note: At any point in the process, a story may be returned to an earlier editor for clarification, amplification or rewriting.

Figure 5.1
Editing and producing a newspaper is a fast-paced and complex process in which editors at different levels review stories. Here is a typical copy-flow pattern for a daily newspaper.

Editors talk about the need to look at a story on both the micro and macro levels. Micro editing is the process of paying attention to detail:

- Are the facts correct?
- Are names spelled correctly?
- Is the grammar sound?

Macro editing, on the other hand, looks at the big picture:

- Will readers understand this?
- Are there unanswered questions or inconsistencies in the story?
- Does this agree with what I know about previous stories on the subject?

All of this, and much more, goes into the editorial process of verification. In the end, the idea is to get it right.

As they strive to get it right, journalists use all types of sources, including interviews, source documents and a variety of other sources ranging from the obvious, such as a Google search, to online sites, computer databases and traditional sources like printed almanacs and encyclopedias. In this chapter, we explore the many possible sources of information. Good reporters make frequent use of them all.

COMPUTERIZED SOURCES OF INFORMATION

Reporters and editors today have a wealth of information available at their fingertips. In addition to making raw data available, computers help reporters organize and analyze information.

From the news library in your local office to national databases of published newspaper, magazine and broadcast stories, the amount of computerized information is staggering. These are the primary sources of computerized information:

- The news library, or morgue, maintained by your own publication or broadcast station.
- Search engines like Google, Yahoo! and MSN Search.
- News sites, portals and content aggregators (USAToday.com, nytimes.com, MSNBC.com, CNN.com, News.yahoo.com, News.google.com).
- Other sites on the World Wide Web. Millions of organizations maintain Web sites with useful information.
- Commercial database services (Dialog, LexisNexis and others).
- Government databases (city, county, state and federal).
- Special-interest databases (those created by organizations with a cause).

- CD-ROMs and DVDs. Not all are entertainment-oriented. Some contain useful factual information.
- Custom databases.

Let's explore the usefulness of each.

Your News Library: The Place to Start

Computer databases are a marvel that good reporters and editors have learned to cherish. Before they were available, doing research for a story was a laborious process that involved a trip to the newspaper, magazine or broadcast station library, or morgue, to sift through hundreds or even thousands of tattered, yellowed clippings. Too often, clippings had disappeared, were misfiled or were misplaced, which made such research a hit-and-miss proposition. Despite those shortcomings, the library was considered a valuable asset. Reporters were routinely admonished to check there first.

You will still hear that advice in news rooms today, but many of today's news libraries are computerized, which almost ensures that an item will not disappear and will be easy to locate. Typically, you can do a check of the computerized library from your own computer. That makes it easier than ever to do good background work on a story. Your ability to search the library is limited only by your skill with search techniques.

News libraries are what computer experts call **full-text databases**, which means that all words in the database have been indexed and are searchable. Such capability gives you great flexibility in structuring searches using what are known as **Boolean search commands**. Boolean operators like AND, OR and NOT allow you to structure the search to find material most closely related to the subject of your research. For example, if you are interested in finding articles on former South African President Nelson Mandela's visits to the United States, you might issue this command on the search line:

    Mandela AND United ADJ States

The computer would then search for all articles that contain the name "Mandela" and also contain the words "United" and "States" adjacent to each other. In this example, AND and ADJ (for "adjacent") are the Boolean operators. This search would produce all articles on Mandela and the United States but would exclude articles involving Mandela and, for example, the United Arab Emirates, despite the presence of the word "United" (it's not adjacent to the word "States"). The result of such a search in most cases would be a report from the computer telling you how many articles match your search criteria:

    Search found 27 articles. Would you like to see them or further narrow your search?

At that point, you would have the option of further limiting the search (by date, for example) or viewing all 27 articles.

Remember that computers don't really think. In our sample search, an article on Mandela's visit to Miami that did not contain the words "United States" would not have been found. Therefore, it is important to understand the limitations as well as the power of computer-assisted database searching. Good reporters quickly learn to take into account such possibilities and learn to recast their searches in other ways.

There are other limitations. Many news library databases do not allow you to see photos, nor can you see articles as they appeared in the newspaper or magazine. Nor do most current systems permit you to hear how a broadcast story was used on the air. Instead, you have access only to a text-based version of what appeared. That limits your ability to learn how the story was displayed in the newspaper or magazine, or how it was read on the air. If necessary, however, you can always resort to looking up the original in bound volumes or on microfilm. Most newspapers save old editions in one or both of those forms. Many radio and television stations maintain tape libraries of old newscasts. While these older forms of storage may be less convenient to use, taking the time to do so is often worth the effort.

Some newer library computer systems overcome the traditional disadvantages of computerization by allowing you to call graphical reproductions of the printed page to the screen. You can view photographs, charts and maps in the same way. In broadcast applications, more and more libraries permit storage of digital video and sound clips. As such systems proliferate, the shortcomings of present computer libraries will disappear.

Despite current limitations, few veteran reporters would be willing to return to the days of tattered yellow clippings. They know that computerization has made the news library a more reliable source of background information.

Thus, the best reporters of today do what good reporters have always done: Check the morgue first. They simply do it with computers.

Search Engines

For many journalists, the first stop after the morgue is Google. Google or one of the other popular search engines—Yahoo!, MSN Search, Dogpile or Ask—can indeed be helpful to a journalist. The key to their successful use is the ability to recognize whether the information contained on the Web site to which the search takes you is accurate and therefore usable.

Information from well-known sites may be reliable; information from Web sites advocating a cause may not be. We discuss how to evaluate such information in the "Evaluating Links" box in this chapter.

News Sites, Portals and Content Aggregators

Some might consider it strange to think of news Web sites, portals and content aggregators as useful sources of information for reporters. Don't tell that to the reporters who use them.

Evaluating Links

The Web is a great resource for reporters, but determining the credibility of information on the Web can be problematic. If the source is a respected media organization like *The New York Times* or *The Washington Post*, chances are the information is solid. But if it is published by an organization promoting a cause, there is ample reason to be wary.

Stan Ketterer, a journalist and journalism professor, tells reporters to evaluate information on the Web by following the same standard journalistic practices that they would use for assessing the credibility and accuracy of any information:

- **Before using information from a Web site in a story, verify it with a source.** There are exceptions to this rule. They include using information from a highly credible government site like the Census Bureau. You might also want to use unverified information when you can't contact the source on a breaking story because of time constraints. An editor must clear all exceptions.
- **In most cases, information taken directly from the Web and used in a story must be attributed.** If you have verified the information with a source, you can use the organization in the attribution — for example, "according to the EPA" or "EPA figures show." If you cannot verify the information after trying repeatedly, attribute unverified information to the Web page — for example, "according to the Voice of America's site on the World Wide Web." Consult your editor before using unverified information.
- **If you have doubts about the accuracy of the information and you cannot reach the source, get it from another source, such as a book or another person.** When in doubt, omit the information.

- **Check the extension on the site's Internet address to get clues as to the nature of the organization and the likely slant of the information.** The most common extensions used in the United States are *.gov* (government), *.edu* (education), *.com* (commercial), *.mil* (military), *.org* (not-for-profit organization) and *.net* (Internet administration). Most of the government and military sites have credible and accurate information. In many cases, you can take the information directly from the site and attribute it to the organization. But consult your editor until you get to know these sites.
- **Treat the sites of colleges and universities as you would other sites.** If college and university sites have source documents, such as the Constitution, attribute the information to the source document. But beware: Personal home pages can have .edu extensions, and the information is not always credible.
- **In almost all cases, *do not* take information directly from the home pages of commercial and not-for-profit organizations and use it without verification.**
- **Check the date when the page was last updated.** The date generally appears at the top or bottom of the first page of the site. Although a recent date does not ensure that the information is current, it does indicate that the organization is paying close attention to the site. If no date appears, if the site has not been updated for a while, or if it was created some time ago, do not use the information unless you verify it with a source.

Such sites are accessible to anyone with a computer and an Internet connection. News sites are those published by established media outlets like *The New York Times* (nytimes.com) and CBS (cbsnews.com), while portals are designed as entry points to the Web, such as America Online (aol.com). Most portals now have news and other information as well as *forums* (electronic bulletin boards) for discussions on topics ranging from genealogy to stamp collecting to sports. Forum participants exchange messages on every conceivable topic. Some even write computer software that facilitates the pursuit of their passion, and they frequently make that software available to others interested in the topic. This makes it simple for reporters to find people knowledgeable about almost any subject.

Online forums provide fertile information to reporters attempting to research a story. For example, if you are assigned to do a story on genealogy and know nothing about the subject, what better way to gauge the pulse of those passionate about the subject than by tapping into their discussions? By logging on to one of these public forums, you can do just that.

If you want to interview those who participated in World War II's Battle of the Bulge, try posting a request for names on one of these services. Chances are you will be inundated with names and telephone numbers of individuals and veterans' groups that would be delighted to help.

The popularity of such services is almost impossible to overstate. What people like about public online forums is that they do what radio talk shows do—give people a place where they can exchange ideas with those who share similar interests. Writing in *Editor & Publisher*, Barry Hollander, a journalism professor at the University of Georgia, contrasts the skyrocketing popularity of talk radio with the continuing decline of newspaper circulation:

> Newspapers used to be an important part of what bound communities together, a common forum for ideas and discussion. But as communities fragmented along racial and demographic lines, newspapers have done a better job of chronicling the decline than offering ways to offset the trend.
>
> A sense of connection is needed. Newspapers, and [their] electronic editions in particular, offer one opportunity to bring people together in ways similar to talk radio.

Over the years, newspapers, magazines and broadcast stations have attempted to connect with their readers and listeners by doing people-on-the-street interviews. Interviewing people at random seldom produces good results because often those interviewed know nothing about the topic or don't care about it. By tapping into the forums on various online sites, you are assured of finding knowledgeable, conversant people to interview.

These services give reporters a way to reconnect with the public and find expert sources for stories. With their huge amounts of easily accessible material, they also are useful sources of information for reporters and editors.

Then there are the news aggregators—sites like Yahoo News (news.yahoo.com) and Google News (news.google.com)—which link to news stories from a plethora of news sites, becoming, in effect, a good place for one-stop news shopping.

Other Sites on the World Wide Web

When a little-known, California-based cult called Heaven's Gate staged a mass suicide, newspapers and broadcast stations had no trouble finding background information on the group. The cult's Web site offered reporters a mother lode of information about the sect and its leader.

ON THE JOB

The Challenges of Editing for the Web

Erik Ulken is among those journalists who have embraced the digital technologies that are changing journalism. After earning bachelor's and master's degrees, Ulken worked as a news producer at NOLA.com, the Web site of the *New Orleans Times-Picayune*, and at the *Columbus Dispatch* before making his way to Los Angeles. He's now managing editor for news of LATimes.com, Web site of the *Los Angeles Times*.

Ulken urges would-be journalists to embrace the Web and to think not just about writing jobs but also about editing:

"If you take a newspaper job two or three years from now, chances are much of the work you do won't be for a newspaper at all, but rather for a Web site. News rooms are reorganizing to meet new challenges as their online editions grow in importance. It's still unclear how many duties copy editors ultimately will juggle, but their new responsibilities almost certainly will transcend the traditional role. (Meanwhile, newspaper gigs aren't the only game in town: Broadcast and online-only sites are hiring more copy editors as their Internet operations grow.)

"In addition to learning basic copy-editing skills (which never go out of style), here's how you can prepare yourself:

- **Learn how to use content management systems.** News organizations use a variety of online content platforms, but there are similarities among them. The simplest content management systems are blogging tools such as TypePad and Blogger. Learning how they work will help you pick up more complex systems much faster.
- **Understand how users find news on the Web.** Many come to your site from search engines and aggregator sites such as Google News, which is one reason why Web heads are so important.
- **Understand audio and video.** It's less important to know how to edit in Final Cut Pro than it is to be able to identify what's missing from a multimedia package.
- **Be flexible and make an effort to adapt to new technologies.** Don't assume that the rules as you've learned them are immutable — even when it comes to style and usage: Technology, and indeed language, are constantly evolving.
- **Use the Web constantly.** The best way to learn how to produce great content for the Web is to experience great content on the Web.

"To answer the question I know you're asking: Yes, you'll probably end up doing more work, and doing it faster, than previous generations of copy editors have done. But, on the plus side, the greater variety of tasks should keep the routine from getting old."

That incident illustrates what a powerful source of information the Internet—and particularly its user-friendly interface, the World Wide Web—has become. The Internet is not a single computer network but rather a series of interconnected networks throughout the world. That arguably makes it the world's first truly international news medium.

For the journalist, the Internet serves two primary purposes:

- It is an increasingly robust source of online information, including federal, state and local government data, and information published by companies on almost any imaginable topic. Need information on a new drug? Chances are you can find it on the Internet, complete with more detail than you ever wanted to know. Need to know about Estonia? Plenty of Web sites are available to tell you what you need to know or to give you the latest news from Tallinn, its capital. Further, most North American newspapers, magazines and broadcast stations have a substantial Internet presence, sometimes complete with archives of previously published stories. Some experts, in fact, now refer to the Internet as the world's largest library. That's good stuff for a reporter who needs to do a quick bit of research to provide background material or context for a news story.

- It is a publishing medium that offers new opportunities for media companies and journalists, and new jobs for journalism and mass communications graduates. In recent years, media companies large and small alike have rushed to establish a presence on the Web in the belief that this is an exciting new medium of increasing interest to the public and one with enormous commercial potential (see Figure 5.2). Media companies also use the Internet to attract readers and viewers to their more profitable traditional products.

Figure 5.2
Established by the *San Jose Mercury News,* the Mercury Center is a substantial Internet resource for both national news and regional coverage of Northern California.

The Internet also serves as an excellent medium for transmitting photos and even audio and video clips. It's possible to tap into the Louvre Museum's Web site and see paintings from that famous collection in full color, for example, and YouTube is a hot site for posting videos. Some of them are quite good.

Many observers of the media industry believe that the Internet, with its ability to give the consumer a choice of full-text, full-motion video and audio, will become the preferred news medium of the future. Indeed, surveys show that it already is the preferred news medium for people under 30. It is possible today to read on your computer the text of a presidential address or to watch video of the address being delivered. On that same computer, you might watch a movie, do holiday shopping or order groceries.

Just a few years ago, slow connections into people's homes made it impossible to play audio or watch video on the Web. Now, however, most telephone companies offer high-speed digital subscriber line service, and cable television companies offer high-speed broadband services. Many are rolling out ever-more-capable services based on fast, high-bandwidth, fiber-optics technology. As the speed of the pipeline into the home increases, so does the popularity and capability of the Web.

As the capability of the Web continues to grow, we see the power and possibilities of the "information superhighway" becoming a reality.

Commercial Database Services

When newspapers and magazines entered the computer era in the early 1970s, publishers were quick to realize the potential value of saving and reselling previously published information. Newspapers and magazines quickly began selling access to their archives by establishing alliances with companies founded for that purpose.

On many topics, searching your own news library will not be sufficient. If U.S. Rep. Barney Frank is making his first appearance in your community and you have been assigned to cover him, your morgue probably won't help; little will have been written about him in your city. It will be much more useful to read recent articles published in Massachusetts, Frank's home state. By doing so, you will be armed with questions to ask about recent events of interest to him. In such situations, the national commercial databases are invaluable.

One of the leading commercial database services is LexisNexis, which provides full-text access to hundreds of newspaper and magazine libraries. It is a rich source of background information for a reporter who wants to see what has already been written on a given subject.

Government Databases

For years, government agencies have maintained large databases of information as a means of managing the public's business. They cover almost every conceivable service that government offers, from airplane registration and maintenance records to census data to local court records. They are maintained not only by the federal and state governments but also by even the smallest of city and county agencies.

The growth of commercial databases is a great asset to reporters, who can easily see what has been written about a subject in other newspapers. But be aware of potential problems.

- Copyright laws must be obeyed. Take care not to use too much material without permission.

- Not all articles that appeared in a newspaper can be found in a database. Wire service and market reports, death notices, box scores, social announcements and items written by freelancers are often excluded.

- Something may have been published, but that doesn't mean it's accurate. History is littered with incidents of newspapers quoting each other's inaccuracies.

- You don't know if the reporter who wrote an account has any real knowledge of the subject matter. If you lift information from that reporter without such knowledge, you may introduce an inaccuracy.

- Databases aren't infallible. The information in them is entered by humans, who are susceptible to mistakes. Databases are occasionally doctored in an attempt to prove a position or promote a cause.

Because most of these databases were begun many years ago, they often reside on large mainframe computers. Data are stored in various file formats, and it is often difficult to access the information. Independent analyses of the data were once impossible because the data were controlled by government agencies. Further, few newspapers had the resources or the computers on which to do independent analyses. After the introduction of personal computers in the early 1980s, however, reporters began finding ways to interpret mainframe data.

A breakthrough technology involved the purchase of nine-track mainframe data tapes from government agencies and subsequent analysis on personal computers equipped with nine-track drives. Newspapers started to win Pulitzer Prizes using this technique, and soon the National Institute for Computer-Assisted Reporting was established at the University of Missouri to spread the word about the technique. Suddenly, reporters had at their disposal the technology to make better use of existing open-records laws, at both state and federal levels.

Among the reporters taking advantage of the technology is Penny Loeb of *U.S. News & World Report*. When she worked for *New York Newsday*, she used a computer analysis of tax and property records to reveal an astounding story: The City of New York owed $275 million to taxpayers as a result of overpayments on real estate, water and sewer taxes. To get that story, Loeb had to analyze millions of computer records. Doing that by hand would have consumed a lifetime, but with the assistance of a computer, she accomplished the task in a matter of weeks.

Still, Loeb cautions against expecting instant stories:

> Don't just go get a computer tape and expect a great story. You need a tip that there is a problem that computerized data can confirm. Or you may have seen a problem occur repeatedly, such as sentencing discrimination. The computer can quantify the scope.

Analyses of this type usually are done with **relational database programs**. Relational database programs, unlike simpler **flat-file databases**, permit you to compare one set of data to another. A classic example would be to compare a database of a state's licensed school bus drivers to another database of the state's drunken-driving convictions. The result would be a list of school bus drivers found guilty of such offenses.

After the introduction of this technology, investigative reporters were among the first to use it. But once such databases are more readily available, you can use them in your day-to-day work just as easily. For example, you might want to analyze federal records on airplane maintenance to produce a story on the safety record of a particular airline. If the records are maintained in an easily accessible format, the next time an airplane crashes it will be possible to call up the complete maintenance record of the aircraft merely by entering the plane's registration number. Such information will be extremely useful, even when writing for a deadline.

Another common use of computers has been to compare bank records on home mortgages to census data. By tracking how many mortgages are issued to homeowners in predominantly African-American or Hispanic areas, reporters have been able to document the practice of redlining, through which banks make it difficult or impossible for minorities to obtain loans.

Again, such records are useful even after the investigation is complete. Access to driver's license records, census data, bank records and other forms of data can be used to produce news stories, charts, maps and other graphic devices. Numbers can be useful in helping to tell a story. They can be particularly effective if used to create charts that illustrate the impact of the numbers.

Special-Interest Databases

Numerous special-interest groups have discovered the usefulness of placing information in computerized databases, and they are eager to make journalists aware of the existence of that information. Some of that material may be quite useful; indeed, it may be unobtainable from other sources. But just as journalists must be wary of press releases issued by organizations promoting a cause, they must be equally wary of information in such databases. It is important to remember that organizations of this type will promote their perspective on a topic, often without any concern for balancing the information with opposing views.

CD-ROMs and DVDs

During the past few years, massive amounts of information have been stored on compact discs and digital video discs, becoming a terrific new source of reference for journalists. Encyclopedias, dictionaries, telephone directories, census data and information of all sorts, ranging from garden plants to armaments, are all available on CD-ROMs and DVDs, which serve as an efficient and inexpensive way to store vast amounts of information. CD-ROM and DVD titles can be quick and effective references for the journalist on deadline.

Custom Databases

When Elliot Grossman of *The Morning Call* in Allentown, Pa., tried to document abuses of parking privileges by local police officers, he sifted through thousands of paper records to prepare his story. Grossman discovered that over the years a scam had allowed hundreds of police officers to park their private cars almost anywhere: They simply signed the backs of parking tickets and sent them to the Allentown Parking Authority, which dismissed the tickets. Any excuse, it seemed, would suffice for Allentown's finest.

Some data on parking tickets were available on computer, but the Parking Authority refused to release the computer tapes necessary for a quick analysis. So Grossman, with the help of a news clerk and reporting interns, decided to do the research the hard way. He set out to build his own database to document the extent of the problem.

For two weeks, Grossman and his helpers sat at laptop computers in the offices of the Parking Authority and entered data on the type of violation, location of the vehicle, date and time of violation, and license plate number. In many cases, other notations were made on the officer's badge number or the reason the officer was parked at the location. The result was a body of information that allowed Grossman to confirm his suspicions that many of the tickets were dismissed without good reason. What had begun as a rule allowing the cancellation of tickets for officers on official business had grown into a local scandal, and Grossman was able to expose it.

Grossman's experience demonstrates how the best reporters have embraced the considerable capability of personal computer technology. Once the domain of investigative reporters, computer skills are now vital in all areas of the news business. Today, no reporter who hopes to succeed in the profession can afford to be without skills in searching internal and external computer databases and building his or her own databases and spreadsheets. These skills, in addition to more traditional library search skills, are among the essential tools of today's working journalist. Like the carpenter who must know how to use a hammer and saw, the journalist must know how to use words and computers.

Like Grossman, reporters occasionally find that the data they want cannot be obtained from government agencies or private businesses. Despite open-records laws at the federal and state levels, public officials often find ways to stall or avoid giving reporters what they want and need. Further, some data aren't available in databases.

Reporters who find themselves in that predicament sometimes resort to analyzing data after entering it into a database themselves. That's a time-consuming process, but it can be effective. If your knowledge of computer programs is limited, consult with computer experts in your news organization. They will be able to recommend an appropriate tool.

If much of what you are indexing contains textual material, you will need a **free-form database**. A program of this type popular among reporters is askSam, adopted by many of the nation's leading investigative reporters. AskSam makes it easy to construct a database of quotations, notes or similar material. Many database programs do not handle such material so easily.

If you need to create a simple list of names, addresses and telephone numbers, a flat-file database might be best. Relational database comparisons, as we have discussed, require more sophisticated programs such as Microsoft's FoxPro.

Many reporters also are turning to **spreadsheet programs** to help them sort through the complexity of government or corporate financial data. A business reporter might use a spreadsheet program to spot trends in the allocation of resources or changes in sources of income. After data covering several years has been collected, a spreadsheet program, which can easily create graphs from the data, makes it possible to notice trends that otherwise might go undetected. Similarly, a government reporter might use a spreadsheet to spot changes in allocations to various city, county, state or federal departments or agencies.

Today's best reporters keep abreast of technological advances and search for new ways to put computers to work in the news room.

TIPS

Ten Sources of Story Ideas

- Other people
- Other publications
- News releases
- A social services directory
- Government reports
- Stories in your own newspaper
- Advertisements
- Wire copy
- Local news briefs
- You

Computer-Assisted Reporting

In this chapter, we describe how some reporters have used computers to produce extraordinary stories. Let's examine one such story from the *Detroit Free Press*:

By Tracy Van Moorlehem
and Heather Newman

Free Press Staff Writers

When it comes to education, the MEAP isn't everything.

It might seem that way, with all the stress in recent years on comparing and improving scores on the MEAP — Michigan Educational Assessment Program — tests, annually given to fourth- and seventh-graders in math and reading and fifth- and eighth-graders in science and writing. School districts use the scores as bragging points; real estate agents for selling points.

The tests, begun in 1969, measure the extent to which each student has learned what the state has defined as basic skills.

By the straight MEAP numbers, schools in affluent areas such as Bloomfield Hills are academic powerhouses while those in relatively poor areas such as Detroit are weaklings.

But consider those MEAP scores in light of other factors beyond the control of the schools, such as poverty, unemployment, the number of single-parent families or parents without a high school diploma in a community.

That's what the *Free Press* did in a computer analysis that produced some surprising results. Detroit schools, for example, are overcoming the odds — doing better than predicted, given the factors working against them.

The analysis shows that students in Bloomfield Hills and some other well-off, high scoring districts could be doing even better.

The study also demonstrates how any straight-up comparison of MEAP scores is inevitably flawed. Consider: Only 49 percent of Detroit fourth-graders pass the MEAP math test, compared with 84 percent of Bloomfield Hills fourth-graders.

Consider: Seventy-one percent of Detroit students are from families poor enough to qualify for a free or reduced-price school lunch; only 2 percent of Bloomfield Hills students qualify.

Yet the test is scored without regard for educational resources, obstacles or opportunity. Educators say MEAP scores brand some schools and entire communities as inferior, creating a cycle that's hard to break.

Mary Anne Bunda, a professor of educational leadership at Western Michigan University, said comparing MEAP scores directly is like rating hospitals based solely on patient death rates: You might think the hospital with the highest numbers gave the worst care.

But what if that hospital specialized in fatal diseases, or was next door to a hospice?

Likewise, schools coping with factors such as severe poverty may be doing a superior job of educating students who start out behind wealthier counterparts. Poor parents, for example, may not be able to afford books, or home computers. Single, working parents may not have as much time to read to children. Parents who dropped out of high school may be too intimidated to approach educators about what's going on with their children in school.

Yet, distorted as MEAP scores may be, they are often used as the sole yardstick of school performance.

Realtors use them to sell one neighborhood over another. Lawyers cite them in child custody battles. State officials use them to accredit schools.

And newspapers, including the *Free Press*, publish them in rank order.

Beginning today, the *Free Press* will take a deeper look at the MEAP, filtering the scores through non-school factors that play a significant role in education.

Researchers and experts say the analysis is a step forward in thinking about the MEAP.

"What you have here is just amazing," said Catherine Taylor, associate professor of educational psychology at the University of Washington in Seattle. She said the "startling" level of correlation between poverty and test scores, especially in urban and suburban districts, illuminates the challenge facing urban educators.

But experts offered a host of cautions, too:

- Poverty and low scores are not inevitably linked.

  "As ammunition for a bigot, it's very, very dangerous," said Harvey Czerwinski, program supervisor in the Office of Research, Evaluation and Testing for Detroit schools.

- Poor schools should not cite adverse circumstances to explain low scores as satisfactory.

  "We are not where we want to be. We are not satisfied with our achievement, even exceeding your model," said Aaron Hedgepeth, also a program supervisor in Detroit's testing department.

- Finally, educators cautioned against making too much of the analyzed MEAP scores, falling into the same trap as with raw scores.

  MEAP tests capture the performance of a small segment of students on one day in a selective curriculum, they said.

"This kind of analysis is better than . . . just looking at the raw numbers, but it's far from ideal," Bloomfield Hills Superintendent Gary Doyle said of the *Free Press* study. "It takes a very limited measure and makes it a little better — but not much."

The *Free Press* story was a complex one that involved taking the raw MEAP test-score data from the Michigan Department of Education and then adjusting the results for factors found to affect school performance. Here's the paper's explanation of how that worked:

To look at MEAP test scores in light of the different challenges facing schools, the *Free Press* used a statistical analysis method called multiple linear regression.

Here's how it works:

Consider MEAP scores against a factor; for example, poverty within the school district. On a graph, you can see that as poverty goes up, MEAP scores go down.

Multiple linear regression is a way of looking at the possible effect of more than one factor. In addition to poverty, the *Free Press* found an impact from six other factors:

- The percent of single parents in a district.
- The percent of households where no one is a high school graduate.
- The local unemployment rate.
- School funds per pupil.
- The percent of students who speak English as a second language.
- Location, specifically city/suburban, midsize town or rural area.

Among city and suburban school districts, more than 62 percent of the differences in scores can be traced to such nonschool factors.

They accounted for 33 percent of the differences among districts in midsize towns, and almost 16 percent of the differences among rural districts.

By using multiple regression to project test scores based on the makeup of the community, we found some disadvantaged districts that are doing better than expected.

The story went on to show that some districts in the inner city are actually outperforming those in richer suburban districts when variables are factored out. Good reporting such as that helps readers sort out the differences between the rhetoric of political candidates and reality. But doing such stories requires reporters to have a working knowledge of statistical analysis and familiarity with basic math. In this case, the *Free Press* enlisted the help of a nearby university professor to analyze the data. Reporters still had to be able to understand the results and translate them into terms readers could understand.

Reporting such as this is known as computer-assisted reporting, and it has become the heart and soul of investigative reporting in the United States. Almost all the recent winners in the annual contest of Investigative Reporters and Editors employed this technique. So, too, did recent winners of the Pulitzer Prize for Investigative Reporting. Organizations like IRE and the National Institute for Computer-Assisted Reporting offer seminars in computer data analysis. Today's best reporters are eager to take advantage of such offerings.

TRADITIONAL SOURCES OF INFORMATION

Accessing information through computerized sources is quick and easy, but more traditional reference sources are also valuable. Some of the following sources of information, such as the newspaper library, are now computerized; others only exist in printed form.

The Newspaper Library

The newspaper library is usually the first stop for a reporter on any kind of assignment. Covering a speech? Look up background information on the speaker. Covering a sports event? What are the teams' records? Who are the coaches? What's the history of the rivalry? Reporters answer questions such as these, and many others, by checking the newspaper library.

Occasionally, there may be no time for such a check. When a fire or accident occurs, for example, the reporter rushes directly to the scene; there's no time for background preparation. But on any kind of story other than a breaking news event, the reporter's first stop should be the morgue.

Another use for the print or broadcast morgue is to search for photos. There you can find photos of a speaker or coach you haven't met. They will help you recognize that person for a possible one-on-one interview before the speech or game begins.

Other Traditional Sources

Traditional sources of information—such as reference books, dictionaries and encyclopedias—still play an important role in the production of the daily news product. Good reporters and editors make a habit of checking every verifiable fact. Here is a list of 20 commonly used reference books:

- **City directories.** You can find these directories in most cities. Like telephone books, they list names, addresses and phone numbers, but they may also provide information on the occupations of residents and the owners or managers of businesses. Useful street indexes provide information on the names of next-door neighbors.

- **Telephone books.** Use telephone books for verifying the spelling of names and addresses. They are usually reliable, but they are not infallible. Remember that people move and have similar names. Almost all telephone numbers in North America are now listed on various Internet-based services, including Switchboard (www.switchboard.com).

- **Maps of the city, county, state, nation and world.** Local maps are usually posted in the news room. Look for others in atlases.

- **State manuals.** Each state government publishes a directory that provides useful information on various government agencies. These directories sometimes list the salaries of all state employees. To date, few are online.

- *Bartlett's Familiar Quotations* (Little, Brown).

- *Congressional Directory* (Government Printing Office). Provides profiles of members of Congress.

- *Congressional Record* (Government Printing Office). Contains complete proceedings of the U.S. House and Senate.

- *Current Biography* (Wilson). Profiles of prominent people, published monthly.

- *Dictionary of American Biography* (Scribner's).

- *Facts on File* (Facts on File Inc.). A weekly compilation of news from metropolitan newspapers.

- *Guinness Book of World Records* (Guinness Superlatives). World records listed in countless categories.

- *National Trade and Professional Associations of the United States* (Columbia Books).

- *Readers' Guide to Periodical Literature* (Wilson). An index to magazine articles on a host of subjects.

- *Statistical Abstract of the United States* (Government Printing Office). A digest of data collected and published by all federal agencies.

- *Webster's Biographical Dictionary* (Merriam-Webster).

- *Webster's New World College Dictionary*, Fourth Edition (Wiley). The primary reference dictionary recommended by both the Associated Press and United Press International.

- *Webster's Third New International Dictionary* (Merriam-Webster). The unabridged dictionary recommended by AP and UPI.

- *Who's Who* (St. Martin's). World listings.

- *Who's Who in America* (Marquis). A biennial publication.

- *World Almanac and Book of Facts* (Newspaper Enterprise Association). Published annually.

These useful publications, and many others like them, enable reporters to verify data and to avoid the embarrassment caused by printing or broadcasting errors. Other traditional sources of information include printed government records, documents from businesses, pamphlets published by government and nongovernment agencies, books, newspapers and magazines.

Be careful, though, when using material from a source with which you are not familiar. Some publications come from biased sources promoting a cause. It's the reporter's job to determine whether the information is biased or reliable. A good way to do that is to balance information from one source with information from another source with an opposing viewpoint. It may not always be possible for you to determine who's correct. Ensuring balance between two viewpoints is the next best thing.

Suggested Readings

Brooks, Brian S., Pinson, James L. and Wilson, Jean Gaddy. *Working With Words: A Handbook for Media Writers and Editors.* New York: Bedford/St. Martin's, 2006. A definitive work on the correct use of language in journalistic writing and editing.

Callahan, Christopher. *A Journalist's Guide to the Internet: The Net as a Reporting Tool.* Boston: Pearson Education, 2002. A useful guide to using the Internet as a reporting resource.

Goldstein, Norm, ed. *Associated Press Stylebook and Briefing on Media Law.* New York: Associated Press, 2006. The definitive work on stylistic matters in journalistic writing.

Houston, Brant. *Computer-Assisted Reporting: A Practical Guide.* New York: Bedford/St. Martin's, 2003. An excellent introduction to computer-assisted reporting by the executive director of Investigative Reporters and Editors.

IRE Journal. This monthly magazine is available from Investigative Reporters and Editors, Columbia, Mo. It offers regular articles on the use of computers in the news-gathering process.

Schlein, Alan M. *Find It Online: The Complete Guide to Online Research.* Edited by Peter Weber and Michael Sandkey. Tempe, Ariz.: Facts on Demand Press, 2004. Basic information on the use of Web resources.

Suggested Web Sites

www.ire.org
Investigative Reporters and Editors maintains an excellent Web site for anyone interested in investigative reporting.

www.nicar.org
The National Institute for Computer-Assisted Reporting conducts seminars for reporters in data analysis with computers.

www.reporter.org
At this Web site you'll find useful links to a variety of news support organizations.

reporter.umd.edu
This Web site, which includes links to a variety of useful sources on the Internet, accompanies the book by Christopher Callahan listed in the Suggested Readings section.

Exercises

1. Choose any story in your local newspaper, and tell how that story could have been improved with a database search. List databases you would have searched.

2. If you were interested in determining where Apple Computer Inc. is located and the name of its chief financial officer, where would you look? What other sources of information might be available?

3. Write a one-page biographical sketch of your congressional representative based on information you retrieve from your library or a database.

4. Using the Internet, find the following information:

   a. The census of Rhode Island in 2000.
   b. The size of Rwanda in land area.
   c. The latest grant awards by the U.S. Department of Education.
   d. The names of universities in Norway that provide outside access via the Internet.
   e. The name of a Web site that contains the complete works of Shakespeare.
   f. The name of a Web site that contains federal campaign contribution data.

Reporting with Numbers

6

Ebony Reed, an education reporter for *The (Cleveland) Plain Dealer*, was talking to a fourth-grade teacher who complained that she had to promote students even though she didn't think they were ready for the next grade. Reed could have simply talked to other teachers and administrators and written a story. But the story would have been anecdotal and unconvincing. Besides, the teachers didn't want to speak on the record for fear of retribution from administrators. So she set about getting the numbers to see if the promotion policy was widespread.

She and Edith Starzyk, education editor, decided to get the standardized math and reading test scores. They focused on the fourth, sixth and 10th grades because state-mandated tests are given to those students.

When they compared the test scores to promotion practices and analyzed the trends by race and gender, they knew they had a significant story. Here is how their startling story began:

> More than 95 percent of Cleveland fourth- and sixth-graders were promoted at the end of last school year, even though better than half the students in those grades failed state reading or math exams, according to a *Plain Dealer* analysis.
>
> The gap between promotion rates and test scores is even more pronounced for black and Hispanic students, who fail the tests more often than their white classmates.

The numbers don't lie. Supported by interviews with parents and students, the story was convincing and readable. Unable to deny the promotion policy, administrators were forced to defend it. Parents were now armed with data. And the Ohio Department of Education said it might begin analyzing school district data by race and gender for the first time.

Journalists have a responsibility to understand numbers so that they are able to report clearly and accurately on everything from schools to polling results. This chapter discusses ways you can help readers to sort through the numbers.

PROPORTION

One of the most important courtesies journalists pay to their readers is to give **proportion** to numbers in the news—explaining things relative to the size or the magnitude of the whole. A municipal budget that is going up by $500,000 would be a windfall for a small town in New Hampshire but a minor adjustment in a metropolis like New York, Chicago or Minneapolis.

Other figures might mean a lot or a little, depending on the context. If you know little or nothing about baseball, you might think that Babe Ruth's career batting average of .342—34.2 hits for every 100 times at bat—indicates that Ruth wasn't a good hitter. After all, he failed almost two out of three times at bat. When you look at the context—other players' averages—you realize that Ruth was exceptional. For instance, in 2006, only three major league players had a higher average—and that was for the year, not for a career.

Percentages and Percentage Change

Percentages are basic building blocks used to explain proportion. Batting averages explain the percentage of hits compared with the number of times at bat. The political strength of a public official is partly reflected in the percentage of the votes won at the polls. Stories about budgets, taxes, wages, retail sales, schools, health care and the environment all are explained with percentages.

To calculate a percentage, take the portion that you want to measure, divide it by the whole and then move the decimal point two places to the right. Say, for example, you want to know what portion of the city's budget is allocated to police services. Divide the police budget by the city budget, move the decimal point two places to the right, and you get the percentage of the budget that pays for police services.

Step 1
Portion (police budget) ÷ whole (city budget) = .xxx
30,000,000 ÷ 120,000,000 = .25

Step 2
Move the decimal point two places to the right: 25%

You can sometimes use percentages to verify whether newsmakers are accurately representing the facts. Frank Gallagher, a reporter at the *San Francisco Independent*, had the same quotes as every other reporter in San Francisco about how the city's Board of Supervisors President Barbara Kaufman had stripped another supervisor of his influential committee assignments. Kaufman said committee chairs were complaining about Supervisor Leland Yee's poor attendance. Yee told reporters that the move occurred because he voted against the board president's proposals so often. All the other media in San Francisco ran stories with the politicians' conflicting claims. Gallagher took the story one step further.

Gallagher walked down to the clerk's office and checked on the supervisors' attendance records for meetings since the beginning of the year. He discovered that Supervisor Yee attended a higher percentage of meetings (91 percent; 48 divided by 53) than many other supervisors, and that Yee had an attendance record that was about the same as that of the political appointee who replaced him (see Figure 6.1).

"This is San Francisco, so everybody pretty much figured the real reason for the committee switch was politics," Gallagher said. "But when you put the numbers down in black and white, there's just no disputing the facts."

Precision in the use of numbers also requires that you ask the basic questions. Reporters need to be careful of percentages that might be used in misleading ways or percentages that tell only part of a story.

If someone is giving you percentages, you must ask what **population** the figures are based on. For instance, a juvenile officer tells a reporter that 70 percent of the juvenile offenders do not have to return to his program. The reporter's first question should be "What population was used to figure the percentage?" Was it all

TIPS

To Calculate a Percentage

● Portion ÷ whole = .xxx

● Move the decimal point two places to the right: .xxx = xx.x%.

Ranking the supes

How often they've attended committee and full board meetings so far in 1997:

Barbara Kaufman

Meetings: 45
Attended: 42

93%

Michael Yaki

Meetings: 43
Attended: 40

93%

Susan Leal

Meetings: 40
Attended: 37

93%

Tom Ammiano

Meetings: 35
Attended: 32

92%

Leland Yee

Meetings: 53
Attended: 48

91%

Gavin Newsom

Meetings: 29
Attended: 26

90%

Sue Bierman

Meetings: 44
Attended: 38

87%

Mabel Teng

Meetings: 42
Attended: 36

86%

Rev. Amos Brown

Meetings: 45
Attended: 36

80%

Jose Medina

Meetings: 55
Attended: 44

80%

Leslie Katz

Meetings: 54
Attended: 37

69%

Figure 6.1
This graphic ran with Frank Gallagher's story in the *San Francisco Independent*. Looking beyond the finger-pointing of politicians, Gallagher investigated the numbers and found that Supervisor Yee had a strong attendance record.

the juveniles in the program during the last calendar year? If so, perhaps the success rate is high because the period being measured isn't long enough. And how are the juveniles who are old enough now to be certified as adults counted? How does your source account for juveniles who may have committed a crime in another jurisdiction?

The officer's answer may be that the figure is based on a sample of the population in the program over 10 years. A **sample** is a small number of persons picked at random so as to be representative of the population as a whole. Using common statistical tables, researchers might draw a sample of the names of all juveniles who were in the program over 10 years and contact them. From those contacts, they can determine the success rate. If the figure is based on a scientific sampling like the one just described, there will also be a margin of error, which will be expressed as "plus or minus x points." Say that the margin of error for this sample is 4. That means that the success rate is between 66 and 74 percent.

The base on which a percentage is calculated is significant. Say a colleague is making $40,000, and you make $30,000. The salary is the base. Your employer decides to give your colleague a 4 percent increase and to give you a 5 percent increase. Before you begin feeling too good about the honor, consider that your colleague's raise is $1,600, and your raise is $1,500. Your colleague won a bigger raise, and the gap between the two of you grew. You spend dollars, not percentages.

So you see that if you have different bases on which to figure the percentages, the comparisons are invalid. Here's another illustration. If you compare the amount of nuclear energy produced by countries on a percentage basis, the United States would rank near the bottom. But if you compare the actual amount of energy produced by nuclear power, the United States produces more nuclear energy than any other country. The reason you can't compare the amount of nuclear energy produced on a percentage basis is that the base—the total amount of energy produced—is different in each country.

More confusion often occurs when people talk about the difference between two percentage figures. For example, say the mayor wins the election with 55 percent of the vote and has only one opponent, who receives 45 percent. The mayor won by a margin of 10 percentage points. Notice we are talking "percentage points," in this case, the difference between 55 and 45. However, the winner won 22 percent more votes (10 divided by 45 equals .22). Because the figures are based on the same whole number—in this case, the total number of voters—the percentages can be compared. But if you compare the percentage of a city budget devoted to law enforcement in consecutive years, you will need to include the actual dollar amounts with the percentages because total spending probably changed from one year to the next.

Another important aspect of percentages is the concept of percentage change. This number explains how much something goes up or down. In Table 6.1 on pages 125–26, look under "Actual Fiscal Year 2006." Total spending was $15,663,029. The proposed budget for 2007 is $19,570,518. What is the percentage increase? If a municipal budget changes, you find the percentage change by doing the following calculation: increase (or decrease) divided by the old budget. In this case, you do the following calculation.

TIPS

To Calculate Percentage Change

- (New number) – (old number) = change.

- Change ÷ old number = .xxx.

- Move the decimal point two places to the right. .xxx = xx.x%.

- Percentage change can be a positive or a negative number.

Step 1	Find the increase (or decrease).
	19,570,518 – 15,663,029 = 3,907,489 (increase)
Step 2	Increase (or decrease) ÷ base amount = .xxx
	3,907,489 ÷ 15,663,029 = .249
Step 3	Move the decimal point two places to the right: 24.9 percent.

Rounded off, this is a 25 percent increase in spending.

Notice that if in the following year (2008) the budget again increases by $3.9 million, you will get a different percentage increase because the base year will be different. Adding $3.9 million to the 2007 budget will yield a 19.9 percent increase. It's a smaller percentage increase because the amount in this new base year (2007) is greater than the amount in the former base year.

When changes are large, sometimes it is better to translate the numbers into plain words rather than to use a percentage figure. For example, suppose the town you are covering decides to put $220,000 for buying parkland into its new budget, while last year it spent $100,000. The percentage change is $120,000 divided by $100,000, or a 120 percent increase. But the change will be easier for readers to understand if you write, "The town next year will more than double the amount of money it will spend buying parkland," and then give the actual dollar amounts.

Averages and Medians

Averages and medians are numbers that can be used to describe a general trend. For any given set of numbers, the average and the median might be quite close, or they might be quite different. Depending on what you are trying to explain, it might be important to use one instead of the other or to use both.

The **average**—also called the arithmetic mean—is the number you obtain when you add a list of figures and then divide the total by the number of figures in the list. The **median** is the midpoint of the list—half the figures fall above it, and half the figures fall below it.

To compute an average:

Step 1	Add the figures.
Step 2	Divide the total by the number of figures:
	Total ÷ number of figures
	The result is the average.

To find the median:

| Step 1 | Arrange the figures in rank order. |
| Step 2 | Identify the figure midway between the highest and lowest numbers. That figure is the median. When you have an even number of figures, the median is the average of the two middle figures. |

As a general rule, you are safe using averages when there are not large gaps among the numbers. If you took an average of 1, 4, 12, 22, 31, 89 and 104, you would get 37.6. The average distorts the numbers because the average is higher than five of the seven numbers. The median, or midpoint, is 22. On the other

When Averages Distort

Take a set of scores from a final exam in a class of 15 students. Students scored 95, 94, 92, 86, 85, 84, 75, 75, 65, 64, 63, 62, 62, 62, 62. Both the average and the median are 75.

The picture can look quite different when the figures bunch at one end of the scale. Consider this example from professional baseball. At the beginning of the 2006 season, the Boston Red Sox baseball team had a payroll of $120,099,824. The median income was $3,023,894. However, the average was only $4,448,141 ($120,099,824 ÷ 27 players).

---

hand, if you had numbers ranging from 1 to 104 and the numbers were distributed evenly within that range, the average would be an accurate reading.

Rates

A **rate** is a term used to make fair comparisons between different populations. One example of a rate comparison is per capita, or per person, spending, such as for school funding. Even though a big-city school budget looks incredibly large to someone in a small community, the money has to stretch over more students than it would in smaller districts. As a result, spending per capita provides a better comparison between districts with different enrollments. Suppose your school district has 1,000 students and spends $2 million. You want to compare spending in your district with spending in another district with 1,500 students and a budget of $3 million. You would use this formula to calculate per capita spending: budget divided by the number of people.

District A: $2,000,000 ÷ 1,000 = $2,000 per capita

District B: $3,000,000 ÷ 1,500 = $2,000 per capita

TIPS

To Calculate per Capita Spending

Divide the budget by the number of people: Budget ÷ population = per capita spending.

School district B spends $1 million more a year than district A, but both districts spend $2,000 per pupil.

In medicine, epidemiology and crime statistics, fair comparisons often come in the form of rates per 100,000 people. So do economic figures. When the Bureau of Economic Analysis released its income report, media throughout the country localized the story. For the *Connecticut Post* in Bridgeport, it was a story about local wealth:

> Connecticut's four major areas all ranked among the top 50 in per capita income. The Bridgeport area, which includes wealthy Fairfield County municipalities, was ranked first. The Hartford-West Hartford-East Hartford area ranked 18th with per capita income of $38,131. New Haven-Milford was 25th with $36,127

and the Norwich-New London area ranked 34th with $35,147.

All of Connecticut's areas beat the nation's per capita income of $31,472.

To compare wealth for municipalities with varying populations, the reporter correctly used per capita figures. She divided the total income by the total population. However, a more thorough analysis would also reveal other aspects of the income story. For instance, the reporter should also look at the median. A few people at the high end of the scale will pull up the per capita figure, but the median shows the midpoint of all incomes.

INTEREST AND COMPOUNDING

Interest is a financial factor in just about everyone's life. Most people have to pay it when they borrow money, and many people earn it when they deposit money at a bank. Consumers pay interest on home mortgages, car loans and credit card balances. Individuals and businesses earn interest when they deposit money in a financial institution or make a loan. Federal regulations require the interest rates charged by or paid by most institutions to be expressed as annual percentage rates so the rates can be compared.

There are two types of interest: simple and compound. *Simple interest* is interest to be paid on the *principal*, the amount borrowed. It is calculated by multiplying the amount of the loan by the annual percentage rate.

Suppose a student borrows $1,000 from her grandfather at a 5 percent annual rate to help cover college expenses. She needs only a one-year loan, so the cost is figured as simple interest. To calculate simple interest, multiply the principal by the interest rate: $1,000 × .05 = $50. To find the amount the student will repay her grandfather at the end of a year, add the principal to the interest. The student will owe $1,050.

If the loan is made over a period longer than a year, the borrower pays *compound interest*. Compound interest is interest paid on the total of the principal and the interest that already has accrued.

Suppose the student borrows $1,000 at an annual percentage rate of 5 percent and pays her grandfather back four years later, after graduation. She owes 5 percent annual interest for each year of the loan. But because she has the loan for four years, each year she owes not only simple interest on the principal but also interest on the interest that accrues each year.

At the end of year 1, she owes $1,050. To see how much she will owe at the end of year 2, she has to calculate 5 percent interest on $1,050: $1,050 × .05 = $52.50.

Here is how to calculate the interest for all four years. (Note that 1.05 is used instead of .05 to produce a running total. If you multiply 1,000 by 1.05, you get 1,050; if you multiply 1,000 by .05, you get 50, which you then have to add to 1,000 to get the principal and interest.)

$$\$1,000 \times (1.05) \times (1.05) \times (1.05) \times (1.05) = \$1,215.51$$

TIPS

To Calculate Simple Interest and Total Amount Owed

- Express the interest rate as a decimal by moving the decimal point two places to the left.

- Multiply the principal by the interest rate: $1,000 × .05 = $50

- Add the principal to the interest owed: $1,000 + $50 = $1,050

The same result can be obtained another way. Multiply the principal by 1 plus the interest rate expressed as a decimal: $1,000 × 1.05 = $1,050

TIPS

To Calculate Compound Interest

- Add 1 plus the interest rate expressed as a decimal:
  1 + .05 = 1.05

- Using a calculator, multiply the principal by (1.xx)*n* (the variable *n* represents the number of years of the loan).
  The result is the total amount owed.

A host of computer programs offer consumers interest formulas and payment plans. Because most consumers pay off student loans, car loans, mortgages and credit card debt over a period of time, and because interest is compounded more often than once a year, calculations usually are far more complicated than those in the example. Many financial Web sites offer such programs. For instance, select Calculator on *USA Today*'s Web site www.usatoday.com in the Money section.

Student loans taken out through federal programs administered by banks, credit unions and universities are a prime example of more complicated transactions. Suppose a student has a $5,000 guaranteed student loan with an interest rate of 8 percent per year. After finishing school, the student has 10 years to pay, and each year she pays 8 percent interest on the amount of the original principal that is left unpaid. If the student makes the minimum payment of $65 on time each month for the 10-year life of the loan, she will pay the bank a total of $7,800. She pays $2,800 in interest on top of the original principal of $5,000. Had she not paid down the balance each month, the interest she owed would have been higher.

Consumers get the benefits of compounding when they put money in interest-bearing accounts, because their interest compounds. The same effect takes place when people make good investments in the stock market, where earnings are compounded when they are reinvested.

INFLATION

Inflation is an increase in the cost of living over time. Because prices rise over time, wages and budgets, too, have to increase to keep up with inflation. A worker who received a 2 percent pay increase each year would have the same buying power each year if inflation rose at 2 percent. Because of inflation, reporters must use a few simple computations to make fair comparisons between dollar amounts from different years.

Let's say the teachers in your local school district were negotiating for a new contract. They claimed that they were falling behind. You knew that the starting salary for a teacher in 1994 was $35,000 and the starting salary in 2004 was $39,000. To determine whether the teachers' claim was true, you converted 1994 dollars to 2004 dollars, and you found that the starting salary in 2004 would have been $43,998 if the district had been keeping up with inflation. In other words, in constant, or "real," dollars, the teachers were earning nearly $5,000 less in 2004 than they had earned in 1994.

Numbers that are adjusted for inflation are called *constant*, or *real, dollars*. Numbers that are not adjusted for inflation are called *nominal*, or *current, dollars*.

The most common tool that is used to adjust for inflation is the Consumer Price Index, which is reported each month by the U.S. Bureau of Labor Statistics of the U.S. Department of Labor. You can get current CPI numbers on the Web at www.bls.gov/cpi. To calculate inflation rapidly, turn to www.minneapolisfed.org and select Inflation Calculator.

TAXES

You not only pay taxes but you also have to report on them. Governments collect taxes in a variety of ways, but the three major categories are sales taxes, income taxes and property taxes.

Sales Taxes

State, county and municipal governments can levy sales taxes on various goods and services. Sales taxes are the simplest to figure out.

To figure a sales tax, multiply the price of an item by the sales tax rate. Add the result to the original price to obtain the total cost.

Take the example of a student buying an $1,800 computer before beginning school at the University of Florida. If he shops in his home state of Iowa, where the sales tax is 5 percent, he will pay a tax of $90, and the computer will cost him $1,890. If he buys the computer after arriving in Florida, where the sales tax is 6 percent, he will pay a tax of $108, and the computer will cost him $1,908.

Sales taxes are an excellent way for you to track sales in your city, county or state. The appropriate government unit will have sales tax revenues, which are a direct reflection of sales and therefore useful for reporting on the economy in your area.

Income Taxes

The government taxes a percentage of your income to support such services as building roads, running schools, registering people to vote and encouraging businesses to grow. Income taxes are paid to the federal government, to most state governments, and to some municipalities.

Calculating income taxes can be tricky because a lot of factors affect the amount of income that is subject to the tax. For that reason, the only way to figure a person's income tax is to consult the actual numbers and to follow tables published by the Internal Revenue Service (www.irs.gov) or the state department of taxation.

Governments use tax incentives to encourage people to undertake certain types of economic activities, such as buying a home, saving for retirement, and investing in business ventures. By giving people and businesses tax deductions, the government reduces the amount of income that is taxable.

A tax deduction is worth the tax rate times the amount of the tax deduction. The most common tax deduction is for the interest people pay on their home loans. Tax deductions are worth more to people with higher incomes. Take the example of two families who own homes. Both pay $2,500 in interest on their home mortgage in a year, the cost of which is deductible for people who itemize. The lower-income family is in the lowest federal income tax bracket, in which the tax rate is 10 percent, so that family saves $250 on its tax bill: $2,500 × .10 = $250. The higher-income family is in the federal income tax bracket with a tax rate of 30 percent, so that family saves $750 on its tax bill: $2,500 × .30 = $750.

Math You Can Count On

Many journalists joke about their mathematical ineptitude. But even for those who are genuinely afraid of statistics, there is no avoiding numbers in journalism. Numbers are at the heart of reporting government, business, sports and investigative issues, and they can surface in areas as diverse as obituaries, food, religion and entertainment.

Journalists who have a fear of numbers these days had better learn to overcome it. That might mean learning some math. Before using figures in your writing, be sure you understand what they mean.

Say you want to describe the volume of a child's screaming. Would you say the child belted out "a 25-decibel roar"? (No. That's barely above a whisper.) Or do you know how many centimeters are in a foot? (30.5.) Or how far it is from home plate to the pitcher's mound? (60 feet 6 inches.) It is vital to check reference books when such questions arise.

Even the most respected journalists can run afoul of numbers. When reporting a Supreme Court case in 1987, *The New York Times* and other media outlets reported that defendants charged in Georgia with killing whites were four times as likely to receive death sentences as were defendants charged with killing blacks. However, reporters — and the Supreme Court itself — confused "probability" and "odds."

Probability represents the likelihood something will happen. For example, the probability of getting heads when flipping a coin is $\frac{1}{2}$ (one of two possible outcomes), or .5. *Odds* represent the likelihood that one thing will happen rather than another. The odds of getting heads — figured as the likelihood of getting heads vs. the likelihood of getting tails — are .5 ÷ .5 ("even money" in betting terms), or 1.

The Georgia reports concluded that the odds of a death sentence when a white was killed were 4.3 times greater than the odds when a black was killed. That doesn't mean the same thing as "four times as likely."

The lessons from that example are that *probability* and *odds* are not synonymous and that math errors can creep into reporting even when your source is the Supreme Court.

Income tax rates are based on your *adjusted gross income*. If you make $7,550 after deductions, you will pay a tax of 10 percent ($755). If you make more than $5,700 but less than $30,650, you will pay $755 (.10 × 7,550) plus 15 percent of the amount over $7,550.

Property Taxes

City and county governments collect property taxes. When people talk about property taxes, they usually mean taxes on the value of houses, buildings and land. In some places, people also are taxed each year on the value of their cars, boats and other personal property.

The two key factors in property taxes are the assessed value and the millage rate. The *assessed value* is the amount that a government appraiser determines a piece of property is worth. The *millage rate* — the rate per thousand dollars — is the tax rate determined by the government. You figure the property taxes by multiplying the assessed value by the millage rate. For example, owners of a house valued at $100,000 taxed at a millage rate of 2.25 would pay $225 in taxes (100,000 ÷ 1,000 × 2.25).

TIPS

To Calculate Property Tax

- Divide the assessed value by 1,000:
  $100,000 ÷ 1,000 = 100

- Multiply that result by the millage rate:
  $100 × 2.25 = $225

Counties and cities hire professional appraisers to assess the value of land and buildings in their jurisdiction, and typically their assessments have been far lower than the actual market value of the property. Because of abuses and public confusion, most states in recent years have ordered revaluations to bring assessments into line with market values, and they have adjusted millage rates accordingly, although assessments can vary widely from appraiser to appraiser.

Appraisals are based on complicated formulas that take into account the size, location and condition of the property. Still, the government may say your house is worth $60,000, even if you know you could sell it for $80,000.

When you are reporting tax rate changes, you should find out how they affect houses in different value brackets to help explain the impact. By talking to the assessor or tax collector, you should be able to report, for instance, that the taxes for a house valued at $100,000 would increase $250.

MAKING SENSE OF BUDGETS

The budget is the blueprint that guides the operation of any organization, and a reporter must learn to read a budget just as a carpenter must learn to read an architect's blueprint. In either case, doing so isn't as difficult as it appears at first glance.

In many cases today, you'll be able to get the budget (and other financial information as well) for your city or school district on computer disk or tape. You can probably also view it on a local Web site, but you probably cannot download that file into a spreadsheet database. However, once you have the budget on a disk, you can create your own spreadsheet and perform analyses that not long ago were only in the power of the institution's budget director. This is one of many ways the computer has become an essential news room tool. However, with or without a computer, first you need to know the basics of budgeting.

Budget Basics

TIPS

Budget Stories Usually Deal with

- Changes.

- Trends.

- Comparisons.

Every budget, whether it's your personal budget or the budget of the U.S. government, has two basic parts: *revenues* (income) and *expenditures* (outgo). Commercial enterprises earn their income primarily from sales; not-for-profit organizations depend heavily on contributions from public funding and private donors. Government revenues come from sources such as taxes, fees and service charges, and payments from other agencies (such as state aid to schools). The budget usually shows, in dollar figures and percentages, the sources of the organization's money. Expenditures go for such items as staff salaries, supplies, utility bills, construction and maintenance of facilities, and insurance. Expenditures usually are listed either by line or by program. The difference is this: A *line-item budget* shows a separate line for each expenditure, such as "Salary of police chief — $150,000." A *program budget* provides less detail but shows more clearly what each activity of the agency costs — for example, "Burglary prevention program — $250,000."

Finding Stories in Budget Changes, Trends and Comparisons

Now let's see what kinds of stories budgets may yield and where to look for those stories. Take a minute to scan Table 6.1, a summary page from the annual budget of a small city. You can apply the skills of reading a city's annual budget to similar accounting documents on other beats—for example, annual reports of businesses and not-for-profit organizations.

The most important budget stories usually deal with changes, trends and comparisons. Budget figures change every year. As costs increase, so do budgets. But look in our sample budget at the line for the Parks and Recreation Department. There's a decrease between Revised Fiscal Year (FY) 2006 and 2007. Why? The summary page doesn't tell you, so you'll have to look further. Sometimes that information will be in the detail pages; other times, you'll have to ask the department director. You might discover, as we did, that the drop results from a proposal by the city staff to halt funding of a summer employment program for teenagers. That's a story.

Another change that may be newsworthy is the increase in the Police Department budget. You'd better find out the reasons for that, too. In this case, we found that most of the increase is going to pay for an administrative reorganization that is adding new positions at the top of the department. The patrol division is actually being reduced. Another story.

Look again at that Police Department line. Follow it back to Actual FY 2006 and you'll see that the increase last year was even bigger. In one year, the budget for police increased by nearly one-third, from $3.3 million to nearly $4.4 million. That's an interesting trend. The same pattern holds true for the Fire Department. More checking is in order. With copies of previous budgets, you can see how far back the growth trend runs. You can also get from the individual departments the statistics on crimes and fires. Are the budget makers responding to a demonstrated need for more protection, or is something else at work behind the scenes?

More generally, you can trace patterns in the growth of city services and city taxes, and you can compare those with changes in population. Are the rates of change comparable? Is population growth outstripping growth in services? Are residents paying more per capita for city services than they paid five or 10 years ago? More good story possibilities.

Another kind of comparison can be useful to your readers, too. How does your city government compare in cost and services with the governments of comparable cities? A few phone calls can add perspective to budget figures. Some professional organizations have recommended levels of service—such as the number of police or firefighters per 1,000 inhabitants—that can help you help your readers assess how well they're being governed.

The same guidelines can be applied to the analysis of any budget. The numbers will be different, as will the department names, but the structures will be much the same. Whether you're covering the school board or the statehouse, look for changes, trends and comparisons.

Table 6.1
General Fund—
Summary

Purpose

The General Fund is used to finance and account for a large portion of the current operation expenditures and capital outlays of city government. The General Fund is one of the largest and most important of the city's funds because most governmental programs (Police, Fire, Public Works, Parks and Recreation, and so on) are generally financed wholly or partially from it. The General Fund has a greater number and variety of revenue sources than any other fund, and its resources normally finance a wider range of activities.

APPROPRIATIONS

	Actual Fiscal Year 2006	Budget Fiscal Year 2006	Revised Fiscal Year 2006	Adopted Fiscal Year 2007
Personnel services	$9,500,353	$11,306,619	$11,245,394	$12,212,336
Materials and supplies	1,490,573	1,787,220	1,794,362	1,986,551
Training and schools	93,942	150,517	170,475	219,455
Utilities	606,125	649,606	652,094	722,785
Services	1,618,525	1,865,283	1,933,300	2,254,983
Insurance and miscellaneous	1,792,366	1,556,911	1,783,700	1,614,265
Total operating	15,101,884	17,316,156	17,579,325	19,010,375
Capital additions	561,145	1,123,543	875,238	460,143
Total operating and capital	15,663,029	18,439,699	18,454,563	19,470,518
Contingency	—	200,000	200,000	100,000
Total	**$15,663,029**	**$18,639,699**	**$18,654,563**	**$19,570,518**

DEPARTMENT EXPENDITURES

	Actual Fiscal Year 2006	Budget Fiscal Year 2006	Revised Fiscal Year 2006	Adopted Fiscal Year 2007
City Council	$75,144	$105,207	$90,457	$84,235
City Clerk	61,281	70,778	74,444	91,867
City Manager	155,992	181,219	179,125	192,900
Municipal Court	164,631	196,389	175,019	181,462
Personnel	143,366	197,844	186,247	203,020
Law Department	198,296	266,819	248,170	288,550
Planning & Community Development	295,509	377,126	360,272	405,870
Finance Department	893,344	940,450	983,342	1,212,234
Fire Department	2,837,744	3,421,112	3,257,356	3,694,333
Police Department	3,300,472	4,007,593	4,139,085	4,375,336
Health	1,033,188	1,179,243	1,157,607	1,293,362
Community Services	50,882	74,952	74,758	78,673

(continued)

Table 6.1
General Fund—
Summary
(continued)

	DEPARTMENT EXPENDITURES			
	Actual Fiscal Year 2006	Budget Fiscal Year 2006	Revised Fiscal Year 2006	Adopted Fiscal Year 2007
Energy Management	—	—	54,925	66,191
Public Works	2,838,605	3,374,152	3,381,044	3,509,979
Parks and Recreation	1,218,221	1,367,143	1,400,334	1,337,682
Communications & Info. Services	532,153	730,129	742,835	715,324
City General	1,864,200	1,949,543	1,949,543	1,739,500
Total Department Expenditures	15,663,028	18,439,699	18,454,563	19,470,518
Contingency	—	200,000	200,000	100,000
Total	**$15,663,028**	**$18,639,699**	**$18,654,563**	**$19,570,518**

Financial Reports

Another document that is vital to understanding the finances of local government is the annual financial report. The financial report may be a few pages long or it may be a book. In any case, its purpose is relatively simple. As its name suggests, the report is an explanation of the organization's financial status at the end of a fiscal year, which often is not the same as the end of the calendar year. Here you will find an accounting of all the income the organization received during the year from taxes, fees, state and federal grants, and other sources. You'll also find status reports on all the organization's operating funds, such as its capital improvement fund, its debt-service fund and its general fund.

Making sense of a financial report, like understanding a budget, isn't as hard as it may look. For one thing, the financial officer usually includes a narrative that highlights the most important points, at least from his or her viewpoint. But you should dig beyond the narrative and examine the numbers for yourself. The single most important section of the report is the statement of revenues, expenditures and changes, which provides important measures of the organization's financial health. Depending on the comprehensiveness of the statement, you may have to refer to the budget document as well. You can check:

- Revenues actually received compared with budgeted revenues.
- Actual spending compared with budgeted spending.
- Actual spending compared with actual revenue.
- Changes in balances available for spending in years to come.

The guidelines offered here should help you shape your questions and understand the answers. With financial statements, as with budgets, look for changes, trends and comparisons. And always look hard at any numbers in parentheses.

MAKING SENSE OF NUMBERS FROM POLLS

Every day, new poll results illustrate what people think about various topics in the news. And just about every day, journalists confuse readers when they try to interpret the results.

The most important thing to keep in mind about polls and surveys is that they are based on samples of a population. Because a survey reflects the responses of a small number of people within a population, every survey has a margin of error. The results must be presented with the understanding that scientific sampling is not a perfect predictor for the entire population.

Suppose your news organization buys polling services and discovers that Candidate Hernandez has support from 58 percent of the people surveyed, Candidate Jones has support from 32 percent, and 10 percent are undecided. The polling service indicates that the margin of error of the poll is plus or minus five percentage points. The margins separating the candidates are well above the margin of error, so you can write that Hernandez is leading in the poll.

Now suppose Hernandez has 50 percent support and Jones has 45 percent. The margin between them is within the margin of error, so you must report that the race is too close to call. If the margin between Hernandez and Jones were less than plus or minus five percentage points, you would only report that one candidate "appears to be leading."

Journalists faced exactly that problem in the elections in the fall of 2006. In Virginia, where Republican George Allen and Democrat Jim Webb were running for the U.S. Senate, poll results in the two weeks before the election showed a tight race. One news organization reported that Webb was leading 50 to 46 percent with 4 percent undecided. They reported, "Because Webb's edge is equal to the margin of error of plus or minus 4 percentage points, it means the Democrat can be considered slightly ahead." The statement is wrong. With a margin of error of plus or minus four percentage points, the race was too close to call. In fact, Allen won with 50 percent of the 2.3 million votes cast.

Lesson number one is not to write that one candidate is ahead of another if the difference is not larger than the margin of error. Lesson two is that if you look at smaller groups within your polling group, the margin of error will be even larger. Subgroups within a sample are subject to a larger margin of error because fewer people are in the subgroup. Fewer respondents means less accuracy. If you wanted to write about how many women supported Allen or Webb, you would have to recalculate the margin of error based on the smaller number of women surveyed. Suppose you wanted to know how women in the survey were going to vote. If women were half the sample, the margin of error would approximately double, to plus or minus 8 percentage points. Being honest about figures that are so unreliable can be difficult, but doing so is the only way to keep your reporting accurate and fair.

The Associated Press Managing Editors Association recommends that you have and share with your audience the following information about any poll on which you are reporting:

- **Identity of the survey's sponsor.** The sponsor's identity is important because it gives some clues to possible bias.
- **Exact wording of the questions.** Question wording is important because responses often depend at least in part on how the question was asked.
- **Makeup of the population.** Here, "population" means the total number of people in the group being studied. For an opinion survey, the population might be all registered voters in the state, black males under 25 or female cigarette smokers.
- **Sample size and response rate.** Sample size is important because—all other things being equal—the larger the sample, the more reliable the survey results should be.
- **Margin of error.** The sampling error, or margin of error, is the allowance that must be made for the possibility that the opinion expressed by the sample may not be exactly the same as the opinion of the whole population. Generally, the larger the sample, the smaller the sampling error.
- **Which results are based on only part of the sample.** The problem of sampling error makes it important to know whether any results are based on only part of the sample. The smaller that part, the greater the margin of error.
- **When the interviews were conducted.** When the interviewing was done may be of critical importance in interpreting the poll, especially during campaigns when the candidates themselves and other events may cause preferences to change significantly within a few days.
- **How the interviews were conducted.** Even when your newspaper does the polling, the obligation remains to let readers know how it was done. It is also incumbent on the paper to reveal how reliable the poll is.

MIXING NUMBERS AND WORDS

Whatever the story and whatever the subject, you probably can use numbers to clarify issues for readers and viewers. All too often, however, numbers are used in ways that muddy the water. Many journalists have some trepidation about working with numbers and often create confusion unwittingly when they work with the volatile mixture of numbers and words.

In *Mathsemantics: Making Numbers Talk Sense*, Edward MacNeal asserts that reporters and editors need to be far more careful in applying numbers in the news by questioning the accuracy and meaning of the numbers they gather and report.

For example, consider the following lead: "Each year 65,000 bicyclists go to the emergency room with injuries. Of those, 70–80 percent die because they weren't wearing helmets."

That means that more than 45,000 bicyclists, and perhaps as many as 52,000, are dying each year, or between about 125 and 140 each day. It's much more likely that the figures meant something else entirely—that 70 to 80 percent of the bicyclists

ON THE JOB

Working with Numbers

Before graduating from the University of Maryland's master's program in public affairs reporting, Sarah Cohen worked as an economist in the federal government, producing some of the statistics journalists report on each month. Early in that job, she had to be reminded how to compute a percentage change, but she learned fast.

In fact, she learned so well that she now is database editor for *The Washington Post*. She sometimes works weeks to find or compute just the right number for just the right place in a story — the number that tells the story best and most accurately.

Before joining the *Post*, she worked as training director for Investigative Reporters and Editors. There, she met many reporters who were terrified of the numbers they were seeing during the computer-assisted reporting seminars.

At a recent seminar of city editors, she heard the managers' side of dealing with numbers-phobia on deadline. Reporters who proudly say, "I don't do numbers" or "I have a problem with numbers" are sometimes viewed by editors in the same way that reporters would be if they said, "I don't do names — it's too scary to get the spelling right."

"The simple fact is, reporters have to overcome their mind-numbing fear of numbers long enough every day to get their stories done. And if they can never get over that fear, they'll find themselves hard-pressed to write any stories more complex than covering a dog show or a council meeting," Cohen says.

"Many reporters had to overcome a natural reluctance to knock on neighbors' doors or call a grieving family. Otherwise they could never be reporters. They have to overcome their fear of numbers to understand the increasingly sophisticated stories expected of us."

She believes the most difficult habit to overcome is the notebook-dumping syndrome.

"We're willing to throw out quotes or anecdotes we've collected. But somehow the carefully selected quote or elegantly crafted lead is sometimes followed by three paragraphs of incomprehensible numbers. So selection of numbers is most important."

There are plenty of devices to help you select the number — you can turn to ratios, rates, percentages or per-person averages, she advises. But remembering that they are guesses, opinions and summaries is the most effective way to reduce the number bloat. Use numbers when they work, not when some other way to convey the same information might work better, she advises.

Cohen is the author of *Numbers in the Newsroom: Using Math and Statistics in News*, published by Investigative Reporters and Editors.

who died of their injuries were not wearing helmets. With the figures given, we still don't know how many bicyclists died.

Journalists can also encourage misunderstandings by describing large increases in percentage terms. For example, a news story reported that Nigerian drivers were quitting the roads because gas prices had increased "more than 300 percent." The headline said, "Tripling of gasoline prices empties roads in Nigeria." They can't both be true. A 300 percent increase would actually be a quadrupling of prices.

Another trouble spot for mixing numbers and words occurs when reporters calculate how much more powerful or expensive something is. For example, a class that grew from 20 students to 100 students is five times as big as it was ($5 \times 20 = 100$), but it has four times as many students as it had before ($4 \times 20 + 20 = 100$).

The lesson to be learned from these examples is not to avoid numbers, but rather to use great care to ensure accuracy. Picking the right numbers to use and using them wisely will help your news stories have the biggest impact.

USING INTERNATIONAL UNITS

If you're writing about travel or international business, you need to understand currency exchange. Currency rates change frequently, though not by much unless there is some significant event that makes a currency more or less valuable. The most popular vacation location for U.S. travelers is Europe, most of which uses the euro. In late 2006, $1 would buy .79 of one euro (79 eurocents). Because you get less than one, you know that euros are more expensive than dollars.

Another popular location to visit and study is England, which, unlike most of its European neighbors, uses the pound. You can exchange $1 for .53 British pound (53 pence), which means London is even more expensive than mainland Europe. You can find dozens of calculators on the Web that will convert currency for you, and you should use them if you are doing stories. If you are traveling, it may be enough to know that it takes approximately two pounds to equal $1.

Suggested Readings

Campbell, Donald and Stanley, Julian. *Experimental and Quasi-Experimental Designs for Research*. Skokie, Ill.: Rand McNally, 1966. A classic guide to field experimentation that is also useful in providing a better understanding of scientific research.

Crossen, Cynthia. *Tainted Truth: The Manipulation of Fact in America*. New York: Simon & Schuster, 1994. An illuminating account of several instances in which public-relations executives manipulated press coverage by twisting the numbers.

Cuzzort, R. P. and Vrettos, James S. *The Elementary Forms of Statistical Reason*. New York: St. Martin's Press, 1996. A basic guide for nonmathematicians in the humanities and social sciences who must work with statistics.

MacNeal, Edward. *Mathsemantics: Making Numbers Talk Sense*. New York: Penguin, 1995. An entertaining and elucidating look into the semantics of numbers.

Meyer, Philip. *The New Precision Journalism*. Bloomington: Indiana University Press, 1991. A step-by-step guide to using social science research methods in news reporting.

Paulos, John Allen. *A Mathematician Reads the Newspaper*. New York: Doubleday, 1996. The book, structured like the morning paper, investigates the mathematical angles of stories in the news and offers novel perspectives, questions and ideas.

Seltzer, Richard A. *Mistakes That Social Scientists Make*. New York: St. Martin's Press, 1996. A useful book about the kinds of errors often made by social scientists during their research.

Suggested Web Sites

www.bls.gov/cpi
The Bureau of Labor Statistics allows you to convert for inflation. In addition, it carries CPI information for the entire nation, broken down by region and type of spending.

www.math.temple.edu/~paulos
You've read his book, *Innumeracy: Mathematical Illiteracy and Its Consequences*. Get more writings from the master of numbers, John Allen Paulos.

www.minneapolisfed.org/research/data/us/calc/
The Federal Reserve Bank of Minneapolis maintains a great Web site that helps you calculate inflation. It also has a clear and simple explanation of how inflation is calculated and how to use the Consumer Price Index.

www.people-press.org
The Pew Research Center offers its own credible polls on politics and public issues. It offers all the data you need to accurately assess the polls.

www.usatoday.com/money/perfi/calculators/calculator.htm
USA Today's site offers calculators to figure everything from interest rates to currency conversions.

Exercises

1. The federal minimum wage began in 1938 at 25 cents. In 1968, it was $1.60. Calculate how much 25 cents in 1938 is worth today and what $1.60 in 1968 is worth today. Compare those numbers with the present minimum wage. Suggest a story idea based on those numbers.

2. Find out from your campus financial aid office how much the graduating class has borrowed in Stafford Loans, the largest category of student loans. Calculate how much debt the average graduate will have in Stafford Loans. Then calculate how much debt the average indebted graduate will have. (The results will probably be quite different.) Find out what the total amount of payments owed will be for the average graduate with loans.

3. Find out how much your college charged for tuition in 1980, 1990, 2000 and today. Adjust those numbers for inflation so they can be compared to this year by going to **www.newsengin.com**. Write a story about the increasing cost of going to college, and use figures adjusted for inflation.

4. Look up numbers in *The Chronicle of Higher Education* that show the incidence of different sorts of crimes on college campuses. Write a story about crime on your campus after comparing rates of crime on different campuses.

5. Get a copy of your city's or town's current budget, and come up with 10 questions a reporter should ask about the changes, patterns and trends the budget suggests. The budget may be available on the Internet.

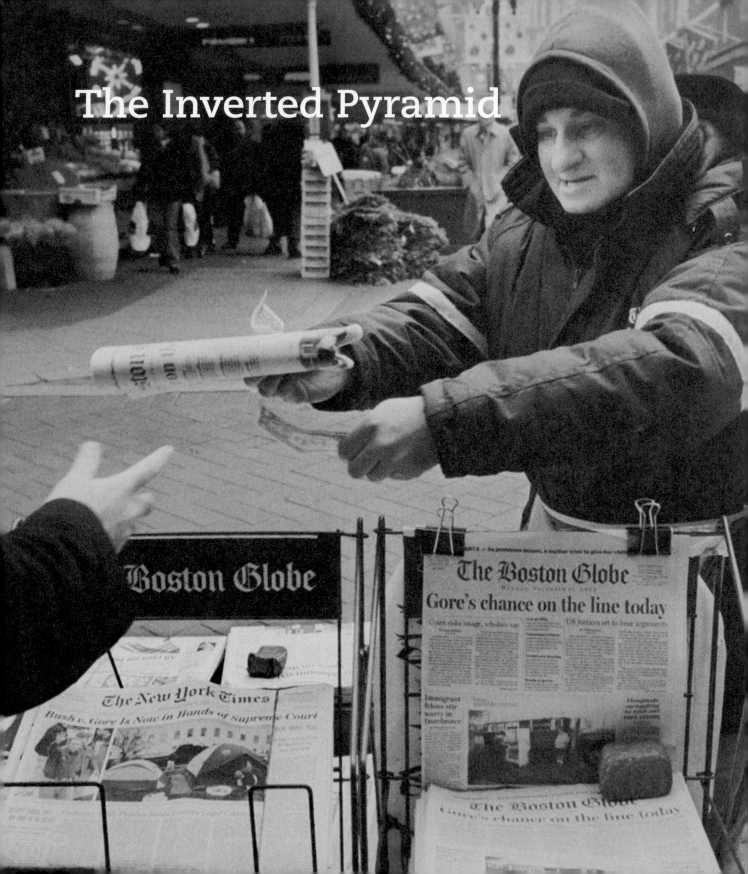

The Inverted Pyramid

IN THIS CHAPTER
YOU WILL LEARN:

1. How to translate news values into leads.

2. How to organize a story using the inverted pyramid.

3. How to increase your accuracy.

The **inverted pyramid**—a news story structure that places all the important information in the first paragraph—has written the first draft of history in the United States for generations. Here is the Associated Press lead on the first use of the atomic bomb in 1945:

> An atomic bomb, hailed as the most destructive force in history and as the greatest achievement of organized science, has been loosed upon Japan.

And here is how the AP started its story of the first moon landing in 1969:

> Man came to the moon and walked its dead surface Sunday.

When terrorists attacked the World Trade Center in 2001, the AP informed the world this way:

> In an unprecedented show of terrorist horror, the 110-story World Trade Center towers collapsed in a shower of rubble and dust Tuesday morning after two hijacked airliners carrying scores of passengers slammed into the side of the twin symbols of American capitalism.

As these examples show, journalists have been using the inverted pyramid for generations to record the daily history of world events. When the country waited for 40 days in 2000 to learn who its next president would be, thousands of journalists recorded every step of the controversy, from the recount to the Supreme Court decision. Mark Barabak, a political writer for the *Los Angeles Times*, worked long hours nearly every day. He told Nardo Zacchino, the *Times* reader representative, "Two or three nights post-election, I called my 9-year-old to tell her I wouldn't be home before she went to sleep because I had to write. I explained this had never happened before, that it was like writing history. She replied, 'Wow, it's really an honor, isn't it?'"

"Yes, it really is," Barabak replied.

Now specialized news delivered to customers online—one of the hottest new services in the new century—relies on the inverted pyramid, one of the most traditional story forms. So do newspapers, despite many editors' emphasis on encouraging new writing forms. So do radio, television and newsletters. Businesspeople often use the inverted pyramid in company memos so their bosses don't have to read to the end to find the main point. Public relations professionals use it in news releases to get the attention of news editors.

IMPORTANCE OF THE INVERTED PYRAMID STORY

Frequently misdiagnosed as dying, the inverted pyramid has more lives than a cat—perhaps because the more people try to speed up the dissemination of information, the more valuable the inverted pyramid becomes. In the inverted pyramid, information is arranged from most important to least important. The king in *Alice in Wonderland* would never succeed in the electronic news service business. When asked where to start a story, he replied, "Begin at the beginning and go on till you come to the end; then stop." Reporters, however, often begin a story at its end. Subscribers to Reuters, Dow Jones News/Retrieval and Bloomberg, for instance, react instantly to news about the financial markets to get an edge over other investors. They don't want narration; they want the news.

So do many newspaper readers, who, on average, spend 15 to 25 minutes a day reading the paper, and online readers, who spend even less time reading than newspaper subscribers. If a reporter were to write an account of a car accident by starting when the driver left the house, many readers would never read far enough to learn that the driver and a passenger were killed. Instead, such a story starts with its climax:

> Two people died Thursday when a backhoe fell off a
> truck's flatbed and sliced the top off an oncoming vehi-
> cle near Fairchild Air Force Base.

The inverted pyramid was fairly common by the turn of the 20th century. Before then, reporters were less direct. In 1869, the *New York Herald* sent Henry Morton Stanley to Africa to find the famous explorer-missionary David Livingstone. Stanley's famous account of the meeting begins:

> Only two months gone, and what a change in my feel-
> ings! But two months ago, what a peevish, fretful soul
> was mine! What a hopeless prospect presented itself
> before your correspondent!

After several similar sentences, the writer reports, "And the only answer to it all is (that) Livingstone, the hero traveler, is alongside of me."

Stanley reported the most important information so casually that today's reader probably would not have learned that Livingstone had been found. Today's reporter would probably begin the story like this:

> David Livingstone, the missionary-explorer missing for six years, has been
> found working in an African village on the shores of Lake Tanganyika.

The inverted pyramid saves readers time and editors space. It saves time by allowing readers to get the most important part of the story first—the climax of the event, the theme of a speech, the key finding in an investigation. It saves space by allowing editors to shorten stories by deleting from the bottom up. But if an editor had cut Stanley's story from the bottom, we would never have had the now-famous lines that end the story:

> "Dr. Livingstone, I presume?"
> And he says, "Yes."

Most journalism history books attribute the introduction of the inverted pyramid to the use of the telegraph during the Civil War. Forced to pay by the word, newspapers supposedly instructed their correspondents to put the most important information at the top. Researchers at the University of Southern California have found that the inverted pyramid was used even earlier. Whatever its origins, the inverted pyramid lead, the first paragraph or two, is presented as simply and clearly as possible. It sets the tone. It advertises what is coming in the rest of the story, and it conveys the most important information.

The lead sits atop other paragraphs arranged in descending order of importance. These paragraphs explain and provide evidence to support the lead. That's why editors can quickly shorten a story; the paragraphs at the bottom are the least important. The need to produce multiple newspaper editions with the same story running different lengths in each one makes it important that stories can be shortened quickly. The inverted pyramid serves that need well. On the Internet, space is not a consideration, but readers' time is. That's why the same inverted pyramid that is used in newspapers is the most common story structure found on such news Web sites as CNN.com, MSNBC.com, CBSNews.com and ABCNews.com.

In Chapter 20, you will learn details about writing news for the Web. You will find that most news Web sites rely on the inverted pyramid to present information quickly. For example, when a bus accident killed three students, CNN used the inverted pyramid as it followed the story the second day:

> HUNTSVILLE, Alabama (CNN)—National Transportation Safety Board investigators were in Huntsville on Tuesday, trying to determine what caused a school bus to plunge off a highway overpass the day before.
>
> The bus, carrying 43 students from Huntsville's Lee High School, fell 30 feet to the street below the overpass and landed on its front end before flipping over.
>
> —CNN

Later that day, however, a follow-up story on the *USA Today* site put casualties back into the lead as another student died. The investigation angle was moved further down into the story:

> HUNTSVILLE, Ala. (AP)—A fourth high school student died of injuries she got when her school bus nose-dived off an interstate overpass, the police chief said Tuesday. The bus driver, who was found critically injured on the overpass, was among 15 who remained hospitalized, authorities said. Four were listed as critical. . . .
>
> Debbie Hersman, a spokeswoman for the National Transportation Safety Board, said investigators were trying to determine how the driver ended up on the overpass, escaping the devastating impact that crumpled the front of the bus.

The inverted pyramid does have some shortcomings. Although it delivers the most important news first, it does not encourage people to read the entire story. Stories stop; they don't end. There is no suspense. In a Poynter Institute study

---

TIPS

The Inverted Pyramid

- Puts the most important information first.

- Arranges the paragraphs in descending order of importance.

- Requires the writer to rank the importance of information.

(www.poynter.org), researchers found that half of the 25 percent of readers who started a story dropped out midway through the story. Interest in an inverted pyramid story diminishes as the story progresses. But the way people use it attests to its value as a quick form of information delivery. Readers can leave whenever their needs are met, not when a writer finishes a story. In an age when time is golden, the inverted pyramid still offers value.

The day when the inverted pyramid is relegated to journalism history is not yet here and probably never will be. Perhaps 80 percent of the stories in today's newspapers and almost 100 percent of the stories on news services for target audiences such as the financial community are written in the inverted pyramid form. The trend is changing, but it's changing slowly. Some of the new media will require other forms. For instance, tailored stories for news-on-demand services that will reach a general audience need not use the inverted pyramid. Nor will those sites devoted to literary journalism (www.Esquire. com). Still, as long as newspaper, electronic and broadcast journalists continue to emphasize the quick, direct, simple approach to communications, the inverted pyramid and modifications of it will have a role.

There are many other ways to structure a story. You will learn about some of the options in Chapter 9. Before you get to the alternatives, however, you should master the inverted pyramid. As you do, you will master the art of making news judgments. The inverted pyramid requires you to identify and rank the most newsworthy elements in each story. That is important work. No matter what kind of stories you write—whether obituaries, accidents, speeches, press conferences, fires or meetings—you will be required to use the skills you learn here.

FINDING THE LEAD

TIPS

The Six Basic Questions

1. Who?

2. What?

3. When?

4. Where?

5. Why?

6. How?

More questions:

● So what?

● What's next?

To determine a **lead**—a simple, clear statement consisting of the first paragraph or two of an inverted pyramid story—you must first recognize what goes into one. As you read in Chapter 1, you begin by determining the story's *relevance, usefulness* and *interest* among readers. One way to measure these standards is to ask "So what?" or "Who cares?" So what if there's a car accident downtown? If it's one of hundreds a month, it may not be news. Any holdup in a community of 5,000 may be news because the "so what" is that holdups are uncommon and some residents probably know the victim. Neither newspapers nor radio or television stations would report the holdup in a metropolitan area where holdups are common. But if the holdup appears to be part of a pattern or if someone is killed, the story becomes more significant. One holdup may not be news, but a holdup that authorities believe is one of many committed by the same person may be news. The "so what" is that if the police catch this robber, they stop a crime spree. To determine the "so what," you have to answer six basic questions: who, what, when, where, why and how?

William Caldwell, winner of a Pulitzer Prize in 1971, remembers the best lead he ever heard. He tells the story in an Associated Press Managing Editors "Writing" report:

One summer afternoon in 1922, I was on my way home from school and my daily stint of work as editor of the village weekly, unhonored and unpaid. Like my father and two uncles, I was a newspaperman.

My little brother came running to meet me at the foot of our street. He was white and crying. A telegram had come to my mother. "Pa drowned this morning in Lake George," he gasped, and I am ashamed to be remembering my inward response to that.

Before I could begin to sense such elements as sorrow, despair, horror, loneliness, anger—before all the desolation of an abandoned kid would well up in me, I found myself observing that the sentence my brother had just uttered was the perfect lead. Noun, verb, predicate, period, and who-what-when-where to boot.

The information from every event you witness and every story you hear can be reduced to answers to who, what, when, where, why and how. If the answers add up to a significant "so what," you have a story. Consider this example of an incoming call at fire headquarters.

"Fire Department," the dispatcher answers.

"Hello. At about 10 o'clock, I was lying on my bed watching TV and smoking," the voice says. "I must have fallen asleep about 10:30 because that's when the football game was over. Anyway, I woke up just now, and my bedroom is on fire. . . ."

That dialogue isn't informative or convincing. More likely, our sleepy television viewer awoke in a smoke-filled room, crawled to the telephone and dialed frantically. The conversation at headquarters would more likely have gone like this:

"Fire Department."

"FIRE!" a voice at the other end yells.

"Where?" the dispatcher asks.

"At 1705 W. Haven St."

When fire is licking at their heels, even nonjournalists know the lead. How the fire started is not important to the dispatcher; that a house is burning—and where that house is located—is.

The journalist must go through essentially the same process to determine the lead. Whereas the caller served himself and the fire department, reporters must serve their readers. What is most important to them?

After the fire is over, there is much information a reporter must gather. Among the questions a reporter would routinely ask are these:

- When did it start?
- When was it reported?
- Who reported it?
- How was it reported?

> **"**Writing is easy; all you do is sit staring at a blank sheet of paper until the drops of blood form on your forehead.**"**
>
> — Gene Fowler, author

- How long did it take the fire department to respond?
- How long did it take to extinguish the fire?
- How many fires this year have been attributed to smoking in bed?
- How does that compare with figures in previous years?
- Were there any injuries or deaths?
- What was the damage?
- Who owned the house?
- Did the occupant or owner have insurance on the house?
- Will charges be filed against the smoker?
- Was there anything unusual about this case?
- Who cares?

With this information in hand, you can begin to write the story.

Writing the Inverted Pyramid Lead

Start by looking over your notes.

Who? The owner, a smoker, Henry Smith, 29. The age is important. Along with other personal information, such as address and occupation, it differentiates him from other Henry Smiths in the readership area.

What? Fire caused damage estimated by the fire chief at $2,500.

Where? 1705 W. Haven St.

When? The call was received at 10:55 p.m., Tuesday. Firefighters from Station 19 arrived at the scene at 11:04. The fire was extinguished at 11:30. Those times are important to gather even if you don't use them. They show whether the fire department responded quickly.

Why? The fire was started by carelessness on the part of Smith, according to Fire Chief Bill Malone.

How? Smith told fire officials that he fell asleep in bed while he was smoking a cigarette.

If you had asked other questions, you might have learned more from the fire department:

- This was the eighth fire this year caused by smoking in bed.
- All last year there were four such fires.
- Smith said he had insurance.
- The fire chief said no charges will be filed against Smith.
- It was the first fire at this house.
- Smith was not injured.

Have you figured out the "so what"?

Assume your city editor has suggested you hold the story to about four paragraphs. Your first step is to rank the information in descending order of importance. There are lots of fires in this town, but eight this year have been caused by smoking in bed. Perhaps that's the most important thing about this story. You begin to type:

> A fire started by a careless smoker caused an estimated $2,500 in damage to a home.

Only 16 words. You should try to hold every lead to fewer than 25 words unless you use more than one sentence. Maybe it's too brief, though. Have you left anything out? Maybe you should include the time element—to give the story a sense of immediacy. Readers would also want to know where the fire occurred. Is it near their house? Is it someone they know? You rewrite:

> A Tuesday night fire started by a careless smoker caused an estimated $2,500 in damage to a home at 1705 W. Haven St.

Just then the city editor walks by and glances over your shoulder. "Who said it was a careless smoker?" she asks. "Stay out of the story."

You realize you have committed a basic error in news writing: You have allowed an unattributed opinion to slip into the story. You have two choices. You can attribute the "careless smoker" information to the fire chief in the lead, or you can omit it. You choose to rewrite by attributing the opinion. You also revise your sentence to emphasize the cause instead of the damage. You write:

> Fire that caused an estimated $2,500 in damage to a home at 1705 W. Haven St. Tuesday was caused by smoking in bed, Fire Chief Bill Malone said.

Now 28 words have answered the questions "what" (a fire), "where" (1705 W. Haven St.), "when" (Tuesday) and "how" (smoking in bed). And the opinion is attributed. But you have not answered "who" and "why." You continue, still ranking the information in descending order of importance.

> The owner of the home, Henry Smith, 29, said he fell asleep in bed while smoking a cigarette. When he awoke about 30 minutes later, smoke had filled the room.
>
> Firefighters arrived nine minutes after receiving the call. It took them about 26 minutes to extinguish the fire, which was confined to the bedroom of the one-story house.
>
> According to Chief Malone, careless smokers have caused eight fires this year. Smith, who was not injured, said the house was insured.

You take the story to the city editor, who reads through the copy quickly. As you watch, she changes the lead to emphasize the "so what." The lead now reads:

A smoker who fell asleep in bed ignited a fire that caused minor damage to his home on W. Haven Street Tuesday, Fire Chief Bill Malone said. It was the city's eighth fire caused by smokers, twice as many as occurred all last year.

The lead is 44 words, but it is broken into two sentences, which makes it more readable. The importance of the "so what" changed the direction of the story. The fire was minor; there were no injuries. However, the increase in the number of fires smokers caused may force the fire department to start a public safety campaign against careless smoking. The city editor continues:

The owner of the home, Henry Smith, 29, of 1705 W. Haven St., said he fell asleep in bed while smoking a cigarette. When he awoke about 30 minutes later, smoke had filled the room.

The editor then checks the telephone book and the city directory and uncovers a serious problem. Both the telephone book and the city directory list the man who lives at 1705 W. Haven St. as Henry Smyth: S-m-y-t-h. City directories, telephone books, and other sources can be wrong. But at least they can alert you to possible errors. Confirm spellings by going to the original source, in this case, Mr. Smyth.

Never put a name in a story without checking the spelling, even when the source tells you his name is Smith.

Look at Figure 7.1 to see the completed fire story.

There are several lessons you can learn from this example:

- Always check names.
- Keep the lead short, usually fewer than 25 words, unless you use two sentences.
- Attribute opinion. (Smoking in bed is a fact. That it was careless is an opinion.)
- Find out the "who," "what," "where," "when," "why" and "how." However, if any of these elements have no bearing on the story, they might not have to be included.
- Write a sentence or paragraph telling readers what the news means to them.
- Report information basic to the story even if it is routine. Not everything you learn is important enough to be reported, but you'll never know unless you gather the information.

When you are learning to write an inverted pyramid story, the process is mechanical. You'll check your notes to be certain you have the six basic questions answered. Eventually, though, you will mentally check through those questions quickly. Of course, you will not always be able to find answers immediately to "how" and "why." Sometimes, it takes experts time to analyze accidents, crimes, fires, and so on.

After you've checked your notes, ask yourself, "What else do readers need to know?" Using the news values of relevance, usefulness and interest, decide which

---

Too many numbers bog down a lead. Focus on the impact of the figures in the lead, and provide details later in the story.

TIPS

When Writing the Lead, Remember

- Always check names.

- Keep the lead short, usually fewer than 25 words, unless you use two sentences.

- Attribute opinion.

- Find out the who, what, where, when, why and how. If any of these elements have no bearing on the story, they might not have to be included.

- Write a sentence or a paragraph telling readers what the news means to them.

- Report basic information even if it's routine. Not everything you learn is important enough to be reported, but you'll never know unless you gather the information.

The Inverted Pyramid Story

The identification of "who" is delayed until the next paragraph because the person is not someone readers would recognize and because his name would make the lead unnecessarily long. Also in the lead are the "what," "when," "how" and, most significantly here, the "so what?"

The performance of the fire department is monitored.

Least important: If someone else had been hurt and charges had been filed, this information would move higher in the story.

A smoker who fell asleep in bed ignited a fire that caused minor damage to his home on W. Haven Street Tuesday, Fire Chief Bill Malone said. It was the city's eighth fire caused by smokers, twice as many as occurred all last year.

The owner of the home, Henry Smyth, 29, of 1705 W. Haven St., said he fell asleep in bed while smoking a cigarette. When he awoke about 30 minutes later, smoke had filled the room.

The fire department, which received the call at 10:55 p.m., had the fire out by 11:30.

Malone said the damage, estimated at $2,500, was confined to the bedroom. The house was insured.

Careless smokers caused only four fires last year in the city. Malone said that he is considering a public awareness campaign to try to alert smokers to the hazards. Those four fires caused total damage of $43,000. This year, fires started by careless smoking have caused total damages of $102,500, Malone said.

No charges will be filed against Smyth because no one other than the smoker was endangered, Malone said.

The "who" is identified. More details on the "how" are given.

Details on the "so what" are given. The impact question is answered with the possible campaign.

Figure 7.1
The inverted pyramid structure dictates that the most important information go in the lead paragraphs. It's the job of the writer and editor to identify the most important information.

answers are the most important so you can put them in the lead. The rest go in the second and third paragraphs.

In the example above, the editor changed the emphasis from the fire, which was minor, to the number of recent fires. She knew that the number of fires was more relevant and more interesting than one minor fire. That angle also answers the question of usefulness by pointing out for readers and public safety officials alike that there is a bigger problem than one minor fire. The angle also answers the "so what" question. There was a minor fire. So what? There are lots of little fires. Eight fires this year caused by smoking is a "so what" that will grab attention.

Compare the fire story in Figure 7.1 with the accident story in Figure 7.2. In what order are the key questions answered in the fire story? In the accident story? Why is the order different?

The Classic Inverted Pyramid Story

The lead identifies the "what," "where" and "when." The "so what" is that people were killed. →

A four-vehicle accident on eastbound I-70 near Stadium Boulevard ended in two deaths on Sunday.

The second paragraph provides details to support the lead and answers "who." →

Barbara Jones, 41, of St. Louis died at the scene of the accident, and Juanita Doolan, 73, of St. Joseph died at University Hospital, according to a release from Springfield police. Two other people, William Doolan, 73, of St. Joseph and Theodore Amelung, 43, of Manchester, Mo., were injured in the accident.

This paragraph shows impact beyond deaths. →

Both lanes of traffic were closed on the eastbound side and limited to one lane on the westbound side as rescue workers cleared the scene.

Authorities said a westbound late-model Ford Taurus driven by Lan Wang of Springfield was traveling in the right lane, developed a tire problem and swerved into the passing lane. A Toyota pickup truck in the passing lane, driven by Jones, was forced over the grassy median along with the Taurus. The two vehicles entered eastbound traffic where the truck struck an Oldsmobile Delta 88, driven by Juanita Doolan, head on.

← The "how" is less important than the "what," "where" and "when," so it appears later in the story.

Wang and the one passenger in his car, Kenneth Kuo, 58, of Springfield, were not injured.

← An eyewitness account adds sensory details that make the scene more vivid.

John Paul, a tractor-trailer driver on his way to Tennessee, said he had to swerve to miss the accident.

"I saw the red truck come across the median and hit the blue car," Paul said. "I just pulled over on the median and called 911."

What's next? This would be higher if the driver, rather than a tire, appeared to be the cause of the accident. →

Jones, who was wearing a seatbelt, died at the scene, Officer Stan Williams said. Amelung, a passenger who had been in the truck, was out of the vehicle when authorities arrived, but it was unknown whether he was thrown from the truck or was pulled out by someone else, Williams said.

No charges have been filed, but the investigation continues.

Figure 7.2
Note how this story, typical of the inverted pyramid structure, delivers the most important news in the lead and provides less essential details toward the end.

Emphasizing Different News Values

In the lead reporting the house fire, the "what" (fire) is of secondary importance to the "how" (how the fire started). A slightly different set of facts would affect the news value of the elements and, consequently, your lead. For instance, if Smyth turned out to have been a convicted arsonist, you would probably emphasize that bizarre twist to the story:

> A convicted arsonist awoke Tuesday to find that his bedroom was filled with smoke. He escaped and later said that he had fallen asleep while smoking.
>
> Henry Smyth, 29, who served a three-year term for . . .

That lead emphasizes the news value of novelty. If Smyth were the mayor, you would emphasize prominence:

> Mayor Henry Smyth escaped injury Tuesday when he awoke to find his bedroom filled with smoke. Smyth said he had fallen asleep while smoking in bed.

What, So What and What's Next

You know that the answer to "what" is often the lead. The preceding examples also illustrate the "so what" factor in news. A $2,500 fire is not news to many people in large communities where there are dozens of fires daily. Even if you crafted a tightly written story about it, your editor probably would not want to print or broadcast it.

In small communities, the story would have more impact because there are fewer fires and because a larger proportion of the community is likely to know the victim.

The "so what" factor grows more important as you add other information. If the fire occurred during a fire-safety campaign, the "so what" would be the need for fire safety even in a community where awareness of the problem had already been heightened. If the fire involved a convicted arsonist or the mayor, the "so what" would be stronger. Oddity or well-known people increase the value of a story. If someone had been injured or if the damage had been $250,000 instead of $2,500, the "so what" factor might even push the story into the metropolitan press. As you've seen above, once you have answered all six of the basic questions, it's important to ask yourself what the answers mean to the reader. That answer is your "so what" factor.

> **"**Selecting the quotes isn't so hard; it's presenting them that causes the trouble. And the worst place to present them is at the beginning. Quote leads deserve their terrible reputation. Yet they still appear regularly in both print and broadcast journalism.
>
> "We can make three generalizations about quote leads. They're easy, lazy, and lousy. They have no context. The readers don't know who's speaking, why, or why it matters. Without context, even the best quotations are wasted.**"**
>
> — Paula LaRocque, former assistant managing editor, *The Dallas Morning News*

In many stories, it is also important to answer the question "What's next?" The City Council had its first reading of its budget bill. What's next? *Members will vote on it next month.* Jones was arrested Monday on a charge of passing bad checks. What's next? *The prosecuting attorney will decide whether there is enough evidence to file charges.*

A reader in a focus group once told researchers that she just wants to be told "what," "so what" and "what's next." That's a good guideline for all journalists to remember.

VARIATIONS ON THE INVERTED PYRAMID LEAD

No journalist relies on formulas to write inverted pyramid leads, but you may find it useful, especially in the beginning, to learn some typical types of leads. The labels in the following sections are arbitrary, but the approaches are not.

The "You" Lead

Regardless of which of these leads journalists use, they are trying to emphasize the relevance of the news to the reader. One good way to highlight the relevance is to speak directly to the reader by using "you." This informal, second-person lead—the "you" lead—allows the writer to tell readers why they should care. For instance:

> You will make more money buying Savings Bonds starting tomorrow.
>   The Treasury boosted the semiannual interest rate on Series EE Savings Bonds to 5.92 percent from 4.7 percent effective Tuesday.

Readers want to know what's in it for them. The traditional approach is less direct:

> The Treasury boosted Savings Bonds interest Tuesday to the highest rate in three years.

As with any kind of lead, you can overdo the "you" lead. You don't need to write "You have another choice in the student president's race." Just tell readers who filed their candidacy. However, you may use those words in writing for radio and television news as a setup for the story to come.

The Immediate-Identification Lead

In the **immediate-identification lead**, one of the most important facts is "who," or the prominence of the key actor. Reporters often use this approach when someone important or well-known is making news. Consider the following example:

> Agence France-Presse
> Former "Seinfeld" star Michael Richards apologized days after unleashing an expletive-laden racist tirade during a stand-up performance at a famous Los Angeles comedy club.

Names make news.

When writing for your campus newspaper or your local newspaper, you would use names in the lead that are known, not necessarily nationally but locally. The name of your student body president, the chancellor, the city's mayor or an entertainer who has a local following would logically appear in the lead. None of these names would be used in a newspaper 50 miles away.

In any accident, the "who" may be important because it is someone well known by name or position. If so, the name should be in the lead.

In small communities, the "who" in an accident may always be in the lead. In larger communities, names are not as recognizable. As a rule, if the name is well-known, it should appear in the lead.

❚❚Language is a very difficult thing to put into words.**❚❚**

— Voltaire, philosopher

The Delayed-Identification Lead

Usually a reporter uses a **delayed-identification lead** because the person, people or organization involved has little name recognition among readers. Thus, in fairly large cities, an accident is usually reported like this:

> MADISON, Wis.—A 39-year-old carpenter was killed today in a two-car collision two blocks from his home.
>
> Dead is William Domonske of 205 W. Oak St. Injured in the accident and taken to Mercy Hospital were Mary Craig, 21, of 204 Maple Ave., and Rebecca Roets, 12, of 207 Maple Ave.

However, in a smaller community, names almost always make news. If Domonske lived in a city of 10,000, his name probably would be in the lead.

By the same token, most people know that IRS stands for "Internal Revenue Service." But many don't know that AARP is an organization for people age 50 and over. This story about AARP features a delayed-identification lead:

> The nation's largest senior citizens organization paid $135 million to settle a dispute with the IRS over the income it earns from royalties.
>
> However, the settlement leaves open the question of whether future income earned by AARP will be taxed, said the group's spokesman, Peter Ashkenaz.

Because so many people over 50 belong to AARP, the reporter could have written the lead using "you":

> If you are one of 33 million members of the nation's largest senior citizens organization, you just settled a bill with the IRS.
>
> AARP has agreed to pay $135 million to settle a dispute with the IRS over the income it earns from royalties.
>
> AARP, which still has $19.6 million in cash reserves, says the settlement will not affect any of your services.

There are two other occasions when the reporter may choose to delay identification of the person involved in the story until the second paragraph. One occurs when the person is not well-known but the person's position, occupation, title or achievements are important or interesting. The other occurs when the lead is becoming too wordy.

As Andy Warhol said, people have their 15 minutes of fame, but fame can be fleeting. While Terry Anderson of the AP was being held captive from 1985 to 1992 by the Islamic Jihad in Lebanon, even casual consumers of the news recognized his name because of daily coverage. By early 2000, when a court ruled that Anderson was entitled to damages, a delayed-identification lead was appropriate.

WASHINGTON—A former AP newsman was awarded $341 million from Iran on March 24 by a federal judge who said his treatment during his nearly seven years of captivity in Beirut was "savage and cruel by any civilized standards."

U.S. District Judge Thomas Penfield Jackson ordered Iran to pay $24.5 million to Terry Anderson, $10 million to his wife, Madeleine Bassil, and $6.7 million to their daughter, Sulome. The judge also ordered the Iranian Ministry of Information and Security to pay the three $300 million in punitive damages.

A name that would appear in the lead in one city would appear in the second paragraph in another. The mayor of Birmingham, Ala., would be identified by title and name in Birmingham and by title only in Bridgewater, Conn.

Some titles are bulky: "Chairman of the Federal Communications Commission" assures clutter even before you add the name. "United Nations ambassador" quickly fills the sentence. When dealing with these types of positions, writers often choose to use the title alone and delay introducing the name until the second or third paragraph. When the title is better known than the name, writers usually use the title alone and delay the name until the second paragraph.

When AP newsman Terry Anderson was released in Lebanon in 1992, his was a household name. Eight years later, during his court case, not many readers would have recognized his name.

ON THE JOB

Thinking in the Inverted Pyramid

Anyone who has stared at a blank screen 15 minutes before deadline knows the importance of the inverted pyramid. It's the quickest, simplest way to organize your notes and thoughts.

When a posh suburban country club caught fire nearly an hour before the early edition's deadline, Stacy St. Clair was assigned to the story. As she drove to the scene — located almost 20 miles away — she wrote a mock story in her head and made mental notes about people she needed to speak with and information she needed to gather. As she drove back to the news room, she filled the holes in her prewrite. It was a classic inverted-pyramid, 12-inch story, which she pounded out in about 15 minutes. She finished the piece with a few minutes to spare and used the extra time to add some color to the story.

"Because the inverted pyramid has become a natural reflex in both my reporting and writing, I had enough time to go back and tell readers about foursomes who finished their rounds rather than seek shelter and panicked members who tried to save their Great Big Berthas from a fiery locker room," she said.

St. Clair, now the chief narrative writer at the *Daily Herald* in the Chicago suburbs, believes the inverted pyramid suffers from an unfair stereotype. "Editors and professors regularly call the writing style uninspired or elementary, but it doesn't have to be. Using the inverted pyramid does not release reporters from the responsibilities of good writing. Pacing, word choice, description, anecdotes — they all have a place in the inverted pyramid. Initial reports of the World Trade Center disaster, for example, were written in the inverted pyramid, yet they contained incredibly powerful anecdotes and heart-wrenching detail," she said.

The inverted pyramid forces you to prioritize and ask yourself, "What's important here? What's the story really about?" As St. Clair notes, "Once it becomes second nature, the inverted pyramid teaches you how to focus on a story, whether it's a 60-inch feature or a 9-inch car crash story."

The Summary Lead

Reporters dealing with several important elements may choose to sum up what happened in a **summary lead** rather than highlighting a specific action. This is one of the few times when a general statement is preferable to specifics.

When Congress passed a bill giving family members with emergencies the right to unpaid leave from work, the writer had to make a choice: to focus on the main provision or to write a summary lead. The writer chose the latter:

> A bill requiring employers to give workers up to three
> months' unpaid leave in family emergencies won Sen-
> ate approval Thursday evening.

Several other provisions in the bill are explained later in the story:

> The unpaid leave can be for medical reasons or to care
> for a new child, and employers would have to continue
> health insurance benefits and restore employees to their
> previous jobs or equivalent positions.

You can also show the readers the "so what" with the "you" lead:

> The Senate voted Thursday to allow you to take up to three months' unpaid
> leave in family emergencies without losing your health benefits.

Likewise, if a city council rewrites city ordinances, unless one of the changes is of overriding importance, most reporters will use a summary lead:

> MOLINE, Ill.—The City Council replaced the city's
> 75-year-old municipal code with a revised version Tues-
> day night.

Summary leads do not appear only in reports of board meetings. A Spokane, Wash., reporter used a summary lead to report a neighborhood dispute:

> An Idaho farmer's fence apparently was cut last week.
> It set off a chain of events Friday night that landed three
> people in the hospital, killed a cow and totaled a vehi-
> cle in the eastern Spokane Valley.

The basic question you must answer is whether the whole of the action is more important than any of its parts. If the answer is yes, a summary lead is in order.

The Multiple-Element Lead

In some stories, choosing one theme for the lead is too restrictive. In such cases the reporter can choose a **multiple-element lead** to work more information into the first paragraph. But you should write the lead within the confines of a clear, simple sentence or sentences. Consider this example:

> PORTLAND, Wash.—The City Council Tuesday or-
> dered three department heads fired, established an ad-
> ministrative review board and said it would begin to
> monitor the work habits of administrators.

Notice that not only the actions but also the construction of the verb phrases within the sentence is parallel. Parallel structures also characterize the following news extract, which presents a visual picture of the scene of a tragedy:

> BAY CITY, Mich.—A flash fire that swept through a landmark downtown hotel Saturday killed at least 12 persons, injured 60 more and forced scores of residents to leap from windows and the roof in near-zero cold.

We are told where it happened, what happened, and how many were killed and injured.

Some multiple-element leads consist of two paragraphs. This occurs when the reporter decides that several elements need prominent display. For example:

> The Board of Education Tuesday night voted to lower the tax rate 12 cents per $100 valuation. Members then approved a budget $150,000 less than last year's and instructed the superintendent to decrease the staff by 25 people.
>
> The board also approved a set of student-conduct rules, which include a provision that students with three or more unexcused absences a year will be suspended for a week.

This story, too, could emphasize the "so what" while retaining the multiple elements:

> The Board of Education lowered your real-estate taxes Tuesday. Members also approved a budget $150,000 less than last year's and instructed the superintendent to decrease the staff by 25 people.

Simpler leads are preferable. But a multiple-element lead is one of your options. Use it sparingly.

Many newspapers are using graphic devices to take the place of multiple-element leads. They use summary boxes to list other actions. Because the box appears under the headline in type larger than text, it serves as a graphic summary for the reader who is scanning the page. The box frees the writer from trying to jam too many details into the first few paragraphs (see Figure 7.3).

Figure 7.3
A summary box can take the place of a multiple-element lead.

Other Council Action

In other action, the council:

- Voted to repave Broadway Ave.
- Rejected a new sign ordinance.
- Hired four school crossing guards.
- Expanded bus hours.

Another approach is to break the coverage of a single event into a main story and a shorter story called a **sidebar**. This approach offers the advantage of presenting the information in short, palatable bites. It also allows the writer to elevate more actions into lead positions. Researchers have found that breaking stories into small segments increases readers' comprehension and retention. For instance, in the example above, the angle about the superintendent's having to decrease staff could be spun off into a short sidebar.

Both methods of presentation have advantages over the more complicated multiple-element lead.

> Breaking stories into small segments increases readers' comprehension and retention.

Danger Signals

Here are some leads that understandably raise red flags to editors:

- **Question leads.** Readers don't know the subject, don't know why they are being asked a question and probably couldn't care less. So the next time you are writing a weather story and are tempted to begin with "So, how hot was it yesterday?" lie down until the temptation passes. Either tell readers the temperature or open with an anecdote of a specific roofer sweating on the job. That's showing how hot it is.

- **Leads that say what might happen or what might have happened.** News organizations try to report what happened. Stay away from leads like this: "Springfield residents may be looking forward to warmer weather." Or they may not. Talk to people. Don't speculate.

- **Leads that overreach.** Report what you know. You may think it's harmless to write, "Springfield residents warmly greeted spring yesterday," but you don't know that *all* Springfield residents were happy about it. Maybe the guy who runs a snow-removal business would rather see winter last longer.

Leads with Flair

Although the inverted pyramid tells readers the news first and fast, not all stories begin with the most important statement. When the news value you want to emphasize is novelty, often the lead is unusual.

When a group of suspected drug dealers was arrested at a wedding, the Associated Press focused on the novelty:

NARRAGANSETT, R.I. (AP)—The wedding guests included drug suspects, the social coordinator was a narcotics agent, the justice of the peace was a police chief, and 52 officers were party crashers.

For the unsuspecting bride and groom, the ceremony Friday night was truly unforgettable—a sting operation set up by state and local police that led to 30 arrests.

That's not exactly your traditional wedding or your traditional lead. Yet the essential information is contained within the first two paragraphs. A less imaginative writer would have written something like this:

> Thirty suspected drug dealers, including a couple about to be married, were arrested at a wedding Friday night.

> **"**The lead should be a promise of great things to come, and the promise should be fulfilled.**"**
>
> — Stanley Walker, city editor

That approach is like slapping a generic label on a Mercedes-Benz. The inverted pyramid approach is not so rigid that it doesn't permit fun and flair.

What is the difference between the two-paragraph, multiple-element lead on the board of education mentioned earlier and the two-step lead on the wedding story? In the first, the reporter was dealing with several significant actions. In the second, the reporter was dealing with only one, so she used the first paragraph to set up the surprise in the second.

STORY ORGANIZATION

Like the theater marquee, the lead is an attention-getter. Sometimes the movie doesn't fulfill the promises of the marquee; sometimes the story doesn't fulfill the promises of the lead. In either case, the customer is dissatisfied.

The inverted pyramid helps you put information in logical order. It forces you to rank, in order of importance, the information you will present.

The One-Subject Story

As we have seen in this chapter, constructing an inverted pyramid news story involves a series of judgments based on classic news values and the specific news outlet. A fire or an accident in a small community is bigger news than a fire or an accident in another, larger area. Earlier events will also influence how a story is written.

Figure 7.4 shows a story about the arrest of a suspect in an assault case. Police say drugs were involved. If there had been a string of assaults or a pattern of drug-related violence, the writer probably would have emphasized different aspects of the story. For instance, the writer could have emphasized the suspect's criminal record with this lead:

> A Columbia man who was convicted of assault three times was arrested again Thursday night for an attack on his girlfriend.

There is almost always more than one way to write a story. The version that is published or broadcast is the result of the judgments of the writer and the editor. If the story in Figure 7.4 had already appeared on the Web or had been on television or radio, the newspaper probably would have chosen another angle, as in the example highlighting the suspect's criminal record, to make the story different.

Anatomy of a Single-Subject Inverted Pyramid Story

Man Arrested in Attack, Charged with Child Endangerment

By Elizabeth Phillips
Columbia Missourian

The arrest, not the assault, is the latest development, so it is emphasized.

Police arrested a Columbia man in connection with an attack on his girl-friend Thursday night.

The lead gives "who," "what" and "when."

Details of the charges are in the second paragraph because the list is too long to put in the lead.

Darrell Vanness Johnson, 37, was arrested on suspicion of second-degree domestic assault, unlawful use of a weapon, felony possession of a controlled substance, misdemeanor possession of a controlled substance and endangering the welfare of a child at about 9 p.m. Thursday in the 1500 block of Greensboro Drive.

The name is not in the lead because most readers would not recognize it.

"Where" is identified. "When" is made more specific than in the lead.

The writer adds details, attributed to the police, on how the assault occurred. This information includes the "why."

Johnson and his girlfriend began arguing over drugs Thursday evening, Columbia Police Sgt. Ken Hammond said. Johnson choked her and held a revolver to her head before she was able to escape and call 911 from a neighbor's house, Hammond said. Three children, two 9-year-olds and a 4-year-old, were in the home during the attack, Hammond said.

Information about the children is pertinent because it adds to the "so what" — the children were also endangered.

This paragraph continues the chronology of the assault and capture.

When Columbia police arrived, Johnson was driving away from the Greensboro Drive home with the three children in the car, Hammond said. When police arrested Johnson, they found marijuana and cocaine, Hammond said.

The victim was taken to an area hospital by ambulance for treatment of bruises and scratches to the hands, neck and back, Hammond said. Her injuries were not life threatening.

The writer offers evidence of the injuries and attributes this information.

Now that the basic facts are established, the writer adds background on the suspect, attributed to a public safety Web site.

According to Missouri Case.net, Johnson has pleaded guilty to third-degree domestic assault three times in the past four years in Boone County Circuit Court, serving close to seven months in jail for those charges. He has also pleaded guilty to theft, first-degree trespass and second-degree property damage in Boone County Circuit Court, serving 75 days in Boone County Jail for the theft charge and receiving two years of unsupervised probation for the trespass and property damage charges.

Johnson violated his probation on the trespass and property damage charges and was scheduled to appear in Boone County Circuit Court for a probation violation hearing in December. He was charged with theft last October in Boone County Circuit Court.

Writer gives the "what's next."

He faces up to 40 years in prison and up to a year in jail in connection with the attack.

Figure 7.4
This typical one-subject story written in the inverted pyramid features a delayed-identification lead.

The Multiple-Element Story

Multiple-element stories are most commonly used in reporting on the proceedings of councils, boards, commissions, legislatures and courts. These bodies act on numerous subjects in one sitting. Frequently, their actions are unrelated, and more than one action is often important enough to merit attention in the story. You have three options:

1. **You can write more than one story.** That, of course, depends on permission from your editor. There may not be enough space.
2. **You can write a summary box.** It would be displayed along with the story. In it you would list the major actions taken by the council or the decisions issued by the court.
3. **You can write a multiple-element lead and story.** Your lead would list all the major actions at the board meeting. The remainder of the story would provide more detail about each action.
4. **You can write a single-element lead and cover the other elements further on in the story.** Your lead would focus on the element you found most interesting, relevant and useful to readers.

Let's go back to a multiple-element lead we saw earlier:

The Board of Education Tuesday night voted to lower the tax rate 12 cents per $100 valuation. Members then approved a budget $150,000 less than last year's and instructed the superintendent to decrease the staff by 25 people.

The board also approved a set of student-conduct rules, which include a provision that students with three or more unexcused absences a year will be suspended for a week.

Four newsworthy actions are mentioned in those two paragraphs: (1) changing the tax rate, (2) approving a budget, (3) cutting staff, (4) adopting conduct rules. In this and all stories that deal with several important elements, the writer highlights the most important. Sometimes several elements are equally important, as in this example. Most of the time, however, one action stands above the rest. When that is the case, it is important to summarize the other, lesser, actions after the lead.

If you and your editor judged that changing the tax rate was more important than anything else that happened at the school board meeting, you would approach the story like this:

Lead

The Board of Education Tuesday night voted to lower the tax rate 12 cents per $100 valuation.

Support for lead

The new rate is $1.18 per $100 valuation. That means that if your property is assessed at $300,000, your school tax will be $3,540 next year.

Summary of other action

The board also approved a budget that is $150,000 less than last year's, instructed the superintendent to cut the staff by 25 and approved a set of rules governing student conduct.

TIPS

Checklist for Assembling the Rest of the Inverted Pyramid

- Introduce additional important information you were not able to include in the lead.

- If possible, indicate the significance or "so what?" factor.

- Elaborate on the information presented in the lead.

- Continue introducing new information in the order in which you have ranked it by importance.

- Develop the ideas in the same order in which you have introduced them.

- Generally, use only one new idea in each paragraph.

Notice that the lead is followed by a paragraph that supports and enlarges upon the information in it before the summary paragraph appears. Whether you need a support paragraph before summarizing other action depends on how complete you are able to make the lead.

In every multiple-element story, the first two or three paragraphs determine the order of the rest of the story. To ensure the coherence of your story, you must describe the actions in the order in which you introduced them.

In Figure 7.5, you see a more detailed example of a multiple-element story. Notice the order in which the writer answers the questions "who," "what," "when," "where," "why" and "how." Do you agree that the lead contains the most important elements? Could the story be cut from the bottom up, if necessary?

CHECKING ACCURACY AND ATTRIBUTIONS

All of us can improve our accuracy. Some improvement comes with experience, but most of the errors journalists make involve routine facts. In Chapter 4, you learned the importance of accurately capturing the words for quotes. Here are additional procedures you should use to produce more accurate stories.

Ensuring Accuracy

This correction is from *The Detroit News*: "Three million Americans are eligible for a low-income subsidy through Medicare Part D. A front-page story on Friday erroneously said 3 million Michigan residents were eligible." Corrections such as this routinely run in newspapers and on Web sites. The errors shouldn't be routine. In *Essay on Criticism*, Alexander Pope wrote, "To err is human, to forgive divine." However, readers are not apt to forgive. We all make errors, but our job as professional journalists is to be as accurate as humanly possible. There are several habits you can develop to improve your accuracy.

One is to go over your notes at the end of every interview. Read back the quotes and the facts as you have written them down. Don't assume anything. As you read earlier in the chapter, if someone tells you his name is Smith, ask how to spell it.

Another is to carefully check your story against your notes and the documents you have collected to be certain you didn't introduce any errors while writing. We all make typing errors. We all make errors because of background noise and interruptions. If you recognize that you are not infallible, you will be a more accurate journalist.

When sources give you facts, if possible, check them. During an interview, the mayor may tell you that the city has 50 police officers. Check with the police department. The mayor may have the number wrong.

Another way to increase accuracy is to perform a prepublication check of some sort with your sources. Some journalists object to such accuracy checks because they believe that it gives sources too much opportunity to object to what

Anatomy of a Multiple-Element Inverted Pyramid Story

U Earns C Average in Student-Access Report

By Norman Draper
Star Tribune

The University of Minnesota does better than most of the nation's major public universities in admitting minority students. But it fares poorly in both graduating them within six years and in admitting low-income students.

Those are among the findings of a report issued Monday by the national Education Trust. The report measured how well the nation's 50 flagship state universities are serving the nation's racial minority and poor students.

Overall, the report's findings described the nation's top state universities as looking "less and less like America—and more and more like gated communities of higher education." Too many, the report stated, aren't pushing hard enough to enroll more minority and poor kids.

The U of M generally fared relatively well in the report, though it earned only a C average based on six criteria. That's better than many state universities, which got Ds and Fs. Other universities in the survey included the University of Wisconsin-Madison, the University of North Carolina-Chapel, the University of California-Berkeley and the University of Texas-Austin.

The U of M got an A in minority student access because the percentage of black, Hispanic and American Indian students in its fall 2004 freshman class—7.7 percent—was identical to the percentage of those students in the state's spring 2004 high school graduating class. Asian students were not counted as minority students in the report because they are not considered underrepresented.

The U got a D in minority student success because of the gap in graduation rates between white students (63.7 percent) and minority students (41.4 percent).

It also got a D in access for low-income students. That's because the number of such students at the U is lower than at all other Minnesota colleges and universities, as measured by the percentage of students who get federal grants.

"The University of Minnesota has long been concerned with issues of access for students from all walks of life," U spokesman Daniel Wolter said

(continued)

Annotations (left margin):

The writer chooses two elements to put in the lead along with "who" and "what."

In order to tell the "what," the writer had to delay revealing the source of the report and the answer to "when."

Having established the most important elements, the writer summarizes the rest of the report.

Now the writer summarizes the local details.

Any of these details could have been in the lead. The writer and editor had to make judgments about the most important details.

Here and in the next two paragraphs is the university's response to the report.

Annotations (right margin):

Are there any elements in the fifth paragraph that you think should be in the lead?

This is the context against which readers can measure the local university's performance.

Note that the writer offers not only the findings but also the reasons for the findings in this and succeeding paragraphs.

Notice that the letter grades used in the report give the reader a way to understand the results.

The terms *black, Hispanic, American Indian,* and *Asian* are preferred by the *AP Stylebook.*

Figure 7.5
The writer for the Minneapolis *Star Tribune* took a national study and localized it for readers. The study produced multiple findings, so the writer and editor had to rank them from most important to least important.

Figure 7.5
(continued)

in an e-mailed response. "The issue of access for underrepresented minorities has been an important one for the U . . . and our A grade underscores that we're doing a good job on that front."

Wolter also cited the creation of a new administrative position—vice president for access and diversity—and the U's raising of $150 million in private gifts to support student scholarships as evidence that the U is committed to academic and racial diversity.

In regard to the two Ds, Wolter said, "We recognize those as areas for improvement," but he added that overall U graduation rates have doubled over the past decade.

The Education Trust is a Washington, D.C. nonprofit organization dedicated to improving student achievement, with a special emphasis on low-income and racial minority students.

← Note how the writer handles the e-mail from the spokesman.

The background helps readers understand who issued the report. →

you will print. In some competitive situations, they are afraid sources may alert other media to get their version of the story out even before you publish. But those situations are rare.

In a study published in the *Newspaper Research Journal*, researcher Duane Stoltzfus found that more newspapers than formerly believed were willing to permit their reporters to check stories or portions of stories with sources before publication. In all cases, sources were told that they were being asked to check the accuracy of the information. No journalist should cede authority for decisions about what goes in a story and what does not. But at the same time, no journalist should be afraid to take every step possible to ensure accuracy. Some read back quotes; some read back facts gathered from that source. Some even describe information obtained from other sources.

The New York Times has a Credibility Group that recommends that the paper encourage "the practice of reporters' interim and final checks with sources to verify specific points." However, the group also says, "We do not advocate having sources look over entire articles." Stoltzfus also reported that *USA Today*, among many other newspapers, permits its reporters to decide whether to check with sources before publication.

If you are at a publication that permits prepublication checks, you do yourself and your profession a favor by performing them. Verify everything you intend to publish or broadcast. In the online world, where speed is king, verification is sometimes sacrificed to be first. Being first and wrong is never right. The bloggers will be the first to tell you that.

How and When to Attribute

Attribution is our way of telling readers that we aren't making this stuff up. Your first obligation is to go to primary sources whenever possible. The mayor is an official source, but he isn't the primary source for how many police officers the city employs. The police chief or someone authorized to speak for the department would be a primary, and more accurate, source. So would someone in the city personnel department. So would city records. However, not all facts need to be attributed. If you are reporting that there was a fire in a five-story building, you do not need to attribute that fact because it is verifiable to anyone who sees it. However, if you are gathering the information about the fire in another community, you should attribute it if you are unable to confirm it.

Witnesses are good sources for firsthand accounts, but they are not always accurate. One witness may say that the Toyota driver hit the Ford. Another may say the Ford hit the Toyota. Your primary source is the police officer. If the officer can't sort it out, you may need to report the conflicting versions with attribution to all the parties. When you are reporting on deadline, you often have to deal with uncertainty. An Associated Press reporter dealt with one such instance this way, "The bus driver was either ejected or escaped from the vehicle before it fell, NTSB investigator Debbie Hersman said Tuesday."

Always attribute opinions. "Augusta is the most livable city in the United States" is an opinion regardless of who says it. If *Money* magazine publishes a list of the most livable cities in the United States, attribute that opinion to the magazine.

Tell readers how you obtained the information. If you are using information from an e-mail sent to you by your source, tell readers that the source gave the information in an e-mail. If you are using instant messaging, tell readers. If someone is revealing something to you from a document that he or she will not let you see because it is confidential, say the source obtained the information from the document. Be transparent about your sources.

Suggested Readings

Brooks, Brian S., Pinson, James L. and Wilson, Jean Gaddy. *Working With Words*, Sixth Edition. New York: Bedford/St. Martin's, 2006. This book, a must for any journalist, provides excellent coverage of grammar and word usage and a strong chapter on "isms."

Gillman, Timothy. "The Problem of Long Leads in News and Sports Stories." *Newspaper Research Journal*, Fall 1994, pp. 29–39. The researcher found that sentences in leads were longer than sentences in the rest of the story.

Kennedy, George. "Newspaper Accuracy: A New Approach." *Newspaper Research Journal*, Winter 1994, pp. 55–61. The author suggests that journalists do prepublication accuracy checks with proper safeguards built in.

Stoltzfus, Duane. "Partial Pre-publication Review Gaining Favor at Newspapers." *Newspaper Research Journal*, Fall 2006, pp. 23–37. The researcher surveyed the 50 largest newspapers to determine policies toward prepublication review. He found that the trend is to permit it.

Suggested Web Sites

www.regrettheerror.com/2006/12/crunks_06_the_y.html
Regret the Error is a Web site that chronicles errors made in all media. It is valuable in that it shows how fallible even professional reporters are.

www.stateofthenewsmedia.com/2006/
The Project for Excellence in Journalism produces an annual "State of the News Media" report that examines journalistic trends and economic trends.

www.wsu.edu:8080/~brians/errors/index.html
Paul Brians, a professor of English at Washington State University, will answer your questions about the English language.

Exercises

1. Identify the "who," "what," "where," "when," "why" and "how," if they are present, in the following lead:

   The United Jewish Appeal is sponsoring its first-ever walk-a-thon this morning in Springfield to raise money for The Soup Kitchen, a place where the hungry can eat free.

2. Here are four versions of the same lead. Which of the four answers more of the six questions basic to all stories? Which questions does it answer?

   a. What began 12 years ago with a federal staff investigation and led to hearings and a court fight culminates today with a Federal Trade Commission rule to prevent funeral home rip-offs.

   b. The nation's funeral home directors are required to offer detailed cost statements starting today, a service they say they are now ready to provide despite nearly a dozen years of debate over the idea.

   c. A new disclosure law going into effect today will make it easier for consumers to determine the cost of a funeral.

   d. Twelve years after first being proposed, a federal regulation goes into effect Monday to require funeral homes to provide an itemized list of services and materials they offer, along with the cost of each item, before a person agrees to any arrangements.

3. Rewrite two of the leads in exercise 2 as "you" leads. Which are better, the third-person or second-person leads? Why are they better?

4. From the following facts, write a lead.

   Who: a nuclear weapon with a yield equivalent to 150,000 tons of TNT.

   What: detonated.

   Where: 40 miles from a meeting of pacifists and 2,000 feet beneath the surface of Pahute Mesa in the Nevada desert.

   When: Tuesday.

   Why: to test the weapon.

   How: not applicable.

   Other information: Department of Energy officials are the source; 450 physicians and peace activists were gathered to protest continued nuclear testing by the United States.

5. From the following facts, write the first two paragraphs of a news article.

   Who: 7-year-old boy missing for three years.

   What: found.

   Where: in Brick Township, N.J.

   When: Monday night.

   Why: not applicable.

   How: A neighbor recognized the child's picture when it was shown after the movie *Adam: The Song Continues* and called police.

   Other information: Police arrested the boy's mother, Ellen Lynn Conner, 27; she faces Alabama charges of kidnapping and interference with a custody warrant.

6. From the following facts, write the first two paragraphs of a news article.

   Who: 40 passengers.

   What: evacuated from a Northwest Airlines jet, Flight 428.

   When: at the LaCrosse, Wis., Municipal Airport.

   When: Monday following a flight from Minneapolis to LaCrosse.

Why: A landing tower employee spotted smoke near the wheels.

How: not applicable.

Other information: There was no fire or injuries; the smoke was caused by hydraulic fluids leaking onto hot landing brakes, according to Bob Gibbons, a Northwest spokesman.

7. Describe picture and information-graphic possibilities for the story in exercise 6.

8. Cut out six leads from newspapers. Determine which basic questions are answered and which are not. Identify the kind of lead used.

9. Read the Education Trust report at **www2.edtrust.org/ EdTrust/Press+Room/Engines+of+Inequality.htm**. Write a local story for your school paper.

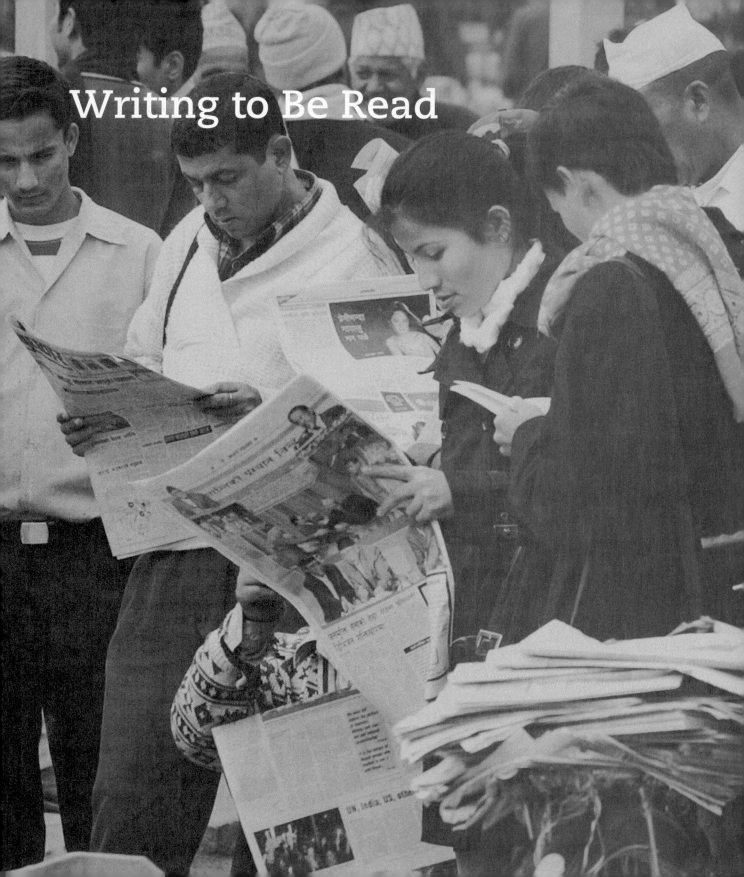

Writing to Be Read

8

Whether you are writing a newspaper story, a television script, a news release or an article for a Web site, a good story told well is important to readers and viewers and to the financial success of your company. Many journalists are getting the message. That is why we see stories like this more often:

By MICHAEL WEINREB
The New York Times
WILMINGTON, Del.— When she was 3 years old, Elena Delle Donne used a wrench to detach the training wheels from her bicycle, then taught herself to ride as her parents watched from inside the house.

This was, her father said, one of the first hints at the extent of the preternatural gifts his daughter possessed. The signs kept coming.

When she was in elementary school, Delle Donne watched a physical-education teacher juggle three balls, then, within minutes, taught herself the trick. She played free safety on a youth league football team. And when she attended a basketball camp in the summer between seventh and eighth grade, she learned that North Carolina Coach Sylvia Hatchell had invited her father, Ernie, into an office to offer a scholarship.

"I thought, does she have the right parent?" Ernie Delle Donne said.

In a way, it all made sense: Ernie Delle Donne is 6 feet 6 inches and played basketball at Columbia. His wife, Joan, is 6-2 and was a swimmer and tennis player. Their son, Gene, is a 6-5 quarterback who recently transferred to Middle Tennessee State from Duke. But their daughter, who is a 6-5 junior at Ursuline Academy, an all-girls Catholic high school here, has emerged as more than just the best women's basketball prospect in the class of 2008 and the latest target of recruiters from N.C.A.A. Division I powers like Tennessee, Duke and Connecticut.

If Delle Donne lives up to her potential, scouts say, she could become one of a handful of talented players in recent years who have helped change the way the women's game is played.

"If you're 6-5 or bigger, you're pretty much set as long as you can walk," said Chris Hansen, the national director of scouting for HoopGurlz.com, which tracks the sport. "But there aren't many people like her who are that big and that mobile."

Delle Donne, 17, has the height of a center, but her skills set her apart. She can play in the paint and on the perimeter. She can pass, run the floor and set screens. Her shooting range extends beyond the 3-point arc, and she set a national record last season by hitting 80 consecutive free throws.

Candace Parker, a 6-4 forward at Tennessee who in March became the first woman to dunk in an N.C.A.A. tournament game, may be more athletic, Hansen said, but Delle Donne appears more versatile. All of that has led some to whisper that Delle Donne could become the LeBron James of the women's game.

"LeBron James, he's unheard of," Delle Donne said.

But just as James blossomed into a celebrity before his senior year of high school, Delle Donne has grown accustomed to giving interviews and playing before sold-out crowds and fighting off double- and triple-teams. During a game against Middletown High School on Thursday, with representatives from Tennessee, Duke and other programs watching from the bleachers of Ursuline's modest gym, she was harassed and thrown off-balance and faced a series of gimmicky defenses.

Despite struggling with her shot, she never seemed particularly bothered by it all and finished with 17 points, 7 rebounds, 4 assists and 4 blocked shots in a 45-29 victory.

[On Monday, at the Nike Tournament of Champions in Chandler, Ariz., she scored 40 points and blocked 11 shots in a victory over Cleveland (Tenn.), the No. 8 team in *USA Today*'s national poll. Ursuline is ranked 10th.]

"In watching her for four years as an observer, I thought she was the best high school player I've seen," said Ursuline Coach Fran Burbidge, a former college assistant coach who took over the program before this season. "But being around her and coaching her, she's better than I thought. This kid is a threat from anywhere on the floor."

It is a philosophy rooted in years of training, beginning in the second grade, when Delle Donne began working with John Noonan, a former high school point guard and physical therapist whom Ernie Delle Donne met while rehabilitating an injured ankle. Ernie Delle Donne and Noonan went to one of Gene Delle Donne's youth-league games, and Ernie was impressed enough with Noonan's basketball advice that he hired him to coach his son.

Eventually, Ernie started taking his daughter along with him, with the notion that he did not want her to be trained as only a post player because of her height. "I thought, what a great idea, to have this tall girl learn the game through the eyes of a point guard," he said.

At their first session, Noonan said, he was so mesmerized by Elena's abilities that they ran through drills for 45 minutes before she tapped him on the shoulder and asked if she could stop for a drink of water. "As a second grader, she played like a freshman in high school," Noonan said. "She's always been looked at as being older than she is, and she acts that way, too. Her composure is well beyond her years."

It is a trait that, if anything, leads people to underestimate her. If there is a knock on Delle Donne, it is her intensity on defense. At times, her effortlessness has been interpreted as laziness. But it was not until he started coaching her, Burbidge said, that he realized Delle Donne was much quicker than he realized.

Ursuline's assistant coach, Peg Desendorf, said Delle Donne's impact was so subtle in last season's state championship game that it seemed almost impossible to believe when she finished with 50 of her team's 68 points. The opponent, St. Elizabeth, scored 51.

"Every aspect of my game can always get better," Delle Donne said. "I just try to ignore all the outside influences and stuff."

Still, it is a great burden for any teenager to handle these intimations that, with players like Parker at Tennessee and Diana Taurasi in the W.N.B.A., she could help alter the way the game is played and viewed.

But Delle Donne has a built-in method of disregarding such heady proclamations: Every afternoon, she returns home and sees her older sister, the one member of her family who will never be an athlete, the one member of her family, she said, who holds them all together.

Elizabeth Delle Donne is 22. She has autism and cerebral palsy. She is blind and deaf and has been through more than 30 operations. She has a full-time caregiver and spends much of her time in bed. When she does make it out, she goes to the Mary Campbell Center, a local home for the disabled.

The residents there have no idea who Elena Delle Donne is, she said. But they see this impossibly tall girl who carries herself without a trace of awkwardness, and they scramble to take her picture.

You've just read a story full of specific examples packed into sentences with proper syntax. The writer invites you to keep reading ("The signs kept coming"), and the story has a surprise ending. Readers don't see that type of writing as often as they should. Some are voting with their feet; they are abandoning newspapers and magazines. Editors are looking at clips more closely for clarity and creativity, not just in feature stories but also in news stories.

There's even some research to support the idea that newspapers are not as easy to read as they should be. Using the Flesch Reading Ease formula, researchers at the University of Texas looked at a century of writing in novels and newspapers. They concluded that novels had become easier to read and newspapers had become harder.

Readability is a measurement of such things as the number of words in a sentence, the number of syllables in a word and the number of ideas in a sentence. In general, the more of them there are, the harder a sentence is to understand. Can we blame readers, then, for reeling when they encounter this typical lead?

> WASHINGTON—A 10-year study of an increasingly popular surgical technique used to correct poor distance vision shows that the method is reasonably safe and effective but that it might lead to an accelerated decline in the ability to see things up close, researchers said Wednesday.

That's 45 words. Hidden somewhere in the thicket is the main idea. In case the readers were still standing, the writer followed this with a 47-word sentence.

If you're thinking that science is a complicated subject calling for complicated writing, how do you explain this lead on a government story?

> Hoping to prevent a recurrence of the wrongdoing uncovered during a recent nine-month undercover investigation at one of its main work sites, the New Orleans Sewerage & Water Board plans to hire a chief of security and devise a plan to prevent crimes by employees.

Writing to inform and entertain is as important for journalists as it is for novelists. Just because newspapers and broadcast reports are done and gone in a day doesn't mean that we should accept a lower level of skill. Comparing the temporal nature of newspapers to a beach, syndicated columnist James Kilpatrick challenged writers: "If we write upon the sand, let us write as well as we can upon the sand before the waves come in."

If Kilpatrick's challenge to your pride is not enough, then the demands of readers and listeners and of editors and news directors who are hiring should be. Editors are looking for those unusual people who can combine reporting and writing talents. The journalist whose prose jerks around the page like a mouse trapped in a room with a cat has no future in the business. The American Society of Newspaper Editors has

> **"**There's nothing to writing. All you do is sit down at a typewriter and open a vein.**"**
>
> — Red Smith, newspaper sports columnist

made improved writing one of its principal long-range goals. Each year, in cooperation with the Poynter Institute of St. Petersburg, Fla., it awards $1,000 to the winners in several categories of the writing competition it sponsors. The winning entries are published annually by the institute in a book series titled *Best Newspaper Writing*. ASNE posts the winning entries and many of its reports on writing at www.asne.org/index.cfm?ID=1469.

Many well-known writers—among them Daniel Defoe, Mark Twain, Stephen Crane and Ernest Hemingway—began their careers as journalists. A more recent list would include John Hersey, Tom Wolfe and Gay Talese. The best-seller list is peppered with the names of journalists: Bob Woodward, Russell Baker, Ellen Goodman, Anna Quindlen, Richard Ben Cramer, Ron Rosenbaum, Tom Brokaw and Edna Buchanan. At newspapers around the country today, small but growing numbers of journalists are producing literature daily as they deal with everything from accidents to affairs of state. If you have respect for the language, an artist's imagination and the dedication to learn how to combine them, you, too, may produce literature.

We should all attempt to bring quality writing, wit and knowledge to our work. If we succeed, our work will be not only informative but also enjoyable, not only educational but also entertaining and not only bought but also read.

GOOD WRITING BEGINS WITH GOOD REPORTING

Without the proper ingredients, the best chef is no better than a short-order cook. Without the proper use of participant accounts, personal observation and detail, the best writer's stories land with a thud. Good writing begins with good reporting. You can settle for a dry police report, or you can go to the scene and gather details. In Chapter 7 we introduced you to this lead:

> Two people died Thursday when a backhoe fell off a truck's flatbed and sliced the top off an oncoming vehicle near Fairchild Air Force Base.

Now let's look at some of the detail writer Alison Boggs of *The (Spokane, Wash.) Spokesman-Review* collected by being there:

> The top of the Suburban, from about hood height, was shorn off by the backhoe's bucket. The front seats were forced backward, and the dashboard, roof and steering wheel were torn off.
>
> Parts of the car lay in a heap of crumpled metal and glass under the overpass. The silver Suburban was identifiable only by a 1983 owner's manual lying in the dirt nearby.
>
> Both victims wore seat belts, but in this case, that was irrelevant, (Sgt. Jeff) Sale said. Both suffered severe head injuries.
>
> Sleeping bags, a Coleman cooler and fishing equipment scattered on the highway and in the back of the Suburban suggested a camping trip. Unopened cans of Pepsi were jammed behind the front seat of the car.

ON THE JOB

Sharing the Experience Through Vivid Writing

By the time she had been out of school only 10 years, Patricia Rodriguez had already worked at the *Springfield (Mo.) News-Leader*, *The Cincinnati Enquirer*, *USA Weekend* and the *Dallas Times Herald*. Now she is the features editor of the *Fort Worth Star-Telegram*, where she oversees the paper's food, travel and daily arts and lifestyle sections. She has freelanced for the *Chicago Tribune*, the *San Francisco Chronicle*, *The Miami Herald*, *The (Baltimore) Sun* and many other publications.

So when she talks about writing, she is speaking from experience.

"The slickest writing can't disguise shallow reporting. Besides just getting the good quotes, that means writing down descriptions, smells, sounds. I also try to write down analogies as I think of them, out in the field or even in the car back to the office. It's easier and more accurate than trying to be clever in front of the computer."

She tries to avoid the temptation to overwrite.

"Don't use stuffy phrases or overload your piece with qualifiers. Tell a story: Write with active words, use natural language, and tie everything together from beginning to end.

"After you finish your interviews, try to remember the anecdotes and facts you couldn't wait to tell your roommate or deskmate. Try to get as many of those in the story as you can, even if you thought they were asides or not the story you set out to get."

She also writes for the ear.

"Read your stuff out loud, at least your lead. Yes, you'll feel goofy, but it gives you a sense of pace and rhythm and tells you which sentences are too complex and wordy."

Notice that the writer built every sentence on concrete detail. Now re-examine the story that opened this chapter. In the first three paragraphs, there are four examples of things Delle Donne did that showed she would be an extraordinary athlete. Good reporting made good writing possible.

ACCURATE, SPECIFIC DETAILS

Good writing is accurate because it is built on concrete details. When you use language to communicate those details precisely, you inform and entertain your readers.

Use Concrete Examples

For lawyers, the devil may be in the details, but for writers, clarity is in the details. Echoing your bureaucratic sources, you can write of infrastructures or facilities or learning pods. But try actually touching any of these. By contrast, you ride on a highway, sit in an arena and learn in a reading group.

Be specific. The speaker is big (compared to what?). The speaker is loud (how loud?). Abstractions are ambiguous. To someone who is 6 feet tall, someone big may be 6 feet 6 inches tall. To someone who is 5 feet 2 inches tall, 6 feet is huge.

Look at the concrete details in the following lead from *The Boston Globe* about an employee who killed five co-workers:

> He was an accountant who had a chip on his shoulder and a bayonet on his kitchen table. He lived with his parents across from a llama farm in a small beige house with a sign informing visitors: "Trespassers will be shot; survivors will be shot again."
>
> As dawn broke over Ledyard yesterday, Matthew Beck, 35, left his folks' home— across town from the casino—got in his car, and drove 1½ hours to his job at Connecticut Lottery headquarters. At some point, he strapped a bandolier of bullets across his chest, over his gray pin-striped shirt but concealed by a brown leather jacket. He carried a 9mm pistol and a knife.

Nearly every sentence contains specific, concrete detail: "accountant," "bayonet," "across from a llama farm," and so on. Here's a student writer at Indiana University who could have reported simply that several things were missing in the apartment. Instead, she used concrete detail:

> When she awoke the next morning, the window was completely open. Random items, including a toaster, a 15-year-old broken VCR, an empty bookbag and the remote control to a stereo were missing.

To be concrete, you must have facts. And you must describe those facts in a way that makes readers able to touch and examine them. Lazy reporters create puffballs. Poke their stories, and you'll stick your finger clear through them. Instead of saying, "Some council members," say, "Five council members." Instead of writing that a business is "downsizing," report that 150 workers will lose their jobs. Avoid abstractions; covet concrete details.

Show, Don't Just Tell

As you chauffeur the reader through the scenes in your story, you can drive down the road or over the green-laced, rolling hills of Kentucky. You can report that a car hit a skunk, or you can convey the nauseating smell. A word here, a phrase there, and you can hear the plane ripping the tin roof off the house, smell the acrid stench of burning tires, feel the boxing glove's leather rasp against the skin. Good writing appeals to one or more of our five senses: sight, hearing, smell, taste and touch.

> **"**There's a time to sow and a time to reap, but there's never a time for seasonal agricultural activities.**"**
>
> — Jack Cappon, Associated Press senior writer and writing coach

In addition to years of anecdotal experience, there is also statistical support for the advice to show rather than tell. For instance, researchers constructed 10 sentences telling information and 10 showing information. College students were divided into two groups and asked to read one of the groups of sentences. Then they were asked to rate the sentences on such qualities as interesting/dull, clear/unclear and engaging/unengaging. The authors concluded, "The experiment found strong evidence that, as many experts have implied, show sentences are seen as more interesting and engaging than tell sentences."

Writer Walt Harrington could simply have told readers that detective V.I. Smith picked up his notebook to leave on a call, but he showed us his preparation:

> "Well, here we go," says V.I., in his smooth, lyrical baritone as he palms a radio, unconsciously pats his right breast coat pocket for evidence of his ID wallet, pats his left breast coat pocket for evidence of his notebook and heads out the door in his athlete's saunter, a stylized and liquid stroll, a modern cakewalk.

Readers can see and hear V.I. because the writer is showing, not telling.

Notice Julie Sullivan's power of observation in her profile of a resident of Spokane in the *Spokesman Review*:

> Joe Peak's smile has no teeth.
>
> His dentures were stolen at the Norman Hotel, the last place he lived in downtown Spokane before moving to the Merlin two years ago.
>
> Gumming food and fighting diabetes have shrunk the 54-year-old man's frame by 80 pounds. He is thin and weak and his mouth is sore.

A student writer used her sense of touch to gather information: "After 40 years of working outside, his skin is as leathery as an alligator's." Did she actually touch him? "Yes," she says. "I kept looking at his skin. Finally, even though I was embarrassed, I asked him if I could touch his face. He laughed. 'You can tell I don't use no fancy lotions, can't you?'"

The writing is better because the reporters didn't just ask questions and record answers. They looked; they touched; they listened. Readers can see and feel along with the reporters.

Translate Numbers

To many journalists and readers, numbers are a foreign language. It is our job as journalists to learn that language of numbers and to translate them so that our readers understand.

TIPS

Avoiding Carelessness in Word Choice

● Know precisely what you want to say.

● Use the conditional mood ("could," "might," "should," "would") when discussing proposals.

● Choose the correct sentence structure to communicate explicitly what you mean.

The most important way to increase comprehension is to compare numbers and sizes. Authorities may announce that forest fires destroyed vegetation over 500 square miles. What does that mean to your readers? One way to make it meaningful is to compare the numbers, the unknown, to something known. Readers in California can understand how large an area that is if they are told the forest fire destroyed an area four times the size of San Francisco. Check your city directory for the size and population of your community.

You can translate large budget numbers on campus by expressing them as spending per student. You can translate a tax increase by expressing it as cost per citizen. You can translate the rate of crime by expressing it as the number of crimes each minute or hour or day in your city or per capita. One newspaper examining the lack of screening for teachers expressed the findings this way:

> Spokane cabbies and Nevada blackjack dealers face tougher screening through background checks than teachers in 42 states.

If every journalist wrote about numbers in plain English, as that one did, more readers would understand.

Use Words Precisely

Words should mean exactly what you intend them to mean. You should never use "uninterested" when you mean "disinterested." Nor should you use "allude" for "refer," "presume" for "assume," "endeavor" for "try," "fewer" for "less," "farther" for "further." If you report that fire destroyed a house, you mean the home needs rebuilding, not repair. If you say firefighters donned oxygen masks to enter a burning building, you are impugning either their intelligence or yours. (Oxygen is dangerous around fire; firefighters use air tanks.) You can make the mayor "say," "declare," "claim" or "growl" — but only one is accurate.

THE TOOLS OF NARRATION

The tools of narration allow you to build interest in stories. When we use scenes, dialogue and anecdotes, we are using narrative tools that help make our stories as entertaining as they are interesting. In exposition, the writer clearly stands between the reader and the information: Journalists have sources, who tell them things. Journalists then tell the reader what they heard and saw. Scenes, dialogue and anecdotes allow the reader to see the action. If you also learn to tease this good stuff with foreshadowing, readers will be more likely to read it. But more about foreshadowing later.

Scenes

Gene Roberts, former managing editor of *The New York Times*, tells about his first job at a daily newspaper. His publisher, who was blind, had someone read the newspaper to him each morning. One day, the publisher called Roberts into his office and complained, "Roberts, I can't see your stories. Make me see."

We should all try to make readers see, smell, feel, taste and hear. One way to do that is to write using scenes as much as possible. To write a scene, you have to be there. You need to capture the pertinent sights, sounds and smells.

A student reporter at South Dakota State University was there to capture this opening scene:

Don Sheber's leathery, cracked hands have been sculpted by decades of wresting a living from the earth.

But this year, despite work that often stretches late into the evening, the moisture-starved soil has yielded little for Sheber and his family.

Sheber's hands tugged at the control levers on his John Deere combine last week as rotating blades harvested the thin stands of wheat that have grown to less than a foot high.

The writer allows the reader to visit Sheber on the farm. We can see and feel the farmer's hands. We can touch the John Deere combine and the stunted wheat.

To create such scenes, you must use all your senses to gather information, and your notebook should reflect that reporting. Along with the results of interviews, your notebook should bulge with details of sights and smells, sounds and textures. David Finkel, winner of the American Society of Newspaper Editors Distinguished Writing Award in 1986 and a Pulitzer Prize in 2006, says, "Anything that pertains to any sense I feel at any moment, I write down." Gather details indiscriminately. Later, you can discard those that are not germane. Because you were there, you can write the scene as if you were writing a play.

"Don Sheber's leathery, cracked hands have been sculpted by decades of wresting a living from the earth." Use descriptive language to paint a vivid picture for readers and to bring a story to life.

TIPS

Moving Your Story Along

● Create vivid scenes.

● Let the actors speak to each other through dialogue. (When the source tells the reporter, who tells the reader, you have a *quotation*. When the reporter records the conversation of two or more people speaking not to the reporter but to each other, you have *dialogue*.)

● Foreshadow important events.

● Relate memorable anecdotes.

Because Bartholomew Sullivan of *The (Memphis) Commercial Appeal* was observing and listening closely at a trial, his readers were able to sit in the courtroom with him:

Helfrich banged an index finger on the rail of the jury box as he recalled Thursday's testimony in which a string of Bowers's Jones County friends testified that he was a solid businessman, a Christian—"a gentleman." One of the witnesses was Nix, who called Bowers a "real, real nice man."

"They talk of gentlemen," Helfrich whispered. Then, shouting, he said: "These people don't have a gentle bone in their bodies. They were nightriders and henchmen. They attacked a sleeping family and destroyed all they owned."

Analyze the detail: banging his index finger, the whisper, the shout. We can see and we can hear.

Another scene from another trial was written by Peter St. Onge, then of *The Huntsville Times*. By creating a scene, he allows readers to watch and listen:

"I not only lost a wife, I lost a best friend, thanks to you two," he said, looking at the boys. "My son looks for his mother to come back. I have to explain to him that his mother's in heaven. I have to explain what you two did."

Johnson rocked back and forth at the

words, nodding his head and wiping his eyes. Golden stared blankly, expressionless as he had been all hearing. When Golden's attorney, Val Price, objected and the judge cautioned Wright not to speak directly to the boys, Wright smiled wryly and continued.

In both of these examples, we are transported to the courtrooms because the writers worked in scenes. Neither writer wrote his entire story in scenes, as it would be in a movie script, but both created scenes when possible. The stories were richer for those scenes.

Dialogue

The use of *dialogue*—conversation between two or more people, not including the reporter—allows the reporter to recede and the characters to take center stage. When you use quotations, you—the writer—are repeating for the reader what the source said, and the reader listens to you relating what was said. But when you use dialogue, the writer disappears, and the reader listens directly to the characters. Dialogue is a key element in creating scenes. Compare these examples:

During the public hearing, Henry Lathrop accused the council of wasting taxpayers' money. "If you don't stop voting for all this spending, I am going to circulate a recall petition and get you all kicked off the council," he said.

Mayor Margorie Gold told Lathrop he was free to do as he wished. "As for us," she said, "we will vote in the best interests of the city."

That is the traditional way of presenting quotations. The reporter is telling readers what was said instead of taking readers to the council chambers and letting them listen. Here is how that account would sound handled as dialogue:

When Henry Lathrop spoke to the City Council during the public hearing, he pounded on the podium. "You folks are wasting taxpayers' money. If you don't stop voting for all this spending, I am going to circulate a recall petition and get you all kicked off the council."

Mayor Margorie Gold slammed her gavel on her desk.

"Mr. Lathrop," she said as she tried to control the anger in her voice. She looked at him directly. "You are free to do as you wish. As for us, we will vote in the best interests of the city."

At the hearing, Lathrop and Gold were speaking to each other. The second version captures the exchange without the intercession of the writer.

Here's another example of dialogue. This conversation took place between Cindy Martling, a rehabilitation nurse, and Mary Jo, the patient's wife, after Martling scolded the patient for feeling sorry for himself:

She wandered around a bit, then saw Mary Jo standing in the hallway. The two women went to each other and embraced. "I'm sorry," Martling said through more tears. "I didn't mean to lose control. I hope I didn't offend you."

"What you did was wonderful," Mary Jo said. "He needed to hear that. Dan is going to work through it, and we're all going to be OK."

Anecdotes

The ultimate treats, anecdotes are stories embedded in stories. They can be happy or sad, funny or serious. Whatever their tone, they should illustrate a point. Readers are likely to remember the anecdotes more readily than anything else in a story. You probably remember the stories that your professors tell regardless of whether you remember the rest of the lecture. Long after you've forgotten this chapter, you will probably remember some of the examples from it. Facts inform. Anecdotes inform and entertain.

Befitting something so valuable, anecdotes are hard to obtain. You can't get them by asking your source, "Got any good anecdotes?" But you can get them by asking for examples so you can re-create the scene.

That's what Kelly Whiteside of *USA Today* did after Michelle Snow of the Tennessee Lady Vols stole the ball, thundered the length of the court and dunked the ball two-handed during a game. Players on her team jumped and screamed; even the opposing team and its fans cheered. Five days later, Whiteside wanted to know what happened in the locker room at halftime after this historic event in women's basketball. It was only the third time in NCAA history that a woman had dunked during a game.

Afterward, the Lady Vols waited for coach Pat Summitt to come into the locker room. They wondered how she would react. After all, Summitt, the John Wooden of the women's game, is a purist who always said that dunking was overrated. At halftime, the locker room door creaked open, and Summitt

"When your reporters feel the innovative Impulse, suggest that they lie down until it goes away."

— James Kilpatrick, syndicated columnist

walked in. Her piercing blue eyes were focused intensely, and a serious look was frozen on her face. Summitt turned toward Snow.

"Nice high-post steal there, Snow," Summitt said. And everyone in the locker room dissolved in laughter as Summitt gave Snow a high-five.

If Whiteside had handled the story in typical expository fashion, she would have quoted Snow or other sources in the locker room something like this:

Snow said she and her teammates wondered if Coach Pat Summitt approved of the dunk.

"We were all sitting quietly in the locker room at halftime," Snow said . . .

Instead, Whiteside called Snow and asked her several specific questions, such as "What did you do when you got in the locker room?" and "What did Pat Summitt say?"

"She needed to be my eyes and ears," Whiteside said of Snow.

Whiteside also needed to talk to others to get more detail and to corroborate the information Snow had given her. Summitt told her that she had come into the locker room with a serious look on her face and had given Snow a high-five, two details Snow hadn't volunteered. Whiteside also talked to Debby Jennings, the Sports Information director, also present in the locker room.

"Each person added something," Whiteside said. As a result, she was able to re-create the scene rather than merely report what happened.

Phrase your questions to get stories. For example, when someone tells you that another person is a practical joker, you want to ask, "Can you give me an example of that?" Some of the best anecdotal examples come from phrasing questions in the superlative: "What's the funniest thing that ever happened to you while you were standing in front of an audience?" "What's the worst case you've ever seen come into this emergency room?"

Foreshadowing

Foreshadowing is the technique of giving hints about what's coming. Moviemakers tease you with the scenes they think will encourage you to buy a ticket. Broadcasters foreshadow to keep you from leaving during a commercial: "Coming up, there's a burglar prowling your neighborhood." Every lead foreshadows the story. The leads that not only tell but promise more good stuff to come are the most successful. Tom Koetting, then of *The Wichita Eagle*, spent nine months observing the recovery of a doctor who had nearly lost his life in a farm accident. He produced a story of about 100,000 words. The simple lead promised great things to come: "Daniel Calliendo Jr. had not expected to meet death this calmly."

A student at Florida A&M University used the same technique to invite readers to continue the story:

A North Carolina family thought the worst was behind them when they were robbed Saturday morning at a gas station just off Interstate 95.

The worst was yet to come.

The worst was yet to come. That's another way of saying, "Read on; the story gets even better."

In the next example, you see a longer opening that is packed with promises of great things to come. It was written by Patricia Rodriguez, then a student at the University of Missouri. (See the "On the Job" box earlier in this chapter.)

> Deena Borman's relationship with her roommate, Teresa, during her freshman year in college had shattered long before the wine bottle.
>
> Weeks had gone by with Teresa drawing further and further away from Deena. Finally, after repeatedly hearing Teresa talk about suicide, Deena says, "I kept telling her how silly she was to want to die."
>
> That made Teresa angry, so she threw a full wine bottle at Deena. It shattered against the wall and broke open the simmering conflict between them. That was when Deena tried to find out what had gone wrong with Teresa's life, and that was when Teresa told Deena that she wanted to do something to get rid of her.
>
> And that was when Deena began to be scared of her own roommate.

The writer is promising a great story. What is wrong with Teresa? Does Teresa really try to hurt Deena? Does Deena really have something to be scared about? There is a promise of great things to come. Would you keep reading?

COHERENCE

When you write coherently, your writing is understandable. Coherence is built on a logical structure, by matching the content to the appropriate sentence structure, by using the correct coordinating conjunctions and by guiding readers with transitions.

Decide on the Order of Elements

A story must have a beginning, a middle and an end. When put in a maze, rats make many wrong turns before they find their way out. So do writers who start a story without knowing where it is going. A coherent story is one in which the information is logically connected.

Chronology is the most easily understood of story structures. You start at the beginning and go to the end. (For more on story structure, see Chapter 9.) Journalists, however, often don't have the luxury of readers' time or publication space to use chronology. That's why it is important to outline a story, even if your outline merely lists the three or four points you expect to make. Your outline is your map. If you know where you are going, your readers will be able to follow.

Here's a simple outline you might make for a story about a city council meeting:

> **"**But I obsess during writing to the point where I can lose sleep over the right word.**"**
>
> — Madeleine Blais, writer

1. Approved one-way streets.
2. Raised parking fines.
3. Bought snowplows.
4. Will study downtown parking.
5. Hired audit firm.

You rank the actions in order of importance. Then you decide whether to focus on one element or write a summary lead or a multiple-element lead. (See Chapter 7 for more on leads.) Once you have done that, you add detail to your outline:

1. Single-element lead: one-way streets
2. Summary of other actions
   a. parking fines
   b. snowplows
   c. parking facilities
   d. city audit
3. Support for lead
   a. the vote
   b. Jones quote
   c. opposition
4. Support for other actions in order introduced in second paragraph
   a. Raised parking fines
      (i) Amount; (ii) reason; (iii) no opposition
   b. Bought snowplows
      (i) Cost; (ii) when delivered
   c. Downtown parking
      (i) Define problem; (ii) when study is due; (iii) who will do it; (iv) Dehaven quote; (v) Chamber of Commerce request
   d. Audit firm
      (i) Who will do it; (ii) cost; (iii) when due

Although outlining may take five minutes, it will save you much more time. The outline also creates a structure that flows logically from one idea to the next. Here's how you could start the story outlined above:

> The Springfield City Council voted Tuesday to make four streets in the downtown area one-way.
>   The council also raised parking fines to $5, voted to buy two snowplows, ordered a study of downtown parking facilities and hired a firm to audit the city.
>   Effective March 1, the four streets that will be one-way are . . .

Select the Proper Sentence Structure

Within each sentence, you must express the proper relationships between ideas. One way to do this is to think about your sentence structure. Simple sentences ex-

---

TIPS

Writing a Coherent Story

- Create logical story structures.

- Express the relationship between ideas properly.

- Use transitions.

- Use language precisely.

press one idea. Compound sentences express two or more ideas of equal importance. Complex sentences subordinate one idea to another. Here are some examples.

Simple	The mayor scolded the council.
Compound	The mayor scolded the council, and she insisted on a vote. (Equates the two ideas.)

Compound sentences equate two or more ideas without commenting on them. Complex sentences allow you to show sequence and cause and effect, among other things:

Complex	After the mayor scolded the council, she insisted on a vote. (Shows sequence.)
Complex	Because the mayor was angry, she insisted on a vote. (Shows cause and effect.)

Each sentence is correct, but the meaning of each is slightly different.

Use the Precise Conjunction

Subordinating conjunctions—such as "if," "since," "while," "after" and "until"—each carry a different and precise meaning. Choose the subordinating conjunction that expresses the idea you want.

Coordinating conjunctions ("and," "or," "but," "for," "nor," "so," "yet") also require careful selection. Observe how the meaning changes with the conjunction in this example:

The mayor insisted that the council vote, and the members ignored her.

The mayor insisted that the council vote, but the members ignored her.

The second example is more coherent because it expresses the council members' reaction more logically.

Use Transitions

Transitions are words, phrases, sentences or paragraphs that show the logical progression of the story structure and the ideas within the structure. Transitions are road signs directing traffic on the information highway. Figure 8.1 shows how transitions can be used in a story.

The reference to memory in the next example directs us from the first to the second paragraph:

Mr. and Mrs. Lester Einbender are using their memory
to project life as it might have been.
   That memory centers around a son named Michael,
a rheumatic disease called lupus and a desire to honor
one while conquering the other.

Using Transitions

On a Monday afternoon, Dr. Glenn Billman pulled back from the autopsy he was performing on a dead girl and stared at the sight before him.

In his seven years at Children's Hospital, he had never seen anything like it. The girl's colon was severely hemorrhaged, ravaged by bacteria that normally lived in a cow's intestine.

Puzzled and quietly alarmed, Billman notified local health officials. It was the first indication that the lethal strain of bacteria, E. coli 0157:H7, was on the loose.

But Billman didn't make his discovery at Children's Hospital in Seattle. He made it at Children's Hospital in San Diego, and he made it three weeks before the E. coli epidemic struck the Northwest, killing three children and sickening about 500 people.

In December, San Diego was hit by a small E. coli outbreak that killed the 6-year-old girl and made at least seven other people sick.

It is now being linked to the Seattle outbreak, but in its early stages, San Diego health officials were slow to recognize the crisis, and they have been sharply criticized for failing to notify the public about the E. coli death and illnesses.

"I really believe we need to be safe and not sorry, and the fact is, a girl died in San Diego," said San Diego County Supervisor Dianne Jacob. "I was outraged. The only way I found out was by reading it in the newspaper" after the Northwest outbreak.

When the first Washington cases were reported in mid-January, authorities there immediately queried neighboring states, including California, but were not told about the E. coli death of the San Diego girl. That information would have alerted them about the bacteria's severity and might have pointed them sooner to the source of the contamination.

Like the patients here, the San Diego girl had eaten a hamburger at a Jack in the Box restaurant days before she got sick and died. The seven other E. coli patients had all eaten hamburgers at fast-food restaurants, among them Jack in the Box.

That information was available in early January, according to Dr. Michele Ginsberg, San Diego County epidemiologist. She would not say how many of the seven patients had eaten at Jack in the Box.

"A variety of restaurants were mentioned," she said. "Naming any one of them would create public reaction and perhaps avoidance of those restaurants."

That reticence angers Jacob, the San Diego County supervisor. "I had a follow-up meeting with county health officials, and I have to tell you, very honestly, I was not pleased with their attitude," she said. . . .

Figure 8.1
Transitions, like road signs, help readers understand where they have been and where they are going.

The word "that" beginning the second paragraph is a demonstrative adjective. Its use is subtle, but its impact is dramatic. If you wrote "A memory," you would not link the reader to the memory already mentioned. If you wrote "The memory," you would be more specific, but by writing "That memory," you point directly to the memory mentioned in the preceding paragraph. Because "a" is good only for general references, "a" is called an *indefinite modifier*. Because "the" is more specific, "the" is called a *definite modifier*. Because "that" is most specific, it is a *demonstrative adjective*; it demonstrates precisely the word or phrase to which you are referring when you couple it with the noun ("memory"). When you move from indefinite to definite modifier, then to demonstrative adjective, you climb the ladder of coherence.

Transitions help you achieve coherence, the logical connection of ideas. They guide you from one sentence to the next, from one paragraph to the next. Writers unfamiliar with transitions merely stack paragraphs, like pieces of wood, atop one another. Transitions keep the story, if not the woodpile, from falling apart.

Repeating a word or phrase also helps to keep the story from falling apart. In the preceding example, the writer used a demonstrative adjective and repeated a word. (Other demonstrative adjectives are "this," "these" and "those.")

Parallelism, repetition of a word or grammatical form, is another way to guide readers through a story. Writers frequently use parallelism to achieve coherence.

Writing about the complicated subject of nuclear-waste disposal in America, Donald Barlett and James Steele, then of *The Philadelphia Inquirer*, relied on parallelism for coherence and emphasis. Notice the parallel use of "They said . . ." to start sentences—and the repeated variations of "It cannot":

This assessment may prove overly optimistic. For perhaps in no other area of modern technology have so many experts in the government, industry and science been so wrong so many times over so many years as have those involved in radioactive waste.

They said, repeatedly, that radioactive waste could be handled like any other industrial refuse. It cannot.

They said that science had most of the answers, and was on the verge of getting the few it did not have, for dealing with radioactive waste permanently. It did not, and it does not.

They said that some of it could be buried in the ground, like garbage in a landfill, and that it would pose no health hazard because it would never move. It moved.

They said that liquid radioactive waste could be put in storage tanks, and that rigorous safety systems would immediately detect any leaks. The tanks leaked for weeks and no one noticed.

Chronology and references to time provide other ways to tie a story together. Words and phrases such as "now," "since then" and "two days later" are invaluable in helping readers understand where they have been and where they are going. Chronology is important in everything from reports of automobile accidents (which car entered the intersection first?) to recaps of events that occurred over months or even years. For instance, Barlett and Steele's stories covered 35 years of efforts to store nuclear waste.

CONCISENESS AND SIMPLICITY

Particularly in newspapers and broadcasting where space and time constraints are severe, conciseness is a virtue. However, even when you write for the Web, you have to respect the readers' time. No one has unlimited time or attention to give you.

Aim for Conciseness

Being concise means saying what you need to say in as few words as possible. Some subjects require more details than others. Here are four ways to shorten your stories. (See also Figure 8.2.)

1. **Eliminate some subject areas.** Always ask yourself whether all of the subjects need to be included. No doubt, your editor will have a more dispassionate view of what's needed than you will.
2. **Eliminate redundancies.** One way is to rid your sentences of cabooses, unneeded words or phrases that hitch themselves, like barnacles, onto other words. Delete the barnacles in italics: remand *back*; gather *together*; consensus *of opinion*; *totally* destroyed; *excess* verbiage; open *up*; fall *down*; my *own personal* favorite and strangled *to death*.
3. **Challenge intensive and qualifying adverbs.** Your job is to select the right word so you don't need two or more. Instead of "really unhappy," perhaps you mean "sad." Instead of "very cold," perhaps you mean "frigid." "Really" and "very" are examples of intensive adverbs. When you say "almost there," you are using a qualifying adverb. Be specific.
4. **Train yourself to value brevity.** Some of the most notable writing in history is brief: Lincoln's Gettysburg Address contains 272 words; the Ten Commandments, 297; and the American Declaration of Independence, 300.

You will use fewer words when you figure out what you want to say and then express it positively. Enter the following thicket of verbiage phrased in the negative at your own risk:

> The Missouri Gaming Commission has 30 days to appeal a judge's temporary order reversing the commission's decision not to grant a gaming license to a firm that wanted to dock a riverboat casino in Jefferson City.

The writer is lost in a maze of reversals of negative findings. The lead tries to cover too much territory. Express it in the positive and strip it to its essential information:

> The state has 30 days to persuade a judge it should not have to license a firm that wants to open a riverboat casino in Jefferson City.

The writer of this sentence also failed to think clearly:

TIPS

Writing Clearly

- Keep sentences short.

- Limit each sentence to one idea.

- Favor subject-verb-object sentences.

- Avoid using more than three prepositional phrases in one sentence.

- Avoid using more than three numbers in one sentence.

- Use plain and simple words instead of jargon, journalese, or clichés.

— Paula LaRocque, assistant managing editor, *The Dallas Morning News*

Editing for Conciseness

"Currently" is usually redundant because the verb tense implies it.

"With" is unnecessary.

The plural form gets around the wordy "his or her."

"Season" isn't required in either sentence in this paragraph.

"Strong" and "too" are unnecessary intensifiers.

Bartholow is ~~currently~~ working on other projects, but he ~~has~~ plans to continue ~~with~~ his video game research. ~~In the future,~~ he hopes to recruit female subjects—a difficult task because far fewer women than men play violent video games. He's also interested in examining how ~~a person's prior~~ *people's* gaming history affects ~~his or her~~ *their* response to a single exposure to a violent video game.

Pumpkins are everywhere ~~during the fall season~~ *in fall*. They ~~serve as a way to~~ help families and friends ~~to get closer~~ *bond* during the ~~holiday season~~ *holidays*. Whether you're ~~taking a trip~~ *traveling* to the local pumpkin patch ~~to search for the perfect pumpkin~~, or baking ~~up some delicious~~ treats ~~for people to enjoy~~, pumpkins are a ~~strong~~ reminder that comfort isn't ~~too~~ far away.

Change "has plans" to "plans" to strengthen verb.

"In the future" is already contained in the verb tense.

No information is lost by eliminating "serve as a way to."

"Traveling" says "taking a trip" in one word.

"Up" is an unnecessary caboose on "baking." Treats are delicious. Whom else do you bake treats for?

Figure 8.2
To be concise, challenge every word or phrase you write. These examples show how to eliminate 36 of the 127 words. (The replacement words are in italics.)

Amtrak, formally the National Passenger Railroad Corp., was created in 1970 to preserve declining passenger train service.

Do you suppose the writer meant to write that Amtrak was created to preserve "declining passenger train service"?

Keep It Simple

The readers of one newspaper once confronted the following one-sentence paragraph:

> "Paradoxically, cancer-causing mutations often result from the repair of a cell by error-prone enzymes and not the 'carcinogenic' substance's damage to the cell," Abe Eisenstark, director of biological sciences at the university, said at a meeting of the Ad Hoc Council of Environmental Carcinogenesis Wednesday night at the Cancer Research Center.

If there is a message in those 53 words, it would take a copy editor, a lexicologist and a Nobel Prize-winning scientist to decipher it. The message simply is not clear. Although the sentence is not typical of newspaper writing, it is not unusual either.

"Short is beautiful. Short and simple is more beautiful. Short, simple and interesting is most beautiful."

— Don Gibb, educator

The scientist is using the vocabulary of science, which is inappropriate for a general audience. The reporter should say, "I don't understand that exactly. Can you translate it for my readers?" The response may produce an understandable quote, but if it doesn't, paraphrase it and check back with your source to be sure you have paraphrased it accurately.

Too much of what is written is mumbo jumbo. For instance:

> Approximately 2 billion tons of sediment from land erosion enters our nation's waters every year. While industrial waste and sewage treatment plants receive a great deal of attention, according to the Department of Agriculture the number one polluter of our waterways is "non-point" pollution.

The writer of that lead contributed some linguistic pollution of his own. The message may have been clear in his mind, but it is not clear in print. Here's another way to approach this story:

> Soil carried into the water by erosion, not industrial waste or sewage from treatment plants, is the number one polluter of U.S. waterways, according to the Department of Agriculture.

One remedy for unclear writing is the short sentence. The following examples introduce the same subject:

> NEW YORK—From measurements with high-precision laser beams bounced off reflectors left at three lunar sites by Apollo astronauts, plus one atop an unmanned Soviet lunar vehicle, scientists believe that the moon is still wobbling from a colossal meteorite impact 800 years ago.

> NEW YORK— The moon may still be wobbling from a colossal meteorite impact 800 years ago.

The writer of the first example drags the reader through some prickly underbrush full of prepositional phrases. The writer of the second has cleared the brush to expose the flowers.

CORRECT AND EFFECTIVE LANGUAGE

Writing to be read is not easy. Reporters become writers by the sweat of their brows. John Kenneth Galbraith, a best-selling author who was able to make economics understandable to the lay reader, commented on the difficulty of writing well. "There are days when the result is so bad that no fewer than five revisions are required," he wrote. "In contrast, when I'm inspired, only four revisions are needed."

Trying the techniques discussed in this chapter is the first step. Mastering them will be the result of repeated practice.

Figures of Speech

Good writers understand how to use literary devices known as figures of speech. Similes and metaphors, two common figures of speech, permit writers to show similarities and contrasts. Similes show similarities by comparing one thing to another, often using the word "like" or "as." Talking about a surgeon fighting massive bleeding, Tom Hallman Jr. of *The (Portland) Oregonian* wrote, "If he plunges ahead, it will be like replumbing a house with the water turned on." Writing about a high-school girls' basketball coach, Madeleine Blais wrote, "At 6 feet 6 inches, Moyer looms over his players. With a thick cap of graying brown hair and bangs that flop down over his forehead, he resembles a grizzly bear on spindly legs."

Metaphor is the first cousin of simile. A simile compares one thing to another, but a metaphor says one thing is another: "Michael is a lion with gazelle legs." A metaphor is a stronger analogy than a simile. Describing the radio personality and writer Garrison Keillor, a reporter once wrote, "And there he is. A sequoia in a room full of saplings." The metaphor works on two levels. Keillor is tall enough to tower over most others in the room. Because he is known internationally, his work towers over that of others, too.

With similes and metaphors, writers draw word pictures. These techniques set the pages of a scrapbook of images turning in each reader's mind.

> **"**The real problem is that misplaced modifiers and similar glitches tend to distract readers. Introduce blunders to an otherwise smoothly flowing story and it's as though a drunk stumbled through a religious procession.
>
> "What's more, while those errors due to carelessness may not permanently damage the language, they can damage a paper's credibility. Botching a small job sows mistrust about the larger enterprise.**"**
>
> — Jack Cappon, Associated Press

Careful Word Choice

Freedom in word choice is exhilarating when the result is a well-turned phrase. Here's Dan Berry of *The New York Times* describing a procession one year after the World Trade Center attacks: "The photographs of the dead bobbed upon the swells of the living." Here's Julie Sullivan of *The (Spokane, Wash.) Spokesman-Review*: "Hand him a soapbox, he'll hand you a homily."

Freedom in word choice is dangerous when it results in nouns masquerading as verbs (*prioritize, impact, maximize*) or jargon masquerading as respectable English (*input, output, throughput*).

Precision, however, means more than knowing the etymology of a word; it means knowing exactly what you want to say. Instead of saying, "The City Council wants to locate the landfill three blocks from downtown," to be precise, you say, "Some members of the City Council . . ." or, better yet, "Five members of the City Council . . ."

Precision means using the conditional mood (*could, might, should, would*) when discussing proposals:

Incorrect	The bill will make it illegal . . .
Correct	The bill would make it illegal . . .

The use of "will" is imprecise because the legislation has not been passed. By using "would," you are saying, "If the legislature passes the bill, it would . . ."

Bias-Free Language

Even when used innocently, sexist and racist language, besides being offensive and discriminatory, is imprecise. Doctors aren't always "he," nor are nurses always "she." Much of our language assumes people are male unless it is shown they are female. Precise writers avoid "policeman" (police officer), "ad man" (advertising representative), "assemblyman" (assembly member) and "postman" (postal worker). In some situations, you can use the plural to eliminate the need for a gender-specific word: "Doctors treat their patients."

Our language is bursting with derogatory racial terminology. You should avoid using derogatory terms not only because they are offensive but also because they are imprecise. They rain inaccurate stereotypes on a class of people. To be precise, use Asian-American, black and American Indian. Check your *Associated Press Stylebook* for the proper terminology.

Some words, perfectly precise when used correctly, are imprecise when used in the wrong context. "Boy" is not interchangeable with "young man," and "girl" is not interchangeable with "young woman." Not all active retired people are "spry," which implies that the writer is surprised to find that the person is active. "Grandmotherly" fails when you describe people in their 40s who are grandmothers. It also fails when you use it indiscriminately. When Nancy Pelosi became the first female speaker of the House in 2007, many accounts identified her as a grandmother. While it is true that she's a grandmother, accounts of new male leaders seldom mention that they are grandfathers. Pelosi's wardrobe also became a subject of stories, something seldom found in accounts of male leaders.

"Dumb," as in "deaf and dumb," is imprecise and derogatory. Instead, use "speech-impaired." When the terms are used in tandem, use "hearing-impaired and speech-impaired" for parallelism. Because alcoholism is a disease, use "recovering alcoholic" instead of "reformed alcoholic." "Handicapped" is imprecise; "disabled" is preferred.

The *Los Angeles Times* uses "lesbian" unless the source prefers "gay woman." *Times* reporters also ask sources their preference for describing their "partner," "companion," "lover," and so on. The Associated Press uses "homosexual" and "gay" and does not permit "queer" and other derogatory terms.

The battle over abortion extends to the terms used in news. One side wants to be described as "pro-life"; the other wants to be described as "pro-choice." The Associated Press prescribes the terms "anti-abortion" and "abortion rights" in an attempt to be neutral.

Some dismiss this concern for language as overly zealous political correctness. That attitude implies that we are afraid to tell the truth. What is the truth about eth-

TIPS

Avoiding Sexism in Language

- Use a generic term ("flight attendant," "firefighter").

- Participate in the movement to drop feminine endings. (Use "comedian," "hero" and "poet" for both sexes.)

- Make the subject plural. (Reporters must not reveal their opinions.)

- Drop the gender-specific pronoun and replace it with an article. (A reporter must not form *a* judgment.)

- Rewrite to eliminate the gender-specific pronoun. (A reporter must not judge.)

- Write the sentence in the second person. (You should not form *your* judgment.)

nic slang? The truth is that many words historically applied to groups of people were created in ignorance or hate or fear. During the world wars, American citizens of German descent were called "Krauts" to depersonalize them. Over the years, pejorative terms have been applied to immigrants from Ireland, Poland, China and Africa. We see the same thing happening to more recent immigrants from Latin America, the Caribbean and the Middle East. The adjective "Muslim" is seldom seen or heard in news reports except to modify "terrorists" or "fundamentalists." As writers concerned with precision of the language, we should deal with people, not stereotypes.

Words are powerful. When used negatively, they define cultures, create second-class citizens and reveal stereotypical thinking. They also change the way people think about and treat others. Writers have the freedom to choose precisely the right word. That freedom can be both exhilarating and dangerous.

Correct Grammar and Punctuation

Far too often, grammar and punctuation errors obscure meaning. Consider this example:

> They spent the afternoon at the mall, buying more clothes than they could fit in the trunk.

Because the participial phrase is misplaced, it sounds as if the mall bought clothes. Write the sentence this way:

> Buying more clothes than they needed, they spent the afternoon at the mall.

No one who aspires to be a writer will succeed without knowing the rules of grammar. Dangling participles, subject-verb disagreement, pronoun-antecedent disagreement and misplaced modifiers are like enemy troops: They attack sentences and destroy their meaning, as the authors of a survey discovered.

The personnel director of an Inglewood, Calif., aerospace company had to fill out a government survey form that asked, among other things, "How many employees do you have, broken down by sex?" After considering the sentence for a few moments, she wrote, "Liquor is more of a problem with us."

Here are some typical errors and ways to correct them:

Pronoun-antecedent disagreement	Each of the boys brought *their* sleeping bags.
Correct	Each of the boys brought *his* sleeping bag.
Subject-verb disagreement	The *mayor* together with the city council *oppose* collective bargaining by the firefighters.
Correct	The *mayor* together with the city council *opposes* . . .
	The *mayor and city council oppose* . . .
Misplaced modifier	*Despite his size*, the coach said Jones would play forward.
Correct	The coach said that Jones, *despite his size*, would play forward.

Improper punctuation creates ambiguities at best and inaccuracies at worst. For instance:

> Giving birth to Cynthia five years earlier had been difficult for Mrs. Davenport and the two parents decided they were content with the family they had.

Without the required comma before "and," a person reading quickly misses the pause and sees this: "Giving birth to Cynthia had been difficult for Mrs. Davenport and the two parents." That's a lot of people in the delivery room. (For more examples of common grammar and punctuation errors, see Appendix 1.)

Most newspapers have two or three people who read each story to catch these and other errors. However, the writer's responsibility is to get it right in the first place.

Suggested Readings

Barzun, Jacques. *Simple and Direct*. New York: Harper and Row, 1975. This excellent rhetoric book explains many of the details of sentence construction.

Hart, Jack. *A Writer's Coach*. New York: Pantheon, 2006. This guide helps you understand the "how" and "why" of sentence, paragraph and story construction.

Osborn, Patricia. *How Grammar Works: A Self-Teaching Guide*. New York: John Wiley and Sons, 1999. This book will do for you what it promises: It will guide you, step by step, through the basics of English grammar. Its goal is to make you feel comfortable with grammar and the way words work.

Strunk, William and White, E. B. *The Elements of Style*, Third Edition. Boston: Allyn and Bacon, 1995. This little book practices what it preaches. For the beginner, it is a good primer; for the pro, it is a good review of writing rules and word meanings.

Tankard, James, and Hendrickson, Laura. "Specificity, Imagery in Writing: Testing the Effects of 'Show, Don't Tell.'" *Newspaper Research Journal*, Winter/Spring 1996, pp. 35–48.

Suggested Web Sites

www.nieman.harvard.edu/reports/contents.html
The *Neiman Reports* are all free online. Several issues have articles about writing and reporting. In addition, you will find examples of narrative writing from newspapers around the country.

http://papyr.com/hypertextbooks/comp1/coherent.htm
Daniel Kies of the Department of English at the College of DuPage explains how to achieve coherence in your writing.

www.poynter.org
Select "Writing and Editing," and you will enter a world full of advice, most of it from writers. This is a site you should check often.

Exercises

1. Choose precisely the right word:
   a. We need to (ensure, insure) a victory.
   b. Stop (aggravating, annoying) your friend.
   c. The attorney won because she (refuted, responded to) the allegations.
   d. The prisoner was able to produce (mitigating, militating) evidence.

2. Rewrite Barlett and Steele's story on nuclear-waste disposal (page 177) to take out the parallelism. Which version, the original or yours, is better? Why?

3. Punctuate the following sentences:
   a. Government officials have come under a newly enacted censorship system and several foreign speakers have been denied permission to enter the country.
   b. It was a Monday night and for the next two days he teetered between life and death.
   c. The council approved the manager's proposals and rejected a tax increase.

4. Use an analogy to explain the following numbers:

   The student council's budget is $350,000. The university has 19,000 students. The local city budget is $3 million. The city has 70,000 residents.

5. In printed or online newspaper articles, find examples of the following:
   a. Incorrect word usage. (Correct it.)
   b. Ambiguous wording. (Correct it.)
   c. Incorrect grammar. (Correct it.)
   d. Incorrect punctuation. (Correct it.)
   e. A nicely worded sentence or paragraph.
   f. Figures of speech.
   g. Analogies that help translate numbers.

6. On the Internet, find at least three versions of the same news event written on the same day. Compare the sentence lengths. Look for transitions. Find figures of speech and analogies. Which, in your opinion, is the most readable? The least readable? Why?

7. Using software that uses the Flesch Reading Ease formula or a similar measurement of readability, compare a story you have written with stories from *The New York Times* and the Associated Press. What are the readability scores? Account for scoring differences and similarities.

Alternatives
to the Inverted Pyramid

9

Newspapers, magazines and Web sites publish some stories that are not suited for the inverted pyramid structure. Here's the opening to a story written as if it were a novel, except that it is all true.

By Helen O'Neill
The Associated Press

LITTLE PRAIRIE, Wis. — It was cold the night Grandma Braun was taken, that bitter dead-of-winter cold when the countryside is sheathed in ice and the stillness is broken only by great gusts of snow that swirl across the fields and back roads, erasing footprints and car tracks and all traces of life.

Eighty-eight-year-old Hedwig Braun was in bed reading when the lights went out but she didn't pay much heed. In her tiny farmhouse on Bluff Road, miles from the nearest town, power outages are not uncommon. Pulling on her dressing gown and slippers, she lit a candle and padded into the kitchen.

She poured a glass of milk, settled at the table and continued her book about angels.

The clock was stopped at 12:50 a.m.

A sudden blast of wind. A shadowy figure in the doorway.

"Eddie!" she screamed as the intruder lurched toward her, throwing something over her head. "Eddie come quick."

But her 88-year-old husband, asleep in the other room, didn't stir.

At 5-foot-2, weighing 80 pounds, Braun is a slip of a woman whose toughness is all inside. She had no strength to fight off her abductor. She didn't even try. She just prayed as she was flung into the trunk of her 1992 white Cadillac, kept praying as they tore down the country road, screeching to a halt beside a ditch, prayed even harder as she was tossed into the trunk of another car and they sped away again.

In the darkness, wedged against the spare tire, she wondered, "Why me? I'm just a nobody. What does he want with me?"

This story about a kidnapping is written as a narrative. You are introduced to Grandma Braun, who is snatched out of her isolated home. What will become of her? Why was she taken? Do you want to read on to find out? Using the inverted pyramid format to tell this story, the reporter would have gotten to the point as quickly as possible. That approach saves readers' and listeners' time, but it's not the way to tell all stories. If you want to engage readers intellectually and emotionally, if you want to inform and entertain, you must use writing techniques that promise great things to come and then fulfill that promise. To that end, you can use alternative story structures as Helen O'Neill does here. In this re-creation of the events, O'Neill tells the story chronologically.

Of course, when the kidnapping actually occurred, the news was told in the inverted pyramid format. (See Chapter 7 for more on the inverted pyramid.) However, during the investigation, there was no resolution. Only after it was all over could O'Neill or any other journalist go back and retell the entire story in chronological order. Readers already knew the broad outlines of the story; what they didn't know was the inside story that only the participants knew. O'Neill interviewed all the participants and scoured court and police files, most of which were not available as the story was developing. O'Neill also used narrative techniques by treating sources as characters, capturing tension and telling the events in chronological order to invite readers to read to the end for the resolution.

O'Neill's story is a full-fledged narrative, but you can and should use narrative techniques in all kinds of writing. Some stories are hybrids of the inverted pyramid and chronology structures. Some use chronology in other ways. These alternative story structures are even suitable for breaking news stories if you are able to gather enough information to write in scenes jammed with pertinent detail, if you are able to confirm the chronology and if you are able to capture the dialogue. These alternate structures also support investigative reports, profiles and issues stories—all genres that allow you more time to gather and write.

If time, detail and space are available, consider the alternative structures we describe in this chapter and summarize in Figure 9.1. Whether you are writing about a car accident, the Boy Scouts jamboree, the campaign for student-government president, corruption in government or the 8-year-old running the corner lemonade stand, writing the story will be easier if you know how to use some of the alternative story forms: chronology, news narrative, focus structure and service journalism formats.

CHRONOLOGY

Stories that work best as a chronology are those that have complications or tension and a resolution worth waiting for. Those elements are present even in events like meetings. When a city council faces a contentious issue, such as a proposed smoking ban in public places, the reporter is presented with controversy (supporters and opponents testifying), tension (how will the council vote?) and a resolution (the vote). Time constraints and tradition often dictate an inverted pyramid structure. But there are other options:

- The newspaper could summarize the vote in a sidebar and allow the writer to use chronology to tell the story of the meeting.
- The reporter could write an inverted pyramid version of the story for both the Web site and the newspaper and then later on write a chronological version for the Web to replace the earlier version.
- A nimble reporter working at an innovative newspaper might use news narrative (see the next section) to report the results and then move to chronology.

Where to Start

Oddly enough, when you use chronology, you don't have to begin at the beginning. Instead, you look for a key moment you can use for the lead to engage readers. To get started, writers often jot down a time line. In the case of the council meeting, it might look like this:

7 p.m.	Opponents and supporters of the smoking ban begin testifying before the council.
	Jones, an opponent, angrily denounces the proposal.
	Smith, a supporter, relates a story about her cancer.
8:15	Council members begin debate.
	Mayor pounds the gavel to break up an out-of-control argument between two council members.
	Council member Rodriguez is nearly in tears as he urges the council to pass the ordinance.
	Council member Jackson says merchants will face financial ruin.
8:47	Mary Solinski, a member of the audience, interrupts the debate and is escorted out of the chambers by city police. Several in the audience boo, but some cheer.
9:10	During a recess, no council members mingle with the public, which irritates several of those who are attending.
9:30	The council votes 5-4 in favor of the smoking ban. There are both jeers and cheers.

A Sample Outline

The writer could begin at the beginning of the time line given above, with the chamber filling with members of the public, but this lead would not attract attention. The writer needs a dramatic scene that captures emotion, is short and does not give away the outcome. The removal of a member of the audience has potential; so does the heated argument within the council. Here is a typical outline for a story using chronology:

1. The lead (the scene with Rodriguez).
2. The nut (theme) paragraph.
3. Foreshadowing.
4. A transition back to the beginning of the meeting to pick up the story from that point.
5. The body highlighting key events found in the time line. (As with any news story, much of the action is left out; this is a news story, not a secretary's report.)
6. An ending that highlights the vote and the audience reaction.

Go back to the story that opened this chapter. O'Neill's four-part narrative begins with the kidnapping and closely follows the chronology of the case. Yet O'Neill takes short detours to talk about Heddie Braun's marriage 68 years earlier and her daughter's marriage. Neither of these events, even though they preceded the kidnapping, would entice readers into the story. (You can find the complete story at www.ASNE.org by clicking on "Archives," then "ASNE Awards" and then "2005 winners.")

News Story Structures

	Inverted Pyramid	Chronology
What is it?	The lead paragraphs have the most important information, and succeeding paragraphs give details in descending order of importance.	Starting at a particular point of interest, the paragraphs tell a story in chronological order.
When should it be used?	It's best used for hard news, where timeliness is essential and the reader wants to know the important facts right away.	It's good for reporting a detailed sequence of events in a story with controversy or tension and resolution, especially as a follow-up to a news story.
How is it structured?	**Traditional news lead** • Give who, what, when, where, why and how. • Frame the story. **Body: support paragraphs in descending order of importance** • Give additional details about the lead. • Summarize other significant actions or elements relevant to the lead. • Give the impact or effect of the event. • Give the "so what" — the story's importance to the reader. • Give background and history. • Describe relevant physical details. • Narrate relevant sequences of events. • Use quotations from relevant sources. • Give sources of additional information, including links to Web sites. **Ending** • End with the least significant information, *not* with a conclusion, summary or tie-back to the beginning. The story can be cut from the bottom up without compromising its effectiveness.	**Narrative lead** • Describe a dramatic point in the story. • Create narrative suspense with foreshadowing. **Nut paragraph** • Give the theme of the story. **Body: narrative support paragraphs** • Use foreshadowing. • Pick up story with a transition back to the beginning of the narrative. • Tell the story in chronological order, highlighting key events found in the time line. • Describe relevant physical details. • Use narrative techniques like dialogue, flashback and foreshadowing. **Ending** • Give a conclusion to the story. • Resolve the tension or conflict in the story.

Figure 9.1
Different structures are useful for different types of news stories.

News Narrative

The story combines elements of inverted pyramid and chronology formats, with an emphasis on either news or narrative.

It's useful for stories where timeliness is somewhat important, but the hard news element is not prominent.

Narrative lead
- Open with an interesting scene or twist that teases the story.

or

Traditional news lead
- Give who, what, when, where, why and how.

Support paragraphs
- Briefly add whatever helps the reader understand the story summarized in the lead.

Body: narrative support paragraphs
- Go back to the beginning, and tell the story in chronological order.

Ending
- Give a conclusion to the story.
- Resolve the tension or conflict in the story.

Focus Structure

The story follows one individual as a representative of a larger group.

It's useful for making complex or abstract stories meaningful to readers.

Narrative lead
- Introduce the subject and describe the person's problem.

Transition
- Create a bridge from the subject to the theme of the story.

Nut paragraph
- Give the theme of the story.

Support paragraphs
- Foreshadow.
- Give the "so what" — the story's importance to the reader.
- Give the "to be sure" — opposing perspectives.

Body: narrative and expository support paragraphs
- Interweave narrative about the subject with facts about the theme to tell the story.

Ending
- Conclude the story, with a summary or with a tie-back that refers to the beginning of the story.

The Nut Paragraph, Foreshadowing and the "To Be Sure"

Like the lead in an inverted pyramid story, a **nut paragraph** (or *nut graf*) is a paragraph that gives the theme of the story and summarizes the key facts. Unlike the lead in the inverted pyramid format, however, the nut paragraph is not the first paragraph in the story. For the council story, after the first (or lead) paragraph describing the scene with Rodriguez, the nut paragraph might look like this:

> In a meeting filled with emotional, sometimes angry testimony, citizens and the City Council debated the proposed smoking ban for nearly three hours. Citizens urged — sometimes threatened — council members. The mayor had to pound his gavel to bring the council to order several times when some members engaged in heated, personal arguments. In the end, council members voted on the landmark legislation amid jeers and cheers and then left through a back door.
>
> From the beginning, it was clear that emotions were running high. . . .

The nut paragraph both defines the story and foreshadows the heated debate. Even though readers will know the results, many will want to read the blow-by-blow account. It also establishes the "so what": This is a divisive issue, involving landmark legislation, that people care about. Notice that the last line "From the beginning . . ." creates a transition back to the start of the story narrative.

In some stories, you might also need to include a **"to be sure" paragraph**. This paragraph, which gives opposing points of view, is a must when you are focusing on one side of an issue. Before the council vote, you could do a story about a restaurant shift from the perspective of a waiter. You could follow that with a story from the perspective of a smoker at a bar. In both cases, you would include a paragraph acknowledging that others disagree, especially if that opposing viewpoint is not included elsewhere in the story. For instance:

> Not everyone agrees with Megan Addison that smoking should be banned. Others, including smokers and business owners, believe that the proposal infringes on their right to smoke or to run their business as they please. But Addison and her fellow servers at the Sports Grill want to work in a smoke-free environment.

A "to be sure" paragraph would not be needed in the council meeting story because all sides are represented in the debate. Nor was it needed in the story of the kidnapping of Grandma Braun. Presumably, no one except the kidnapper believes she should have been kidnapped.

The Ending

Stories written chronologically need strong endings. Here's how the kidnapping story ends:

At the back of the courtroom Heddie Braun clutched the hand of her wheelchair-bound husband, Eddie, and listened. She didn't feel any joy, she said later. She was curious about what her kidnapper looked like without his black face mask. But mostly she felt sad for his wife and children.

Not Eddie. For Eddie, life in prison was not punishment enough for the monster who had taken his wife.

So he gave a grim smile when the judge sentenced Ravesteijn to 45 years for kidnapping, burglary and false imprisonment. Heddie let out a gasp.

Forty-five years? For kidnapping her? But I'm just a nobody, she protested.

"No ma'am," Sheriff Graves said.

Her family thinks she may have suffered a mild stroke, brought on by the ordeal. Heddie says the pain in her foot wears her down, and that is why she seems so frail and tired.

She sleeps a lot these days, more than she used to.

She locks the door now. And she always leaves the lights on.

For both the hypothetical council story and the real kidnapping story, readers want to know the outcome of the narrative. Was justice served in the kidnapping story? How is the victim now? In the council story, how did the meeting end? Readers read a chronology to the end because they want to know the conclusion of the story.

NEWS NARRATIVE

In Chapter 7, you saw examples of inverted pyramid stories that didn't have the news in the first paragraph (see "The 'You' Lead" and "Leads with Flair" in Chapter 7), but as soon as the writer teased the reader, the news lead appeared. Then the writer arranged the rest of the story in the traditional descending order of importance. Further modification, though, offers writers more choices. The **news narrative** structure combines the inverted pyramid and chronology. Here is an outline of its basic elements:

1. An opening with an interesting scene or twist that teases the story.
2. A traditional news lead.
3. Brief paragraphs that add whatever help readers need to understand the story summarized in the traditional lead.
4. A transition back to the beginning to tell the story in chronological order.

The "news" in "news narrative" implies that the story has a time element and that the story is not a feature. **Features**, sometimes called "soft stories," are those that can run nearly any time, such as a profile of a stamp collector, a story on a volunteer at the local food bank or a piece about riding with a police officer for a shift A story with a time element usually has to be published in the next issue of the newspaper or as soon as possible on the Web. The "narrative" in "news narrative" means that the writer can use chronology, one of the most important tools of narrative writing. In the news narrative, you will often find other narrative tools, such as those discussed in Chapter 8: scenes, dialogue, anecdotes and foreshadowing.

News Narrative with News Emphasis

When the local sheriff's department broke an unusual burglary ring, Jane Meinhardt of the *St. Petersburg Times* elected to use the news narrative structure. In Figure 9.2, you can read her story, which follows the outline above. Notice that Meinhardt's story is a news narrative with news emphasis. This format works well for news that is significant but not earth-shattering. You probably wouldn't use it to report the first few hours or perhaps even the first couple of days of an event like Hurricane Katrina. You need to be able to get all the details of how something happened to relate the chronology. Immediately following a disaster or other major event, the authorities don't have all the information, the reporter might not have access to witnesses. The AP's O'Neill was only able to write the story that opens this chapter as a chronology after the trial when all the testimony and investigative records were available.

News Narrative with Narrative Emphasis

When the news is less important, the news narrative structure is also useful, but the emphasis is on narrative rather than news. John Tully, a reporter for the *Columbia Missourian*, was asked to look for a story at a horse-riding competition one Sunday afternoon. Because most of the competitors were not from the newspaper's local area, reporting the results of the competition was not as important as finding a good story.

Tully knew nothing about horse-riding competitions, so he first found people who could explain the judging. He also asked people to suggest interesting competitors. A youth coordinator told him that Cara Walker was competing for the first time since her accident. After gathering more information from the coordinator, Tully found Walker and her mother—and a story that lent itself to news narrative. Through Tully's story (see Figure 9.3), readers learned that Walker, who was seriously injured, was able to recover enough to ride again. What they didn't find out until the end was that she won the competition. Because he had less news to report, Tully was able to go to the chronological format more quickly than Meinhardt. He used the outcome of the competition to reward readers who completed the story.

FOCUS STRUCTURE

For centuries, writers have used the **focus** structure to tell the story of an individual or a group that represents a bigger population. This approach allows the writer to make large institutions, complex issues and seven-digit numbers meaningful. Not many of us can understand—let alone explain—the marketing system for

News Narrative with News Emphasis

The opening paragraphs set the scene with information that informs and is interesting.

PALM HARBOR—They carried knapsacks and bags to tote loot. They had a screwdriver to pry open doors and windows.

They used latex gloves.

They acted like professional criminals, but officials say they were teenage burglars coached and directed by a Palm Harbor woman whose son and daughter were part of her gang.

A traditional news lead gives "who," "what" and "when."

Pinellas County Sheriff's deputies arrested Rovana Sipe, two of her children and two other teens Wednesday after a series of home burglaries.

"She was the driver," said Sheriff's Sgt. Greg Tita. "She pointed out the houses. She's the one who said 'Do these.'"

The writer supports the lead with a quote.

The story continues with the breaking news for the next four paragraphs.

Sipe, 38, of 2333 State Road 584, was charged with two counts of being a principal in burglary. She was held Thursday in lieu of $20,000 bail.

Her daughter, Jackie Shifflet, 16, was charged with grand theft. Her son, Ryan Shifflet, 15, was charged with two counts of burglary.

Charles Ruhe, 17, of 1600 Ensley Ave., in Safety Harbor, and Charles Taylor, 16, of 348 Jeru Blvd. in Tarpon Springs, also were held on four counts of burglary each.

"They were very well-prepared to do burglaries, especially with the guidance they were given," Tita said. "We recovered thousands of dollars of stolen items. Anything that could be carried out, was."

The burglary ring unraveled Tuesday, Tita said. A Palm Harbor woman saw a large, yellow car driven by a woman drop off three boys, he said. The three went to the back of her house.

Now that the news has been established, instead of continuing to present the information in order of importance, the writer presents the rest of the story in chronological fashion. Note the important transition from inverted pyramid to chronology: "The burglary ring unraveled Tuesday, Tita said."

They put on gloves and started to pry open a window with a screwdriver, she said. When she tapped on a window, they ran.

She called 911. As she waited for deputies, other neighbors saw the boys walk through a nearby neighborhood carrying bags.

Deputies chased the boys and caught two. The third got into a large yellow car driven by a woman.

The bags contained jewelry, a shotgun and other items deputies say were taken from another house in the neighborhood.

Tita said the boys, later identified as Taylor and Ruhe, told detectives about other burglaries in Dunedin and Clearwater and who else was involved.

At Sipe's house, detectives found stolen VCRs, televisions, camcorders and other valuables. They arrested the other two teens and Sipe.

The story ends with a quote rather than a tie-back or summary.

"We're very familiar with this family and its criminal history," Tita said. "We have found stolen property at the house in the past and made juvenile arrests."

Figure 9.2
In news narratives with a news emphasis, the writer needs to establish some facts before giving the chronology. This format is associated with breaking news of significance, such as crime.

News Narrative with Narrative Emphasis

The first two paragraphs reveal the news of the injury and the twist that even though doctors were unsure, she recovered enough to compete. The horse show is the news event that generated the story. Note that the second paragraph reveals that she competed but only foreshadows how she did.

About five months ago, Cara Walker, 17, was lying in a hospital recovering from the spinal injury she received when she lost control of her car, rolled the vehicle and was thrown halfway through the side window.

Doctors weren't sure she would ever ride again. On Sunday, in a remarkable turnaround, Walker competed in the Midway Fall Classic Quarter Horse Show at the Midway Expo Center. The results were surprising.

Last July, Walker, a junior at Rock Bridge High School, was taking a lunch break from riding in preparation for the Fort Worth Invitational, where she qualified in five events. Driving with three passengers on a back road near Moberly, she rolled her car at 50 mph where the paved road turned to gravel without warning. Walker was the only one not wearing a seat belt. Her head and upper body smashed through the side window.

"Last July" is the transition to chronology after the news lead.

Fortunately, she was still in her riding boots. Her spurs got caught on the bar under the seat, which Walker says may have saved her life.

At the time of the accident, Walker was nationally ranked in the trail-riding event.

Doctors fused her neck in surgery. During the next couple of weeks, she was able to shed her full upper-body cast. Walker returned home to her parents and twin sisters two days after surgery, but her mother, Jane Walker, said doctors told her to stay away from her sport for a few months until she healed.

This background helps establish that she isn't just any rider and that she had more to lose in this accident than most riders.

For Walker, the top all-around youth rider in Missouri and the president of the American Quarter Horse Youth Association, the four months following the accident was her first time away from riding.

Note that there are no quotes to break the narrative flow. "My spurs got caught on the bar under my seat" (paragraph 4) and "She first started walking, and going to the mailbox wore her out" are paraphrased to stay in storytelling mode.

After returning home she worked to regain strength and mobility from the accident that initially left her right side paralyzed. She walked short distances. Going to the mailbox at the end of the driveway wore her out, her mother recalls.

The story has a surprise ending, which is possible in a chronology. In a straight news story, this would have been the lead.

Walker had to work almost every muscle in her body back into shape. After the accident, the family brought her 10-year-old quarter horse to their barn in Columbia. That motivated Walker to at first walk to the barn and then to start caring for the horse and eventually ride again.

Sunday, the rehabilitation was complete. With ramrod posture and strict horse control, she won first place in the horsemanship class.

Figure 9.3

In news narratives with a narrative emphasis, less space is devoted to the news, and more narrative techniques are used. These types of narratives use fewer quotes and save important information for a strong ending. *(Source: "Horse Power" by John Tully,* Columbia Missourian, *Nov. 27, 2006.)*

wheat, but we could more easily do so if we followed a crop of wheat from the time it was planted until a consumer bought a loaf of bread.

The Wall Street Journal knew that not many of us would be attracted to a story about the interaction between pesticides and prescription drugs. That's why one reporter focused on one person to tell a story of pesticide poisoning:

> Thomas Latimer used to be a vigorous, athletic man, a
> successful petroleum engineer with a bright future.
> Then he mowed the lawn.

Does this opening make you want to read on?

In a quip attributed to him, the Soviet dictator Joseph Stalin summed up the impact of focusing on a part of the whole: "A single death is a tragedy; a million deaths is a statistic." Think about that the next time you hear that a plane crash killed 300 people. You probably won't be emotionally touched by the crash unless you know someone who was on the plane. However, if you write the story of the crash by focusing on a couple of the victims, you will have a better chance of involving your readers emotionally.

Writing the Lead

Issues like health care, budget deficits and sexual harassment don't have much emotional appeal in the abstract. You make them relevant if you discuss the issue by focusing on someone affected by it. For instance, the college student who wrote the following story spoke to Karen Elliott, who willingly told her story to help others with the same disease. The key word is "story." You write articles about diseases; you write stories about people. The lead paragraphs focus on one person in an anecdote that shows her as a character we can relate to:

> Karen Elliott, 44, remembers the phone call from Dr. Jonathen Roberts, a general surgeon, as if it had happened yesterday. Dr. Roberts' nurse called one afternoon two years ago and told Karen to hold the line. She froze. She had just had a biopsy on her right breast because of a new lump. It's never good news when the doctor calls at home. Dr. Roberts cut to the chase.
>
> "You have atypical hyperplasia," he said.
>
> Being a nurse, Karen knew exactly what he meant. No number of breast self-exams could have detected this. Atypical hyperplasia is a life-long condition characterized by abnormal cells. Affecting only 4 percent of the female population, it puts Karen and others at an increased risk for breast cancer. With her family history of the disease, her risk of breast cancer jumps sky-high.

Reporters working on local stories have just as many opportunities to apply this approach as those writing national and international stories. For example, instead of keeping score on the United Way fund drive, focus on the people who will benefit — or will fail to benefit — from the campaign. If the streets in your city jar your teeth when you drive, write about the problem from the point of view of a driver. If Dutch elm disease is killing the trees in your city, concentrate on a homeowner who has lost several. The focus structure offers the writer a powerful

TIPS

Applying the Focus Structure

● Focus on the individual.

● Transition to the larger issue.

● Report on the larger issue.

● Return to the opening focus.

method of reducing institutions, statistics and cosmic issues to a level readers can relate to and understand.

Advertising agencies use the technique, too. That's why instead of being solicited for money to help the poor and starving, you are asked to support one child for only pennies a day. The technique gives poverty and hunger a face. A starving population is an abstraction; one starving child is a tragedy.

Writing the Setup

Once you've completed the opening, you must finish the setup to the story. The **setup** consists of the transition to the nut paragraph, the foreshadowing, the "so what" and the "to be sure." Let's look at each of these.

The Transition and the Nut Paragraph

When you open with a scene or an anecdote, you must construct a transition that explicitly makes the connection to the nut, or theme, paragraph. "Explicitly" is the key word. If you fail to help readers understand the point of the opening, however interesting it is, you risk losing them. The transition in this example is in italics:

> Anita Poore hit the rough pavement of the parking lot with a thud. She had never felt such intense, stabbing pain and could barely lift her heavy head. When she reached for the car door, a police officer stared at her and asked her husband, "Is she drunk?" A wave of nausea swept over her, and she vomited.
>
> "That's it. Get her out of here!" the officer demanded.
>
> Poore was not drunk. She avoided jail, but she faces a life sentence of pain.
>
> Now 25, she has suffered migraine headaches since she was in seventh grade.
>
> *Not that it is much comfort, but she's not alone.* Health officials estimate that Americans miss 157 million workdays a year because of migraines and spend more than $2 million a year on over-the-counter painkillers for migraine, tension and cluster headaches. Researchers haven't found a cure, but they have found methods to lessen the pain.

The italicized transition explicitly places Anita Poore among those who miss work, buy painkillers and are still waiting for a cure. The material that follows the transition is the theme.

Let's return to Karen Elliott, who was diagnosed with atypical hyperplasia. Here is the nut paragraph, the part of the story that states the theme:

> What Karen didn't know was that her pleasant life in New Bloomfield would become a roller coaster of ups and downs for the next two years, a ride that nearly destroyed her. Her husband of 19 years, Bob, and their two children, Bethany, 6, and Jordan, 8, could only watch as she struggled with the decision of whether to voluntarily have her breasts removed because Karen, and only Karen, could make that choice.

Types of Journalistic Writing

News Writing

- News stories emphasize facts and current events. Timeliness is especially important.
- Typical news stories cover government, politics, international events, disasters, crime, important breakthroughs in science and medicine, and sports.

Feature (Soft News) Writing

- Feature stories go into depth about a generally newsworthy situation or person. Timeliness is relevant, but not critical.
- Typical feature stories are profiles, day-in-the-life stories, how-to stories, and background stories.

This is where the writer tells readers what the story is about — in this case, Karen's struggle with her decision. There are many other themes the writer could have pursued.

The nut paragraph, says Jacqui Banaszynski, Pulitzer Prize-winning writer, "is like a secret decoder ring — it lets the hapless reader know what your story is about and why they should read it." When you have involved the reader and successfully written the explicit transition to the nut paragraph, you are ready to build the rest of the setup.

Foreshadowing

Foreshadowing can be done in a single line: "The killing started early and ended late." Or you can foreshadow over several paragraphs. The goal is to assure readers they will be rewarded if they continue reading.

This is what Erik Larson of *The Wall Street Journal* promised readers of his fire investigation story:

> And so began what may well be the most intensive scientific investigation in the history of arson — not a whodunit, exactly, but a whatdunit. So far the inquiry has taken Seattle investigators places arson squads don't typically go, even to the Navy's weapons-testing grounds at China Lake in California. Along the way, the investigation has attracted a team of scientists who, likewise ensnared by the "Twilight Zone" nature of the mystery, volunteered time and equipment. At one point the investigators themselves torched a large building just to test a suspected fuel.

The "So What"

The "so what" tells readers explicitly why they should care. Thomas Latimer was poisoned when he mowed his lawn. Karen Elliott has to decide whether to have surgery. Anita Poore almost got arrested for having a migraine headache. Interesting, but so what? Reporters and editors know the "so what" or they wouldn't spend time on the story. Too often, however, they fail to tell it to readers. Latimer's story is interesting, but it's much more important because the writer added the "so what" (in italics):

The makers of the pesticide, diazinon, and of Tagamet firmly deny that their products had anything to do with Mr. Latimer's condition. The pesticide maker says he doesn't even believe he was exposed to its product. And in fact, Mr. Latimer lost a lawsuit he filed against the companies. *Even so, the case intrigues scientists and regulators because it illustrates the need for better understanding of the complex interactions between such everyday chemicals as pesticides and prescription drugs.*

Neither the Food and Drug Administration nor the Environmental Protection Agency conducts routine tests for such interactions. Indeed, the EPA doesn't even evaluate the synergy of two or more pesticides commonly used together. "We have not developed ways to test any of that," says an EPA spokesman. "We don't know how to do it." And a new congressional report says the FDA lacks both the resources and the enforcement powers to protect Americans from all kinds of poisons.

The "so what" is the impact—the relevance—for people who have no warning that pesticides and prescription drugs may interact to poison them. In other cases, the "so what" may be included in the theme statement. Let's look at the migraine story again:

[1] Not that it is much comfort, but she's not alone.
[2] Health officials estimate that Americans miss 157 million workdays a year because of migraines and spend more than $2 million a year on over-the-counter painkillers for migraine, tension and cluster headaches.
[3] Researchers haven't found a cure, but they have found methods to lessen the pain.

Sentence 1 is the transition. Sentence 2 is the "so what." The reporter is writing about Anita Poore, but the problem is widespread. Sentence 3 is the theme, which includes foreshadowing. The search for a cure, and the intermediate discovery of ways to lessen the pain, will be the focus of the story. The "so what" establishes the dimensions of the problem. When you define the "so what," you are establishing the story's impact.

The "To Be Sure"

To maintain an evenhanded approach, writers must acknowledge that there are two or more sides to a story. We call this the "to be sure," as in "to be sure, there are other opinions." We've seen in the pesticide story that the drug and pesticide makers "firmly deny that their products had anything to do with Mr. Latimer's condition." We see the technique again in an article about the impact of gambling on Tunica, Miss. Writer Jenny Deam opens with a scene in the mayor's store. The mayor says gambling is the best thing that ever happened to the town. At the front counter, a woman is asking for the $85 back she paid on furniture last week because she lost her grocery money gambling. What comes next is a combination theme and "to be sure" statement, highlighted in italics:

And so is the paradox of this tiny Mississippi Delta county, now that the casinos have come to call.

On the one hand, unemployment in a place the Rev. Jesse Jackson once called "America's Ethiopia" has dropped from nearly 24 percent to a low last fall of 5 percent. Anyone who wants a job has one with the casinos. There are more jobs than people to fill them. In a county of about 8,100 people, the number of food stamp recipients fell from 4,218 before the casinos to 2,907 now.

But there is another side. New problems never before seen.

Since the first casino opened in 1992, the number of DUI arrests has skyrocketed by 400 percent. U.S. Highway 61 leading to Memphis is constantly jammed. On a busy weekend as many as 28,000 cars head toward the nine casinos now open. The criminal court system is just as overloaded. In 1992, there were 1,500 cases filed. A year later, 2,400. As of last month there had already been 6,800 cases filed for this year.

"Well," says the mayor, "it's just like anything else in life: You got to take the evil with the good."

The story of Tunica's economic rebirth had been told before. This story focused on the problems that inevitably follow gambling. To be sure, there are benefits, but this story also examined the costs.

Now that you have constructed the setup, you are ready to enter the body of the story.

Writing the Body

Think of readers as people antsy to do something else. To maintain their interest, offer them frequent examples to support your main points. Use anecdotes, scenes and dialogue to move the story line. Mix *exposition* (the facts) with narration (the story line). Let's return to Karen Elliott, who just learned that she has atypical hyperplasia. The writer, Tina Smithers, has been dealing in exposition for a few paragraphs, so she shares an anecdote set in the following scene to keep the readers' interest:

Karen was walking downstairs to get the beach ball out of the summer box for Bethany's Hawaiian swim party at Kindercare. Suddenly, Karen fainted and fell down the stairs. She knew she had broken something. Coming to, she blindly made her way upstairs and lay on the bed.

"The cat was staring me in the eyes," she mumbled as Bob, fresh from the shower, grabbed ice and a pillow.

Karen noticed Bethany crying in the doorway. At this point, Karen realized she had been shouting, "Call 9-1-1! Call 9-1-1!" She didn't want her daughter to see her lose control. She quieted down and told Bethany to come to her bed.

"It's okay, honey. Mommy broke her arm, but they'll be over soon to fix it." In the ambulance, one of the paramedics tried to cut off her yellow Tommy Hilfiger sweater.

"It's brand new," Karen shouted. "Can't you pull it off?"

They gave one small yank, and Karen immediately changed her mind. Every bump along the way was agonizing. Karen pleaded for more morphine. Her wrist, it turned out, was broken in 20 places.

ON THE JOB

Tips for Writing

Ken Fuson, a feature writer and humor columnist at *The Des Moines (Iowa) Register*, has won several national writing awards, including an ASNE Writing Award and the Ernie Pyle feature-writing award. He offers his top 10 tips for improving your writing:

1. **Write stories.** Write real stories — narrative stories that hook readers from the opening scene and transport them to another world. Stories that make people call out to their spouse or roommate and say, "You have got to read this." Remember: You can find these stories in the courthouse, at city hall and on the police blotter. And they can be done on deadline.
2. **Look for conflict or drama.** Most of the best stories have a conflict and a resolution. Jon Franklin, author of *Writing for Story*, says the more basic the conflict — involving love, hate, death, triumph and travail — the better the story. Pared to its essence, the *Wizard of Oz* consists of two parts. Conflict: Dorothy loses home. Resolution: Dorothy finds home. The plot is what happens in the middle.
3. **Be there.** Put people on the scene. "Make me see," editor Henry Belk told his reporters. "You aren't making me see." Belk was blind. Even spending a half-hour with the subject of a quick-hit profile is better than just conducting a phone interview.
4. **Think scenes.** Use dialogue and descriptions to make readers feel as if they're watching the action unfold as it happens. Move your camera shots — from panning the crowd to close-ups.

Writing the Ending

TIPS

Ending the Story

- Use anecdotes, dialogue, scenes and good quotes to end the story.
- Be sure the ending wraps up the whole story, not just the last section of the story.

As in the chronology structure, you need a strong ending in the focus structure. The difference is that in chronology, you are relating the resolution or outcome. In the focus structure, one device is the **tie-back**, a reference to something that appears at or near the beginning of the story. Here is a lead in a *Wall Street Journal* story:

ETHEL, Mo.—Kristin Gall can't look at an old tractor without wondering about the lives it's rolled through. "There's a story behind every one if you can find it," says the 36-year-old farmer. In 2000, he began trying to track down one that belonged to his late grandfather.

By then, Leonard Gall had been dead for 11 years and the tractor had been gone from the family for nearly twice that long. But Kristin Gall's memories were stirred after he stumbled across a tattered notebook in which his grandfather had jotted down the vehicle's serial number, along with the dates of each oil change.

The story goes on to detail Gall's successful search. It even mentions, high in the story, that his grandfather sometimes bought his grandchildren pedal-driven toy tractors. The story ends with this tie-back to the lead and that anecdote:

5. **Write every sentence.** I'm stealing that advice from Susan Orlean, the wonderful writer for *The New Yorker*. She says we shouldn't distinguish between the "writerly" sentences, which we spend all our time on, and the workmanlike sentences that do all the heavy lifting. Think about every sentence. Be the reader's guide through the entire piece, not just the descriptive parts.

6. **Take ownership of a story.** Roy Peter Clark of the Poynter Institute uses music to show that different artists can sing the same song with quite different results. No matter what the assignment — even if it's that hardy perennial, the day-after-Thanksgiving shopping spree story — make it your own.

7. **Search for the universal truth.** The story about a mother who stays by her sick child's bedside isn't about health care; it's a story about devotion. The story of the priest who gives his first sermon isn't about graduating from the seminary; it's a story about faith. The story about the athlete who overcomes childhood arthritis to win an Olympic gold medal isn't about the competition; it's a story about perseverance. Constantly ask yourself: What's this story *really* about?

8. **Look for humor opportunities.** Humor is the most underused tool in our writing kit. Readers love humor almost as much as they love real stories.

9. **Take risks.** I once wrote a one-sentence, one-paragraph weather story that (much to my amazement) has been reprinted several times. It's not just a matter of trying to be clever. It's a matter of doing anything to get read.

10. **Remember Tammy Gaudette.** Tammy is a housewife in Iowa who was invited to appear on a panel of newspaper readers. She was asked what she read. "Oh, I don't like the news," she said. "I like the interesting stories." Always ask yourself: Would I read this?

Mr. Gall's hopes are clearer. Aiming to keep his grandfather's tractor in the family for at least one more generation, he revived a tradition his grandfather started: He bought his toddler son a pedal-driven 1206 for Christmas this year.

The goal in the focus structure is to summarize the theme of the story or tie back to the top of the story. Anecdotes, dialogue, scenes and good quotes can all end the story. Don't just stop writing; construct an ending.

SERVICE JOURNALISM

In Chapter 1, you read that one of the criteria for news is usefulness. Many, if not most, of the magazines you find on the racks appeal to readers by presenting information they might find useful. More than that, they attempt to present this useful information in the most usable way. This approach to presenting information has been called **service journalism**. You often see it labeled "News you can use."

A pioneer in service journalism, James Autrey of the Meredith Corporation, liked to call service journalism "action journalism." Its goal is to get readers to use the information. Magazine publishers know that people are more likely to resubscribe to a magazine if they do some of the things the magazine suggests for them to do.

Service journalism strives to present useful information in the most usable way. One way to think of this is "refrigerator journalism," information presented in such a way that people can cut it out and put it on their refrigerator or bulletin board.

Newspapers, too, are doing more service journalism (see Figure 9.4). Some sections, such as travel, food and entertainment, use many techniques of service journalism. Front-page news stories, too, often contain elements of service journalism, even if it's just a box listing a sequence of events or directing readers to more information. Service journalism is even easier on the Web. You can provide links to lists, how-to information, time-date-place of events, and relevant Web sites.

In this textbook, you see examples of service journalism in the marginal elements that list the learning objectives for each chapter or highlight important points. The techniques of service journalism require that you think about content and presentation even as you are reporting. Ask yourself, "What does the reader need to be able to act on this information?" The answer might range from an address to a phone or fax number to instructions on how to fix a lawnmower or make a loaf of bread. It might include directions on how to travel to a festival or information on where and when to buy tickets. As these examples illustrate, you move from simply talking about something to providing the information the reader needs to act on your story.

Much of the basic service journalism information can be presented as sidebars or lists or boxed material. Figure 9.5 uses common service journalism devices to present more information about this topic.

Figure 9.4
When snow blanketed Seattle, thousands lost their electricity. Trying to heat their homes and apartments with charcoal or generators indoors, six people died from carbon monoxide poisoning and more than 100 others were hospitalized. In response, *The Seattle Times* devoted the top half of its front page to warnings in six languages about the improper use of heating devices. This was service journalism at its finest.

Service Journalism

In today's microwave world, in-a-hurry readers want practical information presented in the most efficient and effective way.

What this means is that you must think not just of a message of words on paper. You also must think of how those words will appear on the page—the presentation.

Basics

Service journalism is:

- **Useful.** You must inform readers, but if you also find ways to demonstrate how the reader can use the information, you will be more successful. Emphasize WIIFM: "What's in it for me?" See how often you can get "you" in the first sentence of your copy.

- **Usable.** Whenever you can, make a list. Lists get more attention and are better understood and more easily retained. You don't have to write sentences. "Tips" is a magical word.

- **Used.** People stop paying attention to information they never use. You should be able to prove that your readers act on information. To get readers to respond, promise them something. Offer a prize; give them something free.

Refrigerator Journalism
10 tips to serve today's readers

1. **Save them time.**
2. **Help them make more money, save money or get something free.**
3. **Address different levels of news interest.**
4. **Address niche audiences more effectively.**
5. **Become more personally useful.**
6. **Make information more immediately usable.**
7. **Become more accessible.** Give readers your name, phone number, fax number and e-mail address.

8. **Become more user-friendly.** Learn to layer the news, use cross-references, put things in the same place, color-code, tell readers where to find things, use page numbers on contents blurbs—even on covers, use glossaries and show readers where to find more information.
9. **Become more visual and graphic.** Use photos and information graphics.
10. **Become more engaging and interactive.** Use contests, quizzes, crosswords, games—make your readers do things. They remember better if they do something. Give awards to those who send answers to you. Give a coffee mug to the reader with the best tip of the month. Readers involved in your publication are more likely to resubscribe.

Figure 9.5
Employing the common presentation devices of service journalism—such as boxes and sidebars—this example shows how to highlight information so readers can easily find it and use it.

Print is a hot, intense medium. Refrigerator journalism cools off a hot medium and invites access and participation.

Other Devices of Service Journalism

1. Use blurbs. After a title and before the article begins, write a summary/contents/benefit blurb. David Ogilvy says no one will read the small type without knowing the benefit upfront. Use the same benefit blurb in a table of contents or menu or briefs column. The best word in a benefit blurb is "how." How to, how you, how I did something. Be personal. Use people in your messages. Also, use internal blurbs, little summaries, pull quotes and tips to tease and coax readers on to the page.

2. Use subheads. Before you write, outline. Put the main points of the outline into the copy. Perhaps a better word than subhead is "entry point." Let readers enter the copy where they find something interesting.

3. Have a question-and-answer column. A Q&A format allows readers to save time by skipping over things they already know or are not interested in.

4. Repeat things in different ways for different people. Don't be afraid to say something in a box or a graphic that you have said elsewhere. Reinforcing a message aids retention.

> "Never be above a gimmick."
> —Dave Orman, ARCO

5. Think more visually. Stop using pictures and graphics that do not contain information. Make them useful. Remember, being effective and efficient is the only thing that matters. We used to write articles and then look for graphics or photos to enhance the message. Now, we put the information in the graphic (where it will get more attention and have more impact) and write a story to enhance the graphic.

The power of the box

When you can, put some information in a box. Boxes or sidebars, like lists, get more attention, increase comprehension and aid retention.

1. A reference box. "For more information, see, read, call . . ."

2. A note box. Take notes from your articles as if you were studying for an exam. Give them to your readers to complement your message.

3. A glossary box. Put unfamiliar or technical terms in a glossary box. Find a way to indicate which words are defined by putting them in color, setting them in a different typeface or underlining them. Also, teach readers how to pronounce difficult words.

4. A bio box. When you need to say something about where a person lived, went to school, and worked, put this information in a box so that your main story is not interrupted. If you have more than one person in the story, bio boxes are even more useful.

The 4 goals of the service journalist:

In a nutshell

1. Attention
2. Comprehension
3. Retention
4. Action

PR Tip

Newspapers, magazines and newsletters are doing more and more service journalism. "News You Can Use" and "Tips & Tactics" have become familiar heads. Both newspapers and magazines are becoming more visual. Yet most news releases sent out by PR professionals look the same as they did five and 50 years ago. Why not try refrigerator journalism techniques in your next news release?

Suggested Readings

Clark, Roy Peter and Scanlon, Christopher, eds. *America's Best Newspaper Writing*, Second Edition. New York: Bedford/St. Martin's, 2006. This is a collection of prizewinners from the annual American Society of Newspaper Editors prestigious competition. The editors deconstruct the stories to help students of writing understand what the writer did and why.

Franklin, Jon. *Writing for Story: Craft Secrets of Dramatic Nonfiction by a Two-Time Pulitzer Prize Winner*. New York: Plume, 1994. If you want to write nonfiction narrative, this book is highly recommended.

Harrington, Walt H., ed. *The Beholder's Eye: A Collection of America's Finest Personal Journalism*. New York: Grove Press, 2006. Harrington offers this collection of personal narratives to make his point that the first-person perspective is the best way to find truth. He adds an introductory essay to argue that the time has come to cast aside objectivity.

LaRocque, Paula. *The Book on Writing: The Ultimate Guide to Writing Well*. Oak Park, Ill.: Marion Street Press, 2003. This great book for new writers covers three main topics: mechanical and structural guidelines, creative elements of storytelling, and grammar, usage and punctuation.

Stewart, James B. *Follow the Story: How to Write Successful Nonfiction*. New York: Touchstone, 1998. Stewart, formerly of *The Wall Street Journal*, won a Pulitzer Prize in 1988 for his reporting on the stock market crash and insider trading. He uses his work to illustrate how to write narration.

Suggested Web Sites

www.asne.org
The American Society of Newspaper Editors conducts a prestigious writing contest every year. Winners from six years are posted on this site. These are the best of the best. At the home page, select "Archives" and then "ASNE Awards" to go to the winning entries.

www.nieman.harvard.edu/narrative/digest/
This site, devoted to explaining narrative writing, displays excellent examples from newspapers and magazines.

www.projo.com/words
The Providence Journal offers an excellent site full of writing and reporting tips from its staff members. Many of their stories are included as examples.

Exercises

1. Write four to eight paragraphs about how you and your classmates learned to be reporters. Use narrative tools. For instance, recreate a scene from one of your classes. Provide the transition into the body of the story and then stop.

2. Interview a student in your reporting class. Ask questions that elicit anecdotes. Write an anecdote about the person.

3. Using a chronology, write about eight paragraphs of a story about some aspect of your experience in your reporting class.

4. Either find a story based on your own reporting or take an inverted pyramid story already published and create a news narrative opening for it.

5. Find two examples in newspapers or magazines of service journalism, and analyze them. Find an example of a story that would have benefited from service journalism techniques. Tell what you would have done to make the information more usable for readers.

6. Analyze focus structure stories. This format is often found in *The Wall Street Journal* and *USA Today*, among other places. How many elements of the setup can you identify? Find all the anecdotes. Identify any dialogue.

7. Write the first two pages of a story describing an event of your life. Try to include as many parts of the setup as you can: scenes, dialogue, foreshadowing and the "so what" statement.

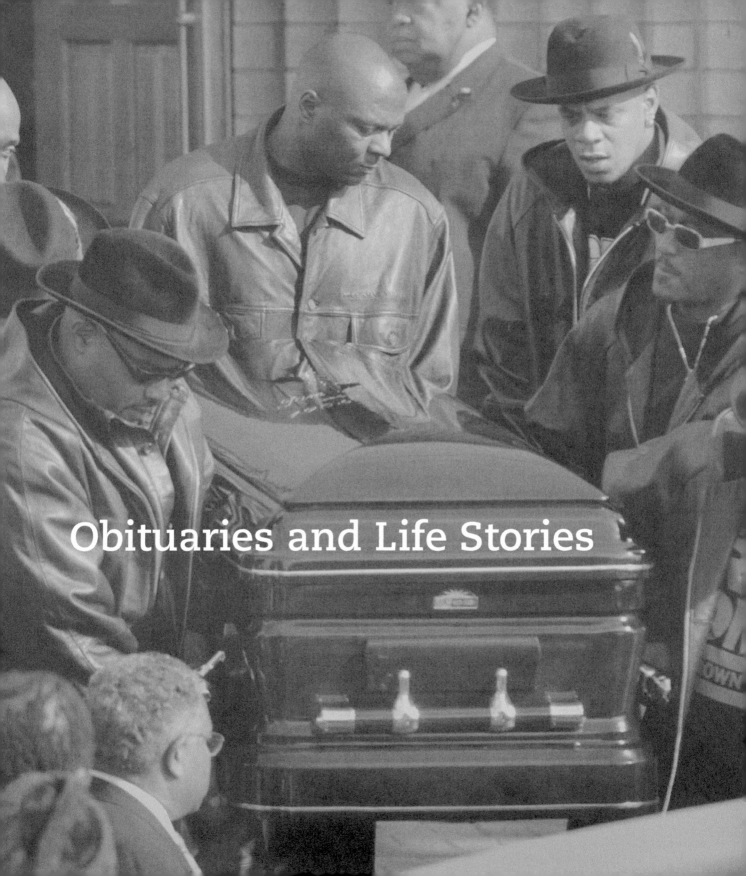

Obituaries and Life Stories

10

While being interviewed on radio about his job as obituary writer for *The Washington Post*, Richard Pearson was asked whether he had written his own obituary.

"No," he answered. "There are too many people in the news room [who] would want to rush it into print."

The *Post* didn't rush his obituary into print, but when he died, colleague Claudia Levy opened his obituary this way:

> Richard G. Pearson, 54, who crafted graceful obituaries
> for Cary Grant, George C. Wallace, Roy Rogers, Andy
> Warhol and thousands of other well-known and virtu-
> ally unknown people, died of pancreatic cancer Nov. 11
> at Virginia Hospital Center–Arlington.

As obituary editor of *The Washington Post*, Pearson chronicled masterfully the lives of movie stars, sports luminaries, senators, prime ministers, mathematicians, generals, sergeants, teachers, bus drivers, beekeepers, barbers, construction workers, cooks and housekeepers. Obit writing, he once observed, "made my life an adventure."

The *Post* has six people who write obituaries about people known and unknown. These obituaries are not formulaic pieces. They are profiles of the person.

In the online world, obituaries are big business. Newspaper Web sites sell advertising to funeral homes and auxiliary services because they have found that readers search for obituaries frequently. Even former residents of a city monitor obituaries. Some Web sites are devoted to obituaries and provide resources for readers and advertisers. One, www.legacy.com, partially owned by a newspaper, provides links and a searchable database to hundreds of newspapers and, in turn, sells advertising to the funeral industry. It also allows readers to post memorials to friends and family members who have died.

Web editors and entrepreneurs are just discovering the drawing power of obituaries, but most newspaper editors have known about obituaries for years. Chuck Ward, publisher of the Olean (N.Y.) *Times Herald*, once told his readers about the time his editor asked whether they should do a special obituary on the father of one of their employees.

"My response was that unless the father (or any relative) of the employee met the criteria for a glorified obituary, the obituary should be treated as 99 percent of our obituaries are."

He then recounted that when he went to the visitation that evening, the line extended 50 yards outside the mortuary. He returned in an hour, and the line was still long. That got Ward thinking about his question earlier in the day: "What did he do?"

"All he did, apparently, was live a wonderful, loving life with a splendid family. During the course of that life, he must have touched the lives of countless people in our community. And they all were there to say goodbye."

Ward learned that people don't have to be public figures to deserve well-reported obituaries. Too many obituaries read as if they were written by a computer program—efficient but lifeless. This tendency persists despite readership surveys that show that about 50 percent of readers look at obituaries, about twice as many as those that look at most other features.

And obituaries are read critically. If the deceased was an Odd Fellow, you'd better not say he was an Elk. If the deceased belonged to the Shiloh Baptist Church, count on a phone call if you say she was a member of Bethany Baptist. Reporting and writing obituaries is important work.

Despite this importance, many newspapers do not publish a news obituary unless the person who died was well-known. At many papers the advertising department handles obituaries as paid notices. Many metropolitan papers have adopted this policy because to publish obits on everyone who died in the area would require a substantial amount of space. *The Kansas City Star* published 14,600 obituaries in one year before it began charging. Where papers publish obits as advertising, the families often write some creative and entertaining obituaries. For instance, one wrote in a Utah paper, "He had his own ideas and some worked." Another wrote, "He devoted his retirement years to amassing a fortune of four dollars and thirteen cents."

Some large papers, such as *The New York Times*, the *Philadelphia Daily News*, *The Cincinnati Enquirer*, *The Detroit News* and *The Des Moines (Iowa) Register*, and some small papers, such as *The (Guntersville, Ala.) Advertiser-Gleam* and the *Columbia Missourian*, take obituaries seriously. Ron Liebau, metro editor of the *Enquirer*, told the *Gannetteer*, "For reporters who shrug them off, I tell them they probably don't have anything more important to do."

Jim Nicholson of the New York *Daily News*, who writes obituaries full-time, won the American Society of Newspaper Editors Distinguished Writing Award. Readers want to know, he said, "How did someone live a good life? How did they get through this world?"

Even if you work at a paper where most obituaries are paid notices or appear as death notices that are written from forms filled out by the family, when a prominent person dies, the news department will want a story. Knowing how to report and write an obit is important because you may make your first impression on an editor by the way you handle the assignment. The editor will examine your work critically. Is the information correct? Is it complete? Did you check additional sources? Did you follow newspaper style? Did you follow newspaper policy? This chapter examines such questions.

BASIC OBITUARY INFORMATION AND STYLE

An obituary is a news story. You should apply the same standards to crafting a lead and building the body of an obituary as you do to other stories.

Crafting a Lead

You begin by answering the same questions you would answer in any news story: who (Michael Kelly, 57, of 1234 West St.), what (died), where (at Regional Hospital), when (Tuesday night), why (heart attack) and how (while jogging). With this information, you are ready to start the story.

The fact that Kelly died of a heart attack suffered while jogging may well be the lead, but the reporter does not know this until the rest of the information essential to every obituary has been gathered. You also must know:

- Time and place of funeral services
- Time and place of burial
- Visitation time (if any)
- Survivors
- Date and place of birth
- Achievements
- Occupation
- Memberships

Any of these items can yield the nugget that will appear in the lead. However, if none of these categories yields notable information, the obituary will probably start like this:

> Michael Kelly, 57, of 1234 West St., died Tuesday night at Regional Hospital.

Another standard approach could be used later in the news cycle:

> Funeral services for Michael Kelly, 57, of 1234 West St., will be at 2 p.m. Thursday at St. Catherine's Roman Catholic Church.

However, good reporters often find distinguishing characteristics of a person's life. It may be volunteer service, an unusual or important job, service in public office or even just having a name of historical significance. Whatever distinguishes a person can be the lead of the obituary. These examples demonstrate engaging leads:

NASHVILLE, Tennessee (AP)—Del Reeves, a country music star who sprinkled his performances with humor and hit No. 1 on the country charts in 1965 with the song "Girl on the Billboard," has died. He was 74.

* * *

Linda Kay Berry didn't flinch when tarantulas, black widow spiders and 3-inch-long cockroaches crawled up her arm.

The slithering sensation of a snake across her neck sent her into smiles. Even a puncture wound from a king snake didn't stop her from loving all things creepy and crawly.

Berry, an animal keeper at the Museum of Discovery in Little Rock, died Tuesday of breast cancer. She was 53 and lived in Little Rock.

TIPS

Five Safeguards for Obit Writers

- Confirm spellings of names on the mortuary form.

- Check the addresses. If a telephone book or city directory lists a different address, contact the mortuary about the discrepancy.

- Check the birth date against the age, noting whether the person's birthday was before or after the date of death.

- Verify with the mortuary or family any obituary phoned or faxed to the newspaper.

- Check your newspaper's library for stories about the deceased, but be sure you don't pull stories about someone else with the same name.

Building the Story Body

You will find most of the obituary information on a standard form from the mortuary. When the reporter relies only on the form, this is usually what results:

Michael Kelly, 57, of 1234 West St., died Tuesday night at Regional Hospital.

Kelly collapsed while jogging and died apparently of a heart attack.

Services will be at 2 p.m. Thursday at St. Catherine's Roman Catholic Church. The Rev. Sherman Mitchell will officiate. Burial will be at Glendale Memorial Gardens in Springfield.

Friends may visit at the Fenton Funeral Chapel from 7 to 9 p.m. Wednesday.

Born Dec. 20, 1950, in Boston to Nathan and Sarah Kelly, Kelly was a member of St. Catherine's Roman Catholic Church and a U.S. Navy veteran of the Vietnam War. He had been an independent insurance agent for the last 25 years.

He married Pauline Virginia Hatfield in Boston on May 5, 1970.

Survivors include his wife; a son, Kevin, of Charlotte, N.C.; and a daughter, Mary, who is a student at the University of North Carolina at Chapel Hill.

Also surviving are a brother, John, of Milwaukee, Wis., and a sister, Margaret Carter, of Asheville, N.C.

WRITING LIFE STORIES

The Kelly obituary is a dry biography, not a story of his life. There is no hint of Kelly's impact on friends, family or community. Good reporting produces stories of life, such as this one:

Jyles Robert Whittler, a World War I veteran and son of a former slave, died Monday at Truman Veterans Hospital. He was 100.

Mr. Whittler helped build the Missouri United Methodist Church in Springfield and served as its janitor for 55 years. In 1986, the church's basement social hall was christened the Jyles Whittler Fellowship Hall in his honor.

"He's a legend in Springfield and rightfully so," said his friend Roy Smith. "He labored hard and lived well. He's in heaven."

The more traditional biographical information, along with information about visitation and funeral services, appears later in the story.

When writing a life story, you ask people what was important to the deceased and what the evidence for that is. If the subject volunteered, find out where and why and talk to the people served. Your goal is to capture the theme of the person's life. If the family and friends recognize the deceased in your story as the person they knew, you have done your job. Amy Rabideau Silvers, the obituary writer for the *Milwaukee Journal Sentinel*, provides such an example in Figure 10.1.

"I don't write about death, I write about life."

— Michael Best, *The Detroit News*

A Life Story

OBITUARY
A life of love was made public in end
Couple came out, testified at Capitol

By Amy Rabideau Silvers, Staff
Milwaukee Journal Sentinel

The opening teases, much like a feature story lead.

For nearly 49 years, Richard Taylor and Ray Vahey did not speak openly about their long and loving relationship.

They did not tell family. They did not tell friends at work.

Two short sentences in a separate paragraph bring attention to themselves.

That changed a year ago, after Vahey was asked if they might speak at PrideFest. Together, they wrote a speech. Vahey gave it, Taylor at his side.

This is the "so what." It establishes the impact Vahey and Taylor had on the state debate. This story is a history of an era told through the experience of two men, one of whom died.

They went on to other appearances, including a state hearing last November in Madison, speaking against the proposed amendment that would ban gay marriage and civil unions in Wisconsin. They spoke at area churches. They were asked to speak at PrideFest in June, but Taylor, hospitalized with cancer, was too ill to go.

"We wrote the speech together at his hospital bed," Vahey said. Then Taylor said something Vahey will never forget.

This strong anecdote motivates the reader to keep on reading.

"Ray, remember, I'm standing right beside you," he said.

"And I feel that now," Vahey said.

News peg. This is a variation of the focus structure.

Richard Taylor died Friday. He was 81.

By chance, his name appeared twice in the *Journal Sentinel* on Sunday. The longtime partners were mentioned in a "Crossroads" opinion piece opposing the proposed amendment. His death notice appeared in the same edition.

"We were from the silent generation," Vahey said. "It was an exaggerated version of don't ask, don't tell."

Vahey is the primary source because they lived together for nearly 50 years.

"I was 18 and he was 31" when they met in 1956, Vahey said. Both grew up in Ohio—Taylor in Cleveland and Vahey in Youngstown.

Taylor's service in the Navy becomes important later in the story.

"When Richard was 17, he convinced his father to allow him to join the Navy during World War II," Vahey said.

Taylor served aboard a naval tanker on convoy duty, first in the North Atlantic and then in the Mediterranean. His tanker next moved into the Pacific.

(continued)

Figure 10.1
This life story uses the basic focus structure. All it lacks is a tie-back.

Figure 10.1
(continued)

"His tanker fueled a cruiser while it bombarded Mount Suribachi on Iwo Jima, and then they went on to Okinawa, where they came under kamikaze attack," he said.

Taylor, who had a high school education, was also self-taught, widely read in economics and philosophy, history and politics. As the two men grew older, they came to see history in a new light.

Here is the impact of his Navy service. →

"Richard voluntarily put himself into harm's way to protect his country and the rights of all Americans of that day, and all of the generations that have followed. Now there is an attempt to separate Richard from society and take away his right to equality under the law."

Over the years, they lived in Ohio, Illinois, California, New Jersey and Virginia. In 2000 they decided to move to Milwaukee, a city they knew from visits to Taylor's brother.

Finally, they decided to step out of the closet for good.

"I never told my sister about us until the night we testified in Madison," Vahey said, adding that she took the news without surprise or judgment. "It was like the elephant in the living room. It was there, but no one addressed it."

← This anecdote reveals the depth of their cover-up.

The official transcripts of hearings and stories in your newspaper library are good sources for quotes. →

"Euphemisms like 'partnership' or 'union' set us apart from society," Vahey said at the Legislative hearing last fall. "Substitute terms that categorize and separate us become our yellow Star of David badges. . . . Here at home, African-Americans learned long ago that 'separate but equal' is not equal."

Taylor and Vahey planned a wedding ceremony for Sept. 16, the 50th anniversary of their life together. But when Taylor became increasingly ill, they had moved up the date, marrying in a religious ceremony at the hospital on Memorial Day. Invitations now will be sent for a special memorial event Sept. 16, which also will be a fund-raiser for Fair Wisconsin's anti-amendment efforts.

Visitation will be from 5 to 7 p.m. today at the Suminski Family Funeral Home, 1901 N. Farwell Ave.

← The story concludes with basic obituary information.

In addition to Vahey, Taylor is survived by brother Robert Morgan, nieces and nephews.

Here is another example built on good reporting:

Ila Watson Portwood died Sunday at the Candlelight Care Center of complications stemming from a stroke she suffered about two weeks earlier. She was 89.

She was born on Aug. 30, 1914, in Boone County. She graduated from Howard-Payne School in Howard County and attended the University of Michigan.

She was the former owner and operator of the Gem Drug Company. She and her late husband, Carl, started as employees in 1935 and bought the business in 1962. They retired in 1981 and sold the company to Harold Earnest.

"She was a total lady," Earnest said. "I've never seen her mistreat anyone. Just the sweetest lady anyone can meet."

Mrs. Portwood volunteered from 1980 to 1986 at the Cancer Research Center's Women's Cancer Control Program and was named volunteer of the year in 1983.

"She was a people person," said Rosetta Miller, program coordinator. "Her caring personalized her commitment to the staff and patients."

Whittler and Portwood were ordinary people whose lives affected others. An obituary should celebrate that life rather than merely note the death.

Writing a life story is like writing a feature story. You seek anecdotes that reveal the person. Your sources include the mortuary form, paid funeral notices, your publication's own library, and family and friends of the deceased.

SOURCES OF INFORMATION

The Mortuary Form

For many newspapers the standard form from the mortuary is the primary source of information. The mortuary can be of further help if you need more information. Does your city editor want a picture of the deceased? Call the mortuary. They can usually obtain one quickly from the family. Is there some conflicting or unclear information on the form? Call the mortuary.

Writing obituaries from the mortuary's information alone is a clerk's work. As a reporter, you should go beyond the form. You should also confirm every fact on the sheet. Mortuary forms are notoriously inaccurate.

Sometimes, what the mortuary form doesn't tell you is as important as what it does. For the writer of the following obit, the first clue that the death notice was unusual was the age. The deceased was 12. That alone was enough for the reporter to start asking questions. The result was an obituary that moved from the records column to the front page:

Sandra Ann Hill, 12, lost her lifetime struggle against a mysterious muscle ailment Wednesday night. The day she died was the first day she had ever been admitted as a hospital inpatient.

Although they knew it was coming, the

end came suddenly for Sandra's family and school friends, said her father, Lester, of 1912 Jackson St.

Just last Friday, she attended special classes at the Parkdale School. "She loved it there," Hill said. "Like at recess, when the sixth graders would come in and read to her. She always wanted to be the center of attention."

"Bright as a silver dollar" was the way one of Sandra's early teachers described her. In fact, no one will ever know. Sandra couldn't talk.

"We didn't know what she knew or didn't know," her father said. Sandra's only communication with the world around her came in the form of smiles and frowns — her symbols for yes and no.

"There were times when I'd come around the corner and kind of stick my head around and say 'boo,'" her father recalled. "She smiled. She liked that."

The care and attention Sandra demanded makes the loss particularly hard for her family to accept, Hill said. "I can't really put it into words. You cope with it the best you can, keep her comfortable and happy. We always took her with us."

Sandra came down with bronchitis Fri-day. Complications forced her to be admitted Wednesday to Lincoln County Hospital, where she died later that night.

Sandra's fight for life was uphill all the way. It started simply enough when she was 4 months old. Her mother, Bonnie, noticed she "wasn't holding up her head" like her other children.

Although her ailment was never firmly diagnosed, doctors found Sandra's muscles held only half the tissues and fibers in a normal child's body. The diagnosis: a type of cerebral palsy. The prognosis: Sandra had little chance to live past the age of 2. Medical knowledge offered little help.

Sandra was born in Springfield on Jan. 15, 1984. She is survived by her parents; one brother, Michael Eugene Hill; one sister, Terrie Lynn Hill, both of the home; and her grandparents, Gordon Hill of Seale, Ala., and Mrs. Carrie Harris of Phoenix, Ariz.

Services will be at 3:30 p.m. today at the Memorial Funeral Chapel with the Rev. Jack Gleason conducting. Burial will follow at the Memorial Park Cemetery.

The family will receive friends at the Memorial Funeral Home until time for the service.

The reporter who wrote this obituary obviously did a great deal of research beyond what was on the mortuary form. Because the girl was not a public figure, the reporter could not consult a reference work such as *Who's Who in America* or a national publication. But the reporter did have access to the newspaper library and could interview the girl's family and friends.

Paid Funeral Notices

Another good source of information is the paid funeral notices in the newspaper. A reporter in Columbus, Ind., spotted an interesting story when he realized that an obituary notice from a funeral home was for the city's "broom man." The resulting story, which appeared on Page One, began this way:

You probably knew him.

Notice of his death Christmas Day almost seemed to fade among the others published Thursday. Ernest W. Ferrenburg, 75, of 1210 California died at 2:50 p.m. Wednesday at Bartholomew County Hospital, the notice said.

"Nobody knew him by his name. He was just the old broom salesman," said one of his six daughters, Irene Michaelis of Greenwood.

Workers and shoppers probably can recall seeing Ferrenburg standing on a street corner downtown on Washington Street, holding a generous stock of brooms of various shapes and sizes. The thin white cane he carried told passersby he had lost his sight. That happened in a gun accident when he was 19.

The story ends this way:

Ferrenburg never considered himself handicapped.

"I can hear birds sing. I can hear little children," Mrs. Michaelis said her father replied when asked whether he would rather see than hear. "I'd rather be blind anytime than deaf."

Hartford Courant reporter Leonard Bernstein wrote about another remarkable life after the obituary notice had already been published. It began this way:

For as long as anyone can remember, David Lowery had two dreams: to buy his own home and raise his own children.

For 23 years, he worked — often two jobs at a time — and finally, on Sept. 1, 1983, he bought a house in Hartford.

Within nine months, the second dream was fulfilled: On June 11, Lowery became a single father, bringing home two brothers from Massachusetts who had been seeking a family for two years.

And then it ended.

On July 8, a cool Sunday evening, Lowery was driving his new family home from church in Middletown when he pulled to the side of I-91 and told the boys he was sick. The 10-year-old flagged down a passing car; the 13-year-old climbed in to go for help.

Seven hours later, David Lowery, 44, was dead of a cerebral hemorrhage.

His death did not make the headlines. No famous people spoke at the funeral.

But David Lowery — a Big Brother for 14 years in Hartford, a member of Shiloh Baptist Church in Middletown where he sang and formed a youth choir, a regular visitor to people whom others had forgotten — was loved by many, and they still mourn.

Each of these last two stories could have been run as a combination obituary and death story if someone had pursued the obituary information when it came to the city room.

The Newspaper Library

In the newspaper library, you may find an interview with the deceased, an interesting feature story or clips indicating activities not included on the mortuary form. In an interview or feature story the person may have made a statement about a philosophy of life that would be appropriate to include in the obituary. The subject also may have indicated his or her goals in life, against which later accomplishments can be measured. You can find the names of friends and co-workers in the clips as well. These people are often the source of rich anecdotes and comments about the deceased.

The New York Times recognized an interesting person when staff members checked the files of Selma Koch. Writer Douglas Martin shared Koch's life story with readers:

> Selma Koch, a Manhattan store owner who earned a national reputation by helping women find the right bra size, mostly through a discerning glance and never with a tape measure, died Thursday at Mount Sinai Medical Center. She was 95 and a 34B.
>
> In the final years of her life, Mrs. Koch appeared on national television and radio programs to discuss her specialty and her occupational longevity. She relished her celebrity, but not as much as she loved guiding the generations of women who visited her store: She worked seven 10-hour days last week instead of her usual six.
>
> Her grandson Danny said he guessed that her only regret would be not dying in the family's store, the Town Shop on Broadway at 82nd Street, something she had often said she hoped to do.

Meyer concluded the life story with this quote:

> Mrs. Koch never stopped wondering why people kept asking her questions. "What's the big deal?" the small woman asked in her raspy, staccato voice. "I'm just selling bras."

Your newspaper's files are not the only source for information on people who have state or national reputations. You or your librarian should also search electronic databases for stories that have appeared in other publications.

Interviews with Family and Friends

Papers treat public figures in more detail than private citizens not only because they are newsworthy but also because reporters know more about them. Even though private citizens are usually less newsworthy, many good stories about them are never written because the reporter did not — or was afraid to — do the reporting. The fear is usually unfounded. Silvers of the *Milwaukee Journal Sentinel* says she always asks family members if it is a good time to talk. It is her way of quickly acknowledging that she knows she is intruding. "It has been fascinating how people want to talk," Silvers says.

That's true even in the worst of circumstances, such as a suicide. Karen Ball, a former reporter for the *Columbia Missourian*, learned that lesson when she was assigned to do a story on Robert Somers, a university professor who had committed suicide. Ball didn't look forward to calling Mrs. Somers. First, Ball talked to students, Somers' colleagues and university staff members. She even obtained a copy of his résumé.

ON THE JOB

Bringing Obituaries to Life

Amy Rabideau Silvers, obituary writer for the *Milwaukee Journal Sentinel* since 2000, says she is still surprised by the amount of feedback she gets. Once she wrote about James Harris, a black bricklayer who had waged a legal fight all the way to the Wisconsin Supreme Court for the right to join the all-white union. His niece called Silvers later to say that a man no one in the family knew asked to speak at the funeral. He had read the obituary in the newspaper, she said, and was touched by Harris' story. A Latino, he told of working with another union in the 1950s and losing his job after being too outspoken about unequal conditions for minority workers.

"I didn't know James Harris, but he was my brother," he told the mourners.

There was hardly a dry eye in the church.

Silvers had been a reporter for more than 20 years when she was asked to assume the obituary-writing duties. Her predecessor had fallen ill. She eventually wrote his obituary and over a thousand others.

"It feels like I'm telling history one person at a time," she says.

Some journalists can't imagine calling the families of the deceased, but Silvers says the reception is positive.

"It has been fascinating how people want to talk," she says. She tells them she is after stories, not just résumé information. "It is really a chance to talk about things that are important in life."

Writing stories about the deceased gives her an opportunity to tell real stories about real people. Once she wrote about the death of a young girl. When the father went to the drugstore to buy copies of the paper, he saw people reading the front-page story. When the mother later called to thank Silvers, she told of hearing strangers talking about her daughter, and of the cards, letters and donations the family had received. That kind of feedback keeps Silvers writing life stories.

"By knowing a lot about him—where he'd studied, what his interests were and where he worked—I knew that I could go into an interview with a bereaved relative and at least have something to talk about," she says.

Ball approached Mrs. Somers in person and explained that her husband was respected and liked. Mrs. Somers agreed to talk. To get her to elaborate on his personality and what he was like away from school, Ball prodded her with questions about their children, where they had lived before and other family matters. She also talked to Somers' mother. Ball told her some of the positive things that students and faculty had said about her son. That helped the mother deal with her sorrow and helped Ball write her story. The story of Somers' life began:

Miko Somers sat at her kitchen table folding and unfolding her youngest daughter's bib as she talked about her husband.

"He could never do anything halfway," Mrs. Somers says. "He set such a high standard for himself. Whatever he did had to be the very best, and he pushed himself to make it that way."

Today Mrs. Somers buries her husband. Monday, Robert Somers, 40, her husband for 17 years, the father of their four daughters and an associate professor in the University's history department, took his life by driving his car head-on into a tree.

Karen Ball didn't know the Somers family, but she still got the story. Even when you know someone, good reporting can improve the story. Tracy Breton of *The Providence Journal* learned early one morning that a judge whom she had covered on and off for 26 years had died. Visiting the judge's home at the invitation of his wife, Tracy learned a good deal more about the man she thought she already knew.

"I was surprised at how modestly he lived," she said, "and learned some things about the judge that I didn't know—like where he played golf with his wife (the judge's golf clubs were stored in the living room, up against a wall behind the TV), the fact that he had attended a computer class that day before watching the NCAA basketball tournament on TV, and that the judge had been stressed over the trial he was presiding over. . . ."

At the judge's wake, two Superior Court judges asked Breton if she would write their obituaries when the time came. That's high praise.

"We write about how people lived, not how they died."

—Kay Powell, *The Atlanta Journal-Constitution*

Allen Green, Fort Wayne — 1923–2000

Allen Green, 77, of Fort Wayne, a member of First Baptist Church, died Saturday, Nov. 11, 2000, at home.

The Indian Mound, Tenn., native was a World War II Army veteran. He had worked for 31 years at Hobby Ranch House as a custodian and also at Trinity Lutheran School for 15 years.

Surviving are his daughters, Frances Green of Oklahoma and Wanda Fay Higgins of Kalamazoo, Mich.; sons Johnny of Ohio and Charles of Tennessee; stepsons George Dahl, Joseph Dahl of Castle Hayne, N.C., and Willard Dahl of Fort Wayne; stepdaughters Aira of Maryland, Audrey Sanders of Hanover, Pa., Sandra Yancey and Margaret McClellen, both of Fort Wayne; sisters Bessie L. Jackson of Pennville and Gladys Keats of Indian Mound, Tenn.; brothers Monroe L. of Zanesville, James A. of Fort Wayne and Horace L. of Hunting; 29 grandchildren; and 19 great-grandchildren.

He was preceded in death by his first wife, Nellie; his second wife, Emma; sisters Gerline Cherry and Della Jones; and a brother, Lester.

Services are 1 p.m. Wednesday at D.O. McComb & Sons Lakeside Park Funeral Home, 1140 Lake Ave., with calling from 2 to 5 and 7 to 9 p.m. Tuesday. Burial will be at Lindenwood Cemetery.

Memorials are to the family.

Figure 10.2
Beginning in 1998, *The News-Sentinel* in Fort Wayne, Ind., doubled the space devoted to obituaries, added information and improved the presentation. Executive Editor Joe Weiler said his goal is "to give all people the dignity and respect they deserve, to make sure that all the vital information is included, and that bureaucratic rule making doesn't stand in the way of doing the right thing."

NEWSPAPER POLICY

Newspaper policy often dictates what will—and will not—be included in an obituary. Newspapers that have written policies may prescribe how to handle everything from addresses to suicides.

Some newspapers, for instance, prohibit a statement such as "In lieu of flowers, the family requests donations be made to the county humane society." This prohibition is in response to lobbying from florists.

Because of threats to the safety of property and the individuals involved, in some cities even information essential to the obituary no longer appears in the paper. Some newspapers specifically tell reporters not to include the address of the deceased. Criminals have used information taken from the obituary columns to prey on survivors. Knowing the time of the funeral and the address of the deceased makes it easy to plan a break-in at the empty residence during the services. Therefore, this information may be withheld.

Two other kinds of information on which newspapers may have restrictive policies are the cause of death and potentially embarrassing information.

Cause of Death

If the person who dies is not a public figure and the family does not wish to divulge the cause of death, some newspapers will comply. That is questionable news judgment. The reader wants to know what caused the death. A reporter should call the mortuary, the family, the attending physician and the appropriate medical officer. Only if none of these sources will talk should the newspaper leave out the cause of death. Many newspapers require that obituaries include the cause of death in the version that the newspaper writes.

> **"**People are drawn to the obit page because they want to know the secret. They want to know, 'How did someone live a good life? How did they get through this world?'**"**
>
> — Jim Nicholson, *Philadelphia Daily News*

A death certificate must be filed for each death, but obtaining it often takes days, and some states do not make the cause of death part of the public record. Even if the state lists the cause of death and the reporter has timely access to the death certificate, the information is often vague.

If the death is caused by cancer or a heart attack or is the result of an accident, most families do not object to including the cause in the obituary. But if the deceased died of AIDS, many families object to mentioning the disease. You can print the cause without the family's consent, but you have to be certain it is correct, and the family is one of the few sources at deadline.

If the deceased was a public figure or a young person, most newspapers insist on the cause of death. If the death is the result of suicide or foul play, reporters can obtain the information from the police or the medical examiner. Some newspapers include suicide as the cause of death in the obituary, others print it in a separate news story, and still others ignore it altogether. This is one way to report a suicide:

Services for Gary O'Neal, 34, a local carpenters' union officer, will be at 9 a.m. Thursday in the First Baptist Church. Coroner Mike Pardee ruled that Mr. O'Neal died Tuesday of a self-inflicted gunshot wound.

Embarrassing Information

Another newspaper policy affecting obituaries concerns embarrassing information. When the *St. Louis Post-Dispatch* reported in an obituary that the deceased had been disbarred and that he had been a key witness in a bribe scandal involving a well-known politician 13 years earlier, several callers complained. The paper's reader's advocate defended the decision to include that history in the obituary:

> One who called to complain about the obit told me it reminded her of the quotation from Shakespeare's *Julius Caesar*, about how the good a man does is often buried with him and forgotten.
>
> Yes, I said, and the first part of that quotation could be paraphrased to say that the news a man makes often lives after him.

When author W. Somerset Maugham died, *The New York Times* reported that he was a homosexual, even though the subject generally had not been discussed in public before. Yet many years later, when Susan Sontag died, few publications included the fact that she had acknowledged her bisexuality in a newspaper interview. When Bill Mauldin, a Pulitzer Prize-winning editorial cartoonist, died in 2003, the *Chicago Sun-Times*, where he had worked for years, wrote, "In his last years, Mr. Mauldin battled alcoholism and Alzheimer's." AIDS is the latest cause of death to trouble editors. Because AIDS still carries a stigma, some go out of their way to make certain people don't think the cause of death was AIDS.

The more AIDS or any other disease is reported as a cause of death, the more people will agree to its publication. Cancer once had a similar stigma. In Boise, Idaho, the newspaper reported that several people requested before they died that AIDS be listed as the cause. They did this to make others more aware of the disease. One professor who has studied AIDS coverage suggests that obituary writers ought not to soften the language or use euphemisms when reporting AIDS-related deaths; they should refer to AIDS "patients" rather than "victims"; and they should try to reach the family for information and confirmation.

The crucial factor in determining the extent to which you should report details of an individual's private life is whether the deceased was a public or private person. A public figure is someone who has been in the public eye. A participant in civic or social activities, a person who spoke out at public meetings or through the mass media, a performer, an author, a speaker—these all may be public figures. A public official, an individual who has been elected or appointed to public office, is generally treated like a public figure.

Whether the subject is a public figure or a private citizen, the decisions newspapers must make when dealing with the obituary are sensitive and complicated. It is your obligation to be aware of your newspaper's policy. In the absence of a clear policy statement, consult the city editor.

CHOOSING YOUR WORDS

Avoid much of the language found on mortuary forms and in obituaries prepared by morticians. The phrasing is often more fitting for a eulogy than for a newspaper story.

Because of the sensitivity of the subject matter, euphemisms have crept into the vocabulary of obituary writers. "Loved ones," "passed away," "our dearly beloved brother and father," "the departed" and "remains" may be fine for eulogies, but such terms are out of place in a news story. Note that a man is survived by his wife, not his widow, and a woman is survived by her husband, not her widower.

Watch your language, too, when you report the cause and circumstances of a death. Unless the doctor is at fault, a person usually dies not "as a result of an operation," but "following" or "after" one. Also, a person dies "unexpectedly" but not "suddenly." All deaths are sudden. Note, too, that a person dies "apparently of a heart attack" but not of "an apparent heart attack," and a person dies of injuries "suffered," not "received."

Be careful with religious terms. Catholics "celebrate" Mass; Reform Jews usually worship in temples, Orthodox and Conservative Jews in synagogues. An Episcopal priest who heads a parish is a rector, not a pastor. Followers of Islam are called Muslims.

Consult *The Associated Press Stylebook* and your newspaper's stylebook when you have a question. Do you use titles such as Mr. and Mrs.? Do you mention divorced spouses, deceased spouses or live-in companions? Do you identify pallbearers? Do you say when memorial contributions are requested? You may need to consult your stylebook often when you are writing an obit.

> **"**People are a lot more open than they were, but I think that they're still not open enough when it comes to AIDS. It's been my experience that nobody will admit it unless they are in the arts. If somebody in business dies of AIDS, we may never know about it.**"**
>
> — Irvin Horowitz, obituary writer, *The New York Times*

TIPS

Choosing Your Words

- Avoid euphemisms; such terms are out of place in a news story.

- Watch your language as you report the cause and circumstances of the death.

- Be careful with religious terms.

Suggested Readings

Hart, Jack and Johnson, Janis. "A Clash Between the Public's Right to Know and a Family's Need for Privacy." *Quill*, May 1979, pp. 19–24. An account of the backlash against a newspaper that printed a syndicated story of how the daughter of a locally prominent family had died a big-city prostitute.

Hipple, John and Wells, Richard. "Media Can Reduce Risks in Suicide Stories." *Editor & Publisher*, Oct. 14, 1989, p. 72. A journalist and a counselor who specializes in treating suicidal young people offer suggestions on handling stories involving suicide.

Johnson, Marilyn. *The Dead Beat: Lost Souls, Lucky Stiffs, and the Perverse Pleasures of Obituaries*. New York: HarperCollins, 2006. Johnson, who has written obituaries of Princess Diana and others and has been an editor at *Esquire*, *Redbook* and *Outside*, writes about the writers who do obituaries. The book is not only informative but also entertaining.

Robins, Wayne. "Obituaries a Staple Offline — and On." *Editor & Publisher*, July 24, 2000, p. 27. A roundup of obituaries on the Web.

Siegel, Marvin, ed. *The Last Word: The New York Times Book of Obituaries and Farewells: A Celebration of Unusual Lives*. New York: Quill, 1998. Examples of well-written and compelling obituaries from *The New York Times*.

Suggested Web Sites

www.legacy.com
This interactive site offers access to thousands of obituaries that have appeared in newspapers across the country.

www.obitpage.com
This site is by and for obituary writers and readers. It includes interesting obituaries, interviews, news about conferences for obituary writers and readers and other interesting information.

www.projo.com/words/index.htm
The Providence Journal's Web site for writers includes an index of stories by staff members describing how they reported and wrote stories. Select "Index of Past Writing Tips," then "Profiles." Scroll down to Tracy Breton's article, "Capturing a Complex Personality in an Obit," May 4, 2000.

Exercises

1. Write a life story of your class professor.

2. Which elements are missing from the following obituaries?

    a. John Peterson died Saturday at Springfield Hospital. Funeral services will be at 1:30 p.m. Tuesday. Friends may call at the Restwell Funeral Home, 2560 Walnut St., from 6 to 9 p.m. Monday. The Rev. William Thomas will officiate at services in the First Baptist Church. Burial will be at City Cemetery.

    b. Richard G. Tindall, Springfield, a retired U.S. Army brigadier general, died at his daughter's home in Summit, N.J. Graveside services will be at 2 p.m. July 3 at Arlington National Cemetery in Arlington, Va.

3. Write a lead for an obituary from the following information:

    Martha Sattiewhite, born July 2, 1986, to Don and Mattie Sattiewhite, in Springfield. Martha was killed in a car accident June 30, 2007. Funeral services will be July 2. She was president of her Springfield High School senior class and of the sophomore class at the University of Oklahoma.

4. An obituary notice comes from a local funeral home. It contains the basic information, but under achievements it lists only "former member of Lion's Club." Your city editor tells you to find out more about the deceased. Whom would you call and why?

5. If George Thomas, private citizen, committed suicide while alone in his home, would you include that fact in his obituary? Why or why not?

6. A few newspapers write obituaries of notable people in advance because the time between the death and publication can be short. Some papers even interview the subject. Write a two-page advance obituary of one of the following: Condoleezza Rice, Henry Cisneros, Colin Powell, Madonna or your university president. At the end, list your sources.

Finding the News in News Releases

11

IN THIS CHAPTER
YOU WILL LEARN:

1. What types of news releases there are.

2. How to handle the news release.

A 2005 news release from Pfizer Inc. began this way:

> Pfizer Inc. said today that the United States Court of Appeals for the Federal Circuit ruled in the company's favor in a lawsuit by generic manufacturer Teva Pharmaceuticals challenging Pfizer's patent for its antidepressant Zoloft.

Just another news release? Is there a story here? What does this mean to perhaps thousands of your readers who take the antidepressant? To Pfizer's shareholders?

"A news release led me to the most important story I ever wrote," says Judd Slivka, a general assignment reporter for *The Arizona Republic*. (See the "On the Job" box later in this chapter.) Reporters do not go out and dig up all the stories they write. Many stories come to them. They are mailed, e-mailed, telephoned, faxed or hand-delivered by people who want to get something in "the news." They come from people or offices with different titles: public-relations departments, public-information offices, community-relations bureaus, press agents, press secretaries and publicity offices. The people who write them call their stories news releases or press releases.

Because good publicity is so important, private individuals, corporations and government agencies spend a great deal of money to obtain it. Much of the money goes for the salaries of skilled and experienced personnel, many of whom have worked in the news business. Part of their job is to write news releases that newspapers, radio and television stations, and syndicated public-relations wire services will use and that will appear on Web sites perhaps throughout the world. PR Newswire, for example, says it issues more than 1,000 news releases every day.

You may very well want to be among the people who write news releases. You may be seeking a career in public relations or advertising, but your journalism department wisely has you begin by studying news and newswriting. Only by studying news and how news organizations handle news will you be successful in public relations or in offices of public information. Knowing how reporters are taught to deal with news releases will help you write better releases if that ever is your job. Of course, studying news also helps you enormously in the advertising world.

Skilled public-relations or public-information practitioners know how to write news, and they apply all the principles of good newswriting in their news releases. A good news release meets the criteria for a good news story.

Nevertheless, as two of the best PR professionals, Carole Howard, formerly of *Reader's Digest*, and Wilma Mathews, formerly with AT&T and now director of public relations at Arizona State University, tell us, news releases are never intended to take the place of reporters. News releases, they write in *On Deadline: Managing Media Relations*, simply acquaint an editor with the basic facts of potential stories. Those who write news releases come to accept that their carefully crafted sentences will be checked and rewritten by reporters.

As a reporter, you must recognize that news releases are both a help and a hindrance to a newspaper. They are a help because without them, newspapers would need many more reporters. They are a hindrance because they sometimes contain incomplete or even incorrect information. Because they are intended to promote the interests and favorable reputation of the individuals and organizations that disseminate them, news releases, by their very nature, are not objective.

Nevertheless, wise editors do not discard news releases without reading them. These editors often give them to reporters, often the newest ones, as sources for stories.

When your editor hands you a news release, you are expected to know what to do with it. You must be able to recognize the news in the release and apply all that you have learned about news values. The release may lead you to a good story. Your resourcefulness may improve your chances of being assigned to bigger things.

TYPES OF NEWS RELEASES

After you have read a number of news releases, you will notice that generally they fall into three categories:

- Announcements of coming events or of personnel matters — hiring, promoting, retiring and the like.
- Information about a cause.
- Information that is meant to build someone's or some organization's image.

Recognizing the types and purposes of news releases (and recognizing that some are hybrids and serve more than one purpose) will help you know how to rewrite them.

Announcement Releases

Organizations use the news media to tell their members and the public about coming events. For example:

> The Camera Club will have a special meeting at Wyatt's Cafeteria at 7 p.m. on Wednesday, March 20. Marvin Miller will present a slide program on "Yellowstone in Winter." All interested persons are invited to attend.

Although the release promotes the Camera Club, it also serves as a public-service announcement. Newspapers that print such announcements are serving their readers. Here is another example:

> The first reception of the new season of the Springfield Art League will be on Sunday, Sept. 8, 3 to 5 p.m. in the Fine Arts Building.
>
> Included in the exhibition will be paintings, serigraphs, sculpture, batiks, weaving, pottery, jewelry, all created by Art League members, who throughout the summer have been preparing works for this opening exhibit of the season.
>
> The event also will feature local member-artists' State Fair entries, thus giving all who could not get to the fair the opportunity to see these works.
>
> The exhibition continues to Friday, Sept. 13. All gallery events and exhibitions are free.

Other news release announcements concern appointments, promotions, hiring and retiring. The announcement of an appointment may read like this:

James McAlester, internationally known rural sociologist at Springfield University, has been appointed to the board of directors of Bread for the World, according to William Coburn, executive director of the humanitarian organization.

McAlester attended his first board meeting Jan. 22 in New York City. He has been on the university faculty since 1999. Prior to that, he served as the Ford Foundation representative in India for 17 years.

The 19,000-member Bread for the World organization is a "broad based interdenominational movement of Christian citizens who advocate government policies that address the basic causes of hunger in the world," says Coburn.

The occasion is the appointment of McAlester, but the release also describes the purpose of the Bread for the World organization. By educating readers about the organization's purpose, the writer hoped to promote its cause.

Companies often send releases when an employee has been promoted. For example:

James B. Withers Jr. was named senior vice president in charge of sales of the J.B. Withers Company, it was announced Tuesday.

Withers, who has been with the company in the sales division for two years, will head a sales force of 23 people.

"We are sure Jim can do the job," James B. Withers Sr., company president, said. "He brings youth, intelligence and enthusiasm to the job. We're pleased he has decided to stay with the company."

Founded in 1936, the J.B. Withers Company is the country's second-largest manufacturer of dog and cat collars.

A release like this one is an attempt by the company to get its name before the public and to create employee goodwill. Written in the form of an announcement, it is an attempt at free publicity.

Cause-Promoting Releases

News releases in this category seek to further a cause. Some of these releases come from organizations whose worthwhile causes are in need of funds or volunteers. The letter reprinted here is from a county chairman of the American Heart Association to the editor of a newspaper. It is not written in the form of a release, but its effect is meant to be the same:

The alumnae and collegiate members of the Alpha Phi Sorority have just completed their annual Alpha Phi "Helping Hearts" lollipop sale. This year Valerie Knight, project chairwoman, led sorority members to achieve record-breaking sales. The lollipop sale is a national project of the Alpha Phi Sorority.

Sunday, March 5, Valerie Knight presented a check for $1,800 to the American Heart Association, Shelby County Unit. The contribution was presented during a reception at the Alpha Phi house. This contribution is an important part of the annual fund-raising campaign of the American Heart Association.

> I wish to extend special thanks to the members of Alpha Phi and in particular to Valerie Knight for this outstanding project.
>
> In addition, I wish to thank the many merchants who participated in the project by selling lollipops in their businesses.

Heads of organizations attempt to alert the public to their message in any way they can. Any release, notice or letter they can get printed for free leaves money for the cause that they represent.

Image-Building Releases

Another kind of news release serves to build up some person's or some organization's image. Politicians seek to be elected or to be re-elected. They desire as much free publicity as they can get. For example:

> James M. Merlin, honorary chairman of the board and director of Merlin Corporation, has been named honorary chairman of the Finance Committee, which will seek city-wide financial support for the campaign to elect Hong Xiang as Springfield's next mayor.
>
> Merlin, a well-known civic leader and philanthropist, termed the election of Xiang "one of the most important and far-reaching decisions the voters of Springfield will make in a long time. The city's financial crisis can only be solved through the kind of economic leadership Xiang has demonstrated the past 10 years as 1st Ward councilperson."

The appointment of Merlin as honorary chairman serves only to promote the image of the candidate. The quote is self-serving.

Organizations and government agencies at all levels often try to build their public image. Many of them have local mayors proclaim a day or a week of recognition, as in the following:

> Mayor Juanita Williams has proclaimed Saturday, May 11, as Fire Service Recognition Day. The Springfield Fire Department in conjunction with the University Fire Service Training Division is sponsoring a demonstration of the fire apparatus and equipment at the Springfield Fire Training Center. The displays are from 10 a.m. to 5 p.m. at 700 Bear Blvd. All citizens are urged to attend the display or visit their neighborhood fire station on May 11.
>
> Our PRODUCT is your SAFETY.

An editor who hands you a release like this has probably decided that it is worth using in some form. The rest is up to you.

HANDLING THE NEWS RELEASE

Regardless of the type of news release, be sure to read the information that appears at the top (see Figure 11.1). All of that information may be useful to you. Even so, many news releases leave unanswered questions. You will probably want to contact

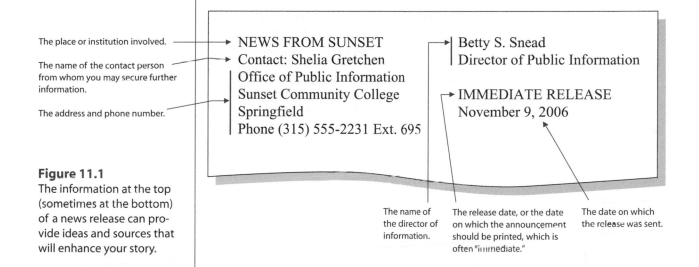

The place or institution involved. ——→ NEWS FROM SUNSET

The name of the contact person ——→ Contact: Shelia Gretchen
from whom you may secure further
information.

Office of Public Information

Sunset Community College

The address and phone number. ——→ Springfield

Phone (315) 555-2231 Ext. 695

→ Betty S. Snead
Director of Public Information

→ IMMEDIATE RELEASE
November 9, 2006

The name of
the director of
information.

The release date, or the date
on which the announcement
should be printed, which is
often "immediate."

The date on which
the release was sent.

Figure 11.1
The information at the top (sometimes at the bottom) of a news release can provide ideas and sources that will enhance your story.

> **"**Desktop publishing has dramatically increased the quantity and enhanced the quality of news releases coming into a news room. News releases from local clubs and organizations that once were written in longhand on notebook paper now rival those of professional public relations firms. The net effect: more news releases with local news than ever before. In a competitive media marketplace, smart newspapers can parlay this additional information into community pages packed with names and faces, reflecting the lives of readers in a way that other media can't.**"**
>
> — Ken Paulson, editor, *USA Today*

people other than the director of information or even the contact person if you have serious doubts about some of the data given. But for routine accuracy checks, the people listed on the release can do the job. They may lead you to other helpful sources, too. Sometimes you may have sources of your own. And sometimes you may uncover the real story only from people who are neither connected to nor recommended by the director of information.

You may have to consult your editor regarding the release date. As a courtesy, most newspapers honor release dates. However, sometimes a morning or evening paper will publish the release early because waiting until the following day would render the information useless. Also, once a release is public knowledge, editors feel justified in publishing whatever information it contains, even prior to the suggested release date. A release date is broken for all when it is broken by one.

Rewriting the Announcement Release

Sometimes directors of information want nothing more than a listing on the record or calendar page of a newspaper. Here is an example of an announcement release:

FOR THE CALENDAR
 Elisabeth Bertke, quiltmaker and designer from Salem, Massachusetts, will discuss her work at 7:00 o'clock p.m. Tues., February 7, in Charters Auditorium, Hampton College. Two quilts designed and constructed

by Bertke are included in the exhibit "The New American Quilt," currently on display at the Smith Art Gallery.

"This is an exciting display," Betty Martin, president of the Smith Art Gallery board of directors, said. "You simply can't afford to miss it."

This simple release may go directly to the copy desk or to a special calendar editor.

If given to you, rewrite it. Some newspapers insist that you rewrite every news release if for no other reason than to avoid the embarrassment of running the same story as a competing newspaper. For some, it is a matter of integrity and professionalism.

First, note all the violations of AP style in the preceding example:

- "Massachusetts" should be abbreviated "Mass."
- "7:00 o'clock P.M." should be "7 p.m."
- "Tues." should be spelled out "Tuesday."
- "February" should be abbreviated "Feb."
- A hyphen should be inserted in "quilt-maker."

Avoid relying on the copy desk to do your work if the rewrite is given to you.

You should check the other points as well. Confirm the spelling of Bertke's name, and see if there is an apostrophe in Charters Auditorium. The Smith Gallery may or may not be on the Hampton campus. Ask how long the exhibit will be at the gallery. Are quilts made by local people included in the exhibit? Perhaps your questions will lead to a feature story on local quilt-making.

In your rewrite, you will drop the quotation of Betty Martin. But you may insert better, less self-serving and less promotional quotes.

Here is another example of an announcement release:

Mr. Richard G. Hernandez has been selected as the Outstanding Biology Teacher of the Year by the National Association of Biology Teachers. He was previously selected as Nevada Science Educator of the Year.

As an outstanding representative of good high-school biology teaching Hernandez will receive a certificate and a series 50 binocular microscope with an engraved citation. Hernandez has been teaching at Hickman High School since 1980.

The story is far from earthshaking, but the honor is statewide. In large newspapers the release may not get much play. A small community newspaper, however, will use it and perhaps enlarge upon it.

A first reading of the release tells you that it is wordy and leaves many questions unanswered. Hernandez may be an interesting fellow, but the release tells us

---

TIPS

How to Approach a News Release

- Finish the reporting. What questions are left unanswered?

- Rewrite it. Make sure that the story adheres to AP style.

little about him. You should approach this release in the same way you approach any news release: Finish the reporting, and then rewrite it. News style demands a new lead to the release:

> A Hickman High School science teacher has been named Outstanding Biology Teacher of the Year by the National Association of Biology Teachers.
>
> Richard G. Hernandez, a Hickman teacher since 1980, will receive a certificate and a series 50 binocular microscope with an engraved citation.
>
> Previously selected as Nevada Science Educator of the Year, Hernandez . . .

There the story runs out of information. You need to ask the following questions:

- Age?
- Degrees from where?
- Local address?
- Spouse, family?
- Annual award? One teacher selected from each state?
- Any previous Hickman winners? Any from local high schools?
- Year he received Nevada Science Educator award?
- Nominated for the award by whom?
- Date and place of bestowal? Public ceremony?
- Value of series 50 binocular microscope?

Then call Hernandez and find out how he feels about the award. Talk to the principal, to fellow teachers and to some of Hernandez's students. Good quotations will spice up your story.

Rewriting the Cause-Promoting Release

Newspapers generally cooperate with causes that are community-oriented. News releases like the following get attention:

> A free tax clinic for low-income persons and senior citizens will be held on Feb. 9 and 10 in Springfield.
>
> The clinic is sponsored by the Central State Counties' Human Development Corporation with the Accounting Department of the Springfield University College of Business.
>
> Senior and graduate accounting students under the direct supervision of accounting faculty members will work with each taxpayer to help that taxpayer complete accurately his or her tax return.
>
> The Human Development Corporation encourages persons especially to use the

ON THE JOB

News Releases: Diamonds in the Rough

A freelance writer since June 2005, Judd Slivka worked for *The Arizona Republic* for five years. He previously worked for the *Arkansas Democrat Gazette, Columbia Missourian*, Minneapolis *Star Tribune* and *Seattle Post-Intelligencer*. His work has twice been nominated for a Pulitzer Prize.

It may surprise you to learn that Slivka says the most important story of his career came out of a news release.

"I get about 400 pieces of mail a week," Slivka says. "E-mail, snail mail, books, letters from people who hate me or hate the stories I write.

"The majority of that mail, though, is news releases. I get them from Democrats and Republicans. I get them from animal shelters. I get them from vintage clothing stores. Every person sending them has a cause to promote, and the truth is that most of the causes don't make good stories for the newspaper."

But now and then, one does, Slivka says. "And that's why I read nearly every news release."

Sometimes that policy pays off. Big time.

An advance copy of a news release from the state health department had come across another reporter's desk. The release detailed the results of a study that found that nearly a dozen deaths over a decade at Lake Powell — a popular vacation spot along the Arizona-Utah line — were caused by a design flaw in the houseboats people were using.

Carbon monoxide from houseboat generators could build up underneath an extended deck at the rear of the boat, and people swimming near it could get poisoned.

clinic who may be eligible for senior citizens' credits or other credits.

This is the fifth year the clinic has operated in Shelby County. Last year more than 275 persons in the eight counties served were assisted.

For information regarding the location of the clinics and to make an appointment, contact the Shelby County Human Development Corporation, 600 E. Broadway, Room 103, Springfield, 555-8376.

Again, you need more information. To begin with, you need to know more about the Human Development Corporation. A background paragraph on its origins, where it gets its money and its other areas of concern will put the story into context.

The release is unclear about who is eligible. What must your income be? How old must you be? Also, you must find out the exact locations of the clinics.

Once you have answers to all your questions, dig for some human interest. Talk to a participating faculty member and to students who helped before and will

"The other reporter had gotten the news release from a friend of hers at the health department," Slivka says. "It was going to be released two days later. To speed things up, I was brought in to help."

The morning the release was officially given to the public, the paper had these four elements: a main story detailing the study, a list of victims, a detailed graphic, and stories of people who survived poisoning, including race-car driver Al Unser Jr.

The news release provided them with a start. "But the other reporter and I went well beyond it. We called experts on carbon monoxide. We called houseboat manufacturers. We called the people who did the study, and we went through the data with them line by line. We asked hard questions.

"If we had just written a story off a news release, it would have been flat and one-dimensional and not served the readers," Slivka says. "Instead, we used it as a starting point to delve into something that was much deeper and more complicated. Over the next three months, we published 25 stories detailing breakdowns in federal government oversight, the industry's ambivalence about the issue, and how families who had lost loved ones were coping."

Over time, the paper published more than 70 stories about the danger of carbon monoxide on recreational boats and followed the path of federal researchers as they've moved from houseboats to cabin cruisers. There have been congressional hearings that have quoted the paper's reports, manufacturers have been forced to change their designs, and the story has been copycatted by every major television network.

"The truth is," Slivka says, "I hate news releases. Most of them are blasted out to lists of reporters without any thought about who's on the receiving end, and thus are wastes of time. But another truth is that I read them, hoping to find a diamond of a story in the rough of unsolicited press releases."

help again. Then talk to some people who were helped in the past and to some who will come for help. In addition, you must talk to those in charge of the joint effort.

Because activities like these are in the public interest, newspapers will give them space. They will be more critical with releases that are merely self-serving.

Rewriting the Image-Building Release

The following is a typical release from a politician:

Sen. John Choi said today that nearly $400,000 in grants have been given final approval by two departments of the state government for interlocking improvements in Springfield and Lincoln County.

Choi said, "This is something I have been working for this past year. It is a chance to show that state agencies are interested in communities. It also demonstrates that two agencies can work together to produce a coordinated, workable solution to improve a blighted area in Springfield."

The grants, Choi said, come from the State Bureau of Outdoor Recreation—$247,000 for purchasing Baltimore and Ohio railroad rights-of-way and developing a strip park—and the Department of Housing and Urban Development—$150,000 for planning the Flat Branch area. The second grant also stipulates that part of the money be used to coordinate the two projects: the B&O strip park and the Flat Branch redevelopment.

"I think residents of Springfield and Lincoln County will have a chance to help out in the planning of these two facilities. I hope this means the entire community will express opinions and come to a conclusion that will see these projects become a reality in the next two years."

The first three words of the release indicate who is being served by the release. A Springfield reporter might write the lead this way to serve the reader:

> Springfield and Lincoln County will receive nearly $400,000 in state grants to fund the B&O strip park and the Flat Branch redevelopment project, Sen. John Choi said today.

The second paragraph of the release is a long and news-less quote from the senator. Probably he did not say those words at all; it's likely they were written by his press agent. You should eliminate them, or if you want a quote from the senator, call him and talk to him yourself.

The second paragraph of your story should indicate the source of the funding:

> The grants come from two state agencies. The State Bureau of Outdoor Recreation granted $247,000 for purchasing the Baltimore & Ohio Railroad rights-of-way and for developing a strip park, and the Department of Housing and Urban Development granted $150,000 for planning the Flat Branch area. The second grant also stipulates that part of the money be used to coordinate the two projects.

You could handle Choi's last quote this way:

> Choi said he hoped Springfield and Lincoln County residents would have a chance to help plan the two facilities. "I hope this means the entire community will express opinions and come to a conclusion that will see these projects become a reality in the next two years."

Like many news releases of this kind, this announcement would trigger other news stories in the local papers. This story would call for local reactions from city and county officials and from local residents. The editor might assign several stories on the matter.

Releases from organizations can also be self-serving—and sometimes misleading. Suppose you were given the following news release.

NEWS RELEASE
Springfield Community Teachers Association
Lillian A. Briggs, President
Contact:
 Tom Monnin, SCTA Salary Committee Chairman
Phone:
 555-555-6794 (Central High School)
 555-555-2975 (home)

For Immediate Release

Springfield—Police officers in Springfield earn a starting salary that nearly equals that of Springfield teachers, as discovered in a recent survey by the Springfield Community Teachers Association. According to their research, a new teacher in the Springfield public school system makes $29,000, while a firefighter starts at $29,725, $725 more than a new teacher. "This is a shameful situation for an educational community," said Tom Monnin, Springfield SCTA Salary Committee chairman.

 The statistics gathered by the Springfield SCTA Salary Committee indicate that police officers with a bachelor's degree make $32,758. A dog catcher with no college education earns just $5,536 less a year than a beginning teacher. Following is a comparison of starting salaries of some Springfield city employees and of public school teachers for the school year:

Occupation	Starting Salary
Police officer with bachelor's degree	$32,758
Firefighter with bachelor's degree	29,725
Meter reader	22,402
Animal control officer	23,464
Bus operator	22,402
Teacher with bachelor's degree	29,000

 "Springfield teachers do not think city employees are overpaid but that teachers are underpaid," Monnin said.

 Even though teachers work under a 9¼-month contract, the workweek is not 40 hours. When the hours for preparing and grading, attending sports events, musical concerts, dances, other after-school activities and PTA meetings are considered, a teacher's workweek is much longer than 40 hours. Summer break is used by many teachers for advanced preparation at the university, at their own expense.

 The Springfield SCTA Salary Committee will present the salary proposal at the next meeting of the Springfield Board of Education.

 The Springfield SCTA represents approximately 523 members in the public school system.

Take special care when news releases cite studies, polls or surveys. Check the source of the figures for accuracy and possible bias. If you can't confirm the figures and their reliability, don't use them.

Your first task is to read the release carefully. The second paragraph cleverly suggests that dogcatchers make as much money as teachers do, although it speaks only of starting salaries. The more you read the release, the more uncomfortable you should feel with it. No one can blame teachers for wanting more money, but there are other factors to consider. What about working conditions? Teachers in Springfield's schools certainly don't have to put their lives on the line the way police officers and firefighters do. And most people do not want to spend their lives chasing stray dogs.

The fact that teachers work for a little more than nine months a year is down in the fourth paragraph. The release fails to mention a two-week break over Christmas and a week off in the spring semester. Most firefighters get two weeks off per year.

Is the release trying to suggest that because teachers actually spend more than 40 hours a week working, they should not have to work more than 9¼ months? Not all teachers spend their summers going to school. You probably know several who have summer jobs or who take long vacations.

Before you turn in a rewrite of the release, you have a lot of checking to do.

You begin by calling the city of Springfield's personnel office. The person answering the phone refers you to the department's Web site. Here you can gather all of the salary information you need, but you still have some questions. You call the personnel office again. When asked about the $29,725 starting salary of a firefighter, the personnel officer replies: "You wouldn't begin at that salary. Everyone is hired at $28,225 for a trial period of at least six months. If you work out OK, you might jump up to $29,725. Again, there are a lot of considerations besides the college degree."

Now you know you are on to something. Comparing starting salaries is one thing. But how much can a person eventually earn in a position?

You then ask about the starting salary for a police officer. "Yes," the director of personnel says, "$32,758 is the beginning salary for a police officer with a B.S. degree."

You then ask whether anyone with a B.S. degree can get hired at that salary.

"Most people wouldn't stand a chance of being hired," he says. "We have more than 100 applicants for every position, so we can be quite choosy. Unless a person has had some real experience as a police officer, I don't think he or she would make it."

Further questioning reveals that a top salary for a police officer is $44,712 after six years of service.

You also find the Web site of the Springfield public school system and check its salary schedule for teachers. Then you call a high school teacher. You ask her if she has to put in more than 40 hours a week at her job.

"Oh, yes," she says. "I teach a section of English composition, and I have a lot of papers to grade. I used to spend a lot of evenings preparing for classes, but once you've taught a course, it gets easier. And then I have to go to all those football games and basketball games."

You then find out that she is indeed required to attend, but only because she is in charge of the cheerleaders. When you express sympathy, the teacher replies, "No, I really don't mind. After all, I get $2,500 a year extra for being in charge of the cheerleaders."

You then learn from someone at the Springfield Schools' personnel office that quite a few teachers receive compensation for after-school activities—coaching, directing plays and musical activities, advising the staffs of the school newspaper and senior yearbook, and chaperoning dances. Teachers sponsoring class and club activities can earn from $500 to $3,000; a sponsor of the pep squad can earn up to $1,300. The top teacher's salary without any of these extras is $57,214.

Now you are ready to call Tom Monnin, the man whose name is on the release, for additional information. You ask if it is fair to compare a new teacher's salary with a new firefighter's salary when the top pay for a firefighter is $40,564 and the top teacher's salary is $57,214. Monnin explains that it takes 17 years for a teacher

TIPS

How to Handle a News Release

- Read the information at the top of the release form.

- Check the news style. Ask questions about missing information. Verify any spellings or information you have doubts about.

- Take for granted that you are to do a rewrite. Fill in missing information. Tighten the copy.

- Watch for self-serving quotations and information. Look for news, and write it.

- Look for other possible news stories — local angles, reactions and the like — that can be triggered by the release.

with a master's degree plus 75 hours to reach that top salary. A teacher with a bachelor's degree can make $44,219 after 11 years of teaching. When you ask about summers off and other vacations, Monnin replies, "I figure I work a 60-hour week. That means I work 51 40-hour weeks a year."

Monnin acknowledges that many teachers got paid extra for extracurricular activities. "But not all of them do," he says. "And there are many activities we do feel the responsibility to attend."

When asked about the argument that teachers do not have to put their lives on the line the way police and fire officials and even dogcatchers do, Monnin replies: "It's debatable who has to put their lives on the line. We're not as bad off as some schools, but we often have to restrain students physically. We read about school shootings all of the time, and we can't help but wonder when that will happen here."

Only now are you ready to write the story. Here's what you might write:

The Springfield Community Teachers Association said Tuesday that new police officers can earn nearly as much as new teachers.

What the teachers did not say was that a teacher eventually can earn $12,502 more a year than a police officer can.

The SCTA statement was included with a survey that lists starting teachers' salaries at $29,000. Other figures listed as starting salaries are: police officer with a bachelor's degree, $32,758; animal control officer, $23,464; meter reader, $22,402; bus operator, $22,402.

"This is a shameful situation for an educational community," said Tom Monnin, the SCTA Salary Committee chairman. "Springfield teachers do not think city employees are overpaid but that teachers are underpaid."

The association officers said that even though teachers work under a nine-month contract, extracurricular activities extend the workweek beyond 40 hours. Summer break, they said, is used for advanced study at the teachers' own expense.

"I figure I work a 60-hour week," Monnin said in an interview. "That means I work 51 40-hour weeks a year."

Some extracurricular activities, such as coaching, directing plays and supervising cheerleaders, earn extra compensation.

Teachers are not compelled to attend after-school functions, but "we do feel the responsibility to attend," Monnin said.

Teachers also feel compelled to continue their education. Top pay for a teacher with only a bachelor's degree is $44,219 after 11 years of teaching. A teacher with a master's degree plus 75 hours of classes can earn $57,214 after 17 years of teaching.

A police officer with a bachelor's degree can reach a top salary of $44,712 after six years of police work. But a person with a bachelor's degree and no police work experience is not likely to be hired, said Phil James, the Springfield director of personnel. James also said all firefighters are hired at $28,225. If a person has a bachelor's degree and stays on, he or she could make $29,725 after a six-month trial period.

Top pay for a dogcatcher is $27,626. "I sure wish I got summers off like those teachers," Tom Merell, an animal-control officer, said. "I got nothing against teachers. But most of them make more money than I'll ever make. . . . Besides, students don't bite many teachers."

The SCTA Salary Committee will present its salary proposal at the next meeting of the Springfield Board of Education.

This story does with a news release what you should do with many of them. You should not be satisfied with the way it was written or with the information it contains. By asking some important questions, you can often put together an informative and more accurate story. Without saying that the news release was dishonest or misleading, a good reporter can correct or clarify some of the information contained in it. Here, the plight of the teacher is told clearly and objectively, but it is placed in a much better perspective than was found in the news release.

Like many news releases, this one was the basis for a story the newspaper otherwise would not have had. That is why editors pay attention to news releases and why reporters look for the real story.

Suggested Readings

Bivins, Thomas H. *Public Relations Writing*, Fourth Edition. Lincolnwood, Ill.: NTC/Contemporary Publishing Group, 1999. You can learn how public-relations professionals approach a wide variety of writing tasks.

Howard, Carole and Mathews, Wilma. *On Deadline: Managing Media Relations*, Third Edition. Prospect Heights, Ill.: Waveland Press, 2000. A practical book on how organizations should deal with the news media.

Wilcox, Dennis L. and Nolte, Lawrence W. *Public Relations Writing and Media Techniques,* Fourth Edition. New York: HarperCollins, 2000. Emphasizes writing, producing and distributing a variety of public-relations materials.

Suggested Web Sites

www.poewar.com
John Hewitt describes techniques that public-relations writers use to capture a publication's attention—techniques that news writers should be aware of. Go to "Writing Business," and then to "Sending Effective Press Releases."

www.pressflash.com/resources_anatomy.php
This is a Web site of a news release distribution service. You will find here a terse description of a good news release.

www.press-release-writing.com/10_essential_tips.htm
Note these 10 essential tips for writing news releases. You'll see how serious professionals go about doing them well.

www.prwatch.org
Web site of the Center for Media and Democracy. The Web site says, "The nonprofit Center for Media and Democracy strengthens participatory democracy by investigating and exposing public relations spin and propaganda, and by promoting literacy and citizen journalism, media 'of, by and for the people.'"

Exercises

1. Read each of the following news releases. First, indicate the type of news release it is. Second, list questions you would have if you were to rewrite it, including the facts you would check and the sources you would turn to for the answers. Finally, correct all departures from Associated Press style rules.

a. NEWS RELEASE

Dennis A. Ausiello to Join Pfizer Board of Directors

NEW YORK, Oct. 26 /PR Newswire-FirstCall/ — Pfizer Inc. announced today the election of Dennis A. Ausiello, M.D. to the Pfizer Board of Directors effective December 1, 2006.

Dr. Ausiello, 61, has deep experience and a distinguished record of leadership and accomplishment in scientific research and medicine, areas of critical importance to Pfizer. He will serve on the Science and Technology Committee of the Pfizer Board which reviews the company's research and development and technology initiatives.

Dr. Ausiello is the Jackson Professor of Clinical Medicine at Harvard Medical School and Chief of Medicine at Massachusetts General Hospital (MGH). He also is an internationally recognized research scientist for his substantial contributions in cell biology.

As chief of medicine at MGH for the last decade, Dr. Ausiello leads one of the most renowned departments of medicine in the United States with an annual clinical, research and education budget of more than $500 million. He oversees the training of graduate and undergraduate medical students, post-doctoral fellows and house officers at Harvard Medical School. He earlier served as chief of MGH's renal unit and oversaw the development of one of the world's leading research and training programs in kidney disease.

Dr. Ausiello currently serves as president of the Association of American Physicians, a leading organization of academic physicians. He was elected to the Institute of Medicine of the National Academy of Sciences in 1999 and the American Academy of Arts and Sciences in 2003. He is the recipient of two MERIT awards from the National Institutes of Health and has served as a member of the National Institute of Diabetes, Digestive and Kidney Diseases Advisory Council and the National Advisory Council on Aging.

Dr. Ausiello serves on the Board of Directors of MicroCHIPS, a drug-sensing and delivery company, and is an advisor to the Chairman of the Board of TIAX (formerly Arthur D. Little).

Dr. Ausiello has published more than 150 papers and book chapters and co-edits Cecil's Textbook of Medicine, now in its 22nd edition. He also has written for *The New York Times, The Wall Street Journal* and *The Boston Globe*.

He is a 1967 cum laude graduate of Harvard College, where he received a Bachelors degree in Biochemical Sciences, and of the University of Pennsylvania School of Medicine where he received his medical degree in 1971.

b. NEWS RELEASE

The teaching faculty, administration and staff of The South Shore Country Day School formally began the school year Friday, August 30, with an all day workshop on curriculum planning.

This year, the School will be involved in a year long task of self evaluation. All aspects of the School's curriculum and student life will be considered and a new five year, long range plan for the curriculum will be written. The School's last major plan was constructed in 1994.

The evaluation process is designed to keep curriculum consistent with the School's educational philosophy and statement of mission. It will identify problems, strengths, and opportunities for expansion. At various stages of the process, all constituencies of the School will have an opportunity to express concerns and opinions. By the end of the school year, a new plan will be ready for integration and implementation by the School's administration.

William R. Lopez, Chairman of the School's Board of Trustees, spoke to the faculty about the upcoming project and the need to change. "We will attempt to make the current school better; we will not be creating a new school," he said.

Thomas B. Lang, the School's headmaster, emphasized the importance of total faculty participation in the formulation and execution of the mission statement. "We're all in this together," Lang said. "Curriculum is the sum of all the parts. No one teaches in a vacuum."

Among topics discussed at the workshop were: the importance of academic excellence; student social service; a need for diversity within the student body; the importance of educating the whole child; providing increased opportunity for students to participate in a variety of academic and nonacademic projects; and the ethical considerations in the School.

2. Assume you are a reporter for the Springfield paper. Your instructor will be your news source for any questions you have. Rewrite each of the following releases.

a. NEWS RELEASE

Nearly 11,000 seat belt violation warnings were issued to motorists by the State Highway Patrol during the first month the new seat belt law was in effect.

Colonel Howard J. Hoffman, Superintendent of the State Highway Patrol, reported today that 10,908 warnings were issued to motorists in passenger vehicles for not wearing their seat belts as required by State Law.

Colonel Hoffman also noted that during this same reporting period, 50 persons were killed in traffic accidents investigated by the Highway Patrol. Only two of the persons killed in these mishaps were found to be wearing seat belts.

"The value of wearing a seat belt cannot be overemphasized," Hoffman said. "We don't know how many of these investigated traffic deaths could have been avoided by the use of seat belts. It is known, however, that seat belts have saved lives and prevented serious injuries to others. We will continue to vigorously enforce the State seat belt law and hopefully more and more motorists will make it a habit to buckle their seat belts."

b. NEWS RELEASE

The Better Business Bureau serving the tri-state area has launched a fund-raising drive to finance the installation of a 24-hour computerized telephone service called Tel-Tips.

James C. Schmitt, President, said Tel-Tips is a unique consumer information and education system designed to give quick useful information about specific goods and services. Consumers would be provided with a number to call and the system will put the caller in contact with a selected pre-recorded message.

A goal of $20,000 has been established to finance installation of Tel-Tips and the physical expansion of the BBB's office.

"Despite efficient telephone communications and computer system, we expect to lose nearly 24,000 calls this year," said Schmitt. "Our operators are trained to limit time given to each caller to avoid losing callers, while at the same time attempting to provide complete information."

The Bureau is unable to respond to inquiries before and after business hours and on weekends, times many customers need BBB services.

Tel-Tips is a computerized information center that allows 114 consumer tip messages to be made instantly available to callers. This system answers incoming calls with a pre-recorded message and instructs the caller to dial the number of the message he or she wants to hear. This unit operates automatically with the use of a Touch-Tone telephone, 12 hours a day. A rotary dial telephone may be used during regular business hours with the assistance of an operator.

c. NEWS RELEASE

"Chest Pains," a film in the HEALTHSCOPE series produced by the American College of Physicians, will be shown from 7-8:30 p.m., Wednesday, Oct. 22, at St. Mary's Health Center. Springfield internist, Dr. Harold Kanagawa, will host a question-and-answer period following the film.

Although most people assume that chest pains signify a heart attack, the public is less aware that other conditions—hiatal hernia, ulcers, viral infections of the heart's membranes—can also cause pains that require prompt diagnosis and appropriate medical treatment. Designed to help increase awareness of these symptoms and their possible significance, "Chest Pains" features an internist and actual patients as they work together to resolve underlying medical problems.

Speeches, News Conferences
and Meetings

12

IN THIS CHAPTER
YOU WILL LEARN:

1. How to prepare to cover speeches, news conferences and meetings.

2. What is involved in covering these events.

3. How to structure and write stories about them.

Speeches, news conferences and meetings rally communities to causes and nations to war. Before President Lyndon B. Johnson's televised address on the Gulf of Tonkin incident in 1964, a Harris Survey showed that less than half of the electorate approved of the president's Vietnam policy. After his address, a second poll indicated that 70 percent approved.

Before President Richard M. Nixon addressed the nation to attempt to justify the invasion of Cambodia in 1970, a Harris Survey showed that only 7 percent of the public supported the decision. After Nixon's television address, more than 50 percent approved. A *USA Today*/CNN/Gallup poll showed that President Bill Clinton's news conference regarding his troubles with the Whitewater real estate deal raised public approval of how he was handling Whitewater from 39 percent to 50 percent.

More recently, no matter how many speeches President George W. Bush made before the 2006 midterm elections, his popularity hovered around 38 percent thanks to massive problems in Iraq. The Democrats, apparently as a result of the president's handling of Iraq, regained control of the U.S. House and Senate. This shows that events are sometimes more important than speeches in shaping public opinion.

Some argue that John F. Kennedy's display of intelligence and wit at news conferences got him elected and earned him respect as president. President Nixon, in contrast, had little flair for give-and-take and less love for reporters. Consequently, his performance at news conferences added little to his popularity. President Ronald Reagan felt at home in front of cameras, and although he disliked news conferences, his televised speeches helped boost his image tremendously. Town meetings helped Bill Clinton get to the White House. Former Vice President Al Gore's perceived stiffness on TV may have helped put President Bush into the White House in 2001.

Because the coverage of speeches, news conferences and meetings is similar, we examine all three in this chapter. But you should keep in mind their distinguishing characteristics.

A *speech* is a public talk. Someone speaks to an audience in person or on radio or television. Regardless of the medium, a speech is a one-way communication. The speaker speaks, and the audience listens.

Speakers are usually invited and sometimes paid to address an audience. That is not the case with those who hold a **news conference**. People "call" a news conference. They do not send invitations to the general public, but they do alert members of the various news media. The media respond because of the importance of the person calling the news conference and because the person may have something newsworthy to say. The person holding the news conference often begins with an opening statement and usually accepts questions from reporters. A news conference is meant to be a two-way communication.

Unlike speeches and news conferences, *meetings* are not held with an audience in mind, although an audience may be present and allowed to participate. A meeting is primarily for communication among the members of a group or organization, whether a local parent-teacher association or the U.S. Congress. Reporters who are permitted to witness a meeting tell the public what is of interest and importance. This task of the news media is especially important if the participants are members of a governmental body that spends or allocates taxpayers' money.

Because you will spend a great deal of time as a reporter covering speeches, news conferences and meetings, you will want to learn all you can about covering them well.

PREPARATION

Professional reporters know that preparation makes covering a story much easier. In all cases, reporters should do their homework. You prepare for speeches, news conferences and meetings in much the same way. Because these events are usually announced in advance, you have time for thorough preparation.

Preparing for the Speech Story

Not every speech will demand a great deal of research. Many speakers and speeches will be dry and routine. The person giving the speech will be someone you know or someone you covered before. At other times you may get an assignment on short notice and be forced to find background information after hearing the speech. In either case, never take the speaker or the topic for granted. Failure to get enough background on the speaker and on the speech almost guarantees failure at writing a comprehensive speech story.

The first step in your research is to identify the speaker correctly. Middle initials are important; sometimes even they are not enough. Sometimes checking the address is not enough. One reporter wrote about the wrong person because he did not know that a father and son with the same name had the same address.

USA Today had to print a "clarification" after reporting that Larry King had made a $1,000 donation to President Clinton's campaign. The donor was Larry L. King, author and playwright, not Larry King the CNN show host.

Be sure you have the right person. Then, before doing research on the speaker, contact the group sponsoring the speech and ask for the topic. You might find you need to do some reading to prepare yourself to understand the subject. If you are lucky, you may get an advance copy of the speech. Also check your newspaper library to see what your paper has written previously about the speaker. If you have access to a databank, use it.

If the speech is important enough, you might want to contact the speaker ahead of time for a brief interview. If he or she is from out of town, you might plan for a meeting at the airport. You might also arrange ahead of time to interview the speaker after the speech. You may have questions and points to clarify.

Not every speech will demand that much effort. But even the most routine speech assignment needs preparation. Do not assume, for instance, that Gene Martin, director of the local library, is addressing the state Writer's Guild to tell members how to use the library to improve their stories. Gene Martin may also be a successful "true confessions" writer, published dozens of times in such magazines as *True Confessions* and *True Romance*. He may be telling guild members how he does it.

TIPS

Preparing for the Speech Story

- Be sure you have the right person.

- Contact the group sponsoring the speech and ask for the topic.

- Check your newspaper library for background on the speaker.

- If the speech is important enough, contact the speaker for a brief interview.

Sooner or later you may be called on to cover speeches by major political figures, perhaps even the president of the United States. For this task, too, you will need background—lots of it. It demands that you read the news and you know what is going on. You must keep up with current events.

Preparing for the News Conference Story

Preparing for a news conference is like preparing for a speech. You need up-to-date background on the person giving the news conference, and you must learn why the news conference is being held. Often the person holding the news conference has an announcement or an opening statement. Unless that statement is leaked to the press, you will not know its content ahead of time, but you can make some educated guesses. Check out any rumors. Call the person's associates, friends or secretary.

You and every other reporter at a news conference will have a line of questions to pursue. Your editor may want certain information, and other editors may want something else. Once the news conference begins, you will not have time to think of questions; recording responses to other reporters' questions will keep you too busy. The better prepared you are, the better chance you will have of coming away with a coherent, readable story.

It may be impossible to arrange an interview before or after the news conference. If the person holding the news conference wanted to grant individual reporters interviews, he or she probably would not have called the news conference. But you can always ask—you might end up with some exclusive information.

Preparing for the Meeting Story

You never know what to expect at a meeting, either. So you must do your best to prepare. Who are the people holding the meeting? What kind of an organization is involved? Who are the key figures? Again, the morgue is your first stop. Then contact some of the key figures.

See if you can find out what the meeting is about. Perhaps the president or the secretary has a written agenda for the meeting. If you know the main subject to be discussed, you will be able to study and investigate the issues before arriving. Knowing what to expect and being familiar with the issues will make covering the meeting much easier.

A reporter with a regular beat—an assigned area of responsibility—usually covers meetings of the most important organizations and groups such as the city council, the school board or the county board. (Beat reporting is discussed in detail in Chapter 14.) A beat reporter has continuing familiarity with the organization and with the issues involved. Often the meetings of important organizations are preceded by an **advance**—a report outlining the subjects and issues to be covered during the upcoming meeting.

COVERING SPEECHES, NEWS CONFERENCES AND MEETINGS

The story is often told of a reporter who prepared well for a speech assignment, contacted the speaker, got a copy of the speech, wrote the story and spent the evening in a bar. Not until after he handed in his speech story did he find out that the speech had been canceled.

And then there's the yarn about a young reporter assigned to cover a meeting who came back and told the city editor there was no story.

"Why not?" the city editor asked.

"Because the meeting was canceled."

"Why was that?"

"Well," replied the reporter, "when the meeting started, some of the board members got into this big argument. Finally, three of them walked out. The president then canceled the meeting because there was no quorum."

A story about a speech, news conference or meeting often requires direct quotes. Whether you use a recording device or not, be sure to take careful notes that you can use while writing your story.

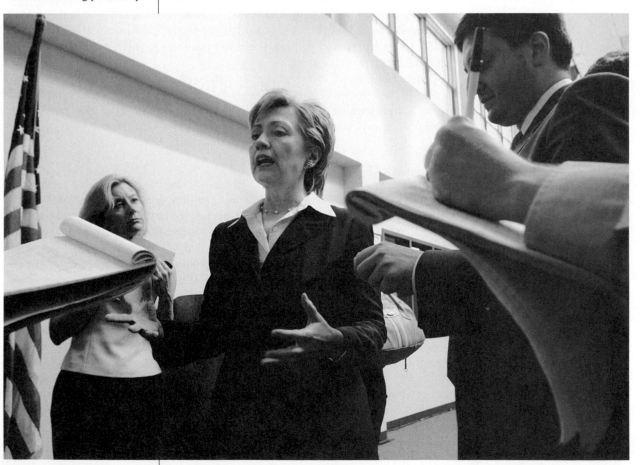

Of course, the canceled meeting and the circumstances surrounding its cancellation probably were of more interest to readers than the meeting itself would have been. Preparing to cover an event is only the beginning. Knowing what to do when you get there is equally important. You must cover the entire event—the content of the speech, news conference or meeting; the time, place, circumstances and number of people involved; and possible consequences of what was said or of the actions taken.

Getting the Content Correct

You may find a digital recorder useful for covering the content of speeches, news conferences and meetings. Digital recorders often intimidate people who don't work in broadcast journalism, but they should not. Practice using a recorder. Use it again and again to become familiar with its idiosyncrasies. Knowing in general how to operate digital recorders is not enough. You need to be comfortable with the one you are using. For example, you must be sure how sensitive the microphone is. It is sound you want, and sound you must get.

The most frequent complaint you may hear about using digital recorders is that listening to the entire recording takes too long. You may have to listen to a whole speech just to find a certain quote you want to check. But if you have a recorder with a digital counter, you can avoid this problem. At any point in a speech or a meeting when something of importance is said, you need only to note the number on the counter. Finding the quotation later will then be easy.

Even if you record an event, take notes in exactly the same way you would if you were not recording. Malfunctions can occur, even with the best machines, at the most inopportune times.

So, with or without a digital recorder, you must become a proficient note taker. Many veteran reporters wish they had learned shorthand or speed-writing early in their careers. You may find it useful to buy a speed-writing manual and learn a few symbols. Sooner or later every reporter adopts or creates some note-taking shortcuts. You will have to do the same. Learn to abbreviate (*wh* for "which," *th* for "that," *bk* for "book," *st* for "street," *bldg* for "building," etc.). Make up signs (*w/* for "with," *w/o* for "without," *acc/* for "according to").

Are you one of those fortunate people with a fantastic memory? Some reporters develop an incredible knack for re-creating whole conversations with complete accuracy without taking a note. Or are you instead someone who takes reams of notes? If you are, take them as neatly as you can. Many of us cannot read our own handwriting at times—a nuisance, particularly when a proper name is involved.

Taking notes is most crucial when you wish to record direct quotes. As you learned in Chapter 4, putting someone's words in quotation marks means only one thing: You are quoting the person word for word, exactly as the person spoke. Speeches, news conferences and meetings all demand that you be able to record direct quotes. Your stories will be lifeless and lack credibility without them. A speech story, for example, should contain many direct quotes.

TIPS

Achieving Total Coverage of Content and Event

- Get the content correct. Recorders can be helpful, but always take good notes. Quote people exactly and in context.

- Note the background, personal characteristics and mannerisms of the main participants.

- Cover the event. Look around the edges—at the audience (size, reactions) and sometimes at what is happening outside the building.

- Get there early, position yourself and hang around afterward.

Whether covering a speech, news conference or meeting, be careful to quote people in context. For example, if a speaker gives supportive evidence for an argument, you would be unfair not to report it. Quotes can be misleading if you carelessly or deliberately juxtapose them. Combining quotes with no indication that something was said in between them can lead to inaccuracies and to charges of unfairness. Suppose, for example, someone said:

> "Cutting down fuel costs can be an easy thing. If you have easy access to wood, you should invest in a good wood-burning stove. With little effort, you can cut your fuel bills in half."

A reporter who omitted the middle sentence of that quote, even inserting an ellipsis, would make the speaker look ridiculous:

> "Cutting down fuel costs can be an easy thing. . . . With little effort, you can cut your fuel bills in half."

There is more to a speaker than the words he or she is saying. Sometimes, quoting a speaker at length or printing a speech in its entirety may be justified. But when you quote a whole speech, you are recording it, not reporting it. The overall content of the speech may or may not be news. Sometimes the news may be what a speaker left unsaid. You must decide what is newsworthy.

Recording speeches, news conferences and meetings is no longer merely something to help the reporter get the story right. Today, many news organizations are asking reporters to bring back audio for their Web sites. That makes it increasingly important for reporters to learn how to do a good job of recording.

Describing the Participants

In addition to listening to what a speaker says, you must watch for other things. A recording does not capture a speaker's facial expressions and gestures. These are sometimes more important than the words themselves.

For example, you may have heard the story of how Soviet Premier Nikita Khrushchev pounded the table with his shoe in the U.N. General Assembly on Sept. 20, 1960. But you probably are unsure about what he was saying or what he was protesting. Similarly, you may remember from your American history class the setting of President Franklin D. Roosevelt's fireside chats, but you probably don't remember the content.

Simply reporting the words of a speaker (or of the person holding a news conference or participating at a meeting) does not indicate volume and tone of voice, inflections, pauses, emphases and reactions to and from those in attendance. You may note that a speaker deliberately winked while reading a sentence. Or you may notice an unmistakable sarcasm in the speaker's voice.

Regardless of who the speaker is or where the speech is taking place, you must always note the speaker's background. A person's words must often be measured against that individual's background. For example, if a former Communist is speaking on communism, this fact may have a bearing on what is said. If a former CIA agent speaks about corruption in the CIA, you would not adequately report the message if you did not mention the person's background.

Sometimes purely physical facts about the speaker are essential to the story. A blind person pleading for funds to educate the blind, a one-armed veteran speaking about the hell of war, a gray-haired person speaking about care for the elderly—these speakers must be described physically for the story to be complete, accurate and understandable.

You also should note what the person who introduces a speaker says. This may help you understand the significance of the speaker and the importance of what he or she has to say.

Covering the Event

Keep an eye on the audience and on what's happening around the edges. You need to measure the mood of the audience by noting the tone of the questions. Are they sharply worded? Is there much laughter or applause? Perhaps members of the audience boo. Does the speaker or the person holding the news conference or the person presiding over the meeting remain calm and in control? Is there casual bantering or joking with the audience? Is the audience stacked with supporters or detractors?

Sometimes the real action takes place outside in the form of a picket line or protest. Sometimes police manage to keep protesters away from the site. Sometimes who is *not* there is news.

Don't overlook the obvious. For example, you should note the size of the audience. Reporting a "full house" means little unless you indicate the house capacity. One way to estimate attendance is to count how many people are sitting in a row or in a typical section. Then you simply multiply that number by the number of rows or sections in the hall. Use good judgment and common sense to adjust for some sections being more crowded than others.

Arriving, Positioning Yourself and Staying On

Most reporters arrive early. At some events they have special seating, but you should probably not count on that unless you know for sure.

At a speech, sitting in the first row is not necessarily the best thing to do. Perhaps you should be in a location that lets you see the reaction of the audience. If there is a question-and-answer period, you may want to be able to see the questioner. And you certainly want to be in a good position to ask questions yourself.

At a news conference, your location may help you get the attention of the person holding the conference. You should have your questions prepared, but preparing them is not enough. You have seen presidential news conferences on television, and you know how difficult it is to get the president's attention. Any news conference presents the reporter with the same difficulties, though on a smaller scale. You have seen how difficult it is for reporters to follow up on their own questions. At some news conferences you will not be called on twice.

But you must do more than try to get your own questions answered. You must listen to others' questions and be able to recognize the making of a good story. Too often a good question is dropped without follow-up because reporters are not listening carefully or are too intent on pursuing their own questions. Listen for what is newsworthy and pursue it. Sticking with an important subject will make the job of writing the story easier. Remember, when the news conference is finished, you will have a story to write. Piecing together notes on dozens of unrelated topics can be difficult, if not impossible.

At a meeting you should be able to see and hear the main participants. Ordinarily, a board or council will sit facing the audience. Before the meeting starts, you should know which members are sitting where. You may want to assign each participant a number so you do not have to write the person's name each time he or she speaks. You also can draw a sketch of where members are sitting. In this way you will be able to quote someone by number and if necessary find out his or her name later. Know who the officers are. The president or the secretary may distribute handouts before the meeting. After a meeting, the secretary may be able to help you fill in missing words or information.

As a general rule, when the speech, news conference or meeting is over, do not rush off unless you are on deadline. Some of the best stories happen afterward. You should have some questions to ask. You may want some clarifications, or you may arrange to interview a key spokesperson. Listen for reactions from those in attendance.

STRUCTURING AND WRITING YOUR STORY

Writing the lead for the speech, news conference or meeting story is no different from writing the lead for any other story. All of the qualities of the inverted pyramid news lead discussed in Chapter 7 are important here as well.

You must be careful not to emphasize something about the event that is of great interest or curiosity but that does not lead into the rest of your story. It is tempting, for example, to lead with a striking quote. But rarely does a speaker or someone holding a news conference highlight the content or the main point in a single, quotable sentence. As always, there are exceptions. As a lead for one of Dr. Martin Luther King Jr.'s most famous addresses, a good reporter might have begun with "I have a dream."

Because of the nature of the inverted pyramid news story, rarely should you follow the chronology of the event you are covering. But the flow of your story may demand *some* attention to chronology (see Chapter 9). If you pay no attention to chronology, you may distort, or cause readers to misinterpret, the meaning of the event.

Writing the Speech Story

Although you may not soon be called upon to cover the speeches of well-known politicians, you can learn a lot from the way the pros handle important political

TIPS

Technical Concerns for the Television Journalist

Speeches, news conferences and meetings present several technical challenges. Here are three to keep in mind:

- Think visuals. What will your backdrop be? Will there be signs, photos, samples, logos or flip-charts to help tell the story?

- Think sound. Will there be one microphone or a multi-box for you to insert your mike, or will you be free to set up your own microphone?

- Think light. Will the event take place outdoors or in a well-lit room, or must you bring your own lighting? How far is the camera throw (the distance from the event to your camera)? Will there be a camera platform or a set space, or will you be free to set up your camera anywhere?

addresses. These speeches can be long and complex, such as President George W. Bush's call for democracy in the Middle East on Nov. 7, 2003. Let's study how Charlene Gubash of NBC covered the speech for the Web site MSNBC.com:

CAIRO, Egypt — President Bush's speech about the need for democracy in the Middle East was met with a mixture of rare praise and skepticism here Thursday.

While commentators condemned the U.S. leader for again, in their view, ignoring Israel's occupation of Palestinian territory, some hailed his remarks as "historic." In fact, analysts and commentators who are usually outraged over the U.S. administration's policy in the region found themselves in agreement on many points.

The president made a plea for democratic reforms in the Middle East the cornerstone of a speech dealing with democratic values across the globe.

And he acknowledged shortcomings in past policy, saying the United States and other nations shared blame for the lack of democratic freedoms in the Middle East.

"Sixty years of Western nations excusing and accommodating the lack of free-

dom in the Middle East did nothing to make us safe because in the long run stability cannot be purchased at the expense of liberty," Bush said.

The president spoke to the National Endowment for Democracy, a group that champions democratic gains around the world, on the same day that he was signing an $87.5 billion package approved by Congress for military and reconstruction operations in Iraq and Afghanistan.

U.S. wars in those two Islamic countries, notably to oust Saddam Hussein in Iraq, have served to seriously damage America's reputation across the Arab world. And what's seen as Washington's bias toward Israel in the conflict with the Palestinians has undermined its credibility in the Middle East.

Consequently words of praise were unexpected.

Notice how Gubash used that last paragraph to put the story into context for her readers. Doing just that is essential in almost any speech story. Also note the focus on the reactions of those who heard the speech:

"It is an historical speech, and I agree with what the president had to say, and this is the first time," said Hafez Abu Se'da, head of the Egyptian Organization for Human Rights.

"It is a new vision from the United States now because they focus on democracy. For a long time, they focused on economy and commercial interests. It is historical because the United States is talking about democracy and the interest of the people in these countries."

The human rights advocate also praised what Bush had to say about democracy's being compatible with Islam and Arab culture.

"I agree with him. Always we hear from the governments of this region saying our culture is not ready for democracy, that we have our own type of democracy. This is not true. Democracy is democracy, freedom is freedom. . . .

Islam is compatible with democracy and is not against democracy," Abu Se'da said.

But Abu Se'da said that just as the area needs democracy and justice, the United States has an important role to play by solving the Israeli-Palestinian problem in a just way. . . .

Campaign speeches, such as this one from Barack Obama, require the reporter to be alert not only to what is said but to the audience reaction.

You also need to get reactions, and you may want to put them in a story separate from the account of the speech itself. Reaction stories often accompany stories about presidential speeches.

Writing the News Conference Story

Writing the news conference story may be a bit more challenging than writing the speech story. Because you will go to the conference with different questions in mind than your fellow reporters, you may come away with a different story. At least, your lead may be different from the leads of other reporters.

A news conference often covers a gamut of topics. Often it begins with a statement from the person who called the conference.

For example, when the mayor of Springfield holds a news conference to announce her candidacy for a second term, you can be sure that she will begin with a statement to that effect. Although her candidacy might be news to some people, you may want to ask her questions about the location of a new landfill that the city is rumored to be planning. Most citizens will admit the need for landfills, but their location is always controversial. And then there's that tip you heard about the possibility of the city manager's resigning to take a job in a large city.

Other reporters will come with other questions. Will there be further cuts in the city budget? Will the cuts mean that some city employees will lose their jobs? What happened to the plans to expand the city jail?

After you come away from a news conference that covered many topics, you have the job of organizing the material in some logical, coherent order. You can choose to write a multiple-element lead (see Chapter 7). But usually you will treat the most newsworthy subject first and deal with the other subjects in the order of their importance. Rarely would you report on them in the chronological order in which they were discussed.

Suppose you decide the location of the landfill is the most important item of the news conference—especially if the mayor revealed the location for the first time. You might begin your story this way:

> The city will construct its new landfill near the intersection of State Route 53 and Route E, four miles north of Springfield, Mayor Juanita Williams said today.
>
> "After nearly a year of discussion and the best advice we could obtain, we are certain the Route E location is best for all concerned," Williams said at a news conference.
>
> The mayor admitted there would be continued opposition to the site by citizens living in the general area, especially those in the Valley High Trailer Court. "No location will please everyone," Williams said.
>
> Williams called the news conference to make the expected announcement of her candidacy for a second term.

Now you have to find a way to treat the other topics of the conference. You might want to list them first in a series of bullet points:

> In other matters, Williams said:
> - City Manager Diane Lushy will not be resigning to take another post.
> - Budget constraints will not permit any new construction on the city jail this year.
> - Budget cuts will not cost any city employees their jobs. However, positions vacated by retiring personnel will not be filled.

After this list, you will either come back to your lead, giving more background and quoting citizens or other city officials on the subject, or go on to treat, one at a time, the matters you listed. Pay particular attention to making proper transitions from paragraph to paragraph so your story is coherent. "On other subjects, the mayor said . . . ," "The mayor defended her position on . . . ," "Again she stressed. . . ."

If one of the subjects is of special interest, you may want to write a sidebar, a shorter piece to go with your main story. For this story, you may want to do a sidebar on the mayor's candidacy, her record, her possible opponents and the like.

With a longer or more complicated story, you may want to make a summary list of all the main topics covered and place it in a box or sidebar.

Remember, your job is to give readers the news, as simply and clearly as possible. Remember, too, to cover the event as well as the content. Perhaps only three reporters turned up for the news conference, or perhaps some pickets protested the mayor's remarks about a local abortion clinic. Sometimes what happens at a news conference is more newsworthy than anything the person holding the conference says. What happens there might well be the lead of your main story, or you may want to place it in a sidebar.

Writing the Meeting Story

Readers also want you to take their place at the meeting you are covering. Let's look at a simple meeting story—in this case, a meeting of a local school board:

The decision of three national corporations to protest a formula used to compute their property taxes is causing more than $264,000 to be withheld from the Walnut School District's operating budget for the 2002–2003 school year.

Superintendent Max Schmidt said at Monday's school board meeting that International Business Machines Corp., ACR Corp. and Xerox are protesting that the method used in computing their 2001 property taxes was no longer valid. Nine California counties are involved in similar disputes.

The taxes, totaling $264,688, are being held in escrow by the county until the matter is resolved. Some or all of the money eventually may be returned to the district, but the administration cannot determine when or how much.

"If we take a quarter million dollars out of our program at this time, it could have a devastating effect," Schmidt said. "Once you've built that money into your budget and you lost it, you've lost a major source of income."

Mike Harper, the county prosecuting attorney, and Larry Woods, the school district attorney, advised board members to take a "wait-and-see attitude," Schmidt said. He said that one alternative would be to challenge the corporations in court. A final decision will be made later.

The board also delayed action on repayment of $80,000 to IBM in a separate tax dispute. The corporation claims the district owes it for overpaid 1999 property taxes. The county commission has ruled the claim is legitimate and must be repaid.

A possible source of additional income, however, could be House Bill 1002, Schmidt said. If passed, this appropriations bill would provide an additional $46 million for state education, approximately $250,000 of which could go to the Walnut School District.

Charles Campbell, the district architect, said plans for the area's new vocational technical school to be built on the Rock Bridge High School campus will be given to contractors in February. Bids will be presented at the March 15 board meeting.

The board voted to have classes on Presidents Day, Feb. 15, to make up for time missed because of the teachers' strike.

ON THE JOB

Speeches, News Conferences and Meetings

After receiving a master's in journalism, Barry Murov worked as an associate editor of a Washington, D.C., newsletter, where he covered federal job programs. Then after working for the *St. Louis Business Journal* for six years, first as a reporter, then as managing editor, Murov became editor of *St. Louis Magazine*. Now he's employed by Fleishman-Hillard Inc., an international public-relations firm.

Murov has written and edited dozens of stories covering speeches, meetings and news conferences. Here are some tips he has for you.

"Always ask for a copy of the speech ahead of time," Murov says. "Even when you are lucky enough to get a copy, don't assume that the speaker will stick to the text."

As a consultant for Fortune 500 corporations, Murov knows that "many executives tend to tinker with their speeches, even making significant changes, up until the final minute."

Murov says you should follow along in the text to note where the actual presentation differs. "You don't want your story to include a statement from the text that the speaker deleted. Also, you may find the real news nugget buried in the speech."

Don't leave a meeting or news conference immediately. "Go up to the spokesperson or the leader of the meeting and ask a question that hasn't been covered during the actual event.

"That can benefit in two ways: One, you will have something extra for your readers. Two, it helps you build a relationship with the spokesperson that may pay off in the future."

The issue of the meeting was money problems — a subject that concerns every taxpayer. The writer jumped right into the subject in the lead, giving the "what" in the first paragraph, and then in the second paragraph giving us the "who," "when" and "where." The reporter then dealt with specifics, naming names and citing figures, and quoted the key person at the meeting. In the last two paragraphs the writer dealt with other matters discussed in the meeting.

The issues discussed at a meeting are not your only considerations in covering a meeting story. Remember, too, to cover the event. Who was there? Who represented the public? Did anyone have reactions after the meeting was over?

One reporter began her meeting story in this way:

Even though they are footing the bill, only one of
Boone County's residents cared enough to attend a
Tuesday night hearing on the county's 2004 budget.

With an audience of one citizen plus two reporters, County Auditor June Pitchford presented her official report on the $21 million budget to the Boone County Commission in a silent City Council chamber.

Even when covering routine, boring events, you are allowed to use your creativity. In addition to getting all the facts, your job is also to be interesting, to get people to read the story. Remember, two of the criteria for news are that it be relevant or useful. Another is that it be interesting.

Finally, you are always expected to write well — even for a common event like a speech, news conference or meeting.

Suggested Readings

Biography and Genealogy Master Index. Detroit, Mich.: Gale Research Co., 1981 to present. A compilation of a large number of biographical directories with names of people whose biographies have been written. Indicates which date and volume of those reference books to consult for the actual biography.

Biography Index. Bronx, N.Y.: H.W. Wilson Co., 1946 to present. Helps you locate biographical articles that have appeared in 2,000 periodicals and journals, as well as in biographical books and chapters from collective biographies.

Current Biography. Bronx, N.Y.: H.W. Wilson Co., 1940 to present. Monthly publication about people in the news, including a photo of each. Excellent source for people not yet or perhaps never included in more formal biographical sources.

Suggested Web Sites

www.pbs.org/greatspeeches/
This site claims it is "one of the most comprehensive online collections of speech texts of contemporary American history." It also gives the backgrounds of many famous speakers and their speeches and puts them in their historical context. Some speeches have audio and video links.

www.rcameron.com/journalism/citycouncil
This Web site takes you step-by-step through the process of covering a city council meeting.

Exercises

1. Journalist Andrea Mitchell is coming to town to speak on the current U.S. president's relationship with the press. Prepare to cover the speech. Record the steps you will take to prepare for the speech and the information you have gathered on Mitchell.

2. You learn that actor Robert Redford is holding a news conference before speaking to a local group about environmental issues. You also learn that Redford is personally and actively involved in these issues. Using appropriate databanks, gather and record background information on Redford.

3. Find out when your university's faculty council or similar faculty representative group is having its next meeting. Record the steps you take to prepare for the meeting and the information you gather as you prepare. Then cover the meeting and write the story.

4. Prepare for, cover and write one of the following:

   a. A speech story.
   b. A news conference story.
   c. A meeting story.

   Then compare your story to the one that appears on your topic in the local paper.

Other Types of Basic Stories

13

When major crimes occur in a community, interest is high among readers and viewers. That gives reporters a chance to deliver compelling accounts of what happened. Consider this example from Leonora Bohn Peter of the *Savannah (Ga.) Morning News*:

Tap. Tap. Tap. Tap. Pause. Tap. Tap. Tap.

Ashley Lewis hit the counter of the oak witness box with his index finger, mimicking what he heard through a crack in the bathroom window . . . as he got ready for bed.

It sounded like a typewriter. But Lewis, testifying on the first day in the death penalty trial of Jerry Scott Heidler for the murder of a family in Santa Claus a year and a half ago, found it hard to believe his mother, a secretary, would break out her typewriter at almost 2 a.m. Just a half hour before, she had told him to turn the television off and go to bed.

Lewis walked to his mother's room and turned on the light. She was asleep in bed. He walked through the house, turning on other lights. Nothing.

"I got this real eerie feeling," Lewis said.

Lewis did not know it yet, but a half-mile away, four of his neighbors lay dead.

Three hours later, Toombs County Sheriff's Department Deputy Mike Harlin arrived at the doorstep of the Daniels family on Dasher Lane in Santa Claus. Just about every light in the one story brick house was on. He thought that was odd for 5:10 a.m.

He knocked on the front door, which was slightly ajar. No answer. Through a window to the left, he noticed the arm of a small child in a bunk bed by the window.

He walked in and announced he was there. He heard a baby crying and a radio playing music. He walked toward the room with the child in it. On the top bunk, he found what was left of 8-year-old Bryant Daniels, who had been shot through the eye.

"I have a small boy myself," Harlin said, swallowing hard as he recalled the image on the witness stand Monday afternoon. "At that point, it was pretty obvious that words wouldn't help."

Harlin moved through the house, running into 4-year-old Corey Daniels near the dining room table. Harlin knelt down beside the child.

"Mama and Daddy are dead. Brother Guy shot them all," Corey said.

A baby continued to cry. The radio, obviously an alarm for early rising postal worker Danny Daniels, continued to play music.

Harlin opened the door of the master bedroom. The first thing he noticed was the gun cabinet with several empty slots where guns had been. Next he noticed a body up against the door, preventing him from opening it further. Corey showed him another entrance to the room, through a laundry room and a bathroom.

Harlin walked into the sunken bedroom and found 10-month-old Gabriel standing between his baby bed and his parents' king-sized bed, hanging onto the sheets. Beneath the sheet lay Kim Daniels, 33, who had been shot in the head. Danny Daniels, 47, also was dead on the bed. And a third body, that of 16-year-old Jessica Daniels, lay over by the door. . . .

This interesting account won the Jesse Laventhol Prize for Deadline Reporting. Stories about crime, accidents, fires and court proceedings are often assigned to beginning reporters. Newspapers, magazines and Web sites record major events in the life of a community, and those events often call for such stories. These stories are also the staple of local news reports on television. As a result, it's likely that as a beginning reporter you will have a chance to cover them. This chapter will help you prepare to do just that.

YOUR PREPARATION

When covering a crime, an accident, a fire or a court proceeding, begin as you would with any other story — by checking the morgue. There you'll learn whether a similar crime has occurred before, whether accidents are common at the location of the latest one, whether similar suspicious fires have occurred or whether the person charged with the crime has been in trouble before.

Preparing for the Crime Story

Meetings, news conferences, speeches and court proceedings are usually scheduled events, so on most occasions you should have ample time beforehand to do background research on the individual or topic to be covered. Obituaries also call for a first stop in the television station or newspaper library, but crime reporting may be different. If the police radio reports a murder in your area, you may be dispatched to the scene as the story is breaking. At that point, no one will know who is involved or what happened. There will be no time to check the library, and you will have to do your initial reporting at the scene.

Most information about crimes comes from three sources:

- Police officials and their reports.
- The victim or victims.
- The witness or witnesses.

The circumstances of the crime may determine which of the three is most important, which should be checked first or whether they should be checked at all. If the victim is available, as a reporter you should make every effort to get an interview. But if the victim and witnesses are unavailable, the police and their report become primary sources.

In the era of convergence, you'll need more than a pencil and notebook to gather information at the scene of a crime. A digital recorder will allow you to record your interviews for publication on your news organization's Web site, and a camera or camera phone might help record what happened at the scene. That's particularly true if you are covering the event alone without the help of a photojournalist or videographer.

The point at which your editor assigns you to a crime story is important. If you are dispatched to the scene of the crime as it happens or soon afterward, you will probably interview the victim and witnesses first. The police report probably hasn't even been written yet. But if you are assigned to write about a crime that occurred the night before, the police report is your starting point.

The timing affects what kinds of material you will be able to gather and which medium might use your information first. A major breaking story might warrant a mobile phone news bulletin or a television report. Something that happened the night before might require more sophisticated work, such as gathering information for a detailed information graphic of a crime scene.

A police officer investigating a crime covers much of the same ground as you. The officer is interested in who was involved, what happened, when, where, why and how. Those details are needed to complete the official report of the incident, and you need them for your story. When you write about crime, always check the police report. It is often the source of basic information, such as:

- A description of what happened.
- The location of the incident.
- The name, age and address of the victim.
- The name, age and address of the suspect, if any.
- The offense police believe the suspect has committed.
- The extent of injuries, if any.
- The names, ages and addresses of witnesses, if any.

The reporter who arrives at the scene of a crime as it takes place or immediately afterward has the advantage of being able to gather much of that information first-hand. When timely coverage is impossible, however, the police report allows the reporter to catch up quickly. The names of those with knowledge of the incident usually appear on the report, and the reporter uses that information to learn the story. See Figure 13.1 for an example of a police report.

Reporters sometimes write crime stories from the police report alone. For routine stories, some editors view such reporting as sufficient. Good newspapers, however, demand more because police reports are frequently inaccurate. Most experienced reporters have read reports in which the names of those involved are misspelled, ages are wrong and other basic information is inaccurate. Sometimes such errors are a result of sloppy reporting by the investigating officer or mistakes in transcribing notes into a formal report. Occasionally, the officer may lie in an attempt to cover up shortcomings in the investigation or misconduct at the scene of the crime. Whatever the reason, good reporters do their own reporting and do not depend solely on a police officer's account. Remember that editors frown on single-source stories of any kind. It's your job to do solid reporting, and you are expected to consult multiple sources.

For crime stories, a background check in the newspaper's morgue is often done after you return to the office. Once you have the names of those involved, for example, you can see whether the morgue reveals relevant information about them. Was the suspect arrested before? Was the store robbed before? The morgue might help answer those kinds of questions.

Figure 13.1
This burglary report is typical of the type of report available to reporters at most police stations.

```
1. OFFENSE                                    BURGLARY                          2. CASE #
   Burglary                                                                        32701
3. OCCURRED AT (ADDRESS)                          4. DATE/TIME OCCURRED   5. DATE/TIME REPORTED   6. DATE/TIME REPORT WRITTEN
   308 Maple St.                                     0100 - 0800             0830                    0945 - 11 March
7. PERSON REPORTING            RAC  SEX  DOB   ADDRESS                       HOME PHONE    BUS PHONE
   Linda L. Mellotti           W    F    9-11-45  308 Maple St.              372-1124      372-9988
8. OWNER OF BUILDING           RAC  SEX  DOB   ADDRESS                       HOME PHONE    BUS PHONE
   VICTIM
9. WITNESS                     RAC  SEX  DOB   ADDRESS                       HOME PHONE    BUS PHONE
   NONE
10. VICTIM (FIRM OR INDIVIDUAL) RAC SEX  DOB   ADDRESS                       HOME PHONE    BUS PHONE

11. RESIDENCE [X]  12. FORCE [X]  13. DAY [ ]   14. TYPE OF BUSINESS   15. POINT OF ENTRY   16. HOW WAS ENTRY GAINED
    NONRESIDENCE       NO FORCE       NIGHT [X]                            Back door          Glass broken to unlock door   TIME/DATE
                                      UNKNOWN [ ]
17. TYPE OF LOCK OR STRUCTURE DEFEATED    18. DAMAGE CAUSED BY ENTRY       19. WHO SECURED BLDG
    Type A                                   Broken window glass              Occupant
STOLEN  20. QUAN  21. TYPE   22. BRAND   23. SERIAL #  24. PHYSICAL DESCRIPTION        25. VALUE  26. DATE   BY  27. DATE    BY
PROP                                                                                              ENTERED         CLEARED
 A       1       Console    GE          Unknown       TV set                          $300

28. SUSPECT NAME               RAC  SEX  DOB   ADDRESS                       HOME PHONE    BUS PHONE
    NONE
HT.  WT.  EYES  HAIR  BUILD  FACIAL HAIR   HAT        COAT       SHIRT      TROUSERS      SHOES

UNUSUAL IDENTIFIERS                        MARKS SCARS & TATTOOS             PHOTO OBTAINED

SUSPECT VEHICLE   YEAR  MAKE   MODEL   STYLE   VIN        LIC YR   LIC STATE   LIC TYPE   LIC NUMBER
COLOR
29. INVESTIGATING OFFICER      DEPT   30. APPROVED BY     31. EVIDENCE COLLECTED BY   32. PHOTOGRAPHY BY   33. REASSIGNED TO   BY

34. NARRATIVE:
    Victim works night shift at Milan Hospital. Residence
    entered while she was working. TV set only item
    known missing.


                              WORK  SHEET
```

Preparing for Accident and Fire Stories

If you are assigned to cover an accident or fire, you can expect some of the same problems you'd encounter if covering a crime. Much depends on whether the police or fire report is available before or after you are assigned to the story. If the accident or fire took place overnight, the official report is the place to start. It will give you most of the basic information you need. It will also lead you to other sources.

If you are sent to the scene of an accident or fire, your job is to collect much of that information yourself. As for crimes, the basic information you'll need includes:

- A description of what happened.
- The location of the incident.
- The name, age and address of the victim or victims.
- The extent of injuries, if any.
- The names, ages and addresses of witnesses, if any.

TIPS

What to Do at the Scene of an Accident

- Question the person in charge of the investigation.
- Try to find and interview witnesses.
- Try to find friends or relatives of the victims.
- If possible, interview the victims.
- Talk with others at the scene.
- Be sensitive to victims and their families.

Preparing for the Court Story

Most court stories you are likely to cover will be follow-ups to earlier stories. If a murder suspect is appearing for a preliminary hearing, details of the crime probably were reported earlier, and a check of the newspaper's morgue may give you ample background information as you prepare for your visit to the courtroom. Otherwise, a chat with the district attorney, the police chief or one of their assistants might provide ample background for writing the story.

Court stories are often difficult for beginners to write because they are unlikely to understand the complex process used in criminal prosecutions. In addition, there are civil court proceedings, lawsuits that charge an individual or company with harming another. Here's our best advice on how to approach court stories: Ask plenty of questions of the judge and attorneys before or after the court proceeding or during recesses. It's much better to admit your lack of knowledge about the court process than to make a serious error in print because you didn't understand what was happening.

WRITING THE STORY

Knowing how to organize stories about crime, accidents, fires and court proceedings is essential. It helps to have a model, and the examples that follow are designed to assist you.

The Crime Story

There is no magic formula for writing crime news. Solid reporting techniques pay off just as they do in other types of reporting; then it is a matter of writing the story as the facts demand. Sometimes the events are most effectively told in chronological order, particularly when the story is complex (see Chapter 9). More often, a traditional inverted pyramid style works best. The amount of time the reporter has to file the story also influences the approach. Let's take a look at how the newspaper accounts of two crimes were developed over time and why different writing styles seemed appropriate for each.

Gathering facts from the many sources available and sorting through conflicting information can be time-consuming tasks. Sometimes the reporter may have to write the story before all the facts are gathered. The result is a bare-bones account written to meet a deadline. Such circumstances often lead to crime stories written like this:

A Highway Patrol marksman shot and killed a Kansas man in a rural area south of Springfield this morning after the victim threatened to blow off the head of his ap- parent hostage. A hitchhiker reportedly told police earlier this morning that his "ride" had plans to rob a service station on Interstate 70. That tip apparently followed an earlier report of a van leaving a station at the Millersburg exit of I-70 without paying for gasoline.

An ensuing hour-long chase ended at 9:30 a.m. in an isolated meadow in the Pierpont area when Capt. N.E. Tinnin fired a single shot into the stomach of the suspect, identified as Jim Phipps of Kansas City, Kan.

Phipps, armed with a sawed-off shotgun, and his "hostage," identified as Anthony

Curtis Lilly, 17, also of Kansas City, Kan., eluded police by fleeing into a rugged, wooded area at the end of Bennett Lane, a dead-end gravel road off Route 163.

Tinnin said he fired the shot with a .253-caliber sniper rifle when it appeared Phipps was going to shoot Lilly. Two troopers' efforts to persuade Phipps to throw down his weapon and surrender were unsuccessful, Tinnin said.

Notice that even in that bare-bones account, the available facts of the story dictated a chronological approach after a summary lead.

The reporter who produced that story for an afternoon newspaper did a good job of collecting information after a puzzling incident. Still, several words and phrases ("apparent hostage," "a hitchhiker reportedly told police," "tip apparently followed") provide tip-offs that the series of events was not entirely clear.

With more time to learn the full story, a reporter for the city's morning newspaper resolved many of those issues. As a result, readers got a more complete account of what occurred:

James Phipps and Anthony Lilly, a pair of 17-year-olds from Kansas City, Kan., were heading west on Interstate 70 at 7:30 a.m. Friday, returning from a trip to Arkansas.

Within the next hour and a half, Phipps had used a sawed-off shotgun stolen in Arkansas to take Lilly hostage, and, after holding that shotgun to Lilly's head, was shot and killed by a Highway Patrol captain on the edge of a rugged wooded area south of Springfield.

As the episode ended, local officials had only begun to piece together a bizarre tragedy that involved a high-speed chase, airplane and helicopter surveillance, a march through a wooded ravine and the evacuation of several frightened citizens from their country homes.

As police reconstructed the incident, Phipps and Lilly decided to stop for gas at the Millersburg exit east of Springfield at about 7:30 a.m. With them in the van was

Robert Paul Hudson Jr., a San Francisco-bound hitchhiker.

Hudson was not present at the shooting. He had fled Lilly's van at the Millersburg exit after he suspected trouble.

The trouble began when Lilly and Phipps openly plotted to steal some gasoline at Millersburg, Hudson told police. He said the pair had agreed to display the shotgun if trouble arose with station attendants.

Hudson said he persuaded Phipps to drop him off before they stopped for gas. He then caught a ride to Springfield and told his driver of the robbery plans he had overheard. After dropping Hudson off near the Providence Road exit, the driver called Springfield police, who picked up Hudson.

Meanwhile, Phipps and Lilly put $8.90 worth of gas in the van and drove off without paying. The station attendant notified authorities.

As he approached Springfield, Phipps

turned onto U.S. 63 South, where he was spotted by Highway Patrol troopers Tom Halford and Greg Overfelt. They began a high-speed chase, which ended on a dead-end gravel road near Pierpont.

During the chase, which included a U-turn near Ashland, Phipps bumped the Highway Patrol car twice, forcing Halford to run into the highway's median.

Upon reaching the dead end, the suspects abandoned the van and ran into a nearby barn. At that point, Phipps, who Highway Patrol officers said was wanted in Kansas for escaping from a detention center, turned the shotgun on Lilly.

When Halford and Overfelt tried to talk with Phipps from outside the barn, they were met with obscenities. Phipps threatened to "blow (Lilly's) head off," and vowed not to be captured alive.

Phipps then left the barn and walked into a wooded area, pressing the gun against Lilly's head. Halford and Overfelt followed at a safe distance but were close enough to speak with Phipps.

While other officers from the Highway Patrol, the Lincoln County Sheriff's De-partment and Springfield police arrived at the scene, residents in the area were warned to evacuate their homes. A Highway Patrol plane and helicopter flew low over the woods, following the suspects and the troopers through the woods.

The four walked through a deep and densely wooded ravine. Upon seeing a partially constructed house in a nearby clearing, Phipps demanded of officers waiting in the clearing that his van be driven around to the house, at which time he would release his hostage. Halford said, "They disappeared up over the ridge. I heard some shouting (Phipps' demands), and then I heard the shot."

After entering the clearing from the woods, Phipps apparently had been briefly confused by the officers on either side of him and had lowered his gun for a moment.

That was long enough for Highway Patrol Capt. N.E. Tinnin to shoot Phipps in the abdomen with a high-powered rifle. It was about 8:45 a.m. Phipps was taken to Boone County Hospital, where he soon died.

The story is as complete as possible under the circumstances. The reporter who wrote it decided to describe the chain of events in chronological order because of the complexity of the story and because the drama of the actual events is most vividly communicated in a chronological narrative.

The story is also made effective by its wealth of detail, including the names of the troopers involved, details of the chase and much, much more. The reporter had to talk with many witnesses to piece together this account. The hard work paid off, however, in the form of an informative, readable story. Notice how the third paragraph sets the scene and provides a transition into the chronological account. Such attention to the details of good writing helps the reader understand the story with a minimum of effort.

If a number of people witnessed or were affected by a crime, you may supplement the main story with a sidebar that deals with the personal impact of the crime—the "so what." The writer of the preceding chronological account also decided to write a separate story on nearby residents, who had little to add to the main story but became a part of the situation nonetheless:

In the grass at the edge of a woods near Pierpont Friday afternoon, the only remaining signs of James Phipps were a six-inch circle of blood, a doctor's syringe, a blood-stained button and the imprints in the mud where Phipps fell after he was shot by a Highway Patrol officer. Elsewhere in the area, it was a quiet, sunny, spring day in a countryside dotted by farms and houses. But inside some of those houses, dwellers still were shaken by the morning's events that had forced a police order for them to evacuate their homes.

Mrs. James G. Thorne lives on Cheavens Road across the clearing from where Phipps was shot. Mrs. Thorne had not heard the evacuation notice, so when she saw area officers crouching with guns at the end of her driveway, she decided to investigate.

"I was the surprise they weren't expecting," she told a Highway Patrol officer Friday afternoon. "I walked out just before the excitement."

When the officers saw Mrs. Thorne "they were obviously very upset and shouted for me to get out of here," she said. "I was here alone and asked them how I was supposed to leave. All they said was, 'Just get out of here!'"

Down the road, Clarence Stallman had been warned of the situation by officers and noticed the circling airplane and helicopter. "I said, 'Are they headed this way soon?' and they said, 'They're here,'" said Stallman.

After Stallman notified his neighbors, he picked up Mrs. Thorne at her home and left the area just before the shooting.

On the next street over, Ronald Nichols had no intention of running.

"I didn't know what was happening," Nichols said. "The wife was scared to death and didn't know what to do. I grabbed my gun and looked for them."

Another neighbor, Mrs. Charles Emmons, first was alerted by the sound of the surveillance plane. "The plane was flying so low I thought it was going to come into the house," she said. "I was frightened. This is something you think will never happen to you."

Then Mrs. Emmons flashed a relieved smile. "It's been quite a morning," she said.

The techniques of writing in chronological order and separating the accounts of witnesses from the main story worked well in the preceding case. More often, however, crime stories are written in the classic inverted pyramid style because of time and space considerations:

A masked robber took $1,056 from a clerk at Gibson's Liquor Store Friday night, then eluded police in a chase through nearby alleys.

The clerk, Robert Simpson, 42, of 206 Fourth St. said a man wearing a red ski mask entered the store at about 7:35 p.m. The man displayed a pistol and demanded that Simpson empty the contents of the cash register into a brown grocery bag.

Simpson obeyed but managed to trigger a silent alarm button under the counter.

The robber ordered Simpson into a storage room in the rear of the building at 411 Fourth St.

Officer J.O. Holton, responding to the alarm, arrived at the store as the suspect left the building and fled south on foot.

Holton chased the man south on Fourth Street until he turned west into an alley near the corner of Olson Street. Holton said he followed the suspect for about four blocks until he lost sight of him.

Simpson said receipts showed that $1,056 was missing from the cash register. He described the robber as about 5 feet 11 inches with a bandage on his right thumb. He was wearing blue jeans and a black leather coat.

Police have no suspects.

Such an account is adequate, and you can write it directly from the police report. That, of course, would be a single-source story. So a good reporter would add to the story by taking time to interview the clerk and police officer.

After filing this story for the first edition, the reporter found time to call the police officer. He had little to add. Then the reporter contacted the clerk, who had plenty to say. This was the result:

"I'm tired of being robbed, and I'm afraid of being shot," says Robert Simpson. "So I told the owner I quit."

Simpson, 42, of 206 Fourth St. quit his job as night clerk at Gibson's Liquor Store today after being robbed for the fourth time in three weeks Friday night.

Simpson said a man wearing a red ski mask entered the store at 411 Fourth St. at about 7:35 p.m. and demanded money. Simpson emptied $1,056 into a grocery bag the robber carried and was ordered into a storage room at the rear of the building.

"He said he'd blow off my head if I didn't cooperate, so I did exactly what he told me," Simpson said. "But I managed to set off the alarm button under the counter while I was emptying the cash register."

Officer J.O. Holton responded to the alarm and arrived as the robber left the store but lost him as he fled through nearby alleys on foot.

"We keep asking the cops to set up a stakeout, but they don't do anything," Simpson said. "I know they've got a lot of problems, but that place is always getting hit."

Police records revealed that Gibson's was robbed of $502 Sept. 10, $732 Sept. 14 and $221 Sept. 24. Simpson was the clerk each time.

"This may have been the same guy who robbed me last time," Simpson said, "but I can't be sure because of that mask. Last time he had a different one."

Police Chief Ralph Marshall said he has ordered patrol cars to check the vicinity of the liquor store more often and is considering the owner's request for a stakeout.

"That's just great," Simpson said. "But they can let someone else be the goat. I quit."

Simpson described the robber as a heavy man about 5 feet 11 inches tall. He was wearing blue jeans and a black leather jacket and had a bandage on his right thumb.

Police have no suspects.

The reporter took the time to get a good interview, and the direct quotes add to the appeal of the story. The reporter also recognized and brought out the best angle: the personal fear and frustration experienced by people in high-crime areas. The result is a much more imaginative use of the basic inverted pyramid formula and a much more interesting story.

The clerk, in the course of his remarks, supplied an important tip about repeated robberies at the store. Two weeks later, police arrested a man as he tried to rob the store. The earlier report was used for background, and a complete story resulted.

Accident and Fire Stories

When you are assigned to cover an accident or a fire, many of the facts and all of the color are gathered at the scene. If the accident has just taken place, a visit to the scene is essential. Being there will give you the best picture of what happened, and you will be able to write a solid story. Too many reporters cover accidents and fires as purely passive observers. Indeed, you must observe. But you must also actively solicit information from those who are present. Many of them, including those directly involved, you may never be able to find again. Keep a digital recorder and camera at hand. You may be asked to prepare stories for multiple media.

When dispatched to the scene of an accident, move as quickly as possible to collect this information:

- The names, ages, addresses and conditions of the victims.
- Accounts of witnesses or police reconstructions of what happened.
- When the accident occurred.
- Where it occurred.
- Why or how it happened or who was at fault, as determined by officials in charge of the investigation.

If that list sounds familiar, it should. You could simplify it to read "who, what, when, where and why." As in any news story, that information is essential. You must gather it as quickly as possible after being assigned to the story. Just as important is knowing what to do when you arrive on the scene. These suggestions will help:

- **Question the person in charge of the investigation.** This individual will attempt to gather much of the information you want. A police officer, for example, needs to know who was involved, what happened, when it happened and who was at fault. If you are able to establish a good relationship with the investigator, you may be able to secure much of the information you need from this one source, though single-source stories are usually inadequate.

  Remember that the spellings of names, addresses and similar facts must be verified later. Any veteran reporter can tell you that police officers and other public officials are notoriously bad spellers and often make errors in recording the names of victims. To avoid such errors, call relatives of the victims or consult the city directory, telephone book or other sources to check your information.
- **Try to find and interview witnesses.** Police and other investigators may lead you directly to the best witnesses. The most accurate account of what happened usually comes from witnesses, and the investigators will try to find them. You should, too. A good way to do that is to watch the investigators. Listen in as they interview a witness, or approach the witness after they are finished. If there is time, of course, try to find your own witnesses. You cannot and should not always rely on investigators to do your work for you.
- **Try to find friends or relatives of the victims.** These sources are helpful in piecing together information about the victims. Through them you often get tips about even better stories.
- **If possible, interview the victims.** Survivors of an accident may be badly shaken, but if they are able to talk, they can provide firsthand details that an official report never could. Make every attempt to interview those involved.

ON THE JOB

Disasters Don't Just Disappear

A year and a half after leaving journalism school, Lisa Arthur found herself covering the rebuilding of South Dade County for *The Miami Herald*. Hurricane Andrew had struck the area on Aug. 24, 1992, and the trail of destruction was still visible 18 months later.

The experience taught Arthur that some of the most important stories in disaster reporting come months after the initial crisis.

"When I arrived, there were still hundreds of people living in trailers, and pockets of the landscape still resembled a bombed-out Beirut," she says. "People were still suffering a great psychological trauma, and they looked to the local media to deliver the message that all was not well yet. They still needed help even though the memory of the hurricane had begun to fade for people not directly affected."

Arthur has this advice for reporters covering the long-term aftermath of any disaster. First, focus on ordinary people and the small battles they are fighting to get their homes and lives repaired. There are still people in South Dade today who are living in trailers because contractors ripped them off or they didn't have insurance. This is fertile ground for stories that are important and can sometimes make a difference. Second, follow the money trail. Tens of millions of federal dollars flow into devastated areas. Track the money and see whether it trickles down to the people who need it. Third, look for heroes. Arthur stumbled upon a Pittsburgh philanthropist who had been quietly pumping millions of recovery dollars into South Dade. His deeds went unnoticed for two years. Arthur's story about him wound up on the front page of the *Herald*.

- **Talk with others at the scene.** If someone died at the scene of the accident, an ambulance paramedic or the medical examiner may be able to give you some indication of what caused the death. At the least you can learn where the bodies or the injured will be taken. That may help, because later the mortician or hospital officials may be able to provide information you need for your story.
- **Be sensitive to victims and their families.** You have a job to do, and you must do it. That does not mean, however, that you can be insensitive to those involved in an accident.
- **Sketch elements of the scene on a piece of paper.** This may be useful in helping an information graphics artist re-create the scene.
- **Record your interviews.** This might be needed for your Web site or to help you make sure the information is correct.

Of course, your deadline will have a major impact on the amount of information you are able to gather. If you must meet a deadline soon after arriving at the scene, you will probably be forced to stick to the basics of who, what, when, where, why and how. Thus it is important to gather that information first. Then, if you have time, you can concentrate on more detailed and vivid information to make the story highly readable.

The following account of a tractor-trailer accident was produced in a race against the clock by the staff of an afternoon newspaper:

A truck driver was killed and a woman was injured this morning when a tractor-trailer believed to be hauling gasoline overturned and exploded on Interstate 70, turning the highway into a conflagration.

Both lanes of I-70 were backed up for miles after an eastbound car glanced off a pickup truck, hurdled the concrete median and collided with a tanker truck heading west.

The explosion was immediate, witnesses said. Residents along Texas Avenue reported the initial fireball reached the north side of the street, which is about 300 yards from the scene of the accident. A wooded area was scorched, but no houses were damaged.

Police evacuated the 600 block of Texas Avenue for fear that the fire would spread, but residents were returning to their homes at 12:35 p.m., about an hour after the collision. Authorities also unsuccessfully attempted to hold back the onlookers who gravitated to a nearby shopping center parking lot to view the blaze.

Police did not identify the driver of the truck, which was owned by a Tulsa, Okla., firm named Transport Delivery Co.

"Apparently it was gasoline," said Steve Paulsell, chief of the County Fire Protection District. "That's what it smelled like." Other officials reported the truck may have been hauling fuel oil or diesel fuel.

For a newspaper with an early afternoon deadline, such a story presents major problems, particularly when it occurs, as this one did, at about 11:30 a.m. Four reporters were dispatched to the scene; all of them called in information to a writer back at the office. There was little time to interview eyewitnesses. Because of the pressing deadline, the reporters were forced to gather most of their information from fire and police officials at the scene.

Writers for the morning newspaper, by comparison, had plenty of time to gather rich detail to tell the story in human terms. Much of the breaking news value was diminished by the next morning because of intense coverage by the afternoon newspaper, radio and television. It was time to tell the story of a hero:

Witnesses credited an off-duty firefighter with saving a woman's life Monday following a spectacular four-vehicle collision on Interstate 70 just east of its intersection with Business Loop 70.

The driver of a gasoline truck involved in the fiery crash was not so lucky. Bill Borgmeyer, 62, of Jefferson City died in the cab of his rig, which jackknifed, overturned

and exploded in flames when he swerved in a futile attempt to avoid hitting a car driven by Leta Hanes, 33, of Nelson, Mo.

Mrs. Hanes, who was thrown from her auto by the impact, was lying unconscious within 10 feet of the blazing fuel when firefighter Richard Walden arrived at the crash scene.

"I knew what was going on," Walden

recalled, "and I knew I had to get her away from there." Despite the intense heat, Walden dragged the woman to safety.

"She had some scrapes, a cut on her knee and was beat around a little bit," Walden said. "Other than that, she was fine."

Mrs. Hanes was taken to Boone Hospital Center, where she was reported in satisfactory condition Monday night.

Smoke billowing from the accident scene reportedly was visible 30 miles away. Westbound interstate traffic was backed up as far as five miles. Several city streets became snarled for several hours when traffic was diverted to Business Loop 70. The eastbound lane of I-70 was reopened about 2 p.m.; the westbound lane was not reopened until 3 p.m.

The richness of detail in the second story, including the account of the rescuer, and the eyewitness descriptions of what happened make the story more interesting. The importance of adding such detail is apparent.

Accidents and fires present similar problems for the reporter, but at a fire of any size you can expect more confusion than at the scene of an accident. One major difference, then, is that the officer in charge will be busier. At the scene of an accident, the damage has been done and the authorities are usually free to concentrate on their investigation. At a fire, the officer in charge is busy directing firefighters and probably will be unable to talk with you. The investigation will not even begin until the fire is extinguished. In many cases, the cause of the fire will not be known for hours, days or weeks. In fact, it may never be known. Seldom is that the case in an accident, except perhaps for air accidents.

Another problem is that you may not have access to the immediate area of the fire. Barriers often are erected to keep the public—and representatives of the

Hazards at the scene of a disaster, such as this fire resulting from a Los Angeles-area earthquake, can make a reporter's job difficult and dangerous.

news media—from coming too close to a burning structure. The obvious reason is safety, but such barriers may hamper your reporting. You may not be able to come close enough to firefighters to learn about the problems they are having or to obtain the quotes you need to improve your story.

These problems usually make covering a fire more difficult than covering an accident. Despite the difficulties, you cover a fire in much the same way, interviewing officials and witnesses at the scene. You also should try to interview the property owner. Moreover, because the official investigation will not have begun, you must conduct your own. When covering any fire, you must learn:

- The location of the fire.
- The names, ages and addresses of those killed, injured or missing.
- The name of the building owner or, in the case of a grass fire or forest fire, the landowner.
- The value of the building and its contents or the value of the land.
- Whether the building and contents were insured for fire damage. (Open land seldom is.)
- When the fire started, who reported it and how many firefighters and pieces of equipment were called to the scene.
- What caused the fire, if known.

As in any story, the basics are who, what, when, where, why and how. But the nature of the fire will raise other questions that must be answered. Of primary importance is whether life is endangered. If it is not, the amount of property damage becomes the major emphasis of the story. Was arson involved? Was the building insured for its full value? Was there an earlier fire at the same location? Did the building comply with fire codes? Were any rare or extremely valuable objects inside? Did any explosives inside complicate fighting the fire and pose an even greater threat than the fire itself?

> **"**The news is no longer the news. . . . It's all about luridness. Body bags will be seen at 7, chasing ambulance at 8, victim's family at 9.**"**
>
> —Oliver Stone, film director

Your job is to answer these questions for your readers or viewers. You will be able to obtain some of this information later on from official fire reports if they are ready before your story deadline (see Figure 13.2). But most information will come from interviews that you conduct at the scene with the best available sources. Finding your sources may not be easy, but you can begin by looking for the highest-ranking fire official. Large departments may have a designated press officer whose job is to deal with you and other reporters.

Another important source is the fire marshal, whose job is to determine the cause of the fire and, if arson is involved, to bring charges against the arsonist. You should make every effort to talk with the fire marshal at the scene, if he or she is available. In most cases, though, the marshal will be the primary source of a second-day story.

Figure 13.2
This casualty report is typical of those available to reporters at most fire stations.

DATE		TIME		ADDRESS	

PAGE   OF   CASUALTY REPORT

FD-500

CHANGE 2 ☐
DELETE 3 ☐   (74)

INCIDENT NO	EXP
8 0 9 0 5 1 3	
1 2 3	7 8 9

NAME
S A N D O Z A   M A N U E L   R   33 | AGE 3 2 | Time of Injury 0 9 4 5 | MONTH 0 2 | DAY 0 8 | YEAR 9 6
LAST, FIRST MIDDLE   33 34 35 36   39 40   45

HOME ADDRESS
307 Banning Ave., Apt. 3   TELEPHONE 555-9088

46 SEX	47 CASUALTY TYPE	48 SEVERITY	49 AFFILIATION
1 ☒ Male	1 ☒ Fire Casualty	1 ☒ Injury	1 ☐ Fire Service
2 ☐ Female	2 ☐ Action Casualty	2 ☐ Death	2 ☐ Other Emergency Personnel
	3 ☐ EMS Casualty		3 ☒ Civilian

FAMILIARITY WITH STRUCTURE		LOCATION AT IGNITION		CONDITION BEFORE INJURY	
Occupant	50	Unknown	51	Unknown	52
CONDITION PREVENTING ESCAPE		ACTIVITY AT TIME OF INJURY		CAUSE OF INJURY	
N/A	53	Leaving building	54	Falling debris	55
NATURE OF INJURY		PART OF BODY INJURED		DISPOSITION	
Broken leg	56	Leg	57	Hospitalized	58

REMARKS:
Occupant was leaving burning structure when burning eave fell and struck his leg.

By   #31   Ambulance to   General   Hospital

NAME
                                          33 | AGE | Time of Injury | MONTH | DAY | YEAR
LAST, FIRST MIDDLE   33 34 35 36   39 40   45

HOME ADDRESS   TELEPHONE

46 SEX	47 CASUALTY TYPE	48 SEVERITY	49 AFFILIATION
1 ☐ Male	1 ☐ Fire Casualty	1 ☐ Injury	1 ☐ Fire Service
2 ☐ Female	2 ☐ Action Casualty	2 ☐ Death	2 ☐ Other Emergency Personnel
	3 ☐ EMS Casualty		3 ☐ Civilian

FAMILIARITY WITH STRUCTURE		LOCATION AT IGNITION		CONDITION BEFORE INJURY	
	50		51		52
CONDITION PREVENTING ESCAPE		ACTIVITY AT TIME OF INJURY		CAUSE OF INJURY	
	53		54		55
NATURE OF INJURY		PART OF BODY INJURED		DISPOSITION	
	56		57		58

REMARKS:

By   Ambulance to   Hospital

Nelson Riley
Supervisor*
*Injury reports for fire personnel,
immediate supervisor to sign here.

SIGNATURE of person completing form/DATE
John R. Sanders.

Printed in U.S.A.

As in covering any **spot news** story—a story in which news is breaking quickly—deadlines will determine how much you can do at the scene of a fire. If your deadline is hours away, you can concentrate on the event and the people connected with it. You will have time to find the little boy whose puppy was killed in the fire or interview the firefighter who first entered the building. But if you have only minutes until your deadline, you may have to press the fire official in charge for as much information as possible. You may have to coax from that person every tidbit, even making a nuisance of yourself to gather the information you need. Through it all, you can expect confusion. There is little order to be found in the chaos of a fire.

The Court Story

Criminal justice proceedings can be very complicated, with a case moving through a number of stages, from occurrence of the crime, to police investigation, to actions by prosecutors and defense attorneys, to actual criminal trials, to legal punishments like incarceration and execution (see Figure 13.3).

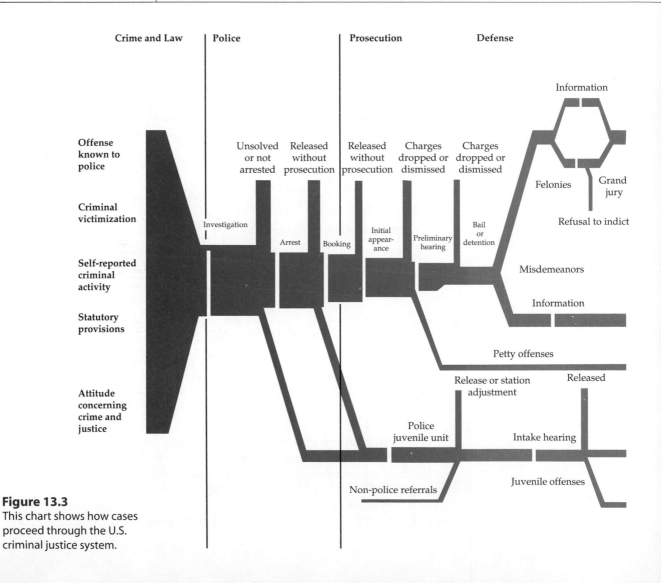

Figure 13.3
This chart shows how cases proceed through the U.S. criminal justice system.

Throughout this cycle of events, a reporter has numerous opportunities to write stories. The extent to which the reporter does so depends on the importance of the case and the amount of local interest in it. In a major case, the filing of every motion may prompt a story; in other cases, only the verdict may be important. As in any type of reporting, news value is the determining factor.

Also, as in any form of reporting, accuracy is important. Perhaps no other area of writing requires as much caution as the reporting of crime and court news. The potential for libel is great.

Libel is damage to a person's reputation caused by a written statement that brings the person into hatred, contempt or ridicule, or that injures a person's business or occupational pursuits (see Chapter 22). Reporters must be extremely careful about what they write. One of the greatest dangers is the possibility of writing that someone is charged with a crime more serious than is the case. After checking clippings in the newspaper library, for example, one reporter wrote:

> The rape trial of John L. Duncan, 25, of 3925 Oak St. has been set for Dec. 10 in Jefferson County Circuit Court.
> Duncan is charged in connection with the June 6 rape of a Melton High School girl near Fletcher Park.

Duncan had been charged with rape following his arrest. However, the prosecutor later determined that the evidence was insufficient to win a rape conviction, the charge was reduced to assault and the newspaper had to print a correction.

Any story involving arrests should raise caution flags. You must have a working knowledge of libel law and what you can and cannot write about an incident. Any reporter who would write the following, for example, is asking for trouble:

> John R. Milton, 35, of 206 East St. was arrested Monday on a charge of assaulting a police officer.

Only a prosecutor, not a police officer, may file charges. In many cases, a police officer may arrest a person with the intent of asking the prosecutor to file a certain charge, but when the prosecutor examines the evidence, the evidence may warrant only a lesser charge. For that reason, most newspaper editors prefer to print the name of an arrested person only after the charge has been filed.

Unfortunately, deadline constraints sometimes make that impossible, and many newspapers publish the names of those arrested before the charge is filed. A decision to publish a name in such circumstances requires extreme caution. If an individual were arrested in connection with a rape and the newspaper printed that information, only to learn later that the prosecutor had filed a charge of assault, a libel suit could result. Many states, however, give journalists a **qualified privilege** to write fair and accurate news stories based on police reports. Once the charge is filed, the lead should be written like this:

> John R. Milton, 35, of 206 East St. was charged Monday with assaulting a police officer. Prosecutor Steve Rodriguez said . . .

By writing the lead this way, the reporter shows that Milton not only was arrested but also was charged with a crime by the prosecutor. Carelessness leads not only to libel suits but also to attacks on a suspect's reputation.

Reporters who cover court news encounter many such pitfalls. They are not trained as attorneys, and it takes time to develop a working knowledge of legal proceedings. The only recourse is to ask as many questions as necessary when a point of law is not clear. It is far better to display ignorance of the law and ask questions than to commit a serious error that harms the reputation of the accused and opens the newspaper to costly libel litigation.

However, it is also important to know that anything said in open court is fair game for reporters. If, in an opening statement, a prosecutor says the defendant is

Many courts handle both civil and criminal cases. Media coverage often focuses on criminal cases, although civil actions — lawsuits involving disputes of one type or another — are often excellent sources of stories.

ON THE JOB

Lessons of the Police Beat

When *The San Diego Union-Tribune* expanded its zoned editions in 1985, the paper hired journalism graduate James Grimaldi to cover El Cajon, Calif. His goal was to go from the suburbs to the city desk.

"The fastest way to the front page was police stories," Grimaldi says.

One Sunday, the El Cajon police discovered a quadruple homicide. Grimaldi volunteered to cover the story. By the end of the day, he had scored an exclusive jailhouse interview with the killer. Within six months, Grimaldi was promoted to police reporter.

He combed through hundreds of police reports looking for trend stories while covering internal policies of the San Diego Police Department. At that time, the force was wracked by a high officer death rate and embarrassed by a sensational, racially divisive trial of a black man acquitted of shooting to death a white police officer in what he said was self-defense.

Once, as coroners removed a charred body from a San Diego Dumpster, Grimaldi was on the scene. He later was the first to report that the death was probably the work of a serial killer. He wrote about police corruption, including the chief's use of city-owned video equipment to tape a TV show on bass fishing.

"There's no better way to learn how to report and write than covering crime," Grimaldi says. "It is the quickest way to explore any community. There's humor and pathos, politics and social issues. Every rookie reporter should spend some time covering crime."

From the *Tribune*, Grimaldi went to *The Orange County Register* in 1989 as a general-assignment reporter. Crime stories taught Grimaldi reporting techniques he used for an investigation of medical deaths, rapes and drug-dealing at the California Institution for Women in Frontera. The Frontera stories won numerous national prizes.

In 1994, Grimaldi was named the *Register*'s bureau chief in Washington. Now at *The Washington Post*, he still relies on the reporting foundation first built on the police beat.

In 2006 Grimaldi, together with Susan Schmidt and R. Jeffrey Smith, two other *Washington Post* journalists, was awarded a Pulitzer Prize for investigative journalism, for a series of articles on congressional corruption involving Washington lobbyist Jack Abramoff.

"nothing but scum, a smut peddler bent on polluting the mind of every child in the city," then by all means report the comment in context in your story. But if a spectator makes that same statement in the hallway during a recess, you probably would not report it. Courts do not extend the qualified privilege to report court proceedings beyond the context of the official proceeding.

Court Organization and Procedure

When a suspect is apprehended and charged with a crime, the reporter's job is only beginning. Because the public wants and needs to know whether the suspect is guilty and, if so, what punishment is imposed, the media devote much time and space to court coverage of criminal charges.

At first glance, reporting court news appears to be simple. You listen to the judicial proceedings, ask a few questions afterward and write a story. It may be that simple if you have a thorough knowledge of criminal law and court procedure. If you do not, reporting court news can be extremely confusing. No journalism textbook or class can prepare you to deal with all the intricacies of criminal law. That is a subject better suited for law schools. You should learn the basics of law, court organization and procedure, however. With this foundation you will be prepared to cover court proceedings with at least some understanding of what is happening. You can supplement this knowledge by asking questions of the judge and attorneys involved.

Court Organization

In the United States, there are two primary court systems: federal and state. Each state has a unique system, but there are many similarities from state to state. The average citizen is most likely to have contact with city or municipal courts, which have jurisdiction over traffic and other minor violations of city ordinances. News from these courts is handled as a matter of record in many newspapers.

Cases involving violations of state statutes usually are handled in the state trial courts that can be found in most counties. These courts of general jurisdiction (often called circuit or superior courts) handle cases ranging from domestic relations matters to murder. "General jurisdiction" is an important designation. It means these courts can and do try more cases, of greater variety, than any other type of court, including federal district (trial) courts. Courts of general jurisdiction handle civil cases, such as contractual disputes, as well as the criminal cases that are the primary focus of news reporters.

Federal district courts have jurisdiction over cases involving violations of federal crime statutes, interpretation of the U.S. Constitution, civil rights, election disputes, commerce and antitrust matters, postal regulations, federal tax laws and similar issues. Federal trial courts also have jurisdiction in actions between citizens of different states when the amount in controversy exceeds $50,000.

Court Procedure

Crimes are categorized under state statutes according to their seriousness. The two primary categories of crimes are misdemeanors and felonies. Under modern statutes, the distinction between a felony and a misdemeanor turns on whether the offense is punishable by imprisonment in a state prison or in a county jail. Most state statutes describe a misdemeanor as an offense punishable by a fine, a county jail term not to exceed one year or both. Felonies are punishable by a fine, a prison sentence of more than one year or death.

Pretrial Proceedings in Criminal Cases

A person arrested in connection with a crime usually is taken to a police station for fingerprinting, photographing and perhaps a sobriety test or a lineup. Statements may be taken and used in evidence only if the person arrested has been informed of and waives what police and lawyers call Miranda rights, so named because the requirement was imposed in a U.S. Supreme Court case involving a defendant named Miranda. Those rights include the right to have an attorney (either hired by the defendant or appointed by the court if the defendant is indigent) and the right to remain silent. Usually within 24 hours a charge must be filed or the person must be released. The time limit may vary from state to state, but all states have some limitation to prevent unreasonable detention.

Initial Appearance

If, after consulting with police and reviewing the evidence, the prosecuting (or state or circuit) attorney decides to file charges, the defendant is usually brought before a judge, informed of the charges and reminded of the Miranda rights. Bail is usually set at this time. If the charge is a misdemeanor and the defendant pleads guilty, the case is usually disposed of immediately, and a sentence is imposed or a fine is levied. If the plea is not guilty, a trial date is usually set.

If the crime is a felony, the defendant does not enter a plea. The judge sets a date for a preliminary hearing, unless the defendant waives the right to such a hearing. A defendant who waives this hearing is bound over to the general jurisdiction trial court. The process of being bound over means simply that the records of the case will be sent to the trial court.

A preliminary hearing in a felony case is usually held before a magistrate or a lower-level judge in state court systems. The prosecutor presents evidence to try to convince the judge that there is probable cause to believe that a crime has been committed and that the defendant committed it. The defendant has the right to cross-examine the state's witnesses, and the defendant may present evidence, but this normally is not done. Thus, because stories about preliminary hearings often are one-sided, care must be exercised to write a story that is well-balanced.

If the judge does find that there is probable cause, the prosecuting attorney must file what is called an information within a short period of time (usually 10 days) after the judge orders the defendant bound over for trial. This information must be based on the judge's findings of probable cause.

Under most state constitutions, it is possible to bring a person accused in a felony case to trial in one of two ways. One is the preliminary hearing; the other is a grand jury indictment. In federal courts, the U.S. Constitution requires indictment by a grand jury in felony cases.

Grand jury hearings are secret in some states. Jurors are sworn not to reveal information about what takes place in the grand jury room, and potential defendants are not allowed to be present when testimony is given concerning them. The prosecuting attorney presents evidence to the grand jury, which must determine whether there is probable cause to prosecute. The prosecutor acts as adviser to the grand jury.

A grand jury returns a true bill when probable cause is found. A no true bill is returned if no probable cause is found. When a grand jury finds probable cause, an indictment is signed by the grand jury foreperson and the prosecuting attorney. The indictment then is presented in open court to a trial judge.

If the defendant is not already in custody, the judge orders an arrest warrant issued for the accused. Arraignment in the trial court follows. This is the first formal presentation of the information or the indictment to the defendant. The arraignment is conducted in open court, and the defendant enters a plea to the charge. Three pleas — guilty, not guilty, and not guilty by reason of mental disease or defect — are possible.

A process known as plea bargaining is sometimes used at this point. Under this process, a defendant may change a plea from not guilty to guilty in return for a lighter sentence than may be imposed if a jury returns a guilty verdict. Typically, in such circumstances the defendant pleads guilty to a lesser charge than the one outstanding. A defendant charged with premeditated or first-degree murder, for example, may plead guilty to a reduced charge of manslaughter. The prosecutor is often willing to go along with such an arrangement if the time and expense of a trial can be saved and if justice is served.

If a guilty plea is entered, the judge may impose a sentence immediately, or a presentencing investigation of the defendant's background may be ordered to help the judge set punishment. Many jurisdictions require presentencing investigations, at least in felony cases. If sentencing is delayed for that purpose, a sentencing date is usually set to allow ample time for completion of the report.

If a not-guilty plea is entered, the judge sets a trial date. Most jurisdictions have statutes or court rules

(continued)

Court Organization and Procedure (continued)

requiring speedy trials in criminal cases and setting time limits from the date of the charge being filed to the date of the trial.

As the prosecutor and defense attorney prepare for trial, motions may be filed for disclosure of evidence, suppression of evidence and similar rulings. Journalists will have a special interest if a defense attorney files a motion for a change of venue, which allows the trial to be conducted in a county other than the one in which the alleged crime occurred. Requests for venue changes often result from pretrial stories in the local media that may prejudice potential jurors. This was the case when the Los Angeles police officers accused of beating Rodney King were tried in Simi Valley.

The Trial

The trial starts as a jury, usually made up of 12 members and at least one alternate, is selected from a group of citizens called for jury duty. During the selection process (called *voir dire*), the prosecutor and defense attorney question the prospective jurors to identify jurors who each side hopes will be sympathetic to its position. In the federal system the judge often asks questions, but the prosecutor and defense attorneys may suggest questions for the judge to ask potential jurors.

Each attorney is allowed to eliminate a certain number of individuals from consideration as jurors without having to state a reason. Thus, either attorney can dismiss a prospective juror believed to be prejudiced against the attorney's view. Elimination of a prospective juror for cause (if, for example, he or she is related to the accused) is also permitted. Each attorney is allowed an unlimited number of challenges for cause.

Once 12 jurors and one or more alternates are chosen and sworn, the prosecutor makes an opening statement. The opening statement outlines how the prosecutor, acting on behalf of the state, expects to prove each of the elements of the crime. The defense attorney may follow with an outline of the defense or may wait until after the prosecution has introduced its

evidence. The defense may also waive an opening statement.

To establish what happened and to link the defendant to the crime, witnesses for the state are called to testify. During this procedure, the prosecutor asks questions, and the witness responds. The defense attorney then has an opportunity to cross-examine the witness. Frequently, one attorney will object to questions posed by the other, and the judge must rule on the objection. When the defense attorney finishes cross-examination, the prosecutor conducts re-direct examination to try to clarify for the jury points that may have become confused during cross-examination and to bolster the credibility of a witness whose credibility may have been damaged during cross-examination. Then the defense attorney may conduct another cross-examination, and the prosecutor may conduct another re-direct examination. This process can continue until both sides have exhausted all questions they want to ask the witness.

After all of the prosecution witnesses have testified and the state rests its case, the defense almost always makes a motion for acquittal, in which it argues that the state has failed to prove its case beyond a reasonable doubt. Almost as routinely as such motions are made, they are denied. A basic tenet of criminal law in the United States is that the prosecution must prove the defendant guilty. The defendant is not required to prove anything or to testify.

The defense then calls witnesses to support its case, and the prosecutor is allowed to cross-examine them. Finally, when all witnesses have testified, the defense rests. The prosecutor then calls rebuttal witnesses in an attempt to discredit testimony of the defense witnesses. The defense then has the right to present even more witnesses, called surrebuttal witnesses. After the various rebuttal witnesses have testified, the judge presents instructions to the jury about the verdicts the jury can return and about points of law that are key to the case. The prosecutor then makes his or her closing argument, usually an impassioned plea for a guilty verdict addressed directly to the jury. The defense attorney's closing argument follows, and the prosecutor is allowed a final rebuttal. In the federal system, closing arguments precede the judge's instructions to the jury. The jury then retires to deliberate.

Because unanimous verdicts are required for acquittal or conviction in a criminal trial, deliberations often are protracted. If the jury fails to reach a unanimous verdict (a hung jury) after a reasonable period of time, the judge may order a mistrial, in which event the entire case will be retried from the beginning of jury selection. If a verdict is reached, the jury returns to the courtroom, where the verdict is read. In some states, juries are permitted to recommend sentences when guilty verdicts are reached. Sometimes a second stage of the trial occurs when the jury must decide, for example, whether to recommend life imprisonment or death. But the final decision is always made by the judge unless a crime carries a mandatory sentence. Sentencing may be done immediately, but more likely a presentencing report will be ordered and a sentencing date set.

The defense often files a motion asking that a guilty verdict be set aside. Such motions are usually denied. A motion for a new trial usually brings similar results. However, in most jurisdictions a motion for a new trial and a denial are prerequisites to the filing of an appeal. Appeals often follow guilty verdicts, so a verdict seldom is final in that sense. Except in extreme circumstances involving serious crimes, judges often permit the defendant to be released on bail pending the outcome of appeals.

With the preceding points in mind, let's trace a criminal case from the time of arrest through the trial to show how a newspaper might report each step. Here is a typical first story:

> An unemployed carpenter was arrested today and charged with the Aug. 6 murder of Springfield resident Anne Compton.
>
> Lester L. Rivers, 32, of 209 E. Dillow Lane was charged with first-degree murder, Prosecuting Attorney Mel Singleton said.
>
> Chief of Detectives E.L. Hall said Rivers was arrested on a warrant after a three-month investigation by a team of three detectives. He declined to comment on what led investigators to Rivers.
>
> Compton's body was found in the Peabody River by two fishermen on the morning of Aug. 7. She had been beaten to death with a blunt instrument, according to Dr. Ronald R. Miller, the county medical examiner.

That straightforward account of the arrest was filed on deadline. Later the reporter would interview neighbors about Rivers' personality and write an improved story for other editions. This bare-bones story, however, provides a glimpse of several key points in covering arrest stories. Notice that the reporter carefully chose the words "arrested and charged with" rather than "arrested for," a phrase that may carry a connotation of guilt.

Another important element of all crime and court coverage is the tie-back sentence. This sentence relates a story to events covered in a previous story—in this case, the report of the crime itself. It is important to state clearly—and near the beginning of the story—which crime is involved and to provide enough information about it so that the reader recognizes it. Clarification of the crime is important even in major stories with ready identification in the community. This story does that by recounting when and where Compton's body was found and by whom. It also tells that she died after being hit with a blunt instrument.

The following morning the suspect was taken to Magistrate Court for his initial court appearance. Here is a part of the story that resulted:

Lester L. Rivers appeared in Magistrate Court today charged with first-degree murder in connection with the Aug. 6 beating death of Springfield resident Anne Compton.

Judge Howard D. Robbins scheduled a preliminary hearing for Nov. 10 and set bail at $10,000. Robbins assigned Public Defender Ogden Ball to represent Rivers, 32, of 209 E. Dillow Lane.

Rivers said nothing during the 10-minute session as the judge informed him of his right to remain silent and his right to an attorney. Ball asked Robbins to set the bail at a "reasonable amount for a man who is unemployed." Rivers is a carpenter who was fired from his last job in June. Despite the seriousness of the charge, it is essential that Rivers be free to help prepare his defense, Ball said.

Police have said nothing about a possible connection between Rivers and Compton, whose body was found in the Peabody River by two fishermen on the morning of Aug. 7. She had been beaten to death.

The reporter clearly outlined the exact charge and reported on key points of the brief hearing. Again, the link to the crime is important to inform the reader about which murder is involved.

Next came the preliminary hearing, where the first evidence linking the defendant to the crime was revealed:

Lester L. Rivers will be tried in Jefferson County Circuit Court for the Aug. 6 murder of Springfield resident Anne Compton.

Magistrate Judge Howard D. Robbins ruled today that there is probable cause to believe that a crime was committed and probable cause that Rivers did it. Rivers was bound over for trial in Circuit Court.

Rivers, 32, of 209 E. Dillow Lane is being held in Jefferson County Jail. He has been unable to post bail of $10,000.

At today's preliminary hearing, Medical Examiner Ronald R. Miller testified that a tire tool recovered from Rivers' car at the time of his arrest "could have been used in the beating death of Miss Compton." Her body was found floating in the Peabody River Aug. 7.

James L. Mullaney, a lab technician for the FBI crime laboratory in Washington, D.C., testified that "traces of blood on the tire tool matched Miss Compton's blood type."

In reporting such testimony, the reporter was careful to use direct quotes and not to overstate the facts. The medical examiner testified that the tire tool *could have been used* in the murder. If he had said it *had been used*, a stronger lead would have been needed.

Defense attorneys usually use preliminary hearings to learn about the evidence against their clients and do not present any witnesses. This apparently was the motive here because neither the police nor the prosecutor had made a public statement on evidence in the case. They probably were being careful not to release prejudicial information that could be grounds for a new trial.

The prosecutor then filed an information, as state law required. The defendant was arraigned in Circuit Court, and the result was a routine story that began as follows:

> Circuit Judge John L. Lee refused today to reduce the bail of Lester L. Rivers, who is charged with first-degree murder in the Aug. 6 death of Springfield resident Anne Compton. Rivers pleaded not guilty. Repeating a request he made earlier in Magistrate Court, Public Defender Ogden Ball urged that Rivers' bail be reduced from $10,000 so he could be freed to assist in preparing his defense.

The not-guilty plea was expected, so the reporter concentrated on a more interesting aspect of the hearing—the renewed request for reduced bail.

Finally, after a series of motions was reported routinely, the trial began:

> Jury selection began today in the first-degree murder trial of Lester L. Rivers, who is charged with the Aug. 6 beating death of Springfield resident Anne Compton.
>
> Public Defender Ogden Ball, Rivers' attorney, and Prosecuting Attorney Mel Singleton both expect jury selection to be complete by 5 p.m.
>
> The selection process started after court convened at 10 a.m. The only incident occurred just before the lunch break as Singleton was questioning prospective juror Jerome B. Tinker, 33, of 408 Woodland Terrace.
>
> "I went to school with that guy," said Tinker, pointing to Rivers, who was seated in the courtroom. "He wouldn't hurt nobody."
>
> Singleton immediately asked that Tinker be removed from the jury panel, and Circuit Judge John L. Lee agreed.
>
> Rivers smiled as Tinker made his statement, but otherwise sat quietly, occasionally conferring with Ball.

The testimony is about to begin, so the reporter set the stage here, describing the courtroom scene. Jury selection is often routine and becomes newsworthy only in important or interesting cases.

Trial coverage can be tedious, but when the case is interesting, the stories are easy to write. The reporter picks the most interesting testimony for leads as the trial progresses:

> A service station owner testified today that Lester L. Rivers offered a ride to Springfield resident Anne Compton less than an hour before she was beaten to death Aug. 6.
>
> Ralph R. Eagle, the station owner, was a witness at the first-degree murder trial of Rivers in Jefferson County Circuit Court.
>
> "I told her I'd call a cab," Eagle testified, "but Rivers offered her a ride to her boyfriend's house." Compton had gone to the service station after her car broke down nearby. Under cross-examination, Public Defender Ogden Ball, Rivers' attorney, questioned whether Rivers was the man who offered the ride.
>
> "If it wasn't him, it was his twin brother," Eagle said.
>
> "Then you're not really sure it was Mr. Rivers, are you?" Ball asked.
>
> "I sure am," Eagle replied.

"You think you're sure, Mr. Eagle, but you really didn't get a good look at him, did you?"

"I sold him some gas and got a good look at him when I took the money."

"But it was night, wasn't it, Mr. Eagle?" Ball asked.

"That place doesn't have the best lighting in the world, but I saw him all right."

The reporter focused on the key testimony of the trial by capturing it in the words of the participants. Good note-taking ability becomes important here, because trial coverage is greatly enhanced with direct quotation of key exchanges. Long exchanges may necessitate the use of the question-and-answer format:

Ball: In fact, a lot of the lights above those gas pumps are out, aren't they, Mr. Eagle?

Eagle: Yes, but I stood right by him.

Q: I have no doubt you thought you saw Mr. Rivers, but there's always the possibility it could have been someone else. Isn't that true?

A: No, it looked just like him.

Q: It appeared to be him, but it may not have been because you really couldn't see him that well, could you?

A: Well, it was kind of dark out there.

Eventually, there is the verdict story, which is usually one of the easiest to write:

Lester L. Rivers was found guilty of first-degree murder today in the Aug. 6 beating death of Springfield resident Anne Compton.

Rivers stood motionless in Jefferson County Circuit Court as the jury foreman returned the verdict. Judge John L. Lee set sentencing for Dec. 10.

Rivers, 32, of 209 E. Dillow Lane could be sentenced to death in the electric chair or life imprisonment in the State Penitentiary.

Public Defender Ogden Ball, Rivers' attorney, said he will appeal.

After the verdict was announced, Mr. and Mrs. Lilborn O. Compton, the victim's parents, were escorted from the courtroom by friends. Both refused to talk with reporters.

Many other types of stories could have been written about such a trial. Lengthy jury deliberations, for example, might prompt stories about the anxiety of the defendant and attorneys and their speculations about the cause of the delay.

Covering court news requires care and good reporting. As in any kind of reporting, you must be well-prepared. If you understand the language of the courts and how they are organized, your job is simplified.

Annual crime statistics are a common source of stories. Reporters must take care when reporting them, however, if they involve small numbers. It is dramatic to say, "Murders increased by 300 percent in 1999," but it is misleading if the increase was from one murder to four.

To provide a more accurate picture, reporters can perform the equivalent of adding apples and oranges. "Unlike" items can be added, subtracted, multiplied and divided, if they are grouped in a category that makes them "like" items. For example, you can group murders, rapes, assaults and armed robberies in the category "violent crimes." That way, you can add murders to rapes to assaults to armed robberies. This technique can be useful if an individual category such as murder isn't large enough to provide much insight (as in many small towns). However, the larger category must be logical and meaningful.

OTHER ISSUES IN CRIME AND COURT REPORTING

Covering crime and the courts is not a simple matter. While the complexity of court proceedings can be baffling to a beginning reporter, there are other pitfalls as well.

The Free-Press/Fair-Trial Controversy

The 1954 murder trial of Dr. Samuel Sheppard in Cleveland was the landmark case involving the perceived conflict between a defendant's right to a fair trial and the public's right to know. Sheppard was accused of murdering his wife. News coverage in the Cleveland newspapers, which included front-page editorials, was intense. In 1966, the U.S. Supreme Court said the trial judge had not fulfilled his duty to protect the jury from the news coverage that saturated the community and to control disruptive influences in the courtroom.

That case more than any other ignited what is known as the **free-press/fair-trial controversy**. This controversy raged during the O.J. Simpson case in the mid-1990s. On numerous occasions, Judge Lance Ito threatened to end television coverage of court proceedings to protect Simpson's rights during his criminal trial. Lawyers charged that the media ignored the Sixth Amendment right of the accused to an impartial jury. The media countered with charges that lawyers ignored the First Amendment.

> **"**To make inroads into the mind-set that 'if the press reported it, it must be true' is the lawyer's most challenging task.**"**
>
> — Robert Shapiro, attorney

Editors realize that coverage of a crime can make it difficult to empanel an impartial jury, but they argue that courts have available many remedies other than restricting the flow of information. In the Sheppard case, for example, the Supreme Court justices said a **change of venue**, which moves the trial to a location where publicity is not as intense, could have been ordered. Other remedies suggested by the Court in such cases are to "continue" (delay) the trial, to grant a new trial or to head off possible outside influences during the trial by sequestering the jury. Editors also argue that acquittals have been won in some of the most publicized cases in recent years.

Gag Orders and Closed Trials

Despite the remedies the Supreme Court offered in the Sheppard case, trial judges continued to be concerned about empaneling impartial juries. Judges issued hundreds of gag orders in the wake of the Sheppard case. Finally, in 1976, in the landmark case of Nebraska Press Association v. Stuart, the Supreme Court ruled that a gag order was an unconstitutional prior restraint that violated the First Amendment to the Constitution. The justices did not go so far as to rule that all gag orders are invalid. But in each case, the trial judge has to prove that an order restraining publication would protect the rights of the accused and that no other alternatives would be less damaging to First Amendment rights.

That ruling, of course, did not end the concerns of trial judges. Rather than issue gag orders restricting the press from reporting court proceedings, some attempted to close their courtrooms. In the first such case to reach the U.S. Supreme Court, Gannett v. DePasquale, the press and public suffered a severe but temporary blow. On July 2, 1979, in a highly controversial decision, the justices said, "We hold that members of the public have no constitutional right under the Sixth and Fourteenth amendments to attend criminal trials." The case itself had involved only a pretrial hearing.

As a result of the decision and the confusion that followed, the Supreme Court of Virginia sanctioned the closing of an entire criminal trial. The accused was acquitted during the second day of the secret trial. The U.S. Supreme Court agreed to hear the appeal of the trial judge's action in a case known as Richmond Newspapers v. Virginia. On July 2, 1980, the court said that under the First Amendment "the trial of a criminal case must be open to the public." Only a court finding of an "overriding interest," which was not defined, would be grounds for closing a criminal trial.

Trials of Sex Offenders

In Massachusetts, a judge excluded the public and press from the entire trial of a man accused of raping three teenagers. A Massachusetts law provided for the mandatory closing of trials involving specific sex offenses against minors. The U.S. Supreme Court held in 1982 in Globe Newspaper Co. v. Superior Court that the mandatory closure law violated the First Amendment right of access to criminal trials established in the Richmond Newspapers case. The justices ruled that when a state attempts to deny the right of access in an effort to inhibit the disclosure of sensitive information, it must show that the denial "is necessitated by a compelling governmental interest." The court indicated in the opinion that in some cases *in-camera proceedings* (proceedings that take place in a judge's chambers outside the view of the press and public) for youthful witnesses may be appropriate.

In Press-Enterprise v. Riverside County Superior Court, the U.S. Supreme Court ruled in 1984 that a court order closing the jury-selection process in a rape-murder case was invalid. The court ruled that jury selection has been a public process with exceptions only for good cause. In a second Press-Enterprise v. Riverside County Superior Court case, the U.S. Supreme Court said in 1986 that preliminary hearings should be open to the public unless there is a "substantial probability" that the resulting publicity would prevent a fair trial and there are no "reasonable alternatives to closure." In 1993, the Supreme Court continued its emphasis on the importance of open court proceedings. It struck down a Puerto Rican law that said preliminary hearings "shall be held privately" unless the defendant requests a public preliminary hearing.

Press-Bar Guidelines

These cases appeared to uphold the right of the press and the public to have access to criminal proceedings. Judges, however, have a duty to protect the rights of the accused. The Supreme Court of the State of Washington, in Federated Publications v. Swedberg, held in 1981 that press access to pretrial hearings may be conditioned on the agreement of reporters to abide by voluntary press-bar guidelines that exist in some states. The decision involved a preliminary hearing in a Bellingham, Wash., murder case tied to the "Hillside Strangler" murders in the Los Angeles area. The state Supreme Court ruled that the lower-court order was "a good-faith attempt to accommodate the interests of both defendant and press." The lower court had required reporters covering the hearing to sign a document in which the reporters agreed to abide by press-bar guidelines. The state Supreme Court said the document should be taken as a moral commitment on the part of the reporters, not as a legally enforceable document.

The U.S. Supreme Court in 1982 refused to hear an appeal of that case. Fortunately, many states have statutes to the effect that "the setting of every court shall be public, and every person may freely attend the same." When such statutes are in place, the closed-courtroom controversy appears to be moot. In states that have no such statute, the result seems to be that:

- A criminal trial must be open unless there is an "overriding interest" that requires some part of it to be closed.
- Judges must find some overriding interest before closing pretrial hearings.

One effect of the Washington decision is that many media groups are withdrawing from state press-bar agreements in the few states that have such guidelines. Their reasoning is that the voluntary guidelines in effect could become mandatory.

Cameras in the Courtroom

In 1994, the U.S. Judicial Conference ended its three-year experiment on cameras in federal courts by banning cameras. In 1996, the Judicial Conference agreed to permit cameras in some lower federal courts. And 47 states do allow cameras in at least some state courtrooms. Only Indiana, Mississippi, South Dakota and the District of Columbia ban courtroom cameras. The fact remains that there are many ways for judges to protect the rights of the accused without trampling on the right of the press and public to attend trials and pretrial hearings. Indeed, most editors are sensitive to the rights of the accused. Most exercise self-restraint when publishing or broadcasting information about a crime. Most have attempted to establish written policy on such matters, although others insist that individual cases must be judged on their merits.

Coverage of Minority Groups

Reporters and editors must share with judges the burden of protecting the rights of the accused. They also must ensure that certain groups within our society are not treated unfairly, either by the courts or in the media. In a study of crime reporting at the Gannett Center for Media Studies, Robert Snyder discovered that minorities tend to be covered by the media mainly in the context of crime news. Crime reporting is a staple of urban news, and urban areas are where minorities are concentrated. In large cities like New York and Los Angeles, some areas of the city often make news only because of crime. As it is reported now, Snyder says, crime is almost always a conversation about race. He concludes that if the media are to change that perception, they must cover minorities more broadly and sympathetically. The real story of crime, Snyder says, should be the "breaking down of communities and the real weakening of the social structure."

Many editors are concerned about the way minorities are portrayed in crime stories. Many newspapers and broadcast stations, in fact, studiously avoid gratuitous mentions of race. Their reporters are allowed to mention the race of a suspect only as part of the complete identification of a fugitive. For many years, it was common to read or hear references to a "six-foot-tall black man" wanted for a crime. Today such a description would be considered unacceptable. There are too many men who fit that description, and the racial reference merely reinforces the stereotype of blacks as criminals. If, however, a complete description of a fugitive might help lead to an arrest, it is appropriate to mention race as a part of that description. Only when race becomes the central theme of a story should it be emphasized.

Similarly, most editors consider a person's sexual orientation off limits unless the story focuses on heterosexuality or homosexuality. Increasingly, though, gays and lesbians are willing to talk openly about their sexual orientation as a means of advancing the cause of gay rights. Such issues cannot and should not be ignored by the media. But tastefully handling crime news involving homosexual murders often proves to be difficult. This was never more true than in the sensational murder trial of Milwaukee's Jeffrey Dahmer, convicted of sexually molesting young boys and men, killing them and eating parts of their bodies. In such cases, the press walks a fine line between responsibly informing the public and pandering to its seemingly insatiable appetite for sensational crime news.

Coverage of Terrorism

Since the 2001 attacks on New York's World Trade Center and the Pentagon in Washington, much has been written about the rights of those arrested as alleged terrorists. Suspects have been held for years without charge at the U.S. naval base at Guantanamo Bay, Cuba, and interrogated by U.S. officials in foreign countries. Rights activists and the suspects' attorneys challenged such actions as unconstitutional, and the courts have agreed. This ongoing battle is likely to be a matter of contention for the foreseeable future.

Megan's Law

Since October 1997, federal law has required each state to have a version of Megan's Law in place. Megan's Law is named for Megan Kanka, a 7-year-old girl raped and strangled in New Jersey in July 1994 by a man who had two prior convictions for sexually assaulting young girls and who moved to a house across the street from Megan. In June 1997, her killer, Jesse Timmendequas, received a death sentence.

The federal Megan's Law requires a person convicted of a violent sexual crime to register a current address with local law-enforcement agencies and to register a change of address within 10 days of moving into a new neighborhood. Failure to register is a crime. The federal law also requires states to perform yearly "verification." But federal law merely requires that a "designated state law-enforcement agency shall mail a nonforwardable verification form to the last reported address of the person" and that person shall sign and return the form within 10 days. While the signed form will say that the person resides there, the federal law requires no independent verification.

In addition, the federal law requires that the designated law-enforcement agencies "release relevant information that is necessary to protect the public concerning a specific person required to register." However, the details of this release of information are left up to the states. Some states release information on all registered sex offenders. Other states allow law-enforcement agencies to release information only when they consider a particular person to pose a risk.

A problem for media organizations trying to decide whether to use information made available under the applicable Megan's Law of their states is the accuracy of the information. Of course, convictions are a matter of public record and verifiable through court records. But addresses are not so easily verified. Even if a state declares that the addresses are a matter of public record, the problem remains that the information may be incorrect. Publication or broadcast of incorrect information may receive protection from libel damages under a qualified privilege to make a fair and accurate report based on public records. Appropriate attribution to the public record, of course, would be necessary. But still, the use of an unverified address might potentially pose a legal problem. For instance, if use of the address posed a reasonable foreseeable risk of physical harm, and that harm occurred, the publisher or broadcaster might be sued for negligence. A reasonable person might foresee a risk of physical harm to Jimmy Jones living at 803 Mill Creek, an address erroneously given as the home of sex offender John Doe.

Even if the legal risks are nonexistent, ethics should dictate careful reporting of addresses of sex offenders. These addresses may be self-reported, may not be independently verified and may change. Such knowledge should give responsible publishers pause about reporting particular addresses, let alone lists of registered offenders' addresses, without first using standard reporting techniques to verify accuracy.

Negligence and Crime Reporting

The key to liability in negligence cases is "foreseeability." If an individual engages in conduct that could foreseeably create harm, and that harm then occurs, the individual may be liable for negligence. Foreseeability refers to what a "reasonably prudent person" would "reasonably" foresee under similar circumstances.

The first major negligence suit against the media for the bodily harm or risk of bodily harm by a third party started in Columbia, Mo. According to Sandra Hyde, as she walked down the main street of Columbia after midnight in August 1980, a man with a red beard and red hair, driving a red Mustang, pulled alongside her. He opened his door, leveled a sawed-off shotgun at her, and ordered her to get in. She did. He then demanded, "You will do what I want you to do or I will blow your brains out." As he drove around a corner, Hyde jumped out of the car and ran to safety in a nearby disco.

Hyde reported the incident to the police. Of course, she gave her name and address—a couple of facts that her assailant didn't have until a *Columbia Daily Tribune* reporter got a copy of the report from the police and the newspaper published her name and address the next day. Then, according to Hyde, the man started terrorizing her, stalking her at her home and workplace and making phone calls to give her messages such as, "I'm glad you're not dead yet; I have plans for you before you die" and "I wanted to refresh your memory of who I am before I kill you tonight."

Hyde sued, alleging negligence by the city in disclosing her name and address. The defendants countered that the information disclosed was a public record under Missouri's Sunshine Law. The trial court ruled in favor of the defendants, accepting the public-record defense. However, on appeal, the Court of Appeals for the Western District of Missouri ruled that Sandra Hyde did indeed have valid grounds to sue for negligence. The Court of Appeals concluded, "[I]t was reasonably foreseeable that the publication of the name and address of the victim, while the assailant was still at large, was a temptation to [the assailant] to inflict an intentional harm upon the victim—a foreseeable risk the . . . defendants had a duty to prevent."

In flatly rejecting the "Sunshine Law" defense, the court used the following argument:

> To construe the Sunshine Law to open all criminal investigation information to anyone with a request . . . courts constitutional violations of the right of privacy of a witness or other citizen unwittingly drawn into the criminal investigation process. . . . Such a construction leads to the absurdity . . . that an assailant unknown as such to the authorities, from whom the victim has escaped, need simply walk into the police station, demand name and address or other personal information—without possibility of lawful refusal, so as to intimidate the victim as a witness or commit other injury.

To avoid what the court called an "absurd" conclusion, it held that "the name and address of a victim of crime who can identify an assailant not yet in custody is not a public record under the Sunshine Law."

In 1983, the U.S. Supreme Court let the Hyde case stand. In doing so, the court sent the message that newspapers could be found liable for printing a news story that exposed a specific victim to an unreasonable, foreseeable risk of harm—even though the defendant arguably was using public records.

A California appeals court cited Hyde when it let a woman sue the *Los Angeles Times* after the paper reported her name in connection with her discovery of the dead, nude body of her roommate who had been beaten, raped and strangled. The reporter, a summer intern, had gotten the name through the coroner's office. Again, the court did not accept the public-record defense.

Issues of Taste and Ethics

Some of the major issues involving taste and ethics in crime and court reporting are these:

- When should the media reveal details of how a murder or another crime was committed?
- When should the media reveal details about sex crimes or print the names of sex-crime victims?
- When should the media reveal a suspect's confession or even the fact that the suspect confessed?
- When should the media reveal a defendant's prior criminal record?
- When should the media reveal the names of juveniles charged with crimes?

None of these questions can be answered to everyone's satisfaction, and it is doubtful whether rules can be established to apply in all such situations. There have been charges that when the media reveal details of a murder, some people use the techniques described to commit additional murders. This charge is directed most frequently at television, but newspapers have not been immune.

Covering Sex Crimes

The reporting of sex crimes often causes controversy. Most editors think of their publications as family newspapers or broadcasts and are properly hesitant about reporting the lurid details of sex crimes. What began as an interesting murder case in one college town turned into grist for the scandal mill. A college professor murdered one of his students who had asked for after-hours tutoring. When police unraveled the morbid tale of the professor, a homosexual necrophiliac, knowing what to write for the family newspaper became a major problem for the reporter. The newspaper provided information to the public on what had happened but deliberately avoided sensationalism. Even during the trial, specifics were avoided in favor of testimony that revealed the nature of the case in general terms:

> "He lived in a world of fantasies," the doctor said. "He
> spent much of his time daydreaming about homosex-
> ual, necrophilic, homicidal, suicidal and cannibalistic
> fantasies."

To have been more specific would have been revolting to many of the newspaper's readers.

A related problem is the question of how to handle rape reports. Too often, rapes are not reported to police because victims are unwilling to appear in court to testify against the suspects. Defense attorneys sometimes use such occasions to attack the victim's morals and imply that she (or he) consented to sexual relations. Many victims decline to press charges because of fear that their names will be made public in newspapers and on radio and television. Both of these things happened to the woman who accused basketball star Kobe Bryant of rape. There is, after all, still a lingering tendency to attach a social stigma to the rape victim, despite increasing public awareness of the nature of the crime.

In some states, "rape shield" statutes prohibit a defendant's attorney from delving into the rape victim's prior sexual activity unless some connection can be shown with the circumstances of the rape charged.

Reporting Confessions and Prior Convictions

Many editors will not publish or broadcast details of a suspect's confession in an effort to protect the suspect's rights. Revealing such information blocks the way for a fair trial perhaps more easily than anything else the media can do. Some newspapers and broadcast stations, however, continue to reveal assertions by police or prosecutors that a confession was signed. Many question whether such information isn't just as prejudicial as the confession statement itself.

Occasionally, the question arises of whether to suppress an unsolicited confession. After a youth was charged with a series of robberies and was certified to stand trial as an adult, a newspaper reporter phoned the youthful defendant, who was free on bail, for an interview. The result was interesting. The defendant admitted to two other robberies in what amounted to a confession to the newspaper and its readers. The editor, who would not have printed a simple statement by police that the defendant had confessed to the crime, printed this one. Why? The editor reasoned that information about a confession to police amounts to secondhand, hearsay information. The confession to a reporter, however, was firsthand information obtained by the newspaper directly from the accused.

Lawyers also view as prejudicial the publication of a defendant's prior criminal record. Even if authorities refuse to divulge that information, much of it may be in the morgue. Should it be published? Most editors believe it should be, particularly if a prior conviction was for a similar offense. Most attorneys disagree.

Identifying Juveniles

Whether to use the names of juveniles charged with crimes is a troublesome issue as well. Most states prohibit law-enforcement officers and court officials from releasing the names of juveniles. The reasoning of those who oppose releasing juveniles' names is that the publicity marks them for life as criminals. Those who hold this view argue that there is ample opportunity for these individuals to change their ways and become good citizens—if the media do not stamp them as criminals. Others argue that juveniles who commit serious offenses, such as rape and armed robbery, should be treated as adults.

Questions such as these elicit divergent views from editors, some of whom regularly seek the advice of their lawyers. Little guidance for the reporter can be offered here. Because the decision to publish or not to publish is the editor's, not the reporter's, consultation is necessary. Each case must be decided on its merits.

Suggested Readings

Buchanan, Edna. *The Corpse Had a Familiar Face.* New York: Random House, 1987. The first of two books by one of America's best crime reporters.

Buchanan, Edna. *Never Let Them See You Cry.* New York: Random House, 1992. An excellent description of covering crime in Miami.

Center on Crime, Communities and Culture and *Columbia Journalism Review. Covering Criminal Justice.* New York: Graduate School of Journalism, Columbia University, 2000. A manual listing resources to help reporters covering crime and the courts.

Giles, Robert H. and Snyder, Robert W., eds. *Covering the Courts: Free Press, Fair Trials and Journalistic Performance.* Piscataway, N.J.: Transaction Publishers, 1998.

Pulitzer, Lisa Beth. *Crime on Deadline: Police Reporters Tell Their Most Unforgettable Stories.* New York: Boulevard Books, 1996. Real stories from nine of the nation's top crime reporters.

Siegel, Marvin, ed. *The Last Word: The New York Times Book of Obituaries and Farewells: A Celebration of Unusual Lives.* New York: Quill, 1998. Examples of well-written and compelling obituaries from *The New York Times.*

Singer, Eleanor and Endreny, Phyllis M. *Reporting on Risk: How the Mass Media Portray Accidents, Diseases, Disasters and Other Hazards.* New York: Russell Sage Foundation, 1993. A critical look at media reporting of accidents and disasters.

Suggested Web Sites

www.fbi.gov
The FBI Web site provides useful information about crime.

www.fema.gov
The Federal Emergency Management Agency, part of the U.S. Department of Homeland Security, provides assistance during major emergencies.

www.ntsb.gov
The National Transportation Safety Board is an excellent source of accident information.

www.supremecourtus.gov
The Supreme Court of the United States is the nation's highest court. The Court's Web site outlines its operation.

Exercises

1. Find an accident story in a local newspaper. List all the sources the reporter used in obtaining information for the story. List additional sources you would have checked.

2. Talk with a firefighter in your local fire department about the department's media policy at fire scenes. Using what you learn, write instructions for your fellow reporters on what to expect at fires in your city or town.

3. Make a list of at least 10 federal agencies that may be of help in reporting accident, fire and disaster stories. Also list the telephone numbers of the agency offices nearest to you.

4. Cover a session of your local circuit court. Write a story based on the most interesting case of the day.

5. Research the coverage of constitutional rights as they pertain to terrorism suspects. Evaluate whether the media have done an adequate job of covering this issue. If you find fault with the coverage, describe what you would have done to improve it.

Covering a Beat

14

IN THIS CHAPTER
YOU WILL LEARN:

1. Basic principles for covering any beat.

2. How to apply those principles to some of the most common beats.

Sophia Maines joined the *Lawrence (Kan.) Journal-World* after working two years in a more conventional news room. This was her second job out of journalism school. Like every new hire in Lawrence, she was told immediately that her responsibilities would stretch beyond putting words on paper. Now, covering higher education in a university town, she understands what that really means.

The basics haven't changed. She cultivates sources, develops story ideas and then writes the stories. Often, they wind up on page one. But just as often, they also show up on the 6 p.m. newscast on the *Journal-World*'s cable television outlet. And invariably they're posted on ljworld.com, frequently along with supporting materials and video that the newspaper alone couldn't accommodate.

"Working in a converged news room requires a spirit of collaboration and a willingness to adapt to new technologies," she says. "This may seem simple, but it does require a change of mind-set for reporters accustomed to working in a traditional news room."

For example, the paper bought MP3 recorders for reporters to use.

"For some stories, we might take a 'man-on-the-street' approach and ask various people what their thoughts or experiences are on a particular issue. And then we simply load the audio onto our Web site.

"I wrote a story about how women traditionally outperform men in higher education. For that story, I went to a campus and gathered audio recordings of men and women voicing their opinions on the college gender divide. So an online reader can click on 'A man's view' to hear a male's take or on 'A woman's view' to get a gal's take."

She's excited about the new tools for storytelling. "I could go on and on about the different ways our reporters use audio, video and photography to tell stories. The possibilities really are limitless."

More than the technology has changed. You saw in Chapter 1 how the definition of news itself is broadening. That change extends the range of beats. Along with such standard beats as local government, police, business and sports, cultural beats reflect the interests and activities of a changing America. Some beat reporters cover shopping malls. Some cover commuting. Some cover spiritual life. Some cover cyberspace.

Increasingly, beat reporters tell their audiences not only what is happening but also how to get involved. Stories include telephone numbers and e-mail addresses along with the names of decision-makers. Much of the most useful reporting is done in advance of public meetings, with the goal of enabling citizens to become participants instead of passive onlookers. Readers are regularly invited to use e-mail or online bulletin boards to speak up on public issues. With all these changes, though, beat reporters remain the eyes and ears of their communities. Surrogates for their readers, they keep track of government, education, police, business and other powerful institutions that shape readers' lives.

The principles of good reporting apply to the coverage of any beat. The same principles also apply to specialized publications, including those aimed at particular ethnic groups, industries or professions. A reporter for *Women's Wear Daily* may cover designers. A reporter for *Diario las Americas* in Miami may cover Cuban exile politics. But each is doing the same job: discovering and writing news that's relevant and useful to the publication's readers.

Many news organizations are responding to audience interests by creating teams of reporters to cover interrelated topics instead of institutions. One team may write about issues of home and family life. Another may cover the arts and popular culture. Another team may focus on the problems and opportunities of urban living.

Editors and audiences expect reporters on these new beats, like those in more traditional assignments, to provide information and understanding that will help readers improve the quality of their lives. That's important work. It's rewarding work. But it's not easy.

PRINCIPLES FOR REPORTERS ON A BEAT

Whether you cover the public library or the Pentagon, the county courthouse or the White House, the principles of covering a beat are the same. If you want to succeed as a reporter, you must be prepared, alert, persistent and wary. And, on any beat, you must be there.

That checklist will help you win the trust of your sources, keep up with important developments on your beat and avoid the trap of writing for your sources instead of your readers. Let's take a closer look at what each of those rules means in practice.

Be Prepared

Where should preparation begin? For you, it has already begun. To work effectively, any journalist needs a basic understanding of the workings of society and its various governments. You need to know at least the rudiments of psychology, economics and history. That is why the best education for a journalist is a broad-based one, providing exposure to the widest possible sampling of human knowledge. But that exposure will not be enough when you face an important source on your first beat. You will need more specific information, which you can acquire by familiarizing yourself with written accounts or records or by talking to sources.

Reading for Background

In preparing to cover a beat, any beat, your first stop should be the newspaper library (see Chapter 5). The newspaper library is likely to have computer access not only to material that has appeared in that newspaper but also to worldwide networks of information on nearly any topic. You can often access the contents of major newspapers, magazines, research publications and other reference libraries without regard to physical distance. Use the Internet to acquire background and to understand the context of local events and issues. For example, if your new beat is

TIPS

The Successful Beat Reporter Is

- Prepared
- Alert
- Persistent
- There
- Wary

medicine, you might begin with the Web site of the Association of Health Care Journalists.

In your local research, make notes of what appear to be continuing issues, questions left dangling in previous stories or ideas for stories to come. Go back several years in your preparation. History may not repeat itself, but knowledge of it helps you assess the significance of current events and provides clues to what you can expect.

Library research is only the start of your preparation. You must become familiar with the laws governing the institution you cover. If a governmental organization is your beat, find the state statutes or the city charter that created the agencies you will be covering. Learn the powers, duties and limitations of each official. You may be surprised to discover that someone is failing to do all that the law requires. Someone else may be doing more than the law allows.

Look at your state's open-meeting and open-record laws, too. Every state has such laws, although they vary widely in scope and effectiveness. Knowing what information is open to the public by law can be a valuable tool for a reporter dealing with officials who may prefer to govern privately.

Talking to Sources

Now you're ready to start talking to people. You should conduct your first interviews in the news room with your predecessor on the beat, your city editor and any veterans who can shed light on the kinds of things that rarely appear in statute books or newspaper stories. Who have been good sources in the past? Who will lie to you? Who drinks to excess? Who seems to be living extravagantly? Whose friends are big land developers? Who wants to run for national office? Who has been hired, fired or promoted? Who has moved to a competing company? Remember that you are hearing gossip, filtered through the biases of those relating it. Be a little skeptical.

Some understanding of the workings of your own news room won't hurt, either. Has your predecessor on the beat been promoted? Has he or she been transferred because of unsatisfactory performance? Will an introduction from your predecessor help you or hurt you with your sources? And what are your city editor's expectations? Is your assignment to report almost every activity of government, or will you have time to do some investigative work and analysis? Trying to live up to your boss's expectations is easier if you know in advance what they are.

Only after gaining as much background as possible are you ready to face the people you will be covering. A quick handshake and a superficial question or two may be all you have time for in the first encounter, but within a week you should arrange for sit-down conversations with your most important sources. These are get-acquainted sessions. You are trying to get to know the sources, but don't forget that they need to know you, too, if they are going to respect and trust you.

You may have noticed that the preparation for covering a beat is similar to the preparation for an interview or for a single-story assignment. The important difference is that preparing for a beat is more detailed and requires more time and

TIPS

Preparing to Cover a Beat

● Use the Internet to acquire background information and understand context.

● Make note of continuing issues or ideas for stories to come.

● Become familiar with the laws governing the institution you cover.

● Look at your state's open-meeting and open-record laws.

TIPS

Talking to Sources

● Talk to your predecessor on the beat, your city editor and veterans in the news room for background.

● Understand your editor's expectations.

● Establish a relationship with sources — demonstrate interest in them.

work. Instead of just preparing for a short-term task, you are laying the foundation for an important part of your career. A beat assignment nearly always lasts at least six months and often two years or more. Understanding that will help shape your first round of meetings with sources.

A story may emerge from those first interviews, but their purpose is much broader. You are trying to establish a relationship, trying to convert strangers into helpful partners in news gathering. To do that, you should demonstrate an interest in the sources as people as well as officials. Ask about their families, their interests, their philosophy, their goals. Make it clear with your questions that you are interested rather than ignorant. (Don't ask if the source is married. You should already know. Say, "I understand your daughter is in law school. Is she going into politics, too?" Similarly, don't ask if your source has any hobbies. Find out beforehand. Say, "So you collect pornographic comic books. Sure takes your mind off the budget, doesn't it?")

And be prepared to give something of yourself. If you both like to fish, or you both went to Vassar, or you both have children about the same age, seize on those ties. All of us feel comfortable with people who have something in common with us. This is the time, too, to let your sources know that you know something about their work and that you're interested in it.

Was your source elected as a reformer? Ask about the opposition she is encountering. Has your source complained that he lacks the statutory power to do a satisfactory job? Ask if he's lobbying to change the law. Has the industry become more competitive? Ask about strategies for meeting the challenge. Is it budget time? Let your source know you're aware of the problems with last year's budget. Nothing does so much to create a warm reporter-source relationship as the reporter's demonstrated knowledge of and interest in the beat.

Be Alert

Lisa Arthur learned her way around schools in three years on the education beat for *The Miami Herald*. When she was assigned to cover the shooting of a teacher, she was ready for any possibility. The shooting had attracted national attention, so a throng of journalists gathered outside the building. School officials announced that only a small group of reporters, called a *pool*, would be allowed inside. Faced with head-to-head competition from a Fort Lauderdale *Sun-Sentinel* reporter, Lisa thought fast.

Let her tell the story:

"So I said, I covered schools in Broward for three years, and there are dozens of schools I have still never seen the inside of. Have you ever actually been to this school?

"She says no. (The mind reels. If there ever was a time to flat-out lie, this was it.)

"I said, Look, no offense, but if you knew them that well, they would have just picked you as the pool reporter and not sent you over here to fight it out with us folks they've never seen before. . . . My suggestion is we flip a coin.

"She said okay. . . .

"I flip. She calls heads. It lands in my palm ever-loving tails side up. . . .

"We ended up being in there for about 30–40 minutes only. The leash was more like a choke chain. But it was understandable. I got lucky because the guy in there coordinating the mental health team was a psychologist from the Miami-Dade school district. So he was extremely helpful and went as far as he could.

"Afterwards I had to give a debriefing to every outlet that wanted it. I literally gave everyone everything in my notebook . . . and all the quotes I used. But nobody could write the inside-the-school story the way we could without giving it a 'from pool report' byline. . . .

"I could have explained not getting in there to my bosses. No one expected me to. Just getting to the coin toss was a major victory for us. I don't know how she explained it."

Sometimes, being alert means thinking fast and seizing opportunity. Sometimes, it means recognizing an important story when others don't. Important stories are seldom labeled as such. In many cases, the people involved may not realize the significance of what they are doing. Probably more often they realize it but hope nobody else will. The motivation for secrecy may be dishonesty, the desire to protect an image or a conviction that the public will misunderstand.

If your beat is a government agency, you will find that many public officials and public employees think they know more about what is good for the public than the public does. The theory of democratic government is that an informed citizenry can make decisions or elect representatives to make those decisions in its own best interests. If you are the reporter assigned to city hall, the school board or the courthouse, you carry a heavy responsibility for helping your readers put that theory into practice. To discharge that responsibility, you must probe beneath the surface of events in search of the "whys" and "hows" that lead to understanding.

When you are presented with a news release or hear an announcement or cover a vote, ask yourself these questions before passing the event off in a few paragraphs:

- **Who will benefit from this, and who will be hurt?** If the tentative answer to the first part suggests private interests, or the answer to the second part is the public, some digging is in order.

- **How important is this?** An event that is likely to affect many people for good or ill usually deserves more explanation than one affecting only a handful.

- **Who is for this, and who is against it?** Answers to these questions are often obvious or at least easy to figure out. When you know them, the answers to the first two questions usually become clearer.

- **How much will this activity cost, and who will pay?** An architect's design for renovating downtown may look less attractive when the price tag is attached. The chamber of commerce's drive to lure new industry may require taxpayers to pay for new roads, sewers, fire protection, even schools and other services for an increased population.

The answers to these questions allow you to judge that most important element of news value—impact.

Be Persistent

Persistence means two things to a reporter on a beat. First, it means that when you ask a question, you do not give up until you get an answer. Second, it means that you must keep track of slow-developing projects or problems.

Insisting on a Responsive Answer

One of the most common faults of beginning reporters is that they give up too easily. They settle for answers that are unresponsive to their questions, or they return to the news room not sure they understand what they were told. In either case, the result is an incomplete, confusing story.

"Why is it that our fourth-graders score below average on these reading tests?" you ask the school superintendent.

He may reply, "Let me first conceptualize the parameters of the socioeconomic context for you."

The real answer probably is "I only wish I knew."

Your job is to cut through the jargon and the evasions in search of substance. Often that is not an easy task. Many experts, or people who want to be regarded as experts, are so caught up in the technical language of their special field that they find it almost impossible to communicate clearly. Many others seek refuge in gobbledygook or resort to evasion when they don't know an answer or find the answer embarrassing. Educators and lawyers are particularly adept at such tactics.

Listen politely for a few minutes while the school superintendent conceptualizes his parameters. Then, when he finishes or pauses for breath, lead him back toward where you want to go. One way is to say, "It sounds to me as if you're saying . . ." and rephrase what he has told you in plain English. At those times when you simply are in the dark—and that may be often—just confess your puzzlement and ask for a translation. And keep coming back to the point: "But how does all that affect reading scores?" "How can the problem be solved?" "What are you doing about it?"

All the while, you must ask yourself, "Does that make sense to me?" "Can I make it make sense to my readers?" Don't quit until the answer is yes. You should not be obnoxious, but you do have to be persistent.

Following Up on Slow Developments

Persistence is also required when you are following the course of slow-developing events. Gardeners do not sit and watch a seed germinate. They do, however, check every few days, looking for the green shoots that indicate that growth is taking place as it should. If the shoots are late, they dig in to investigate.

Beat reporting works much the same way. A downtown redevelopment plan, say, or a revision in a school's curriculum is announced. The story covers the plans and the hoped-for benefits. The seed is planted. If it is planted on your beat, make a note to yourself to check on it in a week or two. And a week or two after that. And

TIPS

Insisting on a Responsive Answer

- Cut through the jargon and evasions in search of substance.

- Rephrase technical language in plain English.

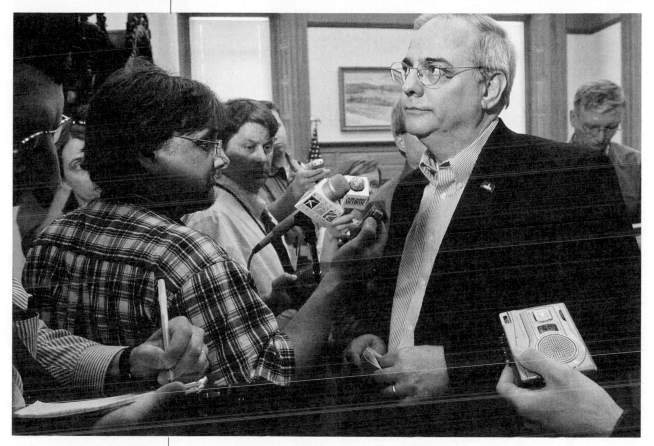

Skilled reporters are persistent interviewers and insist on responsive answers. Make sure your questions are answered satisfactorily.

a month after that. Start a file of reminders so you won't forget. Such a file often is called a **tickler** because it serves to tickle your memory.

Like seeds, important projects of government or business take time to develop. Often what happens during the long, out-of-public-view development is more important than the announcements at the occasional news conferences or the promises of the promotional brochures. Compromises are made. Original plans turn out to be impractical or politically unpalatable. Consultants are hired. Contracts are signed. Public money is spent. The public interest may be served, or it may not.

Sometimes the story is that nothing is happening. At other times the story may be that the wrong things are happening. Consulting contracts may go to cronies of the mayor. Redevelopment may enhance the property values of big downtown landowners. Curriculum revisions may be shaped by some influential pressure groups.

Even if nothing improper is taking place, the persistent reporter will give the readers an occasional update. At stake, after all, are the public's money and welfare.

ON THE JOB

Life of a Happy Beat Reporter

Mary Jo Feldstein was taking a chance when she took a job at a newspaper she'd never heard of in a Pennsylvania city she'd never visited. Less than two years later, she was as happy as a young reporter is ever going to be. Here's her report on life on the beat at the (Scranton) *Times-Tribune*:

"At 10 a.m. you're patiently, compassionately interviewing a patient who overcame the limitations of medical science to prove the spirit of humanity. The next hour, you're analyzing hundreds of pages of Medicare cost reports with a bunch of hospital-finance geeks. In the afternoon, you're schmoozing with politicians, chasing down a tip that the governor met with policy wonks to lay out his medical malpractice reform package.

"At the end of each day, you'll likely have an A1 candidate to write. You always have a story because it's your responsibility to explain the most rapidly changing industry and the most pressing social problem in our nation.

"You marvel at other reporters' ability to focus, work on a project and go for days, maybe weeks, without a fast-breaking story. News happens constantly on your beat, and there's always some issue begging for the clarification and context a more in-depth piece provides.

"You're a health-care reporter."

She admits she's biased, but she argues that no beat is more challenging or complex. Her assignment "requires an understanding of numbers and politics and people," she says. Gaining that understanding took plenty of background reading. As a place to start, Mary Jo recommends the Web site of the Association of Health Care Journalists.

She broke dozens of important stories in Scranton, including one that led an insurer to change its policy on terrorism coverage and a series that inspired merger talks among the community's financially struggling hospitals.

She's proud of that series and warmed by her continuing connection with one of the ordinary people she included in her stories. Joe Piechota's wife, Joyce, died after her cancer treatment was delayed.

Mary Jo says, "Joe and I met about 10 times before the story ran, sometimes for interviews . . . other times because he was lonely and just needed to talk. Joe once told me that having his wife's story told might encourage change, and that helped him heal.

"Joe still calls. He says it's just to see how I'm doing. I say it's to remind me why I'm doing this."

Her good work in Scranton caught the eye of editors at the *St. Louis Post-Dispatch*, where she is now on the business desk but still covering health-related stories.

Be There

In beat reporting, there is no substitute for personal contact. Trying to do it all by telephone or e-mail won't work. The only way to cover a beat is to be there—every day, if possible. Joking with the secretaries, talking politics with council members and lawyers, worrying over the budget or trading gossip with the professional staff—you must make yourself a part of the community you are covering.

Remember that the sources who are most important to you probably are in great demand by others, too. They have jobs to do. Maneuver to get as much of their time as you need, but don't demand too much. Do your homework first. Don't expect a school superintendent to explain basic concepts of education. You can learn that information from an aide or from reading. What you need to learn from the superintendent is how he or she intends to apply those concepts, or why they seem to be inapplicable here. Find out what a "Class I felony" is before asking the police chief why they are increasing. You will get the time you need more readily if busy sources know their time will not be wasted.

There are other simple techniques you can use to build and maintain good relationships with the people on your beat. Here are some of them:

- **Do a favor when you can.** As a reporter, you spend much of your time asking other people to do favors for you—giving you their time, sharing information they need not share, looking up records and figures. If a source needs a favor in return, don't refuse unless it would be unethical. The favors asked are usually small things, like getting a daughter's engagement picture or a club announcement in the paper, procuring a print of a picture taken with the governor to decorate the official's wall, bringing in a few copies of a favorable feature you wrote.

- **Don't shun good news.** One ill-founded but common complaint is that news media report nothing but bad news. Admittedly, there is usually no story when people are doing what they are supposed to do. Sometimes there should be, if they do their duty uncommonly well or have done it for a very long time or do it under the burden of some handicap. Sources like these "good news" stories, and so do readers.

- **Protect your sources.** Many people in government—politicians and bureaucrats alike—are willing to tell a reporter things they are not willing to have their names attached to in print or otherwise. The same is true of people in private business, who may fear reprisals from their employer, co-workers or competitors. Sometimes such would-be anonymous sources are trying to use you to enhance their own positions. You have to protect yourself and your readers against that possibility. Confer with an editor if you have doubts. Most news organizations are properly wary of relying on unnamed sources. Sometimes, though, the requests for anonymity are valid, necessary to protect the source's career. Once you have agreed to protect a source, you must do it. Don't tell anyone but your editor. An inability to keep your mouth shut can cost you more than a source. It can cost you your reputation. (The protection of sources has legal as well as ethical implications. So-called shield laws in some states offer limited exemptions for journalists from legal requirements to disclose sources; see Chapter 21. But there are no blanket exemptions.)

● **Above all, be accurate.** Inaccurate reporting leads first to loss of respect from sources, then to loss of the sources themselves and finally to loss of the job. If you are a good, tough reporter, not all your contacts on your beat will love you. But if you are an accurate reporter, they will respect you.

The best way to ensure accuracy is to check and double-check. Many of the stories you will write are likely to be complicated. You will be expected to digest budgets, master plans, legal opinions and complicated discussions, and to translate these into language your readers can understand. When in doubt, ask somebody. If you are unclear about the city manager's explanation of the budget before the council, arrange a meeting afterward and go over it. If a company's brief in a legal case has you confused, call the lawyer who wrote it. If the new master land-use plan strikes you as vague, consult with the planner. If you are writing a story on a subject you feel tentative about, arrange to read it back to the sources when it is complete. Not all experts relish being asked to translate their jargon into English, so in some cases you will have to insist, politely. The best persuader is the assurance that it is far better for your sources to take a few minutes to explain now than to see themselves misrepresented in print.

Remember, beat reporting is a lot like gardening. Both require you to be in the field every day, cultivating. And in both, the amount of the harvest is directly proportional to the amount of labor invested.

Be Wary

The point of all this effort—the preparation, alertness, persistence and personal contact—is to keep your readers informed. That is an obvious statement, but it needs to be made because every reporter on a beat is under pressures that can obscure the readers' importance. You must be wary of this problem.

You will have little to do with 99.9 percent of your readers. They will not write you notes when you have done a story they like or call you when they dislike what you have written. They will not offer to buy you a cup of coffee or lunch, or stop you in the hall to urge you to see things their way. But your sources will.

If you write that city council members are thinking about raising the property-tax rate, you will probably hear complaints from council members about premature disclosure. If you write that the police department is wracked by dissension, expect a less-than-friendly reaction from the chief. If you write that the CEO of a major business is looking for a new job, the chances are that he or she will deny it even though the story is true.

All sources have points of view, programs to sell, careers to advance, opponents to undercut. It is likely and legitimate that they will try to persuade you of

A TV crew covers a press conference featuring a man who rode his horse from Montana to Crawford, Texas, to protest President George W. Bush's policies.

the merit of their viewpoint, try to sell their programs through the columns of your newspaper, try to shape the news to help their careers.

Be wary of sources' efforts to use you. You can lose the critical distance a reporter must maintain from those being covered. When that happens, you start thinking like a participant rather than an observer. You begin writing for your sources rather than your audience. This is a real danger. No one can spend as much time as a reporter on a beat does with sources or devote as much effort to understanding them without becoming sympathetic. You may forget that you are writing for the outsiders when you associate so closely with the insiders.

ONLINE COVERAGE

Before we apply those principles to specific beats, let's look briefly at the opportunities and challenges online journalism presents to beat reporters. At the beginning of this chapter, you got a glimpse of those opportunities and challenges at the *Lawrence Journal-World*. First is the opportunity for instant reporting. With cell phones, digital cameras and laptop computers, reporters can and do file short stories and even photographs for posting on the Web site as the story unfolds. For newspaper reporters, this is a high-tech return to the distant days of multiple editions, when instead of one deadline a day journalists had many. For radio and television reporters, the online opportunities match those of live reporting over the air. Research shows that increasing numbers of online readers rely on Web sites to stay in touch with news as it happens.

Online, you're expected to gather and present to readers more information, more detail and more points of view than either print or broadcast permits. Readers who care enough to follow an issue online want and expect to see the source documents you use—and that the policy-makers use. They want and expect links to other Web sites that offer related information or further background.

Here's how those needs are met in Lawrence. Sophia Maines and other reporters supplement their standard stories with regular, informal blogs on the paper's Web site. Another Web site, lawrence.com, is intended mainly for younger readers. It features music and coverage of the student culture. It also includes citizen journalism in the form of blogs written by community members on topics ranging from music to politics. Still another Web site is devoted to sports at Kansas University.

One reporter, Joel Mathis, has been named managing editor for convergence. The Web sites have their own staff but are located in the same building as the news rooms for print and television.

All these outlets offer opportunities for what really sets online media apart—interactivity. This term has two practical meanings. First, online journalism permits readers to interact with the information you post. Readers can search your Web site's restaurant reviews, lists of dangerous traffic intersections or any other information that can be tailored to individual needs.

The second type of online interactivity is between journalists and readers. During the Iraq War, for example, www.washingtonpost.com regularly arranged online conversations between reporters in Baghdad and readers anywhere in the world. Such conversations gave readers a chance to ask follow-up questions and reporters a chance to clarify or personalize the news. Some traditional reporters find this prospect terrifying. They're more comfortable in a world of one-way communication, reporter to reader. That world is fast disappearing.

COVERING THE MOST IMPORTANT LOCAL BEATS

Your political science courses will introduce you to the structure of government, but from a reporter's viewpoint, function is usually even more important than structure. You must learn who holds the real power, who has the most influence on the power holders and who are the most likely sources of accurate information. The specifics vary from city to city, but there are some general principles that will help you in covering any form of state or local institution.

- **Information is power.** The holder of information may be a professional administrator (the city manager, school superintendent, police chief or court clerk), or it may be an elected official (the mayor, chair of the county commission or chair of the school board). The job title is unimportant. Find the person who knows in detail how any organization really works, where the money goes and how decisions are made. Get to know that person because he or she will be the most important person on your beat.

- **The budget is the blueprint.** This principle is a corollary of the first. Just as detailed knowledge of how an organization works is the key to controlling that organization, a budget is the blueprint for the organization's activities. The budget tells where the money comes from and where it goes. It tells how many people are on the payroll and how much they are paid. It tells what programs are planned for the year and how much they will cost. Over several years' time, the budget tells where the budget-makers' priorities are, what they see as their organization's role in the community.

So, find copies of the last two or three years' budgets for your beat. Try to decipher them. Learn all you can from your predecessor and from newspaper clips. Then find the architect who drew up this blueprint—the budget director or the clerk or the assistant superintendent—and get a translation. Ask all the questions you can think of. Write down the answers.

When budget-making time arrives, follow every step. Attend every public hearing and every private discussion session you can. In those dollar figures are some of the most important stories you will write—stories of how much your readers will be paying for schools and roads and garbage pickup, stories of what they will get for their money.

- **Distributing power and money is politics.** While looking for your beat's power centers and unraveling its budget mysteries, you will be absorbing as well the most interesting part of beat reporting—politics.

At any organizational level in any form, power and money go hand-in-hand with politics. Politics provides the mechanisms through which limited resources are allocated among many competing groups. Neither elections nor political parties are necessary for politics. You will have to learn to spot more subtle forms of political maneuvering.

If you are covering city hall, for example, pay close attention as the city budget is being drafted. You may find the mayor's pet project being written in by the city manager. Nobody elects the city manager, but it is good politics for him or her to keep the mayor happy. Are the builders influential in town? If so, you will probably find plenty of road and sewer projects in the budget. Are the city employees unionized? Look for healthy wage and benefit increases if they are. Is there a vocal retirees' organization? That may account for the proposed senior citizens' center. None of those projects is necessarily bad just because it is political. But you and your readers ought to know who is getting what and why.

Now suppose an election is coming up, and the builders' campaign contributions will be heavy. A councilman who is running for mayor switches his vote from money for parks to money for new roads. Has a deal been made? Has a vote been sold? That's politics, too. Some digging is in order.

Power, money and politics are the crucial factors to watch in any beat reporting. With this in mind, let's take a closer look at the most important local beats.

City and County Government

Most medium-sized cities have council-manager governments. The mayor and council members hire a professional administrator to manage the day-to-day affairs of the city. The manager, in turn, hires the police and fire chiefs, the public works director and other department heads. Under the city charter, the council is supposed to make policy and leave its implementation to the manager. Council members are usually forbidden to meddle in the affairs of any department.

Some cities have governments in which the mayor serves as chief administrator. Rudy Giuliani, mayor of New York when the terrorists attacked in 2001, became a national hero for his take-charge approach.

Whatever the structure of your city, you will have a range of good sources to draw on:

- **Subordinate administrators.** They know details of budgets, planning and zoning, and personnel matters. They are seldom in the spotlight, so many of them welcome a reporter's attention as long as the reporter does not get them into trouble. Many are bright and ambitious, willing to second-guess their superiors and gossip about politics, again providing you can assure them that the risk is low.

- **Council members.** Politicians, as a rule, love to talk. What they say is not always believable, and you have to be wary of their attempts to use you, but they will talk. Like most of us, politicians are more likely to tell someone else's secret or expose the other guy's deal. So ask one council member about the political forces behind another member's pet project while asking the other about the first's mayoral ambitions. That way you probably will learn all there is to know.

- **Pressure groups.** You can get an expert view of the city's land-use policies from land developers and a different view from conservationists. The manager or the personnel director will tell one side of the labor-management story. The head of the employees' union tells the other. How about the school board's record in hiring minorities? Get to know the head of the NAACP or of the Urban League chapter. Public officials respond to pressure. As a reporter, you need to understand those pressures and who applies them.

- **Public citizens.** Consumer advocate Ralph Nader made the term "public citizens" popular, but every town has people—lawyers, homemakers, business executives, retirees—who serve on charter commissions, head bond campaigns, work in elections and advise behind the scenes. Such people can be sources of sound background information and useful assessments of officeholders.

- **Opponents.** The best way to find out the weaknesses of any person or program is to talk with an opponent. Seek out the board member who wants to fire the school superintendent. Look up the police captain demoted by the

Writing for Readers

What does it mean to write for your readers instead of your sources? It means that you must follow several important guidelines.

Translate

The language of bureaucrats, educators, scientists and lawyers is not the same language most people speak. You need to learn the jargon of your sources, but you also need to learn how to translate it into standard English for your readers. The city planning consultant might say, "Preliminarily, the concept appeared to permit attainment of all our criteria; but, when we cost it out, we have to question its economic viability." Your lead could translate that to:

The proposed plan for downtown redevelopment looks good on paper, but it may cost too much, the city's planning consultant said today.

Make Your Writing Human

In big government and big business, humanity often gets lost in numbers. Your readers want and need to know the impact of those numbers on real people. How many people will be displaced by a new highway? And who are they? Who will be affected by a school closing or a welfare cut? When a police report announced that burglaries were up by 35 percent in the last two months, an enterprising reporter told the story through the eyes of a victim. It began this way:

Viola Patterson picked her way through the shattered glass from her front door, passed the table where her television used to sit, and stopped before the cabinet that had held her family silver.

She wept.

Mrs. Patterson, 72, is one of the more than 75 people victimized by burglars in the last two months.

Think of the Public Pocketbook

If the tax rate is going up 14 cents, how much will it cost the average homeowner? If employees of a firm are seeking a 10 percent raise, how much will that cost the employer? How much of that increase will be passed on to customers? If garbage collection fees are about to be increased, how do they compare to fees in comparable cities?

The city manager proposed "adjusting" the price of electricity to lower the cost to industrial customers and raise rates to private homes. The city hall reporter did a quick survey of comparable cities around the state. Then she wrote:

City residents, who already pay more for their electricity than residents of eight similar-sized cities around the state, would be charged an average of $4 per month more under a proposal announced Tuesday by City Manager Barry Kovac.

Industrial users, whose rate now is about average among the nine cities, would enjoy the second-lowest rate under Kovac's proposal.

Kovac defended his plan as "equitable and necessary to ensure continued economic growth for the city."

Get Out of the Office

City council votes are important, but far more people will have personal contact with government in the form of a police officer, a clerk or a bus driver than with a council member. Go to where government meets its constituents. Ride a bus. Visit a classroom. Patrol with a police officer. Not only will you get a reader's-eye view of your beat, but you may also find some unexpected stories.

Ask the Readers' Questions

"Why?" "How much will it cost me?" "What will I get out of it?" You are the public's ombudsman.

Remember, a good beat reporter has to be prepared, be alert, be persistent and be there. If you always keep in mind the people you are writing *for*, you'll keep the customers — and the editors — satisfied.

new chief. Chat with the leader of the opposition to the new hospital. There are at least two sides to every public question and every public figure. Your job is to explore them all.

Once you have found the sources, keep looking, listening and asking for tips, for explanations, for reactions, for stories. The fun is just starting.

Covering a county government is very much like covering a city government. In both cases you deal with politicians, with administrators, with budgets, with problems. The similarities may be obscured by differences in structure and style, however.

Cities are more likely to have professional administrators, for example. The administration of county governments is more likely to be in the hands of elected commissioners, supervisors or judges. Counties, too, are more likely to have a multitude of elected officials, from the sheriff to the recorder of deeds. City governments are more likely to be bureaucracies. One way to generalize about the differences is to say that city governments are often more efficient and county governments are more responsive.

These differences frequently mean, for a reporter, that county government is easier to cover. More elected officials means more politicians. That, in turn, can mean more talkative sources, more open conflict, more points at which constituents and reporters alike can gain access to the governmental structure.

The principles and the problems of reporting are the same. The budget remains the blueprint whether it is drafted by a professional administrator or an elected officeholder. Knowledge is power whether it is the city manager or the elected county clerk who knows where the money goes. Politics is politics.

The Schools

No institution is more important to any community than its schools. None is worse covered. And none is more demanding of or rewarding to a reporter. The issues that arise on the school beat are among the most important in our society. If it is your beat, be prepared to write about racial tensions, drug abuse, obscenity versus free speech, religious conflict, crime, labor-management disputes, politics, sex—and yes, education.

The process of learning and teaching can be obscured by the furor arising from the more dramatic issues. Even when everyone else seems to have forgotten, though, you must not forget that all those are only side issues. The most important part of the school beat is what goes on in the classroom.

Whether those classrooms hold kindergartners or high school students, the principles for covering education remain the same. For the most part, so do the issues. When the schools are private rather than public, you have fewer rights of access.

The classroom is not an easy place to cover. You may have trouble getting into one. Administrators frequently turn down such requests on the grounds that a reporter's presence would be disruptive. It would be, at first. But a good teacher and an unobtrusive reporter can overcome that drawback easily. Many papers, at the start of the school year, assign a reporter to an elementary school classroom. He or she visits frequently, gets to know the teacher and pupils, becomes part of the furniture. And that reporter captures for readers much of the sight and sound and feeling of education.

There are other ways, too, of letting readers in on how well—or how badly—the schools are doing their job. Here are some of them:

- **Examine standardized test scores.** Every school system administers some kind of standard tests designed to measure how well its students compare either with a set standard or with other students. The results of such tests are or ought to be public information. Insist on learning about them. Test scores are an inadequate measure of school quality, but they are good indicators. When you base a story on them, be sure you understand what is really being compared and what factors outside the schools may affect the scores. Find out what decisions are made on the basis of standardized test scores. For example, do schools whose students' average scores are relatively low get additions to their faculty? Do they get special-education teachers?

- **Be alert to other indicators of school quality.** You can find out how many graduates of your school system go to college, how many win scholarships and what colleges they attend. You can find out how your school system measures up to the standards of the state department of education. Does it hold the highest classification? If not, why not? National organizations of teachers, librarians and administrators also publish standards they think schools should meet. How close do your schools come?

- **In education, as in anything else, you get what you pay for.** How does the pay of teachers in your district compare with pay in similar-sized districts? How does the tax rate compare? What is the turnover among teachers?

- **Get to know as many teachers, administrators and students as possible.** You can learn to pick out the teachers who really care about children and learning. One way to do that is to encourage them to talk about their jobs. A good teacher's warmth will come through.

One reason schools are covered poorly is that the beat often does not produce the obvious, easy stories of politics, personalities and conflict that the city hall or police beats yield. School board meetings usually produce a spark only when a side issue intrudes. Most school board members are more comfortable talking about issues other than education itself, which is often left to the professionals.

The politics and the budgets of schools are very much like those of other institutions. The uniquely important things about the school are the classroom and what happens inside it. Your reporting will suffer if you forget that fact. So will your readers.

Higher Education

Look around you. Relevant and useful stories are everywhere. From the next meeting of the governing board to the classroom of a popular professor, the same principles that apply to coverage of primary schools can be applied on the campus.

Politics, economics and pedagogy—all included as subjects in the course catalog—are also prime prospects for examination. Politics may be partisan, especially in public universities with elected or appointed governing boards, or it may be bureaucratic, as individuals or departments compete for power and prestige. The economics of higher education translates to budgets, salaries and tuition costs. Pedagogy, the art and science of teaching, is often overlooked by reporters, but it is really the point of the enterprise.

The Chronicle of Higher Education and campus newsletters are required background reading—the former for insights into national issues and trends, the latter for the nitty-gritty of local developments.

Suppose, for example, that the *Chronicle* reports a slowdown nationally in the skyrocketing rates of tuition. The obvious local story is what's happening on your campus and how that compares with the situation at peer institutions. A less obvious story may be how students are scraping up that tuition money. And an even better, though more difficult, story would be how rising costs affect who can afford to attend, and therefore the composition—by race, ethnicity, social class, even geography—of the student body.

To cover the campus, you'll have to overcome the natural hesitancy of many students to challenge professors, administrators and other authority figures. Try to think of them, not as superior beings, but as sources and possible subjects of stories. Then treat them respectfully but not obsequiously, as you would any public official. If your campus is state-supported, they are public officials, after all. That means, among other things, that state laws governing open meetings and records apply.

Here are a few of the issues that should yield good stories on most campuses:

- **Politics.** How are members of the governing board chosen? Who are the members, anyway? What's their agenda? Within the campus, which are the favored departments? How strong is the fraternity and sorority system? How much clout does the athletic department wield with the campus administration or alumni? In an institution founded on free inquiry, just how free is speech for students, faculty and staff?

- **Economics.** How much does the president get paid? The faculty? The janitors? Where does the money to support the institution really come from? The state? Tuition? Alumni giving? Research grants and contracts? Where does that money go? How much is spent on intercollegiate athletics? How much on the English and history departments?

- **Pedagogy.** Who are the best (and worst) teachers on campus? Is good teaching rewarded as much as research is? Among the faculty, who gets tenure and who doesn't? Who does the teaching, anyway? Senior faculty? Graduate students? Part-timers?

You can practice good reporting without leaving your campus.

The Police Beat

The police beat probably produces more good, readable stories per hour of reporter time than any other beat. It also produces some of the worst, laziest reporting and generates many of our most serious legal and ethical problems. It is the beat many cub reporters start on and the beat many veterans stay on until they have become almost part of the force. It offers great frustration and great opportunity. All these contradictions arise from the nature of police work and of reporting.

If you are going to be a police reporter—and nearly every reporter is, at least briefly—the first thing you have to understand is what police officers are and what they do. We hire police officers to protect us from each other. We require them to deal every day with the dregs of society. Abuse and danger are parts of the job, as is boredom. We pay police officers mediocre wages and accord them little status. We ask them to be brave but compassionate, stern but tolerant. Very often what we get is less what we ask for than what we should expect. Police work seldom attracts saints. Police officers are frequently cynical, often prejudiced, occasionally dishonest.

When you walk into a police station as a reporter for the first time, expect to be met with some suspicion, even hostility. Young reporters often are perceived by police as being radical, unkempt, anti-authority. How closely does that description fit you or your classmates?

Police departments are quasi-military organizations, with strict chains of command and strong discipline. Their members are sworn to uphold the status quo. The reasons that police and young reporters are mutually suspicious should be clear by now.

Then how do you cover these people?

- **Educate yourself in police lore.** Take a course in law enforcement, if you can, or take a course in constitutional law. You also might read Joseph Wambaugh's novels for a realistic portrait of the police.

- **Try to fit in.** Keep your hair neat, dress conservatively and learn the language. Remember that police officers, like the rest of us, are usually quicker to trust people who look and act the way they do.

- **Lend a sympathetic ear.** You enjoy talking about yourself to somebody who seems to be interested; so do most police officers. They know they have a tough job, and they like to be appreciated. Open your mind, and try to understand even the points of view with which you may disagree strongly.

- **Encourage gossip.** Police officers may gossip even more than reporters do. Encourage such talk over a cup of coffee at the station, while tagging along in

TIPS

Covering the Police Beat

- Educate yourself in police lore.

- Try to fit in.

- Lend a sympathetic ear.

- Encourage gossip.

- Talk with other police-watchers.

a patrol car or over a beer after the shift. The stories will be one-sided and exaggerated, but you may learn a lot. Those war stories are fascinating, besides. Just don't print anything you haven't verified.

- **Talk with other police-watchers.** Lawyers can be good sources, especially the prosecutors and public defenders who associate every day with the police. Other law-enforcement sources are good, too. Sheriff's deputies, for example, may be eager to talk about dishonesty or inefficiency in the city police department, and city police may be eager to reciprocate.

One important reason for all this work is that little of the information you need and want as a police reporter is material you are entitled to under public records laws. By law, you are entitled to see only the *arrest sheet* (also called the *arrest log* or **blotter**). This record tells you only the identity of the person arrested, the charge and when the arrest took place. You are not entitled by law to see the arrest report or to interview the officers involved.

Writing a story depends on securing more than the bare-bones information. Finding out details depends on the goodwill you have generated with the desk sergeant, the shift commander and the officers on the case.

The dangers—of being unfair, of damaging your and your paper's or broadcast station's reputation—are ever-present. Good reporting requires that you know what the dangers are and how to try to avoid them.

The greatest danger arises from the one-sidedness and frequent inaccuracy of police reports. At best, the reports represent the officer's viewpoint. Particularly in cases involving violence, danger, confusion or possible repercussions, there may be plausible viewpoints different from that of the police officer. Conflicting interpretations of the same situation lead many times to the dropping of charges.

To protect yourself, and to be fair to the accused, always be skeptical. Attribute any accusatory statement to the officer who made it. If the room for doubt is great enough, talk to the accused, his or her relatives or lawyer, and any witnesses you can find. The result is almost sure to be a fairer, more complete story.

Sometimes the story is that the police officers themselves are misbehaving. Jo Craven McGinty was fresh out of journalism graduate school and new to the computer-assisted reporting staff of *The Washington Post*. That didn't prevent her from suggesting that the *Post* follow up on something she had spotted at the National Institute for Computer-Assisted Reporting. A first run through the data was promising, and soon a team was studying the rate at which Washington, D.C., police shot civilians. It was far higher than the national average. Before the team was finished, a system of deadly carelessness and corruption was exposed. And the *Post* won a Pulitzer Prize for the rookie's idea.

Religion

If you ever doubted the importance of religion in the world or in the news, just do a quick Google search for the terms "Islamic fundamentalists" and "pedophile priests." Whether your beat is the Pentagon or the police station, you're more likely than ever to find yourself covering stories with a connection to religion. Indeed, the dark side of religion news has become so prominent that it's easy to forget that religion has always been more important to everyday people than many journalists seem to think.

More Americans attend religious services than attend college football games. More Americans are active in religion than in politics. Overwhelming majorities of Americans say that religion is important in their lives. However, you'd never guess any of those realities from reading or viewing most news reports. The typical newspaper offers a weekly Religion page, usually published on Saturday, when circulation and readership are low. The typical television news coverage of religion is even less, often nonexistent.

There are some signs that journalism is waking up. Some papers, large and small, are expanding religion reporting beyond the weekly page. Some have expanded their definitions of the subject to include broader issues of spirituality and ethics. Others are recognizing the role of religion beyond formal worship. That's not surprising. Just consider the stories:

TIPS

Look for Religion Stories In

- Social issues
- Politics
- Law
- International affairs
- Everyday life

- In social issues, religion plays a role in the continuing debate over sex education, AIDS research and treatment, abortion, homosexuality, and an almost-endless variety of other policy questions.

- In politics, religion has become a key to campaigning and to governing. Presidents from both major political parties proclaim themselves born-again Christians. Candidates at all levels solicit the support of the religious right or, in fewer cases, make the most of their independence from it. In campaigns throughout the country, well-organized and well-financed religious organizations, usually conservative in their theology and their politics, exert influence even beyond their numbers. In major cities, candidates court Jewish and Muslim support.

- In law, constitutional questions continue to cloud the relationship of church and state. The U.S. Supreme Court is asked to decide whether inclusion of the phrase "under God" in the Pledge of Allegiance is a violation of the First Amendment. President George W. Bush made news when he urged federal financial support for the social welfare programs of religious organizations. The hierarchy of the Catholic Church angered many of the faithful when it failed to report to law-enforcement agencies accusations of sexual abuse by priests.

Since Sept. 11, 2001, reporters accustomed to writing about international affairs have found themselves required to explain Islam, the religion of one-fifth of the world's population. While political leaders struggled with unfamiliar names and previously unknown organizations, journalists had to learn the differences between Sunni and Shiite, the role of religion in the politics of Pakistan, and the geography and theology of the world's fastest-growing faith.

In everyday life, religion-based charities assume increasing importance as the American economy leaves behind growing numbers of the unskilled and uneducated. The "Religion Calendar" for just one week in a Midwestern college town includes activities that range from the African Methodist Episcopal women's group to the pagan Wiccan circle to meditation practice at the Zen Center.

So how does a reporter cover such a range of issues, personalities and events?

First, prepare. Read as widely as you can. A good place to start is with a booklet called *Deities and Deadlines*. Its subtitle tells its purpose: *A Primer on Religion News Coverage*. Written for the Freedom Forum by a veteran religion news reporter, John Dart, this little guide is full of specific, helpful advice and information. It includes brief descriptions of the major faiths, summaries of issues and a list of sources, complete with telephone numbers. You can order it from the Freedom Forum First Amendment Center at Vanderbilt University in Nashville, Tenn.

The best-informed coverage of religion and related issues can be found in such magazines as *CrossCurrents*, *Christianity Today*, *National Catholic Reporter*, *The Christian Century*, *Worldview* and other publications you'll find indexed at your local public or university library. Every major faith today has a range of Web sites. Look, for example, at iviews.com for news from a Muslim perspective and Jewsweek.com, a weekly webzine devoted to all things Jewish. An all-inclusive source on religion and spirituality is beliefnet.com.

For theological expertise and local comment on major stories about religion, consult faculty members at the nearest Religious Studies department or seminary. But beware of their possible biases. Get to know your local religious activists, in the clergy and outside. Who are the rebels and the questioners? Who are the powers behind the pulpit quietly raising money, directing spending and guiding policy?

Remember that religion is also big business. Public records and computer databases can help you trace property ownership and finances. Religious organizations often own commercial property, housing, parking lots and educational facilities. Typically, they pay no taxes, but their economic impact can be great, and it isn't always positive. Churches have been found to be slumlords.

Religious organizations pay no income taxes, either. But they are required to file federal tax forms — Form 990 — to maintain their tax-exempt status. These Internal Revenue Service forms are the only income tax forms that are public by law. You'll find readers interested in the finances as well as in the good works of religion.

In addition to ignorance, other obstacles impede effective coverage of religion. Many reporters and editors are reluctant to subject religious leaders and institutions to the same scrutiny as their counterparts in business or politics. Remember that religious leaders are human. They are often good, sometimes devious, occasionally corrupt. Be respectful, but remember that a member of the clergy who demands deferential treatment might be hiding something behind that ecclesiastical smile.

Another special problem in covering religion is the emotional intensity with which many people hold to their beliefs. If you do serious reporting, you will not be able to avoid arousing somebody's wrath. You can avoid arousing it needlessly, however, by doing your homework.

Do not confuse a Southern Baptist with an American Baptist, or a Lutheran of the Missouri Synod with a Lutheran of the Evangelical Lutheran Church of America. You will not get very far interviewing a Jesuit if you ask him what denomination he belongs to. But not every Roman Catholic priest is a Jesuit. Don't attribute the same views to Orthodox, Conservative and Reform Jews. And remember that Jews and Christians, although they dominate American religious life, are only a fraction of the world's religious believers.

Some stories about religion are uplifting. They tell of selfless service to the poor, the sick, the forgotten and abandoned. They illustrate values other than money or power. They describe the courage of people who put lives and property on the line for human rights or in opposition to war. Other stories are not so uplifting. Parishes run up huge debts. Parochial schools hire badly trained, poorly paid teachers. Blacks are refused admission. Women and gays are refused ordination.

Stained-glass windows are no barrier to politics. Religious issues, such as abortion, homosexuality and capital punishment, are often also political issues. Churches may use their economic clout to combat injustice or to support it. Belief can be blind.

Whatever side of religion it explores, a good story about religion will wind up on the front page along with the best of the city hall or medical stories. The techniques for getting those stories are no different, either.

Suggested Readings

Dart, John. *Deities and Deadlines: A Primer on Religion News Coverage*, Second Edition. Nashville, Tenn.: Freedom Forum First Amendment Center, 1998. A brief primer on covering news of religion.

Houston, Brant, ed. *The Investigative Reporter's Handbook*, Fourth Edition. New York: Bedford/St. Martin's, 2002. The first comprehensive guide to using public records and documents, written by members of Investigative Reporters and Editors. A must for serious reporters. See also the readings at the end of Chapter 18, "Investigative Reporting." They'll be useful in beat reporting, too.

Royko, Mike. *Boss*. New York: New American Library, 1971. A classic, brilliantly written study of urban machine politics.

Suggested Web Sites

www.journalismnet.com
A great source for journalists. Go to the topics list on the left side of the home page. You'll find sources for almost any subject.

www.poynter.org
We list this site repeatedly because it is so useful in so many ways. One feature is its links to nearly every professional journalism organization. See also the bibliography for sources and examples.

www.scout.cs.wisc.edu
The Scout Report is a weekly publication offering a selection of new and newly discovered Internet sources of interest to researchers and educators.

www.stateline.org
This site provides story tips and background information on state government and state-level issues.

Exercises

1. Spend some time with **www.ljworld.com** or another news Web site. Now compare what you find, and what you can do there, with the content of the newspaper and the television outlet that cover the same area. Which is more useful, more satisfying, more fun?

2. Scout your campus for story ideas. Think of the three broad categories of politics, economics and pedagogy. Write a memo to your editor outlining at least one good idea from each category. What sources will be most useful? What audio or video will you want to accompany your prose?

3. In the library or in a computer database, look up three recent national or international stories about a religious issue. Write a memo explaining how you would localize each story for your city. Include possible sources.

4. Using Nexis or another public computer database, examine how two or three major newspapers cover a national beat, such as Congress or a federal agency. What similarities and differences do you see between that work and local coverage? The topics will be different, but what about sources? Do you see any different focus on reader interests?

5. Analyze a local news story about crime. Identify the sources. If you were reporting this story, what other sources would you consult? What specific questions would you try to get answered?

Business and Commerce News

15

Scandals on Wall Street and a volatile stock market have made business news a Page One staple. Flip on satellite or cable television in any country around the world, and you'll find 24-hour channels like CNBC or Bloomberg devoted to following the world stock markets, and broadcasting that information in English, Chinese, Arabic, Spanish, Portuguese and German. Many major U.S. cities now boast at least one radio station that is devoted to business news or that uses syndicated business news programs, such as Invested Central, a twice-daily live broadcast featuring veteran stock-watchers John Hopkins Jr. and Tom Bowley.

News about business, economics and personal finance is a booming industry, and knowledgeable journalists have their pick of well-paying jobs. Take Jill Woerner, who graduated in 2004 with dual degrees in journalism and business. Just two years later, she became a field producer for CNBC in New York, reporting on energy issues and traveling to oil-drilling sites in Venezuela or OPEC meetings in Vienna. "I wouldn't have gotten the opportunity to move up this fast if I hadn't specialized in business news," says Woerner.

As recently as 20 years ago, the business section was a few columns of stocks and business briefs. But now, stories about Ben Bernanke, of the Federal Reserve, deciding to raise or lower interest rates frequently lead the evening newscasts. Why? Because readers and viewers want to know where interest rates are headed before they buy a car, refinance their home or invest in the stock market.

Because 60 percent of Americans now own stock, often through employee retirement funds, millions of news consumers are focused on the ups and downs of the Dow Jones Industrial Average or the performance of individual stocks or mutual funds.

Because of this surge of interest in business news, it's especially important for political reporters to learn the basics of business. The relative health of the U.S. economy played a major role in the 2000 and 2004 election campaigns, from the debate over the loss of jobs overseas to medical benefits for seniors. And in the 2006 elections, voters decided to take business matters into their own hands by passing amendments increasing the minimum wage in some states. Health issues, as well, are becoming increasingly related to economics, such as whether to advise seniors to sign up for Medicare Prescription Drug plans, on the basis of their personal income and medical needs.

All stories have some sort of business angle. A quick glance at an edition of *The Wall Street Journal* shows the breadth of news with an economic angle — from admissions policies at Ivy League schools to the latest technology employed by Procter & Gamble scientists in the $1.3 billion home hair-coloring industry.

Yet many news directors and editors still struggle with the focus of their business news. Who is their audience? Is it consumers, investors or local business executives? When gasoline prices rise in Texas, should reporters in Dallas emphasize how high prices hurt consumers or how they increase the costs of goods shipped by highway? Or should they write about how higher oil profits will spur more oil exploration off the Texas Gulf Coast? Or should they focus on the potential loss of jobs at refineries hurt by a decline in gasoline consumption? This array of ways to focus business stories provides both a crisis and an opportunity in the field of business journalism.

Business news is changing rapidly. Financial news, including up-to-the-second stock prices, is now available on many Internet sites, and investors can sign up for business news alerts sent to their mobile phones. Most traditional print news outlets are adapting by adding more analysis to their business coverage.

Newspapers are eliminating the pages of stock listings they used to run, in favor of more local business coverage. In 2006, *The Kansas City Star* launched a 24-page weekly business section on Tuesdays to capture the increase in local business advertising and to compete with the successful *Kansas City Business Journal*, which is distributed later in the week.

All major U.S. cities—from Fresno to Louisville to Hartford—now support local business journals. American City Business Journals, based in Charlotte, N.C., continues to expand its business-related titles with the 2005 purchase of *Sporting News*, which covers the growing business of sports.

Pick an industry and there is a magazine, Internet news site, newsletter or newspaper that specializes in covering it. Far from sleepy operations, these publications often find themselves in the midst of breaking news. *CFO* magazine—whose audience is corporate financial experts—doesn't shy away from covering the scandals that have rocked the industry. A weekly trade newspaper, *The Packer*, based in Lenexa, Kan., covered the recall of bacteria-infected fresh spinach, which resulted in several deaths.

And it's a growing global industry. Business newspapers are now prevalent in China's major cities. The *Shanghai Securities News*, founded in 1991, focuses on covering the Shanghai and Hong Kong Stock Exchanges as well as Asian economic news. American business media outlets have bureaus in major Asian cities and often employ multilingual reporters. It was a team of Chinese and American reporters for Dow Jones Newswires, the fee-based industry wire service, that broke the China copper-trading scandal in 2005. Those stories won several distinguished journalism prizes. In 2006, the managing editor of *The Wall Street Journal*'s European edition left to be a co-founder of a new English-language business publication in India. The newspaper will focus on that country's growing economy and increased trade with the U.S. tech industry.

The number of Internet news sites devoted to financial coverage continues to grow. Former newspaper executive Larry Kramer and his partner founded MarketWatch, a Web-based financial news site in 1997. The company went public in 1999, and CBS MarketWatch was sold to Dow Jones for $540 million, which set off a wave of high-profile mergers in the Web-publishing industry. Why the stellar price? Each month, MarketWatch attracted 5 million unique visitors to its free service.

The growing number of business publications is just one reason why business-trained journalists are in high demand. Even in a troubled newspaper industry, these specially trained journalists often command a 20 percent premium in salary, according to Detroit-based recruiter Joe Grimm, who works for news industry giant Gannett Inc.

But business journalism training is also important for those who seek jobs in corporate communications. With the growth of individual American investors in the stock market, many journalists are employed in investor relations or consumer relations, writing news items aimed at customers, employees or investors.

So, how do you get started covering business news? First, you need to understand basic business terminology and basic math. You also need to learn how to read financial statements, which is surprisingly easy. Beyond that, you need the skills of any journalist: perseverance, curiosity and an ability to ask questions and get answers.

PREPARING TO COVER BUSINESS NEWS

The range of business stories can be as broad as the range of business itself. Business stories may be about a company's promotions and retirements. Or they may concentrate on a company's potential profits, of interest to investors and potential investors in that company. Other business stories can cover personal finance issues that are of interest to lay readers rather than investment community insiders. Such stories explore issues such as these: Which are better investments, 15- or 30-year mortgages? Is art a good investment? Which mutual funds are high performers? Personal finance news is so popular that most major newspapers have at least one personal finance columnist. *The Dallas Morning News* has three—all aimed at different aspects of money management or investment. A business story might also be about products, like a new kind of digital camera. The story would interest not just shareholders of the company but potential buyers as well.

In fact, business journalists who work for mainstream organizations must acknowledge the often-conflicting outcomes of economic events. A story about an outbreak of mad cow disease in Washington state could have multiple effects—depressing the earnings of McDonald's, but boosting the price of Brazilian beef and leading to trade restrictions from a nervous Taiwan.

And business journalists must be able to see the big picture. While many Americans have lost jobs that went to workers in India or Mexico, an increasing number of Americans now work for global employers. Workers in South Carolina make small refrigerators for Chinese-owned Haier Inc. Autoworkers in southern Indiana learn Japanese manufacturing techniques while building Tundra trucks for Toyota.

These stories are global and local. Sometimes, though, the local angle is not so obvious. A story about a decision by the Federal Reserve Board's Open Market Committee to expand or tighten the money supply may seem far removed from your audience. But that decision can affect the rate your readers pay for a car or mortgage loan. News of a sizable trade deficit for the United States may weaken the value of the dollar and increase the price of a Sony TV, a Volkswagen car or a bottle of Cutty Sark Scotch whiskey. It takes skill, but a good business journalist can make these seemingly esoteric stories clear and relevant to the audience.

Many major corporate and economic decisions that affect us all are made in Washington, New York, Chicago and a few other major metropolitan centers. But those cities do not have a monopoly on the creation and coverage of business news. Even in towns of a few thousand residents, businesses will be opening or closing, and manufacturing plants will be increasing or decreasing production, hiring or firing employees. Local residents will be spending money for houses, cars, ski trips or new laptop computers, or socking it away in the town's banks or savings and loan associations. There is a business story in every such development.

Increasingly, economics has a strong role in disaster coverage. Hurricane Katrina caused at least $125 billion in economic damage when it swamped coastal areas in Louisiana, Mississippi, Alabama and Florida. Only half of that was covered by insurance, and the region will be hampered by the economic effects of the damage long after the cleanup and rebuilding effort ends.

In fact, the economic risk of natural disaster is of paramount interest to investment professionals, who abide by the investing wisdom "Buy on rumor and sell on news." Two days before Katrina hit, financial news outlets like Bloomberg News were already reporting the potential impact on oil drilling and gasoline refineries in the Gulf.

It's often economics journalists who find the flip side of tragedy—a business boom that often occurs during the recovery and rebuilding process.

On the Friday, Sept. 9, edition of PBS' *Nightly Business Report*—less than two weeks after the hurricane devastated the Gulf, correspondent Darren Gersh detailed the tangled economic issues caused by Katrina that affect workers, consumers and business owners:

SUSIE GHARIB: The clouds of Katrina may have a silver lining for the port of Houston. Traffic there has ramped up in recent days, as shippers look for ways to get their goods in and out of the country. As we continue our ongoing series "Recovering from Katrina," Washington bureau chief Darren Gersh looks at the port and the business boom it's bringing to Houston.

DARREN GERSH, *NIGHTLY BUSINESS REPORT* CORRESPONDENT: The cargo ship "Indotrans" was supposed to dock in the port of New Orleans. And New Orleans native Dave Morici might have been one of the workers unloading it there, had it not been for Katrina. Now Morici and the "Indotrans" are working out of the port of Houston.

DAVE MORICI, NEW ORLEANS LONGSHOREMAN: My attitude is I have a place to work right now, a place to stay, a place to keep on living right now. In New Orleans it will probably be a rough road right now, so I am going to wait until things are up and running good before I make a decision to go back home.

GERSH: That's a key challenge in reopening the port of New Orleans. Its workforce is scattered here and across the southeast. In the meantime, shippers are bringing order to the chaos, offloading cargo originally bound for New Orleans in ports like Tampa and Houston. This ship was supposed to stop in New Orleans. Instead it diverted here to Houston, and it's now filling up with 27,000 tons of grain bound for Veracruz, Mexico. But millions of tons of grain usually [flow] down the Mississippi to the port of New Orleans, and [that] will be expensive to reroute.

JIM EDMONDS, CHAIRMAN, PORT OF HOUSTON AUTHORITY: This port, Galveston, Corpus, Beaumont, all have grain elevators and we're about to approach the end of the harvest season here. [T]here's going to be some decisions that need to be made on how they get that across the country and out into the foreign marketplace.

GERSH: The supply chain disruptions stretch around the world. Coffee from Vietnam and South America is being held up. Houston does a big business importing bags of coffee, but for four or five generations, New Orleans has specialized in bulk coffee and warehouses here say they can only do so much.

TODD STEWART, GULF WINDS INTERNATIONAL: A lot of the coffee that has been displaced that's coming in is actually bulk coffee, so unfortunately, we haven't been able to lend a huge hand on the bulk side.

GERSH: In the long run, shipping traffic may be permanently rerouted, though economist Bill Gilmer says ports like Houston will have a hard time competing with the Mississippi River.

BILL GILMER, SENIOR ECONOMIST, FEDERAL RESERVE BANK OF DALLAS: If you are concerned about infrastructure in the New Orleans area, either because of the levees or its location that close to the Gulf, maybe you just move upstream.

GERSH: That's one reason New Orleans natives like longshoreman Armond Rodriguez are eager to get their port up and running. He says the Houston union local is treating him well, but he has 15 years' experience operating cranes back in New Orleans.

ARMOND RODRIGUEZ, NEW ORLEANS LONGSHOREMAN: I love being a longshoreman. I love doing my job. I just have a little bit more seniority there. I figure that's where my future is.

GERSH: But if the work does not return home, Rodriguez says he may have to start over in Houston as the low man on the totem pole. Darren Gersh, *Nightly Business Report*, Houston.

HOW TO REPORT BUSINESS STORIES

What separates a business story from a soccer story—or, for that matter, a soccer story from a story about atomic particles—is the knowledge and language required to ask the right questions, to recognize the newsworthy answers and to write the story in a way that the reader without specialized knowledge will understand. A reporter who understands the subject can explain what the jargon means.

For example, if banks change their prime rates, the personal finance reporter might be the person to write the story explaining that an increase of one percentage point could result in higher interest rates for car or home loans.

If West Coast longshoremen go on strike, one reporter covering local corporations might explore the impact on the supplies for a local manufacturer, while a retail reporter might talk to store owners about whether they'll have the right toys on their shelves in time for Christmas. With terrorism continuing to affect the airline and travel markets, labor and transportation reporters at the *Orlando Sentinel* often work together on a story about how security alert levels affect local employment.

Business reporters must use understandable language. But oversimplifying can turn readers off. *The Wall Street Journal* avoids both traps by shunning jargon as much as possible and explaining any technical terms essential to the story. In one story, for example, the *Journal* explained the terms "Federal Open Market Committee," "federal funds rate," "M1," "M2" and "free-reserve position." Sophisticated readers might know what those terms mean, but many of the paper's readers would not.

Sourcing presents a major challenge for business reporters: how to get information from someone who does not legally have to tell you anything. It often takes much more clever reporting skills to coax a story out of a business source than out of a government official. After all, almost all government information is open to the public. Many business records are not.

The mistrust that many businesspeople have of the press can make it difficult to cover stories adequately, even when it would be in the business's interest to see that the story is told. Even if executives are willing to talk, they may become angry if the reporter quotes an opposing point of view or points out a wart on the corporate visage.

The best antidote a reporter can use against this animosity is to report fairly and accurately what a business is doing and saying. By always being fair, you can win the trust and confidence of businesspeople—or at least their grudging respect.

Because business executives tend to be cautious when it comes to talking with reporters, it may help you to dress more like a business manager than a concert reviewer. Appearances count, and businesspeople, like reporters, plumbers, generals and linebackers, feel more comfortable with their own kind. The more you can demonstrate that you understand their business, the more likely you are to generate the trust that will draw out the information you seek. Public-relations people are often helpful in providing background information and directing you to executives who can provide other comments and information, but you should try to

ON THE JOB

Translating Business into English

Nik Deogun didn't set out to be a business reporter. It took an internship with *The Wall Street Journal* to change his mind. True, he had studied economics as an undergraduate, but his reporting courses in his master's program in journalism school had emphasized government and education. He sought the internship not because of the *Journal*'s niche in business coverage but because he hoped for the chance to do the kinds of news features that appear on its front page.

He got hooked on business. "This is where the power lies, and not many people are writing about it," he says. "Money is the source of all power, the source of all evil" — and thus the source of good stories.

Deogun thinks his generalist background, both in liberal arts and in journalism, prepared him well. Business writers need to understand the social and political context in which their subjects operate.

"I use here the same reporting skills you'd use on any beat," he says. "If tomorrow I had to go cover fly-fishing, I wouldn't know diddley. But I'd learn. You read a lot and ask people questions."

Too much specialization in a field such as business can even be a handicap. The *Journal* serves an audience more involved in business than the audiences of most daily papers or broadcast outlets, but a reporter's job still includes a great deal of translating from the jargon of the specialist into everyday English.

Now marketing and media editor for the *Journal*, Deogun understands he must be able to speak the technical language without falling into the trap of also writing it. "Most of your readers don't know that much about business," he observes.

Clear thinking and clear writing remain essential.

get to know as many company executives as you can. Sometimes you can do this best through a background interview, one not generated by a crisis but intended simply to provide information about what the company is doing. Perhaps you can arrange to have lunch to see what the managers are thinking about and to give them a chance to see you are probably not the demon that they may have thought you were.

Always remember that a company, government agency or pressure group may be trying to use you to plant stories that serve some special interest. Companies want a story to make them look promising to investors with the hope of driving up the price of the stock or to make them attractive merger partners. If you are suspicious, do some digging; talk to competitors and analysts, and ask detailed questions. Just because a company or some other group is pushing a story does not mean you have to write it.

Conflict-of-interest issues challenge business journalists because they often write stories, some of which are unfavorable, about advertisers. Business editors across the country have become increasingly concerned as advertisers threaten to pull advertising over unfavorable coverage. For instance, in 2003 a story in the *Orlando Sentinel* on the shoddy practices of home builders cost the newspaper $700,000 in canceled advertisements.

Auto dealers and grocers, both traditionally large advertisers, have worked together to pressure other newspapers. While newspapers make a show of not caving in to such pressures, advertiser threats can produce a chilling effect in the news room.

It is challenging to cover business. To do so effectively, a business reporter should be all the things any good reporter is—honest, fair and alert to possible new stories and to new angles on old stories. Business writing can be rewarding, both financially (because specialists usually earn premium pay) and intellectually.

WHERE TO FIND BUSINESS STORIES

The starting point in writing a business story is similar to the first step in reporting any story—understanding the subject you're writing about. For the business reporter, that almost always means some basic research into the subject. For openers, check your organization's archives to learn what's been written locally about your topic or company.

There is a broad spectrum of Internet-accessible databases that provide lists and summaries of stories published on a wide range of subjects. The truly adept can plumb raw data, including stock market transactions, to track the impact of announcements, mergers and promotions on stock. But everyone can use simple Internet searches to access annual reports, stock analyses, press releases and other announcements.

Of growing importance are databases that provide lists and summaries of stories published on a range of topics. Newsearch, Standard & Poor's, Predicasts, F & S Index, Dow Jones and Disclosure Inc. are some of the companies providing these data. Reuters, Dow Jones (Factiva) and Bloomberg Business News also provide background information on companies and securities, historical prices and real-time news on business and economic issues. Likewise, Business Wire, PR Newswire, Tribune Business News, all major newspapers and magazines, and the Associated Press all provide online business information.

Journalists also use Web sites focused on investors, such as Yahoo! Finance, which compiles news on companies and provides links to government-required filings and historical stock-price charts.

Another valuable secondary source for business reporters is *Predicasts' F & S Index of Corporations and Industries*, considered by many to be the best index for company and industry information. *Predicasts* indexes a broad range of business, financial and industrial periodicals, plus a few reports by brokerage houses. For information on foreign companies, see *Predicasts' F & S Index International*. The

Public Affairs Information Service Bulletin is a less inclusive index covering economics, social conditions, public administration and international relations.

Records and Reports

Here are some good sources of information that you will find invaluable when writing business stories. Remember, many of these can be accessed through various online databases. That means you can decide on a question, log on and have the information you need right away.

Corporate Data

Basic information on corporations can be found online, either on the company's own Web site or through government filings. Independent sources include *Dun & Bradstreet's Million Dollar Directory*, a list of U.S. companies worth $1 million or more. The *Middle Market Directory* profiles companies worth $500,000 to $999,999. The three-volume *Standard & Poor's Register of Corporations, Directors and Executives* provides similar information for about 36,000 U.S. and Canadian companies. Volume 2 provides brief biographies of executives and directors. Other directories are the *Thomas Register of American Manufacturers* and the *Thomas Register Catalog File*.

Investment Data

To get specific information about the financial performance of a company or an industry, check reports prepared by Standard & Poor's (especially valuable is S&P's Compustat Services Inc.), Moody's, Dun & Bradstreet, Thomson First Call and Value Line Investment Survey. These reports also discuss company prospects and major trends. Also helpful are annual corporate scoreboards prepared by *Fortune, Business Week* and *Forbes* magazines. *Business Week* uses S&P's Compustat to prepare its scoreboard.

Financial Ratios

To assess a company's financial picture and management, you should compare your subject's financial ratios with the averages for other firms in the same industry. Industry ratios and averages can be found in reports prepared by Dun & Bradstreet, Moody's, and S&P's Compustat and in a number of trade journals.

Company Filings

For years, the Securities and Exchange Commission operated under the guiding principle that companies should make available a maximum amount of information so that stockholders could make the most informed decisions regarding management's performance. The SEC preferred to keep out of corporate affairs and to let the stockholders provide the necessary discipline. Much of that information was made public through SEC filings. In recent years, the SEC has required less information, but corporate filings remain a valuable source of information for reporters. You should start with the annual report, which will give you an attractively packaged overview of the company's operations and finances. The 10-K, a more detailed version of the annual report required by the SEC, also will give you the number of employees, a list of major real estate and equipment holdings, and information on any significant legal proceedings. Many other important documents, such as labor contracts, are listed by reference and can be acquired through the company, a Freedom of Information Act request or a private service such as Disclosure Inc. Annual reports do show up on the bed stands of business reporters. Carol Loomis, the prize-winning reporter for *Forbes* magazine, read 50 years worth of company annual reports while researching a story on Bethlehem Steel.

Most filings are available free of charge through the SEC's online EDGAR system, but journalists often use the pay service 10-K Wizard, which alerts them electronically to SEC filings by the companies they cover. Other outlets, such as Marketwatch and Yahoo! Finance, will let you set up "alerts" to news and filings on companies of interest.

Another SEC filing, the proxy statement, which goes to shareholders before the annual meeting or other important meetings, provides an outline of issues to be voted on, as well as executive salaries and information on the company's board of directors. The proxy also sometimes contains leads about the company's business dealings. Interesting nuggets are found under mundane headings such as "other matters" or "legal proceedings." For example, now-bankrupt Enron Corp. did disclose some hints about its offshore partnerships in the footnotes of the Houston company's SEC filings. Those footnotes did generate some stories, but company officials did not disclose the true extent of the company's financial problems. In any filing, always read anything pertaining to lawsuits. That, in turn, can lead you to public documents regarding a particular suit.

Many companies are quite willing to send you their annual report, 10-K and proxy statement. They may even send you the other documents outlined above. To keep up with SEC filings, you may want to follow the *SEC News Digest* at your local library, or use the SEC's EDGAR service.

Trade Press

Beyond the newspapers and magazines you already know and read is another segment of journalism known as the *trade press*. In these journals and house organs you will find grocers talking with grocers, undertakers talking with undertakers and bankers talking with bankers. You will learn the important issues in a field, how an industry markets its products and services, and what legislation it fears and favors. Interested in health care and physicians? Try *Medical Economics*, where investigative reporter Jessica Mitford predicts you will find "many a crass and wonderfully quotable appeal to the avarice of the practitioners of the healing arts."

A number of trade publications are independent and objective. Among them are *Advertising Age, Aviation Week & Space Technology, Institutional Investor, American Banker, Medical World News* and *Variety*, which covers the entertainment industry. Many more, however, are practically industry public-relations organs. But even they can be valuable for learning about current issues, marketing and lobbying strategies, and even market shares. To find trade publications, consult the *Standard Periodical Directory, Ulrich's International Periodicals Directory, Standard Rate & Data Service: Business Publication Rates and Data*, and *Gale Directory of Publications and Broadcast Media*. Many trade publications offer online versions, like www.ogj.com, the online version of the comprehensive trade publication *Oil & Gas Journal*.

Newsletters

Newsletters have become an important source of inside information in recent years. Some are purely ideological, but others can be valuable. Among the best are *Energy Daily, Nucleonics Week, Education Daily, Higher Education Daily* and the *Washington Report on Medicine*. For example, the *Friday Report*, published by Institutional Shareholder Services, explores proxy issues of U.S. companies and is a must-read for professional investors who need to know what issues corporate boards are facing. Even the media industry has newsletters. Peter Zollman, a former reporter for United Press International, runs a subscription-only print and online newsletter, *Classified Intelligence*, which covers the $6 billion online classified industry, which includes such companies as Monster.com and Craigslist.

Directories

Directories can be an invaluable tool for locating information on companies, organizations or individuals. You can use them to learn who makes a certain product, to identify company officers or directors or to find an expert source for an interview. Basic directories include *Who's Who, Directory of Directories, Guide to American Directories, Consultants and Consulting Organizations Directory, Directory of Special Libraries and Information Centers, Research Centers Directory, Consumer Sourcebook, Statistical Sources* and *Directory of Industrial Data Sources*.

Court Records

Most companies disclose only information required by the SEC. But when a corporation sues or is sued, an extensive amount of material becomes available. Likewise, criminal action against principals in a firm can provide the lead to a good story. It is important to check court testimony and records at all levels, including those of bankruptcy and divorce courts. Information about the pay package and executive perks of former General Electric CEO Jack Welch were found by journalists in Welch's divorce filing.

Local Regulators

Frequently, businesses want to enlarge their facilities or expand into new markets. To do so, a business may seek funds from an industrial bond authority, which helps the company obtain large sums of money at below-market rates. Or when an institution such as a hospital wants to expand its services, often it must make a case for the expansion before a regional or local agency. In either case, documents filed to support the requests may be revealing and may put into the public record information that previously was unobtainable. Local reporters who know how to find business plan filings in the county or city planning commission office get a great insight into their area's economic development. These records are public but are often underutilized by reporters.

Other Sources

The preceding lists are certainly not exhaustive. Other relevant materials may be found at local tax and record-keeping offices, as well as in filings with the Federal Trade Commission, the Federal Communications Commission, the Food and Drug Administration, the Interstate Commerce Commission, the Bureau of Labor Statistics and various state agencies, such as the Secretary of State's office, which compiles information on businesses registered in each state.

Don't overlook the Federal Reserve system, which employs scores of economic analysts at each of its 12 regional banks. Eight times a year, the Fed publishes a

Publicly Held Companies' SEC Filings

The following is a list of places to look for publicly held companies' SEC filings:

- **13-D.** Lists owners of more than 5 percent of the voting stock. Filed within 10 business days. Must report increases and decreases of holdings.
- **13-F.** Quarterly report of ownership by institutional investors. Includes holders of less than 5 percent of the company.
- **8-K.** Report of a significant incident.
- **10-Q.** Quarterly financial statement.
- **10-K.** Annual financial statement. Includes number of employees, lists of major real estate and equipment holdings, significant legal proceedings. Many other important documents, such as labor contracts, are listed by reference and can be acquired through the company, a Freedom of Information Act request or a private service.
- **Proxy statement.** Contains information on executive salaries, director information, shareholder voting issues.
- **Annual report to shareholders.** May lack much of the data found in the 10-K.
- **Securities registration statement/prospectus.** Submitted when new stock is to be issued; usually contains same information as 10-K and proxy but is more up to date.

comprehensive book of regional statistics and analysis, nicknamed the "Beige Book," available online at www.federalreserve.gov. The Consumer Confidence Index, a survey of 5,000 sample households by the Conference Board, gauges consumer sentiment on the U.S. economy. This is an important monthly index, followed by market watchers as well as the Federal Reserve in setting interest rates.

The Department of Commerce's Bureau of Economic Analysis (www.bea.gov) now allows reporters to generate economic data by county, region or state. The BEA uses data from agencies that don't issue public reports, such as the Internal Revenue Service. The Census Bureau has launched an interactive database that allows you to look at an area's employment statistics and population and income demographics. The "dynamic" mapping tool on the site allows journalists to analyze data within specific points on the electronic map. You can find the Longitudinal Employer-Household Dynamics information at http://lehd.dsd.census.gov/led.

Human Sources

Who are the people you should talk to on the business beat? Here are some who are important sources of information.

Company Executives

Although many public-relations people can be helpful, the most valuable information will probably come from the head of the corporation or the heads of its divisions. Chief executive officers are powerful people, either out front or behind the scenes, in your community. They are often interesting and usually well-informed. Not all of them will be glad to see you, although many executives value open communication with the press. In 2000, in an effort to tighten up information that could lead to illegal stock trading based on inside information, the SEC adopted Regulation FD (Fair Disclosure). It governs how corporate executives release information about corporate finances and other material information. Though Regulation FD has an exemption for journalists, it has caused executives to be more cautious in releasing information. As a result of Reg FD and the 2002 Sarbanes-Oxley Act, companies now release quarterly financial information via electronic news services like PR Newswire and Business Wire and discuss those results in Web-based conference calls in which journalists can participate.

Public-Relations Sources

Don't automatically assume the public-relations person is trying to block your path. Many people working in corporate communications are truly professional, and providing information to journalists is part of their job. Remember, though, that they are paid to make the company look good, so they are likely to point you in the direction of the company's viewpoint. Public-relations professionals aren't objective, but that doesn't mean that the information they provide is untrue. Instead, you should assume that it is being packaged to show the company in its best light.

Academic Experts

Your college or university has faculty members with training and experience in business and economics. Often they are good sources of local reaction to national developments or analysis of economic trends.

Associations

Although trade associations clearly represent the interests of their members, they can provide expert commentary on current issues or give explanations from the perspective of the industry. When *The New York Times* reported on the revival of the moving industry, the Household Goods Carriers Bureau, a major trade group, proved to be an important source. To find trade associations, look in the *Encyclopedia of Associations* or the *National Trade and Professional Associations of the United States.*

Chamber of Commerce Officials

Their bias is clearly pro-business, and they will seldom make an on-the-record negative comment about business, but they usually know who is who and what is what in the business community. The chamber may be involved in such projects as downtown revitalization and industry recruiting. State and regional areas all have economic development agencies that receive tax funds and are required to file reports of their recruitment activities.

Former Employees

The best business reporters say that frequently their most valuable sources are former employees of the company they're profiling. Writes business reporter and analyst Chris Welles, "Nobody knows more about a corporation than someone who has actually worked there." He warns, "Many, probably most, have axes to grind, especially if they were fired; indeed, the more willing they are to talk, the more biased they are likely to be." The good reporter will exercise care in using materials thus gained.

Labor Leaders

For the other side of many business stories and for pieces on working conditions, contracts and politics, get to know local union officials. The workings, legal and otherwise, of unions make good stories, too.

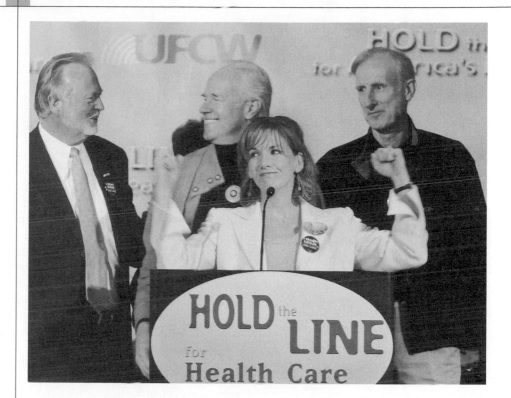

Union meetings, like this one of the United Food and Commercial Workers in Los Angeles, can be excellent sources of labor stories.

Other Sources

Don't overlook the value of a company's customers, suppliers and competitors. You may also want to consult with local bankers, legislators, legislative staff members, law-enforcement agencies and regulators, board members, oversight committee members and the like.

Announcements and Meetings

The source of much business news, and the starting point for many good stories, is an announcement by a company of a new product or the firm's reaction to some action by a government agency. News conferences can take many forms—in person or via a webcast. Companies also send out news releases via electronic outlets like PR Wire or Business Wire, or news might be sent directly by e-mail to a reporter from a company public-relations person.

If you work in a city where one or more corporations are based, you may have the opportunity to cover an annual meeting, which invariably produces some news. Although some meetings are more lively and more newsworthy than others, all say something about the state of the company's business and provide an opportunity for shareholders to ask management questions about the company's performance.

The time leading up to the annual meeting also can produce drama, as key players jockey for position.

Reporter Enterprise

As in other areas of journalism, often the best business news stories are generated by a reporter's initiative, sparked by a hunch or a tip passed along by an editor, a shareholder or a disgruntled employee or customer. Sometimes a self-promoting source can lead to a good story. When the president of a new commodity options firm called *The Boston Globe* to suggest a story on her company, reporter Susan Trausch was dispatched. The reporter quickly became suspicious of some things she saw and was told. The investigation that followed produced a series on abuses in an unregulated industry and won several national prizes. The original caller got her name in the paper all right, but hardly as she had expected.

In other cases, a news release may raise questions that turn into stories. For example, a routine announcement of an executive appointment may lead a curious reporter to a story about the financial problems that produced the change in leadership. A stockholder's question may result in a story about a new trend in corporate financing or a shift in emphasis on operations within the company. Or a former employee's call that a company is quietly laying off workers may produce a story about the firm's declining fortunes.

LOOKING AT THE NUMBERS

An understanding of the numbers that a business generates is essential to any intelligent analysis of a company or an industry. The most complete summary of the financial picture of a business is found in the annual report and the 10-K.

More than 100 million copies of annual reports are pumped out each year at a cost of $1 to $10 each. The annual report can be a sales tool for future investors, and it often looks like a catalog. The 2005 annual report for Limited Brands features a shapely model from Victoria's Secret—a retail chain that's part of the Ohio-based retailer. Others are less flashy. New journalists should look at reports issued by Microsoft, which feature easy-to-read financial statements.

A typical table of contents of an annual report includes:

- Opening Letter from the CEO
- Key Financial Data
- Results of Continuing Operations
- Market Segment Information
- New Product Plans
- Subsidiary Activities
- Research and Development Activities on Future Programs
- Summarized Disclosures from the 10-K Report

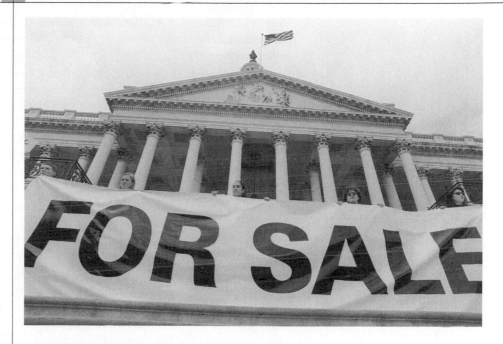

A public consumer activist group holds a sign on Capitol Hill proclaiming that Congress is "For Sale."

Most veteran reporters, like Diana Henriques, investigative business reporter for *The New York Times*, start with the auditor's statement, which is generally located near the back of the annual report, together with basic financial data, footnotes and supplementary financial information. The basic auditor's report, ranging from one long paragraph to three or four paragraphs, states that the material conforms to generally accepted auditing standards and that it fairly presents the financial condition of the company. But read the report closely. Sometimes auditors hint at trouble by deviating from the standard language.

Next, move on to the footnotes, where the seeds of many fascinating stories may be germinating among the innocuous prose and numbers that follow and supplement the company's basic financial data. Then, flip back to the front of the annual report and find the report from the chairman or chairwoman. It is usually addressed "To our shareholders" and should give an overview of the company's performance.

After that you're ready to look at the numbers. Here are a few things to watch for:

- **Balance sheet.** This report is a snapshot of the company on one day, generally the last day of the fiscal year. The left side of the balance sheet lists the assets, or what the company owns. On the right side are the liabilities, or what the company owes, and the shareholders' equity, or the dollar value of what stockholders own. The two sides must balance, so the balance sheet can be summarized with the following equation: assets equal liabilities plus shareholders'

TIPS

Cautionary Tips When Examining an Annual Report

- The numbers on an annual report are not definite.

- Look at the company's numbers in the context of both its industry and several years' performance.

- Use the knowledge you gain in this chapter to reach preliminary conclusions that you can pursue with experts and company officials.

equity. The balance sheet shows how the year in question compares with the previous year. Reporters should note any significant changes worth exploring for a possible story.

- **Income statement.** This report, also referred to as an earnings statement or statement of profit and loss, answers this key question: How much money did the company make for the year? Look first at net sales or operating revenues and determine if they went up or down. If they increased, did they increase faster than they did last year and faster than the rate of inflation? If sales lagged behind inflation, the company could have serious problems.

- **Return on sales.** Company management and financial analysts calculate a number of ratios to gain better insights into the financial health of an organization. One important test of earnings is the relation of net income to sales, which is obtained by dividing net income by sales. This will tell you how much profit after taxes was produced by each dollar of sales. Reporters should remember that average percentages can vary widely by industry.

- **Return on equity.** This ratio, which shows how effectively a company's invested capital is working, is obtained by dividing net income minus preferred dividend by the common stockholders' equity for the previous year. Every year since 1997, Standard & Poor's Equity Research staff has compiled a list of the best returns on equity by U.S. companies of various sizes. Those are available in *Business Week* magazine every January or on www.businessweek.com. *Business Week* and S&P are owned by McGraw-Hill, the information publishing company.

- **Dividends.** These payments to shareholders are declared quarterly and generally are prominently noted in the annual report. Dividends are an inducement to shareholders to invest in the company. Because companies want to see dividends rise each quarter, they sometimes go so far as to change their accounting or pension assumptions so enough funds will be available to increase dividends. Other companies, such as Berkshire Hathaway Inc., declare no dividends because they prefer to reinvest profits internally. Shareholders of Microsoft Corporation complained for years that the software giant was holding on to too much cash and urged the board to return more money to its investors through higher dividends.

Now that you have an idea of how to examine an annual report and its numbers, it is time for some important words of caution. First, the numbers in an annual report, though certified by an auditor and presented in accordance with SEC regulations, are not definite because they are a function of the accounting assumptions used in their preparation. That leads to the second and third points: Look at a company's numbers in the context of both its industry and several years' performance. To understand how well a firm is performing, examine the numbers along with those of other firms in the same industry. Look at how the company has performed for the last five to 10 years. Then you will discern trends instead of basing your conclusions on one year's performance, which may be atypical.

PREPARING TO COVER CONSUMER NEWS

The phrase "consumer news" is in its broadest sense arbitrary and redundant. All news is, directly or indirectly, about consumers. And many business stories could just as easily be called consumer stories. A story about the stock market may affect or be of interest to "consumers" of stocks and bonds even though those items aren't "consumed" in the same sense as corn flakes. A story about the price of crude oil affects consumers of gasoline and many other products refined from crude oil. A story about a drought that may drive up the price of wheat has an impact on consumers of hamburger buns.

Many news outlets, print and broadcast, run "action line" features that respond to consumer complaints of alleged fraud or unfair treatment by merchants or landlords.

Where to Find Consumer News

Sources of consumer news fall into three general categories: government agencies, consumer groups and private businesses. Let's consider each of these groups.

Government Agencies

Many municipalities, especially large cities, have a public consumer advocate who reports to the mayor and calls public attention to problems that affect consumers. Most county prosecuting attorneys' offices also have someone — or even a whole department — to challenge business practices of questionable legality. Cases of consumer fraud — in which people pay for something they do not receive or pay for something of a certain quality and receive something less — are handled by these offices.

At the state level, most states have a consumer affairs office to investigate consumer problems and to order or recommend solutions. In addition, state attorneys general investigate and prosecute cases of consumer fraud. Most states also have regulatory commissions that represent the public in a variety of areas. The most common commissions regulate insurance rates and practices, rates and levels of service of utilities and transportation companies, and practices of banks and savings and loan associations. Another source is your state auditor's office, which may also uncover fraud and wrongdoing within government or government contracts.

At the federal level, government regulatory agencies involved in consumer affairs have the power to make rules and to enforce them:

- The Federal Trade Commission oversees matters related to advertising and product safety.
- The Food and Drug Administration watches over prices and safety rules for food, drugs and a variety of other health-related items.

- The Securities and Exchange Commission oversees the registration of securities for corporations and regulates the exchange, or trading, of those securities.
- The Interstate Commerce Commission regulates prices and levels of service provided by surface-transportation companies in interstate commerce.
- The Federal Energy Regulatory Commission regulates the rates and levels of service provided by interstate energy companies.
- The Occupational Safety and Health Administration has inspectors who routinely visit and report on safety in workplaces and factories and who investigate workplace accidents.

Consumer Groups

Nongovernment consumer groups are composed of private citizens who have organized to represent the consumer's interest. They, too, are often good sources of background information or comment.

Common Cause, which lobbies for federal and state legislation, and Consumers Union, which publishes the popular *Consumer Reports,* are general in nature. Many states have public-interest research groups. Other organizations are advocates, such as the Sierra Club, which concentrates on environmental matters. Still other groups may be more local in scope. They may try to enact legislation that promotes recycling or to fight what they perceive as discrimination in the way banks and savings and loan associations make housing loans.

Private Businesses

Almost all large corporations and many smaller ones have public-relations departments. They try to present their company in the most favorable light and to mask the scars as well as possible when the company is attacked from the outside, whether by the press, the government or a consumer group.

Because of the successes of the consumer movement, a number of companies have taken the offensive and have instituted programs they deem to be in the public interest. Oil companies tell drivers how to economize on gasoline, electric utilities tell homeowners how to keep their electric bills at a minimum, and credit card companies suggest ways to manage money better.

How to Report Consumer Stories

Consumer stories may be exposés, bringing to light a practice relating to consumers that is dangerous or that increases the price of a product or service. Research for such stories can be simple and inexpensive to conduct, and the findings may arouse intense reader interest. The project can be something as simple as buying hamburger meat at every supermarket in town to see if all purchases weigh

A Business Mini-Glossary

Bonds

Governments and corporations issue bonds to raise capital. The bonds pay interest at a stated rate and are redeemable on a predetermined maturity date.

Constant Dollars

Because of inflation, $10 doesn't buy in 2007 what it did in 1987. Constant dollars take inflation into account by figuring their value compared with a base period.

Consumer Price Index

A measure of the relative price of goods and services, the CPI is based on the net change compared with a base period. An index of 115 means the price has increased 15 percent since the base period. Thus, to report the significance of a rise or drop in the CPI, you need to know the base year.

Dow Jones Industrial Average

The DJIA is the principal daily benchmark of U.S. stock prices. It is based on the combined value of 30 major stocks, which are changed on a regular basis. Those stocks, despite the name, are no longer purely indus-

trial, and also represent some companies listed on the NASDAQ and not the New York Stock Exchange. The DJIA exceeded 12,000 for the first time in 2006.

IRA (Individual Retirement Accounts)

IRAs are savings accounts whose earnings (as well as some contributions) are tax-free until withdrawal. They generally can't be accessed until retirement.

Mutual Funds

These funds are collections of bonds, stocks and other securities managed by investment companies. Individuals buy shares in them much as they buy shares of stock, but mutual funds provide more diversity.

Stocks

A share of stock represents a piece of a company. The price varies from day to day. "Blue chip" stocks are generally less volatile stocks that are meant for long-term investing. The price per share of such a stock does not generally increase at any sort of going rate, but is more stable and can give decent or large returns in the long term.

---

what they are marked. Some college newspaper reporters have compared the interest rates and fees of credit cards offered to students. Databases offer ideas for such consumer-focused project stories.

Susan Lundine, a reporter for the *Orlando Business Journal*, scoured Florida state insurance records to detail claims from the hurricanes that crisscrossed the state in 2004 — Charley, Frances, Ivan and Jeanne. Lundine found, for example, that homeowners who lived in 12 counties on Florida's east coast, 370 miles from where Ivan made landfall, claimed more than $65 million in damages from that storm. The *Business Journal* ran a county-by-county map of claims for each of the four storms, which starkly showed how ludicrous some of the claims were. The state reacted, investigating additional cases of potential insurance fraud.

Consumer stories may also be informational, intended to help readers make wiser or less expensive purchases. In 2003, *The New York Times* published a story on what parts of Manhattan were relative bargains for renters. You may want to discuss the advantages and disadvantages of buying a late-model used car instead of a new one. Or you can explore the advantages and disadvantages of buying term life insurance instead of whole life insurance.

Other consumer stories can be cautionary, warning readers of impending price increases, quality problems with products or questionable practices of business or consumer groups. Such stories can have great impact. A Houston television station's reports about Firestone tire deficiencies led to a massive recall. Dozens of magazines and books focus on consumer news, from stories on what to look for when building a new house to how to select a good nursing home.

Consumer stories can put news organizations at odds with advertisers. It was a consumer story about how to get the best deal on a used car that led to a massive advertising boycott—and the loss of $200,000 in ad dollars—at the *San Jose Mercury News*. And it was a consumer story that led to a lawsuit against *The Denver Post* when it published a story about a dry cleaner that consistently lost customers' clothes.

Suggested Readings

Houston, Brant, ed. *The Investigative Reporter's Handbook: A Guide to Documents and Techniques*. New York: Bedford/St. Martin's, 2002. See the chapter on business.

Schmertz, Herbert. *Good-Bye to the Low Profile: The Art of Creative Confrontation*. Boston: Little, Brown, 1986. A Mobil executive touts the merits of public-relations hardball.

Smith, Rebecca and Emshwiller, John R. *24 Days: How Two Wall Street Journal Reporters Uncovered the Lies That Destroyed Faith in Corporate America*. New York: Collins, 2003. An inside-the-news-room account of the Enron scandal, the biggest bankruptcy in recent business history.

Taparia, Jay. *Understanding Financial Statements: A Journalist's Guide*. Chicago: Marion Street Press, 2004. Taparia, a popular trainer in business journalism, walks journalists through complicated financial statements.

Woodward, Bob. *Maestro: Greenspan's Fed and the American Boom*. New York: Simon and Schuster, 2000. A primer on the power of the Federal Reserve and the economic clout of its former chairman, Alan Greenspan.

Suggested Web Sites

www.bea.gov and www.bls.gov
These sites, from the U.S. Department of Commerce and the U.S. Department of Labor, respectively, offer overviews of the U.S. economy and exhaustive studies about each segment of the economy.

www.business.com
This directory of business Web sites offers information about individual companies and industries.

http://finance.yahoo.com
This portal is an accessible and free index of corporate financial filings, stock prices and corporate news.

www.nicar.org
The National Institute for Computer-Assisted Reporting provides access to databases and training in how to use them to analyze business, economic and regulatory information.

www.businessjournalism.org
This Web site, funded by the Donald W. Reynolds Institute, offers tips and tutorials for business journalism professionals and students.

www.investorwords.com
This is one of many commercial sites with reliable definitions of words used in finance.

www.sabew.org
The Society of American Business Editors and Writers can be a good source for contacts, story ideas and student training opportunities. Students can also join the organization.

Exercises

1. Find stories on the same business topic, such as the latest federal employment statistics, in a newspaper, on television and on the Internet. Compare their detail and sources. Which is the most informative? Which is the most interesting?

2. Identify a local business reporter. Study her or his work. Then interview the reporter. Ask about sources, story ideas and career opportunities.

3. Send away for a prospectus on a mutual fund, and study its investment rationale. Or send away for a prospectus on a stock offering, and study its price-earnings ratio, yield dividends and other value indicators. Look up commentary on the fund or stock on the Web, and explain the fund's or stock's performance.

4. Use Nexis or the SEC's EDGAR Online service to find the 10-K report on a publicly traded company with a local operation.

16

Reporting on sports isn't all fun and games. When T.J. Quinn isn't covering major league baseball for the New York *Daily News*, he spends too much time talking to lawyers and worrying about friendly competitors who're facing prison time for their work.

Two of those friends are Mark Fainaru-Wada and Lance Williams of the *San Francisco Chronicle*, whose reporting on the use of illegal drugs, especially steroids, led to national controversy and tightened drug testing in the major leagues. That reporting also led them to the jailhouse door because some of their material came from leaked grand jury testimony. When they refused to reveal their sources, they were held in contempt of court and threatened with heavy fines or imprisonment. The threat was lifted only when a lawyer confessed to having been the source. That case has changed conversations in news rooms across the country.

T.J. said, "We've been told to use personal e-mail and personal computers for any correspondence with sources, to try to use outside phones, to maybe get our own cell phones and then get reimbursed by the paper. All of that makes perfect legal sense, but I'm far more concerned with the confidential meetings we've already had with the lawyers about holding off on certain stories because it isn't worth the risk of a subpoena."

Another disturbing development is the threat of heavy fines against reporters who don't reveal sources. T.J. told his boss, "I'll do 18 months for you, but I can't do $1,000 a day."

That was a joke, but it wasn't the lighthearted humor you'd expect to hear in what is often derided as the toy department of journalism. As the drug scandal and other serious stories demonstrate, writing about sports is writing about life, with all the challenges and satisfactions of any other form of reporting. Both the principles and the techniques of good reporting apply—in the stadium or the courtroom.

More than on most beats, a sports reporter is bound to be in the middle of ongoing electronic conversations. Reporters, readers and athletes write blogs. Specialized Web sites encourage fans to discuss and vent about their teams and the journalists who cover those teams. Your work will be analyzed, debated and challenged as never before. That's exciting, but it's also stressful and time-consuming.

COVERING THE SPORTS BEAT

What young sports fan doesn't dream of someday writing about sports? Not T.J. Quinn. After graduating from journalism school with a news-ed emphasis, he took a job covering local government on a suburban newspaper. Not until four years later, accepting an unexpected job offer, did he turn to sports. Eight years into his career, he was covering major league baseball for the *Daily News*. He considers it a good job but hardly a dream. Here are a few of the lessons he has learned along the way:

- "It's a lot harder to come up with a fresh angle on a mid-August baseball game when the team is out of the pennant race than it is to write about a fire."

- "Stories about sports are stories about the people who play them. Sports writing tells you who won the race. Good sports writing tells you how they got there and makes you care about the people who ran."

- "The best sportswriters are the best sports reporters and hold themselves to the same standard as any political writer worth his or her salt. Journalism is journalism."

- "There are elements in sports writing that are vastly different from news, of course. Talking to large, naked men is one. Having to duck out of the way of foul balls is another. Getting vicious hate mail because you think Greg Maddux is the most successful right-hander since Walter Johnson is yet one more."

A good sports reporter is a good reporter. That's not always obvious, especially to beginners, because the love of sports lures them to the field in the first place. Most sports reporters were sports fans before they were journalists. That's not typical of other specialties. Reporters who cover government seldom attend city council meetings for fun. Medical reporters don't usually spend their days off observing operations. (Instead, they may watch a sports event.)

As a sports reporter and writer, you are likely to find your workplace organized in much the same way as the news department. Typically, in the sports department of a newspaper, there will be reporters, copy editors and an editor. The difference is likely to be the scale. On small papers, the sports editor may double as writer and may even take the photographs, too. On midsized papers, the sports reporters usually don't specialize as the news reporters may. One day you may be covering high school swimming; the next, football or a visiting rodeo.

In broadcasting, at small and medium-sized stations, a "sports department" is likely to consist of one person who serves as writer, photographer and sports anchor at various times of the day or night. The big crews, the "guys in the truck" you hear mentioned on ESPN, are at the network level. At most local stations, you'll be expected to report, to write, to photograph and to deliver your work on camera. Sometimes, when time pressure is great or the game is big, you'll go on the air live, summarizing a game that has just ended or that may even be in progress. Then your skills at ad-libbing will be tested, a challenge print reporters don't face.

One more thing: Don't confuse sports reporters with play-by-play announcers. The latter may be reporters in a literal sense, but they usually aren't journalists. Their skill is in instant description, not the behind-the-scenes digging or the after-the-fact analysis expected of print and broadcast reporters. Often they are hired by the teams they follow or the sponsors they serve instead of by the station carrying their work.

As a new reporter, you'll find that the principles that follow apply to any medium and any sport. In Chapter 14, we discussed the techniques employed by all successful beat reporters. Review them. They apply to the coverage of sports as well as to politics or education or science. Now we will see how they can help you meet the special challenges of reporting sports.

ON THE JOB

Sports Reporting Is Beat Reporting

After graduating from journalism school, T.J. Quinn began his career covering several towns in the southern suburbs of Chicago. He recalls that he wrote about council meetings, murders, fires, politics and "the occasional feature about a spectacular schnauzer."

He became a sportswriter on a whim, his fiancée's whim. After she and T.J. left Chicago for *The Salt Lake Tribune,* she was visiting the old paper when the editor mentioned an opening on the White Sox beat. She said T.J. might be interested. He was. From covering the Sox for the *Daily Southtown,* he moved to the *The (Bergen County, N.J.) Record* to cover the New York Mets. A couple of years later he moved up again, this time to the New York *Daily News,* still on the Mets beat.

Except for "talking to large, naked men" and ducking foul balls, covering baseball isn't so different from covering politics, he has found. "There are two sides; someone is going to win; someone is going to lose; and everyone is going to speak in clichéd sound bites."

He reminds young fans who want to be sportswriters, "Sports entertainment is a multibillion-dollar business that requires some knowledge of local and state governments, taxes and business. There are payrolls to calculate, salary caps to consider and contracts to dissect. And half the time it seems like athletes are covered in the courtroom more often than on the court. It helps if a sportswriter knows how and where to get arrest reports and how to read them."

The special challenge of writing about sports, he says, "is taking a sport like baseball or basketball or volleyball, attending a match and then finding a way to distinguish it from the zillions of games played in that sport before."

The secret: "As the esteemed Rick Reilly says to young writers, 'Never write a sentence you've read before.' Stories about sports are stories about the people who play them. There are plenty of heartwarming tales of athletes who overcame tremendous personal hardship, and there are plenty more who are immature, greedy narcissists. But they are almost all heroes, because they all have to follow a hero's path. They have goals, they seek to achieve them and they have to overcome obstacles to get there. Some make it; some don't."

And a final word of advice: "After a while, those hot dogs get pretty nasty. Better to pack a sandwich."

Be Prepared

Before you even thought about sports reporting, the chances are that you were reading, watching and playing sports. In that sense, at least, preparing to be a sports reporter is easier than preparing to cover city hall. But there is more to preparation than immersing yourself in sports. Competition pushes people to their limits, bringing out their best and worst. So you need to know some psychology. Sports has played a major role in the struggles of blacks and women for equality. So you need to know some sociology and history. Sports, professional and amateur, is big business. So you need a background in economics. Some of our greatest writers have portrayed life through sports. So you need to explore literature.

This paragraph by Grantland Rice, for example, may be the most famous lead ever written for a sports story:

Outlined against a blue-gray October sky, the Four Horsemen rode again. In dramatic lore, they are known as Famine, Pestilence, Destruction and Death. These are only aliases. Their real names are Stuhldreher, Miller, Crowley and Layden. They formed the crest of the South Bend cyclone before which another fighting Army football team was swept over the precipice at the Polo Grounds yesterday afternoon as 55,000 spectators peered down on the bewildering panorama spread on the green plain below.

Rice, the most famous American sportswriter in the first half of the 20th century, graduated Phi Beta Kappa from Vanderbilt University, where he majored in Latin and Greek. His prose may seem overblown by today's standards, but he wrote some memorable poetry, too. And he knew who the Four Horsemen of the Apocalypse were.

Be Alert

Here's T.J. Quinn again: "The myth of the job is that sportswriters sit in the press box, eat hot dogs, live on expense accounts and get to travel all over the country. Mostly true. But covering a beat means keeping track of which players are doing what, who's injured, what a team needs to get better and where they might get it, who wants a contract, who's going to be a free agent, which pitcher is experimenting with a new grip on his slider, which coach is feuding with the owner, which power forward is angry with the point guard because she doesn't pass to the low post enough."

And here's the top of a story that resulted from paying close attention:

Mike Hampton was already a professional athlete the first time he beat his father at basketball.

Until that day, as an 18-year-old minor leaguer, he was oh-for-life against Mike Sr., never walking off the driveway of their Homosassa, Fla., home with so much as a gift win.

When Little Mike was 8 years old, Big Mike blocked his shots. When Little Mike tried to drive the lane, Big Mike would put his body in front of the boy and put him on the ground. The boy bled often but learned to cry less and less. His eyes puffy, his breath short, he would sometimes storm off, but he always came back to play the next day.

"It was gross how tough he was," the new ace of the Mets pitching staff said. "You fall down, get a scratch. 'Get up. It'll stop hurting. Get up; let's go.'"

Big Mike knew it was cruel, and won-

ders still whether he pushed the boy too hard. But the boy needed to learn that winning meant taking something, not waiting for a handout.

This is a story that entertains while it informs. It shows readers something of the character of an athlete and the meaning of tough love. Here are a few tips to help you be alert to stories that go beyond the cliché:

- **Look for the losers.** Losing may not—as football coaches and other philosophers like to assert—build character, but it certainly bares character. Winners are likely to be full of confidence, champagne and clichés. Losers are likely to be full of self-doubt, second-guessing and surliness. Winners' dressing rooms are magnets for sportswriters, but you usually can tell your readers more about the game and those who play it by seeking out the losers.

- **Look for the bench warmers.** If you follow the reporting crowd, you'll end up in front of your local version of Alex Rodriguez or Venus Williams every time. Head in the other direction. Talk to the would-be football player who has spent four years practicing but never gets into a game. Talk to the woman who dreams of being a professional golfer but is not yet good enough. Talk to the baseball player who is growing old in the minor leagues. If you do, you may find people who both love their sport more and understand it better than do the stars. You may find less press agentry and more humanity.

- **Look beyond the crowds.** Some of the best, and most important, sports stories draw neither crowds of reporters nor crowds of fans. The recent and rapid growth of women's sports is one example. Under the pressure of federal law— the "Title IX" you read and hear about— the traditional male dominance of facilities and money in school and college athletics is slowly giving way to equal treatment for women. From junior high schools to major universities, women's teams now compete in nearly every sport except football. With better coaching, and more incentive, the quality of performance is increasing, too. The results of this revolution are likely to be felt far beyond the playing fields, just as the earlier admission of blacks to athletic equality advanced their standing in other areas. Male-run sports departments, like male-run athletic departments, can no longer overlook women athletes.

The so-called minor sports and participant sports are other largely untapped sources of good stories. More Americans watch birds than play football. More hunt or fish than play basketball. More watch stock-car races than watch track meets. But those and similar sports are usually covered—if at all—by the newest or least talented reporter on the staff. Get out of the press box. Drop by a bowling alley, a skeet-shooting range, the local college's Ultimate Frisbee tournament. Anywhere you find people competing—against each other, against nature, against their own limits—you can find good stories.

Be Persistent

It was a big story. A sports agent had told another newspaper that he had given money to and arranged travel for a star college basketball player before and during the player's senior season. The agent saw it as no big deal. He had done the same for players at universities across the country as he tried to win their allegiance for life in the professional leagues. But for the university, his allegations, if true, could mean at least embarrassment and at most the forfeiting of NCAA tournament games in which the player had participated.

It was a big problem. The agent had been willing, even eager, to talk to reporters at the metropolitan newspaper that broke the story. He was available to other reporters at other papers with which he was familiar. But he had no time for student reporters at the newspaper of the university most involved. His attitude was discouraging for the reporters, frustrating for their editors and baffling for their readers.

The reporters refused to give up. They got the agent's home phone number, in a city across the continent, from the reporter who had discovered his role. They left message after message. While they waited for his call, they worked at the story from the edges by talking to people less directly involved but more accessible. The player himself, of course, was unavailable to any reporters. Finally, after a week of reading other versions of the story they wanted, the student reporters got a payoff for their persistence. The agent called. Using what they had gleaned from other interviews and previous stories, the students were able to write a story that offered readers a few new tidbits:

Nate Cebrun on Thursday described prospective agents' year-long courtship of former university basketball player Jevon Crudup as an "out-of-control bidding war."

Cebrun, a self-described middleman, said his dealings with Crudup and his mother, Mary, probably netted them only about $5,000 in cash and other gifts. But sports agents Michael Harrison and Raul Bey must have spent even more money on Crudup, Cebrun said.

"I saw Jevon's mother at Missouri's game against Arizona in tournament action. And I know she wasn't able to afford that with the money she makes," Cebrun said in a phone interview from his Las Vegas home. "But if I were a betting man, I'd almost guarantee Harrison paid for her to go to L.A."

In that case, the reward for persistence was catching up on an important story. In other cases, the reward may be a story that otherwise wouldn't be done at all. That was so when a sports reporter at the *St. Paul Pioneer Press* learned of a university secretary who said she had written term papers for University of Minnesota basketball players. Weeks of cajoling her to talk, checking out her accounts, prying loose supporting documents and withstanding pressure from even the state's governor yielded stories that stunned Minnesota and won for the paper a Pulitzer Prize.

The most important reward of persistence, though, is the loyalty of readers who feel well-served.

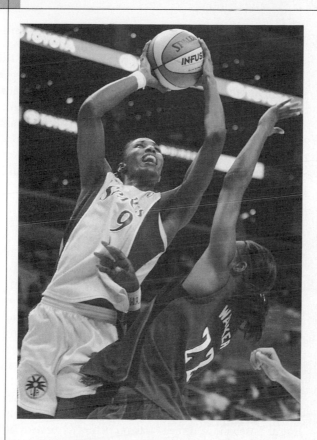

The recent rapid growth of women's sports has generated much public interest and media attention. Here Lisa Leslie of the Los Angeles Sparks goes up for a shot against Demya Walker of the Sacramento Monarchs.

Be There, and Develop Contacts

Being there, of course, is half the fun of sports reporting. You're there at the big games, matches and meets. You're there in the locker rooms, on team buses and planes, with an inside view of athletics and athletes that few fans ever get. And you should be there, most of the time. If you are to answer your readers' questions, if you are to provide insight and anecdote, you must be there, most of the time.

Sometimes you should try being where the fans are. Plunk down $20 (of your boss's money) for an end-zone seat and write about a football game from the average fan's point of view. Cover a baseball game from the bleachers. Cold hot dogs and warm beer are as much a part of the event as is a double play. Watch one of those weekend sports shows on television and compare the way a track meet or a fishing trip is presented to the way it is in person. Join a city league softball team or a bowling league for a different kind of inside view.

A sports reporter must develop and cherish sources just as a city hall reporter must. You look for the same kinds of sources on both beats. Players, coaches and administrators—like city council members and city managers—are obvious sources. Go beyond them. Trainers and equipment managers have insiders' views and sometimes lack the fierce protectiveness that often keeps players, for example, from talking candidly. Alumni can be excellent sources for high school and college

TIPS

Contacts

- Obvious sources: players, coaches, administrators

- Trainers

- Equipment managers

- For high school and college sports, alumni

- Business managers and secretaries who handle money

- Former players

- People who are disgruntled

sports stories. If a coach is about to be fired or a new fund drive is being planned, important alumni are sure to be involved. You can find out who they are by checking with the alumni association or by examining the list of major contributors that every college proudly compiles. The business managers and secretaries who handle the money can be invaluable for much-needed but seldom-done stories about the finances of sport at all levels. Former players sometimes will talk more candidly than those who are still involved in a program. As on any beat, look for people who may be disgruntled—a fired assistant coach, a benched star, a big contributor to a losing team. And when you find good sources, cherish them. Keep in contact, flatter them and protect them. They are your lifeline.

Be Wary, and Dig for the Real Story

It is even harder for a sports reporter than it is for a political or police reporter to maintain a critical distance from the beat. The most obvious reason is that most of the people who become sports reporters do so because they are sports fans. To be a fan is precisely the opposite of being a dispassionate, critical observer. In addition, athletics—especially big-time athletics—is glamorous and exciting. The sports reporter associates daily with the stars and the coaches whom others, including cynical city hall reporters and hard-bitten managing editors, pay to admire at a distance. Finally, sports figures ranging from high school coaches to owners of professional baseball teams deliberately and persistently seek to buy the favor of the reporters who cover their sports.

We are taught from childhood that it is disgraceful to bite the hand that feeds you. Professional teams and many college teams routinely feed reporters. Major-league baseball teams even pay reporters to serve as official scorers for the game. In one embarrassing incident, the reporter-scorer made a controversial decision that preserved a no-hit game for a hometown pitcher. His story of the game made little mention of his official role. The reporter for the opposition paper wrote that if it had been his turn to be scorer, he would have ruled the other way.

Sports journalism used to be even more parasitic toward the teams it covered than is the case now. At one time, reporters routinely traveled with a team at the team's expense. Good newspapers pay their own way today.

Even today, however, many reporters find it rewarding monetarily as well as psychologically to stay in favor with the teams and athletes they cover. Many teams pay reporters to write promotional pieces for game programs. And writing personality profiles or "inside" accounts for the dozens of sports magazines can be a profitable sideline.

Most sports reporters, and the editors who permit such activities, argue that they are not corrupted by what they are given. Most surely are not. But temptation is there for those who would succumb. Beyond that, any writer who takes more than information from those he or she covers is also likely to receive pressure, however subtle, from the givers.

Every sports reporter is given a great deal by high school and college coaches or publicity agents, who feed reporters sheets of statistics, arrange interviews, pro-

TIPS

Digging for the Real Story

- Maintain your distance from the people you cover.

- Keep readers in mind.

- Answer readers' questions about the story behind the story that too often goes unanswered:
  - Money
  - The real "why"
  - The real "who"

vide space on the team bus or plane, and allow access to practice fields and locker rooms. And what do they want in return? They expect nothing more than an unbroken series of favorable stories. Too often, they get exactly that. Only the names have been changed in this excerpt from a metropolitan newspaper:

The State U. troops reported today to begin three weeks' tune-up before the Fighting Beagles invade Western State.

Offensive commander Pug Stanley had some thoughts available Thursday before some 90-odd players arrived.

"We really made some strides this year," Stanley declared. . . . Charlie Walker, he said, is no longer feeling his way around at quarterback. The Beagle pass catchers are hardly old men, but the top four targets are two juniors and two sophomores rather than two sophomores and two freshmen.

State U.'s heaviest artillery is located behind Charlie Walker. Beagle runners ranged from good to outstanding a year ago. Most are back, with a season's more experience.

"Our runners keep on getting better," commented their attack boss. "Our backfield has to be our biggest plus. We're going to burn some people with it this year."

The story did not mention that State U., which had managed only a 6-5 record the previous year against weak opposition, was universally picked to finish in the second division of its second-rate conference. That's not only bad writing, but bad reporting.

Anywhere athletics is taken seriously, from the high schools of Texas to the stadiums of the National Football League, athletes and coaches are used to being given special treatment. Many think of themselves as being somehow different from and better than ordinary people. Many fans agree. Good reporters, though, regard sports as a beat, not a love affair.

Those sports reporters maintain their distance from the people they cover, just as reporters on other beats do, by keeping their readers in mind. Readers want to know who won, and how. But they also want to know about other sides of sports, sides that may require some digging to expose. Readers' questions about sports financing and the story behind the story too often go unanswered.

Money

Accountants have become as essential to sports as athletes and trainers. Readers have a legitimate interest in everything from ticket prices to the impact of money on the actual contests.

The Real "Why"

When a key player is traded, as much as when a city manager is fired, readers want to know why. When athletes leave school without graduating, find out why. When the public is asked to pay for the expansion of a stadium, tell the public why. One of the attractions of sports is that when the contest is over, the spectators can see who won and how. Often that is not true of struggles in government or business. The "whys" of sports, however, frequently are as hard to discover as they are in any other area.

The Real "Who"

Sports figures often appear to their fans, and sometimes to reporters, to be larger than life. In fact, athletics is an intensely human activity. Its participants have greater physical skills, and larger bank accounts, than most other people, but they are people. Probably the two best descriptions of what it is really like to be a major-league athlete were written by athletes—*Ball Four* by Jim Bouton and the novel *North Dallas Forty* by Pete Gent. Still, some of the best sports writing results from the continuing effort by reporters to capture the humanity of games. Roger Kahn, in perhaps the finest baseball book ever written, *The Boys of Summer*, needed only two inches of type to capture Carl Erskine, the old Dodger pitcher, in this scene with his wife and their mentally handicapped son:

> Jimmy Erskine, nine, came forward at Betty's tug. He had the flat features and pinched nostrils of [Down syndrome].
>
> "Say, 'Hello, Roger,'" Betty said.
>
> Jimmy shook his head and sniffed.
>
> "Come on," Carl said.
>
> "Hosh-uh," Jimmy said. "Hosh-uh. Hosh-uh."
>
> "He's proud," Carl said, beaming. "He's been practicing to say your name all week, and he's proud as he can be." The father's strong right hand found Jimmy's neck. He hugged the little boy against his hip.

COVERING THE CONTESTS

A major part of any sports reporter's job is covering the games, matches or meets. That task is harder than it might seem. You have the same problems you would have in covering any event, from a city council meeting to a riot. You must decide what to put in your lead, capture the most interesting and significant developments, find some good quotes, answer as many of your readers' probable questions as you can and meet your deadline. But a reporter covering a football game, for instance, has a major concern that a reporter writing about a council meeting does not have. Most of the readers of your football story already know a great deal about the game. Many were there. Others saw it on television or listened on radio. They know *what* happened. They expect you to tell them *why* and *how*.

In sports writing, as elsewhere in journalism, the inverted pyramid structure has given way in many cases to an alternate approach. (You learned about these alternatives in Chapter 9.) Your goals for the opening of any story about a sports event should be twofold:

"Slowly, but ever so surely, is vanishing the notion that the sports department's job is to cover the games and perpetuate the image that sports are pure, its participants are All-American boys, and its pages [are] places simply to report the game and what was said after it was over.

"And who knows, maybe someday we'll even achieve equal status in job title. Through the years, it has always been 'reporter' on the news side, sports 'writer' in my world."

—Tom Tuley, executive sports editor,
The Cincinnati Post

To get to the "why" and "how" of a game's outcome, reporters need to dig beneath the mere results. Getting out of the press box to find an interesting story angle or to secure compelling quotes from players and coaches can bring a story to life.

- **Focus on the unique element.** No sporting event is quite like any other. A perceptive reporter picks out what made this game different and shares it with the reader. The unique element may be a single play, a questionable ruling by an official, an untimely injury, or a missing player. Find that unique element and you have found the key to your story. Your lead may be a quote, the description of a scene, an analysis by some expert observer or your own summary of the contest's high point. Whatever opening device you choose, be sure the facts support it. A summary or an analysis based on fact is permissible in a news story. Reliance on your own opinion is not.

- **Tell the reader who won.** No description is so compelling and no analysis so astute that a reader will forgive you if you forget to say at the start what the outcome of the event was. The basic "who," "what" and "where" must never be left out or buried in the body of your story. The story is, after all, about the contest.

The body of your story should develop the unique angle brought out in the lead. This writing technique gives a unified focus and maintains the reader's interest. In the course of the story, you should also meet three other objectives:

- **Describe what happened.** In addition to knowing the outcome, your audience will want to read at least the highlights of how it was reached, if only to savor them again. Analysis and background are hollow without the solid descriptive core of what happened.

- **Answer readers' questions.** The story should supply the explanation—or part of it, at least—of why the game turned out as it did. It should tell readers something they could not have discovered easily for themselves. Rarely should you have to rely on your own expertise to answer the questions of why and how. Experts abound at practically every sports event. Assistant coaches or scouts sit in the press box. The coaches and players directly involved are available after the game. Alumni, supporters or former players can be found if you look for them. The most important question for you to ask as a reporter is what your readers will want to know. Then try to find the answers for them.

- **Get the competitors into the story by using good quotes.** Your audience usually wants to know what the competitors think about what they have done. When winners exult, when losers cry, put your audience in the scene. That is part of the attraction of sports. The hours spent getting to know athletes pay off when they share with you—and your audience—what the contest was really like.

The preparation and techniques of interviewing are essentially the same in a locker room as in a politician's office, although you seldom have occasion to interview a mayor who is wearing only a towel. The reward for a good job in either situation is the same, too. You get lively quotes that provide some insight.

FOLLOWING THE MONEY

If your assignment includes a professional team, you'll quickly learn to think in terms of signing bonuses, salary caps and the seven-figure contracts of major-league stars. But even during your student days, while you're covering your college teams, money talks. If you listen, and if you follow the money trail, you'll help your readers understand the business behind the games.

Here's some advice from Mike McGraw of *The Kansas City Star*. McGraw isn't a sportswriter. He's an investigative reporter with a share of a Pulitzer Prize to his credit. He gave these tips to a conference of Investigative Reporters and Editors. He notes that some college football teams are worth more than some pro franchises. He also notes that most major college athletic programs, while earning millions every year, wind up losing money. Inevitably, at least some of those losses are made up from money taken, directly or indirectly, from the academic programs of the institution. McGraw suggests you examine:

- **The perks coaches receive, from free cars to huge shoe contracts.** The NCAA requires that coaches get written permission from their institution's president before making those lucrative deals. Ask to see those records.

- **Budgets.** Athletic departments typically have separate budgets. At state-supported schools, those budgets are public records. Look especially for any subsidies to athletics from academics.

- **Gender equity issues.** Federal law now requires schools receiving federal funds to file reports listing coaches' salaries, athletic budgets, recruiting costs and other expenditures by gender. Those reports are public records.

- **Booster clubs.** Many are incorporated as nonprofit organizations. If so, they're required to file Form 990—the only federal tax form that is open to public inspection. Look for extra payments to coaches and others.

- **Stadium and arena financing.** For tax-supported schools, state open-records laws give you access to numbers on operating costs, financing and such sensitive matters as personal seat licenses.

- **Academics.** Student records are protected by the Buckley Amendment. However, budgets can show spending on the often-elaborate tutoring programs for athletes. You may be able to get documents showing courses or degree programs recommended to the athletes, and you can get statistics on overall academic performance.

- **Enforcement issues.** Open-records laws give you access to documents such as any self-reported violations of NCAA rules.

- **Conferences.** You can also get copies of Form 990 for the athletic conference your school belongs to. These forms show both revenue and such expenditures as salaries of top officials.

McGraw's tips may not win you a Pulitzer, but they will help you help your readers understand the bottom line of sports.

WRITING ABOUT SPORTS

Many sports journalists think of themselves more as writers than as reporters. This chapter is intended to help you become a sports reporter. But good writing is an important part of any top reporter's skills, and the sports beat offers abundant material for good writing.

Good writing is precise, conveying what the author means to say and nothing else. It is descriptive, re-creating for the reader the sights, the sounds, the smells of the event. It is suited in pace and in tone to the story—lively for an exciting game, somber for the reflections of a loser.

Consider, for example, the possibilities offered a writer by one of the most common but least-valued contributors to sports: mud.

> The ball skittered across the cleat-torn field, slithering through the slop of mud and water.
>
> Two players raced after it, but their legs tangled. They fell into the muck and slid out of bounds.

It was a beautiful day for Cougar soccer on Friday. The Cougars are American Midwest Conference champions after defeating Lindenwood 3–1.

Or you could try a summary lead and then let an athlete do the talking:

What a mess.

The Springfield cross-country team knew it would be facing the best runners in the state on Saturday. But the team didn't know the Class 4A state championships would turn into a mudfest.

"It was awesome," said Springfield junior Nathan Mechlin. "I sank into the mud about ankle-high. It was fun. I loved it."

"The ball skittered across the cleat-torn field, slithering through the slop of mud and water." Use descriptive language to re-create the sights, sounds and smells of a sporting event.

You can almost feel the mud between your toes, or in your eyes. The ball went "slithering through the slop." Two players, legs tangled, "fell into the muck." A teenage runner, mud-covered, exults, "It was awesome."

Good writing captures the environment and the emotions. It is based on detailed observation and is full of imaginative word choices. It doesn't require elaborate settings or major-league athletes. It requires you to use the tools of the craft.

TIPS

Producing a Good Game Story

- Do your homework before the game.

- Spot the unique element and build the story on it.

- Tell your readers who won and how.

- Answer readers' questions.

- Get the participants into the story.

Here, for example, is narrative, used to capture the key moment in a championship high school softball game:

The bottom of the 15th inning would be as tense as the rest of the game.

Hickman managed to load the bases with one out on singles by Janet Reilly and Jessica Barton and on an error by Jays third baseman Gretchen Snodgrass.

With junior first baseman Kelly Simmons, who had two hits already, coming up, the Hickman fans sensed imminent victory. However, Simmons was called out on strikes, watching a changeup sneak by her.

This brought up junior second baseman Lauren Kriegbaum, whose day had consisted of no hits, a strikeout with the bases loaded to end the fourth inning and a pop-out with the winning run on second base in the seventh.

With a 1–1 count, Kriegbaum hit a grounder to third. First baseman Chrissy Armstrong was unable to hang onto Snodgrass' throw, allowing pinch runner Denise Brixton to come home with the winning run.

Brixton's run set off a wild celebration among the Hickman players, who piled on one another at the pitcher's mound in a victory scrum.

From the foreshadowing in the first paragraph through the buildup of tension, the unlikely hero and the celebratory term borrowed from the sport of rugby, this writing employs the classic tools of storytelling.

One of the best contemporary sports reporters and writers is Thomas Boswell of *The Washington Post*. He has won the Best Newspaper Writing award of the American Society of Newspaper Editors. Here are a few samples of his work. First, the opening of a story about aging baseball players:

The cleanup crews come at midnight, creeping into the ghostly quarter-light of empty ballparks with their slow-sweeping brooms and languorous, sluicing hoses. All season, they remove the inanimate refuse of a game. Now, in the dwindling days of September and October, they come to collect baseball souls.

Age is the sweeper, injury his broom.

Mixed among the burst beer cups and the mustard-smeared wrappers headed for the trash heap, we find old friends who are being consigned to the dust bin of baseball's history. If a night breeze blows a back page of the *Sporting News* down in the stadium aisle, pick it up and squint at the one-time headline names now just fine print at the very bottom of a column of averages.

Notice the imagery, as gloomy as the subject matter. Notice the pacing, with long, complex sentences slowing the eye to match the mood of sadness. Notice the metaphor: age as the sweeper, injury the broom. But notice, too, the sharp-eyed description that must ring true to anyone who has ever seen or thought about the debris cast aside by a baseball crowd. A little later in the same story:

"I like a look of Agony," wrote Emily Dickinson, "because I know it's true." For those with a taste for a true look, a glimpse beneath the mask, even if it be a glimpse of agony, then this is the proper time of year.

Spring training is for hope, autumn is for reality. At every stop on the late-season baseball trail, we see that look of agony, although it hides behind many expressions.

TIPS

Working with Sports Statistics

- Perspective is vital. A 400-meter dash time of 52 seconds is poor for a collegian but outstanding for a freshman in high school.

- Don't repeat in a story what is included in box scores or other statistical listings.

- If you have a list of figures in your story, consider presenting it in graph or chart form.

- Avoid using statistics you don't understand. If you don't know what earned-run averages are, don't refer to them.

As this quotation from the poet Emily Dickinson shows, familiarity with the classics of literature did not die with Grantland Rice. Boswell not only found the line, he made it work.

From another story, this one about a championship boxing match, comes a short paragraph that is equally powerful but sharply different in tone:

> Boxing is about pain. It is a night out for the carnivore in us, the hidden beast who is hungry.

Later in that story, Boswell returns to the theme:

> But boxing never changes. One central truth lies at its heart and it never alters: Pain is the most powerful and tangible force in life.
>
> The threat of torture, for instance, is stronger than the threat of death. Execution can be faced, but pain is corrosive, like an acid eating at the personality.
>
> Pain, as anyone with a toothache knows, drives out all other emotions and sensations before it. Pain is priority. It may even be man's strongest and most undeniable reality.
>
> And that is why the fight game stirs us, even as it repels us.

From the poetry of aging to the brutality of pain, Boswell matches his images, his pace and his word choice to the subject matter. The principles of careful observation and clear writing cover all occasions.

There is one thing that sets a writer like Boswell apart from many lesser writers. It is his attitude toward his readers. That may be worth copying, too. After winning the ASNE award, he told an interviewer:

> We vastly underestimate our audience in newspapers. In 11 years I have never had one letter from anybody saying, "What's all this highfalutin talk?" I get the most touching letters from people who seem semi-literate but who really appreciate what you're doing. I think the fact that people are capable of understanding the Bible, or sensing the emotion in Shakespeare, just proves how far they are above our expectations.

Suggested Readings

Fainaru-Wada, Mark and Williams, Lance. *Game of Shadows: Barry Bonds, BALCO, and the Steroid Scandal That Shocked Professional Sports.* New York: Gotham Press, 2006. Based in part on leaked grand jury testimony, this book forced drug-testing reforms and led its authors to the jailhouse door.

Feinstein, John. *A Season on the Brink.* New York: Macmillan, 1986. This chronicle of a year with Indiana basketball coach Bobby Knight entertains while explaining much about the high-pressure world of big-time college sports.

Flood, Curt. *The Way It Is.* New York: Trident Press, 1971. The first-person story of the baseball player whose challenge to the reserve clause revolutionized professional sports in America. Also noteworthy are the caustic comments on sportswriters.

Lewis, Michael. *Moneyball: The Art of Winning an Unfair Game.* New York: W. W. Norton, 2004. This behind-the-scenes look at a scientific approach to baseball management changed the conversation among professionals and fans.

Sports Illustrated. Continuously features the best examples of how sports should be reported.

Wolff, Alexander and Keteyian, Armen. *Raw Recruits.* New York: Pocket Books, 1990. A hard look at college basketball recruiting written by two veterans of *Sports Illustrated.*

Suggested Web Sites

www.espn.go.com
The king of sports on television (and on the Web), ESPN shows you the competition, gives you ideas and provides background on every sport that's played for money. (http://sportsillustrated.cnn.com is similar, but it draws content from *Sports Illustrated* magazine and CNN television.)

www.ncaa.org
Here you'll find the rules of the game for upper-level college teams, plus lots of background.

Every college and every pro team now has its own Web site, usually packed with all the trivia a fan or a writer could desire.

Exercises

1. Using the Web, research the BALCO drug controversy reporting. Were the stories worth the price? Where would you draw the line between protecting sources and obeying a judge's order to reveal them? Would you go to jail? Explain your reasoning.

2. You have been assigned to cover your college's football team. Write a memo describing at least five likely sources and listing at least five story ideas.

3. Now do the same for the women's basketball team. Compare facilities, funding, fan interest and actual coverage. Be prepared to discuss your findings.

4. Select a "minor" sports event, such as a wrestling meet or a volleyball game. Prepare for and cover the event. Write the story.

5. Choose one of the story ideas in exercise 2 or 3. Report and write it.

6. Compare the coverage of a major event in your local newspaper and in *Sports Illustrated*. Which seems better written? Why?

7. Compile an inventory of the online sources available to fans and reporters in your area. What story possibilities does your list suggest?

Social Science Reporting

17

Journalists and scholars have long understood that journalism plays an important agenda-setting role in society. That is, the stories journalists tell help determine what issues are discussed by the public and even what readers and viewers think about those issues. This is an important and honorable role, but it raises a serious question: Who sets the agenda for journalists?

Too often, the answer is that sources with their own special interests provide the information on which journalists rely. You've probably heard the saying that a reporter is only as good as her or his sources.

That's a limitation that cuts into journalists' ability to provide their readers and viewers with the best obtainable version of the truth. Increasingly, however, the best reporters are using more reliable tools for gathering and analyzing information. Those are the tools of science. Journalists don't usually regard themselves as scientists. Many would resist the very suggestion. But the best reporting has a great deal in common with the work of political scientists, historians and sociologists. Like social scientists, reporters frame research questions or hypotheses. They seek answers to their questions by the careful accumulation of reliable data and the use of scientific formulas and statistics to analyze the information they've gathered. They double-check their findings for reliability. Then they report clearly and carefully what they have learned.

Here's an example: the *Omaha World-Herald* wanted to reveal the best obtainable version of the truth about one of the most important and least examined institutions of modern life—high school. First, *World-Herald* reporters followed eight ordinary students through a year of school, recounting in narrative form the triumphs and tragedies, academic and social, of teenagers learning to be adults.

Sure, critics said, you may have captured those individual stories, but you haven't told us how well the schools are doing at their main job of educating. So Mike Reilly, assistant managing editor for investigations, and his team persuaded the University of Nebraska to release statistics on the performance of freshmen at the main campus, in Lincoln. No names but thousands of numbers—test scores, university grades, academic status and the Nebraska high schools from which those freshmen had graduated.

Using the skills of computer-assisted reporting, the newspaper staff analyzed all that data and reported the results in a four-day series of front-page stories. The results were stunning: The statistics demonstrated that graduates of some of Omaha's, and the state's, most highly regarded high schools wound up on academic probation at rates far higher than graduates of lesser-known schools. The statistics also showed that female students succeeded at a significantly higher rate than males.

This wasn't just reporting what somebody said, or even what a reporter had observed. This was new knowledge, developed by the newspaper and presented to readers who had no way, on their own, of learning what they, and policy-makers, needed to know. This is social science reporting.

The social science tool that journalists use most often is the public-opinion survey. It is also the tool they misuse most often. Here's an example from the McClatchy Newspapers:

WASHINGTON – Democrats are slightly ahead of Republicans in three election battleground states that will help determine control of the Senate, a series of polls released today showed.

In Montana, Democrat Jon Tester had the support of 47 percent of registered voters while incumbent Republican Sen. Conrad Burns had the support of 40 percent.

In Ohio, Democrat Rep. Sherrod Brown was the choice of 45 percent of registered voters, while incumbent Republican Sen. Mike DeWine had 43 percent.

In Tennessee, Democratic Rep. Harold Ford Jr. got the nod from 43 percent of voters and former Chattanooga mayor Bob Corker, the Republican Senate nominee, had 42 percent.

A few paragraphs later, the story reported that the polls had "an error margin of plus or minus four percentage points." See the problem? Many readers wouldn't. That last phrase—"an error margin of plus or minus four percentage points"—means that the first paragraph is just plain wrong. Any scientist would tell you that a 4 percent margin of error means that the poll really shows that, for example, support is somewhere in the range of 43 percent to 51 percent and Sen. Burns' support is between 36 and 44 percent. Rep. Brown is in the range of 41 to 49 percent, and Sen. DeWine is in the range of 39 to 47 percent. So what the story really should have said is that all three races were too close to call.

These examples show both the power and the pitfalls of using the research tools of social science in reporting. The increasing complexity of the world around us requires the journalists of today and tomorrow to learn to use tools adequate to the task of understanding and explaining that world. Often the most useful tools turn out to be those developed and regularly used by social scientists. In unskilled hands, however, such tools can be dangerous.

COMPUTER-ASSISTED REPORTING

American journalism—print, broadcast and online—relies on computers. Reporters write on computers. Photographers edit and transmit their pictures by computer. The almost unlimited storage capacity of computers and the flexibility of digital technology enable online journalists to combine text and video with links to original documents and to related information stored anywhere in the world. Increasingly, journalists are also using computers to analyze data, to do what the *World-Herald* team did and create knowledge that nobody knew before.

Computers assist reporting in two main ways. First, journalists can access digital information from databases on the Internet. (You learned about these resources and how to tap them in Chapter 5.) Second, journalists become knowledge creators by compiling and analyzing information that was previously not collected or not examined. That's what the Nebraska reporters did.

David Herzog, director of the National Institute of Computer-Assisted Reporting, teaches University of Missouri students and hundreds of practicing journalists from all over the world how to use their computers as more than word processors. His students learn how to acquire data from government agencies, nonprofit organizations and other researchers. Then they learn to use the techniques of statistical analysis to pull important patterns, developing trends and good stories from the numbers.

Take, for instance, the topic of guns. Jo Craven McGinty was a graduate student at Missouri who mastered analytical techniques and worked part-time for NICAR helping professional journalists tell statistics-based stories. She came across an FBI database on the use of weapons by police officers. When she took an internship at *The Washington Post*, she took with her that knowledge and a story idea. Months later, as part of the *Post*'s investigative team, she helped tell the story that Washington, D.C., police used their guns to shoot civilians more often than police in any other city. The story won a Pulitzer Prize for the *Post*.

Not all computer-assisted reporting leads to Pulitzers, but much of it reveals important information that otherwise would remain hidden in bureaucratic files. Sometimes those stories are hidden in plain sight, and the data just demands arranging to be understood. Herzog is an expert in computer mapping, the use of special software programs to display information in maps that reveal significant patterns. Instances of crime, for example, can be mapped to show the truly dangerous areas of a city. Outbreaks of disease can be mapped to help identify sources of infection. Patterns of immigration or unemployment or voting can be demonstrated more clearly by electronic maps than words alone could describe.

To learn more, or to get help with your own reporting, go to www.nicar.org. There you can benefit from computer-assisted learning.

PARTICIPANT OBSERVATION

Audiences around the world watched in real time as America's war with Iraq unfolded. Viewers saw desert terrain spread out across their screens as cameras mounted on military vehicles captured the progress of American and British troops toward Baghdad. Correspondents wearing camouflage uniforms often slipped into the first-person plural as they described the experiences of the soldiers they were accompanying. The military term for those reporters was that they were "embedded" with their units. A social scientist would say that they were engaged in "participant observation."

Participant observation is a tool long used by anthropologists and sociologists to learn about unknown societies by becoming part of the scene they are studying. War correspondents have used it for just as long to provide firsthand accounts of campaigns. Other journalists have employed participant observation for **undercover reporting**, to expose crimes or social ills from the inside. All participant observers get close-up views of their subjects, insights not obtainable from studying statistics or formal interviewing. Facts and feelings can be captured that otherwise would remain unknown.

Along with its unique advantages, participant observation also poses some unique problems. These problems may have no clear solutions, but you and your editors need at least to consider them before you set out to become an ambulance attendant or a migrant worker.

The Problem of Invasion of Privacy

Unless you identify yourself as a reporter, you are, in effect, spying on people—an ethically questionable activity. But if you do identify yourself, the advantages of participant observation can be lost. Sensitivity is essential, especially when the people you write about may be embarrassed or have their jobs placed in jeopardy.

The Problem of Involvement

There are two things to watch out for. First, do not become so involved that you change the course of the events you are observing. You may be on stage, but you are not the star performer. Second, do not assume that the people you are observing feel the same way you do. No matter how hard you work at fitting in, you remain an outsider, a visitor. The view from inside a migrant workers' camp or a psychiatric hospital is different when you know you will be there for two weeks instead of two years or a lifetime. This was the problem that drew the most criticism of the embedded reporters in Iraq. Their perspective on the war was necessarily that of the units to which they were attached. One reporter for *USA Today* even wrote a column in which he described how, during a battle, he was requested to help a medic who was treating a wounded soldier. The reporter told how he put his "objectivity" aside to save the life of a man who might have saved the reporter's life if the fight had turned out differently.

The Problem of Generalizing

Scientists know well the danger of generalizing from limited observations. Reporters don't always recognize that danger, or sometimes they forget it. Keep in mind that although participant observation yields a detailed picture of a specific situation, it tells you nothing reliable about any other situation. Participant observation is a good tool, but it is a limited one. It usually works best as a supplement to the standard techniques of interviewing and examining documents. This, too, was true of the war reporting. As the embedded journalists pointed out, theirs was not the only angle from which the war was reported. Other reporters at military headquarters, back home or even in besieged Baghdad all contributed to the overall account. That's a lesson to keep in mind.

SYSTEMATIC STUDY OF RECORDS

The *World-Herald* example at the beginning of this chapter relied on the systematic study of records. Kathleen Kerr and Russ Buettner of *Newsday* faced the same sort of problem. Their goal was to discover whether New York City's criminal justice system discriminated against the poor. Their method was to acquire computer databases of city and state records on 27,810 prisoners and then to use their own computer to sort those cases by race and other criteria. They found that the poor, especially minorities, were often denied bail and forced to wait in jail for trials that often found them not guilty. No amount of traditional interviewing and observing could have produced such credible stories.

Scholars have long used the systematic study of records in their research. Its use by reporters is still limited but growing. The advantage of detailed analysis of court records, budgets, voting records and other documents is that it permits reporters and readers to draw conclusions based on solid information. The widespread availability of powerful personal computers and easy-to-use analytical programs brings the systematic study of records within the reach of any news organization.

The main obstacles to such study are shortages of time and money. Major projects for a large metropolitan daily often require months of work by one or more reporters. On small papers, especially, you may have trouble freeing yourself for even several days. And reporters' time and computer time both cost money. Editors and publishers must be convinced that the return will be worth the investment before they will approve the project. You probably should have at least some clues that wrongdoing, injustice or inefficiency exists before launching a systematic study.

Once you have begun a study, make sure that it is in fact systematic. Either examine all the pertinent records or choose the ones you examine in such a way that they will be truly representative of the rest. Be sure to ask the right questions, and record the information necessary to answer them. A computer can perform complicated analyses quickly, but it cannot analyze facts that have not been fed into it. People who use computers have a word for that problem: GIGO, an acronym for "garbage in, garbage out."

Don't set out on a systematic study without assurances of time and money, a clear idea of what you're looking for and expert technical advice. If the expertise is unavailable at your newspaper, look to the nearest college.

TIPS

Once You Begin a Study . . .

- Make sure it is systematic. Either examine all the pertinent records or choose the ones you examine in such a way that they are truly representative of the rest.

- Be sure to ask the right questions and record the information necessary to answer them.

- Remember that a computer can perform complicated analyses very quickly but cannot analyze facts that have not been fed into it.

FIELD EXPERIMENTS

Here's a test you can do. Say you want to find out whether landlords in your town discriminate against nonwhite would-be renters. Send out teams of different races to visit the same rental agencies or to respond to the same advertisements. Then compare the results. Did the all-white teams receive more welcoming treatment than others? A scientist conducting that kind of test would call it a **field experiment**. In all such experiments, researchers take some action in order to observe the effects.

Reporters may not think of themselves as scientists, but they conduct a great many experiments. A common one is to examine the honesty of auto mechanics by taking a car in perfect condition to several shops and reporting what "defects" each finds. Consumer reporters also commonly check weights and measures: Does a "pound" of hamburger really weigh a pound? And they test for discrimination by having a black reporter and a white reporter apply for the same insurance policies or mortgages.

ON THE JOB

Computer-Assisted Reporting Wins Awards

Not many reporters win the Pulitzer Prize in their first job after journalism school. Jo Craven McGinty did, as a key member of an investigative team at *The Washington Post*. She'd be the first to tell you that the secret of her success was computer-assisted reporting.

Jo already had several years of experience on small newspapers when she decided to return to graduate school. She began learning computer-assisted reporting and became a graduate research assistant at the National Institute for Computer-Assisted Reporting.

In that job, she recalls, "I implemented my new skills in computer-assisted reporting which I had learned in the classroom. And, while preparing the FBI's annual release of the Uniform Crime Report database, I noticed something: It appeared that the FBI tracked police shootings but did not release the records. I knew that I would pursue those records when the time was right."

That time came when Jo was hired in a temporary position to work on computer-assisted reporting at the *Post*. She picks up the story: "I obtained several years of the FBI records on computer tape. They revealed that D.C. police had shot and killed more people than any other big-city police department at that time."

The *Post* team, led by investigations editor Jeff Leen, discovered that a flood of new police hires had swamped the department's training program and had not received proper instruction. Many officers skipped the required handgun training. Some bad shootings were covered up. Poor record-keeping meant that the police department's top brass didn't even know how many people their officers were killing — until the reporters told them.

The five-day series that resulted saved lives, generated reforms and won for the *Post* the Pulitzer gold medal for public service, the highest award in American journalism.

Now Jo is a member of the *New York Times* team that specializes in computer-assisted reporting. She is still putting to good use the principles and techniques of social science that she learned in grad school.

If reporters' field experiments are to be successful, they must follow the same guidelines—and avoid the same pitfalls—that scientists' experiments must. A little scientific jargon is necessary here. It is fairly straightforward, though, and will be useful if you ever have the opportunity to set up an experiment.

Your field experiment must have a **hypothesis**, a statement of what you expect to find. Your hypothesis must be stated clearly and simply. When it is, it will help focus your attention on the two elements of the experiment: the independent variable and the dependent variable. The **variables**, just as their name implies, are the things that change during the experiment. The *independent variable* is what you think may be a cause. You change it and observe what happens to the *dependent variable*, the effect.

Let's look again at the search for bias in renting. As a social scientist, you would state the hypothesis you're testing: "Landlords in our town discriminate against renters of color." The independent variable is race. The dependent variables are the forms of security, the kinds of identification and the rents charged to each team. You're looking to see how differences in the variable of race affect the dependent variables.

There are two other steps you must take to ensure a successful experiment. First, you must **control** the experiment. Every aspect of the experiment must be carefully structured to make sure that any change you observe is caused only by the independent variable you want to test. For example, your teams of would-be "renters" must be as much alike as possible in the financial details they provide, the way they dress, their gender and their age. Otherwise, any differences in the responses by the landlords might be due to something other than race, the variable you are interested in. Also, the applicants should visit the same landlords and speak to the same officials. Without careful control of the experiment, you may end up being unable to say whether you supported your hypothesis or not. Then you've got no story.

The other step is called **randomization**, or random selection. In a small town you could run your experiment with every landlord. But in a big city that would be impossible. So if you want to be reasonably sure that the results of the experiment apply to all the landlords in town, you must choose at random the ones to approach. Randomization allows you to assume that what you select—10 rental agencies, for instance—is representative of the whole (the total number of landlords in the city).

Choosing anything at random simply means that you employ a method for choosing that gives every person or thing an equal chance of being picked. The procedure for making a random selection is beyond the scope of an introductory reporting text. The Suggested Readings at the end of the chapter include several books in which you can find that and other material relating to the concepts introduced here. Much of that other material deals with statistics. Many experiments require statistical analysis to ensure that what you have found is significant. Most polls and surveys require some statistical analysis, too. Explanations of the fairly simple math involved also can be found in the books listed in Suggested Readings.

PUBLIC OPINION POLLS

Surveying is a powerful journalistic tool. At the beginning of the chapter, we examined an example of its misuse. Despite such problems, more journalists, politicians, businesses and scholars are using poll results because they show more reliably than anecdotes or ordinary interviews what the public thinks about important issues. Many news organizations now go beyond reporting the findings of

Lies, Damned Lies and Statistics

Get your facts first, and then you can distort them as much as you please.

— Mark Twain

Sometimes reporters distort the facts without even trying.

The *San Jose Mercury News* reported that women are "10 times more likely to be represented on the Supreme Court of the United States than on the average board of directors for a company in Silicon Valley." The *Mercury News* based that statement on the fact that 22.2 percent of the justices were women, compared with 2.9 percent of Silicon Valley directors.

But there were about 135 million women in the United States; two of them were Supreme Court justices, and 30 of them were Silicon Valley directors. Thus, despite the paucity of women on Silicon Valley boards, the likelihood of a woman being represented there was actually 15 times greater than on the Supreme Court.

In its effort to illustrate a point, the *Mercury News* stumbled into an error that is common in newspapers. It generalized to the entire population (all U.S. women) from figures that applied only to subpopulations (women on the Supreme Court and Silicon Valley boards). What the *Mercury News* should have said was that the "ratio of women to men on the Supreme Court is nearly 10 times greater than on the boards of directors of Silicon Valley companies."

The lesson from the *Mercury News* story is that even when you think you're comparing apples to apples, make sure you don't have some oranges in there. You must have the same base population for a comparison to mean anything.

Here are some other ways statistics can deceive:

Bias can influence the credibility of a survey. For example, a national survey on sexual behavior indicated that 1 percent of 3,321 men questioned said they were gay, compared with the 10 percent commonly accepted as constituting the gay population. When reporting the survey results, *Time* magazine pointed out that people might be reluctant to discuss their sexual orientation with a "clipboard-bearing stranger."

One year does not a trend make. A large increase in the number of rapes merits a story, but it might represent a fluctuation rather than a trend. Depending on the subject matter, you need to study at least five to 10 years of data to determine whether there is a significant shift.

The way organizations compile figures can change, and that can distort comparisons. In the late 1980s, the formula for compiling AIDS cases among heterosexuals was changed. The figures skyrocketed, as did the number of media reports on the spread of AIDS to the general population. Not all the reports noted the change in compiling the statistics.

Conclusions that sound credible might not hold up under the scrutiny of cause and effect. Advocacy groups that call for less violence on television say studies show TV violence causes violence in children. They cite research at Yale showing that prolonged viewing of violent programs is associated with aggressive behavior among children. But the association could be that children who tend to be aggressive watch more violent programming, not the other way around.

---

national polling firms such as the Gallup and Louis Harris organizations to conducting or commissioning their own surveys. Several journalism schools — including those at the universities of Alabama, Florida, North Carolina and Missouri — have developed scientific polling operations staffed by faculty and students to serve newspapers and broadcasters.

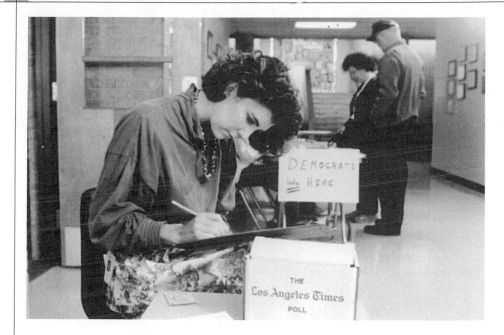

Polling voters on election day is an excellent way to forecast election results. However, polls must be conducted properly and interpreted carefully to produce reliable information.

When polls are conducted properly and reported carefully, they can tell people something they could not know otherwise and perhaps even help to produce wiser public policies. But when they are badly done or sloppily reported, polls can be bad news for journalists and readers alike.

The chances are good that sometime in your reporting career you will want to conduct an opinion poll or at least help with one your newspaper is conducting. The Suggested Readings listed at the end of the chapter will tell you much of what you need to know for that. Even if you never work a poll, you almost certainly will be called on to write about the results of polls. What follows will help you understand what you are given and will help you make sure your readers understand it, too.

Requirements for Sound Polling

The Associated Press Managing Editors Association prepared a checklist of the information you should have and should share with your audience about any poll on which you are reporting. Several of their points require some explanation.

- **Identity of the sponsor.** The identity of the survey's sponsor is important to you and your readers because it gives some clues to possible bias. Most people would put more trust in a Gallup or Harris poll's report that, for instance, Smith is far ahead of Jones in the presidential campaign than they would in a poll sponsored by the Smith for President organization.

TIPS

"Average" Can Mean Different Things to Different People

In reporting statistics, be certain you know the "average" involved. All of the following are averages:

- **Mean.** The arithmetic average, found by adding all the figures in a set of data and dividing by the number of figures. The mean of 2, 4 and 9 is 5 (2 + 4 + 9 = 15; 15 ÷ 3 = 5).

- **Median.** The middle value in a set of figures. If there is no middle value because there is an even number of figures, average the two middle numbers. The median of 2, 4 and 9 is 4. The medians of 5, 7, 9 and 11 and of 3, 7, 9 and 15 both are 8 (7 + 9 = 16; 16 ÷ 2 = 8).

- **Mode.** The most frequent value in a set of figures. The mode of 2, 5, 5, 5, 15 and 23 is 5.

- **Exact wording of the questions.** The wording of the questions is important because the answer received often depends at least in part on how the question was asked (see Chapter 3 on interviewing for more detail). The answer might well be different, for example, if a pollster asked, "Whom do you favor for president, Jones or Smith?" rather than "Wouldn't Jones make a better president than Smith?"

- **Population.** In science, the *population* is the total number of people — or documents or milkweed plants or giraffes — in the group being studied (see Chapter 6). For an opinion survey, the population might be all registered voters in the state, black males under 25 or female cigarette smokers. To understand what the results of a poll mean, you must know what population was studied. The word "sampled" refers to the procedure in which a small number — or sample — of people is picked at random so as to be representative of the population.

- **Sample size and response rate.** The sample size is important because — all other things being equal — the larger the sample, the more reliable the survey results should be. The response rate is especially important in surveys conducted by mail, in which a low rate of response may invalidate the poll.

- **Margin of error.** The *margin of error* of any survey is the allowance that must be made for the possibility that the opinion of the sample may not be exactly the same as the opinion of the whole population. Another name for it is "sampling errors." The margin of error depends mainly on the size of the sample. For instance, all other things being equal, a sample of 400 would have a margin of error of 5 percent, and a sample of 1,500 would have a margin of error of 3 percent. If, with a sample of 1,500, the poll shows Jones with 60 percent of the votes and Smith with 40 percent, you can be confident that Jones actually has between 57 and 63 percent and Smith actually has between 37 and 43 percent. The laws of probability say that the chances are 19 to 1 that the actual percentages fall within that range. Those odds make the information good enough to publish.

- **Which results are based on part of the sample.** The problem of sampling error helps explain why it is important to know which results may be based on only part of the sample. The smaller that part is, the greater the margin of error. In political polls, it is always important to know whether the results include responses from all eligible voters or only from individuals likely to vote. The opinions of the likely voters are more important than others' opinions.

- **When the interviews were collected.** When the interviews were collected may be of critical importance in interpreting the poll. During campaigns, for example, the candidates themselves and other events may cause preferences to change significantly within a few days. Think of presidential primaries. As candidates join or drop out of the race, support for each of the other candidates changes. A week-old poll may be meaningless if something dramatic happened after it was taken. Candidates have been known to use such outdated results to make themselves appear to be doing better than they really are, or their opponents worse. Be on guard.

"Next question: I believe that life is a constant striving for balance, requiring frequent tradeoffs between morality and necessity, within a cyclic pattern of joy and sadness, forging a trail of bittersweet memories until one slips, inevitably, into the jaws of death. Agree or disagree?"

Some pollsters' questions seem designed to elicit a desired response.

- **How the interviews were collected.** When the poll is your newspaper's, the obligation remains to let your readers know how it was taken. It is also incumbent on the paper to reveal how reliable the poll is.

The Need for Caution in Interpreting Polls

Whether you are helping to conduct a survey or only reporting on one produced by someone else, you must exercise caution. Be on guard for the following potential problems:

- **The people interviewed must be selected in a truly random fashion if you want to generalize from their responses to the whole population.** If they are not, you have no assurance that the interview subjects are really representative. The old-fashioned people-in-the-street interview is practically worthless as an indicator of public opinion for this reason. The man or woman in the street probably differs in important ways from all those men and women who are not in the street when the questioner is.

Also invalid are such "polls" as the questionnaires members of Congress mail to their constituents. Only strongly opinionated—and therefore unrepresentative—people are likely to return them. For the same reason, the "question-of-the-day" feature that some newspapers and broadcast stations ask you to respond to online tells you nothing about the opinions of the great mass of people who do not respond. Even worse are the TV polls that require respondents to call a 900 number to register their opinions. Because there is a charge for such calls, these pseudo-polls produce not only misleading results but profits that encourage their use.

- **The closer the results, the harder it is to say anything definitive.** Look again at the example of the Smith-Jones campaign. Suppose the poll showed Smith with 52 percent and Jones with 48 percent of the vote. Smith may or may not be ahead. With the 3 percent margin of error, Smith could actually have only 49 percent, and Jones could have 51 percent. All that you could report safely about those results is that the race is too close to call. Many reporters—and pollsters—are simply not careful enough when the outcome is unclear.

- **Beware of polls that claim to measure opinion on sensitive, complicated issues.** Many questions of morality, or social issues such as race relations, do not lend themselves to simple answers. Opinions on such matters can be measured, but only by highly skilled researchers using carefully designed questions. Anything less can be dangerously oversimplified and highly misleading.

Surveying, like field experiments, systematic analysis and participant observation, can help you as a reporter solve problems you could not handle as well by other techniques. But these are only tools. How effectively they are used—or how clumsily they are misused—depends on you.

Suggested Readings

Campbell, Donald and Stanley, Julian. *Experimental and Quasi-Experimental Designs for Research.* Skokie, Ill.: Rand McNally, 1966. A classic guide to field experimentation that is also useful in providing a better understanding of scientific research.

Demers, David Pearce and Nichols, Suzanne. *Precision Journalism: A Practical Guide.* Newbury Park, Calif.: Sage, 1987. A primer for students and journalists, simply written and complete with examples.

Houston, Brant. *Computer-Assisted Reporting*, Third Edition. New York: Bedford/St. Martin's, 2004. A practical introduction to data analysis and field reporting.

McCombs, Maxwell, Shaw, Donald L. and Grey, David. *Handbook of Reporting Methods.* Boston: Houghton Mifflin, 1976. Offers examples of real-life uses of social science methods in journalism but does not provide enough on statistics to serve as a guide in employing the methods.

Meyer, Philip. *Precision Journalism*, Fourth Edition. Lanham, Md.: Rowman and Littlefield, 2002. A detailed introduction to surveying, conducting field experiments and using statistics to analyze the results, by a reporter who pioneered the use of these methods in journalism. The theoretical justification of the techniques is included as well.

Seltzer, Richard A. *Mistakes That Social Scientists Make.* New York: St. Martin's Press, 1996. A useful book about the kinds of errors often made by social scientists during their research.

Williams, Frederick. *Reasoning with Statistics.* New York: Holt, Rinehart and Winston, 1979. A nonintimidating but sufficiently complex guide to using mathematical tools.

Suggested Web Sites

www.aejmc.org
The Association for Education in Journalism and Mass Communication is the professional organization of journalism teachers and researchers. For a journalist or journalism student, perhaps the most useful feature of this site are the links to the research publications of the organization. Many of the reports in those publications use, and explain, the techniques discussed in this chapter.

www.gallup.com
The Gallup organization is one of the most reputable of the national polling companies. This site contains results of a wide variety of public polls, along with their methodology.

http://people-press.org
This is the site of the Pew Research Center for the People and the Press. Here you'll find not only poll results but explanations of methodology and limitations.

Exercises

1. Go to the **ire.org** or **nicar.org** Web site, and find at least one story that uses one or more of the social science techniques discussed in this chapter. Analyze the reporting and writing. What are the differences from a story that relies on interviewing? What possible sources of practical or ethical problems can you find?

2. Find a newspaper story that reports on the results of a public-opinion poll. Analyze the story using the guidelines discussed in this chapter.

3. Using the technique described by Philip Meyer in *Precision Journalism* (see the Suggested Readings), design a simple survey. Write a memo outlining your plan.

4. Design a field experiment: State your hypothesis, identify the dependent and independent variables, and describe the controls you will use.

5. As a class project, carry out one of the surveys designed in response to exercise 3.

6. Analyze the data you collected in exercise 5 using SPSS or a similar software package. As a final step, write the story of your findings.

Investigative Reporting

18

IN THIS CHAPTER
YOU WILL LEARN:

1. The process of investigative reporting.

2. How to find and use human and written sources.

3. The obstacles you will face as an investigative reporter.

When Howard Kurtz, media reporter for *The Washington Post* and CNN, wanted to illustrate the impact of investigative reporting, all he had to do was scan a few days of headlines. His findings:

- Three *Los Angeles Times* reporters disclosed how U.S. Rep. Curt Weldon of Pennsylvania used his influence on behalf of two Russian companies that paid close to $1 million a year to the lobbying firm of Weldon's daughter. The FBI followed with its own investigation.

- Brian Ross of ABC broke the story of Mark Foley, the Florida congressman who sent sexually suggestive e-mails to teenaged pages in the House of Representatives. Foley promptly resigned his seat.

- *The San Diego Union-Tribune* revealed that another congressman, Randy Cunningham of California, had sold his home for $700,000 above market value to a defense contractor he had helped win Pentagon business. Cunningham pleaded guilty to taking bribes and went to prison.

- *The Washington Post* uncovered questionable lobbying by Jack Abramoff and his ties to two prominent congressmen. Abramoff pleaded guilty to charges of fraud and conspiracy to commit bribery. One of the congressmen, Tom DeLay, resigned his position as majority leader and his seat in the House. The other, Bob Ney, pleaded guilty to conspiracy and making false statements.

And that's just in Washington. Across the country, good reporters use technology and the law, along with shoe-leather reporting, to tell important, hidden stories. The Internet spreads those stories around the world and permits instant response and passionate debate. The public is both informed and involved. Public policy may change. These and thousands of other journalists are doing difficult, important work. They're serving society.

Investigative reporting has a rich tradition in American journalism. The fiercely partisan editors of the Revolutionary era dug for facts as well as the mud they hurled at their opponents. In the early 20th century, investigative reporting flowered with the "muckrakers," a title bestowed angrily by Theodore Roosevelt and worn proudly by journalists. Lincoln Steffens explored the undersides of American cities, one by one, laying bare the corrupt combinations of businessmen and politicians that ran them. Ida Tarbell exposed the economic stranglehold of the oil monopoly. Theodore Dreiser, Upton Sinclair and Frank Norris revealed the horrors of working life in factories and meatpacking plants.

Their professional heirs today bring to the work the same commitment to exposure and reform. They use refinements of many of the same techniques: in-depth interviews, personal observation, analysis of documents. But modern muckrakers have a powerful tool their predecessors didn't dream of. The computer allows reporters today to compile and analyze masses of data, to perform complicated statistical tests, and to create charts and graphs to enhance understanding. This tool, in turn, requires of reporters numeracy as well as literacy. It requires the addition of another set of skills to every serious journalist's repertoire.

Ida Tarbell, one of the original muckrakers, helped set the pattern for investigative reporting with her exposé of Standard Oil.

Computer-assisted reporting gives young reporters the opportunity to be admitted to the major league of journalism. If you develop your computer-research skills and acquire the techniques taught in this chapter, you will be equipped for the 21st century.

THE PROCESS

Most investigations start with a hunch or a tip that something or someone deserves a close look. If a preliminary search bears out that expectation, a serious investigation begins. When enough information has been uncovered to prove or modify the reporter's initial hunch, it's time to analyze, organize and write the story.

Beginning the Investigation

No good reporter sets out on an investigation unless there is some basis for suspicion. That basis may be a grand jury report that leaves something untold or a tip that some public official is on the take. It may be a sudden upsurge in drug overdoses, or it may be long-festering problems in the schools. If you don't have some idea of what to look for, an investigation is too likely to turn into a wild-goose chase.

Acting on the tip or suspicion, together with whatever background material you have, you form a hypothesis. Reporters hardly ever use that term, but it is a useful one because it shows the similarity between the processes of investigative reporting and scientific investigation (see Chapter 17). In both, the hypothesis is the statement of what you think is true. Your informal hypothesis might be "The mayor is a crook" or "The school system is being run incompetently." It is a good idea to clearly state your hypothesis when you begin your investigation. By doing so, you focus on the heart of the problem and lessen the possibility of any misunderstanding with your editor or other reporters who may be working with you.

Once the hypothesis is stated, the reporter—like the scientist—sets out to support it or show that it is not supportable. You should be open to the possibility that your first assumption was wrong. Reporters—like scientists—are not advocates. They are seekers of truth. No good reporter ignores or downplays evidence just because it contradicts his or her assumptions. In journalism, as in science, the truth about a situation is often sharply different from what is expected. Open-mindedness is an essential quality of a good investigative reporter. Remember, too, that you may have a good story even if your hypothesis is not supported.

Carrying Out the Investigation

The actual investigative work usually proceeds in two stages. The first is what Robert W. Greene, a legendary reporter and Pulitzer Prize-winning editor for *Newsday*, named the **sniff.** In this stage, you nose around in search of a trail worth following. If you find one, the second stage, serious investigation, begins.

Preliminary checking should take no more than a day or two. Its purpose is not to prove the hypothesis but to find out the chances of proving it. You make that effort by talking with the most promising source or sources, skimming the most available records and consulting knowledgeable people in your news room. The two questions you are trying to answer at this stage are these: (1) "Is there a story here?" and (2) "Am I going to be able to get it?" If the answer to either question is no, there is little point in pursuing the investigation.

When the answer to both questions is yes, however, the real work begins. It begins with organization. Your hypothesis tells you where you want to go. Now you must figure out how to get there. Careful organization keeps you on the right track and prevents you from overlooking anything important as you go. Many reporters take a kind of perverse pride in their illegible notebooks and cluttered desks. As an investigative reporter, you may have a messy desk, but you should arrange your files of information clearly and coherently. Begin organizing by asking yourself these questions:

- Who are my most promising sources? Who is likely to give me trouble? Whom should I go to first? Second? Last?
- What records do I need? Where are they? Which are public? How can I get to the ones that are not readily accessible?
- What is the most I can hope to prove? What is the least that will still yield a story? How long should the investigation take?

TIPS

Carrying Out the Investigation

- Be organized. Careful organization keeps you on the right track and prevents you from overlooking anything important.

- Draw up a plan of action. Write out a plan; then go over it with your editor.

- Carry out your plan, allowing flexibility for the unexpected twists that most investigations take.

- Be methodical. The method you use isn't important as long as you understand it.

Then draw up a plan of action, such as the one shown in Figure 18.1. Experienced reporters often do this mentally. But when you are a beginner, it's a good idea to write out a plan and go over it with your editor. The editor may spot some holes in your planning or have something to add. And an editor is more likely to give you enough time if he or she has a clear idea of what has to be done.

Allowing flexibility for the unexpected twists that most investigations take, carry out your plan. During your first round of interviews, keep asking who else you should talk to. While you are checking records, look for references to other files or other people.

Be methodical. Many investigative reporters spend an hour or so at the end of every day adding up the score, going through their notes and searching their memories to analyze what they have learned and what they need next. Some develop elaborate, cross-indexed files of names, organizations and incidents. Others are less formal. Nearly all, however, use a code to disguise the names of confidential sources so that those sources will remain secret even if the files are subpoenaed. The method you use isn't important as long as you understand it. What is vitally important is that you have a method and use it consistently. If you fail to keep careful track of where you're going, you may go in the wrong direction, or in circles.

Getting It Right

The importance of accuracy in investigative reporting cannot be overstated. It is the essential element in good journalism of any kind. But in investigative reporting especially, inaccuracy leads to embarrassment, to ruined reputations and, sometimes, to lawsuits. The reputations ruined are often those of the careless reporter and newspaper. Most investigative stories have the effect of accusing somebody of wrongdoing or incompetence. Even if the subject is a public official whose chances of suing successfully for libel are slim (see Chapter 22), fairness and decency require that you be sure of your facts before you put them in print.

During the Watergate investigation, *The Washington Post* followed the policy of requiring verification from two independent sources before an allegation could be published. That is a good rule to follow. People make mistakes. They lie. Their memories fail. Documents can be misleading or confusing. Check and double-check. There is no good excuse for an error.

Writing the Story

Most investigative stories require consultation with the newspaper's lawyer before publication. As a reporter, you will have little or nothing to say about the choice of your paper's lawyer. That lawyer, though, will be an important part of your investigative career. The lawyer advises on what you can print safely and what you cannot. Most editors heed their lawyer's advice. If you are lucky, your paper's lawyer will understand and sympathize with good, aggressive journalism. If he or she does not, you may find yourself forced to argue for your story. You will be better equipped for such an argument—few reporters go through a career without several—if you understand at least the basics of the laws of libel and privacy.

2/28/08   Plan for Mayor Jane Jones story

Hypothesis: Mayor Jones accepted improper campaign contributions from Top Construction as a council member, and as mayor she later awarded the company a contract to build a new high school.

Initial source: During the course of a conversation, XX casually suggested info about the campaign contribution.

Draft: Due 3/7

Questions
--How much of this hypothesis can I prove?
--Is XX trustworthy? What does XX have to gain? Will XX go on record?
--Will documents support the hypothesis? What records are important?
--What other people should I interview—on both sides?
--Will I have at least two credible sources for each fact?
--How can I make sure the story is relevant, useful and interesting?
--Is this one story or a series?

Plan
Request and review relevant documents:
--Any docs from XX.
--Campaign contribution records; get Stacy to help w/this.
--Contract bids for HS; ask Manuel how to compare.

Interview major people:
--XX, to follow up on initial info.
--Schools chancellor about bids.
--Mayor's campaign manager (Roberts?) about contributions.
--Pres. of Top Construction (Smythe?) about contributions.
--Mayor.

Write outline:
--What's the lead?
--Story structure: inverted pyramid?
--Enough facts? details? anecdotes?

Write draft:
--Is the story complete? easy to follow? convincing? compelling?

Next steps:
--Editor? legal document?
--Need more facts? details?
--Revise and finalize draft?

Figure 18.1
A plan of action lists the hypothesis and the steps the journalist will take to gather information and draft a story.

Chapter 22 outlines those laws, and several good books on law for journalists are listed in the Suggested Readings at the end of that chapter.

The last step before your investigation goes public is the writing and rewriting. After days or weeks of intense reporting effort, the actual writing strikes some investigative reporters as a chore—necessary but unimportant. That attitude is disastrous. The best reporting in the world is wasted unless it is read. Your hard-won exposé or painstaking analysis will disappear without a trace unless your writing attracts readers and maintains their interest. Most reporters and newspapers that are serious about investigative reporting recognize this. They stress good writing almost as much as solid reporting.

> **"**Go to the scene of the disaster and don't let the breaking story stop you from thinking ahead. There, you will find almost all of the sources to tell you what went wrong in responding to the disaster. Though you will have to get your proof through public-record requests, you will get your leads at the scene.**"**
>
> —James Grimaldi, *The Washington Post*

How do you write the results of a complicated investigation? The general rule is, as simply as you can. One approach is to use a **hard lead** (an inverted pyramid lead that reports newly discovered facts), displaying your key findings in the first few paragraphs. Another choice, often used, is to adopt one of the alternative approaches to storytelling explained in Chapter 9.

Mei-ling Hopgood helped report and write a *Dayton Daily News* investigation of the dangers of the Peace Corps. Here's how that series began:

AGUA FRIA, El Salvador—On a clear Christmas night near a moonlit stretch of Pacific beach, a man with a pistol came from the darkness and forced Diana Gilmour to watch two of her fellow Peace Corps volunteers being gang-raped while a male volunteer was pinned helpless on the ground.

One of the men—his breath reeking of alcohol—raped Gilmour, too. Then the attackers herded the volunteers at gunpoint to a field of high grass where they feared they would be executed.

"I was constantly waiting to hear a shot in the dark," Gilmour said.

Suddenly another volunteer approached with a flashlight, and the attackers fled.

The best stories are usually about people, and this one is no exception. The drama of one case introduces readers to the bigger story. A few paragraphs later Hopgood and colleague Russell Carollo show that big picture:

Records from a never-before-released computer database show that reported assault cases involving Peace Corps volunteers increased 125 percent from 1991 to 2002, while the number of volunteers increased by 29 percent, according to the Peace Corps.

Last year, the number of assaults and robberies averaged one every 23 hours.

The *Dayton Daily News* spent 20 months examining thousands of records on assaults on Peace Corps volunteers occurring around the world during the past four decades. . . .

Moving from the particular to the general is both a logical progression and an effective way to show readers both the humanity and the full scope of the investigation. Notice that the last paragraph also lets readers know something about how the information was developed. That's important, too, if you want to be believed. (In this case, the paper's editor also wrote a column explaining both the motivation and the methods of the investigation. That's another good idea. You owe it to your audience to be as open as possible about not only what you know but how you know it. In this era of diminished credibility, it's especially important to do everything you can to be honest and open about your work.)

Writing an investigative story so that it will be read takes the same attention to organization and to detail as does any good writing. Here are a few tips that apply to all types of writing but especially to investigative stories:

- **Get people into the story.** Any investigation worth doing involves people in some way. Make them come alive with descriptive detail, the kind we were given in the Peace Corps story.

- **Keep it simple.** Look for ways to clarify and explain complicated situations. When you have a mass of information, consider spreading it over more than one story—in a series or in a main story with a sidebar. Think about how charts, graphs or lists can be used to present key facts clearly. Don't try to print everything you know. Enough to support your conclusions is sufficient; more than that is too much.

- **Tell the reader what your research means.** A great temptation in investigative reporting is to lay out the facts and let the reader draw the conclusions. That is unfair to you and your reader. Lay out the facts, of course, but tell the reader what they add up to. A reporter who had spent weeks investigating the deplorable conditions in his state's juvenile corrections facilities wrote this lead:

  Florida treats her delinquent children as if
  she hated them.

  Then he went on to show the reality that led to that summary. If the facts are there, drawing the obvious conclusions is not editorializing. It is good and helpful writing.

- **Organize.** Careful organization is as important in writing the investigative story as in reporting it. The job will be easier if you have been organized all along. When you are ready to write, examine your notes again. Make an outline. Pick out your best quotes and anecdotes. Some reporters, if they are writing more than one story, separate their material into individual folders, one for each story. However you do it, know what you are going to say before you start to write.

- **Suggest solutions.** Polls have shown that readers prefer investigative stories that show how to correct the problems described in the stories. Many of today's best newspapers are satisfying readers' demands by going beyond exposure in search of solutions. Are new laws needed? Better enforcement of present laws? More resources? Better training? Remember that the early-20th-century Progressive movement (of which the original muckrakers were a part) produced reforms, not just good stories.

Think of writing as the climax of a process that begins with a hypothesis, tests that hypothesis through careful investigation, checks and double-checks every fact, and satisfies the concerns of newspaper editors and lawyers. Every step in that process is vital to the success of any investigative story.

THE SOURCES

Investigative reporters—like other reporters—get their information from people or documents. The perfect source would be a person who has the pertinent documents and is eager to tell you what those documents mean. Don't count on finding the perfect source. Instead, count on having to piece together the information you need from a variety of people and records—some of the people not at all eager to talk to you and some of the records difficult to obtain and, if you do gain access to them, difficult to understand. Let's consider human sources first.

Human Sources

Suppose you get a tip that the mayor received campaign contributions under the table from the engineering firm that just got a big city contract. Who might talk?

- **Enemies.** When you are trying to find out anything bad about a person, his or her enemies are usually the best sources. More often than not, the enemies of a prominent person will have made it their business to find out as much as possible about that person's misdeeds and shortcomings. Frequently, they are happy to share what they know with a friendly reporter.

- **Friends.** Friends are sometimes nearly as revealing as enemies. In trying to explain and defend their friend's actions, they may tell you more than you knew before. Occasionally you may find that someone your subject regards as a friend is not much of a friend after all.

- **Losers.** Like enemies, losers often carry a grudge. Seek out the loser in the last election, the losing contender for the contract, the loser in a power struggle. Bad losers make good sources.

- **Victims.** If you are investigating a failing school system, talk with students and their parents. If your story is about nursing home abuses, talk with patients and their relatives. The honest and hard-working employees caught in a corrupt or incompetent system are victims, too. They can give you specific examples and anecdotes. Their case histories can help you write the story. Be wary, though. One thing enemies, losers and victims have in common is that they have an ax to grind about your subject. Be sure to confirm every allegation they make.

- **Experts.** Early in many investigations, there may be a great deal that you don't understand. You may need someone to explain how the campaign finance laws could be circumvented, someone to interpret a contract, someone to decipher a set of bid specifications. Lawyers, accountants, engineers or professors can help you understand technical jargon or complicated transactions. If they refuse to comment on your specific case, fit the facts you have into a hypothetical situation.

- **Police.** Investigative reporters and law-enforcement agents often work the same territory. If you are wise, you will make friends with carefully selected agents. They can—and frequently will—be of great help. Their files may not be gold mines, but they have investigative tools and contacts you lack. When they get to know and trust you, they will share. Most police like seeing their own and their organization's names in the paper. They know, too, that you can do some things they cannot. It takes less proof for you to be able to print that the mayor is a crook than it may take to convince a jury. Most police investigators want to corner wrongdoers any way they can. You can use that attitude to your advantage.

- **People in trouble.** Police use this source and so can you, although you cannot promise immunity or a lesser charge, as prosecutors can. A classic case is the Watergate affair, in which members of President Richard Nixon's administration recruited five men to break into the headquarters of the Democratic National Committee to wiretap phones illegally. Once the Nixon administration started to unravel, officials trying to save their careers and images began falling all over each other to give their self-serving versions of events. People will react similarly in lesser cases.

As an investigative reporter, you cultivate sources in the same ways a reporter on a beat does. You just do it more quickly. One excellent tactic is to play on their self-interest. Losers and enemies want to get the so-and-so, and thus you have a common aim. (But don't go overboard. Your words could come back to haunt you.) Friends want their buddy's side of the story to be explained. So do you. If you keep in mind that no matter how corrupt your subject may be, he or she is still a human being, it may be easier to deal sympathetically with that person's friends. That attitude may also help ensure that you treat the subject fairly.

Experts just want to explain the problem as you present it. And you just want to understand. People in trouble want sympathy and some assurance that they still merit respect. No reporter should have trouble conveying either attitude.

Another way to win and keep sources is to protect them. Occasionally a reporter faces jail unless he or she reveals a source. Even jail is not too great a price to pay to keep a promise of confidentiality. More often, the threats to confidentiality are less dramatic. Other sources, or the subject of the investigation, may casually ask, "Where'd you hear that?" Other reporters, over coffee or a beer, may ask the same question. Hold your tongue. The only person to whom a confidential source should ever be revealed is your editor.

Human sources pose problems as well as solve them. To hurt an enemy or protect a friend, to make themselves look better or someone else look worse—and sometimes simply for fun—people lie to reporters. No reporter is safe and no source is above suspicion. They may use you, too, just as you are using them. The only reason most people involved on any side of a suspicious situation will talk about it is to enhance their own position. That is neither illegal nor immoral, but it can trip up a reporter who fails to take every self-serving statement with the appropriate grain of salt.

Sources may change their stories as well. People forget. Recollections and situations change. Pressures can be applied. Fear or love or ambition or greed can intrude. A source may deny tomorrow—or in court—what he or she told you today.

Finally, sources will seldom want to be identified. Even the enemies of a powerful person are often reluctant to see their names attached to their criticisms in print. So are friends. Experts, while willing to provide background information, often cite their codes of ethics when you ask them to go on the record. Stories without identifiable sources have less credibility with readers, with editors, even with colleagues.

Written Sources

Fortunately, not all sources are human. Records and documents neither lie nor change their stories, they have no axes to grind at your expense, and they can be identified in print. Many useful documents are public records, available to you or any other citizen on request. Others are nonpublic but still may be available through your human sources.

Public Records

As the examples earlier show, a great deal can be learned about individuals and organizations through records that are available for the asking, if you know where to ask. Let's take a look at some of the most valuable public records and where they can be found.

- **Property records.** Many investigations center on land—who owns it, who buys it, how it is zoned, how it is taxed. You can find out all that information and more from public records. Your county recorder's office (or its equivalent) has on file the ownership of every piece of land in the county as well as the history of past owners. Most such offices have their files cross-indexed so that you can find out the owner of the land if you know its location, or the location and size of the property if you know the owner. Those files also will tell you who holds a mortgage on the land. The city or county tax assessor's office has on file the assessed valuation of the land, the basis for property taxes. Either the assessor or the local zoning agency can tell you for what use the property is zoned. All requests for rezoning are public information, too.

- **Corporation records.** Every corporation must file with the secretary of state a document showing the officers and principal agent of the company. The document must be filed with every state in which the company does business. The officers listed may be only "dummies," stand-ins for the real owners. Even if that is the case, you can find out at least who the stand-ins are. But that is only the beginning. Publicly held corporations must file annual reports with the Securities and Exchange Commission in Washington. The reports list officers, major stockholders, financial statements and business dealings with other companies owned by the corporation. Nonprofit corporations—such as foundations and charities—must file with the Internal Revenue Service an even more revealing statement, Form 990, showing how much money came in and where it went. Similar statements must be filed with the attorneys general of many states. Corporations often are regulated by state or federal agencies as

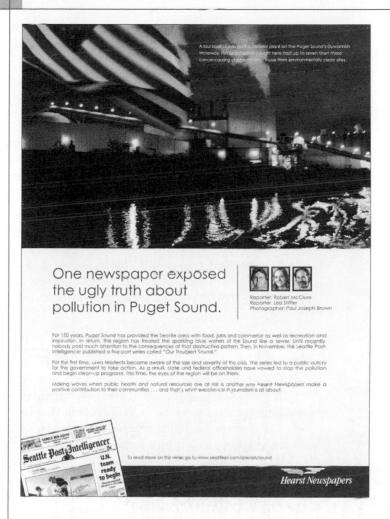

Investigative reporters have uncovered scandals and illegal activity and raised public awareness of issues like water pollution.

well. They file regular reports with the regulating agency. Insurance companies, for instance, are regulated by state insurance commissioners. Nursing homes are regulated by various state agencies. Broadcasters are overseen by the Federal Communications Commission, truckers by the Interstate Commerce Commission. Labor unions must file detailed statements showing assets, officers' salaries, loans and other financial information with the U.S. Department of Labor. Those statements are called "5500 Forms."

Once you have such corporation records, you must interpret them. Your public library has books that tell you how. Or your newspaper's own business experts may be willing to help.

- **Court records.** Few people active in politics or business go through life without some involvement in court actions. Check the offices of the state and federal court clerks for records of lawsuits. The written arguments, sworn statements and answers to questions (interrogatories) may contain valuable details or provide leads to follow. Has your target been divorced? Legal struggles over assets can be revealing. Probate court files of your subject's deceased associates may tell you something you need to know.

- **Campaign and conflict-of-interest reports.** Federal—and most state—campaign laws now require political candidates to disclose, during and after each campaign, lists of who gave what to whom. Those filings can yield stories on who is supporting the candidates. They also can be used later for comparing who gets what from which officeholder. Many states require officeholders to file statements of their business and stock holdings. These can be checked for possible conflicts of interest or used as background for profile stories.

- **Loan records.** Commercial lenders usually file statements showing property that has been used as security for loans. Known as Uniform Commercial Code filings, these can be found in the offices of state secretaries of state and, sometimes, in local recorders' offices.

- **Minutes and transcripts.** Most elected and appointed governing bodies, ranging from local planning and zoning commissions to the U.S. Congress, are required by law to keep minutes or transcripts of their meetings.

Using and Securing Public Records

The states and the federal government have laws designed to ensure access to public records. Many of these laws—including the federal **Freedom of Information Act,** which was passed to improve access to government records—have gaping loopholes and time-consuming review procedures. Still, they have been and can be useful tools when all else fails. Learn the details of the law in your state. You can get information on access laws and their interpretations by contacting the Freedom of Information Center at the University of Missouri, 127 Neff Annex, Columbia, MO 65211.

Nonpublic Records

Nonpublic records are more difficult, but often not impossible, to obtain. To get them, you must know that they exist, where they are and how to gain access. Finding out about those things requires good human sources. You should know about a few of the most valuable nonpublic records:

- **Investigative files.** The investigative files of law-enforcement agencies can be rich in information. You are likely to see them only if you have a good source in a particular agency or one affiliated with it. If you do obtain such files, treat them cautiously. They will be full of unsubstantiated allegations, rumor and misinformation. Be wary of accepting as fact anything you have not confirmed yourself.

- **Past arrests and convictions.** Records of past arrests and convictions increasingly are being removed from public scrutiny. Usually these are easier than investigative files to obtain from a friendly police or prosecuting official. And usually they are more trustworthy than raw investigative files.

- **Bank records.** Bank records would be helpful in many investigations, but they are among the most difficult types of records to get. Bankers are trained to keep secrets. The government agencies that regulate banks are secretive as well. A friend in a bank is an investigative reporter's friend indeed.

- **Income tax records.** Except for those made public by officeholders, income tax records are guarded carefully by their custodians, and properly so. Leaks are rare.

- **Credit checks.** Sometimes you can get otherwise unavailable information on a target's financial situation by arranging through your newspaper's business office for a credit check. Credit reports may reveal outstanding debts, a big bank account, major assets and business affiliations. Use that information with care. It is unofficial, and companies that provide it intend it to be confidential.

Problems with Written Sources

Even when you can obtain them, records and other written sources present problems. They are usually dull. Records give you names and numbers, not anecdotes or sparkling quotes. They are bare bones, not flesh and blood. They can be misleading and confusing. Many highly skilled lawyers and accountants spend careers interpreting the kinds of records you may find yourself pondering without their training. Misinterpreting a document is no less serious an error than misquoting a person. And it's easier to do.

Documents usually describe without explaining. You need to know the "why" of a land transaction or a loan. Records tell you only the "what."

Most investigative reporters use both human and documentary sources. People can explain what records cannot. Documents prove what good quotes cannot. You need people to lead you to documents and people to interpret what the documents mean. And you need records to substantiate what people tell you. The best investigative stories combine both types of sources.

NEW TOOLS, TRADITIONAL GOALS

As you've seen, the computer is the most important new tool of investigative reporting. Once you know how to use it, the computer allows you to obtain, analyze and present information in ways that would have been impossible 20 years ago, let alone in the era of the original muckrakers. But useful as it is, the computer is only a tool. Many modern investigative reporters are guided by goals that their predecessors of a century ago would easily recognize.

Today's investigators, like the original muckrakers, are not satisfied with uncovering individual instances of wrongdoing. They tend to want to look at organizations as a whole, at entire systems. They seek not only to expose but to explain. In many cases, they also seek to change the problems and abuses they reveal. Many, perhaps most, investigative reporters think of themselves as more than chroniclers of fact or analysts. They also see themselves as reformers. This, too, was true of the muckrakers.

ON THE JOB

Leading Readers Through the Maze

Karen Dillon entered journalism through the back door — literally. She began in the back shop of a small paper in Iowa. After working her way into the news room, she decided to go to college, where she earned degrees in political science and journalism. After school, she got a job covering the police in Florida. Now she works at *The Kansas City Star*, on the special projects desk.

"I have noticed one overarching theme," she says. "Many public agencies are doing something their leaders don't want the public to know about. In other words, public agencies can be anything but. The luxury — and the burden — of my job is that I am given the time and means to become the public's microscope. I question the bureaucrats, follow the money and take our readers into the sometimes-working maze of their governments."

She began following the money into the maze of drug-law enforcement after she spotted a case in which the Missouri Highway Patrol stopped a vehicle on Interstate 70 and found a large amount of cash. The Patrol seized the money, saying it was the proceeds from drug sales, even though no drugs were ever found and no one was charged. Then the Patrol turned the money over to the federal Drug Enforcement Administration, which kept 20 percent and returned the rest to the Patrol, which kept it.

The Missouri Constitution, like laws in other states, requires such seized money to be used for public education. Karen decided to investigate the frequency of such financial sleight-of-hand between law-enforcement agencies. "Pulling reports in more than 200 seizure cases in Missouri, we found that the I-70 case was typical — police usually circumvented the law when they seized cash and gave it to the feds without getting court approval."

Her stories prodded Missouri lawmakers to act, filing bills to plug the loophole. The U.S. attorney, embarrassed, called a press conference to attack her work. Karen and the *Star* were not deterred.

Karen broadened her reporting, using the Internet to access forfeiture laws in all 50 states. She used Justice Department statistics to build a database showing that millions of dollars were involved. She learned that local law-enforcement agencies across the country were getting federal help to circumvent state laws and use seized cash to finance their own activities. In 35 states, that was against the law.

The national story, titled "To Protect and Collect," drew widespread public response. Meanwhile, a Missouri appeals court ruled that the police were, indeed, breaking the law.

And Karen is leading her readers through other mazes.

In Chapter 17, you met Jo Craven McGinty, who used her computer-assisted reporting skills to help *The Washington Post* win a Pulitzer Prize for a team investigation of the misuse of firearms by police. In this chapter, the On the Job feature introduces Karen Dillon, whose lengthy investigation of the trickery that allowed police agencies to keep millions of dollars that should have gone to public schools combined the tools of computer analysis with the passion for reform.

This drive to expose abuses is something the public welcomes and expects from journalists. Studies have shown that the consumers of journalism support investigative reporting when it leads to reforms. There's no conflict between investigative reporting and the journalistic standard of objectivity, either. You'll remember from Chapter 1 that objectivity doesn't have to mean neutrality. In journalism as in science, objectivity is the method of searching for the truth. Just as scientists are not expected to be neutral between disease and cure, journalists don't have to be neutral between good and evil. What objectivity requires of both scientists and journalists is honest, open-minded investigation and truthful reporting of the results of that investigation.

THE OBSTACLES

You have seen now why investigative reporting is important and how it can be done. The picture would not be complete, though, without a brief look at the reasons why not every newspaper or broadcast organization does investigative reporting. As a reporter, you will face certain obstacles. You and your editors will have to overcome them if you are to do real investigative reporting. Good newspapers and news broadcasters do overcome such obstacles.

Money and Staffing

The first obstacle is money. Investigative reporting is the most expensive kind of reporting. It takes time, and time is money. When Howard Kurtz listed the investigative projects that began this chapter, he was worrying that continuing cuts in staff and budget in many news rooms are removing the resources required for serious reporting. He pointed to staff cutbacks at *The Dallas Morning News, The (Cleveland) Plain Dealer,* NBC and his own *Washington Post.* Usually, the reporters doing investigations are the paper's or station's best and highest paid. Frequently, fees for experts are involved. Lawyers charge for looking over a story and much, much more if a suit is filed. Space to publish the results costs money, too.

The second obstacle is staffing. Most newspapers and broadcast organizations, large or small, are understaffed even before the budget cuts begin. When a reporter is devoting time to an investigation, somebody else must be found to fill the gap. Many editors are unable or unwilling to adjust for prolonged absences by a key reporter. You may be able to get around that obstacle by doing your investigating in bits and pieces, keeping up with routine assignments all the while. That kind of part-time probing requires a high level of dedication from you and your editor. Such commitment is hard to sustain over long stretches of time.

Lack of Courage

The third obstacle is a lack of courage. This is the great inhibitor. Investigative reporting means disturbing the status quo. It means poking into dark corners, asking hard questions about controversial, sensitive affairs. Investigative reporting upsets people. If you are looking into the right things, the people who get upset are likely to be important.

Violence or the threat of violence directed toward reporters and newspapers in this country is rare. The 1975 murder of investigative reporter Don Bolles in Phoenix was shocking partly because such things hardly ever happen. In many other countries, investigative reporters routinely risk death or imprisonment. The Committee to Protect Journalists (cpj.org) publishes regular reports on reporters killed or harassed. In the United States, economic or social pressure, usually applied to your editor or publisher, is common enough. It takes courage to stand up to such pressure.

The Nixon administration threatened the lucrative television licenses of the Washington Post Co. during the Watergate investigation. The federal government sued *The New York Times*, *The Boston Globe* and *The St. Louis Post-Dispatch* to prevent publication of the *Pentagon Papers*. FBI and CIA agents investigated newspapers and harassed reporters during the era of Vietnam and Watergate. Those were dramatic cases. The papers involved were big and rich, and they resisted.

Other pressures are directly economic. After the *San Jose Mercury News* published a buyer's guide to getting the best deals on cars, automobile dealers pulled ads worth millions of dollars. The paper's publisher issued an apology, although there were no serious inaccuracies in the report. You can imagine how the newspaper's staff felt.

More common and less visible are the social pressures and social influence of editors' and publishers' peers. It is common for the top executive of a newspaper to associate socially with the political and business leaders who may be the targets of investigative reporting. It is also common for the reporters who work for those executives to be pulled off such stories.

If you find yourself on a paper lacking money or staff, you can still find ways to do investigative reporting, at least part-time, if you want to badly enough. But if you find yourself on a paper lacking courage, you have only two choices: give up or leave.

Fortunately, investigative reporting is so important and its rewards are so substantial that more reporters than ever are finding the support to do it. You can, too.

Suggested Readings

Houston, Brant. *Computer-Assisted Reporting*, Third Edition. New York: Bedford/St. Martin's, 2004. Invaluable how-to guide for using the newest and most powerful reporting tool. Houston is executive director of Investigative Reporters and Editors Inc.

Houston, Brant. *The Investigative Reporters' Handbook*, Fourth Edition. New York: Bedford/St. Martin's, 2002. Tells you how to get and how to use the most important records and documents.

The IRE Journal. Publication of Investigative Reporters and Editors Inc., 138 Neff Annex, Missouri School of Journalism, University of Missouri, Columbia, MO 65211. Every issue has articles on investigations, guides to sources and documents, and a roundup of legal developments. Edited transcripts of IRE conferences are also available.

Rose, Louis J. *How to Investigate Your Friends and Enemies.* St. Louis: Albion Press, 1981. Very good on the nuts and bolts of investigating.

Williams, Paul. *Investigative Reporting and Editing.* Upper Saddle River, N.J.: Prentice Hall, 1978. A classic, good on both how and why to investigate.

Suggested Web Sites

www.ire.org
Begin here. Investigative Reporters and Editors, headquartered at the University of Missouri, is the world's leading source of expertise, story ideas and professional and personal support for investigative reporters.

www.nicar.org
The National Institute for Computer-Assisted Reporting, a partnership of IRE and the Missouri School of Journalism, teaches the skills and provides the consulting you'll need to get and analyze the data for richer, more revealing stories.

www.opensecrets.org
The Center for Responsive Politics specializes in collecting, analyzing and making available information on money and politics. The center's handbook, "Follow the Money," is an invaluable resource for any reporter interested in the impact of money on self-government.

Exercises

1. On the **ire.org** Web site, find the stories that have won recent IRE awards. Choose one story from each of at least three categories. Compare the sources and techniques used. What similarities and differences do you find in different media? Which stories seem to you most complete and most satisfying? Why?

2. School board member Doris Hart reported at last week's meeting of the board that major flaws, including basement flooding and electrical short circuits, have shown up in the new elementary school. She noted that this is the third straight project designed by consulting architect Louis Doolittle in which serious problems have turned up. School Superintendent Margaret Smith defended Doolittle vigorously. Later, Hart told you privately that she suspects Doolittle may be paying Smith off to keep the consulting contract, which has earned the architect more than $100,000 per year for the past five years.

Describe how you will investigate:
a. The sniff.
b. Human sources. Who might talk? Where should you start? Whom will you save for last?
c. What records might help? Where are they? What will you be looking for?
d. What is the most you can hope to prove? What is the least that will yield a story?

3. Choose a public official in your city or town, and compile the most complete profile you can, using only public records.

4. Use one or more of the computer databases described in Chapter 5 to learn as much as you can about your representative in Congress. Write the most complete investigative profile you can from the databases. In a memo, explain what additional information you'd need to complete your story and where it might be found.

Writing News for
Radio and Television

19

Hurricane Katrina was a made-for-TV event.

Yes, newspapers carried headlines and stories and graphic photos, Web sites did that and more, and blogs contributed grassroots reporting and monitored the mainstream media, but it was television and, to a lesser extent, radio that did what they do best. They told and showed what was really happening before, during and after the devastation.

Katrina did more than make the news. Nora Gallagher wrote on latimes.com that "the story of New Orleans broke through the gloss of business as usual on television." She added:

> I don't think we are fully aware, no matter how many times it is said, of how television (and print) news creates a bubble in which stories are not actually reported as they are, but to fit a prescribed idea of what news should be.
>
> Katrina blew that away. We got the story of what is really happening in the United States right between the eyes. We got the story of how poor people live and are treated in this country by watching them suffer and die. We got the story because it happened so fast, and right in front of our faces, and no one could put a spin on it quickly enough. We got the story because television reporters were openly outraged on camera. We got the story because reporters asked real questions and demanded real answers, rather than throwing softballs and settling for the fluff and the spin that pass for news. It was raw, it was awful, and it slid under the skin of our sleepy, numb, feel-good lives.

Radio and television did what they do best: They told the world the details of what happened. Moreover, they were able to repeat their reports and update their audience as the news developed. If you tuned in to CNN, you not only saw what happened and listened to commentary, you also saw additional headlines streaming below the picture on a ticker tape. You could pay attention to the news you were most interested in, and you had the feeling you were up-to-date about what was happening. The anchor reminded viewers to go to the network's Web site for more information.

Of course, radio and television reporters are not always present to record the news while it is happening. Much of the time, these journalists must write and report news after it has occurred. Many, if not most, radio and television stations provide at least some news that is written by journalists working for the wire services, such as the Associated Press or Reuters.

Selecting and writing news for these media is different from selecting and writing news for print. This chapter explores the differences and discusses news reporting and writing for television and radio. Even if your primary emphasis is not radio and television news, in this day of converging media in news rooms, you may be called upon to work with radio and television reporters and even to prepare copy for their reports. And if you are writing for radio or television news, almost certainly you will be called upon to contribute to the station's Web site. Radio and television stations have expanded their news operations to give background for stories they don't have time to air. Rather than interrupt programming when new facts arrive on a developing story, they often send listeners and viewers to their Web sites.

CRITERIA FOR SELECTING RADIO AND TELEVISION NEWS

All of the news criteria you have learned so far apply to the selection of print and broadcast news. However, four criteria distinguish radio and television news selection from print news: These newswriters emphasize timeliness above all other news values, information more than explanation, news with audio or visual impact, and people more than concepts.

Timeliness

The radio and television newswriter emphasizes one criterion of news value more than any other: timeliness. *When* something happens often determines whether a news item will be used in a newscast. The breaking story receives top priority.

Radio and television news "goes to press" many times a day. If an event is significant enough, regular programming can be interrupted. The sense of immediacy influences everything in radio news, from what is reported to how it is reported. Often this is true of television news. Even when television and radio air documentaries or in-depth segments, they typically try to infuse a sense of urgency, a strong feeling of the present, an emphasis on what's happening now.

Information

Timeliness often determines why a news item is broadcast; time, or lack of it, determines how it is reported. Because airtime is so precious, radio and television reporters are generally more concerned with information than with explanation. Most stories must be told in 20 to 30 seconds; rarely does a story run longer than two minutes. A minute of news read aloud is only 15 lines of copy, or about 150 words. After you subtract time for commercials, a half-hour newscast has only 22 minutes of news, which amounts to about one-half of the front page of a newspaper. Although radio and television newswriters may never assume that their audience knows anything about a story, they may often have to assume that listeners or viewers will turn to newspapers, newsmagazines or the Internet for further background and details.

Of course, because of the long success of *60 Minutes* and because of relatively low production costs, newsmagazine formats such as *20/20*, *48 Hours* and *Dateline NBC* continue to proliferate. *Dateline NBC* now runs twice a week. These programs represent a somewhat different challenge to television newswriters, but even in a newsmagazine format, the writing resembles that done for television news.

Audio or Visual Impact

Another difference between radio and television and print news results from the technologies involved. Some news is selected for radio because a reporter has recorded an on-the-scene audio report. Some news is selected for television because it is visually appealing or exciting. For this reason, news of accidents or of fires that may get attention only in the records column of the newspaper may get important play on a television newscast. If a television crew returns with good pictures of an event, that event often receives prominence in the next newscast.

People

Another important difference between radio and television and print news selection is that radio and television more often attempt to tell the news through people. They follow the classic writing formula described by Rudolf Flesch in *The Art of Readable Writing*: Find a problem, find a person who is dealing with the problem, and tell us how he or she is doing. These journalists look for a representative person or family, someone who is affected by the story or who is a chief player. Thus, rather than using abstract concepts with no sound or visuals, television in particular humanizes the story. You can't shoot video of an issue.

WRITING RADIO AND TELEVISION NEWS

Radio and television writing emphasizes certain characteristics that newspaper and online writing do not, and story structure may vary.

Characteristics of Radio and Television Newswriting

Because of the emphasis on timeliness, radio and television newswriters, like online writers, must emphasize immediacy and try to write very tightly and clearly. However, radio and television newswriters must work harder at achieving a conversational style.

Immediacy

Radio and television newswriters achieve a sense of immediacy in part by using the present tense as much as possible. Note the use of present-tense verbs (italicized) in this Associated Press story.

WASHINGTON (AP)—More evidence that *there's* room for improvement in urban public schools.

A government study *shows* elementary and middle school children in major cities *perform* worse in science than other students around the country.

Ten urban school districts volunteered to have their students tested and compared with other public school children nationwide. Eighth graders in all ten cities, and fourth graders in all but one, had scores below the national average.

Michael Casserly *heads* a coalition of urban public school districts and *says* more energy *needs* to be devoted to science education. He *says* no one in the country "*has* much bragging rights" when it *comes* to the subject.

The report *underscores* concerns that a lack of scientific achievement could hurt the U-S economy.

Some all-news radio stations serve their communities with news and commentary 24 hours a day. Many allow listeners to voice their opinions.

Notice that, for accuracy, the past tense is sometimes necessary, as in the paragraph beginning "Ten urban school districts . . ." But radio and television writers like to use the progressive form of the verb ("is using," "was using," "will be using") to show continuing action and the present perfect tense ("have used") more than the past tense because, again, the present perfect indicates past action that is continuing.

Sometimes you stress immediacy by saying, "just minutes ago" or, on a morning newscast, "this morning." If there is no danger of inaccuracy or deceit, though, you can omit references to time. For example, if something happened yesterday, you may report it like this:

> The latest rash of fires in southern California is under control.

But if you use the past tense in a lead, you should include the time element.

> The legislature sent a welfare reform bill to the governor late last night. It finished just in time before the spring recess.

The best way to avoid the past tense is to avoid yesterday's story. You can do that by updating yesterday's story. By leading with a new development or a new fact, you may be able to use the present tense.

Remember, radio and television are "live." Your copy must convey that important characteristic.

Conversational Style

Although "write the way you talk" is questionable advice for most kinds of writing, with some exceptions, it is imperative for radio and television writing. "Read your copy aloud" is good advice for most kinds of writing; for radio and television writing, that's what it's all about.

Write so that your copy *sounds* good. Use simple, short sentences, written with transitive verbs in the active voice. Transitive verbs do things *to* things; they demand an object. People rarely use verbs in the passive voice when they talk; it usually sounds cumbersome and awkward. You don't go around saying, "Guess what I was just told by somebody." "Was told" here indicates the passive voice; the subject is being acted upon. Note the preposition "by" also tells you the verb is in the passive voice. "Guess what somebody just told me" is active and more natural, less wordy and stronger. "Told" is in the active voice; the subject is doing the acting.

> **"**Good television journalism presents news in the most attractive and lucid form yet devised by man.**"**
>
> — Bill Small, veteran broadcaster, former president of CBS News

Because casual speech contains contractions, an occasional contraction is OK, too, as long as your pronunciation is clear. The negative "not" is more clearly understood than when you use it as a contraction. Conversational style also permits the use of occasional fragments. Sentences are sometimes strung together loosely with dashes and sometimes begin with the conjunction "and" or "but," as in the following example from the Associated Press:

> (Spring Lake, North Carolina)—Aubrey Cox keeps
> giving police the slip. But he's had lots of practice—
> he's been doing it for 41 years.

Writing in conversational style does not mean that you may use slang, colloquialisms or incorrect grammar. Nor does it mean that you can use vulgar or off-color expressions. Remember that your audience includes people of all ages, backgrounds and sensitivities.

Tight Phrasing

You must learn to write in a conversational style without being wordy. That means you must condense. Use few adjectives and adverbs. Reduce the use of the passive voice to save a couple of words. Make each word count.

Keeping it short means selecting facts carefully because often you don't have time for the whole story. Radio and television newscasters want good, tight writing that is easy to follow. Let's look at how a wire story written for newspapers can be condensed for radio and television. Look at this newspaper wire story.

ST. CHARLES — The husband of a former St. Charles County prosecutor faces a drug charge after police said he was growing 359 marijuana plants in the basement of their Portage des Sioux home.

Max Conley, 42, of the 900 block of Pawnee Drive, was charged Tuesday with producing a controlled substance, a felony. He is married to Ella Boone Conley, who was put on administrative leave on Aug. 25, pending the results of the investigation. She resigned on Sept. 26 and now works for a law firm in St. Peters.

Her attorney has said she didn't know about the marijuana and was only living there part time because of problems between the couple.

The investigation began after the St. Charles County Regional Drug Task Force got information that Max Conley was growing marijuana. A detective went to the house on Aug. 24 and Conley gave him permission to search the home. The detective found the plants in the basement "in various stages of growth," according to court documents, and he also found lights, wiring, chemicals, potting soil and pots being used to grow the plants.

The court documents said Conley admitted growing the marijuana.

A warrant was issued Tuesday for his arrest, and bail was set at $25,000. At the request of St. Charles County Prosecuting

Attorney Jack Banas, a special prosecutor from the St. Louis circuit attorney's office, Jeannette Graviss, headed the investigation.

Graviss said Tuesday that there was not enough evidence to charge Ella Boone Conley and that she was not home when police went to the house. She said Max Conley did not have a job.

Banas did not want to talk about specifics of the case but said it was Boone Conley's decision to resign from his office. He also said the entire situation has been difficult to deal with.

Boone Conley's attorney, Joe Green, said in an interview in September that she resigned to protect the integrity of the St. Charles County prosecuting attorney's office. He also said she was planning to file for divorce. She had filed for divorce in 2002, but the case was later dismissed.

Conley's attorney, Joe McCulloch, said Conley would turn himself in this morning but would not comment further.

Green and Boone Conley could not be reached for comment Tuesday. Conley also could not be reached.

Boone Conley, 44, had worked as an assistant prosecutor in St. Charles County for 13 years and ran unsuccessfully for the Republican nomination for associate circuit judge in the Aug. 8 primary.

Most recently, she had headed the child support enforcement unit.

Here's how the story appeared on the Associated Press *broadcast* wire in its entirety:

ST. CHARLES, Mo. (AP) — The husband of a former St. Charles County prosecutor is accused of growing 359 marijuana plants in the basement of their home.

Forty-two-year-old Max Conley was charged yesterday with felony producing a

controlled substance. Conley's attorney says he plans to turn himself in this morning. He is married to Ella Boone Conley, who resigned from the prosecutor's office September 26th amid the investigation.

She ran unsuccessfully for the Republican nomination for associate circuit judge in the August eighth primary and now works for a law firm in St. Peters.

Her attorney says she was unaware of the marijuana and was only living in the home part time because of domestic problems. Ella Boone Conley has not been charged in the case.

In the broadcast version, listeners are given just the bare facts. They must turn to their newspapers or online news source for the details. One newspaper story is often two or three broadcast stories and can sometimes be a half dozen online stories.

In radio and television news, tight writing is important even when there is more time. These writers usually strive to waste no words, even in documentaries, which provide in-depth coverage of events.

Clarity

Unlike readers of newspaper and Internet news sources, television and radio news audiences can't go back over the copy. They see or hear it only once, and their attention waxes and wanes. So you must try hard to be clear and precise. All of the emphasis on condensing and writing tightly is useless if the message is not understood.

> *Short words are best, and old words, when short, are best of all.*
>
> — Winston Churchill

Clarity demands that you write simply, in short sentences filled with nickel-and-dime words. Don't look for synonyms. Don't be afraid to repeat words or phrases. Oral communication needs reinforcement. Avoid foreign words and phrases. Avoid phrases like "the former" and "the latter." Repeat proper names in the story rather than use pronouns. The listener can easily forget the name of the person to whom the pronoun refers.

When you are tempted to write a dependent clause in a sentence, make it an independent clause instead. Keep the subject close to the verb. Close the gap between the doer and the activity. This version doesn't do that:

> A man flagged down a Highway Patrol officer near Braden, Tennessee, today and told him a convict was hiding in his house. The prisoner, one of five who escaped from the Fort Pillow Prison on Saturday, surrendered peacefully.

The second sentence contains 12 words between the subject, "prisoner," and the main verb, "surrendered." By the time the broadcaster reaches the verb, many listeners will have forgotten what the subject was. The story is easier to understand this way:

> A man flagged down a Highway Patrol officer near Braden, Tennessee, today and told him a convict was hiding in his house. The prisoner surrendered peacefully. He's one of five who escaped from the Fort Pillow Prison on Saturday.

The third sentence is still a complex sentence ("who escaped . . ." is the dependent clause), but it is more easily understood. A complex sentence is often just that—complex—only more so in oral communication.

Clarity also requires that you resist a clever turn of phrase. Viewers and listeners are probably intelligent enough to understand it, but a good figure of speech takes time to savor. If listeners pause to savor it (if they grasped it in the first place), they will not hear what follows. Clever columnists often fail as radio commentators.

Even more dangerous than figures of speech are numerical figures. Don't barrage the listener or viewer with a series of numbers. If you must use statistics, break them down so that they are understandable. For example, it is better to say that one of every four Americans smokes than to say there are 47 million smokers in the United States. You may be tempted to say how many billion dollars a federal program will cost, but you will help listeners understand if you say that it will cost the average wage earner $73 for each of the next five years.

Story Structure

Now that you know the characteristics of radio and television writing, let's examine the story structure. Writers must craft television and radio leads somewhat differently from the way they cast print and online leads. They also must construct special introductions and conclusions to video or audio segments and synchronize their words with taped segments.

Christiane Amanpour is CNN's chief international correspondent. Her authoritative reports from around the world have informed millions.

Writing the Radio and Television Lead

Like newspaper reporters, television and radio reporters must grab the attention of their audience. Much of what you learned in Chapter 7 applies to radio and television leads. But be aware that people tend to be doing other things when listening to radio or watching television, so when you write for them, you strive to attract their attention in different ways.

One way is by preparing your audience for what is to come. You cue listeners to make sure they are tuned in. You introduce the story with a general statement, something that will pique the interest of the audience; then you go to the specifics. For example:

> **General:** Things are far from settled for Springfield's teacher strike.
> **Specifics:** School officials and union representatives did not agree on a contract yesterday. They will not meet again for at least a week.

Sometimes the opening sentence will cover a number of news items:

> There were several accidents in the Springfield vicinity today.

"Cuing in" is only one method of opening a radio or television story. Other leads go immediately into the "what" and the "who," the "where" and the "when." In radio or television news, the "what" is most important, followed by "who" did the "what." The time and place may be included in the lead, but seldom is the "why" or the "how." If time permits, the "why" and the "how" may come later in the story, but often they are omitted.

The first words of the lead are the most important. Don't keep the listener guessing as to what the story is about. Don't begin with a dependent clause or with a prepositional phrase as in this example:

> *With the strong backing of Governor Sebelius,* a second state spending-limit bill is scheduled for final Senate action today.

The opening words are meaningless without what comes later. The listener may not know what you are talking about. Here is a better way to introduce this story:

> The Senate will vote today to make deeper cuts in state spending — with the strong backing of Governor Sebelius.

Be sure to "tee up," or identify, an unfamiliar name. By introducing a person, you prepare listeners for the name they otherwise may miss. Do it this way:

> *Veteran Kansas City, Kansas, businessman and civic leader* Ivar Larson died yesterday in a nursing home at age 83.

Don't mislead. The opening words must set the proper tone and mood for the story. Attract attention; tease a little. Answer questions, but don't ask them. Lead the listener into your story.

Writing Lead-Ins and Wrap-Ups

Radio and television journalists must learn how to write a **lead-in** that introduces a taped excerpt from a news source or from another reporter. The functions of a lead-in are to set the scene by briefly telling the "where," the "when" and sometimes the "what," and to identify the source or reporter. The lead-in should contain something substantive. Here's an example:

> A grand jury has decided not to charge a Springfield teenager in the killing of his father. Jan Morrow reports the panel believes the death was an accident.

Lead-ins should generate interest. Sometimes several sentences are used to provide background, as in the following:

> We'll all be getting the official word this morning on how much less our dollars bought last month. The consumer price index for March is expected to show another sharp rise in retail prices. The rate of inflation was one percent in January and one-point-two percent in February. Here's more on our inflation woes from Bill McKinney.

Be careful not to include in the lead-in what is in the story. Just as a headline should not steal word for word the lead of a newspaper story, the lead-in should not rob the opening words of the correspondent. The writer must know the contents of the audio report in order to write a proper lead-in.

After the recorded report, you may want to wrap up the story before going on to the next item. The **wrap-up** is especially important in radio copy because there are no visuals to identify the person just heard. If the story reported by Evelyn Turner was about a meeting to settle a strike, you might wrap up Turner's report by adding information:

> Turner reports negotiations will resume tomorrow.

A wrap-up like this gives your story an ending and clearly separates it from the next story.

Writing to the Video

Writing for a video report begins with the selection of the subject and deciding how it is to be shot. The writing continues through the editing process and is done with the pictures clearly in mind.

Words and pictures must be complementary, never interfering with each other, never ignoring each other. Your first responsibility is to relate the words to the pictures. If you do not, viewers will not get the message because they will be wondering what the pictures are about.

You can, however, stick too closely to the pictures by pointing out the obvious in a blow-by-blow account. You need to avoid both extremes and use what Russ Bensley, formerly of CBS News, calls the "hit-and-run" technique. This means that at the beginning of a scene or when a scene changes, you must tell the viewer where you are or what is happening. Once you are into the scene, the script may be more general and less closely tied to the pictures.

Suppose the report concerns the continuation of a hospital workers' strike and the opening scene shows picketers outside the hospital. You can explain the tape by saying:

> **"**Writing a silence is as important as writing words. We don't rely on video enough.**"**
>
> —John Hart, veteran NBC broadcaster

> Union members are still picketing Mercy Hospital today as the hospital workers' strike enters its third week.

Viewers now know two things that are not obvious on the video: who is picketing and where. If the video switches to people sitting around a table negotiating, you must again set the scene for viewers:

> Meanwhile, hospital administrators and union leaders are continuing their meetings—apparently without success.

Once you have related the words to the pictures, you may add other details of the strike. You must not only comment on the video but complete it as well. Part of completing it is giving the report a wrap-up or a strong ending. Don't be cute, and don't be obvious, but give the story an ending. Here's one possible ending for the strike story:

> Strikers, administrators, patients and their families agree on one sure effect of the strike—it's a bad time to be sick.

Now that you know some principles of writing radio and television news, let's learn how to prepare the copy.

PREPARING RADIO AND TELEVISION COPY

Preparing copy to be read by a newscaster is different from preparing it for a typesetter. Your goals are to make the copy easy for the newscaster to read and easy for the audience to understand. What follows will help you accomplish these two goals.

Format

Most radio and television news editors want triple-spaced copy. Leave two to three inches on the top of the page and one to two inches on the bottom.

For radio copy, set your computer so that you have 70 characters to a line (see Figure 19.1). Each line will average about 10 words, and the newscaster will average 15 lines per minute. Start each story on a separate piece of paper. That way, the order of the stories can be rearranged, and stories can be added or dropped easily. If a story goes more than one page, write "MORE" in parentheses at the bottom of the page.

Write television copy on the right half of the page in a 40-character line (see Figure 19.2). Each line will average about six words, and the newscaster will average about 25 lines per minute. Use the left side of the copy for audio or video information. This information, which is not to be read by the newscaster, is usually typed in all caps. The copy that is read generally appears upper- and lowercase. In television copy, number the stories, and start each story on a separate page. If a story goes more than one page, write "MORE" in parentheses at the bottom of the page.

Do not hyphenate words, and be sure to end a page with a complete sentence or, if possible, with a complete paragraph. Then if the next page should be missing in the middle of a newscast, the newscaster could at least end with a complete sentence or paragraph.

At most stations, you prepare copy for a teleprompter, an electronic device that projects the copy over the camera lens so the newscaster can read it while appearing to look straight into the lens.

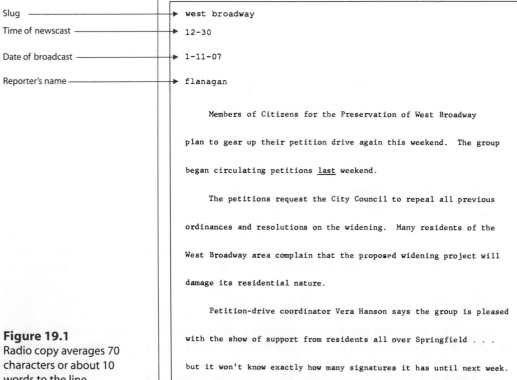

Slug — west broadway
Time of newscast — 12-30
Date of broadcast — 1-11-07
Reporter's name — flanagan

    Members of Citizens for the Preservation of West Broadway

plan to gear up their petition drive again this weekend. The group

began circulating petitions <u>last</u> weekend.

    The petitions request the City Council to repeal all previous

ordinances and resolutions on the widening. Many residents of the

West Broadway area complain that the proposed widening project will

damage its residential nature.

    Petition-drive coordinator Vera Hanson says the group is pleased

with the show of support from residents all over Springfield . . .

but it won't know exactly how many signatures it has until next week.

Figure 19.1
Radio copy averages 70 characters or about 10 words to the line.

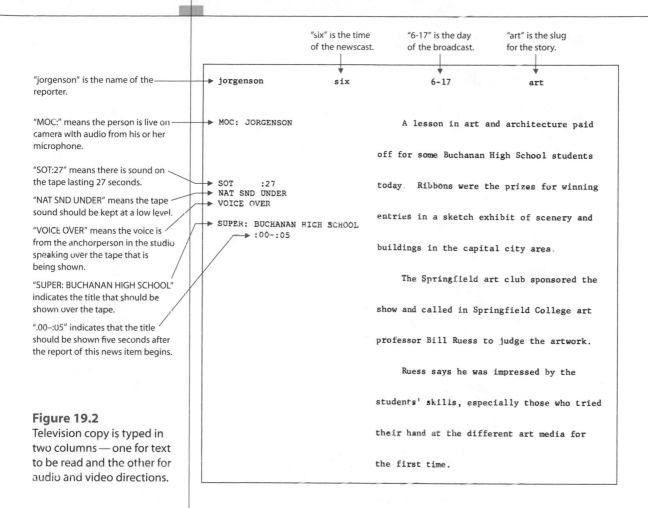

"jorgenson" is the name of the reporter.

"MOC:" means the person is live on camera with audio from his or her microphone.

"SOT:27" means there is sound on the tape lasting 27 seconds.

"NAT SND UNDER" means the tape sound should be kept at a low level.

"VOICE OVER" means the voice is from the anchorperson in the studio speaking over the tape that is being shown.

"SUPER: BUCHANAN HIGH SCHOOL" indicates the title that should be shown over the tape.

":00–:05" indicates that the title should be shown five seconds after the report of this news item begins.

"six" is the time of the newscast.

"6-17" is the day of the broadcast.

"art" is the slug for the story.

```
jorgenson              six              6-17              art

MOC: JORGENSON                    A lesson in art and architecture paid

                          off for some Buchanan High School students

SOT     :27               today.  Ribbons were the prizes for winning
NAT SND UNDER
VOICE OVER                entries in a sketch exhibit of scenery and

SUPER: BUCHANAN HIGH SCHOOL
       :00-:05            buildings in the capital city area.

                              The Springfield art club sponsored the

                          show and called in Springfield College art

                          professor Bill Ruess to judge the artwork.

                              Ruess says he was impressed by the

                          students' skills, especially those who tried

                          their hand at the different art media for

                          the first time.
```

Figure 19.2
Television copy is typed in two columns — one for text to be read and the other for audio and video directions.

Date the first page of your script, and type your last name in the upper left-hand corner of every page. Stations vary regarding these directions. The newscast producer determines the **slug** for a story and its placement. Some producers insist that the slug contain the time of the broadcast. If a story continues to a second page, write under the slug "first add" or "second add," or "page 2," "page 3" and so forth.

Stations with computerized news rooms may use scripting software that alters these formats somewhat.

Names and Titles

In radio and television style, unlike that followed by newspapers, well-known names, even on first reference, are not given in full. You may say Senator Dole of North Carolina or Governor Napolitano of Arizona. Don't use middle initials unless they are a natural part of someone's name (Edward R. Murrow) or unless they are necessary to distinguish two people with the same first and last names, as with George W. Bush.

ON THE JOB

Writing News for Radio and Television

Bernard Choi works as the government reporter and fill-in anchor for KWCH (CBS) in Wichita, Kan. Before that, he spent two years on the education beat at KWCH. During the summer of his sophomore year in college, he interned at WPSD (NBC) in Paducah, Ky. There he won first place in the Randolph Hearst Journalism Awards in television news. He also won first place in the Education Writers Association's Television Hard News category.

"I was a wide-eyed reporter straight out of college," Choi says. "When my new boss offered me a full-time on-air reporting position, I jumped at the chance. The excitement apparently paralyzed my hearing, as I failed to listen to his one condition: I would have to cover a beat, the education beat.

"I had never covered a beat. I never took a beat-reporting class. I didn't know what covering a beat entailed."

Three years, two beats and countless mistakes later, Choi says, "I realized I was in way over my head. But I'm glad no one caught on and that they gave me the chance to discover the most rewarding type of journalism. It allows you to dig the story up from the ground before it appears in a news release or the news wires.

"When other television reporters in the market scrambled when a story hit the newspaper, I was already on it. It's not because I am a better journalist. It's because I did all the hard work and legwork that led up to it."

Covering a beat involves all the mundane tasks: reading city-council agendas, reading planning reports and zoning regulations, trying to decipher state and district test scores, keeping up with boring school newsletters, reading state laws. You don't always get rewarded with a great story, Choi says, but it's the breadth of knowledge and expertise you develop in an area that pays off in the long run.

The most important lesson Choi learned from covering a beat is you have to talk to people. "I'm generally a shy person with people I don't know. In the past two years, I have had to force myself to walk up to strangers and chat. Stories are

Titles should always precede names so that listeners are better prepared to hear the name. When you use titles, omit the first name and middle initial. For example, you would say Federal Reserve Chairman Bernanke and Justice Ginsburg.

Pronunciation

You must help the newscaster pronounce the names of people and places correctly. To do this, write out difficult names phonetically in parentheses. MSNBC has its own reference list, and many individual stations have their own handbooks. Look up difficult names in unabridged dictionaries. If you don't find the name there, about people, and what better way to find a story than to talk to people. More often than not, you will get a story from someone who is plugged in a lot faster than trying to search public records."

A good example came one lazy afternoon. "I already had a story for the day, and I had time to spare at City Hall. I had made a personal resolution to talk more often with the city-council members. Because I had an hour to spare, I went to the council office to hunt a council member down. Once I got there I was told everyone had gone to lunch. Disappointed, I started walking to my car. Then I turned back and headed up to the cafeteria, where I spotted one council member. I hesitated at the door. I had already eaten, and I didn't want to interrupt. After five minutes of internal debate, I bought a lunch and sat next to the council member and started making small talk.

Thirty minutes later, Choi found out the U.S. Attorney's Office was in town covertly investigating former council members for questionable oversight; the city was ready to offer incentives to bring in a major corporation; a top city official was steering business to his wife's firm; and the council member's daughter was headed off to a prestigious college on the East Coast.

"There have been other conversations that netted absolutely nothing," he says. "I've wasted many a precious hour talking with an official and wasted many a night looking through agendas. But I've learned it's that one conversation, it's reading an extra page of a city report, it's that extra phone call that makes the difference. I've learned this because I've also been on the losing end."

The people, the organization and the beat you cover will appreciate the extra work. When you go the extra step to really understand the issue, they know. They can tell when you've done your homework and when you're slacking off. You are dealing with their lives. They don't owe you anything. If you don't take them seriously, they will treat you in kind. It's not just makeup and hairspray. This is a serious enterprise.

Choi's final advice: Journalists should say thanks every now and then.

---

call the person's office, or the consulate or embassy. If the name is of a U.S. town, try calling someone in that town. There is no rhyme or reason to the way some people pronounce their names or to the way some names of places are pronounced. Never assume. Never guess. Find out. Here's an example of how you should write out difficult names:

ZAMBOANGA, Philippines (AP) — There's been another deadly bombing in the Philippines.

A bomb exploded near a Roman Catholic church in the southern city of Zamboanga (zahm-BWAHNG'-gah), killing one person and injuring 12.

Perhaps most people would know how to pronounce Lima (LEE-mah), Peru, but not everyone would correctly pronounce Lima (LIE-mah), Ohio. You must note the difference between NEW-erk, N.J., and new-ARK, Del., both spelled Newark. And who would guess that Pago Pago is pronounced PAHNG-oh PAHNG-oh?

Abbreviations

Generally, do not use abbreviations in your copy. It is easier to read a word written out than to read its abbreviation. Do not abbreviate the names of states, countries, months, days of the week or military titles.

When you do abbreviate a name or phrase, use hyphens instead of periods to prevent the newscaster from mistaking the final period in the abbreviation for the period at the end of the sentence. You may abbreviate United States when you use it as an adjective—U-S would be the correct form. If an abbreviation is well known—U-N, G-O-P, F-B-I—you may use it. Hyphens are not used in acronyms like NATO and HUD that are pronounced as one word.

You may use the abbreviations Dr., Mr., Mrs. and Ms., and a.m. and p.m.

Symbols and Numbers

Do not use symbols in your copy because newscasters can read a word more easily than they can interpret a symbol. Never use such symbols as the dollar sign ($) and the percent sign (%). Don't even use the abbreviation for number (no.).

Numbers can be a problem for both the announcer and the listener. As in newspaper style, write out numbers one through nine. Also write out eleven, because 11 might not be easily recognized as a number. Use figures for 10 and from 12 to 999. The eye can easily take in a three-digit number, but write out the words thousand, million and billion—for example, 3,800,000 becomes three million, 800 thousand. Write out fractions (two-and-a-half million dollars) and decimal points (three-point-two percent).

Some stations have exceptions. Figures often are used to give the time (3:20 a.m.), sports scores (ahead 5 to 2) and statistics, market reports (an increase in the Dow Jones Industrial Average of 2-point-8 points) and addresses (3-0-0-2 Grand Street; in common speech no one would give an address as three thousand two).

Ordinarily, you may round off big numbers. Thus, 48-point-3 percent should be written "nearly half." But when dealing with human beings, don't say "more than one hundred" if 104 people died in an earthquake.

Use *st, nd, rd* and *th* after dates: August 1st, September 2nd, October 3rd, November 4th. Make the year easy to pronounce by using numerals: June 9th, 1973.

Quotations and Attributions

Rarely use direct quotations and quotation marks. Because it is difficult and awkward to indicate to listeners which words are being quoted, use indirect quotes or a paraphrase instead.

If it is important for listeners to know the exact words of a quotation (as when the quoted words are startling, uncomplimentary or possibly libelous), introduce the quote by saying "in his words," "with these words," "what she called" or "he put it this way." Most writers prefer to avoid the formal "quote" and "unquote," though "quote" is used more often than "unquote." Here's an example:

> In Smith's words, quote, "There is no way to undo the harm done."

When you must use a direct quotation, the attribution should always precede the quotation. Because listeners cannot see the quotation marks, they will have no way of knowing the words are a direct quote. If by chance they did recognize the words as a quote, they would have no idea who was being quoted. For the same reason, the attribution should precede an indirect quote as well.

If you must use a direct quotation, keep it short. If the quote is long and it is important to use it, use a tape of the person saying it. If you are compelled to use a quote of more than one sentence in your copy, break it up with phrases such as "Smith went on to say" or "and still quoting the senator." For television, put a longer or more complicated quote on a full-screen graphic display as you read it.

Punctuation

In radio and television copy, less punctuation is good punctuation. The one exception is the comma. Commas help the newscaster pause at appropriate places. Use commas, for example, after introductory phrases referring to time and place, as in the following:

> In Paris, three Americans on holiday met their death today when their car overturned and caught fire.

> Last August, beef prices reached an all-time low.

Sometimes three periods are used in place of a comma. Three periods also take the place of parentheses and the semicolon. They signal a pause and are easily visible. The same is true of the dash—typed as two hyphens. Note the dash in the following example:

> But the judge grumbled about the news coverage, and most prospective jurors agreed -- saying the news coverage has been prone to overstatement, sensationalism and errors.

The only punctuation marks you need are the period, comma, question mark, dash, hyphen and, rarely, quotation marks. To make the copy easier to read, add the hyphen to some words even when the dictionary does not use it: anti-discrimination, co-equal, non-aggression.

Stations vary in writing style and in the preparation of copy. But if you learn what is presented here, you will be well-prepared. Differences will be small, and you will adapt to them easily.

Suggested Readings

Bliss, Edward Jr. and Hoyt, James L. *Writing News for Broadcast*, Third Edition. New York: Columbia University Press, 1994. A classic text that excels in good writing.

Block, Mervin. *Writing Broadcast News—Shorter, Sharper, Stronger*, Second Edition. Chicago: Bonus Books, 1997. An excellent book by a former network newswriter.

Freedman, Wayne. *It Takes More Than Good Looks*. Chicago: Bonus Books, 2003. A book packed with practical, down-to-earth advice by a man called "the best local TV news feature reporter in the country."

Schultz, Brad. *Broadcast News Producing*. Thousand Oaks, Calif.: Sage, 2004. A text that teaches how to put together a newscast.

White, Ted. *Broadcast News Writing, Reporting and Producing*, Third Edition. Boston: Focal Press, 2001. The best book on all aspects of broadcast newswriting.

Suggested Web Sites

www.nab.org
Site of the 75-year-old National Association of Broadcasters. A wonderful resource for all kinds of radio- and TV-related information, including a career center.

www.newscript.com
This site's purpose is to help radio journalists improve their skills as writers and anchors.

www.rtndf.org
The Radio-Television News Directors Association and Foundation promotes excellence in electronic journalism through research, education and professional training. The site features excellent reports and useful links.

www.tvrundown.com
This site describes the latest successful ideas in local news, programming and promotion.

http://writing.umn.edu/docs/publications/Irving%20Fang.pdf
"Writing Style Differences in Newspaper, Radio & Television." A monograph by renowned author Professor Irving Fang of the University of Minnesota. A clear discussion of the differences along with examples of stories in parallel columns demonstrating the differences in style.

Exercises

1. Watch a local evening television newscast. Make a simple list of the news stories. Then try to find those stories in the next morning's newspaper, and compare the coverage.

2. Check to see if the following AP stories written for broadcast follow acceptable broadcast style. Are they technically correct? Do they emphasize immediacy? Change the copy where you think necessary.

   a. ST. LOUIS (AP)—Peabody Energy is suing a Wisconsin power supplier to settle a dispute involving a two-and-a-half-billion-dollar power plant planned in southwestern Illinois. Wisconsin Public Power Incorporated serves 40 municipalities that sought to be a partner in the Prairie State Energy Campus being developed in Washington County, southeast of St. Louis. That company says—under its deal with St. Louis-based Peabody—it is entitled to buy electricity from the plant for 25 years beginning in 2010 at a fixed price.

   Peabody counters that a letter of intent between the parties last year isn't binding. Peabody also says the cited price would result in a massive windfall for Wisconsin Public Power and a financial burden for the project.

   Peabody wants a St. Louis court to enforce Peabody's interpretation. (Copyright 2006 by The Associated Press. All Rights Reserved.) AP-NY-11-15-06 1134EST

   b. NICE, France (AP)—Positive thinking might make cancer patients feel better, but it won't help their chances of surviving the disease.

   A new study finds that a positive outlook won't improve a person's survival rate.

The British study looked at whether psychologist-run support groups kept patients alive.

Researchers analyzed eleven studies that included a total of 15 hundred patients.

The lead researcher says there was no evidence at all that support groups prolong life in cancer patients.

However, experts say it's still worthwhile for patients to try to improve their mindsets, perhaps by joining a cancer support group, because it does make them feel better.

The findings were presented today at a meeting of the European Society of Medical Oncology in Nice, France.

c. ATLANTA (AP)—Before heading to jail, an Atlanta pastor used his last sermon to encourage his flock to continue whipping disobedient children.

The Reverend Arthur Allen Junior—convicted of cruelty to children—took off his belt and waved it behind a 14-year-old boy as part of a mock whipping at the House of Prayer.

Allen and four church members were found guilty Thursday of aggravated assault and cruelty to children for whipping two boys in front of the congregation in February of 2001. The defendants received prison sentences ranging from 20 to 90 days, plus fines and mandatory parenting classes.

The pretend whipping yesterday mocked a judge's order that Allen and his followers use only an open hand on their own children's buttocks.

3. Rewrite the following AP newspaper story in broadcast writing style. Assume that the news is current.

a. DETROIT (AP)—Almost half of Ford Motor Co.'s hourly production workers—38,000 so far this year—have accepted buyouts or early retirement offers as the nation's second biggest automaker shrinks in the face of multibillion-dollar losses and fierce competition from Asian carmakers.

Ford said Wednesday the figure includes approximately 30,000 buyouts during the open enrollment period that concluded late Monday, plus about 8,000 who took deals offered at limited plants earlier this year.

Faced with lower demand for its products, Ford had hoped that 25,000 to 30,000 workers would take one of eight packages so it could reduce manufacturing capacity to better match demand.

A 38,000-worker reduction would amount to nearly 46 percent of the 83,000 unionized employees that Ford had at the start of the year.

Those who accepted the buyout packages will begin to leave the company starting in January, the company said.

The eight packages offered to employees ranged from $35,000 to $140,000 depending on their years of service, age and how close they are to retirement. One four-year package offered up to $15,000 per year for college tuition, plus half of the workers' salaries and health benefits. Another offer paid 70 percent of employees' salaries and tuition for two years.

"One of Ford's priorities, and a large cost component of our 'Way Forward' plan for North America, is our ability to adjust manufacturing capacity with demand, while continuing to reduce operating costs and becoming more efficient," Ford President and Chief Executive Alan Mulally said in a statement. "While I know that in many cases decisions to leave the company were difficult for our employees, the acceptances received through this voluntary effort will help Ford to become more competitive."

Ford shares rose 12 cents to $8.27 in morning trading on the New York Stock Exchange.

The open enrollment period began in October. The offers included traditional packages for employees eligible for retirement, as well as nontraditional packages for employees with at least one year of service.

The company said just more than half of the employees accepted the nontraditional packages, which provided options such as lump-sum payments, tuition reimbursements or scholarship funds for family members.

Ford lost $7 billion in the first nine months of the year, and the company on Monday announced that it plans to get about $18 billion in financing due in part to pay for its restructuring. Ford's share of the market has declined from around 26 percent in the early 1990s to 17.6 percent at the end of October.

The company expects to cut its costs by $5 billion through 2008, with further unspecified reductions in 2009.

Ford has announced plans to close 16 plants as part of the "Way Forward" restructuring plan. Nine of the plants have been identified, but the company has not named the remaining seven.

4. Read a copy of a current newspaper; then write a five-minute newscast. Pay special attention to lead-ins and wrap-ups. (Do not include sports material in your broadcast.)

Writing for the Web

20

When Democrats took control of Congress in the midterm elections of 2006, they did so in a media environment that was quite unlike anything seen in previous elections. Both CNN and Fox News offered Web pages that allowed users to choose and track the races they cared about on one page. VideotheVote.com enlisted people all across the country to chronicle problems in their precincts.

Blogs abounded, and CNN even sponsored a blog party with an open bar. Those who attended blogged about politics and blogged about blogging.

It didn't stop there. Associate Editor Bob Kaiser of *The Washington Post* chatted online with readers during the heat of election-night coverage. The *St. Louis Post-Dispatch* created a Web-based, touch-screen voting guide to acquaint readers with the electronic voting machines being used in the area for the first time. *The Jackson (Tenn.) Sun* published a live webcast of its news room on election night so readers could get the feel of collecting the news. WSB-TV in Atlanta posted video blogs—or *vlogs*—of stories it had no time to air but that some viewers might have found useful.

All of this resulted from media efforts to engage with the public and embrace citizen journalism. Still, at the heart of the coverage were the efforts of professional journalists to make sense of what was happening. And journalists did just that, describing in great detail the shift in direction of the political winds.

There was a big story to tell, and for the most part, the public turned to mainstream journalists to make sense of it all. Journalists responded by writing news for newspapers, magazines, radio, television and the Web. Those who wrote for the Web did so with clarity and purpose and with a newfound sense of what writing for online media is all about.

In this chapter, we examine the peculiarities of writing for online media and what sets it apart from writing for traditional media.

THE LESSON OF KATRINA

It's no stretch to argue that the mainstream media really began to understand the power of online media only when disaster struck in the form of Hurricane Katrina in 2005. No story better illustrates the power of online journalism than that of NOLA.com, the online site of *The (New Orleans) Times-Picayune*, in the wake of Katrina. Floodwaters idled the newspaper's printing plant, making publication impossible, but NOLA.com became a primary source of information. It did so with great distinction.

Mark Glaser writes in *Online Journalism Review*:

> The NOLA.com news blog became *the* source for news on hurricane damage and recovery efforts—including updates from various reporters on the ground and even full columns and news stories.
>
> The blog actually became the paper, and it had to because the newspaper's readership was in diaspora, spread around the country in shelters and homes of families and friends. The newspaper staff was transformed into citizen journalists, with arts

reviewers doing disaster coverage and personal stories running alongside hard-hitting journalism. In a time of tragedy and loss, the raw guts of the organization were exposed for us to see.

Glaser writes that NOLA.com editor Jon Donley turned over his blog to his readers, who sent in dozens of calls for help. Most came through text messaging because mobile telephone towers and landlines were downed and inoperable. The calls were relayed onto the blog, which rescuers monitored to know where to go. As a result, NOLA.com not only provided information but also saved lives.

Across the country, newspapers and other media noticed. They began to realize the power of online journalism and set about the task of giving it its own place in the media landscape.

THE WEB AS ITS OWN MEDIA FORM

Online journalism wasn't always so powerful, and in its infancy few knew how to use it. Indeed, when it first appeared, online journalism followed a familiar pattern—one established when radio began to yield to television. As television arrived for real in the post-World War II era, news reports consisted almost entirely of someone sitting at a desk reading written-for-radio news. Similarly, when the World Wide Web appeared in the mid-1990s, media organizations quickly adopted it but merely regurgitated news written for traditional media—newspapers, magazines, and radio and television stations. Sites operated by traditional media contained little more than this morning's stories, which had already appeared in print or on the air.

As the Internet evolved, that began to change. One reason it changed is that citizen journalism began to flourish—as it did in New Orleans—challenging the dominance of traditional media in the process of disseminating news. Anyone, it seemed, could become a journalist or even a publisher.

Recognizing that the media landscape had changed, traditional publishers began to embrace blogs, instant messaging of news alerts and even citizen journalism itself. Those developments led editors and publishers of traditional media to understand that the Web is an entirely new medium that demands a fresh approach. It's an approach that takes advantage of the Internet's ability to deliver links to other sites, to link people with two-way communication and, with high-speed connections, to provide not only text, photos and graphics but also audio and video on demand.

When the Web first came along, no one knew how to make money with it, an essential ingredient in a country in which the media are not state-supported. All that has changed. In 2006, online advertising revenue was expected to exceed $13 billion, a 30 percent increase from the previous year. No other medium was experiencing revenue growth even approaching that. And *Folio*, the trade publica-

> **"Computers can:**
> - Look things up for us.
> - Navigate for us ('Please turn to page . . .').
> - Link words to other words.
> - Remember where we were and take us back there.
> - Play audio, video and animation.
> - Organize and present information according to a nonlinear structure.**"**
>
> — Andrew Bonime and Ken C. Pohlmann,
> *Writing for New Media*

tion of the magazine industry, reported that some titles were using online revenue to make up for lost print revenue, effectively underwriting their older siblings. Clearly, Web businesses based on news are here to stay, and that requires us to study the best ways of producing both advertising and news for them.

Just as writing for television evolved from its early iterations, so, too, is writing for the Web evolving. Most now recognize that writing for the Web is different from writing for television or newspapers. The Web is clearly a unique medium that requires a new approach, but that approach is still evolving as journalists learn new ways to communicate online. Let's take a look at the conventional wisdom on writing for the Web as we know it today.

HOW TO WRITE FOR THE WEB

Even if you plan to work at a newspaper, magazine, or radio or television station, you will need to know how to write for online media. At a growing number of newspapers, even veteran journalists are being asked to turn in two versions of their stories, one for the newspaper and one for the paper's Web site. At the *St. Paul Pioneer Press*, all print reporters must file a Web story within 30 minutes after witnessing an event or learning about the news. In the old days, newspapers would print several editions a day and would occasionally come out with an "extra." Today, cyberspace has turned newspapers into 24-hour competitive news machines, and "print reporters" are rapidly becoming a disappearing species.

At *The Tampa Tribune*, where convergence is a mantra, Donna Reed, the managing editor, insists that the newspaper's most valuable staffers are those who can produce material for multiple media. "I can send one sports reporter to the Super Bowl, and he can cover for the newspaper, the Web site and even television," Reed says.

Of course, online writing isn't just about writing. It's about determining the best way to tell a story and then using all media forms — text, audio, video and graphics — to deliver it. That requires at least a basic understanding of audio and video production and the use of information graphics. Writing, though, is at the heart of all media, including the Web.

Good online writing has many of the characteristics of other forms of effective writing. Much of what you have read so far about newswriting applies to online journalism; what you've learned about news gathering and reporting, either in print or broadcast, applies here. The demand for accurate, simple, clear and concise writing is the same for all the media.

Nevertheless, the online journalist must be aware of some fundamental differences between online and traditional media. These distinctions increasingly result in stories that look quite different from the stories published on paper or broadcast. One sure way to drive away online readers is to give them *shovelware* — stories as they appeared in print. Hundreds of publications continue to do that, but it's now clear that most online readers refuse to be buried in the dirt created by shovelware — unless they have a real need for in-depth information.

The 69-year-old Associated Press Managing Editors association amended its bylaws in 2001 to fill one seat of its board of directors with a supervisor of an online news operation, and in 2002, Ken Sands, interactive editor of *The Spokesman-Review*, Spokane, Wash., was elected to the board.

To be sure, there are readers who want the stories as they appear in the newspaper and not rewritten in some other form. They want shovelware because they want to know what other readers are seeing. Readers of *The New York Times'* online edition, scattered around the world, undoubtedly want to see what the print readers have read. The *Times* and many other newspapers now produce downloadable versions that look exactly like the newspaper edition. So, there's a market for that. But most readers want stories tailored to take advantage of the Web's considerable power. They want links, and they want graphics, audio and even video to accompany the text.

To write effectively for the Web, you need to learn a unique way of thinking about writing. Let's begin with these three principles:

- The reader rules.
- The writing is nonlinear.
- Structure is everything.

The Reader Rules

Unlike print journalists writing for newspapers and magazines, where narrative works fine, newswriters online should keep no secrets from readers; they should not try to withhold information until later in the story. In short, when writing online you should surrender control of the story's sequence to the reader. Online, authors lose their "position of central authority," writes David Weinberger, author and editor of the *Journal of the Hyperlinked Organization*, a newsletter that considers the Web's effect on how business works. Every reader is different; every reader has different needs. Every reader, therefore, not only will select and choose what to read but also will choose a path that best meets those needs.

Also, readers can come from anywhere in the world, not just from a local audience. And because of the enormous archival capability of the Internet, readers can come in at any time. As Prof. Phil Brooks of the Missouri School of Journalism tells his students, "Today becomes yesterday tomorrow." In other words, he says, when writing for the Web you are writing history for an international audience.

You should think of ways to present different information for different people at different times. Unlike newspapers and magazines, which must decide how long to make a story, online media should layer information in such a way that readers can choose the amount they need at any given time.

You have learned to write the inverted pyramid story. This much of the traditional news story remains the same. The lead in an online story becomes even more important because the lead literally may be all that appears on the screen. Readers may have to click to get more of the story. The lead must nail the "what" or the "so what" to get the full attention of the reader. In fact, it is similar to the anchor's introduction to a television news story.

The lead is also important because for most search engines, the lead will be the only information provided for the link to the story. You would be wise to include

---

Newspaper Web sites are expanding the reach of their publications in unprecedented ways. According to the Newspaper Association of America, in 2005, unique visitors to newspaper Web sites represented on average more than one-third (46 million) of all Internet users over the course of a month.

key words such as "Maine" and "governor" in the lead about a story concerning the Maine governor.

Sometimes the lead appears like an extended headline, followed by two or three statements that also read as headlines. After the lead, little is the same as the traditional news story. Readers can often click on the hyperlinked headlines to read the full version of the story on another page within the Web site.

Note also that the reader is active, not passive. Steve Outing writes on Poynter.org:

> If I gave you an assignment to look at the content of 100 news Web sites, you'd probably find that 95 percent of them don't ever go beyond routine presentation of text, images and the occasional audio or video clip. It's still the rare few that craft content in such ways that go beyond what would be possible in print or broadcast. Rare is the story that uses online interactive techniques that help the user understand the story best by letting him or her interact with and manipulate elements of the story—to experience it, not just read about it.

Outing writes that good Internet writing says to the reader, "Don't read—do!" It does this because it plays to the essential nature of the Internet—it is interactive.

The Writing Is Nonlinear

Because most people don't think linearly, writing online is more in line with the way people think. It's even more in line with the way today's readers read. Break the story into short, digestible pieces. Rather than stringing together a long story and trying to get readers to read the whole thing in the order in which you presented it, keep in mind that many readers don't want to read everything you have to tell them. You must give them choices and let them decide what to read and in what order.

Stories that require multiple continuous screens turn off many readers immediately. Many readers hate to scroll on screen. Some exit even before they get to the bottom of the screen. Few will take the time to read a lot of text in one clump. Note, of course, that this is not true of highly motivated readers who crave your information. At times you may want to send them to reliable databanks where they can read the whole story and get all the facts—preferably, of course, within your own site.

Structure Is Everything

Some who write online forget entirely about structure. That's a huge mistake. Even though an online story takes on an entirely different structure, it still must be organized in a logical, coherent way. The online reader does not revel in chaos. Even though the story may appear on the screen as a mosaic, the way that mosaic is composed will help attract readers, keep readers and help readers follow what for them is the most logical path.

Newspapers own 11 of the top 25 national news and information Web sites and provide a strong draw for younger audiences, according to the Newspaper Association of America.

The online writer must present information in layers. Remember: No two readers are alike. You may present the same information with different degrees of detail and support. The first layer is information that is immediately available to readers—no action or effort is demanded. A second layer, a more substantial read, could be reachable easily by moving the cursor or by scrolling. A third layer may require readers to click on a link that opens up still more information, perhaps audio, video or a source document.

When you write for print, you need to be concerned with continuity, with themes, with working in all aspects of the story while keeping the writing clear and coherent. When you write online, you need to worry not about the structure or flow of the whole piece but rather about the relationships of the levels and parts. You need to help readers navigate from place to place to get the information they want. That means you must have clear entrances and exits.

Sometimes you have to give clear directions. For example, if you include a hyperlink in your story, more readers will "click here" if you tell them to do so than if you don't. Sometimes you may take readers down one path that branches into several others. Some call this technique "threading." The story of a plane crash can lead to various threads—the airline and its safety record, the plane itself and the record of that type of plane, the place of the accident, the people involved, and so forth.

You need not be concerned about some repetition. Remember, readers choose what parts to read. Besides, a certain amount of repetition or of stating things in different ways, perhaps visually, increases retention. Readers, after all, online or elsewhere, process information differently.

> **"**Hypertext and hypermedia have the following characteristics:
>
> - They present ideas nonsequentially.
> - They follow the thought process.
> - They allow users to choose individual pathways through the information.
> - They allow information to transcend individual documents.
> - They link text with pictures, audio and video.**"**
>
> — Andrew Bonime and Ken C. Pohlmann,
> *Writing for New Media*

GUIDELINES FOR WRITING FOR THE WEB

Readers online are surfers or scanners, much more so than readers of print, perhaps because it takes 25 percent longer to read online than it does in print. Researchers Jakob Nielsen and John Morkes found that 79 percent of those they tested scanned a new page they came across; only 16 percent read the copy word for word.

Online expert Shel Holtz says you want readers to dive, not to surf. Surfing is what frustrated readers do. Here are 10 ways to make divers out of surfers—or at least to hold their attention long enough to get your message across.

1. Think Immediacy

Although you must of course make sure what you write is accurate, the Internet can deliver news when it is brand-new. Writing online is like writing for the wire

ON THE JOB

An Online Career

Troy Wolverton says that when he was studying journalism in graduate school, he "quickly fell in love with the Internet." He took every course available in new media, as well as newspaper reporting, basic photojournalism and broadcast journalism. He freelanced for *The New York Times* Web site and taught a class in Internet basics. He left graduate school to take a job at the *San Jose Mercury News* as an online editor.

After two years, he began working as a reporter for CNET News.com, a technology news Web site. There he covered e-commerce companies like Amazon.com, online auctioneer eBay and online brokerage E*Trade. Wolverton is now on his third online job, as a reporter at TheStreet.com, where he covers the retail industry both online and off.

"I was trying to figure out where I wanted to go when I left CNET. Many online reporters I know — the few of us who are left — have a desire to get back to print. In fact that's the route several of my former News.com colleagues have taken.

"I probably wouldn't turn down *The New York Times* if they came calling, but I really enjoy working online. I love the immediacy of the medium. By the time a newspaper is delivered to a reader's door, many of the stories in it have been online for hours.

"Writing for an online publication brings you closer to your readers. When I wrote for a newspaper, I felt as if my stories were floating out into the ether. I had no idea whether people were reading them. I know how much people are reading my News.com articles by how many e-mail responses I receive."

services. Everyone on the Internet now consumes information the way a wire-service subscriber does. Keeping readers with you means keeping readers up-to-the-minute. You must expect to update breaking stories quickly and to add depth whenever it is available. But just because you can easily correct your mistakes, that does not mean you are allowed to make them. Reporter David Broder of *The Washington Post* warned at an annual National Roundtable sponsored by the Scripps Howard Foundation that posting news quickly could sacrifice quality and damage credibility.

While attempting to exercise such care, newspapers are now using their Web sites to break news. For example, when the *Financial Times* learned that Iranian security forces held a son of Osama bin Laden, it reported that news on its Web site on Saturday because it doesn't publish on Sunday. The Ft. Lauderdale, Fla., *Sun-Sentinel* partners with radio and television, and it may break a story on any of those media, occasionally even scooping itself. Time is usually the deciding factor.

2. Save Readers Time

What most readers do not have is time. Whatever you can do to save readers' time is worth *your* time. It's been said by various people in different ways since the philosopher Blaise Pascal first said it: "Excuse me for this long letter; I don't have time to write a short one." For many stories, if not most, perhaps your chief concern should be this: Have I presented this information in such a way as to cost readers the least amount of time?

The best way to save readers' time is to be clear. Choose the simple word; vary the length of sentences, but keep them short; write short paragraphs. Help readers. Emphasize key words by highlighting them or by putting them in color.

Another reason to write simply, using simple words and simple sentences, is to enable the auto-translation programs used by some search engines to translate the page. The simpler the words and sentences, the more likely a foreign-language translation of the story will be accurate and understandable.

3. Provide Information That's Quick and Easy to Get

The overall organization of your story must say to the reader that getting this information is going to be quick and easy. Online readers have zero tolerance for confusion and no time at all to be led astray. It's too easy to click on something else.

Figure 20.1
The Cincinnati Post online edition (www.cincypost.com) uses the inverted pyramid throughout its Web site. In doing so, the site allows readers to find the "what" or the "so what" without reading the entire story.

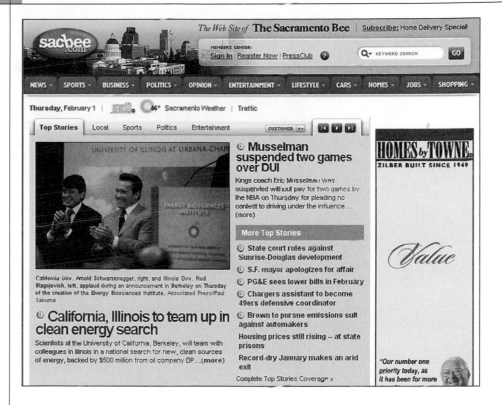

Figure 20.2
This front-page story on *The Sacramento Bee* Web site (www.sacbee.com) has a headline with a long lead. A statement that also reads as a headline accompanies the lead.

Don't get carried away by your own eloquence. Be guided by what your readers want or need to know. Make it easy for them. Write short paragraphs with one idea per paragraph.

4. Think Both Verbally and Visually

In the past, writers for print thought little about how their stories were going to appear. Their job was to write the story—period. The designer's job was to make the story fit on the page in some meaningful way. Writers did not worry about headlines, subheads, summary quotes, photos, illustrations or anything but the story.

Television newswriters know that they must write to the pictures. Good television has good video; the visual medium tries to show rather than to tell. Words complement pictures; they say what the pictures do not. Many times, of course, the writer does not make the pictures and is not responsible for getting them. But the writer still must consider the best way to tell the story; sometimes visuals convey the story as no amount of text could possibly do.

As an online journalist, you may not have to do it all by yourself, but you definitely must *think* both verbally and visually. From the outset, you must be concerned

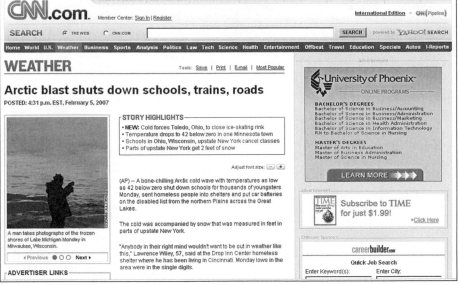

Figure 20.3
This article on CNN.com appears as a lead on the first screen, but readers can click on "Full Story" for more. The complete story follows the lead and has sidebars providing more links for further information on the subject. CNN.com is one of the most popular sites on the Internet.

about the most effective and efficient way for the information to appear on the screen. You have to think not only about the organization of the page, but also about ways to use graphics, to be interactive and to use online tools.

No one doubts that photos and graphics grab readers' attention. That's why you see more icons and infographics in magazines and newspapers, and that's why

A Story Greater Than the Sum of Its Parts

From an interview with Kerry Northrup, executive director of Ifra Center for Advanced News Operations, in *EPN World Reporter*:

"A lot of people who are journalists today simply cannot be journalists tomorrow. They can't grasp the changes in how people get and use news and information. They won't adapt to thinking in terms of multiple media rather than being concerned only about their personal area of specialization. They are media bigots, for want of a better term, insisting past reason that print is print, broadcast is broadcast, Web is Web, and never will they mesh.

"The idea of blending formats to create a story greater than the sum of its parts remains foreign to them. Perhaps the kindest and most effective approach for an editorial organization to deal with this situation is to create new jobs that reflect the new requirements, the new skills, the new compensations, the new realities, and then let those that will evolve into them, and those that won't phase out."

As an interesting side note to the above, Ifra reports that in the United Kingdom, the BBC and its trade union have a new video-journalist classification with salary increases for journalists "who retrain to report, film and edit their own news stories."

you must think, perhaps with the help of graphic designers, of ways to use graphic elements online.

In short, if you are writing online, you have to be much more than a wordsmith. You must have a pocketful of other skills. Writing online demands a great deal of collaboration and not just with other writers. Working closely with those more expert than you in design and photography becomes crucial from the outset.

5. Cut Copy in Half

You probably don't have to be told that writing online must be concise. But you do need to be told to cut your copy in half. Years ago, writing expert William Zinsser recommended that writers take their eight pages and cut them to four. Then, he wrote, comes the difficult part, he wrote—cutting them to three. And that was for print!

Most online readers simply will not read long stories. Even veteran computer users find reading on screen somewhat difficult, even unpleasant, says Jakob Nielsen. Perhaps this will change when larger screens and high-resolution screens become more common by becoming less expensive.

Studies contradict each other about people's aversion to scrolling. In the not-so-distant past, some experts advised getting the whole story on one screen. Because some screens are small, they advised not writing more than 20 lines of text. Now, because of the proliferation of larger and less-irritating screens, some readers are finding it easier and less frustrating to scroll for more information.

As in broadcast newswriting, there's little room online to be cute or even literary. Be crisp and clear.

6. Use Lots of Lists and Bullets

Often you can cut copy by putting information into lists. Whenever you can make a list, do so. Lists get more attention and allow for better comprehension and more retention than ordinary sentences and paragraphs. Bulleted or numbered lists are scannable. Readers can grasp them immediately. Think of information on the Web as a database. That's how people use their computers, and that's how they use the Web.

Nielsen tested five versions of the same information for usability. Look first at the longest version, what he calls promotional writing, his control condition:

> Nebraska is filled with internationally recognized attractions that draw large crowds of people every year, without fail. In 1996, some of the most popular places were Fort Robinson State Park (355,000 visitors), Scotts Bluff National Monument (132,126 visitors), Arbor Lodge State Historical Park & Museum (100,000), *Carhenge* (85,598), Stuhr Museum of the Prairie Pioneer (60,002), and Buffalo Bill Ranch State Historical Park (28,446).

Now look at this same material in list form.

> In 1996, six of the most visited places in Nebraska were:
> - Fort Robinson State Park.
> - Scotts Bluff National Monument.
> - Arbor Lodge State Historical Park & Museum.
> - *Carhenge.*
> - Stuhr Museum of the Prairie Pioneer.
> - Buffalo Bill Ranch State Historical Park.

The list version of the information scored a 124 percent usability improvement over the first version.

7. Write in Chunks

When you can't put material into lists, you can still organize it into chunks of information. Put information into sidebars or boxes. Readers will read more, not less, if you break up the information into small bites. Research has also shown that putting some information in a sidebar can give readers better comprehension of the subject. But the main objective here is to write for diverse readers who want to get only the information they want in the order in which they want to receive it.

Think of your story as having parts. When writing a story for a newspaper, you need to think of ways to join the various parts of the story, you should craft transitions carefully and you may even add subheads. When writing a story online, rather than writing subheads, make each segment of the story a separate story. Be sure that each part can stand on its own enough to be comprehensible and to make your point. Again, remember the importance of a strong lead in the best inverted pyramid form.

Mark Deuze and Christina Dimoudi of the Amsterdam School of Communications Research conclude from their study that online journalism is really a fourth kind of journalism after print, radio and television. Its main characteristic is "empowering audiences as active participants in the daily news." Online journalists have "an interactive relationship with their audience" and a "strong element of audience orientation" and are "more aware of their publics and service function in society than their colleagues elsewhere."

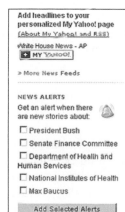

Figure 20.4

Yahoo! News (news.yahoo .com) uses short, concise paragraphs in its articles. This Web site also makes other information easy to get by displaying a sidebar next to the story that contains related news stories, opinions and editorials, and related Web sites.

8. Use Hyperlinks

To understand the Web, think of a spider web. The Web, says David Weinberger, is a place of connection; it is a connective place; it is a place where we go to connect. Users of the Internet feel connected. If you want them to read your copy and come back for more, you must satisfy and enhance that sense of being connected.

Being connected means being interactive. Web users want to be actively involved in what they are reading. They are not passive observers. Like video-game players, they want to be in control of where they are going and how they get there. Your copy must be interactive both internally and externally.

Internal Connections

The most challenging and necessary aspect of online writing is making the copy interactive. You begin that process by streamlining your copy by not including everything. Create **hyperlinks,** and allow readers to click on information elsewhere on your site.

One of the most perplexing problems writers face is deciding when to include the definition of a word. Will you insult some readers by including the definition? Will you leave others behind if you do not define the term? A similar problem is whether to tell who a person is. Many readers may wonder how stupid you think they are for telling them that actor Fred Thompson was a former Republican senator from Tennessee. Other readers may need or want that information.

The online writer can simply make the word or name a hotspot or a link and hyperlink it to a different "page." Readers need only click on the word to find its meaning or read more about it. No longer do writers have to write, "For more information, see . . ." Academic writers use footnotes. Hypertext, or hypermedia, linking readers to audio, video and pictures, are much more convenient.

Writing concisely has never been easier. Rather than defining words, going into long explanations, giving examples or elaborating on the story itself, you can stick to the essentials and make the rest of the story available to readers who need or want it. A story about a homicide can link to a map of where the crime took place, to a chart showing the numbers of homicides this year as compared with last year, to a piece about friends of the victim, to information about violent crimes nationally, and so forth.

Remember, too, that unlike the newspaper where you may be short of space, and unlike radio and television where you may be short of time, online you have unlimited space and time to run photos and aspects of stories that could be of real interest to some readers. Sports fans, for example, would probably enjoy seeing a whole gallery of shots from Saturday's

---

Web expert Jakob Neilsen argues that Web sites must employ scannable text using:

- Highlighted keywords, including hypertext links.
- Meaningful subheads.
- Bulleted lists.
- One idea per paragraph.
- Half the word count of conventional writing.

"We have derived three main content-oriented conclusions from our four years of Web usability studies:

- Users do not read on the Web; instead they scan the pages, trying to pick out a few sentences or even parts of sentences to get the information they want.
- Users do not like long, scrolling pages; they prefer the text to be short and to the point.
- Users detest anything that seems like marketing fluff or overly hyped language ('marketese') and prefer factual information.**"**

— John Morkes and Jakob Nielsen (1997), "Concise, SCANNABLE, and Objective: How to Write for the Web," useit.com

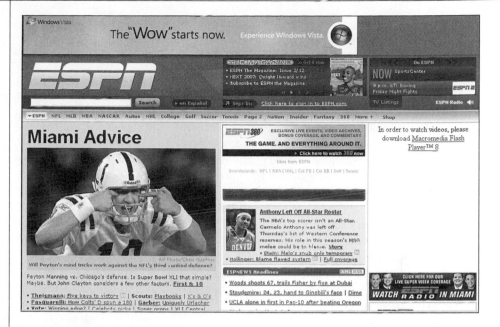

Figure 20.5
Perhaps better than any other site, ESPN.com (espn .go.com) uses hyperlinks throughout its stories. The hyperlinks lead readers to related stories, player profiles and even audio and video files.

championship game. They would read interviews from all of the stars of the victory—or of the defeat.

External Connections

Of course, you can do much more. You can hyperlink to different Web sites. Academic writers include bibliographies. Print journalists often identify sources in their stories. Other writers simply say to readers: That's all I know about the subject, I'm not going to tell you where I obtained my information, and I'm not telling you where you can find more information. Hypertext and hypermedia have changed all that. Not only can you hyperlink online, but readers expect you to do so.

Obviously, you are not expected to draw readers away from your site to a competitor, especially on a breaking story. Nevertheless, readers will come to rely on your site to help them find more information about subjects that interest them greatly.

To find appropriate external hyperlinks, you need to know how to use search engines like Yahoo! (www.yahoo.com) and Google (www.google.com).

9. Give Readers a Chance to Talk Back

A big part of being interactive is allowing readers to talk back. The Internet has leveled the playing field. Everyone is an owner or a publisher. Everyone feels the right, and often the need, to write back—if not to the writer of the piece, then to other

The 3-2-2-1 Format

After spending 25 years as a professional newsman, the last four of those as a general manager, Associate Professor Clyde Bentley now teaches classes in online journalism and other courses at the University of Missouri. In one class, students take stories from the newspaper and rewrite them for the online version. Bentley calls students online "producers" rather than reporters.

"I was surprised at the resistance my students had to changing the copy of reporters," Bentley says. "They preferred the 'shovelware' concept so they would not tamper with the prose of their friends."

In frustration, he instituted what he called a "3-2-2-1" format. "It was a way to force my young journalists to take on a new process."

Here's what the numbers mean.

3 Subheads

By inserting three subheads, the producers "chunk" the story into four pieces. "This is easier to read than one long, scrollable piece of text," Bentley says. The subdivisions can be as simple as "who, what, when . . ."

2 External Links

These are directions to further information posted outside the story. "For instance, in a story about the local dog pound, we might have external links to the ASPCA and the American Kennel Club."

2 Internal Links

These are explanatory links tied to text within the story. "In the pound story," Bentley explains, "the word 'Doberman' might be a link that takes one to a breeder's site that explains the Doberman Pinscher."

1 Piece of Art Not Available in the Print Edition

Print publications limit art primarily because of space limitations. There are no such limits on the Web. "If a photographer shoots 20 shots, we can run more than one," Bentley says. "More commonly, however, the producers insert mug shots of people mentioned in the story. There is no reason not to run mugs of everyone who is mentioned in a story."

Among other rules for writing online, Ellen Schindler, a senior account executive at Berry Associates, recommends the following:

- Double-space between paragraphs. Leave two spaces after periods.
- Avoid serif type. Serifs get lost on the screen.
- Make the text black. It's easier to read.
- Remember that simple is best.

readers in chat rooms or blogs. The wonderful thing about allowing readers to talk back is that they do. When they do, they will revisit the site again and again. Online readers want to be part of the process. Readers love it when newspapers like *The Miami Herald* include the reporter's e-mail address in the byline, and many of them respond.

A word of caution: Including e-mail addresses on the Web leaves you open to operations that use a program called an e-mail syphon that scans Web site pages for e-mail addresses that are then used for spam. Depending on your mail-server provider's antispamming capabilities, putting your e-mail address in a news story or magazine article can subject you to a deluge of spam. One alternative is, rather than your permanent personal address, include in your stories a different address that you change from time to time.

Never has it been easier to find out what is on the minds of your readers. Print and broadcast have always been mainly one-way communication. Now, not only can you get opinions easily and quickly, but you can incorporate them into your story or at least hyperlink to them. Letters to the editor have always been among

Figure 20.6

The *Boston Herald* (www .bostonherald. com) provides several stories on the same subject, separating them with bulleted headlines.

the best-read sections in newspapers and magazines. Many readers, especially those reading online, not only want to express their own opinions but love to read the opinions of others. Be sure, however, that you use the same strict standards for publishing others' remarks on your Web site that you use for publishing in your newspaper or magazine. Even e-mail polls can and have been flooded by advocacy groups. Reporting their results can be meaningless and misleading and certainly unprofessional unless they are monitored carefully.

10. Don't Forget the Human Touch

Veteran correspondent Helen Thomas told a convention of newspaper interactive editors: "I do hope the human touch remains in the robotic scheme of things. Human beings still count."

Remember, people make the news. Facts are just facts unless you relate them to people.

LEGAL AND ETHICAL CONCERNS

Online journalists have the same legal and ethical concerns as other journalists (see Chapters 22 and 23). Libel is still libel, and plagiarism is still plagiarism. Just because you are not "in print" doesn't mean that you can destroy someone's reputation or

Figure 20.7
This article on *The Washington Post*'s Web site (www.washingtonpost.com) discusses the first photos of Mars sent by the rover *Spirit*. To the right are links to more information (shown below), including 3-D images of Mars taken by *Spirit*.

distort the truth. You also must always be aware that what is on the Internet is not yours, even though the very design of it allows you to download words and images. If you use someone else's words, put quotation marks around them, and cite the source.

Although the Internet makes it easier to find and steal someone else's work, it also makes it easier to get caught doing so. Already, there have been several cases where Web readers of local columnists or reviewers have turned in a writer for plagiarism.

Plagiarism is not the only danger. Some areas of ethics are even more touchy and difficult to solve for online journalists.

Privacy

Many Web sites maintain files on almost all their active users. Some allow you to see what anyone has ever posted on a message board. What may journalists use? Most everyone agrees that private e-mail is off limits. But what about material sent to corporate intranets?

Advertising

Newspapers and magazines generally try to label advertising as advertising, and they have rules that require ads to use typefaces different from those the publication uses. There are also rules about the placement of ads. Online ads regularly break up the copy of news stories or pop up over news stories. There is no separation of ads from editorial content and no attempt to make any separation.

Why don't the same rules that apply to print apply online? Note what the code of the American Society of Magazine Editors says:

> The same ASME principles that mandate distinct treatment of editorial content, advertisements, and special advertisements, and special advertising sections ("advertorials") in print publications also apply to online editorial projects bearing the names of print magazines or offering themselves as electronic magazines. The dynamic technology of electronic pages and hypertext links creates a high potential for reader confusion. Permitting such confusion betrays reader trust and undermines the credibility not only of the offending online publication or editorial product, but also of the publisher itself. It is therefore the responsibility of each online publication to make clear to its readers which online content is editorial and which is advertising, and to prevent any juxtaposition that gives the impression that editorial material was created for — or influenced by — advertisers.

The ASME code then goes on to spell out 10 specific ways to carry out these general guidelines.

The code of the American Society of Business Press Editors says simply:

> On all such papers, editors should ensure that a clear distinction is made between advertising and editorial content. This may involve type faces, layout/design, labeling, and juxtaposition of the editorial materials and the advertisement.

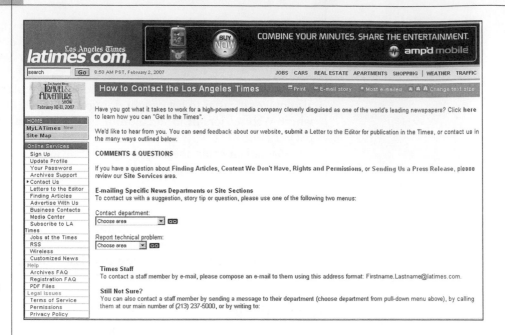

Figure 20.8

Many Web sites offer a chance for reader feedback, whether it's a chance to send a letter to the editor or to report a technical problem. The *Los Angeles Times* (www.latimes.com) encourages feedback with several links to help readers send a letter to specific news departments or to help answer their questions.

The ASBPE code adds this important sentence: "Editors should directly supervise and control all links that appear with the editorial portion of the site."

Manipulating Photos

Print has not dealt with this problem well either. *New York Times* photographer Fred Ritchin proposed using an icon to flag a digitally altered photo. But how will readers know how much it has been altered? Will readers trust what they see?

Concealing Your Identity

It's so easy to conceal your identity as a reporter on the Web. At times, you may be doing undercover investigative reporting, but the time to reveal yourself as a reporter is usually at the outset of your questioning people online, not after you have gotten to a certain point in your story.

Corrections

Some online news sites act as if they never make mistakes. They simply post new stories with updated information. Surely you owe it to readers to tell them that the story has changed or has been updated with new information and how that was done. Such notice of correction or updating will not be done unless the news site has a clear policy requiring it.

Forbes.com erroneously quoted former Disney Chairman Michael Eisner as saying he didn't think his company's network, ABC, would be operating "in four to five years." In the update to the story, the changed headline read, "Clarification: Eisner Discusses the ABC Brand and Other Brands." In addition to correcting the story, Forbes.com put asterisks next to the changed sentences and included explanations at the bottom of the story such as this: "The original version of this story incorrectly stated that Eisner did not see the third-ranked network being around in four to five years." In his column in *The Washington Post*, Howard Kurtz reported that Forbes.com editor Paul Maidment said his reporter had "extrapolated" without the "broader context."

Hyperlinks to External Sites

Is raw data journalism? How much and how often may you use raw data, and with what warnings or interpretations?

There's little doubt that readers appreciate links to source data so they can make judgments for themselves. At the same time, good Web sites help readers navigate that information. Journalists are still trying to find the right balance between the two.

TOMORROW'S READERS

Print has been around for centuries, and we are still figuring out ways to use it effectively. In contrast, writing for the Web is in its infancy. Like all good writers, online journalists must be students of writing. Both writers and readers are still learning the most effective uses of the newest medium. Writing for the Web is more about showing than telling, about the audience experiencing rather than witnessing, about the audience actively participating rather than being passive, about the audience doing rather than merely reading. Perhaps never have writers been more challenged.

Suggested Readings

Craig, Richard. *Online Journalism: Reporting, Writing, and Editing for the New Media.* Stamford, Conn.: Wadsworth-Thomson Learning, 2005. A comprehensive source of information about writing for the Web.

De Wolk, Roland. *Introduction to Online Journalism: Publishing News and Information.* Boston: Allyn & Bacon, 2001. A short, simple and readable text with a wonderful glossary of terms.

Morkes, John and Nielsen, Jakob. "Concise, Scannable, and Objective: How to Write for the Web." Available from www.useit.com/papers/webwriting/writing.html. A wonderful summary of their research regarding effective online writing.

Nielsen, Jakob. "How Users Read on the Web." Available from www.useit.com/alertbox/9710a.html. Practical advice, including research, on the usability of online copy.

Suggested Web Sites

http://news.cincypost.com
Like many daily newspapers, *The Cincinnati Post*'s online edition includes most of the stories from its print edition, along with additional online-only posts.

http://espn.go.com
One of the best Web sites is espn.com. It is probably the most extensive Internet site for sports fans, and it was an early leader in the use of audio and video.

www.mercurynews.com
The Mercury News, one of the first comprehensive local news Web sites, includes area news courtesy of the *San Jose Mercury News.*

www.msnbc.msn.com
This companion site to the cable news channel offers a wealth of news resources. Its opinions section includes, among other things, links to top stories; stories from Slate, another Microsoft Web site; and opinion pieces and blogs—online journals written by pundits and journalists.

Exercises

1. Choose a major national story from a recent newspaper or newsmagazine. Then visit two newspaper Web sites and compare the treatment of the story. Write a 300-word critique of the online writing techniques that the Web sites used.

2. Visit your local newspaper or television station and interview individuals who do the news online. Find out how they were trained and what major challenges they face.

3. Your professor will assign you a newspaper story. Rewrite it for online use, and indicate any hyperlinks that you might include.

4. Visit five newspaper or magazine Web sites. Then pick the one that does the best job of using online writing techniques, and write a 200-word report on your findings.

5. Find a Web site that does a good job of linking readers to original source material. Evaluate the use of that technique, and explain why the technique works in this case.

Writing for Public Relations

VICTORY REPORT 2007

EARTHJUSTICE
Because the earth needs a good lawyer

20 YEARS OF PRESERVING THE PACIFIC NORTHWEST

IN BRIEF SPRING 2007

A three-month trial ends with renewed hope for Florida's Lake Okeechobee. See page 5.

A New Day Has Dawned

THE 110TH CONGRESS that convened on January 4 is unlike any that we have seen in Washington in a very long time. The implications for our environment as a result of the dramatic difference in leadership starts at the very top of both the House and Senate. Speaker Nancy Pelosi has a 92 percent lifetime pro-environmental voting record, a remarkable change from Representative Denny Hastert's near single digit record when he became Speaker of the House. Similarly, Senate Majority Leader Harry Reid's lifetime 75 percent average outshines former Majority Leader Bill Frist's seven percent lifetime average. The number two slots in both the Senate (Majority Whip Senator Dick Durbin) and House (Majority Leader Steny Hoyer) similarly surpass their predecessors.

EARTHJUSTICE
Because the earth needs a good lawyer

EARTHJUSTICE

Because the earth needs a good lawyer

21

You work in public relations for an over-the-counter drug company. Someone walks into your office and tells you that tiny fragments of metal have been discovered in a small number of 500-milligram acetaminophen caplets.

You learn from the company's quality-control manager that about one in 400,000 caplets might contain traces of the particulates. The Food and Drug Administration tells you that the possibility of adverse effects is remote. The company assures you that it has 100 percent of the initial product batch that originally caused the investigation.

Would you advise recalling all 11 million bottles of 500-milligram acetaminophen caplets?

You may confront issues and decisions like this if you choose a career in public relations. You may not be planning a career in news—you may know already that you are headed toward some area of public relations. Or, as happens to many people, perhaps you will work in news organizations for a while, but at some point in your career you may decide to switch to public relations. Or perhaps you are already writing for public relations.

Few disagree that the skill most required of public-relations people is good writing. Your writing skills should include newswriting, and you should be familiar with the way news operations work. That's why journalism schools traditionally require a course in newswriting for students interested in public relations, and that's why many public-relations professionals like to hire people with some news experience. Only by studying news and how news organizations handle it will you be successful in public relations or in offices of public information. Knowing how reporters are taught to deal with news releases will help you write better releases. Of course, studying news also helps you enormously in the advertising world and in what is now frequently called strategic marketing or strategic communications.

Skilled public-relations or public-information practitioners know how to write news, and they apply all the principles of good newswriting to their news releases. A good news release should meet the criteria of a good news story.

These same professionals know that working for an organization and doing internal and external communications demand a perspective different from a news perspective and, in many cases, a kind of writing different from newswriting. In many ways, of course, good writing is good writing, and what you have learned so far about newswriting also applies to public-relations writing. However, in public relations you also will be called upon to do writing that is different from the kinds of writing done by those who work for news organizations.

PUBLIC-RELATIONS WRITING—A DIFFERENT APPROACH

Let's begin with a few definitions and distinctions. Rex Harlow, called by some the "father of public-relations research" and perhaps the first full-time public-relations educator, claimed to have found 472 definitions of "public relations." The

443

1978 World Assembly of Public Relations in Mexico came up with this definition: "Public relations is the art and social science of analyzing trends, predicting their consequences, counseling organizational leaders and implementing planned programs of action which will serve both the organization's and public interest."

According to authors Wilcox, Ault, Agee and Cameron in *Public Relations: Strategies and Tactics*, these key words are found in all the definitions of "public relations":

- **Deliberate:** the "activity is intentional . . . designed to influence, gain understanding, provide feedback, and obtain feedback."
- **Planned:** "organized . . . systematic, requiring research and analysis."
- **Performance:** "based on actual policies."
- **Public interest:** "mutually beneficial to the organization and to the public."
- **Two-way communication:** "equally important to solicit feedback."
- **Management function:** "an integral part of decision-making by top management."

Public relations, then, is not just publicity, which seeks to get the media to respond to an organization's interests. Nor is it advertising, which pays to get the attention of the public, or marketing, which combines a whole host of activities to sell a product, service or idea. Advertising and marketing are concerned with sales.

A Range of Interests

If you wish to write in the field of public relations, you can choose to work in one of many areas. Here are some of the specialties:

- **Media relations:** seeking publicity and answering questions posed by the media.
- **Government affairs:** spending your time with legislatures and regulatory agencies and doing some lobbying.
- **Public affairs:** engaging in matters of public policy.
- **Industry relations:** relating to other firms in your industry and to trade associations.
- **Investor or financial or shareholder relations:** working to maintain investor confidence and good relationships with the financial world.

And the list goes on. Whoever said public-relations writing was dull knew nothing of the various worlds these professionals inhabit.

We must introduce one more term before proceeding. More and more today you see the term "strategic communication" replacing "public relations." Some have said that one simple reason for this is that the term "public relations" has always suffered a "PR" problem. It is true that many people have had a negative view of public relations, but, of course, the problems are much more serious than that.

The demands made of public-relations professionals are greater today than they were a generation ago. As Ronald Smith explains in *Strategic Planning for Public Relations*:

> No longer is it enough merely to know *how* to do things. Now the effective communicator needs to know *what* to do, *why* and how to *evaluate* its effectiveness. Public relations professionals used to be called upon mainly for tasks such as writing news releases, making speeches, producing videos, publishing newsletters, organizing displays and so on. Now the profession demands competency in conducting research, making decisions and solving problems. The call now is for strategic communicators.

In short, the strategic communicator must take a more scientific approach, do some research, make careful choices, and, when finished, evaluate the effectiveness of the completed program. Such a communicator would certainly be expected to write clearly and precisely, but differently from reporters.

Objectivity and Public-Relations Writing

Journalists will debate forever whether anyone can be truly objective when writing a story. Most settle the argument by saying what is demanded is a verifiable method of reporting. Nevertheless, in traditional reporting, writers should strive not to have a point of view. Reporters should not set out to prove something. Certainly they should not be an advocate for a point of view. They should get the facts and let the facts speak for themselves.

By contrast, columnists have a point of view, and good ones find ways to support it convincingly. Editorial writers use facts to persuade people to change their minds, or to confirm their opinions, or to get people to do something or to stop doing something.

That's also what public-relations writers do. Although sometimes they wish only to inform their audiences, more often they want to do what editorial writers do: persuade the audience to adopt a particular position.

However, there's one major difference: Journalists serve the public. Public-relations writers work for an organization or for a client other than a news operation. Their job is to make that organization or client appear in the best possible light. Effective public-relations writers do not ignore facts, even when they are harmful or detrimental to the cause they are promoting. But they are promoting a cause or looking out for the best interests of the people for whom they are working. As a result, they will interpret all news, even bad news, in the most favorable light.

Public-relations writers work much the way attorneys work for clients—as advocates. They don't lie or even distort, but perhaps they play down certain facts and emphasize others. In its "official statement of public relations," the Public

Relations Society of America states: "Public relations helps our complex, pluralistic society to reach decisions and function more effectively by contributing to mutual understanding among groups and institutions. It serves to bring private and public policies into harmony. . . . The public-relations practitioner acts as a counselor to management and as a mediator, helping to translate private aims into reasonable, publicly acceptable policy and action."

The preamble to the Public Relations Society's code of ethics (Figure 21.1) stresses a commitment to ethical practices. For a good discussion of what public relations is, check the Web site of the Public Relations Student Society of America at www.prssa.org. The Public Relations Society of America has a "Code of Professional Standards for the Practice of Public Relations." The code requires members to "adhere to the highest standard of accuracy and truth, avoiding extravagant claims or unfair comparisons and giving credit for ideas and words borrowed from others." It also requires members not to "knowingly disseminate false or misleading information." See www.prsa.org/profstd.html for the rest of the code.

Preamble

Public Relations Society of America Member Code of Ethics

- Professional Values
- Principles of Conduct
- Commitment and Compliance

This Code applies to PRSA members. The Code is designed to be a useful guide for PRSA members as they carry out their ethical responsibilities. This document is designed to anticipate and accommodate, by precedent, ethical challenges that may arise. The scenarios outlined in the Code provision are actual examples of misconduct. More will be added as experience with the Code occurs.

The Public Relations Society of America (PRSA) is committed to ethical practices. The level of public trust PRSA members seek, as we serve the public good, means we have taken on a special obligation to operate ethically.

The value of member reputation depends upon the ethical conduct of everyone affiliated with the Public Relations Society of America. Each of us sets an example for each other—as well as other professionals—by our pursuit of excellence with powerful standards of performance, professionalism, and ethical conduct.

Emphasis on enforcement of the Code has been eliminated. But, the PRSA Board of Directors retains the right to bar from membership or expel from the Society any individual who has been or is sanctioned by a government agency or convicted in a court of law of an action that is in violation of this Code.

Ethical practice is the most important obligation of a PRSA member. We view the Member Code of Ethics as a model for other professions, organizations, and professionals.

Figure 21.1
The preamble to the Public Relations Society's code of ethics stresses the value of ethical practice for members of the society.

PUBLIC-RELATIONS WRITING—A DIVERSITY OF TASKS

Like all good communicators, public-relations personnel are concerned with three things: the *message*, the *audience* and the *media* to deliver the message.

The Message

Like a good reporter writing a well-written story, you must know the message your organization wants to send. That message may be about a product, a program or the organization itself. For every message you work on, you must first know what you hope to accomplish, even if your purpose is just to inform.

That's why it is so important for you to be a reporter first, to know how to gather information and to do so quickly. Like any reporter, you may be called upon in an instant to help make strategic decisions.

The scenario that opened this chapter, about metal fragments found in acetaminophen caplets, was based on a real story. How did the Perrigo Company respond?

First, Perrigo notified the Food and Drug Administration. The FDA's investigation concluded that the possibility of any adverse effects was remote. Nevertheless, Perrigo announced a voluntary recall of 11 million bottles of 500-milligram acetaminophen caplets.

Moreover, Perrigo listed on its Web site all of the stores that sold the drug and showed pictures of the bottle and the box with the batch number that consumers should look for.

Regardless of the cost, Perrigo's quick and decisive action gained the public's goodwill and reinforced the company's credibility.

Another incident that called for quick and decisive action occurred when the Crown Princess cruise ship left Port Canaveral for New York at 3:25 a.m. on July 18, 2006. Suddenly she listed 15 degrees to the right and injured 240 of her 3,450 passengers, 94 of them seriously enough to be sent to the hospital. To make matters worse, a similar incident had involved another of the cruise line's ships, the Grand Princess, the previous February. That one was blamed on human error.

One can only wonder what was done or said to calm the passengers as the ship headed back to Cape Canaveral. If you looked under "News" on the Crown Princess Web site on July 18, you would have found a letter, not a news release, about the incident. The letter, posted at 5:30 p.m. by the Public Relations Department of Princess Cruises in Santa Clarita, Calif., contained only general information about "a number of passengers" who sustained injuries and "numerous reports of injuries such as cuts, bruises and fractures." But follow-up messages were much more specific once reliable information became available.

The Crown Princess was on a nine-day Western Caribbean sailing, a roundtrip out of New York, with Port Canaveral as its last stop. The July 18 letter noted that passengers would be returned home and would receive a full refund and full reimbursement of any additional expenses. The cruise line was frank about the cause of the listing—again it was human error. These prompt and honest decisions and announcements were public relations at its best.

The Audience

Almost as important as knowing all you can about the message is knowing the audience to whom you are directing it. The better you target your audience, the more effective you will be. As in advertising, demographics and psychographics determine the way you write your message, the language you choose, and the simplicity or complexity of the piece you are creating (see Figure 21.2 for an example of a news release).

Who are those people, what are their attitudes, and what do they do for work and recreation? You will answer these questions somewhat differently if you write for internal audiences (employees or managers) or external audiences (the media, shareholders, constituents, volunteers, consumers or donors).

The first concern of the Crown Princess public-relations staff was the people on the ship. They needed to communicate with the passengers, of course, but just as crucially, they needed to communicate with the staff to tell them how to deal with the situation, not to panic and to assure passengers that the Crown Princess was sound and in no danger of sinking. And then there were all of the media bombarding them with questions, and it wasn't just the general news media, but travel magazines, Web sites, newsletters and cruise magazines.

USA Today, for example, ran a front-page story with the headline " 'We Thought We Were Gone' after the Cruise Ship Tilts." The story quotes various passengers, one of whom described how people were washed out of the pool. "It was like Niagara Falls," he said.

And, of course, there were the moment-by-moment decisions of what to do with the people on board. How were they going to get home? What sort of compensation would be appropriate?

The Media

Once you have mastered the message or product and targeted the audience, you then have to choose the best media by which to deliver the message to the audience. For a message that nearly everyone wants or needs to know, television may be your best medium. Procter & Gamble spends millions advertising soap on television because everyone needs soap. Television offers color and motion; television can show rather than just tell.

Radio listeners are usually loyal to one radio station. They will listen to your message over and over. The more often they hear it, the more likely they are to retain it.

Print is better for complicated messages and sometimes for delicate messages. Some argue that print still has more credibility than other media and that people can come back again and again to a print message.

More and more people are getting the information and products they need online, where you have all the media in one medium. People who are online are generally better educated and more affluent than those who are not. They love the

Microsoft Partners with Local School Districts to Improve Math Education
Increasing awareness of challenges and expanding teaching skills seen as vital to success.

REDMOND, Wash. — Nov. 1, 2006 — Microsoft Corp. today launched the Microsoft® Math Partnership, a public-private initiative to enable educators and encourage Washington state businesses and state government to focus new attention and resources on improving middle-school math education. Brad Smith, Microsoft's senior vice president and co-chair of the Prosperity Partnership, announced the initiative during his keynote speech at the Prosperity Partnership Fall Luncheon in Seattle.

Smith noted the following:
- Barely half of Washington's 10th graders passed the latest WASL math exam. A passing score on the WASL exam becomes a requirement for high-school graduation in 2008.
- Forty-seven percent of high-impact job openings that require a bachelor's degree require high proficiency in math.
- Fewer than 20 percent of the students receiving a bachelor's degree in Washington each year, however, get their degrees in one of these high-demand fields.
- Only 53 percent of Washington state secondary teachers teach the subject they majored in.

Math Is at the Center of Global Competitiveness
Despite an increased insistence on critical thinking, technology and competitiveness in today's global economy, the United States, and especially the state of Washington, lags behind the rest of the world in preparing the future workforce with math fundamentals.

Consequently, businesses in Washington must recruit people from out of state with bachelor's and advanced degrees to fill the jobs created by the growing economy. This leaves Washington's economic future partly in the hands of decision-makers in other states and regions across the country and around the world.

"Clearly it is time for us to invest even more in our math teachers so they can invest even more in our students," Smith said. "It starts at the middle-school level so that the students are interested in and prepared for the math that's needed in high school and college. And then it means filling the pipeline by finding the space for these motivated students in our colleges and universities."

"We must invest in Washington students if we want our state to remain globally competitive," said Washington Gov. Chris Gregoire. "Microsoft understands the business sense behind this investment and knows that there are significant reasons for private businesses to partner with our public institutions."

"Our state is a major force in the international economy," said Terry Bergeson, state superintendent of public instruction for Washington. "Mathematics is essential to the jobs that drive that economy. And it is also essential to successfully managing our daily, complex lives. The world has changed. It is time to face facts: Mathematics is for everyone."

The key finding in research conducted by the American Institutes for Research is that algebra is the "gatekeeper" for student access to the upper-level high-school courses in mathematics that drive high-school graduation, college readiness and college completion. Students who pass algebra by the ninth grade and geometry by the 10th grade more than triple their odds of attending college.

"We feel so strongly about the importance of higher math at the middle-school level that we are investing our resources to help make some solid, measurable strides to help our teachers improve our students," Smith said.

Figure 21.2
Traditional news releases can be found online at companies' Web sites. This excerpt was taken from such a site.

control they have over the messages they find there. They can select only the information they want, and they can get it in any order they choose.

What is so wonderful (and so frightening) about "new media" is that you are dealing with a mass medium that is highly individualized; you are in the world of what has been called "mass customization." You must present the message at different levels to different people so that they feel they have choices, so that everyone feels as if you are writing only to him or her. It's all about individual choices and involving your readers so they interact with you. Communicating online ideally means that you have all the advantages and disadvantages of communicating all in one medium.

If you work in internal communications, you may decide to publish a newsletter or magazine. A large number of corporations communicate with employees throughout the day by an intranet, an internal online service accessible only to them. As a result, a surprisingly large number of organizations have ceased to publish internal print publications.

For messages that need more explanation, such as healthcare matters, perhaps a printed brochure will best do the job. Externally, for matters that may concern the community, you may want to use billboards in addition to paid ads in publications or on radio or television. Or you may choose to write news releases and leave it to others to interpret your message.

Sometimes, however, there's no quick fix. What took a long time to build can come tumbling down quickly, and then a long rebuilding process is necessary.

Many corporations and organizations have newsletters and magazines for internal and external audiences. These outstanding publications are published by Staffing Industry Analysts Inc. in Los Altos, Calif.

Common Public-Relations Activities

Public Relations: Strategies and Tactics, by Wilcox, Ault, Agee and Cameron, lists these activities as common to those who work in public relations. Notice how many of these involve writing either directly or indirectly.

Advise management on policy

Participate in policy decisions

Plan public-relations programs

Sell programs to top management

Get cooperation of middle management

Get cooperation from other employees

Listen to speeches

Make speeches

Write speeches for others

Obtain speakers for organizational meetings

Plan and conduct meetings

Prepare publicity items

Talk to editors and reporters

Hold press conferences

Write feature articles

Research public opinion

Plan and manage events

Conduct tours

Write letters

Plan and write booklets, leaflets, reports and bulletins

Attend meetings

Plan films and videotapes

Plan and prepare slide presentations

Plan and produce exhibits

Take pictures or supervise photographers

Make awards

Design posters

Greet visitors

Screen charity requests

Evaluate public-relations programs

Conduct fund-raising drives

The Media Campaign

Research shows that the more media you use, the better chance you have to succeed. That's why effective public-relations people, like those in advertising, think in terms of campaigns and strategies. A campaign assumes that you can't just tell an audience only once what you want them to learn, retain and act on. You need a strategy to reach a goal that may take days, weeks, months or even years to attain. Which medium do you use to introduce the subject, which media will you engage for follow-up and details, which aspects of the message are best suited for which media? You accomplish little by sending out the message once and in only one medium. If you send the message in a mix of media, in a carefully timed or orchestrated way, the results will be exponentially greater.

Public-relations writers adapt messages to the whole spectrum of media available. To do this, you must learn what each medium does best. Perhaps Marshall McLuhan was exaggerating when he wrote that the medium is the message, but no one doubts there is a great deal of truth to his statement.

You may be hired as a speechwriter or do something as specialized as writing an organization's annual report. Corporations and institutions such as hospitals

Creating News

Journalists, especially television journalists, are sometimes accused of creating stories by their very presence or, at least, of exacerbating situations, of fanning the flames. However, it is not in their job description to "create" news. A large part of doing public relations is to do just that — to create news. Here's a list of how to do that from the text of Wilcox, Ault, Agee and Cameron:

1. Tie in with news events of the day.
2. Cooperate with another organization on a joint project.
3. Tie in with a newspaper or broadcast station on a mutual project.
4. Conduct a poll or survey.
5. Issue a report.
6. Arrange an interview with a celebrity.
7. Take a part in a controversy.
8. Arrange for a testimonial.
9. Arrange for a speech.
10. Make an analysis or prediction.
11. Form and announce names for committees.
12. Hold an election.
13. Announce an appointment.
14. Celebrate an anniversary.
15. Issue a summary of facts.
16. Tie in with a holiday.
17. Make a trip.
18. Make an award.
19. Hold a contest.
20. Pass a resolution.
21. Appear before a public body.
22. Stage a special event.
23. Write a letter.
24. Release a letter you received (with permission).
25. Adapt national reports and surveys for local use.
26. Stage a debate.
27. Tie in to a well-known week or day.
28. Honor an institution.
29. Organize a tour.
30. Inspect a project.
31. Issue a commendation.
32. Issue a protest.

and universities hire thousands of communicators to get their messages out to the public. Or you may work for a public-relations agency that is hired to do this work for organizations.

Regardless of the means or media you choose to use, your job is to have good relations with the public. You do that best by trying to establish mutually beneficial relationships and by trying to set up win-win situations. All of this is best achieved when you make two-way communications possible. You must allow and encourage your various publics to have a voice in what you are trying to achieve. If you involve your audience in what you are trying to achieve, your chances of achieving it increase. Establishing a Web site is an excellent way to get people's ideas and reactions. Of course, you must find ways (notices on bulletin boards, brochures, newsletters, etc.) to make your Web site known.

PUBLIC-RELATIONS WRITING— A MATTER OF PERSUASION

Most of the time, your writing will attempt to persuade people. You need to study the techniques of persuasion and use them carefully. To persuade people, you need to believe three things:

1. **People are essentially good.** You need to be convinced of that and to appeal to people's basic goodness and fairness.
2. **People are intelligent or at least educable.** Don't talk down to people; don't assume that you can trick or fool them.
3. **People are changeable.** You must believe not only that people are changeable but also that you can change them.

First, more than anything else, you need to establish and maintain your credibility and the credibility of the organization you represent. Aristotle wrote that the character of the speaker is the most essential and powerful component of persuasion. Without a doubt, character is the most important thing public-relations people need to have and to develop. A sterling reputation takes a long time to build—and can be lost in an instant.

Second, you must assume goodwill on the part of your audience. You cannot persuade people by beating up on them, by calling them names or by considering them the enemy. This is particularly true regarding your attitude toward the press. Too many public-relations professionals consider the press the enemy, not to be trusted with the truth, to be stonewalled at every opportunity. Not everyone agrees with this approach.

Bill Huey, president of Strategic Communications in Atlanta, writes: "The next time you become incensed about something the media has done—or you want to go on a crusade, call your travel agent and go on a golfing vacation instead."

Here's an example of trusting the press. The University of North Carolina-Chapel Hill trusted the press when it learned that People for the Ethical Treatment of Animals had planted a spy in one of its animal-research facilities. The woman had worked there for eight months and secretly videotaped animals and the staff at work. PETA's goal was to defeat the Helms amendment to the 2002 farm bill that would have extended USDA authority for animal welfare to cover laboratory mice, rats and birds. That change, according to those opposed to it, would have meant a great deal more paperwork for the research team and little improvement in animal care. PETA held a press conference and set up a Web site showing lurid photos and making claims of animal cruelty and neglect.

The university's response was rapid, candid and forthright. On the same day PETA broke the story, Tony Waldrop, vice chancellor for research, and other university officials held a press conference, promised a thorough investigation and opened the facility in question to reporters. The university did not attempt to deny or discredit the PETA claims. With no hint of a coverup to feed upon, the story faded from the news in just a couple of days and university officials, at least, considered the media coverage to be fair and factual. The farm bill passed with the Helms amendment intact.

> **"**Desktop publishing has dramatically increased the quantity and enhanced the quality of news releases coming into a news room. News releases from local clubs and organizations that once were written in longhand on notebook paper now rival those of professional public-relations firms. The net effect: more news releases with local news than ever before. In a competitive media marketplace, smart newspapers can parlay this additional information into community pages packed with names and faces, reflecting the lives of readers in a way that other media can't.**"**
>
> — Ken Paulson, former senior vice president, The Freedom Forum, and now editor, *USA Today*

Meanwhile, the university lived up to its promise to investigate. It spent several thousand hours in internal investigations, and Waldrop commissioned a panel of three outside experts to do an independent review. The university then presented a 40-page report to the federal Office of Laboratory Animal Welfare, and the local press summarized it—again, in a fair, evenhanded manner. The report was then published in the university's research magazine: a candid account of what PETA claimed, what the university found in its investigations, and what it did to correct the problem.

That's how public relations can, should and does work.

WRITING NEWS RELEASES THAT GET ATTENTION

Earlier in this chapter, you read that good writing is the most important skill you can acquire as a public-relations professional. You also read about various positions available in the public-relations field, each demanding writing skills directed at different audiences. Whether you write brochures or annual reports; articles for your organization's newsletter or magazine or Web site; or copy for print or broadcast or film, the quality of what you produce will reflect directly on your organization.

> **❙❙** If you don't understand good journalistic style and format (who, what, when, where and why) for writing a press release, you harm your company and yourself.**❙❙**
>
> —G. A. Marken, president of Marken Communications, Inc., *Public Relations Quarterly*

Perhaps nothing that you will be called upon to write is more important than news releases. Even the smallest newspaper and radio or TV station gets dozens of news releases daily. How do you break through the clutter to grab the attention of the gatekeepers on the news desks? If you send news releases for the PR wire services or online, your problem is still the same. Here are some guidelines to help you get your message to your intended audience:

Know What News Is and How to Write It

If you are headed toward a career in public relations or public information, you are probably taking this newswriting course to help you understand the principles of news. The news media will not pay attention to copy that is laced with opinion or self-serving quotations. Worse, they will ridicule your work and discard it immediately.

Avoid statements like this: "Monroe College is recognized as the foremost and most prestigious college of liberal arts in the entire Midwest." Who says?

To write for most publications, certainly for newspapers, you need to know Associated Press style. Correct spelling, usage and grammar are essential, of course, but just as important is AP style. Why should news editors take you seriously if you do not bother to write in the style of their publications?

News releases are notoriously inaccurate and inconsistent in style and grammar. How ironic that people so concerned with image are so careless in how they present themselves to the public.

Know the Structure and Operations of News Rooms

If you do not get actual experience in a news room in college, find ways to spend some time in one. In Chapter 2, you studied how news rooms are organized. Now use your public-relations skills to get inside one and to experience what goes on there.

The most simple and important thing you can learn about news rooms is that they have deadlines. Learn the deadlines of the media in your area, and respect those deadlines. That means you cannot call in a story to a television news station a half hour before broadcast time. Not only will the station not use your story, but station employees will resent you and not forget the interruption at a critical time. News organizations will tell you what time you must submit a story to make the news that day.

Know the People in the News Media and the Jobs They Hold

This is especially true of newspapers. Sending a release addressed simply to a newspaper can be a waste of your time and make you look as if you do not know what you are doing. Sending a release to the business editor or to the features editor makes more sense. Addressing by name the editor of the section in which you wish the release to appear works best.

At a packed meeting of the Publicity Club of New York, features editor of the *New York Post* Faye Penn told her audience to stop sending her news releases. First, she said she could not possibly read them all, and second, many of them were about things her section never covered. Later, she backed down from her position and admitted that she looked to see who sent the release.

If people in the news media know and trust you, they are more likely to read your releases, and you can sometimes call them with a story and let them write their own stories. There's nothing writers like more than to get wind of a good story. At the Publicity Club of New York meeting, however, features editor Barbara Schuler of *Newsday* warned that she never answers her phone but does read all news releases and faxes. She stressed the importance of getting the release into the right hands, and she handed out a sheet with the names, phone numbers and beat assignments of the reporters on *Newsday*. You need that list for each medium you cover.

Just remember, your job is to help reporters write good stories. If you can help them do that and at the same time serve your client's interests, you will be a successful public-relations practitioner.

Know the Style of Writing That Fits the Medium

Do not make the mistake of sending the same news release to the radio or TV station that you send to the newspaper. Do not expect busy newspeople to translate your newspaper release into broadcast copy. If you can write radio or television copy (see Chapter 19), you have a much better chance of getting the copy read over the air. And if you can supply video, many stations will use it in their newscasts.

News Releases That Get Used

In Chapter 11, you read about the three general categories of news releases — announcements, cause-promoting releases and image-building releases. Fraser P. Seitel, author, communications consultant and teacher, writes that research reveals eight categories of news releases that are most likely to be used. They deal with

1. New products or projects
2. Personnel promotions — at least of important people
3. Trends
4. Conflict
5. Topicality — "relating your news to pressing issues of the day"
6. Local heritage — tying news to community roots or history
7. Human interest
8. Insanity — the truly bizarre or unusual

"Employers want people who can write and communicate ideas — who can pull complex or fragmented ideas together into coherent messages. This requires not only technical skill but also intelligence. It also requires a love of writing."

— Thomas H. Bivins, *Public Relations Writing*

Of course, none of the above media, including the largest newspapers or radio or television networks, can reach as many people as online media. Millions of Web sites know practically no limits. First, you must establish your own credible, up-to-date, interactive Web site. Second, you must be thoroughly familiar with Web sites like www.online-pr.com, www.prnewswire.com or www.medialink.com so you can distribute your releases online and keep up with what's happening in public relations. Third, you must become expert yourself at using the new media to get across your organization's messages.

Just as some newspapers will use your news releases almost verbatim, some radio and television stations will use your audio and video. The Center for Media and Democracy's 2006 report of a six-month investigation revealed that 46 stations in 22 states inserted video news releases, known as VNRs, into their newscasts. Moreover, nearly 90 percent did not reveal to viewers that these were VNRs, even though some of them dealt with controversial subjects such as global warming.

APPROACHES TO WRITING THE NEWS RELEASE

The Inverted Pyramid

The straight, no-nonsense inverted pyramid news release remains the staple of the public-relations professional (see Chapter 7). Many believe that any other approach will not be taken seriously by news professionals.

Here's an example. Notice the address and phone number of the organization putting out the release and the name of a contact person. If the news is for immediate release, say so. Otherwise, indicate a release date.

NEWS RELEASE

Missouri Department of Natural Resources

P.O. Box 176, Jefferson City, Missouri 65102 (573-751-3443)

For further information, contact: Mary Schwartz

(For immediate release)

JEFFERSON CITY, MO., FEB. 26, 2007— The winter solitude of Roaring River, Bennett Spring and Montauk state parks will be shattered by about 8,000 fishing enthusiasts expected to participate in the annual trout opening March 1 in Missouri State Parks.

The start of trout-fishing season in these parks marks the beginning of the vacation season in Missouri state parks, which are administered by the Missouri Department of Natural Resources. The Department also administers 30 other state parks and 22 historic sites, which officially open on April 15.

"Trout opening is definitely a big event for fishermen in Missouri," said John Karel, director of state parks. "But, it's also a big day for state parks since it traditionally marks the beginning of the upcoming vacation season."

Karel notes that park visitors to Montauk, Roaring River and Bennett Spring state parks will be greeted by a number of new construction and major renovation projects. . . .

The release goes on to talk about the projects and about how many trout tags were sold. It's a traditional approach, although the lead attempts to be a bit creative with the "winter solitude" being "shattered." The lead jumps to a quote from an authority, John Karel, the director of the state parks, and uses him as the source throughout.

Beyond the Inverted Pyramid

Let's look now at a different approach; some would call it a feature approach. The information at the top of the release is the same.

When the siren sounds at 6:30 a.m., March 1 in Bennett Spring State Park near Lebanon, Bill Brooks will be there. He'll be standing knee-deep in icy water as he's done every March 1 since 1985.

Brooks, known in fishing circles as Big Trout, will join an expected 8,000 other Missouri fishing enthusiasts for the opening of trout-fishing season in Missouri State Parks. Missouri's other trout-fishing state parks are Roaring River, near Cassville, and Montauk, near Salem.

Brooks can't imagine anything, short of a death in the family, that would keep him away. "This is just a tradition for me, I'm already making wagers and getting together my equipment."

As an extra measure, Brooks has made a special trip from his Marshfield home to the park just to check stream conditions.

After 22 years of opening days, Brooks has seen some changes. "I guess you could say they've gotten stricter on us. Things used to be a lot wilder down there in the old days, until they stopped us from gambling and stopped selling beer. . . ."

A Day in the Life of a Public-Relations Professional

Wilma Mathews is the consummate public-relations professional. Her 30-year career includes 15 years with AT&T and 10 years with Arizona State University. Her background includes work with a magazine and newspaper and at a medical center and chamber of commerce. She is a Fellow of the International Association of Business Communicators. She now serves as director of constituent relations for ASU and also as a faculty associate in the Walter Cronkite School of Journalism and Mass Communication.

In her former position as director of public relations at Arizona State University, her work crossed the borders of legislative affairs, community relations, media relations, events planning, marketing, advertising, employee communication, presidential support and the ever-famous "other duties as assigned."

Here she speaks of a typical day. This particular day points out the variety of problem solving and opportunity snatching that comes with a job of this scope.

A Wednesday . . .

Four meetings crowded this day and took precedence over the smaller issues that came up between them.

A colleague at one of our campuses had noticed that the advertising rate issued to us at *The Arizona Republic*

newspaper was based on the nonprofit status that assumed about $150,000/year in advertising. Since that rate was set, some years ago, many things have changed, and it appeared that ASU's cumulative advertising is closer to about $500,000/year, an amount that would qualify the university for a better rate.

I presided at a meeting that included the advertising manager and two representatives from the newspaper and representatives from the major Arizona State University advertiser organizations: athletics, public events (Broadway and other performances), extended education and the College of Business and Public Affairs.

The hour-long meeting confirmed that (a) university units are collectively advertising far more than realized; (b) there is no single representative for the university at the newspaper, so individual departments are quoted rates by whatever representative they happen to get; (c) the university had not done a good job of routinely working with the newspaper's advertising department.

Results of the meeting: We agreed to get a three-year look at ASU's advertising, allow the advertising manager and staff to present next month to all ASU public relations people both the new rate and other advertising opportunities, to have one advertising rep to serve as the coordinator among reps at the newspaper, and to help the paper develop a more accurate list of ASU advertisers.

The release then introduces fishing expert Jim Rogers, who runs concessions at both Bennett Spring and Roaring River. Rogers tells with specific numbers how he has sold more than double the number of trout tags that he sold just eight years ago.

In this approach, the writer uses a "real person," a long-time fisherman, to introduce the story—rather than a person in authority. By using Brooks and Rogers, the writer tells a story and still gives important information, but in an interesting and appealing way.

Now suppose the writer accompanied this story with a photo from the year before of Big Trout standing knee-deep in icy water. Public-relations professionals know that releases accompanied by photos or art of some kind get more attention and more play.

Some professionals have also begun to place attention-grabbing headlines on top of their releases. Others accompany the head with a summary/contents/benefit blurb. Why should the editor or the intended audience have to read the entire release to find out what it's about?

From that meeting, I went to one of the Sun Devil Advocates, an organization run by the ASU Alumni Association, to help build support for ASU's legislative agenda. The conversation focused on the need to have more face-to-face presentations within the university to departments and leadership about the serious and critical situation the university will be in for the second half of this fiscal year as well as fiscal '04 and '05. It appears that other channels of communication about the situation have not worked, and only face-to-face is getting people's attention.

I had to leave that meeting early in order to drive to a meeting in downtown Phoenix with Arvizu Advertising and Public Relations, an agency selected just a few days before to help ASU reach the Hispanic and other minority audiences in January and February with face-to-face and print presentations about the state universities' request to increase tuition by 44 percent while also increasing financial aid significantly. The agency is being asked to turn around an estimate in less than three working days and a draft plan in six working days in order to get as much accomplished as possible during the year-end holidays. I will be coordinating this program and working with the agency.

After returning to the office, I e-mailed a summary of the meeting to the provost, vice presidents and directors who are part of the planning group on this issue.

I then left the office for a meeting in Scottsdale with United Blood Services, the organization that conducts blood drives on our campuses. ASU is large enough to warrant a single representative from UBS to schedule the drives, find volunteers to help with the drives, develop blood drive "sponsors" from within the university to host drives, and report functionally to me about the program. ASU is one of the largest suppliers of blood in the Valley and has the ability to conduct two to three drives each month at various locations. This meeting approved the development plan and goals for the coming year.

In between meetings, I made appropriate notifications within the university and with police regarding two young men soliciting funds in various neighborhoods in the Valley who claimed to be students from our West campus. This required multiple voice mails and explanations and carried over into the next day while I was traveling to Chicago.

I also completed work as a survey participant for a graduate student's paper on crisis communications involving racial disturbances, wrote thank-you notes to two speakers who had presented at the monthly internal public relations meeting, and wrote and got approved a letter from the president regarding the United Way campaign.

At day's end, I completed what I needed to do for a trip to Chicago and a presentation I was to make there.

A normal day? Yes.

— Wilma Mathews, IABC, Former Director
of Public Relations, Arizona State University

❞Promotions into high office are newsworthy not just to the business, financial or trade press, but also to the person's hometown papers, alumni magazines and professional society journals. Notices of service anniversaries, training courses completed, retirements and honors received are welcome at various publications; the trick is to match the medium with the message. Some of these items, depending on visual appeal, could interest television as well.❞

— Carole Howard and Wilma Mathews, *On Deadline:
Managing Media Relations*

You might want to go a step further. Why not do some service journalism? Put the parks, their locations and the opening dates in a separate box. How about a map of how to get there? Perhaps you could make a list of the top-10 things to remember on opening day. Maybe you could create an infographic indicating where to get trout tags. Some news organizations will use just one sidebar or graphic of what you send. But the important thing is that if you give them choices, you have a better chance of getting some of your information used.

In the past, some public-relations professionals shied away from what they thought of as gimmicks, for fear that editors would not take them seriously. What they didn't see was the way newspapers were changing, especially some sections.

Why not experiment? Attention is harder and harder to get. Don't be afraid to try a "you" lead or even a question — for

ON THE JOB

News Releases

Jo Johnston has gone from reading news releases to writing them and sending them to the media.

After college, Johnston worked as a reporter and managing editor for the *Maryville (Mo.) Daily Forum* before becoming editor of *The Examiner* in Independence, Mo. She then left newspapers for corporate public relations with AT&T, where she's worked for more than 10 years.

In late 2004, she retired from AT&T to found her own firm, Johnston Public Relations, a public-relations and public-affairs consultancy in Dallas.

Back when she was in the news room, she says, "We opened and read every release in the daily mail." That's not the way it is today. One reporter told her recently he doesn't have enough time to open all the overnight-delivery packages he receives.

Today's reporters are more likely to receive releases by wire service. Only a grabbing headline or lead will get the reporter to take a second look before hitting the delete key.

Once you get the reader's attention, Johnston says, your job has just begun. Reporters are usually on deadline. "So anything you can do to make the reporter's job easier will increase the odds of getting ink or airtime," Johnston says.

She tries to give technical information in simple language. "First, what's new, and so what, followed by simple descriptions and a complete story that doesn't leave the audience with unanswered questions."

Most of all, she says, "We absolutely refuse to bow to the company's pressure to include 'fluff' in a news release. After all, we're building relationships with reporters, and our reputations are at stake."

example, "Are you ready for opening day at Bennett Spring?" Remember to get to the "so what" quickly—not your organization's but the audience's. What's in it for the reader or listener? Most readers don't care whether Comcast has announced the purchase of another company. (Some companies seem never to do anything but "announce" things in news releases.) Readers do care about how this sale might affect them and their cable bills.

Remember, too, that a film clip of Big Trout will more likely be used by a television news producer than will a written release, and a recorded interview might get played on your local radio station.

Even if none of these media uses your material the way you presented it, perhaps you will succeed in grabbing the attention of an editor or reporter. If that person is inspired to pursue the story, you'll still get the information to the public.

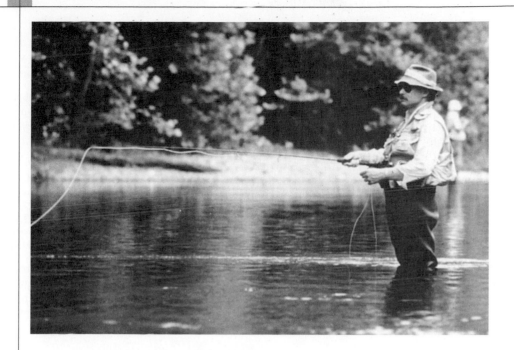

Photos like this one, provided by the Missouri State Department of Conservation, can accompany press releases promoting trout fishing in Missouri.

    Be sure that you make yourself available—by cell phone, e-mail, fax, Web site, in person—24 hours a day. A reporter on deadline will write the story with or without you. It's better that you talk—it's *always* better that you talk—to the reporter.

    Remember, your job is not just to write news releases. Your job is to get information from your organization to the public. Writing news releases is only one means to that end. As a public-relations writer, you will use your writing skills in myriad ways in all media to serve your clients well.

Tips for Writers of News Releases

1. Follow an accepted journalistic style of writing. Use AP style.
2. Go easy on length. Hold it to two double-spaced, typewritten pages.
3. Avoid breaks. Don't hyphenate words at the ends of lines, and don't split a sentence at the bottom of a page.
4. Write clearly. Avoid corporate jargon, legalese or other alien language.
5. Remember the pyramid. But don't put all the w's in the lead.
6. Beware of adjectives. Especially avoid superlatives.
7. Make it local.
8. Attribute news to a person, not to a company or an organization.
9. Indent the paragraphs.

                                       —Carole Howard and Wilma Mathews,
On Deadline: Managing Media Relations

Suggested Readings

Bivins, Thomas H. *Public Relations Writing*, Fourth Edition. Lincolnwood, Ill.: NTC/Contemporary Publishing Group, 1999. This useful book covers the wide variety of writing expected of public-relations professionals.

Holtz, Shel. *Public Relations on the Net*. New York: Amacom, 1999. Anything Shel Holtz says or writes about online subjects is worth paying attention to. See also www.holtz.com.

Horton, James L. *Online Public Relations*. Westport, Conn.: Quorum Books, 2001. This superb primer begins by explaining terminology and ends with 85 industry and general information topics on placing news and gathering information.

Howard, Carole and Mathews, Wilma. *On Deadline: Managing Media Relations*, Third Edition. Prospect Heights, Ill.: Waveland Press, 2000. This is a practical book on how organizations should deal with the news media.

Huey, Bill. "'Incensed' about Something the Media Has Done? Get Over It." *O'Dwyer's PR Report*, October 2006, p. 37. This article offers excellent advice to public-relations professionals on how to deal with what they perceive as bad press.

Newsom, Doug and Carrel, Bob. *Public Relations Writing, Form and Style*, Sixth Edition. Australia: Wadsworth, 2001. A truly thorough classic, it even has a section on grammar, spelling and punctuation.

Seitel, Fraser P. *The Practice of Public Relations*, Tenth Edition. New York: Prentice Hall, 2006. You can tell Seitel has been a teacher. He writes simply, clearly and engagingly.

Seitel, Fraser P. "'Used' News Releases." *O'Dwyer's PR Report*, September 2006, pp. 31, 42. Seitel's columns on "Professional Development" appear regularly in this publication.

Wilcox, Dennis L. *Public Relations Writing and Media Techniques*, Fourth Edition. New York: Longman, 2001. Filled with practical tips in all areas of public-relations writing, this text includes handy boxes and sidebars.

Suggested Web Sites

www.instituteforpr.com
Provides information about public-relations research, measurement, programs, seminars, publications, scholarship, etc., from the Institute for Public Relations.

www.odwyerpr.com
Subscription to this Web site includes *O'Dwyer's PR Report*, an excellent monthly that devotes each issue to a public-relations specialty field.

www.online-pr.com
An amazingly helpful site for anyone interested in public relations. Offers links to many useful Web sites.

www.prnewswire.com
This site sends out more than a thousand news releases each day.

www.prsa.org
Has general information about the Public Relations Society of America, lists its chapters and sections, has publications, membership and accreditation information, recognitions and awards, conferences and seminars.

www.prsa.org/awards/silveranvil
Site of the Silver Anvil awards—annual awards to organizations that have successfully addressed a contemporary issue with exemplary professional skill, creativity and resourcefulness."

www.prssa.org
Contains news for members and leaders of the Public Relations Student Society of America, as well as job listings and a calendar of events.

www.prwatch.org
Web site of the Center for Media and Democracy. Investigates "public-relations spin and propaganda."

Exercises

1. Obtain a magazine published by a corporation. Study it, and write a brief report on how it differs from a consumer magazine.

2. A classmate was killed in a car accident. Some money has been raised to set up a scholarship to honor his memory, but much more is needed to endow the scholarship. Several students in the class have been training to run in the Chicago marathon. A group decides to solicit money for each mile the students complete. Organize a campaign on your campus to get people to pledge or to donate money. Answer these questions:

   a. What are your target audiences?
   b. Which media will you use?
   c. What print materials will you develop?

   Then write a news release for the local media.

3. Read the following news release, and note any deviations from AP style. Also note any content that news organizations might object to.

   NEWS RELEASE
   "Chest Pains", an excellent film in the HEALTHCARE series produced by the American College of Physicians, will be shown from 7:00–8:30 P.M., Wednesday, October 22, at St. Mary's Health Center. Springfield internist Dr. Harold Kanagawa will host a question-and-answer period following the film.

   Although most people assume that chest pains signify a heart attack, the public is less aware that other conditions—hiatal hernia, ulcers, viral infections of the heart's membranes—can also cause pains that require prompt diagnosis and appropriate medical treatment. Designed to help increase awareness of the symptoms and their possible significance, "Chest Pains" features an internist and actual patients as they work together to resolve underlying medical problems.

   Through a warm and engaging human-interest style of presentation, each twenty-five-minute documentary encourages people to take an increased responsibility for their own well-being by establishing healthy habits and assuming a more active role in disease prevention.

   The HEALTHCARE series is produced under an educational grant from the Elsworth Company of Midland, Michigan. Other films in this superb, highly acclaimed series cover "Aches, Pains and Arthritis", "Diabetes", and "Abdominal Discomfort".

   Doctor Kanagawa, a renowned specialist in internal medicine, is 1 of fifty-thousand members of the American College of Physicians. Founded in 1915, the College is the largest medical specialty society in the U.S. and one of the most prestigious. It represents doctors of internal medicine, related non-surgical specialists, and physicians-in-training.

   To register or for more information, contact the Women's Life Center.

4. Interview a student from a small town. Then write a news release about his or her life and activities at the university, and send it to the town's newspaper.

5. Study the Web site of the college or university you attend. List five aspects of the Web site that you think are excellent and five aspects that you would like to see improved.

Media Law

22

The First Amendment states:

> Congress shall make no law respecting an establishment of religion, or prohibiting the free exercise thereof; or abridging the freedom of speech, or of the press; or the right of the people peaceably to assemble, and to petition the Government for a redress of grievances.

Read that again: "Congress shall make no law . . . abridging the freedom of . . . the press." No other business in the United States enjoys that specific constitutional protection, unless you consider religion a business.

Why should there be such protection for the press? The Supreme Court gave an eloquent answer to that question in a 1957 obscenity decision. The press is protected, the court ruled, to ensure the "unfettered interchange of ideas for bringing about the political and social changes desired by the people."

The free flow of ideas is necessary in a democracy because people who govern themselves need to know about their government and about those who run it, as well as about the social and economic institutions that greatly affect their day-to-day lives. Most people get that information through newspapers, the Internet, radio and television. Increasingly, citizen journalists are communicating through blogs. While professional journalists debate whether blogs should be considered "real" journalism, the legal system is grappling with the issue of how to apply constitutional protection and law to them.

In 1966, Congress passed the Freedom of Information Act to assist anyone in finding out what is happening in federal agencies. This act, which was amended in 1996 by the Electronic Freedom of Information Act to improve access to computerized government records, makes it easier for you to know about government business. All 50 states have similar **open-records laws**. Though of great assistance to the press, these laws are also used by individuals and businesses to gain information previously kept secret by the government. There are other laws ensuring access to government transactions. The federal government and all the states have **open-meetings laws**—often called "sunshine laws"—requiring the public's business to be conducted in public. However, all of these access laws contain exemptions that keep some meetings private.

The First Amendment, the Freedom of Information Act and the sunshine laws demonstrate America's basic concern for citizen access to information needed for the "unfettered interchange of ideas." Nevertheless, there are laws that reduce the scope of freedom of the press.

LIBEL

Traditionally, most of the laws limiting the absolute principle of freedom of the press have dealt with libel. These laws result from the desire of legislatures and courts to help individuals protect their reputations. Their importance was explained by U.S. Supreme Court Justice Potter Stewart in a 1966 libel case.

465

The right of a man [or woman] to the protection of his [or her] own reputation from unjustified invasion and wrongful hurt reflects no more than our basic concept of the essential dignity and worth of every human being—a concept at the root of any decent system of ordered liberty.

Protection for reputations dates back centuries. In 17th-century England, individuals were imprisoned and even disfigured for making libelous statements. One objective was to prevent criticism of the government. Another was to maintain the peace by avoiding duels. Duels are rare today, and government is freely criticized, but the desire to protect an individual's reputation is just as strong.

A case concerning a general is helpful in understanding libel. The extensively covered trial was held in the winter of 1984–1985 in the federal courthouse in Manhattan. The case was based on a 1983 *Time* magazine cover story, "Verdict on the Massacre," about Israel's 1982 judicial inquiry into the massacre of several hundred civilians in two Palestinian refugee camps in Lebanon.

The *Time* article suggested that Ariel Sharon, then Israel's defense minister and later its prime minister, had ordered the massacre. The general sued *Time*. His attorneys knew they would have to show that their client had suffered hatred, contempt or ridicule because these statements were serious attacks on his reputation and not just unpleasant comments.

> **❝The government's power to censor the press was abolished so the press would remain forever free to censure the government.❞**
>
> —Hugo Black, Supreme Court Justice

The jury's decision was in three parts. The first part of the verdict was in answer to this question: Was the paragraph concerning Sharon defamatory? The jury said it was. This meant the *Time* article had damaged Sharon's reputation and exposed him to hatred, contempt or ridicule.

The second question for the jury was this: Was the paragraph concerning Sharon and revenge false? Again the jury answered affirmatively. If the answer had been no, the case would have ended there. Truth is a complete defense for libel.

The third question for the jury was: Was the paragraph published with "actual malice"—with knowledge that it was false or with reckless disregard of whether it was false ("serious doubt" that it was true)? The jury answered no. Thus the trial ended in favor of *Time* magazine, despite the jury's ruling that the article was defamatory.

Courts use four categories to help jurors like those in the Sharon case decide if someone's reputation has been damaged because he or she has been brought into hatred, contempt or ridicule. They are:

1. **Accusing someone of a crime.** This may have been the basis for the Sharon suit.
2. **Damaging a person in his or her public office, profession or occupation.** If the statements by *Time* against Sharon did not accuse him of crimes, they did damage him in his profession as a military man.
3. **Accusing a person of serious immorality.** The example lawyers often use is accusing a woman of being unchaste. Many states have statutes that make an accusation of unchastity a cause of action in a libel suit.

4. **Accusing someone of having a loathsome (i.e., contagious) disease.** This category was fading as a source of defamation until the AIDS epidemic helped it reappear.

This does not mean you can never say a person committed a crime, was unethical in business, was adulterous or had a loathsome disease. It does mean you must be certain that what you write is true.

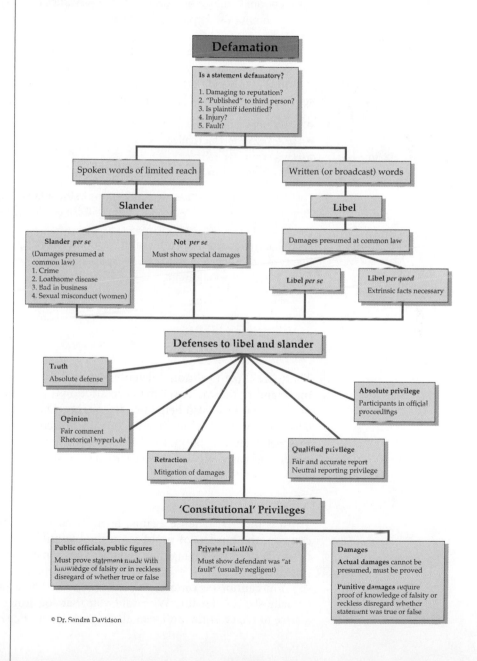

Figure 22.1
An understanding of libel and related concepts is essential for journalists.

ON THE JOB

The Keys to Avoiding Libel

Ken Paulson earned a law degree after graduating from journalism school. He then practiced journalism for 18 years. After serving as senior vice president of the Freedom Forum in Arlington, Va., and executive director of The First Amendment Center at Vanderbilt University, he returned to the news room as editor of *USA Today*.

"Having a law degree has been helpful as a journalist," he says, "but the key to avoiding libel suits really boils down to a few fundamentals."

The keys to avoiding a libel suit are rooted in professionalism and common sense. He suggests that journalists ask themselves these questions:

- Have I reported fully?
- Have I reported factually?
- Have I reported fairly?
- Have I reported in good faith?

"If you can answer those four questions in the affirmative, the law will take care of itself," he says. Paulson joined the Gannett Co. in 1978. He has been executive editor of *Florida Today* in Melbourne, Fla.; editor of the *Green Bay (Wis.) Press-Gazette*; managing editor of the Bridgewater, N.J., *Courier News* and executive editor of Gannett Suburban Newspapers in the New York counties of Westchester, Rockland and Putnam.

Libel Suit Defenses

There are three traditional defenses against libel: truth, privilege, and fair comment and criticism. Two other constitutional defenses—the **actual malice** and negligence tests—also help libel defendants. The court case clarifying these standards involved traditional media, but the principles are now being applied to the Internet, including blogs. In 2006, a blogger in Georgia lost the first of these electronic libel cases. He was ordered to pay $50,000 to a lawyer he had criticized.

Truth

Truth is the best defense against libel. In libel cases involving matters of public concern, the burden of proof is on the plaintiff. This placement of the burden, however, does not change the reporter's responsibility to seek the truth in every possible way.

You cannot be certain, for example, whether a person charged with arson actually started the fire. Who told you that Joe Jones started the fire? The first source to check is the police or fire report. If a police officer or fire marshal says that Jones started a fire, you can report not that Jones did it but that he has been accused of doing it. Unless you have information you would be willing to present in court, you should go no further. Be sure you report no more than what you know is true.

When a newspaper in Oklahoma reported that a wrestling coach had been accused of requiring a sixth-grader, who wanted to rejoin the team, to submit to a whipping by his fellow students while crawling naked through the legs of team members, the coach sued. He claimed damage to his reputation.

In cases like this, the reporter has to be certain not just that one or more participants told of the incident but also that the statements were true. In court, some participants might testify to an occurrence and others might testify the incident never took place. A jury would have to decide on the credibility of the participants.

Although you must always strive for absolute truth in all of your stories, the courts will settle for what is known as **substantial truth** in most cases. This means that you must be able to prove the essential elements of all you write.

The Georgia case and others show that the courts are holding bloggers to the same standard established for traditional media. In the Georgia case, a disappointed client accused his former attorney, in a blog, of bribing judges. The lawyer sued and won when the blogger couldn't show that his charge was true.

Privilege

In addition to truth, the courts traditionally have allowed another defense against libel: **privilege**. This defense applies when you are covering any of the three branches of government. The courts allow legislators, judges and government executives the **absolute privilege** to say anything—true or false—when acting in their official capacities. The rationale is that the public interest is served when an official is allowed to speak freely and fearlessly about making laws, carrying them out or punishing those who do not obey them. Similarly, a participant in a judicial proceeding, such as an attorney, court clerk or judge, is absolutely privileged to make false and even defamatory statements about another person during that proceeding.

In the executive branch it isn't always clear whose statements are privileged and when. The head of state and the major officers of executive departments of the federal and state governments are covered. However, minor officials might not enjoy the protection of absolute privilege.

As a reporter, you have a qualified privilege, sometimes called *neutral reporting* or *conditional privilege*, to report what public officials say. Your privilege is conditioned on your report's providing full, fair and accurate coverage of the court session, the legislative session or the president's press conference, even if any one of the participants made defamatory statements. You can quote anything the president of the United States says without fear of losing a libel suit, even if the president is not acting in an official capacity. Reporters have a qualified privilege to report unofficial statements. But there are many other levels of executives in federal, state and local government. Mayors of small towns, for instance, often hold part-time positions. Although you are conditionally privileged to report on what those officials say when they are acting in their official capacities, a problem can arise when the part-time mayor says something defamatory when not acting in an official capacity. Courts in some jurisdictions might grant a qualified privilege; some might not.

Fair Comment and Criticism

In some types of writing, you may be commenting or criticizing rather than reporting. The courts have protected writers who comment on and criticize the public offerings of anyone in the public eye. Included in this category are actors and actresses, sports figures, public officials and other newsworthy people. Most often, such writing occurs in reviews of plays, books or movies, or in commentary on service received in hotels and restaurants.

The courts call this **fair comment and criticism**. You are protected as long as you do not misstate any of the facts on which you base your comments or criticism, or as long as you do not wrongly imply that you possess undisclosed, damaging information that forms the basis of your opinion. Merely labeling a fact as an opinion will not result in opinion protection, the U.S. Supreme Court ruled in 1990.

The Actual Malice Test

It was a small but momentous step from fair comment and criticism to the case of *The New York Times* v. Sullivan. In 1964, the U.S. Supreme Court decided that First Amendment protection was broader than just the traditional defenses of truth and privilege and that the press needed even greater freedom in coverage of public officials.

The case started with an advertisement for funds in *The New York Times* of March 29, 1960, by the Committee to Defend Martin Luther King Jr. and the Struggle for Freedom in the South. The advertisement contained factual errors concerning the police, according to Montgomery, Ala., Commissioner L.B. Sullivan. He thought the errors damaged his reputation, and he won a half-million-dollar judgment against *The New York Times* in an Alabama trial court.

The Supreme Court said it was considering the case "against the background of a profound national commitment to the principle that debate on public issues should be uninhibited, robust and wide open." Thus Justice William Brennan wrote that the Constitution requires a federal rule prohibiting a public official from recovering damages from the press for a defamatory falsehood relating to his or her official conduct, unless the public official can prove the press had knowledge that what was printed was false or that the story was printed with reckless disregard of whether it was true or not. The justices called this the **actual malice test**.

The actual malice test was applied later in a case involving a story on CBS's *60 Minutes* about a retired Army officer. Col. Anthony Herbert contended the broadcast falsely portrayed him as a liar. He tried to prove that producer Barry Lando recklessly disregarded whether or not it was a false broadcast. Herbert asked some questions that Lando claimed were protected by the First Amendment because they inquired into his state of mind and into the editorial processes during the production of the program.

The decision in the Sharon case discussed earlier in the chapter is an example of the burden of proving actual malice against the press. The jury decided that *Time* did not know when the article in question was printed that its statement about Gen. Sharon was false.

In 1991, the Supreme Court decided Masson v. *The New Yorker*, the so-called "fabricated quotes" case. Masson, a psychologist, had sued the magazine and journalist Janet Malcolm, accusing them of making up quotes he never said. Overruling a lower court's decision that journalists could fictionalize quotations by making rational interpretations of speakers' remarks, the Supreme Court protected the sanctity of quotation marks. But the court also made clear that not every deliberate change in a quotation is libelous. Only a "material change in the meaning conveyed by a statement" poses a problem.

Although Masson won the right to try his case, he lost against all defendants. Malcolm won in 1994.

Standards Applicable to Public Figures

The actual malice protection was expanded in two cases in 1967 to include not only public officials but also public figures—people in the public eye but not in public office.

The first case stemmed from a *Saturday Evening Post* article that accused Coach Wally Butts of conspiring to fix a 1962 football game between Georgia and Alabama. At the time of the article, Butts was the athletic director of the University of Georgia. The article, titled "The Story of a College Football Fix," was prefaced by a note from the editors of the *Post* stating:

> Not since the Chicago White Sox threw the 1919 World
> Series has there been a sports story as shocking as this
> one. . . . Before the University of Georgia played the
> University of Alabama . . . Wally Butts . . . gave (to
> Alabama's coach) . . . Georgia's plays, defensive pat-
> terns, all the significant secrets Georgia's football team
> possessed.

The *Post* reported that, because of an electronic error about a week before the game, George Burnett, an Atlanta insurance salesman, accidentally had overheard a telephone conversation between Butts and the head coach of Alabama, Paul Bryant.

Coach Butts sued Curtis Publishing, publishers of the *Post*, and won a verdict for $60,000 in general damages and $3 million in punitive, or punishment, damages. Curtis Publishing appealed the case to the Supreme Court and lost. The trial judge reduced the amount of the damages to $460,000.

The second case was decided the same day. Gen. Edwin Walker sued the Associated Press for distributing a news dispatch giving an eyewitness account by an AP staffer on the campus of the University of Mississippi in the fall of 1962. The AP reported that Gen. Walker personally had led a student charge against federal marshals during a riot on the Mississippi campus. The marshals were attempting to enforce a court decree ordering the enrollment of a black student.

Walker was a retired general at the time of the publication. He had won a $2 million libel suit in a trial court. However, the Supreme Court ruled against him.

In both cases, the stories were wrong. In both, the actual malice test was applied. What was the difference between the Butts and Walker cases?

The justices said the football story was in no sense "hot news." They noted that the person who said he had heard the conversation was on probation in connection with bad-check charges and that *Post* personnel had not viewed his notes before publication. The court also said, as evidence of actual malice on the part of the *Post*, that no one looked at the game films to see if the information was accurate; that a regular staffer, instead of a football expert, was assigned to the story; and that no check was made with someone knowledgeable in the sport. In short, the *Post* had not done an adequate job of reporting.

The evidence in the Walker case was considerably different. The court said the news in the Walker case required immediate dissemination because of the riot on campus. The justices noted that the AP received the information from a correspondent who was present on the campus and gave every indication of being trustworthy and competent.

In the Butts and Walker cases, the court used two definitions of public figure. The first is a person like Butts who has assumed a role of special prominence in the affairs of society—someone who has pervasive power and influence in a community. The second is a person like Walker who has thrust himself or herself into the forefront of a particular public controversy in order to influence the resolution of the issues involved.

In the 1970s, the Supreme Court decided three cases that help journalists determine who is and is not a public figure. The first case involved Mrs. Russell A. Firestone, who sued for libel after *Time* magazine reported that her husband's divorce petition had been granted on grounds of extreme cruelty and adultery. Mrs. Firestone, who had married into the Firestone Tire and Rubber Co. family, claimed that those were not the grounds for the divorce. She also insisted that she was not a public figure with the burden of proving actual malice.

The Supreme Court agreed. Even though she had held press conferences and hired a clipping service, the court ruled that she had not thrust herself into the forefront of a public controversy in an attempt to influence the resolution of the issues involved. The court admitted that marital difficulties of extremely wealthy individuals may be of some interest to some portion of the reading public but added that Mrs. Firestone had not freely chosen to publicize private matters about her married life. The justices said she was compelled to go to court to "obtain legal release from the bonds of matrimony." They said she assumed no "special prominence in the resolution of public questions." The case was sent back to Florida for a finding of fault, and a new trial was ordered. Eventually, the case was settled out of court.

The second case involved Sen. William Proxmire of Wisconsin, who had started what he called the Golden Fleece Award. Each month he announced a winner who, in his opinion, had wasted government money. One such winner was Ronald Hutchinson, a behavioral scientist who had received federal funding for research designed to determine why animals clench their teeth. Hutchinson had published articles about his research in professional publications. In deciding that Hutchinson was not a public figure, the court ruled that he "did not thrust himself or his views into public controversy to influence others." The court admitted there may have been legitimate concerns about the way public funds were being spent but said this was not enough to make Hutchinson a public figure.

The third case concerned an individual found guilty of contempt of court in 1958 for his failure to appear before a grand jury investigating Soviet espionage in the United States. Ilya Wolston's name had been included in a list of people indicted for serving as Soviet agents in a 1974 book published by the Reader's Digest Association. Wolston had not been indicted, and he sued.

The Supreme Court, in deciding that he was not a public figure, found that Wolston had played only a minor role in whatever public controversy there may have been concerning the investigation of Soviet espionage. The court added that a private individual is not automatically transformed into a public figure merely by becoming involved in or being associated with a matter that attracts public attention.

As a journalist, do you have the same protection from a libel action when you write about a person somewhat connected with a news event as you do when you are certain a person is a public figure or public official? A 1974 Supreme Court decision says the answer is usually no. In the landmark Gertz v. Welch case, the justices said states may give more protection to private individuals if a newspaper or radio or television station damages their reputations than if the reputations of either public officials or public figures are damaged. Generally, you have protection from a libel action when you write about people who have thrust themselves into the forefront of a controversy or event.

Standards Applicable to Private Citizens

Private citizens who sue for punitive damages must meet the same actual malice test as public officials and public figures do. Because of the Gertz case, states have been allowed to set their own standards for libel cases involving private citizens who sue only for actual damages. A majority of states and the District of Columbia have adopted a **negligence test**, which requires you to use the same care in gathering facts and writing your story as any reasonable reporter would use under the same or similar circumstances. If you make every effort to be fair and answer all the questions a reasonable person may ask, you probably would pass the negligence test.

One state, New York, has adopted a gross irresponsibility test. A few states have established a more stringent standard that requires private citizens to prove actual malice. Some states simply require a jury to find "fault."

Libel Remains a Danger

Despite all the available defenses, libel remains a serious risk to journalists' financial health, as the following example demonstrates: In 1997, a Texas jury awarded a record $222.7 million to a defunct bond-brokerage firm against Dow Jones & Co., which owns *The Wall Street Journal*. The judge threw out $200 million in punitive damages but let stand the $22.7 million in actual damages for a *Journal* story about "bond daddies."

For citizen journalists, such as bloggers, even awards that are much smaller could be devastating. If you blog, you should meet the same standards of fairness and accuracy that are expected of traditional media.

Libel and the Internet

As we have seen, individuals who libel others over the Internet can be held liable. But the Internet raises the interesting question of whether an online service provider like America Online or Microsoft Network can be held liable for the libelous messages of their users.

In 1991, CompuServe successfully defended itself against a libel suit in a New York federal trial court. CompuServe had made a contract with another company to provide an electronic bulletin board in the form of a newsletter about journalism. The second company then used a third company to create the newsletter. Because CompuServe did not try to exercise any editorial control over the newsletter, the court let CompuServe off the hook for libel. The court also reasoned that no library can be held responsible if a book that the librarian has not reviewed contains libel. CompuServe, the court said, was providing an "electronic, for-profit library."

In 1995, however, Prodigy lost a libel case. In order to promote itself as a family-oriented Internet service provider, Prodigy controlled the content of its computer bulletin boards by using screening software to look for forbidden words, and its editorial staff blocked allegedly offensive posts. Unfortunately for Prodigy, no screening software could identify libelous material. A New York trial court said that by holding itself out as exercising editorial control, Prodigy was "expressly differentiating itself from its competition and expressly likening itself to a newspaper." Thus the court treated Prodigy like a newspaper and held it liable for libel posted on one of its bulletin boards.

Congress did not agree with the Prodigy decision, however, and effectively overruled the case in 1996 by passing "protection for 'Good Samaritan' blocking and screening of offensive material." Congress obviously did not support the idea that the failure to screen meant protection from libel but that limited screening could lead to liability.

INVASION OF PRIVACY

Libel is damage to an individual's reputation. **Invasion of privacy** is a violation of a person's right to be left alone.

As a reporter, you may be risking an invasion of privacy suit under any of these circumstances:

- You physically intrude into a private area to get a story or picture—an act closely related to trespass.
- You publish a story or photograph about someone that is misleading, and thus you portray that person in a "false light."
- You disclose something about an individual's private affairs that is true but that is also offensive to individuals of ordinary sensibilities.

Invasion of privacy may also be claimed if someone's name or picture is used in an advertisement or for similar purposes of trade. Called appropriation, this does not affect you when you are performing your reporting duties.

Consent is a basic defense in invasion of privacy suits. Make sure, however, that your use of the material does not exceed the consent given.

Another basic defense in an invasion of privacy suit is that you're a reporter covering a newsworthy situation. The courts usually protect members of the press against invasion of privacy suits when they are reporting matters of legitimate public interest. There are three exceptions, however.

> *"There are only two occasions when Americans respect privacy. . . . Those are prayer and fishing."*
>
> —Herbert Hoover, 31st U.S. president

Trespassing

One exception arises when you invade someone's privacy by entering private property to get a story. You cannot trespass on private property to get a story or to take a picture, even if it is newsworthy. The courts will not protect you when you are a trespasser.

Two *Life* magazine staffers lost an invasion of privacy suit because, posing as patients, they went into a man's home to get a story about a faith healer. They lost the case even though they were working with the district attorney and the state board of health.

You may enter private property only when you are invited by the owner or renter.

Portraying in a "False Light"

The courts also will not protect you if you invade someone's privacy by publishing misleading information about that person. For example, a legal problem arises if a photograph or information from a true story about a careful pedestrian struck by a careless driver is used again in connection with a story, say, about careless pedestrians. The pedestrian who was hit could file a lawsuit charging libel, "false light" invasion of privacy or even both in some states.

Some states do not recognize "false light" invasion of privacy and insist that libel is the appropriate form of suit. But "false light" suits can cover situations where a picture or story is misleading but not defamatory. Even flattering material can place a person in an unwanted, false light.

Causing Unwanted Publicity Offensive to a Person of Ordinary Sensibilities

The third type of invasion of privacy that the courts recognize—unwanted publicity—arises from stories about incidents that, because they are true, are not defamatory but can be offensive to a person of ordinary sensibilities. The courts say that in order for privacy to be invaded, there must be a morbid and sensational prying into private lives. Merely being the subject of an unflattering or uncomfortable article is not enough. An example is a picture published by *Sports Illustrated* in which a football fan's pants zipper was open. The fan sued for invasion of privacy but lost.

Also in the area of unwanted publicity, the Supreme Court held in 1975 and again in 1989 that truthfully reporting the name of a rape victim is permitted. In 1976 and in 1979 the justices upheld the right of the press to publish the names of juveniles involved with the law because the information was truthful and of public significance.

You may be committing invasion of privacy by:

- Trespassing on private property.
- Portraying someone in a "false light."
- Causing unwanted publicity that is offensive to a person of ordinary sensibilities.

PROTECTION OF SOURCES AND NOTES

Another area you must know about is your ability—or inability—to protect your sources and notes. The problem may arise in various situations. A grand jury that is investigating a murder may ask you to reveal the source of a story you wrote about the murder. Or you may be asked to testify at a criminal or a civil trial.

The conflict that arises is between a reporter's need to protect sources of information and the duty of every citizen to testify to help the courts determine justice. Your work as a reporter will take you to events that are important and newsworthy. Anyone wanting the facts about an event can subpoena you to bring in all the details. Journalists usually resist. They work for their newspaper or radio or television station, not a law-enforcement agency. Their ability to gather information would be compromised if sources knew that their identities or their information could go to the police.

By 2005, some protection against testifying—shield laws—had been adopted by these 31 states and the District of Columbia. The states are:

[The media] seek to maintain a balance on the constantly shifting tightrope of personal privacy, access to information and government accountability.

—John R. Finnegan Sr., former newspaper editor

Alabama	Kentucky	North Carolina
Alaska	Louisiana	North Dakota
Arizona	Maryland	Ohio
Arkansas	Michigan	Oklahoma
California	Minnesota	Oregon
Colorado	Montana	Pennsylvania
Delaware	Nebraska	Rhode Island
Florida	Nevada	South Carolina
Georgia	New Jersey	Tennessee
Illinois	New Mexico	
Indiana	New York	

Shield law protection is important because without it, journalists do go to jail. In 2001–2002, Vanessa Leggett, a freelance journalist in Houston, spent a record 168 days in jail for refusing to hand over notes and interview tapes she had made while writing a book about the murder of a Houston socialite. Texas has no shield law. In 2004–2005, Jim Taricani, a broadcast reporter in Providence, R.I., spent four months under house arrest for refusing to tell who gave him an FBI videotape that showed a Providence official taking a bribe from an undercover FBI agent. A federal judge had ordered Taricani to reveal his source. Although Rhode Island has a shield law, the federal government does not.

Perhaps *New York Times* reporter Judith Miller has garnered the most publicity for being jailed. Her saga started when conservative columnist Robert Novak revealed the name of a CIA undercover agent, Valerie Plame. Plame's husband, retired diplomat Joseph Wilson, had said the Bush administration misrepresented the facts when it claimed that Saddam Hussein had tried to buy depleted uranium from Niger. The disclosure about Plame came after Wilson's assertions.

Miller did not write about Plame, but she went to jail on July 6, 2005, for refusing to reveal the source who had provided her with information about Plame. Because it is a violation of federal law for an official to reveal the identity of an undercover CIA agent, a special prosecutor was assigned to investigate that leak. Several other journalists did testify, after receiving permission from their sources. Miller and her bosses at the *Times* took the position that her promise to hold confidential her sources' names was not one she could break. The U.S. Supreme Court refused to hear her appeal. Although her imprisonment inspired bills in Congress calling for a federal shield law, Congress has not yet passed such a law.

Miller was released after serving 85 days in jail. Her source gave permission for her to reveal his identity. The only criminal charge to result from the investigation was a charge against Lewis "Scooter" Libby, assistant to Vice President Dick Cheney, of lying to investigators. Libby was convicted in federal court.

In 1980, Congress did pass the Privacy Protection Act. Under that act, federal, state and local law-enforcement officers generally may not use a search warrant to search news rooms. Instead, they must get a subpoena for documents, which instructs reporters and editors to hand over the material. Officers may use a warrant

After refusing to disclose to a judge his source for a 1971 article about the trial of mass murderer Charles Manson, reporter William Farr was taken to jail in a police van.

to search news rooms only if they suspect a reporter of being involved in a crime or if immediate action is needed to prevent bodily harm, loss of life or destruction of the material.

The difference between a search warrant and a subpoena is great. Officers with a search warrant can knock on the door, enter the news room and search on their own. A subpoena does not permit officers to search the news room. A subpoena for specific documents requires reporters to turn over the material to authorities at a predetermined time and place. In addition, it gives reporters time to challenge in court the necessity of surrendering the material.

Even in states with shield laws, judges in most criminal cases involving grand juries will not allow you to keep your sources secret. In other criminal cases, courts may allow confidentiality if a three-part test is met. Supreme Court Justice Potter Stewart suggested this test in his dissent in Branzburg vs. Hayes, decided in 1972:

> Government officials must, therefore, demonstrate that the information sought is clearly relevant to a precisely defined subject of government inquiry. . . . They must demonstrate that it is reasonable to think the witness in question has that information. . . . And they must show that there is not any means of obtaining the information less destructive of First Amendment liberties. . . .
>
> In civil litigation you may be permitted to keep sources confidential in most cases unless the court finds that the information sought is unavailable from other sources and highly relevant to the underlying litigation or of such critical importance to the lawsuit that it goes to the heart of the plaintiff's claim.

If you are sued for libel, you will find it difficult both to protect your sources and to win the lawsuit. The court might well rule against you on whether a statement is true or false if it came from a source you refuse to name.

The best way to avoid such confrontation with the courts is not to promise a source you will keep his or her name confidential. Only for the most compelling reason should you promise confidentiality.

In 1991, the U.S. Supreme Court ruled in Cohen v. Cowles Media Co. that the First Amendment does not prevent a source from suing a news organization if a reporter has promised the source confidentiality but the newspaper publishes the source's name anyway.

ACCESS TO COURTS

The Supreme Court held in 1979 that "members of the public have no constitutional right" under the Sixth Amendment to attend criminal trials. In a reversal exactly one year later, the justices held that the public and the press have a First Amendment right to attend criminal trials. The justices said the right was not absolute but trial judges could close criminal trials only when there was an "overriding interest" to justify such closure. The basic concern of judges when they close trials is to protect the accused person's Sixth Amendment right to an "impartial jury"—often translated by attorneys as "a fair trial."

In addition, the First Amendment prevents the government from conducting business—even trials—in secret. In the Richmond Newspapers case in 1980, Chief Justice Warren Burger traced the unbroken and uncontradicted history of open judicial proceedings in England and the United States. He concluded that there is a "presumption of openness" in criminal trials and pointed out the important role of the news media as representatives of the public.

By 1984, the Supreme Court had decided that openness in criminal trials "enhances both the basic fairness of the criminal trial and the appearance of fairness so essential to public confidence in the system." Public proceedings vindicate the concerns of victims and the community in knowing that offenders are being brought to account for their criminal conduct "by jurors fairly and openly selected." Proceedings of jury selection could be closed, the chief justice said, only when a trial judge finds that closure preserves an "overriding interest" and is narrowly tailored to serve that interest.

Judges are using that option. For instance, when John Gotti was convicted of Mafia activities in New York, the jurors' names were kept secret. Gotti's attorneys unsuccessfully challenged their anonymity. Jurors' names in the Rodney King case, which resulted in riots in Los Angeles in 1992, also were withheld.

In 1986, the Supreme Court said that only an overriding interest found by a trial judge can overcome the presumption of openness of criminal proceedings. Today, 47 states allow cameras in at least some state courtrooms. Cameras are permitted in some lower federal courts but are excluded from the U.S. Supreme Court.

COPYRIGHT AND FAIR USE

The purpose of copyright law is to ensure compensation to authors for contributing to the common good by publishing their works. The Constitution provides for this in Article 1, Section 8, by giving Congress the power to secure "for limited times to authors and inventors the exclusive right to their respective writing and discoveries." The same section indicates that this provision is intended "to promote the progress of science and useful arts" for the benefit of the public. Copyright laws protect your work and prohibit you from using significant amounts of others' writings without permission and, in some cases, a fee.

Key elements of copyright law include the following:

- Copyrightable works are protected from the moment they are fixed in tangible form, whether published or unpublished.
- Copyright protection begins with a work's "creation and . . . endures for a term consisting of the life of the author and 70 years after the author's death."
- Works for hire and anonymous and pseudonymous works are protected for 95 years from publication or 100 years from creation, whichever is shorter.
- There is a "fair use" limitation on the exclusive rights of copyright owners. In other words, it may be permissible to quote small excerpts from a copyrighted work without permission. According to the Supreme Court, these factors govern fair use:
  1. The purpose and character of the use.
  2. The nature of the copyrighted work.
  3. The substantiality of the portion used in relationship to the copyrighted work as a whole.
  4. The effect on the potential market for or value of the copyrighted work.

Although a work is copyrighted from the moment it is fixed in tangible form, the copyright statute says certain steps are necessary for the work to receive statutory protection. The author or publisher must:

- Publish or reproduce the work with the word "copyright" or the symbol ©, the name of the copyright owner and the year of publication.
- Deposit two copies of the work with the Library of Congress within three months of publication. Failure to do so will not affect the copyright but could lead to the imposition of fines.
- Register the work at the Library of Congress by filling out a form supplied by the Copyright Office and sending the form, the specified number of copies (usually one copy of an unpublished work and two copies of a published work), and a $30 fee to the Copyright Office. The copies and registration fee may be sent together and usually are.

Copyright law has a special provision for broadcasters of live programs. Broadcasters need only make a simultaneous tape of their live broadcasts in order to receive copyright protection. The tape fulfills the requirement that a work be in a "fixed" form for copyright protection. Because a digital form is a "fixed" form, editors of online newspapers already meet that copyright requirement.

Some aspects of U.S. copyright law changed in 1989, when the United States finally joined the 100-year-old Berne Convention, an international copyright treaty, primarily to prevent the pirating of American film productions in other countries. The changes include the following:

- Placing a copyright notice on a work is no longer necessary to protect a copyright after publication. This is in line with the Berne Convention principle that the copyright protection should not be subject to formalities. The copyright notice, however, is still widely used because it acts as a bar to an infringer's claim of innocent infringement.

- Copyright registration is no longer a prerequisite for access to the federal courts for an infringement action. But registration is required for a copyright owner to recover statutory damages. (Without registration, the copyright owner can recover only the damages he or she can prove, court costs and "reasonable" attorney's fees.) The amount of statutory damages, generally between $750 and $30,000, is determined by the judge. If the infringer was not aware he or she was infringing a copyright, the court may award as little as $200. If the infringement was willful, the court can award up to $150,000. Thus, like the copyright notice, copyright registration remains highly advisable.

Suggested Readings

Carter, T. Barton, Franklin, Marc A. and Wright, Jay B. *The First Amendment and the Fourth Estate*, Eighth Edition. Westbury, N.Y.: Foundation Press, 2000.

Holsinger, Ralph and Dilts, Jon Paul. *Media Law*, Fourth Edition. New York: McGraw-Hill, 1997.

Middleton, Kent R., Trager, Robert and Chamberlin, Bill F. *The Law of Public Communication*, Sixth Edition. Boston: Allyn & Bacon, 2003.

Overbeck, Wayne. *Major Principles of Media Law*. Toronto: Thomson Wadsworth, 2004.

Pember, Don R. *Mass Media Law*, Thirteenth Edition. Dubuque, Iowa: McGraw-Hill, 2003.

Teeter, Dwight L. Jr., Le Duc, Don R. and Loving, Bill. *Law of Mass Communications*, Tenth Edition. New York: Foundation Press, 2002.

Suggested Web Sites

www.freedomforum.org
The Freedom Forum has online yearly "State of the First Amendment" reports, also published on paper. Discusses the public's ambivalence about First Amendment issues.

www.firstamendmentcenter.org
At this Freedom Forum site you'll find the "State of the First Amendment" report by Donna Demas, which discusses the public's ambivalence about First Amendment issues.

www.medialaw.org
This is the site of the Media Law Resource Center, "a non-profit information clearinghouse organized in 1980 by lead-ing media groups "to monitor developments and promote First Amendment rights in the libel, privacy and related legal fields." The site features a 50-state survey of media libel law.

www.rcfp.org
The Reporters Committee for Freedom of the Press maintains online publications and guides on First Amendment and freedom of information issues. Here you'll find current hot stories, plus archives and much more.

Exercises

1. Which defense against libel discussed in this chapter would you have used to defend *Time* magazine in the lawsuit filed by Gen. Ariel Sharon? Why?

2. *The New York Times* v. Sullivan, 376 U.S. 254 (1964), was a landmark decision in favor of the press. Discuss what the consequences for the press might have been if the decision had been different.

3. You are on an assignment with your photographer, who enters a house without permission and photographs the sale of illegal drugs. Discuss the issues raised by the circumstances and explain why you would or would not publish the pictures.

4. Using the LexisNexis database, determine how the U.S. Supreme Court has used Richmond Newspapers v. Virginia, 448 U.S. 555 (1980), in later cases dealing with openness in criminal proceedings.

Ethics

23

● Shinika Sykes, who reported on higher education for *The Salt Lake Tribune*, plagiarized material from the University of Utah's student newspaper. She was fired.

● Editor Larry Hackett of *People* magazine paid Angelina Jolie and Brad Pitt $4 million for pictures of their baby. A spokesperson for CNN denied that the deal included Jolie's agreeing to an interview with CNN newsman Anderson Cooper. *People* and CNN are both part of the Time Warner family.

● *The (Spokane, Wash.) Spokesman-Review* reported that it used a forensic computer expert posing as an 18-year-old man in a gay chat room to ascertain whether Spokane Mayor Jim West was using his public position to proposition young men on a gay Web site.

● The *Corpus Christi Caller-Times* used a reporter to pose as a prostitute to lead police to the arrest of several johns. Said editor Libby Everyt, "Having a reporter become involved in law enforcement activities was a mistake and will not happen again."

● Incoming CBS Evening News anchor Katie Couric appeared several dress sizes smaller in the promotional magazine *Watch!*, the result of a digitally altered photo. Couric said she did not know about the altered photo. "I liked the first picture better because there's more of me to love," she said.

● Griego Erwin quit her position as a three-times-a-week columnist for *The Sacramento Bee* when, among other things, editors were "unable to verify the existence of 43 people she named in her columns."

● Popular *Detroit Free Press* columnist Mitch Albom, author of *Tuesdays with Morrie* and *The Five People You Meet in Heaven*, wrote that two former Michigan State Spartan stars flew to St. Louis to see their alma mater play in the Final Four. He also wrote that the two sat next to each other at the game. He wrote his Sunday column on Friday because that's when the section was printed. Guess what? The two NBA players didn't make it to St. Louis.

● In her third column in the UNC-Chapel Hill *Daily Tar Heel*, Jillian Bandes wrote: "I want all Arabs to be stripped naked and cavity-searched if they get within 100 yards of an airport. I don't care if they're being inconvenienced. I don't care if it seems as though their rights are being violated." She was fired.

● Cultural critic Lee Siegel of *The New Republic* magazine started using a pseudonym for a culture blog at the magazine's Web site in which he praised himself and attacked others. When readers got on him concerning what he had written about comedian Jon Stewart, Siegel wrote: "Siegel is brave, brilliant, and wittier than Stewart will ever be. Take that, you bunch of immature, abusive sheep."

● *The New York Times* did not publish a story for an entire year about the government's engagement in domestic spying. The *Times'* editors said they gave in to national security arguments by the Bush administration.

This is just a small list of recent, well-known decisions of journalists that have ethical implications. No wonder that Cherie Blair, wife of British Prime Minister Tony Blair, could say to an audience of students at Roehampton University that there "is no professional morality in journalism," that journalism is "not a noble calling" and that it has "no ethics."

And yet, arguably, journalism has never been practiced in a more ethical way in this country and in a host of other countries around the globe. How can that be? Some of the credit belongs to bloggers who are serving as watchdogs of the press and to many other citizens on the Internet who are calling attention to every irregularity they see in journalism. As a result, journalists have responded by becoming much more transparent, by openly discussing their mistakes and failings. It's safe to say, unlike in the past, nearly every practicing journalist is concerned about ethics.

Nevertheless, journalism as a profession has been slow to establish a mandatory and enforced code of ethics because of a fear that it might in some way infringe upon freedom of the press.

In other professions, enforcing a code means the profession must have the power to keep people from practicing unless they have membership or a license to practice. That also means that the profession must have the power to suspend a license and to keep members from practicing if they violate the code of the profession.

For some professions, the state requires a license to practice. If as a condition of keeping that license, people may not express certain ideas, that is a form of censorship. Because journalists are not licensed by states, it is difficult to determine who is a journalist. In fact, the Supreme Court has said that it does not want to define a journalist.

Therefore, government does not keep anyone from practicing journalism, although individual news organizations have established and enforced codes of ethics that have restricted journalists from practicing journalism in their organizations. For example, some journalists who have plagiarized have been suspended or fired from their news organizations.

Because of the wide range of the First Amendment and its relatively few legal restraints, perhaps no profession has a greater need to discuss proper means of conduct than journalism. As the Commission on Freedom of the Press concluded in 1947, unless journalists set their own limits on what is acceptable and responsible, government will eventually and inevitably do it for them. Journalists too often and too easily justify all of their actions by citing the First Amendment.

Associations of journalists, such as the Society of Professional Journalists, do have codes of conduct. Of course, journalists do not have to belong to such organizations to practice journalism, but at least half of all newspapers and television stations now have written codes of ethics. Larger news organizations are more likely to have them. Associations of magazines, such as the American Society of Magazine Editors, the American Business Press, the American Society of Business Publication Editors and dozens of others, all have codes of ethics in place. CyberJournalist.net

---

The "Statement of Shared Purpose" from the Committee of Concerned Journalists states, "The central purpose of journalism is to provide citizens with accurate and reliable information they need to function in a free society." The committee lists nine principles to accomplish this:

1. Journalism's first obligation is to the truth.
2. Its first loyalty is to citizens.
3. Its essence is a discipline of verification.
4. Its practitioners must maintain an independence from those they cover.
5. It must serve as an independent monitor of power.
6. It must provide a forum for public criticism and compromise.
7. It must strive to make the significant interesting and relevant.
8. It must keep the news comprehensive and proportional.
9. Its practitioners must be allowed to exercise their personal conscience.

has a model bloggers' code of ethics that is similar to the code of the Society of Professional Journalists.

Critics of journalism codes of ethics condemn codes for being hopelessly general and therefore ineffective or for being overly restrictive. Advocates argue that strict codes might improve journalists' credibility. Those who disagree say they merely make journalists easier targets for libel suits.

Whether your organization has a code of ethics or not, you should develop your own ethical values and principles. Your upbringing, and perhaps your religious training and education, have already helped prepare you to do that.

THREE ETHICAL PHILOSOPHIES

Your personal ethics may derive from the way you answer this fundamental question: Does the end ever justify the means? Should you ever do something that is not good in itself in order to achieve a goal that you think is good?

If you answer "no" to that question, you are in some sense an absolutist or a legalist, and you are likely to subscribe to *deontological* ethics. If you answer "yes" to that question, you are more of a relativist and are likely to subscribe to *teleological* ethics. If you answer "maybe" or "sometimes," you subscribe to *situation* ethics.

Don't be put off by the philosophical jargon. To understand ethical thinking, to be able to discuss ethics and to solve ethical dilemmas that arise on the job, you need to learn the vocabulary of ethicists.

Deontological Ethics

Deontological ethics is the ethics of duty. According to this philosophy, you have a duty to do what is right. Deontologists believe that some actions are always right and some are always wrong, that there exists in nature (or, for those with religious faith, in divine revelation) a fixed set of principles or laws from which there should be no deviation. For a deontologist, the end never justifies the means. That belief is why some refer to this ethical philosophy as **absolutism** or legalism.

An absolutist or legalist sees one clear duty: to discover the rules and to follow them. If it is wrong to lie, it is always wrong to lie. Suppose a stranger comes to your door and asks where your roommates are so that he can murder them. If you were an absolutist, you would not lie to save their lives. An absolutist or legalistic ethical philosophy could induce a conscientious objector not only to refuse to take up arms but also to refuse to go to war even as a medic. The deontologist believes that if war is absolutely wrong, to participate in war in any way is absolutely wrong.

One such absolutist was Immanuel Kant (1724–1804). Kant proposed the "categorical imperative," a moral law that obliges you to do only those things that you would be willing to have everyone do as a matter of universal law. Once you make that decision, you regard it as "categorical" and without exception, and it is imperative that you do it.

Many people draw support for their absolutism or legalism from their religious beliefs. They cite the Bible, the Koran or some other book they believe to be divinely inspired. If they themselves cannot resolve an ethical dilemma, they turn to their minister, priest, rabbi or imam for the answer. The absolutist is concerned only with doing the right thing and needs only to discover what that is.

The absolutist journalist is concerned only with whether an event is newsworthy. If it is interesting, timely, significant or important, it is to be reported, regardless of the consequences. The duty of the journalist is to report the news. Period. Walter Cronkite once said that if journalists worried about what all the possible consequences could be for reporting something, they would never report anything.

What happens when journalists have knowledge of something, some corruption in government or marital infidelity of a political candidate, and do not report it? What happens when the public learns that journalists knew but did not let the public know? What happens to public trust? The public relies on the news media to keep them informed. That is why journalists enjoy First Amendment privileges.

This deontological philosophy was best enunciated by Charles A. Dana, who in 1868 began a 29-year career as editor of *The New York Sun*. Dana said, "Whatever God in his infinite wisdom has allowed to happen, I am not too proud to print."

Absolutists discount any criticism of the press for printing or broadcasting certain stories. Stop blaming the messenger, they say. We don't make events happen; we just report them.

When a television news producer was asked why he telecast the confession of a suspect, he replied, "Because it's news."

Many journalists find the deontological philosophy attractive because it provides a rationale for full disclosure, for never withholding anything newsworthy from the public. In the end, these journalists believe, journalists are unethical only when they withhold the news. Publishing without fear of the consequences or without favoring one group's interests over another's is, to them, highly ethical behavior.

Teleological Ethics

Teleological ethics is the ethics of final ends. According to this philosophy, what makes an act ethical is not the act itself but the consequences of the act. Teleologists believe that the end can and often does justify the means. In this philosophy, ethics are more relativistic than absolutist or legalistic.

From a teleological perspective, stealing, for example, may not always be wrong. In some cases, it may be the right thing to do. A mother who steals food for her starving child would be performing a good act. A person who lies to save someone's life would be acting ethically. A person who kills to protect his or her own life would be acting morally.

An important consideration in teleological ethics is the intention of the person performing the act. What one person would declare unethical, another person

People magazine reportedly paid Brad Pitt and Angelina Jolie $4 million for pictures of their baby. Did the deal include a guarantee for an interview for CNN with Anderson Cooper? Not according to CNN. Both *People* and CNN are a part of Time Warner.

would do for a good purpose or a good reason. For example, police often work undercover, concealing their identity in order to apprehend criminals. If in the course of that work they must lie or even get involved in criminal activity, the teleological response would be: So be it. Their purpose is to protect the public; their intention is to work for the good of society. The end justifies the means.

Some journalists would not hesitate to do the same. Some would require certain conditions be in place before they would steal or use deceit, but then they would proceed. They believe their purpose is to be the watchdog of government, to protect the common good, to keep the public fully informed. Whatever they must do to accomplish these goals, they argue, is clearly ethical.

The most extreme expression of the notion that the end justifies the means was written centuries ago by the Italian political theorist Niccolò Machiavelli (1469–1527). In the 20th century, the American philosopher and educator John Dewey (1859–1952) revealed teleological leanings in his philosophical pragmatism—whatever works is ethical.

A pragmatic approach is common in business generally and in the business of journalism. If a proposed negative story about a local grocery brings threats of withdrawing advertising, some editors will decide against publishing it. If a proposed favorable story brings pledges of more advertising dollars, they will publish the story. They'll generally do whatever works.

Situation Ethics

Situation ethics is the ethics of specific acts. When asked whether the end justifies the means, a person subscribing to situation ethics would reply, "It all depends." Here are eight philosophies that use some form of situation ethics.

Antinomianism

Antinomianism is the belief that there are no moral absolutes and that there is only one operative principle—namely, that every person and every ethical situation is unique, and to solve an ethical dilemma by applying principles held by others or principles that apply in other cases is unethical. An antinomian believes that because each situation is unique, each ethical problem must be judged entirely on its own merits.

This does not mean that an antinomian has no core values. It does not mean that an antinomian is always willing to lie or cheat or steal. In some instances, an antinomian journalist would not hesitate to pose as someone else in an attempt to gather information. In other instances, the antinomian would decline to do so. The determining factor would be the situation itself, because no two situations are alike.

John Merrill's Deontelics

Other proponents of situation ethics are not as extreme as the antinomians. Some ethicists shy away from absolutism and say that one must consider both the act and the consequences of the act. Journalism scholar and ethicist John Merrill calls

Jayson Blair may forever be the symbol of unethical journalism. He not only disgraced himself and one of the world's greatest newspapers, but he also brought about the resignation of *The New York Times'* top bosses, Executive Editor Howell Raines and Managing Editor Gerald Boyd.

such ethics deontelics—a word he coined combining deontological and teleological ethics. To act responsibly, Merrill says, journalists must consider more than just the ethics of the act, although they dare not ignore that some acts are by their very nature unethical in most cases.

For a journalist, telling the truth is paramount, and lying is unethical—in most cases. According to deontelic theory, there may be a rare time when lying is justifiable for a good purpose. For example, an investigative reporter might justify lying about his or her identity as a journalist if that is the only way to get information for an important story.

When *The New York Times* chose not to run the story about domestic spying, the editors chose to withhold the news because the government said it would endanger national security. The *Times* refrained from publishing the news for what it considered a justifiable reason.

Mixed-Rule Deontology

Similar to deontelics is what other ethicists, such as Edmund Lambeth, call mixed-rule deontology. These ethicists believe that journalists have a duty to consider both the act itself and possible consequences of the act. Although not claiming to be a relativist, Lambeth sets forth certain guidelines that make some acts, usually considered unethical, ethical in certain situations. We'll see some of those guidelines and the guidelines of the Society of Professional Journalists when we discuss journalists' use of deceit later in this chapter.

Love of Neighbor

A fourth type of situation ethics has been described by Joseph Fletcher, author of *Situation Ethics*. Fletcher bases his philosophy on love of neighbor as articulated in the Golden Rule and the maxim "You shall love your neighbor as yourself." He presents his ethics from a Christian perspective with roots in Judaic teaching, but one need not profess Christianity to share the conviction that all principles are relative to one absolute: love of neighbor. Indeed, many religions, as well as secular humanism, hold human values as the highest good.

Although those who subscribe to this belief understand and accept other ethical maxims and weigh them carefully when facing an ethical decision, they must be prepared to set them aside completely if love of neighbor demands it. In a broad sense, followers of Fletcher's form of situation ethics always place people first. In every ethical dilemma, they always do what is best for people. Sometimes they must choose between love for one person and love for a larger community of people.

Utilitarianism

The thinking that Fletcher advocates leads to another form of situation ethics: utilitarianism. From the utilitarian perspective, your choices are ethical if you always choose the action that is likely to bring the most happiness to the greatest number

From the Society of Professional Journalists' professional code of ethics:

Journalists should:

- Avoid conflicts of interest, real or perceived.

- Remain free of associations and activities that may compromise integrity or damage credibility.

- Refuse gifts, favors, fees, free travel and special treatment, and shun secondary employment, political involvement, public office, and service in community organizations if they compromise journalistic integrity.

- Disclose unavoidable conflicts.

- Be vigilant and courageous about holding those with power accountable.

- Deny favored treatment to advertisers and special interests, and resist their pressure to influence news coverage.

- Be wary of sources offering information for favors or money; avoid bidding for news.

Ethical Guidelines

"The primary function of newspapers is to communicate to the human race what its members do, feel and think," stated the American Society of Newspaper Editors in 1923. To do this, the ASNE issued the following guidelines (quoted from *Digital Dilemmas: Ethical Issues for Online Media Professionals* by Robert I. Berkman and Christopher A. Shumway):

Responsibility. The right of a newspaper to attract and hold readers is restricted by nothing but considerations of public welfare.

Freedom of the press. Freedom of the press is to be guarded as a vital right of mankind.

Independence. Freedom from all obligations except that of fidelity to the public interest is vital.

Sincerity, truthfulness, accuracy. Good faith with the reader is the foundation of all journalism worthy of the name.

Impartiality. Sound practice makes clear distinction between reports and expressions of opinion. News reports should be free from opinion or bias of any kind.

Fair play. A newspaper should not publish unofficial charges affecting reputation or moral character without opportunity given to the accused to be heard; right practice demands the giving of such opportunity in all cases of serious accusation outside judicial proceedings.

Decency. A newspaper cannot escape conviction of insincerity if, while professing high moral purpose, it supplies incentives to base conduct, such as are to be found in details of crime and vice, publication of which is not demonstrably for the general good.

---

of people. This theory, formulated by John Stuart Mill (1806–1873) and Jeremy Bentham (1748–1832), was later modified to emphasize the greatest good rather than the greatest happiness. Some utilitarians also add the words "over a long period of time," because some actions may seem wrong if one looks merely at the present situation.

Most journalists probably do subscribe to a utilitarian philosophy. They know, for example, that publishing a story about the infidelities of a public figure may destroy the person's reputation, hurt his or her family and perhaps even lead to suicide, but—taking a utilitarian view—they would decide that for the greater good, the public should have this information. The decision to publish would seem even more justifiable if the public official were involved in embezzlement or bribery.

Former Cleveland talk-show host Joel Rose committed suicide the same day *The Plain Dealer* published a story that he was being investigated for harassing several women. The public overwhelmingly blamed the newspaper for Rose's death, but *The Plain Dealer* maintained that Rose was a public figure and that the paper merely reported the fact that Rose was a suspect.

Some journalists who would agree that publishing pretrial publicity may endanger a defendant's right to a fair trial also believe that by keeping an eye on the police and the courts, they are ensuring that, in the long run, all people have a better chance for a fair trial.

Critics of journalists and utilitarianism say this philosophy is too easy to practice and too vague to be useful. Some journalists respond that it is the only practical philosophy in a hurry-up, deadline-focused world. They believe that achieving the greatest good for the greatest number calls for a general operating principle: When in doubt, unless some clear circumstance dictates against it, it is best to report the news. Otherwise, the public will not be able to rely on its news agencies, the role of the press in a democracy will be undermined, and perhaps democracy itself will be abolished. Democracy, after all, practices a form of utilitarianism—one called majority rule.

Ayn Rand's Rational Self-Interest

Ayn Rand's ethics of rational self-interest is the opposite of utilitarianism and certainly of Christianity or any form of altruism. Someone subscribing to her notion of ethical egoism would never sacrifice himself or herself for the good of others. An ethical egoist always looks out for his or her own self-interest first, believing that if everyone acted in this manner, everyone would be better off.

> **"**Ethics is a system of principles, a morality or code of conduct. It is the values and rules of life recognized by an individual, group or culture seeking guidelines to human conduct and what is good or bad, right or wrong.**"**
>
> — Conrad C. Fink, professor of media ethics

Journalists who are ethical egoists would not mind using people for stories, even if the people they use have no idea how embarrassing the story may be to them. Photographers would take pictures of dying or dead children and of their grieving parents. Broadcasters would not hesitate to telecast people committing suicide. In their opinion, whatever helps them get good stories and thus advance in the profession is ethical.

Some critics accuse journalists of embracing rational self-interest merely to sell newspapers or to increase ratings. However, on many occasions journalists report stories that anger both their readers and their advertisers.

John Rawls' Veil of Ignorance

A different form of rational self-interest is manifested in the ethical philosophy of John Rawls. His "veil of ignorance" would have you treat all people the same, as if there were no differences in social or economic status. Race, gender, age, looks—behind the veil, all people are equal; all are to be treated the same. If there is any unequal treatment, it must benefit the least advantaged.

Rawls argues that these considerations would make people act more in tune with their rational self-interest. People would be more likely to look out for themselves if they placed themselves in the position of others.

In our society, research indicates that wealthy white men and poor African-American men who commit the same crimes seldom receive the same sentences. This disparity is especially apparent among those who receive the death penalty. The "veil of ignorance" would help judges and juries to disregard racial and other differences.

The Spokesman-Review employed a forensic computer expert to pose as an 18-year-old on a gay chat room. Spokane Mayor Jim West responded. West had been accused of using his office to offer jobs and gifts to young men on a gay Internet chat room. He lost his office in a recall election on Dec. 6, 2005, and he lost his life to cancer surgery on July 22, 2006.

Journalists often treat famous people—especially politicians—more harshly than they treat average citizens. If journalists placed themselves with politicians behind the veil, perhaps their adversarial attitude would dissipate somewhat.

Aristotle's Golden Mean

Another form of situation ethics derives from Aristotle's notion of the golden mean, a moderate moral position that avoids extremes. Aristotle believed that after considering the extremes, a person is likely to find a rational and moral position somewhere in between—and not necessarily in the middle.

Journalists make choices ranging from running no photographs of a tragedy to running the most graphic display of violent death. A person who subscribes to the ethics of the golden mean would try to run a photo that indicates the horror of the tragedy without offending the sensibilities of the audience or of the family involved.

> **❝I tell the honest truth in my paper, and I leave the consequences to God.❞**
>
> — James Gordon Bennett, newspaper publisher, 1836

The *Detroit Free Press* tried to do this when it ran a front-page photograph of a Wayne County Medical Examiner's Office worker holding a plastic bag with the body of a 7-month-old baby inside. The story ran on Sept. 15, 2000, and the paper received many calls and letters protesting the photo. The strong criticism lessened once the paper explained its reason for running the photo. Deputy photography director J. Kyle Keener said the photo was chosen because it showed "the extent of how poorly our children are treated." In a letter to readers the following day, executive editor Robert G. McGruder stated, "It was not our intention to offend, alienate and even lose some readers, but we knew that might happen. We weighed that against telling our readers about a horrific story that took place in our community."

RESOLVING ETHICAL ISSUES

Unless you are an absolutist, ethical reasoning can take many forms. You may adopt one or more of the ethical stances just discussed, and they will guide your day-to-day ethical decision making. What is paramount is that you engage in what Lambeth and others have called *principled reasoning*. You must deliberate by reflecting on ethical principles—principles that will help you decide proper or moral ways to act.

Principled reasoning assumes that you are not acting ethically if you do something simply because you have been told to do it or because that's what everyone else does. You are not ethical if you report the story just to beat the competition.

To help journalists and others make ethical decisions, ethicists Clifford Christians, Kim Rotzoll and Mark Fackler have adapted a model of moral reasoning devised by Dr. Ralph Potter of the Harvard Divinity School. Called the **Potter Box** (see Figure 23.1), the model has four elements:

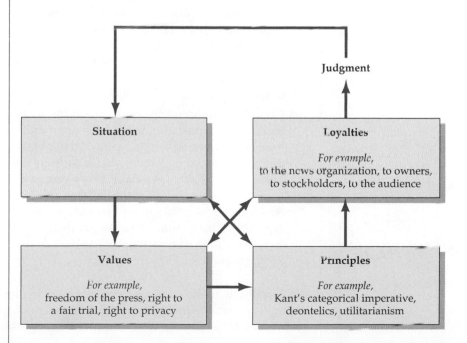

Figure 23.1
Journalists can use the Potter Box to analyze and try to resolve ethical problems.

Judgment

Situation

Loyalties

For example,
to the news organization, to owners, to stockholders, to the audience

Values

For example,
freedom of the press, right to a fair trial, right to privacy

Principles

For example,
Kant's categorical imperative, deontelics, utilitarianism

- **Appraising the situation.** Making a good ethical decision begins with good reporting. You need all the facts from a variety of sources. Reaching a decision without trying to know all the facts makes any ethical decision impossible.

  Did ABC News have all the facts when it risked mentioning an e-mail from a 16-year-old congressional page in Brian Ross' "The Blotter"? All Ross and ABC had was the e-mail from the page who was concerned about the appropriateness of an e-mail exchange with Congressman Mark Foley. Other news agencies did nothing with that e-mail. After appraising the situation, they apparently thought they needed more facts.

- **Identifying values.** What are your personal values, your news organization's values, your community's values, the nation's values? You may place high value on your personal credibility and that of your news organization. Certainly, freedom of the press is a value prized by this nation. You value your audience's right to know, but you may value a person's right to a fair trial more. You also value your independence and not being used by the police department or by the prosecution or by the defense.

- **Appealing to ethical principles.** You need to look at the ethical principles discussed previously. The principles are not meant to be a shopping list from which you pick and choose items that serve your personal interest. To be ethical, you may have to choose a principle or principles that are far from expedient. Even if you choose a utilitarian solution, Aristotle's golden mean may keep you from going to extremes, and Kant's categorical imperative may keep you from doing anything at all.

  You have a duty to your audience to present them with the news. Ignoring the memo from the youth who mentioned Foley's contacts was what some newspapers chose to do. ABC could have gone on the air and had a sensational story but chose instead to mention it in a blog. Once Foley's Democratic opponent called for an investigation, the story could no longer be ignored. It was news — especially in the heat of an important election, regardless of what the opposition had to say about releasing it so close to the actual date of the elections.

- **Choosing loyalties.** You owe a certain loyalty to your news organization, it is true, but you must also be loyal to your own principles and to your readers, listeners or viewers. Some argue that that's where all loyalty begins and ends.

  People depend on you to keep them fully informed. Besides, ignoring the Foley story, for example, might cause people to turn elsewhere for the news. Can you completely ignore the fact that another station chose to broadcast it? And what about loyalty to your sources and to the people about whom you are reporting? Finally, some would argue that you also must consider your loyalty to your station's owners and stockholders. If your newspaper is not profitable, it will go out of business.

Usually, there is no one clear answer to a difficult ethical dilemma. Seldom do the most reasonable and experienced news veterans agree completely. But principled reasoning at least makes an ethical decision possible.

The four elements in the Potter Box need not be considered in any particular order. Also, don't stop reasoning after you have touched upon the four elements. Principled reasoning should continue, even to another discussion of another ethical dilemma.

This continuing ethical dialectic or dialogue helps create ethical journalism and ethical journalists. Journalists should not simply reflect society. They should present a reasoned reflection. Journalism should be done by people who make informed, intelligent and prudent choices.

The main objection to the Potter Box is that using it takes too much time and is impractical in the deadline-crazed business of journalism. However, as you become better acquainted with ethical principles and more practiced at principled reasoning, you will be able to make ethical decisions much more quickly and reasonably.

Although each case is different and you must always know the situation, you need not always start from the beginning. After a while you know what your values are, where your loyalties lie and which principles will most likely apply.

> **"**Journalists demean themselves and damage their credibility when they misrepresent themselves and their work to news sources and, in turn, to the public at large.**"**
>
> — Everette E. Dennis, executive director, Freedom Forum Media Studies Center

ETHICAL PROBLEMS FOR JOURNALISTS

Journalism ethicist Ralph Barney says that journalists must always be concerned with protecting the First Amendment, "which allows them to push the envelope for the good of society." Because of the First Amendment, society has fewer "rules" for journalists in spite of the special problems they face. The following sections discuss some of those problems.

Deceit

Perhaps the most bothersome of ethical problems facing journalists involves using deceit of some kind to get a story. Deceit covers a wide range of practices. When may you lie, misrepresent yourself, use a hidden digital recorder or camera? When may you steal documents? When may you hire someone to lay a trap to verify a rumor, as *The Spokesman-Review* did to find out whether the mayor was using his position to lure young men on a gay Web site? For the absolutist, the answer is simple — never! But for the rest of us, the answer is not easy.

A group of journalists in an ethical decision-making seminar at the Poynter Institute for Media Studies devised a list of criteria to justify the use of deceit. The accompanying box summarizes their conclusions.

Ethicist Edmund Lambeth has written that for deceit to be used the abuse must be in immediate need of correction and the news media must be the only means to correct it.

Obviously, police often work undercover. Many journalists do the same — especially if it is to expose police malfeasance. But shouldn't journalists, like other

Conditions Justifying Journalists' Use of Deceit

- Issue of profound public importance:
  - of vital public interest, revealing system failure at high levels
  - a preventive measure against profound harm to individuals
- All alternatives exhausted.
- Full disclosure of deception and reason for it.
- Full commitment to the story of everyone involved.
- Harm prevented outweighing any harm caused.

- Meaningful, collaborative and deliberative decision-making process, taking into account:
  - short- and long-term consequences of deception
  - impact on credibility
  - motivations for actions
  - deceptive act in relation to their editorial mission
  - legal implications
  - consistency of reasoning and action

citizens, call the police when they see that the law is being broken, rather than broadcast a story about it on the evening news?

Journalists use deceit most often in consumer reporting. For example, the journalists who exposed a computer repair shop that charged $500 for minor repairs could hardly have done so by revealing that they were journalists. Is there any way other than deceit to expose a crooked dentist who puts unnecessary crowns on people's teeth?

Conflicts of Interest

Reporting generally assumes that the reporter starts out with no point of view, that the reporter is neither out to get someone nor to get something out of the story. This basic tenet is the foundation for any and all credibility.

Ethicist Jay Black reports that most news-media ethics codes devote the bulk of their substance to determining what constitutes a conflict of interest. And well they should.

Friendship

Perhaps the most obvious, the most frequent and yet the most overlooked source of a conflict of interest confronting journalists is friendship. Professor Paul Fisher, founder of the Missouri Freedom of Information Center, called friendship the greatest obstacle to the flow of information. No one knows whether friendship causes more stories to be reported or more stories to be killed. Either way, it sets up a powerful conflict of interest.

Sometimes reporters get too close to their sources. That's why, in some news organizations, beat reporters are shifted around.

Friendship can involve one's family, or a friend of one of the family. In smaller communities especially, editors and producers dine with members of the chamber

Popular *Detroit Free Press* columnist and author Mitch Albom wrote that two former Michigan State basketball players flew to St. Louis to see their team play in the final four and sat next to each other at the game. Albom wrote his column on Friday; the game was on Sunday. The two players never made it to St. Louis.

of commerce, the Kiwanis, the Kings Daughters, the country club. Sometimes a story involves a close acquaintance of a co-worker or a member of one's church.

When U.S. Rep. Chaka Fattah decided to run for mayor in Philadelphia, his wife, Reneć Chenault-Fattah, the co-anchor of NBC 10 in the city, announced that her co-anchor would handle any news about the mayoral race and from City Hall. The veteran newscaster even volunteered to use her maiden name while the race was on.

Nevertheless, Kelly McBride, the ethics guru at the Poynter Institute, asked whether Chenault-Fattah would cover anything the Democrats were doing. Tom Rosenstiel, director of the Project for Excellence in Journalism, says problems of conflict of interest are even more confusing on a local level. The mayor, he says, is responsible for the police force, the fire department, public safety, and so on. How could Chenault-Fattah report on these parts of city government without involving the mayor?

If you ever find yourself covering a story that involves a personal acquaintance, ask your supervisor to assign the story to someone else.

Payola

Journalists may not accept payment for writing a story from anyone other than their employer. *The Honolulu Advertiser* suspended a freelance columnist when it learned he had accepted $500 to write an article favorable to the dairy industry. *The Kansas City Star* fired a veteran outdoors writer for mentioning the name of a van he had received for free.

News organizations frown on reporters doing promotional work for people they cover. For example, when Lou Dobbs was managing editor of Cable News

ON THE JOB

A Healthy Ethical Process

"Every journalist must 'do ethics' in every story," says Kelly McBride. "Young journalists make a common mistake when they fail to identify everyday decisions as ethical choices. Journalists of all experience levels make an even bigger mistake: They assume they should know the answer to every ethical question. Both mistakes undermine a healthy ethical process."

As a teacher of ethics at The Poynter Institute, McBride spends most of her time fostering "a healthy ethical process." McBride has an undergraduate degree in journalism (1984) and a master's degree in religion from Gonzaga University (2000). She spent 14 years as a reporter at *The Spokesman-Review* in Spokane, Wash.

"Young journalists have more power than they imagine in this process," McBride says. "As a newcomer to the profession, or to a particular news room, you are expected to figure out how things get done."

The best tool to accomplish this? "Curiosity," McBride says. "Use your reporting skills to understand the ethical climate of your news room. Observe the signs. Where do the important conversations occur and who is involved?

"Test your observations. Ask colleagues involved in a specific decision to describe the process. In your own work, bounce your decisions off your supervisor and your peers. Invite key editors to tell you what they like about the best stories in the paper or on the air.

"Ask this question over and over again: Why do we do it this way? This simple question will force your co-workers to articulate their news rooms' values. It may

Network business news, he was reprimanded by CNN for making promotional videos for Wall Street firms.

Other conflicts of interest are not so obvious. The *San Jose Mercury News* prohibits its business news reporters and editors from owning stock in local companies.

Will news agencies prohibit journalists from accepting speakers' fees? Will Congress attempt to legislate full disclosure of journalists' income and associations? Ken Auletta quoted then-Sen. Robert G. Torricelli of New Jersey in *The New Yorker* magazine: "What startles many people is to hear television commentators make paid speeches to interest groups and then see them on television commenting on those issues. It's kind of a direct conflict of interest. If it happened in government, it would not be permitted."

What about the reporters who spout their opinions on Sunday morning talk shows and then "objectively" report on those same matters on Monday?

help some people see the gaps between the way things are and the way they ought to be."

These are the things McBride did while a reporter. She observed. "From my desk in the back corner of the news room," she says, "I could see decisions being made. In fact, I could see through the decisions to the very structure, the skeleton if you will, that supported the decision-making process."

She learned that in a healthy news room, reporters constantly turn to each other for exchanges, McBride says. The pathways between the editors' and reporters' desks are busy, two-way streets. At the intersections, journalists cluster in conversation. The most encouraging sign of all occurs when a huddle briefly loosens up and more people are invited into a discussion.

"When the news room is sick, decisions are made in secret, behind closed doors," McBride says. "Surprises show up in the paper or on the air without explanation, and no one knows how the decisions were made. People are afraid to ask questions. There is very little talking."

Now from her desk at the Poynter Institute, McBride gets a larger view. "I get to peer into news rooms around the country," she says. "Part of my job is to offer counseling to journalists trying to make better decisions."

The phone calls and visits reinforce what she first learned about ethical decision making by sitting in the back of the news room and watching the process. "There are three components to any decision in the news room: the individual, the institutional values and the culture," McBride says. People call her when one of these components is out of kilter.

You can e-mail questions to her at kmcbride@poynter.com and sign up for her regular columns at www.poynter.org.

Freebies

- "Whoever said there's no free lunch was obviously not a sports reporter," writes Laura Shutiak in the *Calgary Herald*. Sports reporters are not the only journalists who are wined and dined by those seeking publicity.

- "Put a movie star in a room with 100 journalists armed with knives and forks and some might say you've got a fair fight," writes Dan Cox in *Variety*. "If you're a studio chieftain, however, those are the kind of odds you like, because you know that when the day is done, your latest pic is in for a stupendously inordinate amount of 'safe' press coverage — or, as some marketing whizzes maintain, free advertising." Cox quotes a senior vice president of marketing for a film company saying, "Now it seems they have a press junket for nearly every film." Why? As advertising costs increase, executives work harder for free advertising.

- Auto shows, like the North American International Auto Show, provide valuable press kits and sometimes other keepsakes for journalists. Not only do journalists accept them, but they have begun selling them on eBay. *Detroit News* reporter Mark Truby quotes journalism ethics professor William McWhirter: "It's probably a new low for all of us."

Probably the most egregious accepters of freebies are travel writers. Unless you work for a large paper like the *Chicago Tribune*, which has paid as much as $6,000 to send one writer to Europe, you may be asked to participate in "fam" trips— "familiarization" trips that take travel writers to places and destinies their news organizations say they can't afford to send them. Generally, writers on these trips are expected to recommend that people take the trips, not find fault with them. Douglas Hanks III quotes British travel writer Christopher Warmoil as saying, readers "want to know from you what's good. If it's crap, you just don't write it."

"Many travel writers have long accepted free trips in return for writing favorable stories," writes James S. Hirsch in *The Wall Street Journal*, "but now a new twist has emerged in the cozy ties between the travel industry and the trade press. International journalists attending a travel conference in Miami . . . have been issued an edict: Submit published stories about the conference or forfeit your place at the table next year."

A new twist indeed. But freebies have always come with a price:

- Can reporters remain objective?
- Do reporters write stories they would otherwise not write?
- Does the public perceive the reporter who has accepted or is suspected of accepting freebies as objective?

It is the perception of conflict that bothers most news organizations. Some argue that the least reporters must do is disclose prominently in their stories any freebies they have accepted. As in any case of deceit, reporters must disclose how they were able to get the story and why accepting freebies was necessary. For example, small news outlets cannot afford to send their travel writers on expensive tours.

When the Poynter Institute's Kelly McBride did a workshop for members of the American Association of Sunday and Feature Editors, she mentioned that she refused to accept freebies. She reports: "I was losing the battle. They were ready to string me up by the chandeliers, toss me into the Gulf of Mexico. They thought I was nuts." Even when she told them to tell the readers about the freebies, she received resistance. The reason? "Many editors thought such disclosure would further undermine credibility, not strengthen it. Others said the readers already know." It was clear that they thought the features department was different from the city desk.

Nevertheless, most news organizations have rules against accepting freebies. The Scripps-Howard newspaper group says, "When the gifts exceed the limits of propriety, they should be returned." The Society of Professional Journalists says,

TIPS

Three Guidelines for the Working Journalist

- Be free of obligations to anyone or to any interest except the truth. As scholar John Merrill has written, the primary obligation of the journalist is to be free.

- Be fair. Even children know when you treat them unfairly or when they are being unfair. So do you.

- Remember good taste. Some actions and stories may be ethical, but they may be in bad taste.

"Nothing of value shall be accepted." Is a cup of coffee something of value? The Associated Press expects its staff members to return gifts of "nominal value." Is a baseball cap of nominal value?

The ethics code of *The Orange County (Calif.) Register* says reporters may accept free meals and drinks only if the meal itself or the events surrounding it are of news value. The code also allows tickets or passes to cultural and athletic events only for the purpose of covering those events.

At the *Chicago Tribune*, staff members can accept nothing over the value of a simple keychain.

The *San Jose Mercury News* "will pay for meals and drinks shared with news sources, for luncheons or dinners which are covered as news events and for restaurant meals reviewed." It prohibits free tickets to sports events, movies, fairs, amusement parks and all entertainment that has a charge.

Some news organizations allow reporters to accept freebies—but the reporters turn them in for an annual auction with the proceeds going to charity.

You must learn the ethics code of your news organization. Sometimes, your personal code may be more stringent than that of your organization. In that case, follow your own code. Remember, you may not think a freebie will influence your reporting. But does your audience think it might?

And if you choose a career in public relations, remember that the code of the Public Relations Society of America states that you are to do nothing that tempts news professionals to violate their codes.

Checkbook Journalism

Is it ethical to pay a source for an exclusive story? Will the audience believe your story if you paid your source for it? Should you always report that you had a paid source? Should newspeople be in the business of keeping other newspeople from getting a story?

In the O.J. Simpson case, "journalists" paid witnesses for their stories. Those deals subsequently caused the witnesses' testimony to be tossed out of court. Are paid sources likely to have an ax to grind? Do they come forward only for financial gain?

The terrible consequence of checkbook journalism is that even legitimate news professionals may be cut off from sources who want and expect pay. Some sources have begun asking for a fee even for good news. The increase in tabloid journalism, both in print and in radio and television, has brought the opportunists out in droves. Few news agencies could outbid *People* magazine's reported $4 million fee to get first and exclusive rights to the photo of Brad and Angelina's baby.

In Boston, Sports Radio 850 WEEI obtained a sports appearance contract with Red Sox pitcher Curt Schilling. Schilling would speak to no other news outlet. The fee from his partnership with WEEI benefited a charity to fight Lou Gehrig's disease. Nevertheless, cutting off access to Schilling at a time when he was undergoing rehabilitation for an injury did not sit well with the other Boston media.

The networks say they do not pay for interviews, but the tabloids say payments to the networks are disguised as consultant fees, writes Richard Zoglin in *Time* magazine. He reports that the traditional stigma against checkbook journalism may be fading away. He quotes Everette Dennis, senior vice president and executive director of the Freedom Forum International Consortium of Universities, who says, "It's hard to argue that the ordinary person shouldn't share in the benefit of what's going to be a commercial product."

> **"But I don't believe that paying sources is unethical, as long as it's disclosed to the reader; in some cases I think it makes for better journalism. It gives a fair share of the profits to sources who spend time and take risks."**
>
> — John Tierney, from "Newsworthy," reprinted from the New York Times Company

The New York Times reported what NBC, ABC and CBS offered for an exclusive interview with Pfc. Jessica Lynch after she had been rescued from an Iraqi hospital. CBS dangled a two-hour documentary—and more. The *Times* quotes a letter from Betsy West, a CBS News senior vice president, to Lynch's military representatives: "Attached you will find the outlines of a proposal that includes ideas from CBS News, CBS Entertainment, MTV networks and Simon & Schuster publishers." A possible movie, book, guest appearances—who could resist?

CBS did some of the same with Aron Ralston, the hiker in Utah who had to cut off his arm to get out from under a boulder.

Good reporting demands that you pay sources only when necessary and only if you can get other sources to corroborate your findings. You'd also better be sure that your bosses know that you're doing it.

Participation in the News

You'd also better let your bosses know which organizations you belong to. When the *Fairfield (Iowa) Ledger* fired two reporters who had joined a local church-sponsored pro-life group, the two reporters filed a $250,000 lawsuit charging the paper with religious discrimination and with violation of their civil rights.

The Washington Post issued a memo to staffers that barred any reporters who had participated in a pro-abortion rights march in Washington "from any future participation in coverage of the abortion issue." Don Kowet reported in *The Washington Times* that the same memo prohibited any "news room professional" from participating in such a protest.

But what about participating in a political campaign? Or running for office? William J. "B.J." Laurie, editor of the *Courier Journal* in Crescent City, Fla., opted to run for city commissioner.

And must a religion reporter be an atheist? Must reporters set aside personal religious convictions?

According to Kowet, Richard Harwood, *Washington Post* ombudsman at the time, told a conference of journalists: "You have every right in the world to run for office, or participate in a political activity or lobbying activity. You don't have the 'right' to work for *The Washington Post*."

Nevertheless, some worry that uninvolved journalists will be uninformed journalists, an unconnected group of elitists. The problem is compounded when editors and even news organizations are involved in community projects. May the editor join the yacht club? May the station support the United Way? Is *The New York Times*' coverage of the Metropolitan Museum of Art influenced by its generous support of that institution? May an HIV-positive journalist report on AIDS?

The second war in Iraq gave the word "embedded" a new meaning for journalists. Those covering the war underwent Pentagon training for their work there. When in Iraq, they accompanied soldiers in an officially sanctioned role never experienced by reporters covering previous wars. Most of those who participated felt they benefited from the training and that they were better reporters for it. Will we ever know?

Jules Crittenden, an embedded reporter for the *Boston Herald*, called American soldiers' attention to a bevy of Iraqis who were firing at a U.S. battalion. In his *Embedded Journal* written for Poynter, Crittenden said he was sure that some would question his ethics or objectivity. His answer: "Screw them, they weren't there. But they are welcome to join me next time if they care to test their professionalism."

> **"** If you're not involved in the community at all and you're totally neutralized, you end up not knowing enough about the community, not being able to get enough leads and so on in order to do your job. **"**
>
> — Tony Case, quoting ethicist Louis W. Hodges
> in *Editor & Publisher*

Reporters have accompanied police on raids for years, but when the World Trade Organization met in Miami in December 2003, Associated Press reporter Rachel La Corte wrote that Police Chief John Timoney wished to embed journalists in order to place "them on the front lines of a protest expected to draw tens of thousands of people." Would you have participated? Under what circumstances?

Should journalists demand of themselves what they demand of politicians—full disclosure of their financial investments and memberships, as well as public knowledge of their personal tastes, preferences and lifestyles?

Surely if you own stock in a company, you must at least tell your editor and make a full disclosure. Better, you should not report on the stock at all. Mark Glaser reported in the *USC Annenberg Online Journalism Review*:

> CNBC glamour anchor Maria Bartiromo recently took flack for an on-air disclosure that she owned stock in Citigroup—just before interviewing Sanford Weill, the company's CEO.
>
> Then, before you could say "online angle," CBS MarketWatch star columnist Thom Calandra touted stock in Ivanhoe Energy Inc. on "CBS MarketWatch Weekend" while making an on-air disclosure of stock ownership. Then the show's anchor, Susan McGinnis, disclosed that she owned shares in Ivanhoe as well. The Monday after the report aired, Ivanhoe's stock shot up 26.7 percent to a new 52-week high.

Advertising Pressure

It's quite possible that you won't work long at a news organization before you realize some subjects are taboo and others are highly encouraged. If you are lucky, you will work for a paper, station, magazine or Web site that still has a solid wall of separation between editorial and advertising.

However, in some places, advertising salespeople are allowed to peek over that wall and see what the publication, station or Web site is planning to run. That information might help sell some advertising. Some say, what could be wrong with that?

The next step is for the advertising manager to climb over the wall and suggest that editorial do a story on some subject so that advertising can be sold.

And then the next step isn't far away. Advertising sits at your desk and begins to dictate what must or must not be printed or broadcast and even what must and must not be said. In print and online media, advertising may want the layout, design and type of ads or sections to look like the publication's normal layout, design and typefaces. They may also insist that the label "Advertisement" be omitted or be displayed so small as to be hardly noticeable.

Seldom does a paper have a policy as blatant as that of the *Palo Alto Daily News*, a free paper: "In addition to covering business as a news beat, (the reporter) must also cover local business from the perspective of the business owner, or, as their partner. This means promoting the business as their own. This is the key to early and continued success. If we embrace our advertisers and help them promote with good writing and photos, they will become our strongest supporters."

Probably, on a day-to-day basis, advertising has more to do with what stories will *not* be run. You may learn quickly that you are not to do a story critical of the local grocery store. Chinese journalist Y.Y. Zhang reports that the oral decree of the *Guangzhou Daily*'s publishers has been carried out loyally: "Never write any stories about the shortcomings of our city's real estate developers because they provide us with 30 percent of advertising."

One small paper lost $50,000 a year in advertising for criticizing a local theater that was part of a big chain of theaters and owner of several other theaters in town. Research has shown that magazines that continue to receive millions in cigarette advertising have carried few or no articles about the health hazards of tobacco. Car buff magazines carry more articles about the cars they advertise than about unadvertised vehicles.

Although some newspaper companies have allowed advertising and news personnel to become a bit chummier, some magazines have gone much further. The Southern Progress Corp., for example, a big moneymaker for Time Warner and publisher of *Southern Living, Southern Accents, The Progressive Farmer, Cooking Light* and other successful magazines, has stopped worrying about the separation of advertising and editorial. In a *Wall Street Journal* story by Matthew Rose, former Southern Progress editor Michael Carlton said, "There is no church and state. They all sit in the same church, maybe in different pews." In the same story, another former chief executive of the Southern Progress unit is quoted as saying, "For me, the acid test was: Am I serving the reader well?"

Not only does Southern Progress tip off advertisers as to what editorial is going to do, but it also sometimes allows advertisers into planning sessions and to make suggestions.

With Southern Progress boasting high renewal rates and high profits, is this the future? In the *Nashville Scene,* Matt Pulle quotes from the Meredith Corp.'s 2003 annual report: "Now everyone at each station, including news anchors and other on-air personalities, is playing a role in generating advertising revenues or supporting sales operations."

Even the tabloids check with Wal-Mart, reports AdAge.com. David Pecker, chairman-CEO of American Media, publisher of the *Star, Globe,* and *National Enquirer,* tabloids that sell a combined 2.8 million copies on newstands weekly, says, "We work with Wal-Mart." If there is "a very controversial cover, we will call and say, 'This is what we are doing.'" That's to keep those tabloids selling at Wal-Mart and not banned like *Maxim* and *Stuff.* When someone approached Jack Kliger, president-CEO of Hachette Filipacchi Media, with "a somewhat sexy idea for a magazine," the person had a solution to "the Wal-Mart-sex question" — use "toned-down covers for copies that Wal-Mart will sell." That example, reports AdAge.com, shows the power of Wal-Mart, the largest single retailer for magazines' on-the-rack sales.

The question of advertisements online is dealt with in Chapter 20. Radio newscasters generally separate themselves from the commercials. Yet popular long-time commentator Paul Harvey and, more recently, Rush Limbaugh and Charles Osgood, have not refrained from reading the commercials with the same gusto with which they say everything else. What has it done to their credibility? Television suffers the same advertising pressures as print with the added problems that there are only so many minutes in a newscast. How ethical is it to cut a complicated international story to 90 seconds just to make time for one more commercial?

It's only fair to point out, of course, that news media have rejected advertising pressure, sometimes at the cost of millions of dollars. For example, during Super Bowl XXVIII in February 2004, which boasted the highest television advertising fees of the year, CBS decided not to air an ad by the political activist group MoveOn.org that criticized President Bush, saying they wouldn't run "issue" ads.

On the flip side of this issue, if you are going into advertising, you need to look at advertising codes of ethics that sometimes state explicitly that enticing or pressuring news media to violate their codes is unethical.

Invasion of Privacy

Most journalists would cry out against an invasion of their own privacy. Yet many of them argue for a vague "right to know" when they report on others, especially if those others are public officials or public figures. The head-on collision of the right to know and the right to privacy will confront you every day of your reporting lives. The Constitution mentions neither "right."

The most obvious and talked-about issue pertaining to the right to privacy is naming crime victims, especially rape and abuse victims. Florida legislated against publishing rape victims' names, only to have the law struck down by a Florida District Court. The U.S. Supreme Court has held that news agencies cannot be punished for publishing lawfully obtained information or information from a public record. Meanwhile, state legislators are looking for ways to close the records on rape and to punish police, hospitals, court clerks and other officials for releasing victims' names.

So it comes down to a matter of ethics, and, as usual, there is no complete agreement. But most news outlets will not publish a rape victim's name without the victim's permission. The same is true of the names of juvenile victims of sex crimes. The obvious reasons are that the victim has suffered greatly and that public knowledge of the crime may stigmatize the victim. Even though the reporting of incidents of rape has risen from 10 percent of all such crimes to 20 percent, most victims do not come forward because of the stigma attached.

Some argue that it is equally unfair to name the accused as it is the accuser. Here are some possible guidelines:

- Name the accuser and the accused only when charges are filed, not at the accusation or arrest stage. This stage at least says the prosecuting attorney believes there is enough evidence to support going forward.

- Name the accuser only if the person agrees. That requires that you make contact directly or through intermediaries to ask the question.

Many disagree. Charles Gay, editor and publisher of the *Shelton-Mason County Journal* in Washington State, is one of them. Reporter Beth Kaiman quotes Gay in seattletimes.com: "I just can't bring myself to be part of a journalistic fraternity that says there's something wrong with you and we're not going to print your name. I want to get rid of the stigma, not perpetuate it."

Geneva Overholser, former editor of *The Des Moines Register,* former ombudsman of *The Washington Post* and now a professor at the Missouri School of Journalism, has long believed in revealing the names of rape victims. In her electronic newsletter from the Poynter Institute, she argues that most discussions about this matter center on broader sociological questions, not on journalistic questions. She writes:

> While I recognize the good intentions of those who seek to protect rape victims, I believe that much of the effort has had contrary results—and that there is little evidence that it has helped rape victims or furthered social understanding. But these views of mine—and the views of others—on these questions are fundamentally beside the point journalistically.
>
> When it comes to asking whether to use people's names, the journalistic ethic is clear: We name names. We do this for reasons of credibility and fairness. To my mind, protecting children is the one valid exception.

But even the question of naming juvenile offenders has no easy or universal answer. Traditionally, news organizations have held that juveniles are juveniles and are entitled to make juvenile mistakes, even if those mistakes are crimes. Juvenile court records are, after all, sealed. But the courts have upheld the right to publish juvenile offenders' names on the public record.

Some media critics, such as former *Fresno Bee* ombudsman Lynne Enders Glaser, applaud the publication of the names of juvenile offenders. Glaser writes: "It doesn't take a rocket scientist to figure out that more and more violent crimes are being committed by young people. And in increasing numbers, *Bee* readers have challenged the law and the media to stop protecting the identity of criminals because of their age."

Regardless of the stigma forever attached to the juvenile offender's name and the embarrassment of his or her parents and family, some worry that in some groups a youth's notoriety will encourage other young people to violate the law. Others argue that the prospect of public humiliation will make other juveniles think twice before committing crimes.

Reporting on crime victims and reporting on juvenile crimes are just two of the myriad privacy issues you will face. Journalists are still protected when writing about public officials and public figures—most of the time. But what about the children of politicians or celebrities?

Photographers and videographers must be especially concerned with privacy. "Lead with blood" is not an uncommon dictum in TV news rooms. But how much blood? And how often and under what circumstances should they stick cameras into people's grieving and anxious faces? When may they ask, if at all, "How did you feel when you saw your daughter get hit by a car?" And when should they comply with government requests not to photograph?

The media were forbidden to take pictures of coffins of troops returning from Iraq, and the Federal Emergency Management Agency asked the media not to photograph the dead in Hurricane Katrina's wake. No one stopped *The New York Times* and the *Los Angeles Times* from running photos of dead babies in what was used as a morgue after the Dec. 26, 2004, tsunami in the Indian Ocean, but many readers strongly objected.

Sometimes matters of privacy and ethics are more just a matter of good taste. When contract photographer Rick Wilking took a picture of President George Bush writing a note at the United Nations, he did not know what the note said. Gary Hershorn, a Reuters' news editor for pictures, zoomed in on the page and found the message: "I think I may need a bathroom break. Is this possible?" The note, written to Secretary of State Condoleezza Rice, was transmitted to Reuters' clients. Hardly unethical, but in good taste?

When a reporter asked former President Harry Truman how he felt when he heard that President John Kennedy was killed, Truman answered, "It's none of your damn business."

When is privacy paramount, and under what circumstances do you fail as a journalist to keep your audience informed?

You should keep one thing in mind: Is secrecy better than disclosure? Is it better to have people whispering names to each other, even guessing who the involved person is, than dispelling all rumors with the facts?

Withholding Information

May you ever withhold information from the news organization for which you work? If you are writing what you hope to be a best-selling book, may you save some "news" until the book is published?

If you work as a journalist, are you ever off-duty? A doctor isn't. Doctors take an oath to treat the sick. If you witness something at a friend's house or at a party, do you tell your news director about it?

One reporter was fired when his boss discovered that he attended a post-concert party of a rock band where lines of cocaine were openly available. The reporter did not include this information in his coverage of the band. His defense was that if he reported the drug abuse, he would never get interviews or get close to other rock groups, and he would be finished as a music critic. His defense didn't work.

If you learn that a political candidate is "sleeping around," would you withhold that information? Would you do so even if you knew that if the public had that information, the candidate would not be elected? Suppose after the election it became clear that you had had the information before the election but did not publish it? *The (Portland) Oregonian* apologized to its readers for not publishing reports about Sen. Bob Packwood's alleged sexual-harassment charges until after he was re-elected.

When do you withhold information because the police ask you to or because it may jeopardize a case? When a suspect in the BTK serial murder case in Wichita, Kan., was finally arrested, *Seattle Times* reporter Cathy Henkel recalled seeing a copy of a two-page memo that BTK had sent to the police in the 1970s. Henkel was working for the weekly *Wichita Sun* at the time. The letter, filled with graphic content and bad grammar, discussed four types of knots he used to strangle his victims. The paper thought it best to do nothing with that information. *The Wichita Eagle* and ABC affiliate television station KAKE had even more information about BTK the year before his arrest, and both said nothing.

> *Journalism, to a considerable degree, has ceased to be the profession of intelligent, idealistic and charming gentlemen. It has become the profession of public office seekers, title hunters, social pushers, dollar diddlers, mountebanks and cads.*
>
> —Columnist H.L. Mencken, 1924

Poynter Institute columnist Kelly McBride says, "Cutting deals to withhold information is dangerous. It should be done with great caution, much forethought and only in rare circumstances." She warns that "we too readily agree with police and keep information from the public."

McBride also says we should pay more attention to children, especially when they tell us about inappropriate behavior of adults. The *St. Petersburg Times* and *The Miami Herald* both had copies of e-mails sent to a 16-year-old Louisiana boy by Florida Rep. Mark Foley. Perhaps other news media had the memos as well. Indications are that those who did check into it were told by congressional staffers that the memos were simply "overly friendly."

The *Los Angeles Times* received all kinds of criticism (one reader wrote about the *Times*' "sleazy hatchet job") for publishing the sexual-harassment complaints of 16 women against then candidate-for-governor Arnold Schwarzenegger in the final week of the campaign in California's special recall election in 2003. Eleven of the women went on record with their names. Schwarzenegger won anyway.

Sometimes there's more than an election at stake. St. Louis WKBQ general manager Bill Viands did not apologize when a popular St. Louis meteorologist committed suicide after WKBQ aired intimate messages left on the answering machine of a woman who said he had been harassing her. In a *Chicago Tribune* story by Staci D. Kraemer, WKBQ producer Courtney Landrum said, "I couldn't believe [the airing of messages] was unethical in any way, shape or form."

Leading politicians in France blamed negative reporting that questioned the integrity of Prime Minister Pierre Beregovoy for his suicide. Press critics blamed the media treatment of Vince Foster, counselor to President Bill Clinton, for his suicide. Foster's suicide note lamented that ruining people's lives was sport in our nation's capital.

Sometimes the press withholds information. In El Paso, Tex., the media held a story of the kidnapping of two boys for two days because of threats, relayed by the FBI, that the kidnappers would kill the boys if the kidnapping were publicized. The boys were eventually freed unharmed.

Sometimes a news organization withholds information to protect its reporters and to maintain access to news sources. Eason Jordan, CNN's chief news executive, shocked the journalistic world with his candid admission in a *New York Times* op-ed piece that CNN often did not report Iraqi government atrocities in Iraq—even when its own reporters were the victims. Reporter Peter Johnson quoted CNN spokesperson Matthew Furman as saying that "you do what you have to do to protect your people." Columnist Eric Fettmann wrote in the *New York Post:* "It's like saying that the best interests of journalism would have justified suppressing stories on the Holocaust in order to keep a U.S. news bureau in Berlin to tell Nazi Germany's side."

Sometimes the press doesn't withhold anything. Sometimes it comes down to what ethicist Edmund Lambeth calls "humaneness." You never do needless harm to an individual or inflict needless pain or suffering. It is better that you do the least harm possible. You certainly don't do harmful stories deliberately to harass someone or without a good reason. No one likes a bully.

Plagiarism

No one wants you to use his or her work as if it were your own. No one condones plagiarism. The problem is defining what constitutes plagiarism. You probably know when you are consciously using someone else's work word for word. But what about when you use only a few phrases or sentences? Claiming any amount of text as your own when you haven't written it is plagiarism.

If you read Jim Romenesko's blog (and you should) on the Poynter Web site (www.poynter.org/medianews), it seems that nearly every other day there is a story about some reporter admitting to plagiarism.

Perhaps it's even more of a temptation to plagiarize material published online. Lloyd Grove wrote in the New York *Daily News* that Lisa Tortoreti Pezzolla, publisher of the 115-year-old weekly New Jersey *Observer*, lifted whole sentences, exact phrases and full paragraphs from online sources. Even *New York Times* Hollywood correspondent Bernard Weinraub admitted to "screwing up." A graduate student in the Gaylord College of Journalism and Mass Communication at the University of Oklahoma lifted several paragraphs from a Web site. Lauren Cavagnolo, writing in hub.ou.edu, quoted the editor of *The Oklahoma Daily*, where the column ran, as saying, "This is troubling news. There is nothing more damaging to a paper's credibility than to have a reporter plagiarize and have it published."

Beware of Plagiarism!

- **Taking material verbatim (word for word) from the newspaper library.** Even when the material is from your own newspaper, it is still someone else's work. Put it in your own words or attribute it.
- **Using material verbatim from the wire services.** Sometimes writers take Associated Press material, add a few paragraphs to give some local flavor, and publish it as their own work. Even though it is a common practice, it is not right.
- **Using material from other publications.** Some blame electronic databases for a whole new explosion of plagiarism. Sometimes writers steal the research of others without attribution. And sometimes they use others' work without realizing it.

- **Using news releases verbatim.** The publicists are delighted, but you should be ashamed — especially if you put your name on an article. Rewrite it, except perhaps for the direct quotations, and use them sparingly. If you use a whole release, cite its source.
- **Using the work of fellow reporters.** If more than one reporter works on a story, if you use a byline on top, put the other names at the end of the story.
- **Using old stories over again.** Columnists, beware! Your readers have a right to know when you are recycling your material. Some of them might catch you at it, and there goes your credibility.

— Roy Peter Clark, The Poynter Institute

In the daily practice of journalism, reporters, consciously or unconsciously, deal with many situations that could involve plagiarism. Roy Peter Clark of The Poynter Institute has listed them (see the "Beware of Plagiarism!" box above). It is not unusual for a writer to plagiarize and have absolutely no idea that he or she is doing it. Apparently, sometimes something one has read becomes so familiar to the reader that the reader later considers it his or her own.

When the *Indianapolis Star/News* fired TV writer Steve Hall in 1999 for plagiarism, Hall stood by his work and maintained that if he had in fact plagiarized, he had done so unconsciously. Hall said he might have unknowingly used information he had read elsewhere. He also said that if plagiarism occurred, it was because of his heavy workload.

Some writers mistakenly believe that incorporating just a few of someone else's sentences or phrases into their own writing is acceptable as paraphrase. It is not. To write a paraphrase, you need to completely digest a text and then restate its contents in your own words. Any of the original wording that remains in the paragraph should be put in quotation marks and attributed. See Figure 23.3 for examples of plagiarism masquerading as paraphrase.

You must fight every impulse, question and check any doubts, avoid any hint of plagiarism. As William A. Henry III wrote in *Time* magazine, a reporter has a First Amendment bond with the public. "Plagiarism," he wrote, "imperils that bond, not because it involves theft of a wry phrase or piquant quote, but because it devalues meticulous, independent verification of fact — the bedrock of a press worth reading."

That bond is not just with the public. It's with your fellow workers and the news organization for which you work. Your personal ethics will safeguard and nurture that bond. Once it is broken, so are you.

Plagiarism, Quotation and Paraphrase

Using an Attributed Quotation — Acceptable
The story fully identifies the source of the quotation and puts the exact words in quotation marks.

As William A. Henry III wrote in *Time* magazine, a reporter has a First Amendment bond with the public. "Plagiarism," he wrote, "imperils that bond, not because it involves theft of a wry phrase or piquant quote, but because it devalues meticulous, independent verification of fact — the bedrock of a press worth reading."

Paraphrasing a Quotation — Acceptable
The story identifies the source and restates the source's original idea in the writer's own words.

William A. Henry III writes about the destructive effect on journalism that plagiarism can have, suggesting that it compromises the integrity of the reportorial research process.

Plagiarizing — Unacceptable
Even though the source is identified, the writer errs by using the source's original words (in bold) without putting them in quotation marks. Simply using distinctive words and phrases without quotation marks can constitute plagiarism.

In writing about how plagiarism **imperils** the reporter's bond with the public, William A. Henry III says the practice goes beyond stealing **a wry phrase or piquant quote**. It **devalues the meticulous, independent verification of fact** that journalism depends on.

Plagiarizing — Unacceptable
The source is not identified, and the source's original words (in bold) are not put in quotation marks. Changing the occasional word (for example, "striking" rather than "piquant") or the structure of a sentence is not sufficient to avoid plagiarism.

Plagiarism damages the reporter's bond with the public. It goes beyond the **theft of a wry phrase or [striking] quote** and diminishes the foundation of journalism — **the meticulous, independent verification of facts**.

Figure 23. 3
Writers sometimes misunderstand the nature of paraphrase. Simply altering a few words of a quotation, with or without attribution, often results in plagiarism rather than paraphrase.

Columnist Lizette Rabe wrote, "Of all our journalistic sins, plagiarism might be the most unforgivable." And just as unforgivable is making up people, fabricating events and inventing quotations from people you make up. A reporter on *The Sacramento Bee* did that, and he was fired. An AP Washington reporter did that, and he was fired.

It's hard to say what's worse — making up material or stealing it. Don't do either. Ever.

Suggested Readings

Beckman, Robert I. and Shumway, Christopher A. *Digital Dilemmas: Ethical Issues for Online Media Professionals.* Ames: Iowa State Press, 2003. A superb review of ethical principles for journalists of all kinds, including a discussion of who is a journalist in the Internet age, privacy, speed and accuracy, advertising and editorial independence.

Christians, Clifford, Rotzoll, Kim and Fackler, Mark. *Media Ethics, Cases and Moral Reasoning,* 7th Edition. New York: Longman, 2004. Applies the Potter Box method of principled reasoning to dozens of journalism, advertising and public-relations cases.

Day, Louis Alvin. *Ethics in Media Communications,* 5th Edition. Belmont, Calif.: Wadsworth, 2005. Begins with a superb discussion of ethics and moral development, ethics and society, and ethics and moral reasoning, and goes on to discuss nearly every problem facing journalists. Includes actual cases.

Fletcher, Joseph. *Situation Ethics: The New Morality.* Philadelphia: Westminster Press, 1966. A classic work on Christian situation ethics.

Lambeth, Edmund B. *Committed Journalism,* Second Edition. Bloomington: Indiana University Press, 1992. Creates an ethics framework specific to the practice of journalism.

Merrill, John. *The Imperative of Freedom: A Philosophy of Journalistic Autonomy.* New York: Hastings House, 1974; Lanham, Md.: University Press of America, 1990. Establishes freedom as the primary imperative of the journalist.

Merrill, John. *Journalism Ethics: Philosophical Foundations for News Media.* New York: St. Martin's Press, 1997. Provides in-depth understanding of the philosophical and theoretical underpinnings of journalism morality.

Wilkins, Lee and Patterson, Philip. *Media Ethics: Issues and Cases,* 6th Edition. Dubuque, Iowa: McGraw-Hill, 2005. An excellent discussion of journalism ethics with up-to-date cases.

Suggested Web Sites

www.elon.edu/andersj/ethics.html
This Web site for online news ethics was put together by Janna Quitney Anderson, from the Elon School of Communications.

www.journalism.indiana.edu/ethics
This Web site from Indiana University School of Journalism provides an extensive database of ethics cases in journalism.

www.poynter.org
The Poynter Institute provides a file of articles written about ethical issues in journalism.

www.poynter.org/medianews
Poynter Online, Jim Romenesko's blog, provides "your daily fix of media industry news, commentary, and memos."

www.rtnda.org/ethics/coe.shtml
The Radio-Television News Directors Association Journalism Ethics program put together this site.

www.spj.org
Follow the "Ethics" link to find the Society of Professional Journalists' code, ethics teaching tools, ethics case studies, an ethics hotline, resources for reporters, suggested readings and other organizations' codes of ethics.

Exercises

1. A student from the law school tells you that journalists should be required to adhere to a code of ethics in the same way that lawyers who are members of a bar association must. Do you agree? Why or why not?

2. You learn that the daughter of a local bank president has been kidnapped. The family has not been contacted by the kidnappers, and police officials ask you to keep the matter secret for fear the abductors might panic and injure the child. Describe how a deontologist, a teleologist and a situation ethicist would make their decisions about how to handle the situation.

3. Would a travel writer ever be justified in accepting a free trip? Explain your answer by using various theories of situation ethics.

4. You are a photographer for a newspaper. On your way back from a track meet, you see a man who looks as if he is thinking about jumping off a bridge. You have a camera with motor-drive action, which permits you to take pictures in rapid-fire sequence. Which of the following would you do? Justify your response.

   a. Shoot pictures from a distance.
   b. Approach the man slowly, take pictures and try to talk him out of jumping.
   c. Step out of his sight and call the police.
   d. Take some other action.

5. For at least a year, on four or five occasions, reporters on your paper have heard rumors that a residence for the aged is negligent in its care of the elderly. Your editor asks you to get a job there as a janitor and report what you find. What would be your response?

6. A Christian minister is running for mayor of your city, which is a conservative, traditional community. You learn that he and his wife of 18 years have a son who was born four months after they were married. Using the Potter Box (Figure 23.1), decide whether you would release that information.

7. Do a computer search of articles written in the past three years on whether journalists should publish the names of rape victims. Then write a brief summary of your findings.

APPENDIX 1

Twenty Common Errors of Grammar and Punctuation

Grammar provides our language's rules of the road. When you see a green light, you proceed on faith that the other driver will not go through the red light. Drivers have a shared understanding of the rules of the road. Writers have a shared understanding of the grammar rules that ensure we understand what we are reading. Occasionally, as on the road, there is a wreck. We dangle participles, misplace modifiers and omit commas. If we write "Running down the street, his pants fell off," we are saying a pair of pants ran down a street. If we write "He hit Harry and John stopped him," the missing comma changes the meaning to "He hit Harry and John."

To say what you mean— to avoid syntactic wrecks—you must know the rules of grammar. We have compiled a list of 20 common errors that we find in our students' stories and in the stories of many professionals. Avoid them, and you'll write safely.

To take quizzes based on this list of 20 common errors of grammar and punctuation, go to Exercise Central for Associated Press Style at bedfordstmartins.com/apexercises. There you will find advice and activities that go beyond grammar; the updated Exercises Central offers much more on Associated Press style—the style that makes news writing distinctly journalistic.

1. Incorrect comma in a series in Associated Press style

Use commas to separate the items in a series, but do not put a comma before *and* or *or* at the end of the series unless the meaning would be unclear without a comma.

INCORRECT COMMA BEFORE "AND"	**The film was fast-paced, sophisticated, and funny.**
CLEAR WITHOUT COMMA	**The film was fast-paced, sophisticated and funny.**
UNCLEAR WITHOUT COMMA	**He demanded cheese, salsa with jalapeños and onions on his taco.**

A comma before *and* would prevent readers from wondering if he demanded salsa containing both jalapeños and onions or if he wanted the salsa and the onions as two separate toppings.

COMMA NEEDED BEFORE "AND"	**He demanded cheese, salsa with jalapeños, and onions on his taco.**

No comma with an *and* before *salsa* would mean salsa with both jalapeños and onions.

NO COMMA "AND" BEFORE "SALSA"	**He demanded cheese and salsa with jalapeños and onions on his taco.**

517

2. Run-on sentence

An independent clause contains a subject and a predicate and makes sense by itself. A run-on sentence—also known as a *comma splice*—occurs when two or more independent clauses are joined incorrectly with a comma.

RUN-ON   **John Rogers left the family law practice, he decided to become a teacher.**

You can correct a run-on sentence in several ways. Join the clauses with a comma and one of the coordinating conjunctions—*and, but, for, nor, or, yet* or *so*—or join the clauses with a semicolon if they are closely related. Use a subordinating conjunction such as *after, because, if* or *when* to turn one of the clauses into a dependent clause. Or rewrite the run-on as two separate sentences.

CORRECTING A RUN-ON WITH A COMMA AND A COORDINATING CONJUNCTION

John Rogers left the family law practice, <u>for</u> he decided to become a teacher.

CORRECTING A RUN-ON WITH A SEMICOLON

John Rogers left the family law practice; he decided to become a teacher.

CORRECTING A RUN-ON BY MAKING ONE INDEPENDENT CLAUSE A DEPENDENT CLAUSE

John Rogers left the family law practice <u>when</u> he decided to become a teacher.

CORRECTING A RUN-ON BY WRITING TWO SEPARATE SENTENCES

John Rogers left the family law practice. He decided to become a teacher.

3. Fragment

A fragment is a word group that lacks a subject, a verb or both, yet is punctuated as though it were a complete sentence. Another type of fragment is a word group that begins with a subordinating conjunction such as *because* or *when*, yet is punctuated as though it were a complete sentence.

FRAGMENTS   **After she had placed her watch and an extra pencil on the table.**

                                Without feeling especially sorry about it.

Correct a fragment by joining it to the sentence before or after it or by adding the missing elements so that the fragment contains a subject and a verb and can stand alone.

CORRECTING A FRAGMENT BY JOINING IT TO ANOTHER SENTENCE

After she had placed her watch and an extra pencil on the table, the student opened the exam booklet.

CORRECTING A FRAGMENT BY TURNING IT INTO A SENTENCE

She apologized to her boss for the outburst without feeling especially sorry about it.

4. Missing comma(s) with a nonrestrictive element

A nonrestrictive element is a word, phrase or clause that gives information about the preceding part of the sentence but does not restrict or limit the meaning of that part. A nonrestrictive element is not essential to the meaning of the sentence; you can delete it and still understand clearly what the sentence is saying. Place commas before and (if necessary) after a nonrestrictive element.

UNCLEAR	**The mayor asked to meet Alva Johnson a highly decorated police officer.**
CLEAR	**The mayor asked to meet Alva Johnson, a highly decorated police officer.**
UNCLEAR	**His wife Mary was there.**
CLEAR	**His wife, Mary, was there.**

5. Confusion of *that* and *which*

The pronoun *that* always introduces restrictive information, which is essential to the meaning of the sentence; do not set off a *that* clause with commas. The pronoun *which* introduces nonrestrictive, or nonessential, information; set off a nonrestrictive *which* clause with commas.

INCORRECT	**The oldest store in town, Miller and Co., <u>that</u> has been on Main Street for almost a century, will close this summer.**
CORRECT	**The oldest store in town, Miller and Co., <u>which</u> has been on Main Street for almost a century, will close this summer.**
INCORRECT	**The creature, <u>which</u> has been frightening residents of North First Street for the past week, has turned out to be a screech owl.**
CORRECT	**The creature <u>that</u> has been frightening residents of North First Street for the past week has turned out to be a screech owl.**

6. Missing comma after an introductory element

A sentence may begin with a dependent clause (a word group that contains a subject and a verb and begins with a subordinating conjunction such as *because* or *when*), a prepositional phrase (a word group that begins with a preposition such as *in* or *on* and ends with a noun or pronoun), an adverb such as *next* that modifies the whole sentence, or a participial phrase (a word group that contains a past or present participle, such as *determined* or *hoping*, that acts as an adjective). Use a comma to separate these introductory elements from the main clause of the sentence.

DEPENDENT CLAUSE	<u>**After the applause had died down,**</u> **the conductor raised his baton again.**
PREPOSITIONAL PHRASE	<u>**Without a second thought,**</u> **the chicken crossed the road.**

ADVERB	**Furthermore, the unemployment rate continues to rise.**
PARTICIPIAL PHRASES	**Waiting in the bar, José grew restless.**
	Saddened by the news from home, she stopped reading the letter.

Although it is always correct to use a comma after an introductory element, the comma may be omitted after some adverbs and short prepositional phrases if the meaning is clear:

Suddenly it's spring.

In Chicago it rained yesterday.

Always place a comma after two or more introductory prepositional phrases.

In May of last year in Toronto, Tom attended three conventions.

Here are more examples of prepositional phrases:

INCORRECT	**Shaking her head at the latest budget information the library administrator wondered where to find the money for new books.**
CORRECT	**Shaking her head at the latest budget information, the library administrator wondered where to find the money for new books.**
INCORRECT	**After a week of foggy, rainy mornings had passed he left Seattle.**
CORRECT	**After a week of foggy, rainy mornings had passed, he left Seattle.**

7. Missing comma(s) between coordinate adjectives

Adjectives are coordinate if they make sense when you insert *and* between them or place them in reverse order.

COORDINATE ADJECTIVES	**The frightened, angry citizens protested the new policy.**
	The frightened and angry citizens protested the new policy.

The adjectives make sense with *and* between them, so they are coordinate.

The angry, frightened citizens protested the new policy.

The adjectives make sense in reverse order, so they are coordinate. Separate coordinate adjectives with commas.

INCORRECT	**The gaunt lonely creature was also afraid.**
CORRECT	**The gaunt, lonely creature was also afraid.**

8. Missing comma(s) in a compound sentence

Two or more independent clauses—word groups containing a subject and a verb and expressing a complete thought—joined with a coordinating conjunction (*and, but, for, nor, or, yet* or *so*) form a compound sentence. Place a comma before the conjunction in a compound sentence to avoid confusion.

UNCLEAR	**She works as a pharmacist now and later she plans to go to medical school.**
CLEAR	**She works as a pharmacist now, and later she plans to go to medical school.**

9. Misused semicolon

In a compound sentence that has a coordinating conjunction joining the clauses, place a comma before the conjunction, not a semicolon.

INCORRECT	**The Chicago Cubs did not play in the World Series; but they did win their division.**
CORRECT	**The Chicago Cubs did not play in the World Series, but they did win their division.**

10. Misplaced or dangling modifier

Modifiers are words or phrases that change or clarify the meaning of another word or word group in a sentence. Place modifiers immediately before or directly after the word or words they modify. A *misplaced modifier* appears too far from the word or words it is supposed to modify in the sentence. A *dangling modifier* appears in a sentence that does not contain the word or words it is supposed to modify. A modifier at the beginning of a sentence should refer to the grammatical subject of the sentence.

	subject
MISPLACED MODIFIER	**Having predicted a sunny morning, the downpour surprised the meteorologist.**
	subject
CORRECT	**Having predicted a sunny morning, the meteorologist did not expect the downpour.**
	subject
DANGLING MODIFIER	**Working in the yard, the sun burned her badly.**
	subject
CORRECT	**Working in the yard, she became badly sunburned.**

11. Missing or misused hyphen(s) in a compound modifier

A compound modifier consists of two or more adjectives or an adjective-adverb combination used to modify a single noun. When a compound modifier precedes a noun, you should hyphenate the parts of the compound unless the compound consists of an adverb ending in *-ly* followed by an adjective.

INCORRECT	**His over the top performance made the whole film unbelievable.**
	The freshly-printed counterfeit bills felt like genuine dollars.
	The local chapter of Parents without Partners will sponsor an open toga party on Saturday.

CORRECT	His over-the-top performance made the whole film unbelievable.
	The freshly printed counterfeit bills felt like genuine dollars.
	The local chapter of Parents without Partners will sponsor an open-toga party on Saturday.

12. Missing or misused apostrophe

Do not confuse the pronoun *its*, meaning "belonging to it," with the contraction *it's*, meaning "it is" or "it has." The possessive form of a noun uses an apostrophe; possessive pronouns never take apostrophes.

INCORRECT	The car is lying on it's side in the ditch.
	Its a blue 2006 Ford Taurus.
	That new car of her's rides very smoothly.
CORRECT	The car is lying on its side in the ditch.
	It's a blue 2006 Ford Taurus.
	That new car of hers rides very smoothly.

For clarity, avoid using the contraction ending in -*'s* to mean "has" instead of "is."

UNCLEAR	She's held many offices in student government.
CLEAR	She has held many offices in student government.

13. Incorrect pronoun case

A pronoun that is the subject of a sentence or clause must be in the subjective case (*I, he, she, we, they*). A pronoun that is the direct object of a verb, the indirect object of a verb, or the object of a preposition must be in the objective case (*me, him, her, us, them*). To decide whether a pronoun in a compound construction—two or more nouns or pronouns joined with *and* or *or*—should be subjective or objective, omit everything in the compound except the pronoun and see whether the subjective or objective case sounds correct.

INCORRECT	He took my wife and I to dinner.

(Try that sentence without the first part of the compound, *my wife and*.)

CORRECT	He took my wife and me to dinner.
INCORRECT	Her and her family donated the prize money.

(Try that sentence without the second part of the compound, *and her family*.)

CORRECT	She and her family donated the prize money.

The pronouns *who* and *whom* often cause confusion. *Who* (or *whoever*) is subjective; *whom* (or *whomever*) is objective. If the pronoun appears in a question, answer the question using a pronoun (such as *I* or *me*) to determine whether to use the subjective or objective form.

INCORRECT	**Who does Howard want to see?**

Answering the question—*Howard wants to see me*—reveals that the pronoun should be objective.

CORRECT	**Whom does Howard want to see?**

When *who* or *whom* is not part of a question, it introduces a dependent clause. Determine the case of the pronoun in the clause by removing the clause from the sentence and replacing *who* or *whom* with *I* and *me* to see which form is correct.

INCORRECT	**She welcomed whomever knocked on her door.**

The dependent clause is *whomever knocked on her door*. Replacing *whomever* with *I* and *me*— *I knocked on her door; me knocked on her door*—reveals that the subjective form *whoever* is correct.

CORRECT	**She welcomed whoever knocked on her door.**

14. Lack of agreement between pronoun and antecedent

Pronouns must agree in number (singular or plural) and person (first, second or third) with their *antecedents*—the nouns or pronouns to which they refer. Do not shift, for example, from a singular antecedent to a plural pronoun, or from a third-person antecedent to a first- or second-person pronoun.

INCORRECT	**The class meets on Thursdays to check their work.**
CORRECT	**The class meets on Thursdays to check its work.**
	Class members meet on Thursdays to check their work.

15. Biased language

Avoid stereotypes and biased language. Take special care to avoid gender-specific pronouns.

BIASED	**A reporter must always check his work.**
ACCEPTABLE	**Reporters must always check their work.**
	If you are a reporter, you must always check your work.
BIASED	**Local politicians and their wives attended a dinner in honor of the visiting diplomat.**
ACCEPTABLE	**Local politicians and their spouses attended a dinner in honor of the visiting diplomat.**

16. Lack of agreement between subject and verb

Subject and verb must agree in number. Use the form of the verb that agrees with a singular or plural subject. Be especially careful to identify the subject correctly when words separate subject from verb.

| INCORRECT | The bag with the green stripes <u>belong</u> to her. |
| CORRECT | The bag with the green stripes <u>belongs</u> to her. |

A compound subject with parts joined by *and* is always plural. When parts of a compound subject are joined by *or*, make the verb agree with the part of the compound closest to the verb.

INCORRECT	A mystery writer and her daughter <u>lives</u> in the house by the river.
CORRECT	A mystery writer and her daughter <u>live</u> in the house by the river.
INCORRECT	Either Mike or his sisters <u>has</u> the spare key.
CORRECT	Either Mike or his sisters <u>have</u> the spare key.

17. Incorrect complement with linking verb

A linking verb such as *be, appear, feel* or *become* links a subject with a word or words that identify or describe the subject. When the identifying word—called a *subject complement*—is a pronoun, use the subjective case for the pronoun.

| INCORRECT | That was <u>him</u> on the telephone five minutes ago. |
| CORRECT | That was <u>he</u> on the telephone five minutes ago. |

When a word or words describing the subject follow a linking verb, the word or words must be adjectives.

| INCORRECT | She feels <u>terribly</u> about the things she said. |
| CORRECT | She feels <u>terrible</u> about the things she said. |

18. Incorrect use of subjunctive mood

Conditions contrary to fact require a verb to be in the subjunctive mood. Apply this rule in stories about all pending legislation at all levels of government. Use the subjunctive mood in "that" clauses after verbs of wishing, suggesting and requiring; in other words, use the subjunctive in clauses, dependent or independent, that do not state a fact.

INCORRECT	The bylaws require that he <u>declares</u> his candidacy by April 10.
CORRECT	The bylaws require that he <u>declare</u> his candidacy by April 10.
INCORRECT	The bill <u>will</u> require everyone to register for the draft at age 18.
CORRECT	The bill <u>would</u> require everyone to register for the draft at age 18.

19. Wrong word

Wrong-word errors include using a word that sounds similar to, or the same as, the word you need but means something different (such as writing *affect* when you mean *effect*) and using a word that has a shade of meaning that is not what you intend (such as writing *slender* when you want to suggest *scrawny*). Check the dictionary if you are not sure whether you are using a word correctly.

INCORRECT	**Merchants who appear <u>disinterested</u> in their customers may lose business.**
CORRECT	**Merchants who appear <u>uninterested</u> in their customers may lose business.**
INCORRECT	**The guests gasped and applauded when they saw the <u>excessive</u> display of food.**
CORRECT	**The guests gasped and applauded when they saw the <u>lavish</u> display of food.**

20. Incorrect verb form

Every verb has five forms: a base form, a present-tense form, a past-tense form, a present-participle form used for forming the progressive tenses, and a past-participle form used for forming the passive voice or one of the perfect tenses.

Dropping the ending from present-tense forms and regular past-tense forms is a common error.

INCORRECT	**The police are <u>suppose</u> to protect the public.**
CORRECT	**The police are <u>supposed</u> to protect the public.**

Regular verbs end in *-ed* in the past tense and past participle, but irregular verbs do not follow a set pattern for forming the past tense and past participle, so those forms of irregular verbs are frequently used incorrectly. Look up irregular verbs if you are uncertain of the correct form.

INCORRECT	**The manager was not in the restaurant when it was robbed because he had <u>went</u> home early.**
CORRECT	**The manager was not in the restaurant when it was robbed because he had <u>gone</u> home early.**
INCORRECT	**The thieves <u>taked</u> everything in the safe.**
CORRECT	**The thieves <u>took</u> everything in the safe.**

APPENDIX 2

Wire Service Style Summary

Most publications adhere to rules of style to avoid annoying inconsistencies. Without a stylebook to provide guidance in such matters, writers would not know whether the word *president* should be capitalized when preceding or following a name, whether the correct spelling is *employee* or *employe* (dictionaries list both), or whether a street name should be *Twelfth* or *12th*.

Newspapers use the wire service stylebooks to provide such guidance. For consistency, the Associated Press and United Press International collaborated in establishing style, and rules of the two services differ in only minor ways. Most newspapers follow one of those stylebooks, although the Associated Press dominates.

This section is an abbreviated summary of the primary rules of wire service style. This summary should be helpful even for those without a stylebook, but we provide it assuming that most users of this book have one. Why? Because this section includes only the rules used most frequently, arranged by topic to make them easier to learn. Only about 10 percent of the rules in a stylebook account for 90 percent of the wire service style you will use regularly. You will use the rest of the rules about 10 percent of the time. It makes sense, therefore, to learn first those rules you will use most often.

ABBREVIATIONS AND ACRONYMS

Punctuation of Abbreviations

- Generally speaking, abbreviations of two letters or fewer have periods:
  600 B.C., A.D. 1066
  8 a.m., 7 p.m.
  U.N., U.S., R.I., N.Y.
  8151 Yosemite St.
  EXCEPTIONS: *AM radio, FM radio, 35 mm camera, the AP Stylebook, "LA smog," D-Mass., R-Kan., IQ, TV, EU*
- Generally speaking, abbreviations of three letters or more do not have periods:
  CIA, FBI, NATO
  mpg, mph
  EXCEPTION: *c.o.d.*

Symbols

- Always write out % as *percent* in a story, but you may use the symbol in a headline.
- Always write out & as *and* unless it is part of a company's formal name.
- Always write out ¢ as *cent* or *cents*.
- Always use the symbol $ rather than the word *dollar* with any actual figure, and put the symbol before the figure. Write out *dollar* only if you are speaking of, say, the value of the dollar on the world market.

Dates

- Never abbreviate days of the week.
- Don't abbreviate a month unless it has a date of the month with it: *August 2007*; *Aug. 17*; *Aug. 17, 2007*.
- The five months spelled with five letters or fewer are never abbreviated: *March*; *April 20*; *May 13, 2007*; *June 1956*; *July of that year*.
- Never abbreviate *Christmas* as *Xmas*, even in a headline.
- *Fourth of July* is written out.
- *Sept. 11* is preferred over *9/11*.

People and Titles

- Some publications still use courtesy titles (*Mr., Mrs., Ms., Miss*) on second reference in stories, although most seem to have moved away from them as sexist. Many publications use them only in quotations from sources. Others use them only in obituaries and editorials, or on second reference in stories mentioning a husband and wife. In the last case, other newspapers prefer to repeat the person's whole name or, especially in features, use the person's first name. The Associated Press suggests using a courtesy title when someone requests it, but most journalists don't bother to ask.
- Use the abbreviations *Gov., Lt. Gov., Rep., Sen.* and *the Rev.*, as well as abbreviations of military titles, on first reference; then drop the title on subsequent references. Some titles you might expect to see abbreviated before a name are not abbreviated in AP style: *Attorney General, District Attorney, President, Professor, Superintendent*.
- Use the abbreviations *Jr.* and *Sr.* after a name on first reference if appropriate, but do not set them off by commas as you learned to do in English class.

Organizations

- Write out the first reference to most organizations in full rather than using an acronym: *National Organization for Women*. For *CIA, FBI* and *GOP*, however, the acronym may be used on the first reference.
- You may use well-known abbreviations such as *FCC* and *NOW* in a headline even though they would not be acceptable on first reference in the story.
- Do not put the abbreviation of an organization in parentheses after the full name on first reference. If its abbreviation is that confusing, don't use an abbreviation at all but rather call it something like "the gay rights group" or "the bureau" on second reference.
- Use the abbreviations *Co., Cos., Corp., Inc.* and *Ltd.* at the end of a company's name even if the company spells out the word; do not abbreviate these words if followed by other words such as "of America." The abbreviations *Co., Cos.* and *Corp.* are used, however, if followed by *Inc.* or *Ltd.* (and, by the way, these latter two abbreviations are not set off by commas even if the company uses them).
- Abbreviate political affiliations after a name in the following way:
  Sen. Christopher Bond, R-Mo., said . . .

Note the use of a single letter without a period for the party and the use of commas around the party and state.

- Never abbreviate the word *association*, even as part of a name.

Places

- Don't abbreviate a state name unless it follows the name of a city in that state:
  Nevada; *Brown City, Mich.*
- Never abbreviate the six states spelled with five or fewer letters or the two noncontiguous states:
  Alaska, Hawaii, Idaho, Iowa, Maine, Ohio, Texas, Utah
- Use the traditional state abbreviations, not the Postal Service's two-letter ones:
  Miss., not *MS*

  EXCEPTION: Use the two-letter postal abbreviations when a full address is given that includes a ZIP code.

  Here are the abbreviations used in normal copy:

Ala.	Fla.	Md.	Neb.	N.Y.	Tenn.
Ariz.	Ga.	Mass.	Nev.	Okla.	Vt.
Ark.	Ill.	Mich.	N.C.	Ore.	Va.
Calif.	Ind.	Minn.	N.D.	Pa.	Wash.
Colo.	Kan.	Miss.	N.H.	R.I.	W. Va.
Conn.	Ky.	Mo.	N.J.	S.C.	Wis.
Del.	La.	Mont.	N.M.	S.D.	Wyo.

- Use state abbreviations with domestic towns and cities unless they appear in the wire service dateline list of cities that stand alone. Many publications add to the wire service list their own list of towns well-known in the state or region. Use nations' full names with foreign towns and cities unless they appear in the wire service dateline list of cities that stand alone. Once a state or nation has been identified in a story, it is unnecessary to repeat the name unless clarity demands it. The lists of cities in the U.S. and the rest of the world that the wire services say may stand alone without a state abbreviation or nation are too lengthy to include here. Consult the appropriate stylebook. A handy rule of thumb is if it's an American city and has a major sports franchise, it probably stands alone. Likewise, if it's a foreign city most people have heard of, it probably stands alone.
- Don't abbreviate the names of thoroughfares if there is no street address with them:
  Main Street, Century Boulevard West.
- If the thoroughfare's name has the word *avenue, boulevard, street* or any of the directions on a map, such as *north* or *southeast*, abbreviate those words with a street address:
  1044 W. Maple St., 1424 Lee Blvd. S., 999 Jackson Ave.
- In a highway's name, always abbreviate *U.S.* but never abbreviate a state's name. In the case of an interstate highway, the name is written in full on first reference, abbreviated on subsequent ones:
  U.S. 63 or U.S. Highway 63, Massachusetts 2
  Interstate 70 (first reference), *I-70* (second reference)
- Never abbreviate *Fort* or *Mount.*
- Always use the abbreviation *St.* for *Saint* in place names. Exceptions: *Saint John* in New Brunswick, *Ste. Genevieve* in Missouri, *Sault Ste. Marie* in Michigan and Ontario.
- Abbreviate *U.S.* and *U.N.* as both nouns and adjectives.

Miscellaneous

- Use the abbreviation *IQ* (no periods) in all references to *intelligence quotient.*
- Abbreviate and capitalize the word *number* when followed by a numeral: *No. 1.*
- Use the abbreviation *TV* (no periods) only in headlines, as an adjective and in constructions such as *cable TV.* Otherwise, spell out *television.*
- Use the abbreviation *UFO* in all references to an *unidentified flying object.*
- Use the abbreviation *vs.,* not *v.,* for *versus,* except in court cases.

CAPITALIZATION

- Proper nouns are capitalized; common nouns are not. Unfortunately, this rule is not always easy to apply when the noun is the name of an animal, food or plant or when it is a trademark that has become so well-known that people mistakenly use it generically.
- Regions are capitalized; directions are not:
  We drove east two miles to catch the interstate out West.
  - Adjectives and nouns pertaining to a region are capitalized: *Southern accent, Western movie, a Southerner, a Western.*
  - A region combined with a country's name is not capitalized unless the region is part of the name of a divided country: *eastern United States, North Korea.*
  - A region combined with a state name is capitalized only if it is famous: *Southern California, southern Colorado.*
- When two or more compound proper nouns are combined to share a word in common made plural, the shared plural is lowercased:
  Missouri and Mississippi rivers, Chrisman and Truman high schools
- Government and college terms are not always as consistent as you might think.
  - *College departments* follow the animal, food and plant rule: Capitalize only words that are already proper nouns in themselves: *Spanish department, sociology department.* By contrast, always capitalize *a specific government department,* even without the city, state or federal designator, and even if it's turned around with *of* deleted: *Police Department, Fire Department, State Department, Department of Commerce.*
  - *College and government committees* are capitalized if the formal name is given rather than a shorter, descriptive designation: *Special Senate Select Committee to Investigate Improper Labor-Management Practices*; *rackets committee.*
  - *Academic degrees* are spelled out and lowercased: *bachelor of arts degree, master's degree.* Avoid the abbreviations *Ph.D., M.A., B.A.,* etc., except in lists.
  - Always capitalize (unless plural or generic) *City Council* and *County Commission* (but alone, *council* and *commission* are lowercased). *Cabinet* is capitalized when referring to advisers. *Legislature* is capitalized if the state's body is formally named that. *Capitol,* the building, is capitalized, but *capital,* the city, is not.
  - Never capitalize *board of directors* or *board of trustees* (but *Board of Curators* and *Board of Education* are capitalized). *Federal, government* and *administration* are not capitalized. *President* and *vice president* are capitalized only before a name.
  - Military titles (*Sgt., Maj., Gen.*) are capitalized before a name, as are *Air Force, Army, Marines* and *Navy* if referring to U.S. forces.

- *Political parties* are capitalized, including the word *party*: *Democratic Party, Socialist Party*. Be sure, however, to capitalize words such as *communist, democratic, fascist* and *socialist* only if they refer to a formal party rather than a philosophy.
- Some Internet and electronics terms are capitalized; some are not:
  - *Internet* and the *Net* (acceptable in later references) are capitalized.
  - *World Wide Web, the Web, Web site* and *Web page* are capitalized. But *webcam, webcast* and *webmaster* are lowercased.
  - *E-mail* and other similar terms (*e-book, e-commerce, e-business*) are lowercased.
- Some religious terms are capitalized; some are not:
  - *Pope* is lowercased except before a name: *the pope, Pope Gregory*.
  - *Mass* is always capitalized.
  - Pronouns for *God* and *Jesus* are lowercased.
- Names of religious figures are capitalized: *Prophet Muhammad, Buddha*.
  - Names of holy books are capitalized: *Talmud, Quran* (preferred to *Koran*); *Bible* is capitalized when meaning the Holy Scriptures and lowercased when referring to another book: *a hunter's bible*.
  - Sacraments are capitalized if they commemorate events in the life of Jesus or signify his presence: *Holy Communion* but *baptism, communion*.
- Actual names of races and nationalities are capitalized, but color descriptions are not: *Arab, Asian* (preferred to *Oriental* for people), *Caucasian, Cherokee, Chinese* (singular and plural), *French Canadian, Negro* (used only in names of organizations and quotations), *white, black*
- Formal titles of people are capitalized before a name, but occupational names are not: President George W. Bush, Mayor Laura Miller, Coach Roy Williams, Dean Fred Wilson, astronaut Ellen Ochoa, journalist Fred Francis, plumber Phil Sanders, pharmacist Roger Wheaton

Some titles are not easy to recognize: *managing editor, chief executive officer*. When in doubt, put the title behind the name, set off with commas, and use lowercase.

- Formal titles that are capitalized before a name are lowercased after a name:
  George W. Bush, president of the United States
  Laura Miller, mayor of Dallas
  Roy Williams, coach of the Kansas Jayhawks
  Fred Wilson, dean of students
- Formal titles that are abbreviated before a name are written out and lowercased if they follow a name:
  Gov. Eliot Spitzer; Eliot Spitzer, governor of New York
  Rep. Lindsey Graham of South Carolina; Lindsey Graham, representative from South Carolina
- The first word in a direct quotation is capitalized only if the quote meets both of these criteria:
  - It is a complete sentence. Don't capitalize a partial quote.
  - It stands alone as a separate sentence or paragraph, or it is set off from its source by a comma or colon.
- A question within a sentence is capitalized:
  My only question is, When do we start?

NUMBERS

- Cardinal numbers (numerals) are used in:
  - Addresses. Always use numerals for street addresses: *1322 N. 10th St.*
  - Ages. Always use numerals, even for days or months: *3 days old*; *John Burnside, 56.*
  - Aircraft and spacecraft: *F-4, DC-10, Apollo 11.* Exception: *Air Force One.*
  - Clothes sizes: *size 6.*
  - Dates. Always use the numeral alone—no *st, nd, rd* or *th* after it: *March 20.*
  - Decades: *the '80s.*
  - Dimensions: *5-foot-6-inch guard* (but no hyphen when the word modified is one associated with size: *3 feet tall, 10 feet long*).
  - Highways: *U.S. 63.*
  - Millions, billions and trillions: *1.2 billion, 6 million.*
  - Money. Always use numerals, but starting with a million, write like this: *$1.4 million.*
  - Numbers: *No. 1, No. 2.*
  - Percentages. Always use numerals except at the beginning of a sentence: *4 percent.*
  - Recipes. All numbers for amounts take numerals: *2 teaspoons.*
  - Speeds: *55 mph, 4 knots.*
  - Sports. Use numerals for just about everything: *8–6 score, 2 yards, 3-under-par, 2 strokes.*
  - Temperatures. Use numerals for all except *zero.* Below zero, spell out *minus*: *minus 6*, not *–6* (except in tabular data).
  - Times: *4 a.m., 6:32 p.m., noon, midnight, five minutes, three hours.*
  - Weights: *7 pounds, 11 ounces.*
  - Years: Use numerals without commas. A year is the only numeral that can start a sentence: *1988 was a good year.*
- Numerals with the suffixes *st, nd, rd* and *th* are used for:
  - Political divisions (precincts, wards, districts): *3rd Congressional District.*
  - Military sequences: *1st Lt., 2nd Division, 7th Fleet.*
  - Courts: *2nd District Court*; *10th Circuit Court of Appeals.*
  - Streets after *Ninth.* For *First* through *Ninth,* use words: *Fifth Avenue, 13th Street.*
  - Amendments to the Constitution after *Ninth.* For *First* through *Ninth,* use words: *First Amendment, 16th Amendment.*
- Words are used for:
  - Numbers less than 10, with the exceptions noted above: *five people, four rules.*
  - Any number at the start of a sentence except for a year: *Sixteen years ago . . .*
  - Casual numbers: *about a hundred or so.*
  - Fractions less than one: *one-half.*
- Mixed numerals are used for fractions greater than one: *1½.*
- Roman numerals are used for a man who is the third or later in his family to bear a name and for a king, queen, pope or world war:
  John D. Rockefeller III, Queen Elizabeth II, Pope John Paul II, World War I

Suggested Web Site

www.ap.org
The Associated Press provides wire news through the sites of its member newspapers.

APPENDIX 3

Society of Professional Journalists' Code of Ethics

PREAMBLE

Members of the Society of Professional Journalists believe that public enlightenment is the forerunner of justice and the foundation of democracy. The duty of the journalist is to further those ends by seeking truth and providing a fair and comprehensive account of events and issues. Conscientious journalists from all media and specialties strive to serve the public with thoroughness and honesty. Professional integrity is the cornerstone of a journalist's credibility. Members of the society share a dedication to ethical behavior and adopt this code to declare the society's principles and standards of practice.

SEEK TRUTH AND REPORT IT

Journalists should be honest, fair and courageous in gathering, reporting and interpreting information.

Journalists should:

- Test the accuracy of information from all sources and exercise care to avoid inadvertent error. Deliberate distortion is never permissible.
- Diligently seek out subjects of news stories to give them the opportunity to respond to allegations of wrongdoing.
- Identify sources whenever feasible. The public is entitled to as much information as possible on sources' reliability.
- Always question sources' motives before promising anonymity. Clarify conditions attached to any promise made in exchange for information. Keep promises.
- Make certain that headlines, news teases and promotional material, photos, video, audio, graphics, sound bites and quotations do not misrepresent. They should not oversimplify or highlight incidents out of context.
- Never distort the content of news photos or video. Image enhancement for technical clarity is always permissible. Label montages and photo illustrations.
- Avoid misleading re-enactments or staged news events. If re-enactment is necessary to tell a story, label it.

Sigma Delta Chi's first Code of Ethics was borrowed from the American Society of Newspaper Editors in 1926. In 1973, Sigma Delta Chi wrote its own code, which was revised in 1984 and 1987. The present version of the Society of Professional Journalists' Code of Ethics was adopted in September 1996.

- Avoid undercover or other surreptitious methods of gathering information except when traditional open methods will not yield information vital to the public. Use of such methods should be explained as part of the story.
- Never plagiarize.
- Tell the story of the diversity and magnitude of the human experience boldly, even when it is unpopular to do so.
- Examine their own cultural values and avoid imposing those values on others.
- Avoid stereotyping by race, gender, age, religion, ethnicity, geography, sexual orientation, disability, physical appearance or social status.
- Support the open exchange of views, even views they find repugnant.
- Give voice to the voiceless; official and unofficial sources of information can be equally valid.
- Distinguish between advocacy and news reporting. Analysis and commentary should be labeled and not misrepresent fact or context.
- Distinguish news from advertising and shun hybrids that blur the lines between the two.
- Recognize a special obligation to ensure that the public's business is conducted in the open and that government records are open to inspection.

MINIMIZE HARM

Ethical journalists treat sources, subjects and colleagues as human beings deserving of respect.

Journalists should:

- Show compassion for those who may be affected adversely by news coverage. Use special sensitivity when dealing with children and inexperienced sources or subjects.
- Be sensitive when seeking or using interviews or photographs of those affected by tragedy or grief.
- Recognize that gathering and reporting information may cause harm or discomfort. Pursuit of the news is not a license for arrogance.
- Recognize that private people have a greater right to control information about themselves than do public officials and others who seek power, influence or attention. Only an overriding public need can justify intrusion into anyone's privacy.
- Show good taste. Avoid pandering to lurid curiosity.
- Be cautious about identifying juvenile suspects or victims of sex crimes.
- Be judicious about naming criminal suspects before the formal filing of charges.
- Balance a criminal suspect's fair trial rights with the public's right to be informed.

ACT INDEPENDENTLY

Journalists should be free of obligation to any interest other than the public's right to know.
Journalists should:

- Avoid conflicts of interest, real or perceived.
- Remain free of associations and activities that may compromise integrity or damage credibility.

- Refuse gifts, favors, fees, free travel and special treatment, and shun secondary employment, political involvement, public office and service in community organizations if they compromise journalistic integrity.
- Disclose unavoidable conflicts.
- Be vigilant and courageous about holding those with power accountable.
- Deny favored treatment to advertisers and special interests and resist their pressure to influence news coverage.
- Be wary of sources offering information for favors or money; avoid bidding for news.

BE ACCOUNTABLE

Journalists are accountable to their readers, listeners, viewers and each other.
Journalists should:

- Clarify and explain news coverage and invite dialogue with the public over journalistic conduct.
- Encourage the public to voice grievances against the news media.
- Admit mistakes and correct them promptly.
- Expose unethical practices of journalists and the news media.
- Abide by the same high standards to which they hold others.

Crisis Coverage: An Interactive CD-ROM Journalism Simulation

A s mentioned in Chapter 13, crime and accidents, fires and disasters are staples of news reporting. Almost every journalist working on a newspaper will write these types of stories, and many cover such stories frequently. Unfortunately, gaining real-world experience with this type of reporting is almost impossible in the introductory newswriting class. Robberies, house fires and car accidents do not fit neatly into a syllabus, nor does listening to a police scanner and driving to such events fit neatly into a student schedule.

The exercises in Chapter 13 of the *Workbook for News Reporting and Writing* provide a good starting ground for learning the fundamentals of crime and accident, fire and disaster reporting, but they can't simulate the news-gathering process. To help prepare you better for both the crime and the accident, fire and disaster genres, we provide a CD-ROM simulation of an actual tragedy, the shooting of a police officer and four bystanders in St. Joseph, Mo.

TIPS FOR USING THE PROGRAM

The simulation program puts you in the news room the night of the shooting. After a brief introduction and opening segment, you begin your news-gathering at your desk in the news room. Your job is to get information from paper, human and electronic sources as the night progresses and then write a story as more information becomes available. (See the section "Types of Articles and Assignments" for possible assignments.) The simulation progresses from approximately 5 p.m. until deadline at 11 p.m.

The main interface is the news room cubicle. On and around your desk are items to click on to get information, as the accompanying screen capture illustrates.

Clicking on the Desk Items

Just as in real-world reporting, sources develop over the course of the story, and some will not be immediately available to you. For example, when the scenario first begins, the reporters dispatched to the scene (under Map of Area) will not be ready to talk to you yet, nor will a phone call to the police station or hospital give you any information. Be sure to check back with these sources multiple times as the night progresses and more bits of news become available. The sources include the following:

- **Television.** You will watch actual news broadcasts from the night of the shooting.
- **Phone book.** Good reporters use the phone extensively. You will call some of your sources, and they will give you quotes and information.
- **Phone.** Sources will call you with updated information throughout the night.

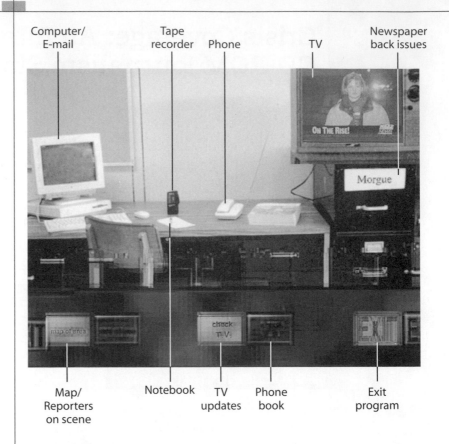

Computer/E-mail   Tape recorder   Phone   TV   Newspaper back issues

Map/Reporters on scene   Notebook   TV updates   Phone book   Exit program

- **Morgue.** Background research is crucial to quality reporting, and you will want to check to see if there are any related articles from back issues of the newspaper.
- **Map/Reporters.** Three reporters will be on the scene, and they will give you updates and quotes from eyewitnesses.
- **Notebook.** Reporters will bring back their notebooks with interview notes for you to use in your story.
- **Tape recorder.** One reporter will bring back a tape-recorded interview from the scene.
- **Computer/E-mail.** There will be e-mail and Web sources for you to use. In addition to the information provided on the CD-ROM, you may wish to do additional Web research.

Because these sources will be available at different times, be sure to click on all of the buttons in the time periods between the TV clips.

Pacing Yourself

The simulation covers a period of approximately six hours, but it will likely take you only between 30 and 60 minutes to run through the scenario. If you are running the program during a 75-minute or longer class, you should not have much difficulty in finishing the simulation during a full class period. If you are trying to complete the program within a

50-minute class period, be sure to be in class on time or early, take notes quickly and make good decisions about what information you will likely not need to copy down. Remember the principles of newsworthiness and definitions of "news" outlined in Chapter 1, and consider what information your readers will be interested in knowing.

Taking Notes

We pointed out in Chapter 1 that accuracy is a cornerstone of good journalism. Accuracy is especially important—and difficult—in breaking news stories about tragedies, stories that are often at the top of Page One and will be read by almost all of your audience. So be sure to take very careful notes. This is not like a book exercise for which you can easily copy down notes and double-check them at a later time. Just as in real-world reporting, for many of these sources you will have only one opportunity to get the information right and to decide what information and quotes to include in your notes. If you're using the TV sources, you won't be able to replay those segments, so take good shorthand and reconstruct your notes after each segment, as we suggested in Chapter 3.

For your notes, you may wish to use a legal pad or a reporter's notebook. Depending on your writing and typing skills, you may prefer to take notes on the computer, especially since you can later cut, copy and paste segments from your computer notes into your final draft. In order to take the computer notes, you'll want to open up a word processing program before starting the simulation and move the program's window to the side of the screen so you can click back and forth between the simulation program and the word processing window when taking notes. Be sure to save your computer notes often in case your computer crashes.

Using the TV

Good news reporters watch their broadcast colleagues—and competitors—all the time, especially during tragedies. You'll be watching several clips from the local TV station, which include selections from the local 6 p.m. and 10 p.m. newscasts and cut-ins with breaking news before and after those newscasts. In all, there are 10 video clips, some of which play automatically and some that play when you click on the *Check TV* button. Be sure to try all of your other sources before you click on the Check TV button, since the TV segment will jump you to a later part in the scenario.

Typically, a print journalist will not use quotes from radio or TV broadcasts. Before you begin the simulation, be sure to check with your instructor about using quotes from the TV in your story. Your instructor may forbid you from using any TV quotes or may allow you to cite such quotes sparingly (ex: "In an interview with KQ2 TV last night, witness James Smith said, . . ."). He or she may allow you to quote the sources (not the reporters or anchors) as if you were interviewing them yourself. You need to know your instructor's wishes *before* you start the simulation so you know how carefully to take notes during the TV segments. You won't have a chance to hear and see those segments again.

Adjusting Sound and Using Headphones

Before you begin the scenario, you'll want to test the sound levels of your computer and make sure the sound is working because you'll need to hear all the audio and video clips in order to write your story. In addition, you may want to bring headphones that fit your computer port, to keep sound levels in the room down and to muffle the sound coming from nearby computers. Then again, the wide array of sounds and voices coming from a dozen or more computers does help mimic the bedlam found in a news room near deadline.

Quitting/Restarting the Program

Because the program replicates the timing and flow of information in a tragedy, you will not be able to jump around in the program or quit and later restart the program where you left off. If you have to restart the program, you will be placed back at the very beginning of the scenario. So be absolutely sure you want to quit before you click on the red EXIT button. Likewise, to prevent the program from crashing and thus prevent you from needing to start over, make sure you are working on a reliable computer with sufficient RAM available.

For this assignment, your instructor may want you to run through the program only once because you would get only one shot at gathering information under deadline in any crime or accident, fire or disaster story. Or your instructor may allow you to run through the program multiple times to make sure you find all of the sources.

TIPS FOR WRITING YOUR ARTICLE

Keep in mind one key tip in newswriting: Listen carefully to your editor — or in this case, your instructor — about what type of article he or she wants you to write. For a spot news story like this, neither you nor your editor would have time to do a rewrite.

In addition, make sure you understand the nature of the publication and your audience. If you wish to replicate the actual situation, assume you are writing for the *St. Joseph News-Press*, an independently owned daily that has a circulation of approximately 40,000 and serves the 70,000 residents of St. Joseph as well as people in the surrounding counties in northwest Missouri. Your instructor may prefer you to write the story for a larger paper, such as *The Kansas City Star*, or for a small, nearby weekly or for the Associated Press or another wire service. Which publication you write for will help determine how you write your story and what information you include.

Because most people will be writing an inverted pyramid account of the main story, the majority of the other tips in this section are geared toward that type of story. If you are writing a different type of story, you may want to refer to the sections of the book that address that type of story in more detail.

Rank Your Information in Order of Importance

You will have a lot of information to deal with and try to fit into your story. To write an inverted pyramid story, you may want to rank or mark each fact or quote to help you decide what material will go near the beginning, the middle and the end of the story and what information you probably won't need to use.

Prepare Information for a Summary Lead

You may not end up using a summary lead in your final draft, but drafting such a lead will help you write the rest of the story. Using the ranking mentioned above, write down the key answers to these questions:

Who?
What?
When?
Where?
Why?
How?

Decide which of these items need to be in the lead (the "why," for example, might not be necessary or may be unknown). Put the most important of the 5W's and H at the beginning of the lead. As mentioned in Chapter 7, try to keep the lead to 25 or 30 words and preferably to one sentence.

Write Several Alternate Leads

Even if you think you are going to use a straight summary lead, you should try other types of leads as well because you may discover one of those other leads works much better. Given the complexity of the situation, you may decide to use a multiple-element lead. Maybe the best choice will be a delayed identification. If you are writing for the St. Joseph community, you may find that an immediate-identification lead is most appropriate. After trying several lead types, you may find that a flair lead that contains elements of description or narration would work best.

Draw a Map

Drawing a map of the scene or the area on a piece of paper can help you organize your thoughts and better understand what happened, especially if you are a visually oriented person.

Make a Chronology

Even if you don't use a chronological format for your article, a timeline of the events will help you understand the events and write your article.

TYPES OF ARTICLES AND ASSIGNMENTS

In a situation like this tragedy, the entire reporting and editing staff is mobilized. Those who were off for the day or who had already put in their hours are called back, and the whole staff works together to produce the in-depth coverage the readership will want and expect. Some reporters go to the scene and collect information. Others are stationed at the police department, city hall or hospital, while still other staffers may research information in the morgue or online. Using all of these resources, the staff produces not only one main article but also three, four or more sidebars to accompany it.

The simulation program lends itself well to writing a variety of different stories and sidebars. Before you begin the simulation, you'll need to be clear about exactly what type of article or articles your instructor wants you to write because the article's focus will affect what notes to take and what sources to pay especially close attention to.

The most typical assignment is covering the main story and using the inverted pyramid, the organizational format most often used for hard news stories like crime and accidents, fires and disasters. Before you write such a story, be sure to reread Chapter 7 to review the principles for writing inverted pyramid stories. Carefully consider what information is most important, and put that information early in the story. Don't bury key information that may end up getting cut or not getting read.

Using the inverted pyramid is not the only way to tell the story. In Chapter 13, the example of the Kansas man who was killed by a police marksman illustrates how a chronological approach sometimes works better. Your instructor may choose to have you write a chronological story instead of—or in addition to—an inverted pyramid account. To do this, you probably will want to reconstruct a timeline and reorganize your notes to represent the order in which events happened instead of the order in which the information became available to you. Your instructor may also assign you or give you the freedom to use one of the other alternatives to the inverted pyramid outlined in Chapter 9.

Regardless of which story type you are assigned, you'll want to remember to include the key information and sources for crime and accident, fire and disaster stories:

- Eyewitnesses.
- Police or other officials in charge of handling the situation.
- Victims, friends and relatives of the victims (when possible and appropriate).

Chapter 13 also stresses the importance of obtaining official documents for these types of stories, such as an accident report, a fire marshal's casualty report or a police report. For this simulation, however, an official document is not available before your deadline.

Your instructor may give you a word limit for your article, in the same way a managing editor, news editor or copy editor might tell a reporter in this situation, "Make it x inches, no more, no less," because the number of column inches allotted to the story might already be set by the time the writer finishes the story. The editors and layout personnel would likely have been scrambling to assemble all of the new shooting-related articles, photos and informational graphics. The main story may be held until the last minute so that the most current information will appear in the next day's paper. Consequently, there may be precious little leeway given for the length of the article.

A word or inch limit is a restriction for the print newspaper only, of course. Chapter 1 illustrates how the space limitations of the physical newspaper don't apply in an online environment. The print newspaper may have space for only a 700-word article and two photos, but the online edition could have 1,000-plus words and virtually unlimited photos and graphics.

Your instructor may choose one of the following articles or exercises or may choose yet another possible assignment.

Main Story

Inverted Pyramid

Write a main news story that contains all of the important facets of the story. This is the story to run under the headline at the top of Page One if you were writing for the local newspaper (see notes in the previous section about what publication you are writing for).

Alternative Organization

Consulting Chapter 9, use a different organizational method for writing the story, such as narration (chronological), vivid scenes, a focus structure or anecdotes.

Early Online Edition

Readers in the community and across the state or country who hear about the shooting are not going to be content to wait until the next morning to find out more. As suggested on the first page of this book, the reporter will need to create text —and perhaps prepare multimedia—for the newspaper's Web site so readers can access that information shortly after the incident. They may return several times in the next 24 hours, expecting updates.

There are two places in the CD-ROM simulation where you will be able to stop and write a story and an update for the online edition.

Wire Story

Assume that you are responsible for writing a story that will go out on the Associated Press wire and will likely be picked up by many of the daily newspapers across the state. Write a 750-word story.

Sidebar Stories

Shooting Injuries

Write a sidebar about the people injured. As detailed in Chapter 13, be sure to include the names, ages, addresses and conditions of the victims.

Neighbor/Witness Accounts

Write a sidebar that focuses on the eyewitnesses and includes quotes and anecdotes about the shooting and the shooter.

Killing the Shooter

Write a sidebar about the killing of the shooter, making sure to include details about the event, eyewitness quotes and information about police procedures and policy during and after a shooting.

Historical/Contextual Piece

This type of sidebar could take one of several different paths. It could look at the history of officers killed in the line of duty in the area. It could look at other mass shootings in the area. Or it could look at police officer deaths from a national perspective, requiring you to go online and research statistics.

Practice and Follow-Up

Writing Leads

Write a variety of leads for a main story, following the advice in Chapter 7 when composing an immediate-identification lead, a delayed-identification lead, a multiple-element lead and one or more flair leads.

Interviewing

Pick two sources mentioned in the simulation that you would like to be able to interview in greater depth, and write up 10 questions for each person. As you learned in Chapter 3, you'll want to phrase and order those questions carefully because this situation is sensitive. Because you will be wanting detailed quotes, make sure that at least seven of the questions are open-ended.

Ethics

Interviewing

After reading Chapter 23 and the section in Chapter 13 about victims/witnesses in the accidents, fires and disasters section, write a pro or con essay about calling to interview the wife of the slain police officer. If you would call the wife, explain why, and describe the approach you would take. If you would not call the wife, explain why, and cite examples from the ethical codes to support your decision.

Photos

On the CD is a folder titled "Photos." Look at the photos and put yourself in the position of a managing editor who has to decide which photos to include in the newspaper. Which photo would you put on the front page? Which photo(s) would you not print at all, and why? If the shooting had happened in another part of the state, would that location affect which photos you would not print? Write an essay explaining your choices.

GLOSSARY

absolute privilege The right of legislators, judges and government executives to speak without threat of libel when acting in their official capacities.

absolutism The ethical philosophy that there is a fixed set of principles or laws from which there is no deviation. To the absolutist journalist, the end never justifies the means.

accuracy check A prepublication check with sources to go over the facts in the story.

actual malice Reckless disregard of the truth. It is a condition in libel cases.

actual malice test Protection for reporters to write anything about an officeholder or candidate unless they know that the material is false or they recklessly disregard the truth.

ad An advertisement.

add A typewritten page of copy following the first page. "First add" would be the second page of typewritten copy.

advance A report dealing with the subjects and issues to be dealt with in an upcoming meeting or event.

advertising department The department of the newspaper responsible for advertisements. Most advertising departments have classified and display ad sections.

anchor One in the television studio who ties together the newscast by reading the news and providing transitions from one story to the next.

anecdotal lead A newspaper story beginning that uses humor or an interesting incident.

anecdote An informative and entertaining story within a story.

angle The focus of, or approach to, a story. The latest development in a continuing controversy, the key play in a football game, or the tragedy of a particular death in a mass disaster may serve as an angle.

antinomianism The ethical philosophy that recognizes no rules. An antinomian journalist judges every ethical situation on its own merits. Unlike the situation ethicist, the antinomian does not use love of neighbor as an absolute.

AP The Associated Press, a worldwide news-gathering cooperative owned by its subscribers.

APME Associated Press Managing Editors, an organization of managing editors and editors whose papers are members of the Associated Press.

arraignment A court proceeding at which a defendant is informed of the charge. At the proceeding, the defendant is asked to enter a plea, and bail may be set.

average A term used to describe typical or representative members of a group. In mathematical terms, it refers to the result obtained when a set of numbers is added together and then divided by the number of items in the set.

background Information that may be attributed to a source by title, but not by name; for example, "a White House aide said."

backgrounder Story that explains and updates the news.

beat A reporter's assigned area of responsibility. A beat may be an institution, such as the courthouse; a geographical area, such as a small town; or a subject, such as science. The term also refers to an exclusive story.

blog A Web page produced by a group or an individual. The writing is primarily opinion-based but sometimes includes original reporting.

blotter An old-fashioned term for the arrest sheet that summarizes the bare facts of an arrest. Today this information is almost always kept in a computer.

books Assembled sheets of paper, usually newsprint, and carbon paper on which reporters prepare stories. Books are not used with modern computerized processes.

Boolean search commands A form of searching full-text databases in which the operators AND, OR and NOT are used to narrow the search.

brightener A story, usually short, that is humorous or pleasing to the reader. It is also called a *bright*.

bureau A news-gathering office maintained by a newspaper at a place other than its central location. Papers may have bureaus in the next county, in the state capital, in Washington, D.C., or in foreign countries.

bureau chief The director of a newspaper's news operations in a remote site or bureau.

business department The newspaper department that handles billing, accounting and related functions.

byline A line of text identifying the author of a story.

chain Two or more newspapers owned by a single person or corporation. Also known as a group. The American chain owning the most newspapers is Gannett.

change of venue An order transferring a court proceeding to another jurisdiction for prosecution. This often occurs when a party in a case claims that local media coverage has prejudiced prospective jurors.

circulation department The department responsible for distribution of the newspaper.

citizen journalism Journalism produced by people who are untrained as journalists. Also known as *participatory journalism*.

city editor The individual (also known as the *metropolitan*, or *metro*, *editor*) in charge of the city desk, which coordinates local news-gathering operations. At some papers the desk also handles regional and state news done by its own reporters.

civil law Statutes under which an individual or a group can take action against another individual or group.

clips Stories clipped from your own or other newspapers.

closed-ended question A direct question designed to draw a specific response; for example, "Will you be a candidate?"

conditional privilege See *qualified privilege*.

Consumer Price Index A tool used by the government to measure the rate of inflation. CPI figures, reported monthly by the Bureau of Labor Statistics of the U.S. Department of Labor, compare the net change in prices between the current period and a specified base period. Reporters should use this data to accurately reflect the actual costs of goods and services.

contextual advertising Advertising on a Web site directed to likely users of that site based on demographic profiles.

contributing editor Magazine columnist who works under contract and not as an employee of the magazine.

control The process of structuring an experiment so that the only forces affecting the outcome are the variables you are observing.

convergence The melding of two or more forms of communication from among print (usually a newspaper or magazine); radio, broadcast or cable television; the Internet; and mobile phones or other wireless devices.

copy What reporters write. A story is a piece of copy.

copy desk   The desk at which final editing of stories is done, headlines are written and pages are designed.

copy editor   A person who checks, polishes and corrects stories written by reporters. Usually copy editors write headlines for those stories, and sometimes they decide how to arrange stories and pictures on a page.

cover   To keep abreast of significant developments on a beat or to report on a specific event. The reporter covering the police beat may be assigned to cover a murder.

criminal law   Statutes under which a grand jury or an officer of the court can take action against an individual.

cub   A beginning reporter.

cutline   The caption that accompanies a newspaper or magazine photograph. The term dates from the days when photos were reproduced with etched zinc plates, called *cuts*.

database   A computerized information bank, usually accessed by newspapers on a subscription basis.

deadline   The time by which a reporter, editor or desk must have completed scheduled work.

deep background   Information that may be used but that cannot be attributed to either a person or a position.

delayed-identification lead   Opening paragraph of a story in which the "who" is identified by occupation, city, office or any means other than by name.

dependent variable   See *variable*.

desk   A term used by reporters to refer to the city editor's or copy editor's position, as in, "The desk wants this story by noon."

desk assistant   Entry-level position in television news rooms. Desk assistants handle routine news assignments such as monitoring wire services and listening to police scanners.

developing story   One in which newsworthy events occur over several days or weeks.

dialogue   A conversation between two or more people, neither of whom normally is the reporter.

dig   To question or investigate thoroughly, as in, "Let's do some digging into those campaign reports."

documentary   In-depth coverage of an issue or event, especially in broadcasting.

editor   The top-ranking individual in the news department of a newspaper, also known as the *editor in chief*. The term may refer as well to those at any level who edit copy.

editorial department   The news department of a newspaper, responsible for all content of the newspaper except advertising. At some papers this term refers to the department responsible for the editorial page only.

editorialize   To inject the reporter's or the newspaper's opinion into a news story or headline. Most newspapers restrict opinion to analysis stories, columns and editorials.

editorial page editor   The individual in charge of the editorial page and, at larger newspapers, the op-ed (opposite editorial) page.

executive producer   The television executive with overall responsibility for the look of the television newscast.

fair comment and criticism   Opinion delivered on the performance of anyone in the public eye. Such opinion is legally protected if reporters do not misstate any of the facts on which they base their comments or criticism, and it is not malicious.

features   Stories that have little or no breaking news.

felony   Serious crime punishable by death or imprisonment.

field experiment   A research technique in which the reporter deliberately takes some action to observe the effects. For example, a perfectly tuned automobile could be taken to several repair shops to find out if the mechanics would invent problems that required fixing.

field producer   Behind-the-scenes television reporter who often does much of the field work for a network's on-camera correspondents.

flat-file databases   Simple databases that do not permit sophisticated searches. An address database is an example.

follow   A story supplying further information about an item that has already been published; *folo* is an alternate spelling.

foreshadowing   A technique of teasing readers with material coming later in the story as a way of encouraging them to keep reading.

Freedom of Information Act   A U.S. law passed in 1966 to make it easier to obtain information from federal agencies. The law was amended in 1974 to improve access to government records.

free-form databases   Unstructured data depositories into which any kind of data or any type of element may be placed.

free-press/fair-trial controversy   The conflict between a defendant's right to an impartial jury and a reporter's responsibility to inform the public.

full-text databases   Sophisticated databases that permit the user to search for any word or phrase that appears. Newspaper and television text libraries are examples.

futures file   A collection, filed according to date, of newspaper clippings, letters, notes and other information to remind editors of stories to assign.

general manager   The individual responsible for the business operations of a newspaper. Some newspaper chains award this title to the top-ranking local executive.

graf   A shortened form of *paragraph*, as in, "Give me two grafs on that fire."

graphics editor   Usually, the editor responsible for all nonphotographic illustrations in a newspaper, including information graphics, maps and illustrations.

handout   See *news release*.

hard lead   A lead that reports a new development or newly discovered fact. See also *soft lead*.

hard news   Coverage of the actions of government or business; or the reporting of an event, such as a crime, an accident or a speech. The time element often is important. See also *soft news*.

human-interest story   A piece valued more for its emotional impact or oddity than for its importance.

hyperlink   A navigation element on a Web site that takes the reader to a related Web site, usually for the purpose of providing additional information.

hypothesis   In investigative reporting the statement a reporter expects to be able to prove, as in, "The mayor took a bribe from that massage parlor." In an experiment the statement of what a researcher hopes to find.

immediate-identification lead   The opening paragraph of a story in which the "who" is reported by name.

independent variable   See *variable*.

indictment   A document issued by a grand jury that certifies there is sufficient evidence against a person accused of a crime to warrant holding that person for trial.

inflation   A term that describes the rising cost of living as time goes by. See also *Consumer Price Index.*

information graphic   A visual representation of data.

invasion of privacy   Violation of a person's right to be left alone.

inverted pyramid   The organization of a news story in which information is arranged in descending order of importance.

investigative reporting   The pursuit of information that has been concealed, such as evidence of wrongdoing.

IRE   Investigative Reporters and Editors, a group created to exchange information and investigative reporting techniques. IRE has its headquarters at the University of Missouri School of Journalism.

lay out (v.)   The process of preparing page drawings to indicate where stories and pictures are to be placed in the newspaper.

layout (n.)   The completed page drawing, or page dummy.

lead   (1) The first paragraph or first several paragraphs of a newspaper story (sometimes spelled *lede*); (2) the story given the best display on Page One; (3) a tip.

lead-in   An introduction to a filmed or recorded excerpt from a news source or from another reporter.

lead story   The major story displayed at the top of Page One.

libel   Damage to a person's reputation caused by a false written statement that brings the person into hatred, contempt or ridicule, or injures his or her business or occupational pursuit.

maestro   The leader of a news-gathering team. Reporters, copy editors, editors and graphic designers work with a maestro to create special reports.

managing editor   The individual with primary responsibility for day-to-day operation of the news department.

margin of error (also called sampling error)   In surveys, the range within which you can be confident of accuracy. A survey with a margin of error of 3 percent, for example, typically has a 95 percent chance of being accurate within 3 percent above or below the exact result. An allowance must be made in any survey for the possibility that the sample questioned may not be exactly like all other members of the population. The margin of error varies with the size of the sample population, and should be reported in every news story about a survey.

median   The middle number in a series arranged in order of size; it is often used when an average would be misleading. (If the series has an even number of items, the median consists of the average of the two "middle" numbers.)

misdemeanors   Minor criminal offenses, including most traffic violations, which usually result in a fine or brief confinement in a local jail.

more   Designation used at the end of a page of copy to indicate there are one or more additional pages.

morgue   The newspaper library, where published stories, photographs and resource material are stored for reference.

multiple-element lead   The opening paragraph of a story that reports two or more newsworthy elements.

narration   The telling of a story, usually in chronological order.

negligence test   The legal standard that requires reporters to use the same care in gathering facts and writing a story as any reasonable individual would under similar circumstances.

network correspondent   A television reporter who delivers the news on camera. Network correspondents may or may not do the actual news-gathering for their stories.

new media The emerging forms of computer-delivered news.

news conference An interview session, also called a *press conference*, in which someone submits to questions from reporters.

news director The top news executive of a local television station.

news editor The supervisor of the copy desk. At some newspapers, this title is used for the person in charge of local news-gathering operations.

news narrative   A story that sums up the news in the first paragraph or two and then goes to chronology rather that ranking the information in descending order of importance.

news release   An item, also called a *handout* or *press release*, that is sent out by a group or individual seeking publicity.

news room   The place, sometimes called the *city room*, where reporters and editors work.

news story   A story that emphasizes the facts, often written in inverted pyramid style.

news value   How important or interesting a story is.

not for attribution   Information that may not be ascribed to its source.

nut paragraph   A paragraph that summarizes the key element or elements of the story. Usually found in a story not written in inverted pyramid form. Also called a *nut graf*.

obscenity   A word or phrase usually referring to sexual parts or functions in an offensive way.

off-camera reporter   One who gathers news for television but does not report on the air.

off the record   Usually means, "Don't quote me." Some sources and reporters, however, use it to mean, "Don't print this." Phrases with similar, and equally ambiguous, meanings are "not for attribution" and "for background only."

op-ed page   The page opposite the editorial page, frequently reserved for columns, letters to the editor and personality profiles.

open-ended question   One that permits the respondent some latitude in the answer; for example, "How did you get involved in politics?"

open-meetings laws   State and federal laws, often called *sunshine laws*, guaranteeing access to meetings of public officials.

open-records laws   State and federal laws guaranteeing access to many—but not all—kinds of government records.

page designer   One who designs newspaper or magazine pages.

parallelism   A technique of presenting ideas in similar grammatical forms.

paraphrase   A paraphrase digests, condenses and clarifies a quotation to convey the meaning more precisely or succinctly than the way in which the speaker's words express it. Quotation marks are eliminated.

participant observation   A research technique in which the reporter joins in the activity he or she wants to write about.

payola   Money or gifts given in the expectation of favors from journalists.

per capita   Latin term meaning "by heads." It is determined by dividing a total figure—such as a budget—by the number of people to which it applies.

percentage   Mathematical way to express the portion of a whole—a given part of every hundred. Determined by taking the number of the portion, dividing by the number of the whole, and moving the decimal two places to the right.

personal digital assistants   Devices such as the PalmPilot that permit users to organize data and usually send and receive textual information.

photo editor   The individual who advises editors on the use of photographs in the newspaper. The photo editor also may supervise the photography department.

piece   See *story*.

plagiarism   Use of any part of another's writing and passing it off as one's own. To avoid plagiarism, a writer must attribute all direct and indirect quotations, as well as paraphrases, to the original source.

play   A shortened form of *display*. A good story may be played at the top of Page One; a weak one may be played inside.

poll   The measurement of opinion by questioning members of some small group chosen at random so as to be representative of the entire group. A poll is also referred to as a *survey* or *public opinion poll*. See also *randomization*.

population   In scientific language, the whole group being studied. Depending on the study the population may be, for example, voters in St. Louis, physicians in California or all residents of the United States.

preliminary hearing   A court hearing held to determine whether there is probable cause that a defendant committed a crime and whether the defendant should be bound over for grand jury action or trial in a higher court.

press   The machine that prints the newspaper. Also a synonym for *journalism*, as in the phrase "freedom of the press." Sometimes used to denote print journalism, as distinguished from broadcast journalism.

press agent   A person hired to gain publicity for a client. The tactics used, often called *press agentry*, might include the staging of interviews or stunts designed to attract the attention of reporters.

press box   The section of a stadium or arena set aside for reporters.

press conference   See *news conference*.

press release   See *news release*.

primary source   A person who witnesses or participates in an event or an authentic document from an event.

privilege   A defense against libel that claims the right to repeat what government officials say or do in their official capacities.

production department   The department of the newspaper that transforms the work of the news and advertising departments into the finished product. The composing room and press room are key sections of this department.

profanity   A word or phrase contemptuously referring to the deity or to beings regarded as divine; a sacrilegious expression.

profile   A story intended to reveal the personality or character of an institution or person.

proportion   Puts something in proper relation to something else—explains specific numbers in the news by relating them to the size or magnitude of the whole.

public figure   A person who has assumed a role of prominence in the affairs of society and who has persuasive power and influence in a community or who has thrust himself or herself to the forefront of a public controversy. Courts have given journalists more latitude in reporting on public figures.

public journalism   The new (or rediscovered) approach to journalism that emphasizes connections with the community rather than separation from it. Among the newspapers best known for practicing public journalism are the *Wichita* (Kan.) *Eagle* and *The Charlotte* (N.C.) *Observer*.

publisher   The top-ranking executive of a newspaper. This title often is assumed by the owner, although chains sometimes designate as publisher the top local executive.

Pulitzer Prize   The most prestigious of journalism awards. It was established by Joseph Pulitzer and is administered by Columbia University.

qualified privilege   The right to report what government officials say or do in their official capacities if the report is full, fair and accurate. Also called *conditional privilege*.

quote   As a noun, the term refers to a source's exact words, as in, "I have a great quote here." As a verb, it means to report those words inside quotation marks.

randomization   The mathematical process used to assure that every member of a population being studied has an equal chance of being chosen for questioning or observation. See also *poll*.

rate   The amount or degree of something measured in relation to a unit of something else or to a specified scale. In statistics, rate often expresses the incidence of a condition per 100,000 people, such as a murder or suicide rate. Rate also can reflect the speed at which something is changing, such as inflation or the percentage increase in a budget each year. See also *per capita*.

records column   The part of the newspaper featured regularly that contains such information as routine police and fire news, births, obituaries, marriages and divorces.

relational databases   Technology that permits users to compare data in two separate databases. Journalists have used this to win many Pulitzer Prizes. Relational databases permit a reporter to do such operations as match lists of school bus drivers with drunk-driving convictions.

reporter   A person whose job it is to gather and write the news for a publication or a broadcast outlet.

rewrite   To write a story again in an effort to improve it. It also means to take information over the telephone from a reporter in the field and mold it into a story.

roundup   A story including a number of related events. After a storm, for example, a reporter might do a roundup of accidents, power outages and other consequences of the storm.

RSS feed   Really simple syndication permits the delivery of Web updates to a user's computer. The information is usually a blog entry, a news item or a podcast.

sample   A portion of a group, or population, chosen for study as representative of the entire group.

scenic lead   A lead that concentrates on a description of an environment.

secondary source   One who talked to witnesses, such as a public safety official investigating a crime. The witness would be a primary source.

second-cycle story   A second version of a story already published, also called a *second-day story*. It usually has new information or a new angle.

senior editor   One who edits sections of major magazines.

senior writer   A title reserved for a magazine's best and most experienced reporters.

series   Two or more stories on the same or related subjects, published on a predetermined schedule.

service journalism   An aspect or type of journalism that recognizes usefulness as one of the criteria of news. Taking into consideration content and presentation, service journalism presents useful information in a usable way, for instance, placing key information in a list or graphic box.

set-up   In broadcasting, an introductory statement to pique the interest of listeners or viewers.

shield laws   Legislation giving journalists the right to protect the identity of sources.

show producer   Television news specialist who produces individual newscasts and reports to the executive producer.

sidebar   A secondary story intended to be run with a major story on the same topic. A story about a disaster, for example, may have a sidebar that tells what happened to a single victim.

situation ethics   The philosophy that recognizes that a set of rules can be broken when circumstances dictate the community will be served better by it. For example, a journalist who believes it normally unethical to deceive a news source may be willing to conceal his or her identity to infiltrate a group operating illegally.

slug   A word that identifies a story as it is processed through the newspaper plant. It is usually placed in the upper left-hand corner of each take of the story. See also *take*.

sniff   The preliminary phase of an investigation.

soft lead   A lead that uses a quote, anecdote or other literary device to attract the reader. See also *hard lead*.

soft news   Stories about trends, personalities or lifestyles. The time element usually is not important. See also *hard news*.

sound bite   An audio to accompany a story in television or, more recently, that is available even on newspaper Web sites as a supplement to the printed product.

sources   People or records from which a reporter gets information. The term often is used to describe persons, as opposed to documents.

spot news   A timely report of an event that is unfolding at the moment.

spreadsheet program   Computer program adept at managing numbers. Often used for budgets.

story   The term most journalists use for a newspaper article. Another synonym is *piece*, as in, "I saw your piece on the mayor." A long story may be called a *takeout* or a *blockbuster*.

stylebook   A book of standard usage within newspaper text. It includes rules on grammar, punctuation, capitalization and abbreviation. The AP and UPI publish similar stylebooks that are used by most papers. (Important elements of AP and UPI style are reprinted in Appendix 2 of this book.)

substantial truth   The correctness of the essential elements of a story.

summary lead   The first paragraph of a news story in which the writer presents a synopsis of two or more actions rather than focusing on any one of them.

sunshine laws   See *open-meetings laws*.

take   A page of typewritten copy for newspaper use.

30   A designation used to mark the end of a newspaper story. The symbol # is an alternate designation.

3G technology   Third-generation mobile phone technology, which permits the transmission of television images over the wireless telephone network. More common elsewhere in the world than in the U.S.

tickler   A file of upcoming events kept on paper or computer at the assignment desks of most news organizations. See also *futures file*.

tie-back   The sentence or sentences relating a story to events covered in a previous story. Used in follow-up or continuing stories or in parts of a series of stories. Also, the technique of referring to the opening in the ending of the story.

tip   A fragment of information that may lead to a story; also called a *lead*.

to-be-sure paragraph   In stories focusing on one person or perspective, writers include a statement reflecting the opinions of those who disagree with the person you are featuring, as in "To be sure, not everyone agrees."

transition   A word, phrase, sentence or paragraph that moves the reader from one thought to the next and shows the relationship between them.

undercover reporting   A technique in which a reporter pretends to be someone else in order to gain access to otherwise unobtainable information.

universal desk   A copy desk that edits material for all editorial departments of a newspaper.

update   A type of follow that reports on a development related to an earlier story.

UPI   United Press International, a worldwide news-gathering organization that is privately owned.

variable   In an experiment, one of the elements being observed. The *independent variable* is what is thought to be a cause; the *dependent variable* is the effect of that cause.

videographer   A television camera operator.

videoprompter   A mechanical or electronic device that projects broadcast copy next to the television camera lens so that a newscaster can read it while appearing to look straight into the lens.

vulgarity   A word or phrase dealing with excretory matters in a less-than-polite way.

webcast   A video report available on a Web site.

wikis   Web applications that permit readers to add, remove and edit content on a Web site. Wikis are a form of collaborative writing.

wrap-up   The completion of commentary that comes at the end of a taped segment in broadcasting; a strong ending to a report.

Acknowledgments

Amos Bridges. "As If High School Freshmen Didn't Have It Hard Enough." From *Columbia Missourian*. Copyright © Columbia Missourian. Reprinted by permission of the publisher.

"TIPS: Audiences of the 21st Century." From *Undercovered: Reaching the New U.S.A.* Published by New Directions for News. © New Directions for News 2001. Funded by The Freedom Foundation. Reprinted by permission.

Dan Gillmor. "We Watched—Again and Again." Originally published in *We the Media: Grassroots Journalism By the People, For the People* by Dan Gillmor. Reprinted by permission of the publisher. www.wethemedia.oreilly.com.

Figure 2.1. MSNBC.com. "MSNBC Is Looking for Your Help." Posted on www.microsoft .com/presspass/press/2006/nov06/11-01msmatheducationpr.mspx. Reprinted by permission of MSNBC via Copyright Clearance Center.

J. D. Lasica. "Six Types of Citizen Journalism." From *What Is Participatory Journalism? Online Journalism Review*, August 7, 2003. Copyright © 2003. Reprinted by permission of the author.

Bill Reiter, *The Des Moines (Iowa) Register* reporter. Comments on one of his first interviews, with Mrs. Edith McClinton, shortly after graduating from journalism school. Reprinted with permission of the author.

Wright Thompson. Comments on a memorable interview with Heisman Trophy winner Eric Crouch. Reprinted with permission of the author.

Sandra Davidson. "Masson v. Malcolm: A Cautionary Tale." Reprinted with permission of the author.

Jeffrey Zeleny. "Pressure Grows for Republicans Over Foley Case." From *The New York Times*, October 3, 2006. Copyright © 2006 by The New York Times Company. Reprinted with permission.

George Dorhmann, *Pioneer Press* Staff Writer. Extensive list of sources noted in story on academic fraud in University of Minnesota Basketball Program. Published in the *St. Paul Pioneer Press*, March 10, 1999. Copyright © 1999. Reprinted by permission of the publisher.

Stan Ketterer, journalist and journalism professor. "Guidelines for Evaluating Information on the Web." Reprinted with permission of the author.

Tracy van Moorlehem and Heather Newman, *Free Press* Staff Writers. MEAP story from the *Detroit Free Press*, January 19, 1998. Copyright © Detroit Free Press. Reprinted by permission of the *Detroit Free Press*.

"Fourth Student Dies from Bus Crash," Huntsville, Ala. (AP), November 22, 2006, Copyright © 2006 The Associated Press. All rights reserved. Reprinted by permission of The Associated Press.

Elizabeth Phillips. "Man Arrested in Attack, Charged with Child Endangerment." From *Columbia Missourian*, November 17, 2006. Copyright © 2006 Columbia Missourian. Reprinted by permission of the publisher.

Norman Draper. "U Earns C Average in Student-Access Report." From Minneapolis *Star Tribune*, updated on Web site November 20, 2006, 8:49 pm. Reprinted with permission of the Minneapolis *Star Tribune*.

Michael Weinreb. "She's 6-5 and 17, with the Potential to Alter the Game." From *The New York Times*, December 20, 2006. Copyright © 2006 The New York Times Company. Reprinted by permission.

Helen O'Neill. "Kidnapping Grandma Braun." From *The Associated Press*, four-part series, March 21, 22, 23 and 24, 2005. Copyright © 2005 The Associated Press. Reprinted with permission of The Associated Press.

Jane Meinhardt. "Mother Accused of Being Criminal Ringleader." From the *St. Petersburg Times*, October 21, 1994. Copyright © 1994 by the St. Petersburg Times. Reprinted by permission of the *St. Petersburg Times*.

Ken Fuson, *The Des Moines Register* feature writer. "Tips for Writing." From *The Des Moines Register*. Reprinted with permission of the author.

John Tully. "Horse Power." From *Columbia Missourian*, November 27, 2006, p. 1. Copyright © 2006 Columbia Missourian. Reprinted by permission of the publisher.

p. 418, bottom: Courtesy of *The Cincinnati Post*

p. 426: Courtesy of *The Cincinnati Pos*t

p. 427: *The Sacramento Bee*, 2007

p. 428: CNN Image Source

p. 428: Darren Hauck/Getty Images

p. 428: Colin Archer/AP Photos

p. 431: Logo courtesy of Yahoo!

p. 431: Charles Dharapak/AP Photo

p. 433: Reprinted with permission of ESPN.com

p. 435: Courtesy of Herald Interactive

p. 436: Washingtonpost.Newsweek Interactive Company

p. 438: © 2007 *Los Angeles Times*. Reprinted with permission.

p. 442: Courtesy of Earth Justice

p. 461: Missouri State Department of Conservation

p. 464: Alan Schein/Corbis

p. 478: Corbis

pp. 484 and xxiii: Domenico Stinellis/AP Photo

p. 489: Jeff T. Green/Getty Images

p. 490: *The New York Times*/Redux Pictures

p. 494: Charley Gallay/Getty Images

p. 499: Kevork Djansezian/AP Photo

INDEX

Page numbers in *italics* indicate material presented in boxes. Page numbers followed by an italicized *f* or *t* indicate figures and tables, respectively. Page numbers in **boldface** indicate terms that appear in the Glossary.

Copy Editing and Proofreading Symbols

Writing and editing for today's media are done almost exclusively on computers. Only in the book industry are most manuscripts still prepared on paper. Nevertheless, at some small newspapers and magazines, editors prefer to edit on paper. For that reason, failure to learn the copy editing symbols used in manuscript preparation is a mistake. There is a good chance you will need to use those symbols at some point in your career, if only to satisfy the occasional editor who prefers doing things the old-fashioned way.

You are even more likely to use proofreading symbols, which are used on galley proofs and page proofs to correct typeset copy. While there are some similarities in the two sets of symbols, there also are differences. The chart on the inside back cover shows the most common copy editing symbols (used in manuscript preparation) and the chart below illustrates the most common proofreading symbols (used to correct typeset copy).

Proofreading Symbols

Symbol	Meaning	Symbol	Meaning
ʌ	Insert at this point.	⌄⌄	Space evenly.
⊥	Push down space.	⌒	Close up entirely.
ℓ	Take out letter, letters or words.	⊏	Move to left.
ꝺ	Turn inverted letter.	⊐	Move to right.
lc	Set lowercase.	⊔	Lower letter or word.
wf	Wrong font letter.	⊓	Raise letter or word.
ital	Reset in italic type.	out, see copy	Words are left out.
rom	Reset in roman (regular) type.	∥	Straighten lines.
bf	Reset in boldface type.	¶	Start new paragraph.
⊙	Insert period.	no ¶	No paragraph. Run together.
⌄	Insert comma.	tr	Transpose letters or words.
⌃	Insert semicolon.	?	Query; is copy right?
H	Insert hyphen.	⊢⊣	Insert dash.
∨	Insert apostrophe.	▢	Indent 1 em.
⌄ ⌄	Enclose in quotation marks.	▢▢	Indent 2 ems.
≡	Replace with a capital letter.	▢▢▢	Indent 3 ems.
#	Insert space.	stet	Let it stand.